Multicultural Origins of th

CW00746749

Westerners on both the left and right overwhelmingly conflate globalisation with Westernisation and presume that the global economy is a pure Western-creation. Taking on the traditional Eurocentric Big Bang theory, or the 'expansion of the West' narrative, this book reveals the multicultural origins of globalisation and the global economy, not so as to marginalise the West but to show how it has long been embedded in complex interconnections and co-constitutive interactions with non-Western actors/agents and processes. The central empirical theme is the role of Indian structural power that was derived from Indian cotton textile exports. Indian structural power organised the first (historical-capitalist) global economy between 1500 and c.1850 and performed a vital, albeit indirect, role in the making of Western empire, industrialisation and the second (modern-capitalist) global economy. These textiles underpinned the complex inter-relations between Africa, West/Central/East/Southeast Asia, the Americas and Europe that collectively drove global economic development forward.

John M. Hobson is Professor of Politics & International Relations at the University of Sheffield and is a Fellow of the British Academy. He has previously written eight books, including *The Eastern Origins of Western Civilisation* (Cambridge University Press, 2004), and *The Eurocentric Conception of World Politics* (Cambridge University Press, 2012).

Multicultural Origins of the Global Economy

Beyond the Western-Centric Frontier

John M. Hobson

University of Sheffield

CAMBRIDGE
UNIVERSITY PRESS

University Printing House, Cambridge CB2 8BS, United Kingdom

One Liberty Plaza, 20th Floor, New York, NY 10006, USA

477 Williamstown Road, Port Melbourne, VIC 3207, Australia

314–321, 3rd Floor, Plot 3, Splendor Forum, Jasola District Centre, New Delhi – 110025, India

79 Anson Road, #06-04/06, Singapore 079906

Cambridge University Press is part of the University of Cambridge.

It furthers the University's mission by disseminating knowledge in the pursuit of education, learning, and research at the highest international levels of excellence.

www.cambridge.org
Information on this title: www.cambridge.org/9781108840828
DOI: 10.1017/9781108892704

First published 2021

Printed in the United Kingdom by TJ Books Limited, Padstow Cornwall

A catalogue record for this publication is available from the British Library.

ISBN 978-1-108-84082-8 Hardback
ISBN 978-1-108-74403-4 Paperback

In memoriam:

Tim and Nora Hobson, my life mentors

Yves Laframboise, my alter-life mentor

Lily (L. H. M.) Ling and John Atkinson Hobson, critics of racism, my academic mentors

السلام عليكم ورحمة الله وبركاته

שלום עליכם

Contents

Figures

Tables

Acknowledgements

This book has been thirty-seven years in the making and is the culmination of much that I have learned in that time. It took me on an odyssey that returned me to the second year of my undergraduate studies in Political Economy, when I was first introduced to the original Marxist debate on the transition from feudalism to capitalism. And from there I moved forward in time through my Political Sociology MSc on to my historical–sociological PhD years of study and thence into the world of International Relations (IR) and International Political Economy, all the while developing ideas, themes and issues that would come to fruition in this book. There are obviously far too many names that I owe a debt to in the early years, but I remain deeply grateful to Monika Beutel, Alan Hooper, Tom Nossiter, Linda Weiss and Michael Mann.

Moving forward to the last decade I would like to express my sincerest thanks to members of my current Sheffield department who have in so many ways provided help, support and advice to me over the many years that I have spent researching and writing this book. I am privileged to work in a department whose profile in political economy is world leading. From the pioneers of 'New Political Economy' and the original directors of the two world-leading political economy research centres (PERC and subsequently SPERI), Tony Payne and Andrew Gamble, through to its present and equally impressive leadership under Colin Hay and Genevieve LeBaron, as well as numerous and highly impressive members of SPERI including Andrew Baker, Matt Bishop, Graham Harrison, Andy Hindmoor, Scott Lavery, Allister McGregor, Owen Parker, Nicola Phillips, Liam Stanley and Burak Tansel, I have learned a great deal, some of which is contained in this book. I am also most grateful to a number of my IR colleagues for the many conversations, advice and kind support they have provided me, including Ross Bellaby, Ruth Blakeley, Ben Docherty, Adrian Gallagher, Jonna Nyman, Simon Rushton, Lisa Stampnitzky, Joanna Tidy, Joe Turner, Peter Verovšek and, above all, Jonathan Joseph, Burak Tansel and Helen Turton.

Regarding the last five years of intensive research and writing, I want to thank a number of people who provided excellent advice on particular parts of the manuscript: Audrey Alejandro, Genevieve LeBaron, Michelle LeBaron, Burak Tansel, Bryony Vince and Peer Vries. Following on from the tragic passing of Lily (L. H. M.) Ling, Bryony has joined me as co-editor in the Rowman & Littlefield International Book series, 'Global Dialogues: Non-Eurocentric Visions of the Global'. Bryony is following in Lily's giant footsteps … so no pressure then! I also feel that this book is in keeping with the core theme of the series that Lily and I set up along with the excellent help provided by Anna Reeve and, more recently, by Dhara Snowden at R&LI. Warm thanks also go to David Blaney and Kaveh Yazdani who read significant chunks of the manuscript and provided timely and invaluable feedback.

Special thanks go to my brilliant PhD student, Zhang Shizhi, with whom I have had the wonderful pleasure of engaging in our shared, quirky interest in China's economic history. I've deeply enjoyed our utterly fascinating and absorbing conversations on the seemingly endless historical ins and outs of China's foreign trade and cotton textile industry in the pre-1911 era. Moreover, his unflinching support and extraordinarily generous help in translating many Chinese books and archival documents that I have relied upon is equally deeply appreciated. Warm thanks also go to Benjamin de Carvalho and Halvard Leira given that parts of the research for this book have been made possible through support from the 'Privateers and the Sea (EMPRISE)' Project at the Norwegian Institute of International Affairs (NUPI), funded by the Research Council of Norway through Grant Number 262657.

Above all, I am enormously grateful to four kind souls – three of whom are Alex Anievas, Eric Helleiner and Andrew Linklater. Not only did they most generously give up their time to read the entirety of the manuscript but, in aggregate, their input has served to improve the book immeasurably and, mercifully, saved me from making various howlers. The fourth kind soul is Lily (L. H. M.) Ling, from whom I have learned so many things postcolonial – so much more than she had the personal capacity of ever realising let alone acknowledging. Her departure is as much a loss for IR as it is personally, professionally and intellectually for me. I believe that her irrepressible spirit weaves its way across the pages of this book, even if she might still have taken issue with some of what I argue here … in her own inimitable way, of course! Her soul has whispered gently in my ear throughout the writing of this book, though neither she nor any of the other people mentioned here should be held responsible for the final product.

Deep thanks go to David Farrow, above all for his friendship but also for his heroic computer skills and efforts, which quite literally saved the book manuscript when my old computer died on me late in the day. Not many things shake my current Head of Department (HoD), Andy Hindmoor, though this one might well have, had it not been for David's technological wizardry! And special thanks go to Andy for helping me navigate (and navigating me) through the rapids of gaining the time to get this book over the finishing line, and whose patience and tenacity in the whole process is as much appreciated as it was truly impressive. The same thanks go to our previous, equally as brilliant, HoD, Nicola Phillips, for the exact same reason. In this vein too, I also want to acknowledge my debt to John Haslam in the Edinburgh Building at Cambridge University Press who has remained especially patient and helpful throughout, for which I am no less truly grateful. Special thanks also go to the two anonymous readers for their invaluable suggestions on how to improve the manuscript. Thanks too go to Toby Ginsberg and Robert Judkins at CUP as well as to Tim Hyde at Sunrise Setting for overseeing the index. And, in this production context, I want to express my deepest thanks to Teena Lawrence for her heroic efforts and for going way beyond the call of duty in steering this book through to publication, for which I am humbly grateful.

Last, but not least, my most heartfelt thanks go to my family for their support – Evangeline, Gabby, Michael, Olivia and, above all, my partner Celia – for their, albeit increasingly but quite understandably fraying, patience in the face of my long absences, given the seemingly endless trials and tribulations in bringing this book to completion. I promise to make it up to you … honestly!

1 Mapping a *New* Global Political Economy
Taking Stock for the Journey Ahead

Introduction

For most scholars, the idea that globalisation is essentially 'Westernisation' and that the global economy has been 'made by the West' is so axiomatic that it requires little or no reflexive interrogation. Indeed, it likely constitutes one of the most unifying themes, and surely comes close to being a cardinal or universal axiom, across the Social Sciences. All scholars seem to be in agreement, from the neoliberal pole on the right to the neo-Marxist and even the postcolonial-Marxist on the left. For many neoliberals, globalisation and the global economy represent the 'glorious and inevitable triumph of the magnificent West',[1] while for neo-Marxists, various postcolonialists and postcolonial Marxists, they constitute but the 'tragic and inevitable triumph of the malevolent West'.[2] Moreover, both poles echo those pre-1945 scientific racist thinkers, including Theodore Roosevelt, Henry Cabot Lodge, Karl Pearson, Woodrow Wilson, Benjamin Kidd and Josiah Strong to name but a few, who (re)present globalisation as but the 'inevitable triumph of the supremacist West'.[3] Indeed, both poles subscribe to the idea of globalisation as constituting, to quote the title of Theodore von Laue's book, 'The World Revolution of Westernization'.[4] Accordingly, in highlighting Western supremacism, they produce variations on a West-side story of the global economy.

It is true that not all Eurocentric scholars conflate globalisation with the universalisation of the West, with some, such as Samuel Huntington and William Lind, in effect rehabilitating the scientific racist cultural realism of Lothrop Stoddard and Charles Henry Pearson by viewing

---

[1] Most notably, Fukuyama (1992), Friedman (1999) and Wolf (2005).
[2] For example, Wallerstein (1974, 1980, 1984, 1989), Chase-Dunn (1989), Arrighi (1994), Gill (1995), Cox (1996), Robinson (2004), Saurin (2006), Dirlik (2007), Ashman (2010), Davidson (2009) and Krishna (2009).
[3] See Hobson (2012) and Vitalis (2015).
[4] von Laue (1987).

globalisation as issuing a rising and rampaging 'barbaric Asian threat' to Western civilisation. But the key to their *shared* Western-centrism, given that neither Huntington nor Lind subscribe to scientific racism, lies in their prime concern to defend the 'purity' of Western civilisation against the non-Western barbaric threat, especially that which they associate with China and Islam.[5]

It is often said that since the buzzword of 'globalisation' exploded onto the social science research agenda some three decades ago, its *intellectual* time has now passed in that there is nothing fresh left to say about it, such that all we can do now is to refine it or, at best, to fill in various missing details. That is, its Western origins, contours and functions are settled such that in this respect, at least, it is considered to be a *finished* project. But this book's core claim is that analyses of globalisation and the global economy settled merely on a Eurocentric foundation, leading me to conclude that the study of this twin phenomenon is an entirely *unfinished* project. Thus, my task in this book is to begin the analysis afresh by re-tracking it onto an alternative non-Eurocentric path.[6]

This book navigates the *origins* of the global economy – or more specifically, the two global economies that I identify in this book – by taking us on a journey that explores a complex series of *multicultural* passages that propel us beyond the exclusive Western-centric frontier. Here, however, it is important that I iron out any potential confusion that the word 'multicultural' plays in the title of this book. First, this is not to be conflated with an approach that focuses only on the *Eastern* origins of the global economy because I include Western alongside non-Western contributions. Second, some critics of multiculturalism view it as a thinly racialised discourse because it promotes separate and distinct ethnic communities within nation-states in which non-white groups live in ghettos on the Other side of an invisible line of racialised cultural apartheid.[7] Rather than a racial–cultural segregationism, in which the dominant culture begrudgingly 'tolerates' the existence of the Other, this book examines how they integrate and mutually entwine, not in some rosy cosmopolitan way, but through 'competitive cooperation' (on which more below). Thus, a core theme of this book, as I explain more fully in the penultimate section of this chapter, is to get at the key point that Edward Said originally made in the 2003 preface to his seminal

---

[5] See Hobson (2012: 142–9, 279–84).
[6] See also the important non-Eurocentric historical studies of *globalisation*: Flynn and Giráldez (1995a, 1995b, 2004, 2006), Bentley (1996), Hopkins (2002), Bayly (2002), Marks (2002), Gills and Thompson (2006) and Beaujard (2019).
[7] For example, Malik (1996).

book, *Orientalism*: '[r]ather than the manufactured clash of civilizations [East *versus* West], we need to concentrate on the slow working together of [non-Western *and* Western] cultures that overlap, borrow from each other, and live together'.[8] In the process, this book produces, to borrow the phrase of Jeremy Prestholdt, 'an inclusive genealogy of globalization' and the global economy.[9]

My primary complaint with the vast majority of the literature on globalisation and the global economy is *not* the assumption that the West has been given a place of importance, but that it has been reified into a fetish such that the myriad non-Western contributions have been air-brushed out of our received picture, as is found most acutely within the discipline of International Political Economy (IPE). To counter this, to borrow the felicitous phrase from Nicola Phillips,[10] we need to properly '*globalize* the study of globalization' and the global economy by shifting our gaze away from the pure Western-centric or 'North-West passage' conception towards one that brings into focus the many non-Western passages that link together Africa, the Americas, India, West and Southeast Asia, China and East Asia as well as Britain and Europe. This is urgently required, I believe, because prevailing (Eurocentric) approaches produce an exclusivist or monological vision of globalisation as but a Western provincialism masquerading as the universal.

This book's voyage of rediscovery entails replacing Eurocentric Global Political Economy (GPE) and IPE with what I shall call a non-Eurocentric *New* Global Political Economy (NGPE). And this, in turn, necessarily propels us across a series of disciplinary frontiers. For while this book is aimed primarily at the disciplines of IPE, Historical Sociology and the historical sociology of International Relations (IR), as well as various cognate disciplines such as Economic Geography, Development Studies and Global Economic History/Global History, it is only through a trans-disciplinary approach that we can move beyond the Eurocentric conception of global economy and globalisation.

But why do I call it 'new' GPE rather than postcolonial political economy (PPE)? I choose this as a play on those terms that were originally pioneered in the 1990s by my departmental colleagues, Anthony Payne and Andrew Gamble on the one hand, and Craig Murphy and Roger Tooze on the other. And, at the risk of embarrassing the 'founding fathers' of these two inter-related approaches, I maintain that they are 'giants' of IPE. The former pair called for a 'New Political Economy'

---

[8]   Said (1978/2003: xxii).
[9]   Prestholdt (2008).
[10] Phillips (2005: chs. 1–2).

(NPE), after which the well-known journal was named,[11] while the latter pair called for a 'New International Political Economy' (NIPE).[12] These approaches share in common a return to the big-picture, historically–sociologically informed focus of classical political economy, especially, though not exclusively, that of the critical theory of Karl Marx. And, certainly, both approaches are open to the critique of Eurocentrism. Still, although my own conception shares a great deal in common with these approaches, we cannot get around the point that classical political economy was ultimately Eurocentric or Western-centric;[13] note that I define 'Western-centrism' later. Nevertheless, this is a paradox rather than a contradiction in my logic. For it is precisely the wide framework that classical political economy represents that allows me to ask critical questions of modern IPE as much as it furnishes me with the mega-canvas that this book works on. Moreover, rather than representing my approach as instigating a radical break with NPE and NIPE, I view my contribution as one that stands on their shoulders.

But why not simply call my approach 'Global Political Economy (GPE)'? This term, which has been circulating for a good while now, is most closely aligned with Marxist IPE that seeks to move away from statist neorealism towards an analysis of capitalist globalisation. In this respect, it clearly enters the terrain of this book. But I find that this approach also suffers from Eurocentrism or 'Eurofetishism' (to be defined later), with the deepest paradox of GPE being that it is an insufficiently 'global' approach, given that its focus is essentially a Western provincialism that masquerades as the global. Thus, I opt for the label of '*New* GPE' simply because its resolute focus on non-Eurocentrism marks it out as distinctive to the present conception of GPE. Above all, though, the term 'global' within NGPE does not so much connote an approach that focuses on globalisation and the global economy, for GPE already does that. Rather, what distinguishes my approach's conception of the global is its focus on the multiple Western *and* non-Western sources of the global economy.

The chapter is divided into five sections which, in aggregate, map out the contours and underpinnings of NGPE. Certainly, this chapter is longer than ideally I would have liked, but there is much theoretical and conceptual brush-clearing that needs to be undertaken before we can begin our journey. I begin by laying out the first of NGPE's twin corefeatures – the need to develop a big-picture (non-Eurocentric)

---

[11] Gamble (1995), Gamble *et al.* (1996) and Payne (2006).
[12] Murphy and Tooze (1991); cf. Hay and Marsh (1999).
[13] Hobson (2012, 2013a).

'global historical sociological' framework that focuses on the deep-historical *origins* of the two global economies that I identify in this book. The second section explores the foundations of a specific brand of Eurocentrism – what I call 'Eurocentrism I' – within which prevailing orthodox conceptions of globalisation and the global economy are embedded. The third section then explores what I call 'Eurocentrism II' and its non-Eurocentric antidote that I call critical 'Eurofetishism', which is a common approach that underpins the analyses of many critical and postcolonial IPE and GPE scholars. The fourth section presents the second core property of NGPE: specifically, my non-Eurocentric antidote to both these modes of Western-centrism, while also presenting a sympathetic critique of the non-Eurocentric California School (CS) of global economic history. And in the fifth and final short sections, I lay out my definitions of the two global economies – historical capitalism (c. 1500–c. 1850) and modern capitalism (c. 1850–2020).

NGPE (I): Bringing 'Big-Picture' (Non-Eurocentric) Global Historical Sociology Back into IPE

In 2013, the journal *Review of International Political Economy* (*RIPE*) most generously published a two-part article of mine. The first part revealed the Eurocentric foundations of classical liberal and neoliberal IPE theory as well as Listian and modern neorealist IPE theory – to which I added classical and modern neo-Marxism in my book *The Eurocentric Conception of World Politics*.[14] My task in this present book is to advance a non-Eurocentric conception of IPE by revealing the multicultural origins of the global economy. Although there are racial undertones that exist within Eurocentrism and need to be confronted, nevertheless I believe that Eurocentrism will likely remain hegemonic until we find a more persuasive alternative empirical account of the world – even, or particularly, in the face of the in-built biases among Western (and all-too-often non-Western) populations towards Eurocentrism and what I call critical 'Eurofetishism'. Which is why this book's critique of Western-centrism takes the form of a fully fledged non-Eurocentric historical–sociological *empirical account* of the rise of the global economy and of modern capitalism. But why 'historical–sociological'?

IPE's narrow focus on the here and now – or IPE's great retreat into the present – verges on a 'presentist pathology'. This plays out in the analyses of the post-1945 global economy that is usually presented as

---

[14] Hobson (2012, 2013a).

temporally *sui generis* such that the pre-1945 world constitutes in effect 'ancient history' – or what amounts to a '1945-as-year-zero' conception of globalisation and the global economy. But sequestering the global economy from its deep-historical origins means that such analyses often fall into the trap of what the rightly celebrated Gramscian-Marxist IPE/ IR scholar, Robert Cox, calls 'problem-solving theory'.[15] In this vein, the task of scholars is to accept the existence of the 'Western' capitalist global economy and fine tune it normatively so that it can run either more smoothly (as in neoliberalism) or more fairly (as in many left-wing critiques, bar Trotskyists and Leninists of course). As Cox originally argued, 'critical theory' is vital if we are to *de-naturalise* capitalism and the global economy. And this requires rethinking the historical *origins* of these processes in order to show that they were neither the abstract realisation of some fictitious notion of human nature – as Cox argues – nor were they the product of factors that were generated solely within Britain, given that they were also partially created by social forces and pressures/opportunities that emanated from the non-Western world, as I argue in this book. All in all, thinking critically by revealing the multicultural origins of the global economy serves to unsettle the prevailing 'commonsense' views that it was made by the West on the one hand and that Western global dominance is natural and inevitable, if not eternal, on the other.

Given that these empirical topics are, of course, amenable only to very large-scale, macro-historical sociological analysis, so this feeds directly into the argument that is advanced by Benjamin Cohen in his seminal book, *International Political Economy: An Intellectual History*. There he laments the fact that 'US-school' IPE – specifically in the guise of the leading neoclassical liberal paradigm known as 'Open Economy Politics' (OEP) – has engineered a massive contraction of the intellectual borders of American IPE into an extremely narrow empirical and economically reductive research agenda.[16] Indeed, it is particularly telling that Robert Keohane, who is viewed as the standard bearer of methodologically narrow rationalism by constructivists and poststructuralists, complains that OEP is far too rationalist, narrow and reductive![17]

This is why Cohen calls specifically for a 'bridge-building' exercise in which US-school IPE scholars should reach out to, and join hands with, their 'British-school' IPE cousins on the basis that the latter advances a much broader, big-picture approach to that of the far

[15] Cox (1996).
[16] Cohen (2008: 41–3, 82–3).
[17] Keohane (2009: 38).

more parsimonious and more methodologically rigorous approach of the former.[18] But, despite its promise to develop a broad-based approach that is interpretive, more social in focus and ultimately more historical–sociological, lamentably Brit-school scholarship has become increasingly more narrow in focus and highly presentist in orientation, particularly in its analysis of the global economy. For one of the points that I problematise is the ahistorical assumption held by British- and American-school scholars that the post-1945/79 era is both entirely new and temporally *sui generis*.

To counter the ever-contracting temporal and analytical borders of US-school IPE – to which I would add those of the British School – Cohen calls for a *return* to the 'big-picture IPE' that was in vogue in the 1970s and 1980s during first-wave American- and Brit-School-IPE.[19] For him the 'really big question' focuses on *systemic transformation*, by which he means 'globalisation'.[20] This focus is, of course, also central to the present book. But it seems to me that Cohen's 'really big question' can only be answered sufficiently by asking an 'even bigger question', which requires us to explain the origins of modern capitalism given that the present global economy rests on a modern capitalist base. Indeed, as Larry Summers puts it, '[i]n many respects the history of capitalism is the history most relevant to our times'.[21] *Inter alia*, this requires us to return to the whole discussion of the transition from feudalism to capitalism that began with the famous Dobb/Sweezy debate in the 1950s and 1960s before we move forward through various historical sociological debates up to the present.[22] And to my perplexed IPE reader who wonders why all this needs to be undertaken, on the assumption that the issue has surely been settled by historical sociologists, it turns out that their explanations settled merely on a Eurocentric foundation (as I explain in the next section). Accordingly, I believe that we need to go back to the drawing board and begin our analysis again from scratch.

Thus, while I agree entirely with Cohen's prescription for a big-picture, historical–sociological approach, nevertheless, I disagree that Brit-school IPE in its present incarnation holds the candle for such a vision.

---

[18] Cohen (2008: ch. 7).
[19] Most notably, Wallerstein (1974, 1980, 1989), Cox (1987), Chase-Dunn (1989) and Gilpin (1981).
[20] Cohen (2008: ch. 3).
[21] Larry Summers cited in Inikori (2020: 251, n. 1).
[22] See Sweezy and Dobb (1950), Dobb (1959), Wallerstein (1974) and Brenner (1977, 1982). For key neo-Weberian-inspired analyses, see Giddens (1985), Mann (1986), Tilly (1990), Landes (1998), Ferguson (2011), Duchesne (2012) and Vries (2013, 2015).

For ultimately what bridges the US and British schools, in addition to their ever-narrowing analytical and temporal visions, is a *Eurocentric* understanding of the global economy.[23] In this sense, then, we do not need to build bridges between the US and Brit schools because they are already connected by an ahistorical Eurocentric tunnel that runs deep beneath the floor of the Atlantic Ocean. And here I must confess to sharing in Heloise Weber's 'astonishment' concerning the debate surrounding Cohen's book, which was conducted in the prominent journals of *RIPE* and *NPE* by equally prominent IPE scholars, given its failure to engage in a sustained critical analysis of the Eurocentrism of IPE.[24] This is precisely why I wrote my two-part *RIPE* article in the first place. And, while the 'postcolonial turn' has occurred in various cognate disciplines – including International Relations,[25] as well as Historical Sociology, Development Studies and Economic Geography,[26] IPE in contrast has been a clear laggard and has yet to reach this critical stage given that only a minority of scholars has been mining this vein.[27] In this respect, my vision of big-picture, non-Eurocentric IPE dovetails with much of Heloise Weber's.[28]

Still, this is not to say that IPE's current preference to drill down ever deeper into narrow research silos is unimportant, for certainly this enables the excavation of more specialised knowledge. And I remain deeply impressed by some of the most detailed and finely grained

---

[23] Hobson (2013a, 2013b).

[24] Weber (2015). Nevertheless, the pieces by Craig Murphy (2009), Anna Leander (2009) and Nicola Phillips (2009) certainly went some way to raising this issue.

[25] Instead of citing the many relevant references that are far too numerous to include here, I shall instead point my reader to some of the key edited volumes: Chowdhry and Nair (2004), Long and Schmidt (2005), Gruffydd-Jones (2006), Kanth (2009), Shilliam (2011), Tickner and Blaney (2012), Katzenstein (2012a), Seth (2013), Suzuki, Zhang and Quirk (2014), Anievas, Manchanda and Shilliam (2015), Bilgin and Ling (2017), Epstein (2017), Zarakol (2017), Sajed and Persaud (2018), Adelman (2019) and Bell (2019); cf. Dunne and Reus-Smit (2017) and Go and Lawson (2017).

[26] A smattering of this literature includes: Meek (1976), Amin (1989), Wallerstein (1997), Pieterse (1990, 2006, 2020), Munck and O'Hearn (1999), Power (2003), Slater (2004), Kapoor (2008), McCarthy (2009), Bhambra (2007, 2014), McEwan (2009), and Go (2011, 2016).

[27] Frank and Gills (1996), Persaud (2001), O'Brien and Williams (2004: chs. 2–3), Hobson (2004, 2012, 2013a, 2013b), Bowden and Seabrooke (2006), Pasha (2006), Hobson and Seabrooke (2007), Harrison (2013), Krishna (2009), Blaney and Inayatullah (2010, 2021), LeBaron (2012), Halperin (2013), Halperin and Palan (2015), Anievas and Nişancioğlu (2015), Tansel (2015a, 2015b), Helleiner (2014, 2015, 2018, 2021), Weber (2015), Selwyn (2015), Stuenkel (2016), Helleiner and Rosales (2017), Singh (2017), Shilliam (2018), Mantz (2019) and Zhang (2020); cf. Phillips (2005).

[28] Weber (2015).

analyses of IPE, far too numerous to reference here. But my point is simply that when these silos are being drilled down ever deeper into Eurocentric ground, ultimately this serves to provide us with yet more detailed Eurocentric knowledge. And, of course, such drilling is inherently precarious given the unstable nature of the meta-narratival ground that it plumbs.

Cohen's preferred macro-focus – or what is synonymous with what the historical sociologist, Charles Tilly, famously referred to as 'big structures, large processes and huge comparisons' – feeds naturally into the remit of historical sociology/global history and the historical sociology of IPE/IR.[29] Here, I deploy, to borrow the term that has been developed by the leading scholars, Julian Go and George Lawson, a '*global* historical sociological' account, in order to build up a big global picture so that we can transcend the familiar Eurocentric narrative. Note that their definition of global historical sociology refers to the study of

two interrelated dynamics: first, the transnational and global dynamics that enable the emergence, reproduction, and breakdown of social orders whether these orders are situated at the subnational, national, or *global* scales; and second, the historical emergence, reproduction, and breakdown of transnational and *global* social forms.[30]

It is important to understand that my pursuit of the historical–sociological global big-picture does not produce a *history* of the global economy in the traditional sense of the term. For the role of conceptual analysis that I undertake here does not fit within the remit of traditional history. Indeed, my central task of critiquing Eurocentric world history and countering it with a non-Eurocentric empirical account would be viewed by traditional historians as an exercise in mere 'polemics'. Moreover, traditional historians' core *modus operandi* is to particularise the past by dissecting it into highly detailed micro-scale snapshots that are taken even deeper into the historical–empirical ground through archival research. Still, none of what follows is intended to denigrate their 'deep-drilling research exercises', not least because I rely on a wealth of their many excellent findings throughout this book. And I also draw on many inspirational

---

[29] Tilly (1984).
[30] Go and Lawson (2017: 2), my emphases. Still, my big-picture approach falls short of the kind of 'mega history' that is produced by the likes of David Christian (2004) and others (Zinkina *et al.* 2019), and nor can I match the kind of 'big history' that is found in the magisterial works of Michael Mann (1986) and Andrew Linklater (2016). Serendipitously, my argument concerning the point that the FGE emerged around 1500 gets me off that particular hook and enables me to focus on the global *longue durée* of some 400–500 years.

global–historical works from which I have learned so much, to name but a few: Pedro Machado, David Northrup, Prasannan Parthasarathi, Kenneth Pomeranz, Jeremy Prestholdt, Rajat Kanta Ray, Giorgio Riello, David Washbrook, Kaveh Yazdani and Zhao Gang.[31]

My opting for a global historical sociological approach has advantages and disadvantages vis-à-vis traditional history, and I make no claim for the inherent superiority of my choice – merely to say that such an approach is best placed to reveal the extensive *horizontal linkages*, whether they be cooperative or competitive or both, which bind the many peoples of the world together within the global *longue durée*.[32] And clearly, micro-scale analysis cannot reveal the origins and reproduction of the two global economies. In turn, this reveals a further key point of differentiation between NGPE and PPE. For postcolonialism's postmodern variant adopts a resolute focus on the micro-level, given its disdain for 'grand narratives'.

Finally, it might be objected that some of my arguments reiterate those that have long been known by specialist historians, while equally some of those historians whom I target for their Eurocentrism are now outdated. But my ultimate target is not historians but those many political scientists, IR and most especially IPE and historical–sociological scholars as well as those found in a range of complementary social science disciplines, who continue to default to the hegemonic Eurocentric narrative of globalisation and the global economy (which I describe in the next section). Thus, my critical discussion of some outdated Eurocentric (a)historians at various places serves merely as a proxy to challenge the Eurocentric historical assumptions that are held by so many IPE, IR and historical–sociological scholars more generally.

The key task ahead is to ascertain the core components of Eurocentrism. And, as we shall see, the next two sections take us not on a journey across a serene and smooth lake, but one that requires us to hold on tight as we navigate through a complex series of intellectually challenging rapids.

Mapping 'Eurocentrism I'

Even four decades on since the publication of Edward Said's seminal book, *Orientalism*,[33] I am struck by the fact that there remains a great deal of confusion surrounding, if not more often sheer ignorance

---

[31] Machado (2014), Northrup (2009), Parthasarathi (2011), Pomeranz (2000), Prestholdt (2008), Riello (2013), Washbrook (1988, 1990, 2007, 2020), Yazdani (2017), Zhao (2013), and Ray (1995).

[32] Cf. Halperin (2013).

[33] Said (1978/2003).

about, the concept of Eurocentrism, or what Said calls Orientalism, especially in IPE. For example, the common assumption that an analysis is Eurocentric if it focuses *only* on the West misses the point that it is perfectly possible to write a Eurocentric book that focuses only on Africa or Asia, given that it is the categories of analysis that matter, not the geographical focus of enquiry. Because I discern two differing definitions of, and antidotes to, Eurocentrism so I shall sketch out the four key moves or categories of 'Eurocentrism I' before considering 'Eurocentrism II' in the following section.

The First Two Moves of Eurocentrism I: Constructing the New Jim Crow Laws of the Global Economy

I define 'Eurocentrism I' as a discourse/metanarrative that reifies Western agency in the global economy and demotes the non-West to a passive entity that is only ever acted upon and never acts as an agent while also silencing the dark side of Western imperialism.[34] To understand this, I shall go through the four key moves that Eurocentrism I performs – a discourse/metanarrative that emerged after about 1750 – the first of which entails the forcing or bludgeoning of the world in all of its complexity into a facile binary conception, wherein the East and West are viewed as entirely separate and self-constituting entities. In particular, this constructed division between the East and West is marked by an imaginary 'civilisational frontier' or line of 'civilisational apartheid' that is reflected in Rudyard Kipling's well-known proclamation, 'Oh East is East and West is West and ne'er the twain shall meet'.

The second move entails an elevation of the West to the superior zone of 'civilisation' on the basis that it has *exceptional, rational* institutions and culture. Conversely, the East is demoted to the inferior zones or ghettos of either 'barbarism' (Asiatic Oriental despotisms found in China, India and the Middle East) or 'savagery' (anarchic/stateless societies found in Africa, the Americas, Australasia and Polynesia). Constructed as constituting the West's opposite Other, these societies are discounted on the basis of their *irrational* institutions and cultures. That is, the 'civilised West' is defined through a series of 'rational presences', the barbaric and savage East through 'rational absences'. Moreover, Eurocentrism in effect projects a 'passage to India syndrome' (which

---

[34] Of the many scholars who subscribe to this definition, see, for example, Blaut (1993), Goody (1996), Frank (1998), Ling (2002, 2014), Bhambra (2007: 5), Agathangelou and Ling (2009), Suzuki et al. (2014), Tansel (2015a), Anievas and Nişancıoğlu (2015), Go (2016), Acharya (2018), and Alejandro (2019).

constitutes a core theme of E. M. Forster's famous novel *A Passage to India*), in which the East is constructed as exotic, irrational but above all strange and confusing on the grounds that it deviates from the rational and normal, if not dour but entirely predictable and stable, West. All in all, these two key moves entail a 'segregation' of the East and West that is analogous to the Jim Crow laws, with the inferior Eastern peoples and societies being separated out and kept apart from the pristine West in analytical/ontological ghettos.

But for all this, my critic would reply by arguing that all I have done here is relate the ideas that dominated much of Western thinking and scholarship *before* 1945. And that, as such, they are merely intriguing artefacts that are best placed in the historiographical museum of Western international thought, to be visited from time to time so that Westerners can marvel at just how far they have come since those bizarre and dark days of their lamentable, deep past. For, it is commonly believed that after 1945, the Social Sciences moved away from explicit/manifest Eurocentrism and scientific racism in the light of the West's acknowledged revulsion of the racist horror of the (Jewish) Holocaust as well as the shame of Western racism and empire. The ensuing 'colonial racist guilt syndrome' is thought to have terminated the *dark old world* and created a *bright new world* in which the post-1945 Academy has come to embrace a tolerant cultural pluralism and positivistic posture, through which the pernicious values of racism and empire have been finally and mercifully exorcised.

The reality, however, has seen the creation of a *brave new world* in which scientific racism and manifest (or explicit) Eurocentrism died out in the halls of the Academy, only to be substituted by 'subliminal' Eurocentrism that appears on first blush to be more socially acceptable.[35] For on a closer inspection, it turns out that although Western academics came to distance themselves from the old scientific racist and *manifest* or explicit Eurocentric tropes of white supremacism, civilisation, barbarism, savagery and imperialism, they ended up reaffirming them in new and sanitised guises. Thus, in *subliminal* Eurocentrism, all references to these aforementioned tropes disappear from view but re-appear in terms that dare not speak their name. So 'white supremacism' was replaced by 'Western supremacism', 'civilisation versus barbarism/savagery' was replaced by 'tradition versus modernity' or 'core versus periphery', while Anglo-Saxon 'imperialism' morphed into *benign* 'hegemony', 'IFI intervention' and 'humanitarian interventionism'. And, since 1989 in particular, 'barbaric Oriental despotisms' morphed into the tropes of

---

[35] Hobson (2012: 185–6, 319–24).

'rogue states' and the 'axis of evil' on the basis that they *would* not reciprocate according to the (civilised) norms of international law and (Western-based) 'international society', while 'savage anarchies' morphed into 'failed states' on the basis that they *could* not reciprocate. In sum, all that has really changed since 1945 is that the old Jim Crow laws morphed into the '*New* Jim Crow laws' of modern academic analyses of the global economy.

The Third Key Move of Eurocentrism I: Constructing the Big Bang Theory of Capitalism and the Global Economy

The third key move performed by Eurocentrism I constructs the Big Bang theory (BBT) of development and globalisation, or what IR scholars refer to as 'the Expansion of the West' narrative.[36] This is typified by the famous assertion made by Marx and Engels in *The Communist Manifesto* that '[t]he [Western] bourgeoisie, by the rapid improvement of all instruments of production, by the immensely facilitated means of communication, draws all, even the most barbarian, nations into civilization ... In one word, it creates a world after its own image'.[37] And, as Hedley Bull and Adam Watson announced in the opening sentence of their prominent edited volume, *The Expansion of International Society*: '[t]he purpose of this book is to explore the expansion of international society of European states across the rest of the globe, and its transformation from a society fashioned in Europe and dominated by Europeans into the global international society of today'.[38] Because the BBT and the 'Expansion of the West' trope are essentially identical two-stage narratives, in what follows I shall take each step in turn.

The First Stage of the Eurocentric BBT: The 'Logic of Immanence' In the first stage, capitalist (and international political) modernity explodes spontaneously into existence in the West as a result of its exceptional, rational institutions. This rests on the Eurocentric 'logic of immanence', for having identified Europe as primed for development, this conception was then extrapolated back in time to (re)present Ancient Greece as the birthplace of what much later would be called modern 'Europe'. Significantly, as Samir Amin and Martin Bernal rightly point out, a considerable amount of intellectual acrobatics had to be performed in order to (re)present Ancient Greece as 'European', given

---

[36] Bull and Watson (1984a).
[37] Marx and Engels (1848/1977: 84).
[38] Bull and Watson (1984b: 1).

that it had been part of the Hellenistic Orient and that Ancient Greeks recognised this at the time.[39] And from there Western academics and thinkers traced the long developmental path forward to modernity as it unfolded solely within Europe. Overall, in the process, Western political economists and philosophers – from Smith through Malthus to Comte, Spencer and Rostow and from Hegel through Mill to Marx and Brenner – constructed *stadial* models of development in which the rise of modernity unfolded through discrete stages over a very long period in a unilinear and teleological fashion within Europe. In this imaginary, then, the breakthrough to industrial capitalism is deemed to be *immanent* from the historical outset – i.e., Ancient Greece – because at no point did the non-Western world help or influence this *auto-generative* European process.

By analogy, in this imaginary, the European developmental train, or what James Blaut originally called the 'Orientalist Express',[40] having pulled out of the station of Ancient Greece, shunts slowly through Ancient Rome and thence 'European' feudalism before steaming forward gathering pace all the while, wending its way through a series of 'European' wayside halts comprising the Italian financial and commercial revolutions (c. 1000) as well as the Renaissance (c. 1450), before tracking northwestwards up through the Reformation (1517), Dutch hegemony and thence the Enlightenment (eighteenth century), pulling finally into the terminus of modern British and thence European industrial capitalism – though for Marxists, of course, this constitutes the penultimate station before the train pulls into the terminus of socialism, whereupon the passengers disembark to enjoy the communist good life. All in all, arriving at the terminus of modernity is (re)presented as but a historical *fait accompli* that is celebrated as a *European* rite of passage – that it was pre-ordained or foretold. As such, this is a linear journey on an exclusive tour of Europe, where passengers alight only to see the most important sights. At no point do the passengers seek to alight in non-Western space. For given its irrational institutions and culture that ensure a permanently unproductive wasteland, the passengers take heed of the conductor's warning: 'nothing to see there'. And because this linear teleological framework elides the manifold forms of non-Western contributions to Europe's breakthrough into capitalist modernity, so we are treated to a story not of the Rise, but of the *Ruse* of the West.[41]

---

[39] Bernal (1991) and Amin (1989: 90–4).

[40] Blaut (1993).

[41] With the exception of a small minority, the overwhelming majority of scholars produce Eurocentric accounts of the rise of capitalism, the list of which is far too large to reference here. Still, a representative sample of such names is referenced in the relevant parts of this book.

The Second Stage of the Eurocentric BBT: The Expansion of the West Having pioneered capitalist modernity in the first stage, the second stage of the BBT cuts in immediately, wherein the modern exceptional 'Promethean' West, to borrow the phrase of David Landes,[42] expands outwards to remake the Earthly universe in its own image so as to cure the ailment of 'Eastern deviancy' for the benefit of *all* peoples. Interestingly, this approach dovetails largely with that of Hedley Bull and Adam Watson's IR account of the second stage of the 'expansion of the West' narrative, though it should be noted that for them the rise of Europe and its expansion across the globe occurred simultaneously.[43] But for this chronological discrepancy, the approaches remain identical. This expansionist process takes the initial guise of formal empire in the Americas and trading-post empires in Afro-Asia after 1492, progressing on to formal imperialism and the full incorporation of the latter during the nineteenth century, which was accompanied by proto-globalisation culminating in full or 'thick' globalisation after 1945 as the West expanded to complete the cultural conversion of the Rest.[44] All of which can be captured in a variation on the Orientalist Express metaphor – that of the Western 'global relay race' idiom – in which the baton of global power is passed from one Western runner to the next, beginning with the Iberians who were followed by the Dutch, the French and the English before culminating with the American anchor man who ran the final leg to cross the finishing line in 1945 in record time. Such a position is standard fare among liberal, Weberian, neorealist and Marxist scholars.[45]

The essential task performed by the 'proto-global' Western runners in the period between 1492 and 1945 was, in effect, to prepare the world for Western global-universalism by smashing down the obstructive walls or barriers that surrounded the barbaric/savage and backward, irrational East. This proto-globalisation is, in effect, equivalent to *primitive global accumulation* – to adapt Marx's notion of the primitive accumulation of capital. And all along, the passive Eastern spectators have been festooned around the Western-made global running track, watching on either in horror (according to neo-Marxism and many postcolonial-writers) or cheering on and applauding the superior Western runners (according to liberalism). All of which culminates in the conclusion

---

[42] Landes (1969).
[43] Bull and Watson (1984a, 1984b).
[44] On this, see Hobson (2012: ch. 9).
[45] For example, Cox (1987), Arrighi (1994), Wallerstein (1974, 1984), Gilpin (1981) and Kindleberger (1996).

that both developmental and global agencies are monopolised initially by Europe and later the United States, with non-Western agency all but disappearing from view, lost in the dark shadows that are cast by the blinding light that is emitted from the pioneering, hyper-agential actions of the imperial/neo-imperial West. In aggregate, the BBT rests on the Eurocentric trope of what Dipesh Chakrabarty calls 'first the West and then elsewhere'[46] or 'first the West then the global Rest'. In sum, it is within the *New* Jim Crow laws of the Eurocentric BBT that contemporary academic understandings of the global economy and globalisation-as-the-expansion of the West are framed.

Thus, to return to my earlier metaphor, in standard narratives of globalisation and the global economy, we receive a West-side story of progressive global history in which the West occupies the lead character, given that it has the (exceptional) means to break through into modern capitalism and the necessary world-agency to spread this form of production around the world. Conversely, Eastern societies are, in effect, portrayed as mere extras, being side-lined by the Western lead actor and being only ever acted upon by the West, never performing agency in their own right and remaining confined to the wings of 'progressive history'. Accordingly, to deploy Chakrabarty's felicitous phrase, in the Eurocentric imaginary, the non-Western peoples are confined to 'the waiting room of history',[47] where they sit patiently in the hope of being emancipated or rescued from their self-imposed plight by the merciful global civilising mission of their dashing Western saviour – a trope that feeds directly into the fourth property of Eurocentrism.

However, before proceeding to reveal the fourth and final move of Eurocentrism I, it is necessary to pause and deal with one potential objection that might be raised here: specifically, that the BBT is *not* embraced by the overwhelming majority of scholars on globalisation and the global economy in what is clearly a very extensive literature on the subject, precisely because they view these phenomena as born *after* 1945 (i.e., the 1945-as-year-zero birth-conception of the global economy). Thus, because they are not concerned with the *pre*-1945 era, which contained the rise of modern capitalism in Europe and its expansion across Afro-Asia after about 1850, so by definition they cannot be said to adhere to the BBT. No less problematic is the point that the scholars whom I single out as embracing the BBT were working largely before 2000 and, as such, their analyses are now largely outdated.

---

[46] Chakrabarty (2000: 6–11).
[47] Ibid. (8).

But here, we confront a profound paradox wherein those analyses that presume globalisation only really emerged after 1945 almost invariably turn out to embrace an implicit *historical trace* that informs a vitally important role within their analyses – usually behind their backs. For on the one hand, many such scholars explicitly posit a profound temporal *discontinuity* between the pre- and post-1945 eras, where 'internationalisation' – or connections between nation-states – predominated before 1945 while 'global relations' dominated thereafter;[48] an empirical assumption that I challenge head-on in the second section of Chapter 14. But, behind this headlining claim lurks the Eurocentric assumption, often more implicit than explicit, that the contemporary Western-led global economy is merely the extension of Western-made modern capitalism, thereby allowing for an important element of economic *continuity* with the pre-1945 era.[49]

Critically, almost all IPE and IR scholars equate globalisation and the global economy with the global spread of modernity. And because it is almost invariably assumed that modernisation is a uniquely Western creation, so globalisation is conflated with Westernisation. Moreover, on those rare occasions when linkages are explicitly made, we encounter, for example, Malcolm Waters' definition of globalisation as 'the direct consequence of the expansion of European [capitalist] culture across the planet via settlement, colonisation and cultural mimesis'.[50] Equally, as Anthony Giddens put it, modernity 'refers to modes of social life or organization which emerged in Europe from about the seventeenth century onwards and which subsequently became more or less worldwide in their influence [via globalization]'.[51] Oliver Stuenkel summarises my point nicely, to wit: 'European and US-American thinkers and policy makers [have] found it difficult to distinguish between modernization and Westernization.'[52] And, as Rhoads Murphey put it, '"Westernization" and "modernization" have been confused by Western pride'.[53] In short, modernisation and globalisation are thought of as but two sides of the same Westernisation coin. More generally, the litmus test for my claim would be to ask whether globalisation theorists bring non-Western

[48] For example, Burton (1972), Giddens (1985, 1990) and Camilleri and Falk (1993).
[49] For example, Wallerstein (1974, 1980, 1989), Roberts (1985), Giddens (1985), Cox (1987, 1996), von Laue (1987), Camilleri and Falk (1993), Hoogvelt (1997), Held *et al.* (1999) and Dirlik (2007).
[50] Waters (1995: 3–4).
[51] Giddens (1990: 1).
[52] Stuenkel (2016: 32–3).
[53] Murphey (1977: 27).

agency into their analysis, the answer to which is almost invariably a resounding negative.

Thus, to return to my discussion of the BBT, I note that this historical trace reflects the construction of a unilinear, teleological Westernline that is drawn between the creation of modernity in Britain around 1780/1850 and the modern global economy today (i.e., the second stage of the BBT/expansion of the West narrative). And, *implicitly*, this historical trace is extrapolated much further back in time given that the rise of industrial capitalist modernity in Britain is viewed almost invariably as the realisation of a long, Western teleological-cumulative developmental process that reaches back to Ancient Greece (i.e., the long first stage of the BBT and the European logic of immanence). All of which means that even those scholars who date the global economy's birth to 1945/73 tend for the overwhelming part to embrace the Eurocentric BBT. And so, finally, I turn to the fourth property of Eurocentrism.

The Fourth Key Move of Eurocentrism I: The Slippery Issue of Western Imperialism

The final key move of Eurocentrism I refers to the treatment of Western imperialism. Here, we find either that Western empire is conjured away through a Eurocentric sleight of hand as if it never happened or, if its existence is conceded, it is put through a Eurocentric laundering process wherein the West's exploitative and repressive imperial practices are cleaned and filtered out, leaving a pristine vision of Western imperialism as the 'benign civilising mission' (à la 'liberal empire'). The latter tendency derives from standard 'paternalist' Eurocentric logic, which in turn derives from the point that because the non-West is said to be saddled with irrational institutions and cultures so its societies are unable to auto-generate into political and capitalist modernity. Accordingly, in this Messianic imaginary, the West assigns itself the 'altruistic duty' to deliver the requisite institutions that can kick-start non-Western societies and thereby re-track them on to the progressive path of capitalist modernisation. Such a paternalist mindset quite literally dovetails with the (in)famous conception of the 'white man's burden', which was the title of the imperialist poem that Rudyard Kipling read out to his American audience in 1899. It is simultaneously paternalistic and Eurocentric because it portrays non-Western peoples as but innocent children or helpless women who are 'therefore in need' of rescuing by the altruistic, paternal West. And, it finds its manifestation not just in nineteenth-century European empire, as is found for example in Bull and Watson's 'expansion of the West' narrative before 1945, but also after 1989 through the Western policies of humanitarian interventionism and structural adjustment programmes more generally.[54]

However, it also needs to be appreciated that not all Eurocentric thinkers are imperialist. Adam Smith's thought was, in my view, anti-imperialist. There was no conception of the civilising mission in his writings and he also believed that non-Western societies are capable of auto-generating into capitalism. Nevertheless, what makes Smith's position Eurocentric is his claim that non-Western societies *can* develop but only by following the natural path that had been trailblazed by the pioneering European societies.[55]

Mapping 'Eurocentrism II': Swinging Westward – Critical Eurofetishism and the Re-segregation of East and West?

However, while most postcolonial discussions of Eurocentrism would end here, it turns out that what I have considered thus far does not get us all the way when trying to understand the discourse of Eurocentrism. For I have come to realise that a second non-Eurocentric antidote exists which, in turn, operationalises a very different definition of Eurocentrism to the one I presented above – what I shall call 'Eurocentrism II'. In what follows, I apologise in advance to my anxious reader who might well, quite understandably, be deeply perplexed if not confused by the admittedly unedifying spectacle of non-Eurocentrics accusing each other of being Eurocentric, or some variant therein. All of which will, no doubt, conjure up the equally dismaying and bemusing image of 'fifty-seven varieties' which has, of course, long dogged Marxist politics. And, I fully recognise that such left-wing internecine debates have done much harm to the greater cause. But there are two points that I want to signal here: first, that while I depart from postcolonial Marxism's approach, this does not mean that it is not a legitimate form of anti-Eurocentrism, even though I view it as problematic in so many respects. And second, as I explain later, there is, paradoxically as it turns out, one aspect of the postcolonial-Marxist approach that I believe *is* important – so much so that I incorporate it, albeit in heavily modified form, into my own solution to Western-centrism. Note that I also treat this present section as a dress rehearsal for the discussion of my antidote to Eurocentrism I and II in the next.

---

[54] See Bowden (2009: chs. 7–8) and Hobson (2012: ch. 12).
[55] Hobson (2012: 74–83).

Defining 'Eurocentrism II' and Its Antidote

Many critical IR/IPE scholars, most especially postcolonial Marxists, have advanced a specific definition of, and antidote to, 'Eurocentrism II'. Here, I interrogate two journal articles, one published in 1997 by the well-known world-systems theorist, Immanuel Wallerstein, and the other published in 2016 by the well-known postcolonialists Alina Sajed and Naeem Inayatullah – with the latter scholar being heavily influenced by world-systems theory (WST). While it is certainly the case that the high tide of WST has, albeit somewhat curiously, long receded within the social sciences, nevertheless I single these scholars' statements out for two inter-related reasons: first, because they constitute the clearest and most well-thought-out representative illustrations of what I call critical Eurofetishism; and second, because I believe that many critical scholars within IPE and IR and elsewhere very much echo their arguments but are likely unaware of their link to Eurofetishism.

In certain respects, the definition of Eurocentrism II and its antidote overlaps with, but also radically departs from the conception of Eurocentrism I and its antidote. In essence, Eurocentrism II comprises a discourse or metanarrative that serves to deny, elide or normatively justify the central role that Western imperialism plays in the global economy, the non-Eurocentric antidote to which lies in revealing the centrality of Western empire/neo-empire in all its abhorrent brutality within the global economy. In this approach, the global economy is said to be dominated completely by the West at the direct expense of the non-West. Or, it might be said that this conception of Eurocentrism constructs a binary division between the 'civilised and the damned'.[56] Bringing back the dark role of Western imperialism is also important to my own analysis as a counter to Eurocentrism I. So far so good.

Eurofetishism's Rejection of 'Non-Western Agency'
and Its Embrace of the Eurocentric 'BBT'

But where such scholars depart significantly from my own perspective – which emphasises, albeit not exclusively, the key role that non-Western agency plays in the making of the global economy (as I explain in the next section) – lies in their insistence that any focus on non-Western agency as an important component of the antidote to Eurocentrism *must be avoided at all costs*. The reason for this is straightforward. For their

---

[56] Persaud (2019: 266). Recall too that Frantz Fanon (1965/2001) talked of the 'damned of the earth', though this was mistranslated as the 'wretched' of the earth.

sole task is to prosecute the West in the Western academic-postcolonial court of social justice for its brutal imperial-capitalist crimes against global humanity. Critically, this means that the creation of capitalism and the malevolent capitalist global economy must be credited *wholly* to the imperialist West. As Wallerstein puts it, '[b]y denying Europe credit [for the creation of the capitalist global economy] we deny European blame [for its crimes committed against global humanity]'.[57] He argues that an approach that brings in non-Western agency in the making of modern capitalism and the global economy, as I do in this book, serves merely to get the West off the moral hook, while also implicating the non-West in the creation of this exploitative and brutal system that is, paradoxically, pointed squarely at the non-Western peoples.

Accordingly, in this imaginary, if the Eurofetishist prosecution lawyer's Black and Brown witnesses turn out to have been fundamental agents who were involved in the creation of capitalism and the global economy, as becomes clear from a deep interrogation by the West's defence lawyer, then the case against the West collapses. As Wallerstein puts it, '[i]f we insist too much on non-European agency as a theme, we end up by whitewashing all of Europe's sins, or at least most of them'.[58] Or as Sajed and Inayatullah put it in their critique of my approach, Hobson's 'insistence on a specific vision of Eastern agency may end up diluting the responsibility of the violence behind Western colonialism, all the while bringing forward the East as a historical agent'.[59] Thus, it is precisely for this reason that Wallerstein would accuse me of being an 'avatar of Eurocentrism',[60] or in the context of my analogy here, of acting as the West's defence lawyer.

A core paradox here is that this anti-Eurocentric approach swings resolutely westward, dovetailing in various respects with the ontological *modus operandi* of Eurocentrism I. For not only does it insist that the focus of analysis *must* be on the exceptional West's creation of modern capitalism and the capitalist global economy, but equally it dovetails with the two-stage BBT concerning the European 'logic of immanence' and 'globalisation-as-Westernisation' – both of which I view as hallmark tropes of Eurocentrism I. Thus, Sajed and Inayatullah affirm that '[w]e can be comfortable with capitalism as the internally generated European creation, because it makes Europe unambiguously guilty and responsible

---

[57] Wallerstein (1997: 104).
[58] Ibid. (102).
[59] Sajed and Inayatullah (2016: 207).
[60] Wallerstein (1997).

for the devastation of the third world'.[61] And Wallerstein expresses the two-stage BBT thus:

> The European world-economy of the sixteenth century became irremediably capitalist. And once capitalism consolidated itself in this historical [European] system, once this system was governed by the priority of the ceaseless accumulation of capital, it acquired a kind of strength as against other historical systems that enabled it to expand geographically until it absorbed physically the entire globe.[62]

Paradoxically, therefore, for Wallerstein the title of my book is a Eurocentric misnomer and should properly be called 'Western Origins of the Global Economy'.

Overall, I characterise this postcolonial-Marxist approach as 'critical Eurofetishism', while Audrey Alejandro calls it 'postcolonial Eurocentrism'.[63] For though highly critical of the West, it subscribes to a 'substantialist' conception of the West. That is, the imperialist West is purposefully reified as a self-made, all-powerful and *self-constituting fetish*, such that it is awarded the status of the 'hyper-agential subject' and prime- or sole-mover of the global economy. For politically this *must* be done precisely so that the West can be prosecuted for the many crimes that Western-made global capitalism has inflicted upon non-Western peoples. Conversely, the non-Western peoples are relegated to the status of irrelevant, helpless and 'passive objects/victims' who cannot, therefore, be blamed for the atrocities that global capitalism imparts. In this critical conception, globalisation is viewed, in effect, as a Western capitalist-imperial project of *Drang nach Osten* and nothing should detract from this. Nevertheless, an acute paradox emerges here, for as I explain in Chapter 9, this focus on the exceptional West and the Eurocentric logic of immanence means that *the imperial origins* of Britain's shift to modern capitalism are whitewashed. But I shall not pursue this further here.

Retrieving and Inverting the East–West Binary: The Eurofetishist 'Western Villains versus Eastern Victims' Discourse

In reifying the West and denying agency to the non-West, so Eurofetishism simultaneously retrieves and inverts the Eurocentric binary of East versus West. Here, we find the hyper-agential and brutal imperialist

---

[61] Sajed and Inayatullah (2016: 206).
[62] Wallerstein (1997: 105). See also Wallerstein (1984: 153, also 6, 29, 37).
[63] Alejandro (2019: ch. 5).

West residing in splendid ontological isolation while the helpless and hapless non-West ekes out a miserable and impoverished existence in the ontological ghetto on the other side of the Western-civilisational frontier, stripped of all agency. Crucially, the Eurocentric binary of the 'morally superior/benevolent West versus the inferior brutal/barbaric/evil East' is inverted into that of the 'morally inferior brutal/barbaric West versus a morally superior, innocent non-West'. As Alejandro puts it in her superb book, *Western Dominance in International Relations?*, these two discourses, Eurocentrism and Eurofetishism (or what she calls Eurocentrism and 'Postcolonial Eurocentrism'), perform 'the West as the main actor capable of organising the world in its image. European exceptionalism remains the same – although, from the postcolonial Eurocentric view, Europe is not considered to be the best actor ever, but the worst'.[64]

Accordingly, in this imaginary, we encounter, in effect, an 'epistemically violent' re-segregation of the East and West. Note that I deploy the term 'epistemic violence' to connote the process by which the non-Western peoples are viewed as passive and weak, thereby impacting non-Western peoples in a negative way. Paradoxically, such a conception of the non-West is not uncoincidentally reminiscent of the role that was played by the old 'noble savage' trope, given that it served as a vehicle for some Europeans to reflect back critically on the West – though clearly the scientific racist base of this concept is absent in critical Eurofetishism. And, most significantly, in retrieving this, albeit inverted, binary so the prime Eurocentric categories of 'Western supremacism' and the 'agency-less East' remain fully intact. Notable here is Sajed and Inayatullah's candid point:

[h]ere is the dilemma: a complex, nuanced, accurate assessment of encounter ... allows for Eastern agency but also may reduce Western responsibility. On the other hand, the not so complex, not so nuanced, not so accurate assessment of the domination of the West over the East [à la dependency theory and World Systems theory] also has its own risks. Such views infantilise non-Western societies/actors who tend to be seen as victims that are always acted upon.[65]

What emerges from all this is the construction of an alternative, epistemically violent binary of 'Western villains and Eastern victims' in which the supremacist West is shoehorned in all of its complexity into the former category while the supine non-West is hammered like a square peg into the round hole of the latter category. In the process,

---

[64] Ibid. (163).
[65] Sajed and Inayatullah (2016: 203, also 206).

we enter into an 'either/or conception' in which agency is equated with power and 'winning' such that this approach replicates the Eurocentric trope of 'the triumph of the West'. And because non-Western peoples are thought of as always losing, so by definition they have *no* agency. To the extent that non-Western agency is allowed into the postcolonial-Marxist vision at all, it is skewed through a Eurofetishist lens into a praxis of non-Western *complicity* with Western imperialism. As Sajed and Inayatullah put it:

> Hobson's highlighting of Eastern agency troubles us because it permits a kind of complicity to creep into the actions of the East—or rather it assumes the East to be equally complicit in its own exploitation and devastation. And while no one could or should deny a certain degree of complicity, Hobson's emphasis might unintentionally vitiate indictments of the West.[66]

As I explain in detail in Chapter 4, this is why the likes of W. E. B. Du Bois and Walter Rodney engage in the 'anti-racist refusal' to recognise the *agency and power* of the African slavers, Muslims and Indians in the multiple African slave trades, insisting – in accordance with the Western villain/Eastern victim world-view – that the entirety of the moral blame (and power/agency) be placed at the door of the Europeans. And, as I also explain there, the upshot of this anti-racist refusal is that the eleven to fourteen million Black slaves – men, women and children – who were carried away in the West Asian slave trade are swept under the world-historical carpet as if the whole process never happened.

The key that unlocks the door into my alternative universe concerns the way in which we conceive of agency. For I reject viewing agency *purely* in terms of a melodramatic, Manichaean headlining 'clash of civilisations' and 'head-on conflict', where one side (the supreme West) always wins out at the expense of the other (the supine non-West). Still, this is not to whitewash various conflicts and nor is it to ignore non-Western resistance in the face of Western imperialism and neo-imperialism, not least because it was this resistance that in large part succeeded in bringing an end to colonialism (as I note in Chapter 14). But more generally, I view agency as existing along a continuum wherein Western and non-Western agency co-exist and such actors can have greater or lesser degrees of agency over time whether or not they 'win' such a 'contest'. Equally, as signalled earlier, I focus on the entwining of these agential interconnections rather than separating them out through an approach that highlights only 'head-on' conflict within a 'victims

---

[66] Ibid. (202–3).

and villains' or 'winners and losers' ontology. All of which requires us to shift from the monological categories of 'substantialism' into the more complex, co-constitutive processes of 'relationalism' (which more below).

None of my critique is designed to deny the not-inconsiderable levels of violence that the West has inflicted upon the non-West either in the past or in the present. And, nor is it to deny the fact of Western dominance since the late-nineteenth century. Rather, my problem with the Western villains/non-Western victims conception is that all of the agential contributions that non-Western peoples have made in enabling the global economy and modern capitalism that I reveal in this book are erased or whitewashed for the politically expedient sake of maintaining an exclusive focus on the brutal imperial actions of the autonomous West. In the process, all of these co-constitutive interconnections are conjured away into thin air before our very eyes, hidden in plain sight as it were. And, even after 1850, at the time when the West begins to assume global hegemony this, I believe, should not occlude the presence of continuing and manifold instantiations of non-Western agency that played out both inside and outside the shadow of Western empire – as I explain in Chapter 13. For in their absence, Western imperialism would likely have been far more limited in its scope, while the rise of the second global economy (SGE) might not have been a forgone conclusion. In essence, power and agency should not be conflated such that the latter is awarded only to the 'winners'.

Nevertheless, it is precisely at this point that various neo-Marxists intervene by taking on an approach such as that of the non-Eurocentric CS (on which more below), which gives pride of place to non-Western agency in global economic history. As the innovative non-Eurocentric neo-Marxist scholar, Eren Duzgun, puts it (joining hands with Wallerstein and Sajed and Inayatullah), 'by trying to narrate an *all-inclusive* [i.e., multicultural] history of the transition to [modern] capitalism, that is, a narrative purporting that everyone was or could have been capitalist, non-Eurocentric accounts reproduce perhaps the most Eurocentric assumption that capitalism represents a superior and better [or natural or universal] mode of organising human relations'.[67] I offer three responses. First, I side with Karl Marx who, if I may be permitted some interpretive license here, was not unlike Winston Churchill in believing that capitalism was the worst economic system except for all the previous ones. Second, while I certainly see what the

---

[67] Duzgun (2018: 27). See also Wallerstein (1997: 103) and Sajed and Inayatullah (2016: 205–6).

neo-Marxist critics are getting at, nevertheless I am talking merely about *developmental agency* which, in my formulation, is conceived of in *a-moral* terms. Thus, I make *no* claims concerning the morality or immorality of modern capitalism. Third, this neo-Marxist critique hinges on the CS's assumption that other parts of the world were developing into modern capitalism – an assumption that I confess to having slipped into, erroneously, in my 2004 book. But in this present book, I find myself in agreement with Wallerstein, Duzgun as well as Sajed and Inayatullah, when they insist that the breakthrough into modern capitalism occurred in Europe – specifically in Britain in the first instance – given my argument in Chapters 11 and 12 that neither India nor China in the eighteenth century was on a spontaneous path into modern capitalism. This point alone renders me far closer to their argument than one might assume, though clearly some fundamental differences remain.

Potential Political Pitfalls and Contradictions of Critical Eurofetishism

Finally, I want to highlight various potential political dangers and contradictions of Eurofetishism, the first of which is that this approach, albeit unwittingly, can reinforce the old imperial trope that 'the sun never sets on the Western empire' and that all 'non-Western resistance is futile'. By fetishising the West and denying agency to non-Western peoples so, albeit inadvertently, there is a real danger that Eurofetishism ends up by eternalising and naturalising Western imperial domination. Accordingly, the approach can end up by painting the non-West as imprisoned permanently within a Western iron cage while global liberal-capitalism marks, in effect, the 'end of history'.[68] This is another reason why I label this approach 'Eurofetishism', given that it is analogous to Marx's famous claim that liberal political economy falls into the trap of 'bourgeois' *fetishism* by reifying objects that are divorced from their underlying class relations, the ultimate upshot of which is the eternalisation and naturalisation of capitalism. Thus, the antidote to Eurofetishism is to factor in the co-constitutive relations between Western and non-Western actors that move and ricochet backwards and forwards across the 'Western-centric frontier' (as I explain later).[69] The Eurofetishist reply here, though, is that bringing in non-Western agency alongside Western agency in effect creates the liberal illusion that the 'world is flat', thereby

[68] Fukuyama (1992).
[69] See also, for example, Pieterse (1990), Ling (2002), Bala (2006), Hobson (2004) and Alejandro (2019).

conjuring the presence of Western imperial/neo-imperial hierarchy into thin air. But Western imperial hierarchy came late to Afro-Asia, emerging globally after the mid-nineteenth century and even then non-Western agency continued both inside and outside the shadow of empire.

Second, Eurofetishism's insistence on awarding the West a monopoly of evil/brutality and power/agency means that those instances in which Afro-Asian forms of power and oppression have played out *within* the non-Western world are silenced and are, albeit unwittingly, condoned and thereby given a free pass. In this way, Eurofetishism can be appealed to and used by those non-Western states that oppress their own populations but cynically blame the imperial West for *all* the human wrongs that are inflicted upon their own populations – with one of the most egregious examples being, as ironic as it is tragic, that of Robert Mugabe. Critically, postcolonial Eurofetishism's ethic of pure ideological conviction renders it all-but-politically paralysed, such that any criticism of the likes of Mugabe or Islamic State of Iraq and al-Sham (ISIS) today is completely shut down because they are excused as but innocent by-products of Western imperialism, much as the exploitation of African slave labour in Zanzibar by the Omani Sultanate after 1840 is explained away by the impact of the 'demands' of the Western capitalist system and the Western imperial powers. Critically, because such non-Western people are denied agency, by definition, they need not take any responsibility for their actions. It is as if the face of the Eurofetishist social conscience has had one eye amputated such that its vision, which is locked on to the West, necessarily overlooks those human wrongs that are, and have been, committed by non-Western states and peoples.

This problem can, at the extreme, be sometimes reflected in postcolonial academic conferences hosted in the West. In such extreme instances there is a danger that the delegates focus exclusively on Western imperialism and all of its many (undeniable) horrors as if the Chinese under the Qing dynasty between 1683 and 1760, or the Japanese between 1894 and 1945, or the Omani Sultanate after 1840, never imperially expanded. Equally, there is a tendency to conflate the African slave trade with the Western-led Atlantic system without acknowledging that this was a *variant* that existed alongside its West Asian and Indian instantiations, which long preceded and post-dated it. Then again, we might hear a lot about White racism but nothing about Japanese patriarchal racism, which took a highly potent form in the first half of the twentieth century. Critically, it was only when Kim Hak-sun finally came forward in 1991 as a victim to bear witness to the Japanese atrocities perpetrated against the Korean Comfort Women during World War II that Eurofetishist attention was finally brought to bear. And, last but not least, reference to Western imperial genocides might well be made, though the Armenian and Zunghar Mongol genocides that were perpetrated, respectively, by the Ottomans and Chinese, are conspicuous for their absence, as if they never happened. In aggregate these lacunae mark, in the words of Choi Jung-Bong 'the poignant silence of postcolonial studies'.[70] And, as he goes on to say, the horrors of Japanese imperialism 'illustrate the need to insert Japanese imperialism into the consciousness and inventory of postcolonial studies'.[71]

All in all, these non-Western episodes of oppression and many others like them are conjured away or swept under the carpet by Eurofetishism for the politically expedient purpose of condemning the West in the Eurofetishist academic court of social justice. And, most cynically of all, on the rare occasions when such episodes *are* recognised, they are used merely as political pawns to condemn the West once more. Ultimately, then, all roads lead back inevitably to the West. In this way, Eurofetishism is in real danger of moving from the progressive to the sometimes patronising and regressive Left via its poverty, or soft bigotry, of low expectations vis-à-vis non-Western states and peoples (whereby Western states and societies are held to an extremely high ethical standard while their non-Western counterparts that 'can do no wrong' are, therefore, subjected to no ethical standard). It would surely be lamentable to find that the only Black and Brown lives who mattered and should be remembered are those that have been taken by the Europeans and Americans.

Importantly, this political posture in effect doubles down through the additional Eurofetishist assumption that a White Western person criticising a non-White person, group or harmful practice is deemed to be a racist or Eurocentric move. And so the profound paradox emerges, as Audrey Alejandro, a rising star in postcolonial IR, put it to me in private conversation at the 2019 British International Studies Association annual conference, that Western postcolonial academic conferences can, at the extreme, devolve into Eurocentric echo-chambers (girded by groupthink) in which White people talk about White people. Thus, as Oliver Steunkel puts it most aptly, '[b]oth sides—those [Eurocentrics] enamored with the West and the postcolonial [Eurofetishist] thinkers who blame every misfortune in history on the West—suffer from a Western-centric fixation'.[72]

Clearly, if our sole political task is to critique the West, then a binary Eurofetishist approach is undoubtedly a powerfully emotive

[70] Choi (2003: 325).
[71] Ibid. (326–7).
[72] Stuenkel (2016: 15).

weapon. But at the extreme it runs the danger of constructing over-simplified representations of 'reality' in which everyone, in all their myriad ambiguities and complex shades of grey, are shoehorned and re-segregated into black and white binary conceptions of non-Western victims and Western villains, precisely so as to make a radical political critique of the West more compelling and urgent. My preference for recognising a world full of greys is rejected by Eurofetishism on the grounds that being 'overly sensitive to nuance' serves merely to sacrifice critical-ideological conviction and thereby dilute the critique of the Western villains – as Sajed and Inayatullah argue in the quote cited above – though this simply returns us full circle to the binary approach that I am interrogating here. But, most interestingly, this same quote also expresses the (refreshingly) candid concession that their approach leads to the 'infantilisation of the non-Western peoples'.

All of which, in turn, leads me to pose two rhetorical questions: first, has the imperialist West really had a monopoly of global agency as Eurofetishism (and Eurocentrism) would have us believe, at least before 1850 and indeed even after that date? And equally, has the non-West really been as powerless, agency-less and irrelevant as they tell us? To assume so is, albeit entirely unwittingly, to flirt with, if not conform to, the Eurocentric propensity of affirming the narcissism of the West while simultaneously demoting non-Western peoples to the status of a mere 'empath' or 'noble savage'.

If truth be told, when confronted by an undergraduate student who wants to do a postcolonial dissertation on the violence of European colonialism, I shudder inside not because this is an unimportant topic – for it is surely very important – but because I dread the ensuing potential voyage into a world of 'imperial porn'. For on this deeply depressing journey, we will visit sites full of sad non-Western peoples who are but hapless and pathetic losers, stripped of all agency by the supremacist West – all of which, most ironically, serves ultimately to naturalise imperialism.

Nevertheless, for all of this critique, I want to close this discussion by making two important qualifications, both of which might well come as a considerable surprise to my reader. First, my critique of Sajed and Inayatullah's Eurofetishism should not be taken as a (hostile) dismissal of their overall work, for I remain extremely impressed by their pioneering book scholarship and, my reader might be even more surprised to learn, of the many impressive subtleties of their analyses.[73] And second, I do *not* seek to discount the 'Eurofetishist' approach outright given that its

[73] See especially Inayatullah and Blaney (2004), Blaney and Inayatullah (2010, 2021) and Sajed (2013).

focus on Western agency, though in my view overblown, needs to some extent to be retrieved within the non-Eurocentric CS of world economic history. Thus, as I explain below, while my own antidote to Eurocentrism and Eurofetishism seeks to bring non-Western agency back in, this does not entail kicking Western agency (and Western imperialism) back out.

NGPE (II): Provisioning the Conceptual Nautical Techniques to Navigate beyond the Eurocentric and Eurofetishist Frontiers

Before I sketch the contours of my antidote to Eurocentrism I and II, it is important to preface it by considering very briefly my approach in the light of what Jack Goldstone has called the 'California School' of global economic history. Noteworthy here is that Goldstone includes my 2004 book within this non-Eurocentric School.[74] But by way of introductory background to my IR and IPE readers, most of whom have probably never heard of this School, it emerged in the late 1980s, with perhaps the most notable contributions comprising James Blaut's *The Colonizer's Model of the World*, Andre Gunder Frank's *ReOrient*, Jack Goldstone's *Why Europe?*, and Kenneth Pomeranz's *The Great Divergence*.[75] However, it turns out that there have been two waves of the CS, the first of which (between roughly 1989 and 2011) focused particularly on China,[76] while the second (between 2011 and the present) focuses more on the great divergence between Britain and India.[77]

This revisionist, non-Eurocentric School seeks largely to bring back the role of non-Western agency into global economic history, mainly in the context of the 'great divergence' between Britain and China, to which India has been added in the last decade. This refers to the industrial over-taking of China and India as the leading economies before about 1800 by Britain during the nineteenth century. One of the lowest common denominators of much of the School is the revealing of many 'surprising resemblances' between China, India and Europe – a move that acts as a direct counterweight to Eurocentrism's central focus on the many core differences that allegedly separate the East from West. In the process many, though by no means all, such scholars account for the

---

[74] Goldstone (2008: viii).
[75] Blaut (1993), Frank (1998), Pomeranz (2000) and Goldstone (2008).
[76] For example, Abu-Lughod (1989), Blaut (1993), Flynn and Giráldez (1995a, 1995b, 2004, 2006), von Glahn (1996a), Goody (1996), Bin Wong (1997, 2002), Goldstone (2000, 2002, 2008), Marks (2002), Lieberman (2003), Hobson (2004) and Rosenthal and Bin Wong (2011).
[77] Most notably, Parthasarathi (2011) and Yazdani (2017).

'great divergence' by ignoring or black boxing the domestic institutional and social properties of China, India, Britain and Europe in favour of a focus on either exogenous contingency (good or bad luck)[78] or external changes in the global economy.[79] All in all, if we are to understand the origins of modern capitalism upon which the modern global economy rests, then we have little choice, I believe, but to reconsider the School's arguments on the grounds of its oft-exclusive focus on non-Western agency. And, in any case, where we stand on the issue of non-Western and Western agencies constitutes the core theme of this present book.

Filling in the Lacuna of the CS

While certainly my approach in this book overlaps to an important extent with the CS, I now find myself in agreement with the criticism, articulated succinctly by Jan Nederveen Pieterse, that 'at times [the School] reverses the current of Eurocentrism by centring the East and marginalizing the West, thus replaying East-West binaries in reverse'.[80] And, certainly, I would concede that this problem infected my 2004 book. This is the first limitation of the CS – the downplaying, if not eradication, of Western agency – though it is noteworthy that Goldstone's own work constitutes a laudable exception.[81] Second, and flowing on directly from this problem, is the point that without some kind of focus on Western agency, we are necessarily *robbed of an explanation* of the rise of modern capitalism. Thus, some of the most prominent CS scholars refuse to countenance the point that there was *anything* internal to Europe – which is read as the old bugbear of Eurocentric 'exceptionalism' – that could account for the rise of modern capitalism such that the notion of Western agency all but disappears from view in this vision.

Typical here is Gunder Frank's assertion in his penultimate (non-Eurocentric) book, *ReOrient*, that 'Europe did not pull itself up by its own economic bootstraps, and certainly not thanks to any kind of European "exceptionalism" of rationality, institutions, entrepreneurship, technology, geniality, in a word – of race.'[82] And, insisting that domestic factors were entirely irrelevant, for fear of retreating back into the Eurocentric *cul-de-sac* of the exceptional logic of immanence, Frank answers his central question as to why Europe broke through to modern

---

[78] Blaut (1993) and Pomeranz (2000).
[79] Abu-Lughod (1989) and Frank (1998).
[80] Pieterse (2006: 64–5).
[81] For example, Goldstone (2008).
[82] Frank (1998: 4); see also Abu-Lughod (1989: 18).

capitalism by asserting that the 'Europeans *bought* themselves a seat, and then even a whole railway car, on the Asian train', which they managed to do by imperially plundering gold and silver from the Americas.[83] While this echoes part of my own argument, nevertheless in a move that is reminiscent of his earlier 'dependency-theoretical' ontology, 'Gunder Frank 2.0' once again erased from view the domestic social properties of Europe as well as those of China and India, this time around by focusing on a world full of 'surprising resemblances' and isomorphic domestic properties.[84] Poignantly, as noted above, this propensity to black box the domestic properties of the world's leading economies in Asia and the West runs through much of the CS.[85] And, one of the most glaring omissions lies in the tendency to ignore the mode of production, such that we learn nothing from the CS about the ways in which the forces and social relations of production play out as much as we lose sight of one of the key social drivers of systemic economic and global change.

To this end, Burak Tansel's perceptive Marxist critique of my 2004 book has it, to which I now plead guilty:

[w]hile correctly pinpointing the 'Eastern origins' of a number of 'resource portfolios' that transformed the trajectory of European development, Hobson ultimately disregarded the question of which [domestic] social forces and processes led Europe to diverge from the East, wherein the initial mechanisms of the ensuing 'European miracle' originated.[86]

Joe Bryant, a key critic of the CS, argues that if the world's leading societies (or certain parts therein) were on a par as late as 1800, with no discernible *internal* differences in evidence such that domestic properties become irrelevant to explaining the British and European creation of modern industrial capitalism (as per the CS), then the upshot must be that there are

no causal mechanisms to explicate the European breakthrough. The conundrum is inescapable: a world flattened of determinant social differences makes the local emergence of any historical novelty structurally inexplicable and restricts explanatory options to conjunctures aleatory [random/contingent] or incidental.[87]

---

[83] Ibid. (277), emphasis in the original.
[84] Frank (1998).
[85] For example, Abu-Lughod (1989: 18, 354), Blaut (1993: 208, n. 2) and Pomeranz (2000); cf. Hobson (2004: esp. ch. 13).
[86] Tansel (2013: 300).
[87] Bryant (2006: 418). See also Vries (2010: 736–41) and Anievas and Nişancioğlu (2015: 249).

Which, in turn, feeds into the criticism levied by Peer Vries, who concludes more sardonically than I would, that 'the quite depressing implications for the poor of the world of the "fact" that the rich would have become rich by sheer luck, apparently escapes' the CS revisionists.[88]

Accordingly, as I argue in Parts III and IV of this book, if we are to overcome this major problem, then we also need to take into account *differing* domestic social contexts and 'surprising differences' if we are to provide a satisfactory *explanation* as to why Britain industrialised and why China and India did not. Focusing *only* on global factors or ecological contingencies – as is the wont of much of the CS – important though these undoubtedly are and upon which a good part of my argument hinges, nevertheless turns out to be a necessary but insufficient solution. All of which means that CS scholars need to take Western agency much more seriously than they have hitherto. And it is precisely this point that I retrieve from critical Eurofetishism though, of course, I reject its fetishised conception of the West in the creation of capitalism and the first and second global economies. What, then, are the foundational principles that inform my own antidote to Western-centrism in its various guises? Here, I build on some of the critique of Eurofetishism that I made in the previous section.

Countering Eurocentrism and Eurofetishism: De-segregating the 'New Jim Crow Laws of the Global Economy'

Table 1.1 provides a summary juxtaposition of the key properties of Eurocentrism, critical Eurofetishism and my own antidote to Western-centrism. And note that I use the term 'Western-centrism' to connote both Eurocentric and critical Eurofetishist analyses.

If the first core property of NGPE comprises the need to develop a 'big-picture' global historical sociology of the global economy/ economies, the second core property comprises my non-Eurocentric antidote to the Western-centric approaches of Eurocentrism and critical Eurofetishism. My antidote comprises two core prongs, the first of which dismantles the New Jim Crow Laws of the global economy by de-segregating our prevailing conception that reifies the West-as-subject and dismisses the non-West-as-object. In the process, I focus not just on the many mutual or co-constitutive interactions and interconnectivities between West and non-West, but I also bring back into focus the multiple roles and instantiations of non-Western

---

[88] Vries (2010: 737).

Table 1.1 *My non-Eurocentric antidote to Western-centrism (Eurocentrism and critical Eurofetishism)*

Core moves	Eurocentrism	Critical Eurofetishism	My non-Eurocentric antidote
No. 1	Splits/segregates East from West (i.e., the New Jim Crow laws of the global economy)	Re-segregates West from non-West	De-segregates West and non-West (i.e., liberates the non-West from the New Jim Crow Laws of the global economy)
No. 2	The West is the supreme 'rational' agent/ subject that has global hyper-agency while the 'irrational' East has none (Western supremacism and Eastern passivity)	The West is the brutal hyper-agential villain of the world, the non-West is a passive *agency-less* victim (Western supremacism and non-Western passivity)	West and non-West have agency even though after 1850 the West gradually came to stand atop of the Eurocentric global hierarchy (Western and non-Western agency)
No. 3	Advances the Big Bang theory: the West pioneers single handedly capitalist modernity and then expands outwards to create a capitalist world	Advances the BBT: the West pioneers single-handedly capitalist modernity and then expands outwards to create and dominate a capitalist world	Rejects BBT: the West makes capitalist global modernity with non-Western help under conditions of *global* uneven and combined development
No. 4	Either celebrates Western imperialism or obscures imperialism's role in the world altogether	Sole focus on Western imperial-capitalism that forces the non-Western victims into the periphery of the ghetto	Focuses on Western imperialism *alongside* co-constitutive Western and non-Western actors and processes

and Western agency that simultaneously de-fetishises the West and rehabilitates the non-West. That is, such agential interconnections have been vital in making the West and non-West as well as Western imperialism and the global economy, all of which I signalled in my critique of Eurofetishism in the last section.

In these ways, I seek to operationalise what the historian, Sanjay Subrahmanyam, refers to as 'connected histories' and what the postcolonial historical sociologist, Gurminder Bhambra, calls 'connected sociologies'.[89] And, at all times, I place Western and non-Western agencies into what the equally prominent postcolonial historical sociologist, Julian Go, refers to as a globally connected *relational context*.[90] This approach is fundamental to the seminal analyses of Lily (L. H. M.) Ling, Qin Yaqing and Emilian Kavalski.[91] Rather than focusing solely on the 'logic of rationality', as is the preference of Eurocentric theory in IPE, IR and elsewhere, we need to think about the 'logic of relationality'. Ling and Qin draw on Daoist dialectics in which the forces of *yin* and *yang* – the two poles of nature and human affairs – are mutually imbricated and overlapping rather than separate and autonomous. Transposing this conception into the international and global realms means that neither West nor non-West can be understood as separate and self-constituting entities (as in 'substantialist' Eurocentrism and Eurofetishism's 'substantialist' conception of the West) but are mutually overlapping and co-constituting. Such a relational conception dovetails broadly with the kind of 'postcolonial actor network' theory that Julian Go also advocates.[92] For in this book, I reveal the vast network of lines and connections (or passages) that run between Western and non-Western actors in the making of modern capitalism as well as the first and second global economies. And, while prominent Marxists such as Jonathan Joseph might see in this a reversion to 'bourgeois fetishism',[93] I argue in this book that global trade and the two global economies are inherently linked to differing forms of capitalist production that are based in part on differing modes of production (as I note at the end of this chapter).

Such a position also serves as an antidote to what Go most usefully refers to as the Eurocentric method of 'analytical bifurcation', which echoes Edward Said's notion of the Eurocentric 'law of division',[94] wherein the West is analysed as an autonomous entity *in isolation* of its relations with the non-Western world. A good example of which concerns the Marxist and neo-Weberian emphasis on the geopolitical relations that existed between European states that in turn constituted a vital driver of the rise of European capitalism. For what is missing in this conception is the point that the great powers, most especially Britain and France, fought to a considerable extent over empire. In this way, imperial relations with the non-Western world and their constitutive impact on

---

[89] Subrahmanyam (1997) and Bhambra (2014).
[90] Go (2016: 118–23).
[91] Ling (2002, 2014), Qin (2018) and Kavalski (2018).
[92] Go (2016: 131–9).
[93] Roberts and Joseph (2015).
[94] Said (1994).

the rise of British industrialisation are conjured away in favour of a one-eyed focus on the anarchic properties of the European multi-state-system (as in the Eurocentric logic of immanence). By contrast, I adhere to Said's solution to Eurocentrism, which draws out the *interconnections* between West and non-West, to wit:

The worst thing ethically and politically is to let [Eurocentric-binary] separatism simply go on, without understanding the opposite of [binary] separatism, which is connectedness.... What I am interested in is how all these things work together. That seems to me to be the great task—to connect them all together—to understand wholes rather than bits of wholes.... In a wonderful phrase, Disraeli asks, 'Arabs, what are they?' and answers: 'They're just Jews on horseback'. So underlying this separation is also an amalgamation of some kind.[95]

The critical word in this quotation is not simply 'connections' but 'amalgamation'. For the logic of relationality and 'entangled relations' serves to produce amalgams or hybrid societies – all of which are whitewashed by Eurocentrism's focus on the self-constituting and wholly autonomous nature of the West and the East that are separated by an imaginary line of civilisational apartheid. In short, a relational approach to agency reveals a world full of multi-layered interactions – some, though not all of which, are imperialist – between Western and non-Western agents that are necessarily obscured by Eurocentric and Eurofetishist monological, binary zero-sum conceptions.

In response to Jeremy Adelman's fascinating and beautifully written critique of 'global history',[96] I argue that my emphasis on 'interconnections' should not be read as a project which seeks to smuggle in a rosy cosmopolitan picture of an increasingly harmonious world since 1500. For the second core prong of my non-Eurocentric antidote rehabilitates the dark role of empire not just in the context of the origins and development of the SGE but also as an important factor that informed the origins of modern capitalism upon which the present global economy is largely based. But as I also emphasise in the final section of this book, both prongs of my approach converge on the point that it has been the fact of entangled Western and non-Western agencies that played such an important role in helping to make Western empire throughout Afro-Asia possible in the first place. For it is a Western-centric illusion to presume that the West was powerful enough to create its various empires single-handedly. Moreover, it is important to recognise the point that my

---

[95] Said (2004: 260–1, 424).
[96] Adelman (2017).

highlighting of interconnectedness and entangled relations of Western and non-Western agencies is not unique to my own non-Eurocentric *modus operandi*, for it is embraced by many non-Eurocentric, postcolonial scholars working across the Social Science disciplines, some of whom I have singled out in this chapter.

All of which comes together through my inversion of the Eurocentric BBT. Part I of the book reveals the first global economy (FGE) before 1850 within which Britain's transition to modern industrial capitalism was situated (as I explain in Part III). That is, the (first) global economy and globalisation as well as Britain's Atlantic empire came first, with Europe's rise to capitalist modernity and its later imperialist thrust into Afro-Asia following on subsequently. In this way, the book complements Dunne and Reus-Smit's excellent edited volume, *The Globalization of International Society*, as well as Andrew Linklater's superb book, *The Idea of Civilization in the Making of the Global Order*, in that we all seek to critique the Eurocentric 'expansion of the West' narrative.[97] I also seek to advance further the superb analysis in Alex Anievas and Kerem Nişancioğlu's non-Eurocentric Marxist book, *How the West Came to Rule*.[98] I build on their analysis of 'regional whips of external necessity' that they reveal for the pre-1800 period by bringing into focus a *global* whip of external necessity – specifically the Afro-Indian global cotton whip – in the making of both the FGE (as I explain in Part I of the book) and British industrial capitalism as well as the SGE (as I explain in Parts III through V). And while I agree with Barry Buzan and George Lawson's key claim made in their excellent historical sociology of IR book *The Global Transformation* – that the nineteenth century was indeed a key turning point in the history of the global system – nevertheless, I countenance against reifying the 1850–2020 period as *sui generis* because, as I explain in Chapters 13 and 14, without the presence of the FGE the second might not have emerged on the one hand, and there are all manner of continuities between the first and second global economies on the other.[99]

One additional point needs to be appreciated. For in recent years, the 'decolonial' approach has emerged within IR, which is perhaps nowhere better represented than in Robbie Shilliam's seminal book *The Black Pacific*.[100] This seeks to reveal how non-Western peoples find their own ways of retrieving their culture and identity, and with it their sense of

---

[97] Dunne and Reus-Smit (2017) and Linklater (2020).
[98] Anievas and Nişancioğlu (2015).
[99] Buzan and Lawson (2015).
[100] Shilliam (2015).

self and dignity in the aftermath of Western empire. Though certainly an important approach it cannot, however, reach into the kind of analysis that this present book undertakes. For while both Shilliam and I are concerned with the issues of Western imperialism and non-Western agency, my task is to rethink the origins of the global economy and Western empire, whereas Shilliam's presupposes, or takes as a given, their prior existence. And so, I turn to the final conceptual issue that needs to be considered before we can begin our journey.

Defining Capitalisms – Historical and Modern

While Immanuel Wallerstein famously argued that the capitalist world economy (CWE) emerged in the sixteenth century,[101] I argue that he was at best half right. In this book, I claim that after about 1500, the *historical capitalist* world economy emerged and, in further contrast to Wallerstein's conception, this one was truly global. For Wallerstein, the global economy only starts to emerge after 1750 when Asia was 'incorporated' into the Western-driven CWE.[102] But, I argue that to an important extent, it was the European East India Companies that were incorporated into the historical capitalist global economy after 1500, in large part because the FGE was structured and organised around 'Indian structural power' – a concept that I advance in Chapter 3 and develop further in subsequent chapters. Then, after about 1850, the Asians to an extent helped pull the Europeans into, and thereby made possible the advent of, the second (modern capitalist) global economy, as I explain in Chapter 13. All of which, in turn, requires me to lay out my definitions of these two different forms of global economy and their various capitalist properties. While I consider this in conceptual detail in Chapters 8 and 14, here I want to signal that discussion to complete my introduction to this book.

Much of my analysis in this book provides a critique of 'fundamentalist' Marxism, typified most clearly by Political Marxism.[103] One of the key points of difference concerns the definition of capitalism. Political Marxism's rigid and exclusive focus on the social relations of production that in turn are reduced down yet further to free-wage labour (and capital), I believe, deviates from Karl Marx's more eclectic approach. Instead, when defining *capitalisms*, I draw from Marx and various unorthodox neo-Marxists (as well as Fernand Braudel). My looser

---

[101] Wallerstein (1974).
[102] Wallerstein (1987, 1989: ch. 3).
[103] For example, Brenner (1977, 1982) and Wood (2002).

definition incorporates not one but four interdependent properties: the forces of production along with *hybrid* social relations which, in turn, are linked to global trade and rational economic institutions.

Specifically, I define modern capitalism as a global system wherein *mechanised* productive technologies that are subjected to constant upgrading (technological accumulation), which may be labour-saving (in the West) or labour-augmenting (in Asia), are deployed within a *hybrid* set of social relations that comprise part unfree/forced labour and part free wage labour that produce for the domestic and global market and where global trade is supported by rational economic institutions. I define historical capitalism as a global system in which *non-mechanised* productive technologies, which are *not* subjected to constant upgrading, are deployed within a complex portfolio, or *hybrid* set, of social relations that comprise part unfree/forced labour, part free-wage labour, part wage labour (which is not fully dispossessed from the land) and part agrarian/household peasant labour, all of which produce to varying extents for domestic and global markets and where global trade is supported by rational (modern) economic institutions. Thus, dismissing the existence of the global economy before 1800 on the grounds that agrarian relations and thin commercial linkages predominated across the world does not hold (as I explain in Chapter 8).

Moreover, as alluded to above, I argue that the 'Afro-Indian global cotton whip' in conjunction with Indian structural power not only guided and wove together the FGE, but that these forces also played an important part in the rise of Britain's capitalist industrialisation, which in turn helped usher in the SGE and the thicker, modern global capitalist whip after about 1850. Also of note in relation to Part I of the book is that the Marxist (and Weberian) assumption that *historical* capitalist global trade was undertaken by simple, small-scale non-Western 'pedlar' merchants misses the point that many were not only involved within large-scale firms but many were capitalists in the modern sense. For example, Indian merchants were often more akin to financial capitalists than simple merchants. In East Africa, for example, they lent money by financing mortgages that Africans and Portuguese took out on land and property.[104] Then again, in Central Asia Indians lent money to rulers and local agricultural producers, where the latter paid their creditors back in terms of produce that the Indians then sold on.[105] Moreover, it is likely that they made more, if not far more, money from their financial investment activities than from their trading activities.

---

[104] See Machado (2014).
[105] Levi (2016).

The book proceeds through five parts, the first of which reveals the trading relations and Western and non-Western interactions and agencies that wove together the FGE. Part II defends my claim concerning the presence of the FGE after 1500 by revealing most of the structural properties of the FGE, while also showing how the major global trading commodities were produced under partly modern capitalist social relations within the historical capitalist global economy. Part III reveals how the FGE alongside the role of British developmental agency promoted the transition to modern industrial capitalism. Part IV answers the question as to why Britain industrialised and why China and India did not, which leads into a complex analysis that focuses on differing 'developmental architectures' and places developmental agency in the wider contexts of the global economy and regional inter-state-systems in order to account in part for these different outcomes. Finally, Part V serves to rehabilitate and simultaneously provincialise the role of Western imperialism in the transition from the first to the second global economy. There I argue that Western and non-Western agencies entwined to make Western empire in Afro-Asia and the rise of the SGE possible.

Thus, with this introductory conceptual stock-take exercise concluded such that we now know of what Eurocentrism and Eurofetishism as well as (global) capitalisms comprise, coupled with the conceptual nautical techniques that I have equipped us with in tandem with a very rough route map of the journey ahead, we can now finally begin our voyage beyond the Eurocentric and Eurofetishist frontier to discover the multicultural origins and development of the FGE.

Part I

Multicultural Origins of the First (Historical Capitalist) Global Economy, 1500–1850

2   Going Global 1.0
Chinese Agency in the Making of the First Global Economy

Introduction

Key parts of the literature on the position of China in what I am calling the first global economy (FGE) (c. 1500–c. 1850) are divided into a binary set of narratives. In the first position, traditional Eurocentric scholars argue that to the extent that China was involved in world trade at all, the Ming dynasty instituted a ban on foreign trade in 1371, the effect of which saw China undertake a great leap backward by turning inward into its regressive and economically irrational tribute system. This supposedly left a vacuum into which first the Iberians and subsequently the English, Dutch, French and other Europeans poured, the result of which saw a gradual battering down of the walls of isolation that regressive Asiatic despotisms had built up around themselves – though the great trading wall of China would not be dismantled until 1842. The second position swings ontologically hard to the east. For while Eurocentrism and Eurofetishism place European global agency front and centre, various California School revisionist accounts – which include my own 2004 book – have countered by raising China to the centre of the early global economy while significantly downgrading, if not doing away with, Western global agency.[1] This chapter makes the case that China was certainly important to the fortunes of the FGE, but that neither Sinocentrism nor Eurocentrism/Eurofetishism provides satisfactory approaches. This is because Sinocentrism exaggerates Chinese agency and underestimates European global agency, while Eurocentrism and Eurofetishism err by inverting this binary.

Contemporary Western thinking today views the Chinese government's announcement of its 'Going Global' strategy, just prior to its joining the World Trade Organization in 2001, as an entirely novel departure

All Chinese-written texts and archival information have been supplied and translated by Zhang Shizhi, for which I am extremely grateful.
[1] Most especially Frank (1998), Flynn and Giráldez (1994, 1995a, 1995b), Pomeranz (2000) and Hobson (2004). See also Hamashita (1994).

in China's 'long protectionist and isolationist history'. With the 'self-reliance' and 'isolation' of the Mao period as the immediate backdrop, it is commonly assumed that since 1978 the Chinese state has opened up through export-oriented industrialisation. In short, this 'going global' initiative is placed along a temporal continuum that reaches back to Deng Xiaoping's 'open and reform' programme and which views 1978-as-year-zero with regards to the 'rise of China'.

But this familiar narrative ignores the Kangxi Emperor's open and reform initiative that expressed itself through the open door policy of 'freer trade' (to be defined later), which was initiated about three centuries earlier in 1684. Likewise, this initiative also sought to move beyond the previous period of 'self-reliance' and 'isolation' as it allegedly manifested itself through the Qing ban on foreign trade (1661–83). Moreover, Kangxi's open and reform initiative in effect reached back to '960-as-year zero' when the outward-looking and impressive commercial posture of the Song dynasty first emerged. All of which means that what we are witnessing today is neither the *rise* of China nor a new course of global opening but, rather, a *return* of a more open China that in effect takes us back to the future when it stood near the centre of the FGE.[2] And, in turn, this means that China today is not 'going global' for the *first* time in her long history because it had already 'gone global'. This emerged after 1571 when silver flowed in from the New World and then intensified with Emperor Kangxi's 'open and reform' policy in 1684. Thus, the post-1571/1684 era could be described as 'going global 1.0', which was followed by 'going global 2.0' just over three or four centuries later. Moreover, the deep irony here is that while Britain claimed the mantle of free trading industrialiser par excellence, it turns out that after 1684 it was China that was far closer to 'free trade' (as I explain in the final section of this chapter). Overall, I argue that China was not only open but that it also played a major rather than the central role in the FGE.

The chapter proceeds through five sections, all of which provide rebuttals to the core Eurocentric/Eurofetishist myths of China's closed economy, specifically the state's official bans on foreign trade (section 'Countering the Eurocentric Myth of the Chinese State's Ban on Foreign Trade'), the dominance of the Europeans in Chinese trade as in Eurocentrism (though I also critique the Sinocentric conception of China's dominance over Britain (section 'Maintaining Chinese Trade: European Interstitial Agency and Competitive–Cooperative Sino–European Relations')), the economically regressive Chinese

---

[2] See also Zhang (2020).

tribute system (section 'Eurocentric and Sinocentric Myths of the CTS'), the highly regulated Canton system (section 'Confronting the Four Eurocentric Myths of the 'Canton System') and finally, China's heavily protectionist trade regime (section 'The Twin Myths of Britain's Laissez-Faire Free Trade Posture and Qing China's Interventionist Protectionist Stance'). And while much of my analysis overlaps with the California School, nevertheless at various points I provide a critique of Sinocentrism, which is developed much further in Chapters 3–6 and 11 and 12.

Countering the Eurocentric Myth of the Chinese State's Ban on Foreign Trade

To many academic observers, the image of China's long trading history is mired in the fog of a series of extensive official bans and heavy state regulations, all of which generate the familiar conclusion that China was largely closed off to foreign trade before 1842. To problematise this common Eurocentric image, I begin by laying out the brief history of these bans before considering the manifold ways in which the Chinese circumvented them.

Typical here is the Eurocentric view that after 1371 and especially after 1434 following the termination of (Islamic) Admiral Zheng He's seven epic transcontinental voyages, China vacated its position within the 'international' trading system as it retreated voluntarily into self-imposed isolation. Or, as it was officially pronounced at the time of the enunciation of the *Hajin* policy: 'even a one-inch plank will not be allowed to show up in the ocean' (*Cunban Buxu Xihai*).[3] This official pronouncement is widely perceived as the epitome of China's isolationist stance. David Landes speaks for many when he declares that after 1434 '[i]solationism became China. Round, complete [i.e., self-sufficient], apparently serene, ineffably harmonious, the Celestial Empire purred along for hundreds of years more, impervious and imperturbable. But the world was passing it by'.[4]

Interestingly, such a view is equally as common among critical, and even some non-Eurocentric, scholars. Notably, Janet Abu-Lughod repeatedly claims that after 1500, in the aftermath of the 'decline of the East' and the 'withdrawal' of China from the world economy, Europe 'swept' the Asian waters in the face of 'minimal resistance' and gradually

---

[3] Cited from the 'History of the Ming', Vol. 205 (*Mingshi*). Text available online: https://ctext.org/wiki.pl?if=gb&chapter=209129&remap=gb

[4] Landes (1998: 98).

created a global economy through European hegemony thereafter.[5] Moreover, Fernand Braudel asserts that

when in 1421 the Ming rulers ... changed their capital city—leaving Nanking, and moving to Peking [Beijing], in order to face the [military] dangers of the Manchu and Mongol frontier—the massive world-economy of China swung round for good, turning its back on a form of economic activity based on ease of access to sea-borne trade.... In the race for world dominion, this was the moment when China lost her position.[6]

Overall, much emphasis is accorded to the point that shortly after the Ming dynasty took over from the old Mongol Yuan dynasty in 1368, the new Hongwu emperor initiated the *hajin* ban on foreign trade in 1371, which lasted almost two centuries before it was terminated in 1567, albeit with a brief pause in 1505–21. About a century later the Qing state instigated two relatively brief bans, one in 1661–83 and a second in 1717–27. However, although there were significant periods in which the Chinese state proclaimed official bans on foreign trade, these have been exaggerated both in terms of their actual effect and their temporal extensity across the whole 1368–1911 era (which covered the duration of the Ming and Qing dynasties). Critically, as I explain later, it was not long after the termination of Zheng He's voyages in 1433 that China moved not away but near to the centre of the FGE. How, then, are such radically different readings possible? Part of the difference derives from the confusion surrounding the nature and purpose of the bans. First to the Qing bans.

The opening Qing ban (1661–83) was a symptom *not* of an endemic Chinese aversion to trade, which is one of the most enduring of the Eurocentric myths on China, but was a product of the need to solve the *temporary* problem of Zheng 'piracy' (as I explain later). And, in any case, the ban was not absolute given that trade continued between China and Japan, and Annam (Vietnam) and the Ryūkyūs. The second and final Qing ban (1717–27) applied only to trade with Southeast Asia and, even then, the Qing allowed Southeast-Asian ships to dock in China.[7] Once again, the 'ban' was informed not by an aversion to foreign trade but by a security logic. For, this was aimed at preventing 'renegade' Chinese living in Southeast Asia from linking up with Chinese 'pirates' who could then undermine China's control over the maritime shipping waters.[8] But what of the Ming's *Hajin* ban?

---

[5] Abu-Lughod (1989: 4, 18, 19–20, 259, 274–6, 286, 313, 340–8, 354, 361).
[6] Braudel (1992: 32).
[7] Hui (1995: 47).
[8] Schottenhammer (2010: 108).

For two core reasons the 1371 ban turns out to be the exception that virtually proves the rule that China had long been relatively open to foreign trade: first, because under the T'ang, Song and Yuan dynasties (618–1368) as well as under the Qing dynasty (1644–61, 1684–1911), China was largely open to foreign trade. True, the T'ang dynasty set up the Maritime Trade Commission to supervise imported trade in Guangzhou, which was extended to many other ports by the subsequent Song dynasty. However, while there were various regulations concerning the sale of imports, tariffs were generally low.[9] And, while it would be wrong to present a picture of a free-trading China, equally it would be highly problematic to present a picture of a permanently closed China that Eurocentrism constructs, which is derived largely from the Ming dynasty's ban of 1371–1567 then extrapolated both backwards and forwards in time. Indeed, between 1567 and 1911 China was officially closed, and only partially at that, for a mere 6 per cent of the time. The second reason is that even during the period of the ban between 1371 and 1567, foreign trade continued in numerous ways as this and subsequent sections explain.

The first rebuttal to the Eurocentric myth is that the official bans did not succeed in closing down foreign trade given that Chinese merchants found various ways of circumventing them. One strategy that emerged, especially after 1371, was the emigration of many Chinese merchants into Indo-China, Siam, Malaysia, Sumatra, Timor and the Philippines, whence they traded goods with China and the region.[10] In particular, they imported Chinese silk fabrics as well as coarse fabrics, sugar, porcelain, iron pans, nails and needles. Of further note is that the southern Chinese coastal regions depended for their livelihood on overseas trade such that they had every incentive to ignore the ban. The bans also directly stimulated massive projects of smuggling and private trade that were dubbed by the Chinese state as illegal 'piracy' – but, in reality, was a euphemism for the continuation of Chinese trade by other means. Moreover, Chinese historical archives lament that 'this smuggling can be found everywhere. The size of these groups was from hundreds to thousands of people'.[11] But this was also made possible by the fact that smugglers often formed strong and symbiotic relations with local officials in order to carry on their activities. And, paradoxically, the Zheng He voyages had done much to stimulate regional trade, especially

[9] Zhao (2013: 117–18).
[10] Hui (1995).
[11] *Huangming Jingshi Wenbian* (Article Collection of Ming Dynasty), Vol. 332, cited in Xu Mingde (1995: 31).

with Southeast Asia such that trade relations and activities *deepened* rather than contracted following the termination of these voyages in 1433. Even so, these voyages merely built upon previous private commercial initiatives that show 'how important the tremendous achievements of navigation during the Song-Yuan period made by private traders were to the success of Zheng He's explorations in the early Ming'.[12]

Another strategy saw Chinese merchants circumventing the ban by purchasing Portuguese *Cartazes* (passports) in order to masquerade as Portuguese shipping – a point that raises the competitive–cooperative nature of Sino-European relations (to which I return later). More generally, as I explain in the third section, a good deal of private trade was carried on within the Chinese tribute system (CTS) and by about the mid-fifteenth century this private trade began to exceed the official trade. As I also explain in Chapter 3, silver began to flow into China from Japan beginning in the 1530s, which provides a further rebuttal to the claim that the trade ban was all pervasive between 1371 and 1567. And the fact that the Ming state had to reaffirm the ban some thirty times between 1451 and 1533 suggests that it was not only violated frequently but also that the rhetoric of the ban was belied by reality.

Overall, it would be fanciful to presume that the Chinese state had anywhere near the levels of infrastructural power (or bureaucratic reach) required to enforce its proclaimed prohibitionist policy. Thus, despite the official proclamation that not even a little plank would be allowed to drift to sea, the fact is that this was negated in practice by the humdrum reality of private merchants and 'pirates' carrying on their trade through everyday agency. Circumstantial proof of this thriving trade lies with China's trading relations with Southeast Asia. Notably, the Javanese had been trading as far west as East Africa from the second century CE, while the kingdom of Śrīvijaya in Sumatra was a vital nodal point, if not one of several linchpins, of Afro-Eurasian regionalisation during the seventh through thirteenth centuries before it was replaced by the Melakan Sultanate.[13] Notable here is that both Śrīvijaya and Melaka owed much of their prosperity to Chinese traders and the Chinese market.[14] The irony, though, is that although Śrīvijaya benefited greatly from its trade with China nevertheless, when from the twelfth century onwards Chinese ships made regular voyages through the Melakan Strait, this served to marginalise Śrīvijaya while simultaneously preparing the way for the rise of Melaka.

---

[12] Zhao (2013: 22).
[13] Wolters (1967).
[14] Ibid., Meilink-Roelofsz (1962), Wink (1990: 331–5) and Bentley (1996: 764).

Of course, Melaka springs to mind in the Eurocentric imagination as a key port in the Portuguese and Dutch 'seaborne empires' after 1511 and 1641, respectively. But this obscures the point that Melaka developed strongly in the early-fifteenth century owing to the boost that it was given following the visit of Zheng He's armada. And by the mid-fifteenth century, Melaka became the meeting point where Indian and Chinese traders alighted to both drop off their wares and collect new ones. These comprised spices, of course, but also more importantly a whole range of everyday, high-bulk mass-based consumer products (as I note later). However, all of this is whitewashed by Eurocentrism on the grounds that Southeast-Asian traders were supposedly small-scale 'pedlars' who traded mainly in low-bulk, luxury goods.[15] But this ignores the importance of the large-scale *nakhodas*, who were moderately wealthy junk owners and who constituted the main carriers of foreign trade from Southeast Asia. They transported on large ships numerous low-value, high-bulk goods that comprised rice, salt, pickled and dried fish, palm wine, cheap textiles and metal wares – such that spices, despite all the Eurocentric hyperbole, turned out to be only a marginal trading item.[16]

Equally, it would be problematic to assume that there was little, if any, Chinese overseas trade before 1567 and its inception thereafter. For it seems clear that the ban was terminated in that year because it

constituted official recognition of an *established fact*: foreign silver had become so important to the Chinese economy that the country's merchants would do almost anything to procure it.... Fortunately for the Chinese, of course, foreign demand for Chinese goods was equally intense and an extra-ordinary expansion of commercial activity ensued.[17]

This is reinforced by the point that silver was the medium of exchange for foreign trade. Testimony to this lies in the contemporary local proverb of Manila, which described silver as *plata sa sangue* – the lifeblood of China.[18] Indeed,

few other places [bar India] produced the commodities that were universally in demand in greater quantity or variety, and few others attracted foreign traders in the same number. The deepening of China's involvement was shown most visibly in the continuous influx of foreign silver.[19]

[15] Steensgaard (1974) and van Leur (1955).
[16] Chaudhuri (1985: 186–7).
[17] Atwell (1982: 69), my emphasis.
[18] Chaudhuri (2006: 155).
[19] Lee (1999: 14–15).

All of which undermines the claim that foreign trade was stymied by the 1371 ban.

While some argue that it was the Ming state that stimulated foreign silver imports, given its initiation of the 'single whip tax' in the early sixteenth century that required taxes to be paid in silver,[20] it was in fact the private economy that drove demand for silver. For a large proportion of Chinese taxes continued to be paid either in copper cash or 'in-kind'.[21] Thus, as Richard von Glahn notes, 'even at their peak [silver taxes] accounted for less than 10 per cent ... of the total supply of silver circulating in China. Demand for silver was driven by the private economy, not public finance'.[22] Moreover, silver currency was the major medium for foreign transactions, while copper was used for domestic trade.

While trade was significant before 1567, the fact is that the lifting of the ban enabled a further expansion, with some 50 large Chinese junks trading between Fujian and Southeast Asia each year, and by 1597 this number had increased to 117 junks per annum. Moreover, between 1580 and 1680 Chinese private merchants carried their trade back and forth to Manila on some 1,800 private ships, totalling some 5,000 trips. Notable too is that the China–Manila trade was only one part of China's overall foreign trade network. Further proof that Ming and Qing China were open to foreign trade even during the 'official ban periods' is provided in subsequent sections. For the moment, though, I want to consider Sino–European relations, which comprised a further means by which China maintained its openness to foreign trade more generally.

Maintaining China's Foreign Trade: European Interstitial Agency and Competitive–Cooperative Sino–European Relations

As noted, one of the means by which Chinese merchants carried on overseas trade during and outside of the official ban periods was by forming competitive–cooperative relations with the European Companies. Equally, for their part, having tried to dominate the region through military power, the Europeans soon learned a good dose of humility and found that forming competitive–cooperative relations with Chinese merchants was the only way that they could maintain their trade in East Asia. For the immediate problem they faced was that East Asian

---

[20] Frank (1998: 112), Hung (2001: 498–500) and Arrighi (2007: 325).
[21] Deng (2008: 346) and Vries (2015: 139).
[22] von Glahn (2003: 188).

political power structures were too powerful to conquer and subdue. At the same time, as Hui Po-keung notes, when the Europeans first arrived in Southeast Asia 'in the early sixteenth century they discovered that Chinese merchants were everywhere and soon saw them as valuable assets and strong competitors'.[23] And, moreover, 'they found that they increasingly relied on, and hence tried to encourage the development of, the extensive private overseas Chinese business networks'.[24] Thus, *contra* Eurocentric and Eurofetishist conceptions of European primacy and autonomy, the Europeans followed an 'interstitial trading strategy' by working within the complex interstices of the East Asian order wherein entangled Sino–European relations rapidly became the order of the day.

This strategy proved to be mutually beneficial when cooperation came to the fore. Thus, European demand for Chinese silk, tea, porcelain and foodstuffs helped stimulate Chinese production. New World silver was their principal means of paying for Chinese products. Moreover, because the Europeans were never able to penetrate the Chinese interior, not even after 1842,[25] so they became dependent upon Chinese merchants to carry this trade. Accordingly, the arrival of the Europeans in East and Southeast Asia acted as a catalyst for yet more Chinese trade such that before the nineteenth century 'much of the activity we have parochially thought of as the "expansion of Europe" was European participation in the expansion of East Asia'.[26]

One illuminating example of the complex acrobatics that the Europeans unexpectedly found themselves performing in East Asia concerned their relations with the Zhengs and the Qing state. Chinese 'pirates' sought to collaborate with the Europeans in order to circumvent both the Qing state's bans and its specific attempts to stifle so-called piratical trade. In the process, this led to *temporary* symbioses with European Companies.[27] The most famous and powerful of the Chinese pirates was the Zheng family, headed by Zheng Zhilong, who was followed by his son, Zheng Chenggong (known as Koxinga to the Europeans), who in turn was succeeded in 1662 by his son, Zheng Jing. The Zhengs were at the heart of the so-called pirate trade that the Qing state was so anxious to quash and they built up a massive sphere of commercial influence that spread outwards from Guangdong and Fujian – the southern Chinese coastal port regions – to Japan, Taiwan, Manila and Southeast Asia.[28] The story

[23] Hui (1995: 45).
[24] Ibid. (9).
[25] Murphey (1974).
[26] Jansen (1992: 25).
[27] Zhao (2013: 23–9).
[28] See especially Hung (2000) and Hui (1995: ch. 2).

of the Zhengs provides a window into the complex networks of relations that existed between Chinese traders and the Europeans, on the one hand, and the Qing state and the Europeans on the other.

Zheng Zhilong moved to Macao in his teens and learned Portuguese while working for another major Chinese trader, Li Dan. This was linked to Zheng's strategy of maintaining trade by forming close relations with the Portuguese traders in Macao and in Japan. But when the Portuguese were ejected from Japan in 1639 on account of their desire to spread Catholicism, the Zhengs sought a new European partner. Paradoxically, just prior to this 'divorce' the Dutch had set out to destroy the Zhengs, whom the Vereenigde Oostindische Compagnie (VOC) saw as their single greatest trading rival in East Asia. The paradox is that the Zhengs' defeat of the VOC in 1633 was resolved in 1641 when the two signed a peace treaty and cooperated subsequently in trade, though it was on the Zhengs' terms given that the VOC had to make annual tribute payments for this trading privilege. Ultimately, the partnership between the Zhengs and the Dutch was important to the success of this most prominent of Chinese 'pirates',[29] not least because they were able to take this opportunity to arm their ships with European weaponry.

However, while the Zhengs used the VOC to enhance their power vis-à-vis the Qing, nevertheless these two trading groups were also rivals. For in 1661 the Zhengs turned on their VOC allies, defeating and then expelling the Dutch from Taiwan, which was then used as their home base. The military power of the Zhengs was so significant that even the Qing state was unable to defeat them outright, which is why the latter came to a temporary *modus vivendi* with them. For in 1661, the Zhengs had an army of 250,000 well-armed troops and some 2,300 ships.[30] Moreover, the Dutch governor of Taiwan was so impressed by the power of the Zhengs that he compared them as a seaborne power to that of the Dutch in Europe a century earlier.[31]

But these were truly complex acrobatics given that Chinese rulers sometimes used European and other foreign merchants in order to weaken native Chinese piratical merchants. And, in yet another twist to this story, when the Zhengs took over Taiwan in 1662 the Dutch courted the Qing and were granted yet more extended tributary relations, given that the state wanted to use them as a counterweight to their 'piratical' enemy. For the Zhengs desired to reinstate the Ming dynasty, thereby coming into fundamental conflict with the new Manchu Qing dynasty.

[29] Zhao (2013: 27–9).
[30] Hung (2000: 9).
[31] Arrighi (2007: 333).

Thus, after 1661, the Qing enhanced the VOC's tributary status in return for its support in attacking the Zhengs on Taiwan. It is true that after repeated requests the Dutch had been finally granted tribute/vassal status in 1654, though they were allowed to send tribute missions only once in every eight years. After 1661 they were 'privileged' in that they were allowed to send a mission once every two years.[32] Accordingly, although Dutch trading activities were determined largely by the whims and exigencies of various public and private Chinese forces, the VOC was prepared to conform to these for the trading benefits that they brought. And it was through the prism of entangled competitive–cooperative relations that this played out. Still, once the Zhengs had been defeated by the Qing in 1683 and Chinese merchants had been demilitarised, the Qing's rationale for dealing with the Dutch waned so that the VOC struggled to maintain a direct trading link with China. Instead, 'in 1690 [the VOC] left this trade to Chinese junks which visited Batavia in yearly growing numbers'.[33] But even in Batavia, the capital of their seaborne trading 'empire', the Dutch had no choice but to form competitive–cooperative relations with the resident Chinese.

Competitive–Cooperation Outside China: Entangled Dutch and Chinese Business Diasporic Relations

Although we tend to imagine the Dutch ruling much of the Indian Ocean trade from their Indonesian 'imperial capital' in Batavia (modern-day Jakarta on Java), it turns out that commercially they ruled neither the high seas nor even Java. The only places where they could assert imperial sway was in the tiny Molucca Islands and Ceylon, where they created plantations for spice production – nutmeg, cinnamon and mace – which were based on slavery that was backed up by very high levels of imperial coercion. But what needs to be factored in here are the highly important roles that the Chinese performed on Java. First, not only were the Dutch dependent on Chinese help but they also benefited from Java's trading links with China. Junks from China arrived each year delivering silk fabrics, sugar, porcelain, iron pans, nails, needles and coarse (everyday mass-based) textiles, and subsequently tea. Moreover, not only was an effective division of labour struck between the Chinese and Dutch VOC in Java, with the latter acting as a wholesale dealer and the former

---

[32] Zhang (2020: ch. 2).
[33] Gaastra (2007: 189).

monopolising the retail trade, but the Dutch relied heavily on many services that were performed by the Chinese.[34]

The Chinese dominated various key Javan industries. One such industry was the salt business,[35] though the Chinese also acted as tax revenue farmers (*Towkays*), who gained monopolies over coining, customs and gambling. Nevertheless, the most significant was the Javanese sugar industry. A VOC report of 1711 stated that there were approximately 131 sugar production factories or workshops in Batavia. Of the 84 owners, 1 was Javanese, 4 were European and 79 were Chinese. Although the number of local Chinese decreased following the massacre of the resident Chinese by the Dutch in 1740, nevertheless the former continued to occupy the key ownership role in local sugar production.[36] For, It is important to note that after the various massacres of resident Chinese, the Dutch learned very quickly that they had little choice but to court fresh Chinese residents as they could not survive without them.[37] Thus by 1762, the total number of sugar production factories in Batavia was 82 with 24 of them owned by Europeans and 26 owned by the Chinese.[38] And, as I explain in Chapter 8, these were run along the lines of historical capitalism that embodied, in part, modern capitalist social relations. Nevertheless, the competitive–cooperative nature and entangled agencies of Sino–Dutch relations on Java were reflected in the fact that all of the employees, including those of the Chinese-owned factories, came under the supervision of the Dutch sheriff and his men.[39]

Sir Stamford Raffles, the famous British colonial agent, stated in the nineteenth century that 'throughout the whole of Java, trade is usually conducted by the Chinese: many of them are very rich, and their means are increased by their knowledge of business, their spirit of enterprise, and their natural confidence'.[40] Moreover, there were considerable synergies between the Dutch and Chinese in terms of developing and conducting inter-regional trade. As Zhang Shizhi notes, 'Chinese sampan [boats] and ships were everywhere. In this region [Southeast Asia] they actively shuttled among the various islands for trade.'[41] Critical here was the Chinese junk trade, with a large number of Chinese ships trading with Batavia and thereby nourishing Dutch and Chinese

[34] Dobbin (1996: 47–8).
[35] Hui (1995: 59).
[36] Mazumdar (1998: 89).
[37] Hui (1995: 71–2).
[38] Zhang (2020: ch. 2) and Shinjiro (1960/1983: 107).
[39] Shinjiro (1960/1983: 107).
[40] Sir Stamford Raffles cited in Dobbin (1996: 69).
[41] Zhang (2020: ch. 2).

trading opportunities.[42] Indeed, between 1681 and 1793 the number of Chinese junks that arrived in Batavia averaged eleven per annum.[43] Moreover, the Dutch peace treaty that was signed with Spain in 1648 ensured that the Dutch could not visit Spanish harbours and nor could the latter extend their existing trade. Accordingly, it was the Chinese who traded with Manila upon whom the VOC, as well as the Spanish, came to rely.[44] The considerable Chinese presence there is confirmed by the point that in Parian (in Manila), the number of Chinese retail stores increased from approximately 400 in 1602 to 800 in 1628 and as many as 1,200 by 1645.[45] All of which qualifies Fernand Braudel's Eurofetishist claim that '[o]nce Holland had conquered the trade of Europe, the rest of the world was a logical bonus, thrown in as it were'.[46] The reality, it turns out, was quite different.

Europe's 'Voluntary Dependency' vis-à-vis East Asian Emperors

Finally, it is worth noting the intriguing paradox that while Western conceptions of the CTS view the vassal states as dependent – though I reveal this as a myth in Chapter 12 – a more accurate example of dependency is found with respect to the East India Companies' relations with the Chinese state. It is equally notable that the Europeans *chose* to accept the dependency status in their relations with the Chinese and Japanese emperors. Indeed, in contrast with the Eurocentric and Eurofetishist mantra of the Europeans' arrival in East Asia – that they came, they saw, they conquered – the reality is that 'they came, they saw, they kow-towed'. Portuguese traders offered large tribute payments to the Chinese emperor as did the Dutch, especially after 1661 (as noted earlier). The same was true with respect to their relations with the Japanese emperor before 1639 (viz. the Portuguese) and after 1641 (viz. the Dutch). The VOC's participation in the Japanese 'tribute system' (JTS) is particularly instructive – though it should be noted that Japan's 'system' was more informal than that of China.[47]

Having expelled the Catholic Portuguese in 1639 for the presumed cultural threat that they posed, the Tokugawa shogunate/Bakufu state granted the Protestant Dutch – who were far more interested in plying trade than proselytising – the right to trade with Japan. But the price that

---

[42] Zhao (2013: 5).
[43] See Hui (1995: 43).
[44] Gaastra (2007: 189).
[45] Zhang (2020: ch. 2).
[46] Braudel (1992: 207).
[47] See Toby (1984).

the Dutch paid for this trading privilege was severe limitations to their autonomy and an affront to their dignity. For there they were confined to the tiny island of Deshima (which measured a mere 236 by 82 paces), which was located in the port of Nagasaki. For a long time

[t]he Dutch were spied on by their Japanese servants and controlled by a 150-strong official interpreter corps. Just one ship a year was allowed to call and its officers were usually 'beaten with sticks as if they were dogs'. They were allowed to visit the mainland once a year in order to pay homage to the shogun.[48]

Critically, the deployment of Dutch military power was simply not an option. As Jason Sharman notes, 'in 1707 a Dutch official in Japan reported: "[t]o show our teeth and use violence is completely impossible, unless we want to leave this land and never come again."'[49] Indeed, the Dutch were prepared to undertake this humiliation because it enabled them to carry on their lucrative trade with Japan which in turn enabled them to expand within the wider Indian Ocean system.[50] This humiliating situation was recognised and indeed embraced by the VOC directors who, in 1650, instructed the Dutch traders to 'look to the wishes of that bold, haughty, and exacting nation, in order to please them in everything'.[51]

To sum up this overall section, I argue that it is the *connected* though above all *interactive histories* and entangled agential relations that are significant. But Sino–European relations were never rosy or cosmopolitan in nature because they existed within the complex, oscillating modalities of cooperation and conflict that played out within a broader relationship of economic interdependence and not infrequent political dependence. And this, once more, points up my claim that this was a thoroughly polycentric global system as opposed to one that was dominated by any one particular country or region.

Eurocentric and Sinocentric Myths of the CTS

Even if foreign trade continued in all manner of ways despite the various official bans, Eurocentric world history presumes that as a result of the 1371 ban the state retreated into the 'imperial' CTS. And equally as 'well known' is the point that the CTS was economically regressive for two reasons: first, because foreign trade was sacrificed on the altar of

[48] Ponting (2000: 525).
[49] Sharman (2019: 79).
[50] See especially, Toby (1984: 194) and Suzuki (2014: 88–9).
[51] Pearson (1991: 115).

the state's irrational obsession with symbolic ritual; and second, because of the Confucian state's aversion to mercantile culture and merchants coupled with the desire to portray China as self-sufficient in the eyes of its population. So-called proof of this lies in the point that nineteenth-century European observers

ridiculed the tribute system for forcing the practical matters of trade into a straitjacket of ritual. To a nineteenth-century Western European, convinced that humans naturally sought economic gain above all, no further proof could be needed that China stifled normal human impulses and would be better off if it was 'opened up' to laissez faire – even by violence.[52]

However, what this common(sense) Western view misses is that foreign trade was not only an important part of the CTS but that Chinese trade also continued outside of it. Indeed, the notion that China retreated into an 'anti-commercial' CTS following the 1371 trade ban needs to be turned inside out. Paradoxically, in at least one key respect, Sinocentrism fares no better and reinforces much of the Eurocentric analysis, not least in terms of viewing the CTS as a coherent system that dominated the politics and economics of the East- and Southeast-Asian region. For when we de-centre the CTS, a series of trading relations emerges from the hitherto shadowy, recessive background.

Trading inside the CTS

There are three core reasons why the CTS enabled rather than stifled foreign trade. First, its relationship to trade was far more conducive than has been recognised by Eurocentrism. There were various forms of trade within the tribute system: first, 'tribute trade' (the exchange of gifts between vassal emissaries and the emperor); second, 'official trade' (conducted between officials and the tribute missions in the 'official markets' within Beijing) and third, 'commercial/private trade' that was conducted between private merchants on the borders and entry ports. The irony of the tribute trade is that it was financially onerous upon the Chinese state, for in order to maintain the ritualistic myth of China's superiority the tribute gifts that the vassals presented to the emperor had to be of a lesser value than those that they received in return.[53] Moreover, the 'vassals' also enjoyed asymmetric gains through

---

[52] Pomeranz and Topik (2006: 11–12). See also: Zhang (2009: 574), Song (2012) and Perdue (2015: 1002).
[53] Fairbank (1942: 135).

the official trade. This was conducted over five days between tribute-envoys and Chinese officials at a special market set up at the Residence for Tributary Envoys.[54]

Under the *Geijia shoumai* (official purchasing system), the Chinese state paid well above market prices for the vassals' goods,[55] thereby helping to 'lock' the vassal states into the CTS. Indeed, the official trade was extremely lucrative for the vassals, yielding spectacular profit margins. Examples abound: in Java 100 lbs of black pepper might fetch one (silver) tael but twenty taels in the official Chinese market – i.e., a price ratio of 20:1. Equally, because Japanese knives sold between two and five times more in China than at home, so the Japanese increased their sale of knives in the Chinese official trade from 3,000 in 1400 to some 50,000 in 1550. Moreover, the price ratios for ivory were 20:1, while sappanwood from Southeast Asia stood at 80:1.[56] And, because the missions' expenses were paid for entirely by the Chinese court prior to the Qing period the envoys' profits on official trade were enhanced yet further. Not surprisingly, this comprised a major incentive for states to join the system as 'vassals', which explains why the CTS expanded after the mid-fifteenth century. Thus, for example, the Japanese resumed tribute missions in 1453 because of the super-normal profit margins that ensued – which ranged from 500 to 600 per cent. Moreover, the Oirat Mongols who resided in western Mongolia tended in general to send missions of a few hundred men but then increased the numbers to 2,524 in 1448, though they falsely claimed that there were some 3,598 men in order to gain more profit from the more expensive gifts that they received from the Chinese state. Interestingly, in this instance the Chinese state became aware of this deception and reduced the return gifts to only 20 per cent of those requested.[57]

The economic trading dimension of the CTS can be revealed by the personnel who formed the tribute team. For while we generally assume that these were *political* envoys, the fact is that the vast majority of them were merchants. For example, with the growing numbers sent by Japan, the Chinese state was forced to restrict the size of the Japanese tribute team. Chinese historical archival records point out that '[i]n 1550, the state stipulated that each team at most includes 2 envoys, 6 officials, 7 monks and 60 merchants'.[58] Overall, not inconsiderable trade was

[54] Ibid. (138).
[55] Hui (1995: 39).
[56] Zhao (2013: 103–4) and Kang (2010: 114–16).
[57] Wang (2011: 148).
[58] *Daming Huidian* (Collected Statutes of the Ming Dynasty), Vol. 105. Text available online: https://ctext.org/wiki.pl?if=gb&chapter=605445&remap=gb

conducted at the official level even though it conferred significant economic losses upon the Chinese state.[59] But the Chinese state endured these losses because, in the words of Stuart Martin-Fox, '[t]he symbolism of ritual submission took precedence over economic benefit' so far as the Chinese emperors were concerned.[60]

Of course, this would appear to confirm the Eurocentric assumption that the CTS was economically irrational. Two replies are noteworthy. First, private trade that was conducted by vassal-based private merchants on the border came to increasingly outweigh the size of official and tribute trade after about the mid-fifteenth century.[61] Most importantly, Hamashita Takeshi estimates that by the late-seventeenth century about ten times as many private merchants engaged in this border trade when compared with those engaged in official and tribute trade;[62] though this ratio in favour of private trade would escalate rapidly after 1684 (as I note shortly). Thus, the notion that the 1371 ban put an end to private trade is clearly incorrect precisely because it was enshrined as a core function of the CTS. Indeed, as David Kang notes, the 'tribute system was the official veneer behind which much larger volumes of private trade occurred'.[63] Or as Kent Deng puts it, '[t]he tributary system was a form of disguised staple trade'.[64] And, in any case, as John Fairbank originally argued, gaining access to China's extremely lucrative domestic economy was the principal reason why foreign states sought to join the CTS as vassals.[65] All of which suggests that the CTS expanded during the Ming period as states were attracted to it in large part for the trading benefits it furnished as opposed to the Sinocentric and Eurocentric views that they were forced to join through Chinese bullying and coercion.[66]

Not only was the tribute system 'often, in effect, only an outward form for very considerable [private] trade', but more important is the point that in 'many cases foreign merchants ... presented themselves as the bearers of fictitious tribute from imaginary states solely for the purposes of conducting trade'.[67] Such was the extensity and seriousness of this problem that the Ming government issued certificates to vassal-based

[59] For example, Pomeranz and Topik (2006: 13) and Kang (2010: 70, 114).
[60] Martin-Fox (2003: 76).
[61] Hui (1995: 40), Zhao (2013: 115) and Zheng (2014: 52).
[62] Hamashita (2003b).
[63] Kang (2010: 110); see also Zhao (2013) and Zheng (2014: 52).
[64] Deng (1997: 254).
[65] Fairbank (1942).
[66] Wade (2004) and Wang (2011: ch. 6). For a rebuttal, see Levathes (1994) and Snow (1989: ch. 1).
[67] Rodzinski (1979: 179). See also: Hamashita (1994, 2003a: 20–3), Flynn and Giráldez (1995b: 438), Deng (1997: 256–61) and Frank (1998: 114).

merchants so as to prevent foreigners arriving in China and posing as emissaries. Overall, as Jacques Gernet aptly notes, '[t]here was a big gap between the official regulations and the reality of the commercial situation; the official [tribute] restrictions [and the official ban] imposed on trade might lead us to suppose that China was isolated at the very time when maritime trade was ... intense'.[68] All in all, then, the considerable amount of private trade that occurred within the CTS goes under the Eurocentric radar given that only official and tribute trade register.

The second problem is that as much as it is incorrect to assume that the presence of foreign trade – especially private trade – was a casualty of the CTS, it is also the case that after about the mid-fifteenth century Chinese emperors began increasingly to question the 'economic irrationality' of its ritual dimension.[69] Thus as more and more 'Geijia products' were brought by foreign envoys and merchants, the Qing state and officials struggled to purchase them all. Eventually, the state allowed them to conduct trade freely in the market. To this end, the official record states that, '[e]xcept for tribute goods ... [if] there are extra products, they are allowed to trade in the market freely'.[70]

All of which culminated in the 1684 Open Door policy (to be discussed later), which entailed the formal separation of private from tribute trade. That is, private merchants wishing to trade with China no longer needed official vassal status to carry out their business. And, moreover, from 1684 onwards the Qing insisted that the vassals bore the costs of their missions to Beijing.[71] Which, in turn, means that the core of the tribute trading system was *de facto* abolished in 1684.[72] But as we have seen earlier, it seems that the Kangxi Emperor was really only formalising a pattern that had been established on an informal basis previously, given that many countries had maintained trading relations with China even in those times when they were not part of the tribute system;[73] and moreover, that the link was being eroded steadily after about the mid-fifteenth century. Indeed, after 1684 the gap widened and escalated at an exponential rate. Thus, for example, between 1685 and 1722, the Ryūkyūs (present-day Okinawa) sent 120 tribute ships to China, but some 2,500 private ships to China and Japan.[74] And by the turn of the

---

[68] Gernet (1999: 420).

[69] Wang (2011: 148).

[70] *Daming Huidian* (Collected Statutes of the Ming Dynasty), Vol. 111. Text available online: https://ctext.org/wiki.pl?if=gb&chapter=232497&remap=gb

[71] Zhao (2013: 109–10, 113–14).

[72] Arrighi (2007: 324–5) and Zhao (2013: 110–11).

[73] Zheng (2014: 51–2).

[74] Zhao (2013: 111–13).

eighteenth century one estimate suggests that the annual value of official trade comprised a mere 3 per cent of total private trade.[75]

Following on from the second is a third inter-related problem that I signalled earlier, in that while the 'vassal states' often went for long periods in which they did *not* send tribute missions to China – as was the case with the Japanese as well as various Mongolian tribes when they were formally part of the tribute system – nevertheless they were often able to maintain trading relations with China regardless. Moreover, Japan maintained trading relations with China even after it had set up its own rival 'tribute system' after 1603, as I explain below. All of which suggests that *informally* the link between vassal status in the CTS and maintaining trading relations with China did not always hold even before 1684 – that trading relations with China could be maintained *outside* of the formalities of the CTS in the T'ang through Ming eras.[76] And this is reinforced much further given that the link was broken by the Qing in 1684.

De-centring the CTS: The Development of Trade beyond Its Boundaries

There was, however, much more to China's foreign trade than that which was conducted within the CTS.[77] For much intra-regional trade was conducted outside of it, which means that it would be wrong to assume that regional trade was filtered through the CTS as if they were one and the same thing. In short, Eurocentric and Sinocentric readings have imputed far too much power, coherence and singularity to the CTS within the region.[78] William Callahan dubs this reified conception of the tribute system as a product of (Sinocentric) 'Sinospeak'.[79] For one of the major reasons why conflating the East/Southeast-Asian region with the CTS is an exercise in mythology lies in the complexities that the rival JTS brought to bear after 1603. And it is at this point that we confront the most bizarre aspect of the CTS when viewed through either a Eurocentric or Sinocentric lens.

Most significant is that the JTS, which had Korea as its number one vassal as well as the Ryūkyūs as its number two were also vassals of China within the CTS's prized 'inner zone of manifest civility'. Having

---

[75] Kisimoto Mio cited in Zhao (2013: 113).
[76] Zhang (2009: 561–2).
[77] See Frank (1998: 115, 116) and Zhao (2013: 189).
[78] Callahan (2012) and Perdue (2015).
[79] Callahan (2012).

to recognise both Japan and China as cultural superiors reveals the complex realities and tangled webs that the region's international politics entailed. Most striking of all is that China was not only a vassal of the JTS after 1603 but it was the lowliest one at that, standing below the 'Dutch barbarians'.[80] Given that this wreaks havoc with the notion of a Sinocentric regional system so this raises the question as to why China joined the JTS. And the answer is that China most likely tolerated this position because it enabled it to carry on its vital trade with Japan from which it gained considerable benefits. Of particular note here is that even after 1557 when Japan left the CTS, Sino–Japanese trade continued and in fact increased right through to about the 1730s before it declined thereafter.

Here, we need to factor in the role of Japanese silver and copper exports to China, which reveals simultaneously both China's and Japan's important trading roles in the FGE. As is the case with China, so Eurocentrism presumes that Japan was isolated from world trade following the 1639 trade ban via the policy known as *Sakoku* (or 'closed county'). Rather than revealing in detail how Japan was indirectly open to overseas trade until at least the 1730s,[81] here I shall merely emphasise what was perhaps the key contribution that Japan made to the FGE – specifically, its supply of silver and copper to China. For this was very important in maintaining the Chinese economy and its overseas trade which in turn was one of the key drivers of the global trading system.

The Japanese supply of bullion to China was particularly important from the 1530s on, and remained so even following the official Japanese 'silver ban' with China in the 1680s. For the reality is that the Tokugawa's initial efforts to restrict the outflow of precious metals proved to be unsuccessful.[82] After 1668 Japan also exported large amounts of gold and silver, but mainly copper, well into the first half of the eighteenth century so as to maintain levels of external trade.[83] As Zhang Shizhi explains, because in 1695 the Tokugawa initiated the 'substitution payment' by which Japanese merchants were required to buy foreign goods with copper only, so copper flowed out of the country to pay predominantly for Chinese imports such as silk and sugar.[84] Moreover, the not-inconsiderable size of the bullion exports in themselves reveals

---

[80] Suzuki (2007).
[81] But see Toby (1984), Jansen (1992), Ikeda (1996), Hobson (2004: 93–6) and Suzuki (2014).
[82] Kang (2010: 125–7).
[83] Ikeda (1996: 55), Frank (1998: 127) and Miyamoto and Shikano (2003: 176–7).
[84] Zhang (2020: ch. 2).

that Japan relied heavily on foreign imports, especially from China, thereby revealing that both these economies were open to foreign trade.

Finally, it is notable that one way in which the Japanese state maintained significant levels of external trade, having banned Japanese merchants from trading abroad, was by relying on Chinese merchants to export goods from, and import goods into, Japan.[85] And while it is certainly the case that the Tokugawa Bakufu restricted trade with China after about the 1730s as it sought to limit the outflow of specie, though Mazumdar argues that Japanese copper exports to China carried on well into the nineteenth century,[86] nevertheless Chinese trade increased with other countries within Europe and Southeast Asia as I explain in the next section.[87] All in all, joining the JTS proved to be a lucrative commercial option for the Chinese.

A second major reason why conflating the East- and Southeast-Asian region with the CTS turns out to be an exercise in mythology lies with the interstitial role that the Southeast-Asian 'mandala systems' performed. Although these were partially linked to the CTS, they also had their own autonomy as well as their own numerous vassals – with the Majapahit empire having some ninety-eight at its peak. Paradoxically, this is relevant for understanding the continuity of trade with China. Critically, the Majapahit Empire, which was the principal Mandala system of the region, neither submitted to, nor sought recognition from, the Chinese emperor. Thus, for example, when the Ming state approached Brunai – as it was known at the time – to become a vassal, the Majapahits overruled this and Brunai remained their vassal. According to the traditional Sinocentric conception of the CTS, one would anticipate, therefore, that trading relations would have been terminated between China and the Majapahits. But, in fact, the Majapahits maintained close trading relations even though they did not have vassal status. Indeed, their ability to retain trading relations with China reflects one of the lowest common denominators of the Southeast-Asian Mandala systems – for as with the northern Mongols, the Mandalas forged links with China principally to enhance their economic power by gaining access to the lucrative Chinese economy, possibly to an even greater extent than did the polities of the Chinese 'inner tribute zone of manifest civility'.[88]

In sum, then, both the Sinocentric and Eurocentric assumptions of a China-centred regional system and economy err by obscuring the

---

[85] Ikeda (1996: 55) and Lee (1999: 9).
[86] Mazumdar (1998: 99).
[87] Zhang (2020: ch. 2).
[88] See Manggala (2013) and Dellios (1996).

presence of a good deal of regional trading relations that escaped the so-called confines of Chinese tributary regulatory constraints. But equally, a good deal of foreign trade occurred within the CTS. Such were the complexities involved in inter-state regional political economy that one might even go so far as to say that the only problem with the term 'Sinocentric tribute system' are the words 'Sinocentric', 'tribute' and 'system'; a point I return to in Chapter 12. Nevertheless, for all this, my sceptical Eurocentric reader will remain unconvinced by my claim that China was open to global trade. For it is 'very well known' that after 1757 China retreated once more by forcing all imported foreign trade through one single port – Canton (Guangzhou) – which, in turn, saw foreign traders heavily regulated and supervised by the notorious Cohong. In this way, the Canton system is viewed, in essence, as a giant non-tariff barrier.

Confronting the Four Eurocentric Myths of the 'Canton System'

The first of the four Eurocentric myths that I identify here concerns the two double standards that underpinned the British 'construction' or 'invention' of the so-called *Canton system* as being indirectly protectionist. The first double standard concerns the point that while the British were highly critical of China's 'effective trade protectionism', which the Canton system supposedly represented, it was in fact Britain and Europe that were the most protectionist countries/regions in the FGE (as I explain in the next section). The second British double standard emerges in the point that although the Europeans proclaimed to stand for free trade while instigating very high protectionism at home, it turns out that the British demanded not free trading access to, but *privileged monopoly* trading rights with, China. Thus, as Zhao Gang points out perceptively,

China's disregard, denial, and rejection of British commercial privileges [was twisted around into] a challenge to 'civilization' and, more important, clearly reflected the isolationist and controlling nature of China's trade policy as well as the backwardness and closed quality of the Chinese empire.[89]

The rebuttal to the second Eurocentric myth of the Canton system is that rather than declining after 1757, British, European and American trade with China *took off*. According to Zhang Shizhi,

---

[89] Zhao (2013: 8).

In the first stage of the Qing's opening (1684–1757), the total number of European and American ships trading with China was approximately 314, which averaged 7.3 ships per year. But this figure surged upwards after the instigation of the 'Canton system'. From 1757 to 1838, some 5,107 trading ships from Europe and America arrived in China, which averaged out at approximately 63 ships per year.[90]

This approximate nine-fold increase in trade is reinforced by the point that when measured in silver, British trade with China increased thirteen-fold between 1760–64 and 1804.[91] And, moreover, within just three years of the establishment of the Canton system, Britain's major import product from China, tea, had grown in volume by 66 per cent,[92] while by 1784 it had grown by 535 per cent over the 1757 figure.[93] And, because tariffs were kept to low levels in Guangzhou, so this problematises the claim that the Canton system restricted foreign trade with Britain. All in all, the system was based on Chinese 'managed liberal trade'.

The third Eurocentric myth concerns the claim that only one Chinese port, Guangzhou, was open to foreign trade. For this whitewashes the point that these 'restrictions' did *not* apply to non-Western merchants given that they were not viewed as a cultural threat and were, accordingly, granted access to many Chinese ports.[94] In fact, specialist research by Chinese scholars now reveals that there were at least fifty large and small ports within these four southern provinces that were open to overseas trade.[95] Which means that the European perception of a 'closed China' derived from the Europeans' limited access to China via Guangzhou is a misreading that appears when viewing it through a one-eyed Eurocentric lens.[96]

Finally, the fourth Eurocentric myth concerns the assumption that it was only the Opium War (1839–42) and the subsequent British-imposed (unequal) Treaty of Nanjing (1842) that forced open China to world trade 'for the first time' by creating five treaty ports – Guangzhou (Canton), Xiamen (Amoy), Ningbo, Shanghai and Quanzhou. But this misses the point that these five ports had become significant well before 1842. Of note here is that the port of Guangzhou became a critically important trading centre as early as the ninth century, when it attracted

---

[90] Zhang (2020: ch. 2).
[91] Archival data calculations made by Yao Xingao cited in Zhao (2013: 230, n. 142).
[92] Chaudhuri (2006: 539).
[93] Calculated from data in de Vries (2010: 721) and Chaudhuri (2006: 539).
[94] Zhao (2013: 186).
[95] Huang (1999) and Zhao (2013: 6, ch. 9).
[96] See also Zhao (2013: 6–7).

some 100,000 foreign merchants annually from Southeast Asia, India and the Arab world. Then, during

the next six centuries, Guangzhou, the capital of Guangdong remained among the most prosperous ports in China, and Guangdong's economy relied on foreign trade to a greater extent than that of any other country [in the world]. The local government worked diligently to attract foreign businessmen, even consciously disregarding the official ban during the time it was in effect.[97]

Like Guangzhou, the other four treaty ports 'established' by the British-imposed treaty had, in fact, all been vibrant centres of trade since at least 1684, if not centuries before they were made customs headquarters. Shanghai, which was selected as the headquarters of the Jiangsu customs in 1684, became a centre for trade with Japan in the late-seventeenth century and with Manchuria in the eighteenth. But it had become a port as far back as the tenth century. Moreover, by 1850, it took in more foreign trade by volume than did Guangzhou. Quanzhou in Fujian came to prominence during the Song dynasty back in the tenth century, and by the thirteenth century Marco Polo described it as 'one of the two greatest havens in the world for commerce'.[98] It had also become a more significant port than Guangzhou during the Song period.[99] Fuzhou (also in Fujian), though reaching back to the pre-Common Era, came to prominence as a port in Song times (c. tenth and eleventh centuries) as did the Fujian city of Xiamen. Ningbo in Zhejiang became a trading port on the Silk Road back in Han times before the Common Era and, along with Quangzhou, became a major port as early as the T'ang dynasty (618–906). In short, then, rather than springing into life as a result of the British treaty in 1842, these five 'treaty' ports – in addition to many others – had all flourished many centuries earlier,[100] all of which goes under the Eurocentric radar.

In sum, because non-Western merchants gained access to China via other 'non-treaty' ports after 1757 – much as they had done long before then – so the assumption that the Europeans 'opened up China to world trade' and thereby 'battered down the walls of barbarism' misses the point that China had long been open to foreign trade, either unofficially between 1371 and 1567, 1661–83 and 1717–27, or officially between 1567 and 1661, 1684–1717 and 1727–1911. Given this, we can detect traces of the argument that is deployed especially by Americans today with

---

[97] Ibid. (178).
[98] Yule (1875: 217).
[99] Finlay (2010: 109).
[100] Zhao (2013: 193–4).

respect to their trade deficit with China, as was the case, viz. Japan in the 1980s: that the British justified their forced intervention in 1839 on the grounds that China was 'closed' to global trade. However, not only was China open to *global* trade after 1571 but the reality was also that '[w]ithout China [and I would add India] the birth of world trade would have been delayed to some unknowable extent'.[101] Or as Robert Marks puts it, '[a]s the largest and most productive economy in the world, China [along with India] was the engine that powered much of the world economy, with New World silver [and Indian cotton textiles] providing the energy'.[102] Nevertheless, for all this there remains one final hurdle to overcome, which concerns the common Eurocentric perception that China could not have been a significant global trading power given that the 'Oriental despotic' Chinese state engaged in very high levels of tariff protectionism.

The Twin Myths of Britain's Laissez-Faire Free Trade Posture and Qing China's Interventionist Protectionist Stance

The familiar Eurocentric claim is that Britain was the free-trading industrialiser par excellence as much as China was the world's most interventionist state that controlled not only the domestic economy but also stifled foreign trade through heavy tariff protectionism. I agree that the two countries developed radically different foreign trade policies, but it was China that moved to freer trade after 1684, whereas Britain moved simultaneously to high protectionism between 1684 and 1796 and exceptionally high protectionism in 1796–1846. This section begins by considering Qing China's freer trading policy before engaging in a comparative analysis to explain the 'great trade-policy divergence' between Britain and China after 1684.

The Qing's Post-1684 'Open Door' Freer Trade Policy

Of all the facts that bust the myth of a closed China that I have dealt with thus far, the most notable one is the Qing's initiation of the Open Door freer trade policy in 1684. The immediate backdrop to this was the Qing ban on foreign trade (1661–83) which, as noted earlier, was initiated as a means of defeating the Zheng 'pirates'. In the process, the state instigated a complete evacuation of the people from the southern

---

[101] Flynn and Giráldez (1995a: 218).
[102] Marks (2002: 80).

coastal region – the policy of *qianjee* – in order to starve out the trading activities of the Zhengs.[103] In tandem with the Dutch, with whom the Qing had formed an alliance in 1661, albeit on Chinese terms, the Zhengs were finally defeated in 1682. And with 'mission accomplished' it then became a matter of some urgency to terminate the ban given that it had come at some economic cost. For the resulting silver shortage had created deflation that had led not only to economic hardship but also to reduced tax revenues.

To solve the so-called Kangxi depression, the Kangxi Emperor instructed the country's merchants in 1684 as follows: '[n]ow, as China ... is united and the world ... is at peace, as Manchu and Han people form one uniform body ... I order you to go abroad to trade, in order to display the good rule of the wealthy and numerous, and by imperial decree open the seas for trade'.[104] Still, while I noted in the introduction to this chapter that the Kangxi reform comprised a vital part of 'going global 1.0', nevertheless this was an extension of previous foreign trading initiatives, though this time with official backing. Moreover, Kangxi believed that foreign trade could enrich the state, which was to be achieved not through high tariffs (customs taxes), unlike in Britain, but more often through tax exemptions. And while local officials often tried to increase customs revenue, Kangxi 'rebuked them insisting that "you will comply with my wish to cherish both merchants and the people"'.[105]

Critically, the Manchu Qing state, which was obviously less Confucianised than the Ming, was well disposed to commercial capitalism while the Kangxi Emperor heralded the turn to near-open trade as a vital means of enriching the country. Notable too is that Kangxi's successor, Qianlong (r. 1735–96), proclaimed that 'some like to work in the fields, but others pursue business. If some people find they excel in commerce, they should stay with it. Commercial successes contribute greatly to the improvement of social practices'.[106] Moreover, the Qing court consistently instructed officials to 'assist merchants', to 'enrich development' and to 'enrich the people'.[107] All foreign merchants were allowed in, including the English East India Company in the late-seventeenth century. And all four coastal provinces were fully opened – Jiangsu, Zhejiang, Fujian and Guangdong – while the *key* ports that foreign merchants could enter, eleven of which hosted

---

[103] Schottenhammer (2010: 107) and Zheng (2014: ch. 2).
[104] Kangxi Emperor cited in Schottenhammer (2010: 126).
[105] Schottenhammer (2010: 110).
[106] Emperor Qianlong cited in Zhao (2013: 183).
[107] Schottenhammer (2010: 108); also Perkins (1967).

customs houses, comprised: Ningbo, Dinghai, Wenzhou, Quanzhou, Chaozhou, Guangzhou, Shanghai, Chongge, Huatingxian, Fuzhou, Nantai, Xiamen (Amoy), Xianshanxian and Aomen (Macao).[108]

Zhang Shizhi makes the important argument that the Qing state's shift to freer trade was in significant part enabled through what he calls 'managed (economic) liberalism'. This is a mode of intervention that is reminiscent of, though not identical to, Karl Polanyi's well-known claim that free (and freer) trade and liberalism rest on a state-regulatory base.[109] First, Zhang highlights the role that the Qing state played in bringing about an end to *corvée* labour by 1711, which enabled the liberalisation of various industries, especially the cotton textile putting out industry. And, in responding to merchant requests for help, the state, for example, ensured the end of the old brokerage system that the putting out merchants had become opposed to.[110]

It is also noteworthy that according to Zhang Shizhi, China's *effective* average tariff rate stood at about 6 per cent.[111] This 'effective' rate aggregates tariff levels with the 'vessel tax' that was paid on entry into a port while it remained docked. It also adds in those amounts that local officials charged. Here, it is important to note that I define *freer* trade as comprising an average tariff across all imports to lie between 5 and 10 per cent *ad valorem*. This contrasts with 'moderate' protectionism (between 10 and 15 per cent *ad valorem*) and high protectionism (over 15 per cent). Interestingly, Qing China's average rate of 6 per cent on all imports after 1684 is close to the European era of freer trade (1860– c. 80), when average tariffs stood at about 8 per cent. China's freer trade regime is brought into further relief by the fact that British tariff rates averaged 31 per cent during its long industrialisation period (1700–1850) and as much as 39 per cent in the main phase of 1796–1850, which was the highest average tariff levied by any European industrialiser. Indeed, it even outpaced Tsarist Russia's average 30 per cent rate in its industrialisation phase (1880–1913), which is striking given that Russia is generally reckoned to have been the most protectionist industrialiser of any European country.[112]

The results of the new Open Door policy were immediate. As Robert Marks notes, 'the explosive growth of Chinese coastal and foreign trade

---

[108] Schottenhammer (2010: 126) and Zhao (2013: 111).
[109] Polanyi (1944/2001).
[110] Zhang (2020: ch. 3).
[111] Ibid. (ch. 2). See also Hung (2001: 480).
[112] The sources for all the calculations made in this paragraph (bar China's) are reported in Hobson (2004: 209). Note that these figures are based on average rates on *all* imports.

immediately follow[ed] the lifting in 1684 of the ban'.[113] Thus, while only 12 private Chinese vessels sailed from China to Japan between 1680/84, the number rose to 467 in the following 1685/89 period.[114] And in 1685/1701 more than 1,167 ships traded between Southeast Asia, Japan and 25 coastal Chinese ports.[115] This was recognised at the time with an official governor's report asserting in 1724 that 'Kangxi's opening since 1684 significantly benefited both state and society.'[116] However, important though such evidence is, it is nevertheless anecdotal and unsystematic. For what the literature has lacked hitherto is some kind of numerical figure for China's total foreign trade. It is for this reason that Gunder Frank spent so much time discussing the Chinese silver sink, for this served as his proxy measure for revealing China's trade surplus with the rest of the world, which underpins his claim that China stood at the centre of the global economy.[117] Fortunately, however, recent and detailed Chinese archival research undertaken by Zhang Shizhi has gone a long way to filling this important gap in the literature.

Zhang's estimates of Chinese foreign trade are based on a series of calculations that are derived from the recorded tariff revenues that were collected in the four southern provinces, Guangdong, Jiangsu, Zhejiang and Fujian. And from these, he makes various adjustments to derive three final estimates of the size of China's overseas trade – what he calls a 'minimum', a 'maximum' and an 'average' (of the two). Running with his 'average estimate', Zhang reveals that when calculated in constant sterling equivalent, China's overseas trade in 1735–95 was on average just under 20 per cent higher than Britain's.[118] If we run with his 'minimum estimate' China's was about 7 per cent lower than Britain's, and if we run with his 'maximum estimate' China's was about 40 per cent higher.[119] Nevertheless, if we include China's overland trade these estimates would increase by at least 5 per cent – which means that even if we were to run with Zhang's 'minimum estimate' of China's foreign trade it would still be very roughly equal to, or very marginally below, that of Britain's.

This discussion has two key ramifications: first, that China's economy was clearly significant within the wider global economy. Interesting here

---

[113] Marks (1999: 104).
[114] Zhao (2013: 35, 55).
[115] Ibid. (134–5); see also Mazumdar (1998: 96–7).
[116] Huang Guosheng (1999: 87), taken from the records of the Palace Museum.
[117] Frank (1998).
[118] British data from Mitchell (2011: 448–50) and then deflated into constant values using the price data given in Mitchell (2011: 719–20).
[119] Zhang (2020: ch. 2).

is Peer Vries's dismissal of China's foreign trade as comprising a mere 1 or 2 per cent of GDP and that it was significantly out-sized by Britain's overseas trade.[120] Ironically, while his guesstimate is reasonably close to Zhang's 'average estimate' that comprised just under 3 per cent of national income (1735–95), nevertheless this obscures the point that China's national income was vastly larger than Britain's. And second, while British trade was likely somewhat lower than China's, nevertheless it was more significant than Sinocentrism presumes. Britain traded with all parts of the world, though as Vries rightly notes, '[t]he most important of those intercontinental trade flows and the one that grew fastest was that across the Atlantic. In the 1770s it was about three times as big as that between Western Europe and the whole of Asia'.[121] All of which serves to de-centre Britain within the Eurocentric framework but to upgrade it within the Sinocentric narrative, as much as it de-centres China within the Sinocentric framework but upgrades it within the Eurocentric narrative. All of which, in turn, reinforces my claim that the FGE was polycentric.

Inverting Eurocentrism: Why China Shifted to 'Freer Trade' and Britain Moved to High Protectionism after 1684

Why, then, did China move to freer trade after 1684, whereas Britain moved in the opposite direction culminating in exceptionally heavy average tariffs between 1800 and 1846? I focus on three core differentials between Britain and China:

1. modes of warfare, military pressures connected to their respective multi-state systems and levels of military expenditures;
2. levels of taxation and modes of taxation;
3. differing state–society relations and differing modes of production.

It is noteworthy that before 1945, tariff protectionism and foreign trade policy were deeply embedded within states' taxation regimes – though this remains the case in the very low-income developing countries today. This is because tariffs are a form of taxation – specifically 'indirect taxation' – which is generally fiscally regressive in that it disproportionately penalises the low-income groups. While land taxes predominated in India and China, most Western states resorted to taxing trade via tariff protectionism as a key source of government revenue

---

[120] Vries (2015: 170–2).
[121] Vries (2010: 735).

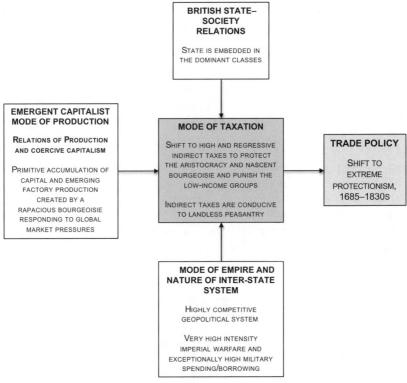

Figure 2.1 'Developmental architectures' and the great trade regime divergence, post-1684: China versus Britain.

before 1945.[122] In turn, this fiscal focus requires an analysis of levels of government spending and taxation as well as different modes of warfare/empire/taxation/production and state–society relations, all of which is captured in my complex concept of a 'developmental architecture' (see Figure 2.1).

Differing Modes of Warfare/Empire and the Huge Fiscal Expenditure Gap between China and Britain   As I explain in Chapter 12, the notion that China was a world-unto-itself and was not part of a multi-state system is one of the more confounding of the Eurocentric myths. Perhaps two of the reasons for this mistaken conception lie in the point that warfare between *most* states in the East and Southeast-Asian system was

[122] Hobson (1997).

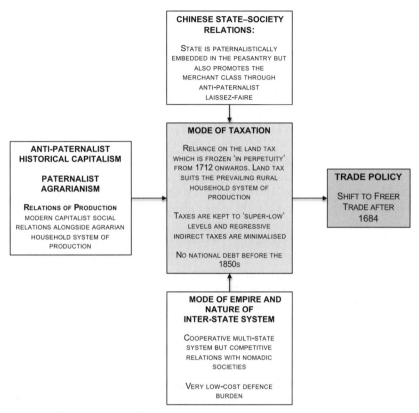

Figure 2.1 (*cont.*)

very rare and that the region is wrongly conflated with the CTS. Either way, the conclusion I draw here is that the near absence of geopolitical competition within the wider multi-state system meant that China's military expenditures were very low (as I explain shortly). However, it would be untrue to say that China did not engage in wars as much as it would be untrue to say that Britain created an empire whereas China did not (as I also explain in Chapter 12). For the fact is that the Qing nearly tripled its landmass between 1683 and 1760 as it colonised large (nomadic societal) areas to the north and west through warfare. But having done so, high military expenditures were not required to maintain its empire since other states in the regional multi-state system did not seek to compete over imperial territory. By contrast, the European great powers competed fundamentally over empire, which was the major reason why British imperial military spending was so high in the long eighteenth century (1684–1815). All of which means that military spending in China could be maintained at very low levels particularly by comparison with Britain, where the latter was embedded within a geopolitically *competitive* multi-state system in which the constituent European great powers were looking constantly to upgrade their military machines as well as develop their economies to fund them.

However, various experts on Chinese history claim that the Qing state engaged not only in regular warfare but also that its military spending levels were very high.[123] They argue that the wars that were prosecuted during the Qianlong Emperor's 'Ten Great Military Campaigns' constituted a 'huge drain' on the treasury, with Peter Perdue claiming that between 1747 and 1805 the state spent a 'very considerable' £100 million (or just under £2 million per annum).[124] But the paradox here is that while Perdue vastly *understates* the amounts that the Qing state allocated to military spending, nevertheless in *real* terms these were strikingly, almost incredibly, low. Thus, while Perdue is correct to argue that the wars cost about £100 million in total – or roughly £2 million per annum – nevertheless this figure omits the amounts that were spent on provisioning the troops in the provinces and cities. When taking these into account, military expenditures averaged about £10.5 million (1747–1805),[125] which came to a total of £609 million across the period.

Interestingly, Peer Vries undertook a critique of Perdue's argument in which he guesstimated a final average Chinese military spending figure of £12 million per annum. Thus, in order to affect the right direction of bias against my argument I shall run with the Vries figure. Coincidentally, this is interesting because across this period the average British figure for D1 was £12 million and D2 was £19.5 million (see following paragraph for the definitions of D1 and D2). But the relevant procedure for comparison requires us to calculate the *real military burden* – that is, military spending as a percentage of national income. Such a calculation is necessary because it informs us of the ability of a population to pay for such spending. For example, in comparison to Saudi Arabia today the United States spends vastly larger amounts when expressed in dollars, but the former's *real burden* based on its ability to pay turns out to be higher than the latter's. Given that Qing China's national income was vastly greater than Britain's, so we find that the former's military burden was striking only for its near-incredibly low levels.

---

[123] For example, Bartlett (1991: 127).
[124] Perdue cited in Vries (2015: 189, 235).
[125] Chen (1992: 194–201).

In comparing the Chinese and British burdens for the period of 1747 through 1815, I provide two calculations of military expenditure (Milex): first, D1, which comprises total ordinary and extraordinary Milex; second, D2, which comprises D1 plus the interest payments that are made on the military-derived national debt. In this period, British D1 was seven times higher, while D2 was eleven times higher than that of China's burden. And for the period 1760–1815, British D1 was nine times higher while D2 was thirteen times higher.[126] If nothing else, these differentials certainly give the lie to the vision of a highly militaristic Chinese Oriental despotic state and a peaceful, fiscally prudent, laissez-faire British state. All of which means that there were considerable pressures for the British state to raise high levels of tariffs to fund such spending while, conversely, no such pressures existed in the Chinese context. That said, though, there is nothing inevitable about choosing tariffs and indirect taxes as the principal form of taxation – a point that requires us to consider differing modes of taxation.

Differing Modes of Taxation and the Colossal Tax-gap between Britain and China   A core Eurocentric trope holds that China's all-powerful Oriental despotic state crushed civil society by extracting crippling rates of taxation, whereas the weak, laissez-faire British state kept taxes low, especially on capitalists. But if the differentials in military spending were huge, the differentials in taxation were colossal. And, revealing this tax gap leads, once more, to an inversion of the standard Eurocentric formulation. Here, it is necessary to compare levels of per capita taxation given that in 1800 China's population was around 320 million compared with around 10 million in Britain. According to Debin Ma, in the 1750/99 period per capita tax revenue was 4.2 grams of silver in China and 158.4 grams in Britain – or a per capita tax burden that is just under 3,800 per cent higher in Britain.[127] Thus, Kent Deng is surely right to say that Qing taxation 'was so light that people "barely noticed the tax system, almost as if they suffered no tax burden at all"'.[128]

One might ask whether China's extremely low tax burden was achievable only because it borrowed large amounts, whereas Britain's high tax burden was the result of the state's fiscal prudence that entailed low public borrowing. But, Britain ran colossal public deficits in

---

[126] Chinese national income data: Liu (2009) and British national income data: Weiss and Hobson (1995: 130). Chinese Milex: Chen (1992: 194–201, 288) and British Milex: Mitchell (2011: 578–80, 587).
[127] Ma (2013: 489).
[128] Deng (2012a: 17).

1715/1850, with interest payments alone comprising an average 6 per cent of national income in this period, which was larger than China's total central government revenues! Moreover, China's much lower overall tax burden was achieved alongside fiscal *surpluses* and it was only as late as the 1850s that the Qing state finally turned to public borrowing.[129] Even so, by 1898 China's national debt comprised a mere 2 per cent of national income,[130] which was a mere 1 per cent of Britain's national debt in 1815 when it comprised 180 per cent of national income.[131]

It is, however, necessary, to break these taxes down into their core constituent parts in order to understand why Britain moved to tariff protectionism and China moved in the opposite direction. Critically, although the Qing government relied on land taxes for about 75 per cent of its revenues,[132] nevertheless it extracted a mere 3.2 grams of silver in per capita land taxes, which comprised only 3 or 4 per cent of the value of farm output.[133] By contrast, the British state relied on indirect taxes for about 66 per cent of its revenues in this period, which comprised some 7.8 per cent of national income and exceeded the Chinese total central government income. Moreover, land taxes averaged less than 20 per cent of British central government revenues. Even after the introduction of the *Likin* tax, which was first levied on internal trade in 1853, Qing per capita *indirect* taxes comprised less than a gram of silver,[134] whereas by my extremely rough calculations the equivalent British figure (1750/99) would have been about 105 grams. Which means that Britain's per capita indirect tax burden was somewhere in the region of 10,500 per cent that of China's.

More generally, British customs revenue comprised 39 per cent of ordinary and extraordinary defence spending in 1760–1815 and 3.2 per cent of national income whereas, by contrast, Chinese tariffs comprised about 10 per cent of defence spending and very roughly 0.2 per cent of national income between 1685 and 1812.[135] Thus, in *real* aggregate terms Britain's customs revenue was about 1,600 per cent that of China's. Nevertheless, the Chinese customs houses significantly under-reported the revenues they took, probably by about two-thirds given that they retained the difference for themselves.[136] But even allowing for this means that the actual amount of customs revenue extracted would have been around 0.6 per cent of national income – or about a fifth of the

[129] Vries (2015: 94, 123).
[130] Chinese national income in Maddison (2007: 379).
[131] Weiss and Hobson (1995: 115).
[132] Rosenthal and Bin Wong (2011: 175) and Vries (2015: 167).
[133] Perkins (1967: 481, n. 9).
[134] Deng (2012a: 17).
[135] Calculated from Chen (1992: 36) and Liu (2009: 144–55).
[136] Hui (1995: 48).

British burden. Overall, Peer Vries captures this comparative paradox nicely, 'what we see are an agrarian state, China, supposed to be anti-merchant, that primarily taxes land, and a mercantile state, Britain, that primarily taxes trade'.[137]

To explain this crucial difference requires a comparative analysis of modes of production, class relations and state–society relations. Western concepts of fair taxation focus on the *individual* burden and how progressive it is. But the Qing sense of fair taxation referred to collective burdens imposed on a village, a county, a prefecture or a province. Individual wealth did not normally concern the Qing. As Kent Deng explains,

food deficit provinces paid proportionally more cash (Zhili, Shanxi, Henan, and Shaanxi, Anhui and Fujian), while food surplus regions paid more in grain (Guangxi, Guizhou and Yunnan). Overall, Zhili, Shandong, Henan, Hunan, Guangdong and Yunnan paid less than the national average. Only Shaanxi, Zhejiang, Fujian, Guizhou and Guangxi contributed more. ... This was very different from the Ming pattern which taxed the Yangtze Valley overwhelmingly heavily.[138]

Nevertheless, Peer Vries points out that the land tax was regressive in China such that in the nineteenth century, peasants paid somewhere between two and five times as much land tax per mu as gentry landowners. (There are 6 mu in an acre). And he reckons that in the eighteenth century, gentry households paid 33 per cent that of poor households.[139]

In Britain, as noted, the land tax was relatively marginal, given that the majority of revenues comprised indirect taxes. And these were highly regressive, designed to penalise the poorer income groups and protect the aristocracy and nascent bourgeoisie (as I explain in Chapter 9). Thus, China's reliance on the land tax enabled it to move to, and maintain, freer trade, whereas the British state's reversion to regressive indirect taxes led it to hike tariffs time and time again between 1684 and the 1820s. Important too, as I explain in Chapter 12, is that the British state's fiscal bureaucracy was vastly superior to that of the Qing. This meant not only that it could extract much larger sums of money but also that it could extract very high amounts of excise tax, the significance of which is that this requires a more effective fiscal bureaucracy to one that relies principally on the land tax. This is because the latter was levied on whole villages in China, whereas indirect taxes are levied on individual acts of consumption.

[137] Vries (2015: 167).
[138] Deng (2012a: 18).
[139] Vries (2015: 138).

The key fiscal epistemic or normative formula of the Chinese state was that 'government expenditure should adapt to government revenue, not the other way round, as was the case in Europe'.[140] Maintaining low taxes was a central political prerogative of the Qing, and expenditures had to conform to this. Li Yesi stated in the seventeenth century that the 'hallmark of good ruling is to keep the number of officials low; the hallmark of good government is to keep the burden of taxation light'.[141] Similarly, Roy Bin Wong notes that Chinese governments 'believed that light taxation allowed the people to prosper, and since a prosperous people was held to be crucial for the maintenance of a powerful state, tax rates were [kept] low'.[142] Most importantly, in 1712 the Kangxi Emperor decreed 'freezing [tax] revenues despite future population growth and prosperity [i.e., economic-growth]' (*shengshi ziding, yongbu jiafu*).[143] And, in turn, this derived from the state's desire to embed itself within the peasantry. For the Qing's obsessive focus on internal order meant that it was anxious not to alienate the peasantry, especially given the latter's perception of the Manchu rulers as an 'alien' race. All in all, the Chinese state, therefore, advanced 'historical capitalism' (as I explain in Chapters 8, 11 and 12) through its freer trade policy while, at the same time, it maintained its social base within the peasantry. The latter was connected to its agrarian paternalism, whereas the former was connected to its anti-paternalist conception of merchant capitalism. Or as Rosenthal and Bin Wong conclude, merchants 'specifically benefited from state policies that facilitated long-distance trade, and their riches … could usually be protected from extraordinary state exactions'.[144]

A different social structure coupled with a radically different fiscal philosophy in Britain was apparent. For, as noted, the British state sought to punish the lower income orders with high levels of regressive indirect taxes – tariffs and excises. Moreover, Britain's emergent modern capitalist mode of production was more conducive to indirect taxes, whereas in China the historical capitalist system, which was based in part on the agrarian household system of production, made the land tax a more natural fit. And a key paradox in the face of the Eurocentric Oriental despotism thesis emerges in the point that it was Britain's trade policy that was embedded fundamentally in the geopolitics of imperial militarism. For while tariffs were hiked time and again during the

---

[140] Ibid. (210).
[141] Li Yesi cited in Vries (2015: 122).
[142] Bin Wong (1997: 90).
[143] See especially Deng (2012a: 16).
[144] Rosenthal and Bin Wong (2011: 212).

long eighteenth century and right up to about 1830 in order to pay for the state's imperial wars and the related interest on the national debt, after 1684 the Qing's trade policy was free of such political 'distortions'. For the Qing sought to enact relative *wu-wei* – i.e., (managed) laissez-faire political economy – which was connected to the Qing state's anti-paternalist posture vis-à-vis the merchants. And here we encounter a key paradox in that while both Chinese and British military spending were at their height between 1683 and 1800/15, nevertheless, the Qing was able to maintain very low tariffs in this period, whereas the British state relied for a significant source of its revenue on high tariffs. But this, in turn, leads us to the most acute paradox of all.

Compared with the philosophy and practice of the British state, Chinese rulers conformed far more closely to Adam Smith's liberal maxim concerning the need to keep taxes and tariffs low;[145] a point which he made in the *Wealth of Nations*.[146] Thus, it was China rather than Britain that came closer to Dugald Stewart's famous maxim that was derived from Adam Smith's conception: for a nation 'to be transformed from the lowest state of barbarism into a state of the highest possible prosperity needs nothing but bearable taxation, [free trade,] fair administration of justice, and peace'.[147] Moreover, this Smithian maxim had wider import. Most paradoxically, in the Eurocentric vision the absence of trade that was backed up by Chinese sea power became misread as an *absence* of private trade per se. The irony here, though, is that it was European states that organised state-sponsored explorations and chartered state monopolies. Moreover, the British state also imposed the protectionist/mercantilist Navigation Acts that began in 1651 whereby colonial trade would be carried only in British ships. The Qing, by contrast, prohibited the deployment of weapons on private Chinese ships, thereby once again conforming far more closely to Adam Smith's liberal prescriptions than did the British state. And to the reply that the seven epic voyages of Zheng He (1405–33) were state sponsored, this example turns out to be the exception that proves the rule that the Chinese state relied on private entrepreneurs rather than chartering foreign trading monopolies.[148] For in the aftermath of these voyages in 1434 no such ventures were ever undertaken. Added to this is the point that after 1684, regulated tribute trade was superseded by the Chinese economy's reliance on market principles with regard to the surging levels of private trade, though this trend had begun in the

---

[145] See Vries (2015: 347–50).
[146] For a discussion, see Millar (2017: 185–6).
[147] Dugald Stewart cited in List (1841/1885: 120).
[148] Zhao (2013: 2).

mid-fifteenth century as I explained earlier. In Britain, by contrast, after 1684 the state engaged in high levels of intervention and protectionist regulation, as I explain in more detail in Chapters 7, 9, 10 and 12.

Conclusion

Before the second half of the eighteenth century, Europeans often, though not always, looked to China as a higher civilisation.[149] And many had viewed China as open to foreign trade.[150] But during the second half of the eighteenth century, China was suddenly reimagined as backward, stagnant and highly protectionist.[151] This *volta face* had various dimensions, though the shifting imaginary from an open to a closed China is a function of Eurocentric construction. For European observers misconceived the post-1757 Canton system as much as they mis-read the CTS in the nineteenth century. And, from there, China's so-called formal and informal protectionism was then retrospectively drawn so as to (re)present China as closed to overseas trade for many centuries, if not millennia, not least by constructing the image of a permanent set of official bans on foreign trade. Linked into this vision is the common trope that China sought self-sufficiency, nowhere more clearly represented than the supposed retreat into its 'regressive' tribute system. As the contemporary observer, Gaspar da Cruz put it, 'one of the greatest and best kingdoms of the world ... [has] need of none other nation for that they have sufficient of all things necessarie [sic] to the mainteining [sic] of human life'.[152] But even the tribute system was not isolationist, not simply for its trading links with the outside world but also because the Chinese emperors were as much dependent on external 'barbarian' state recognition to secure their legitimacy as were the vassal-state rulers vis-à-vis the Chinese emperor's powers of investiture.

All in all, while I have argued against these Eurocentric misconceptions by revealing China to have been not only open to global trade for many centuries but also an important contributor to the FGE, nevertheless I also seek to qualify various California School scholars by showing how it was rather less significant than Sinocentrism would have us believe. The purpose of Chapters 3–6 is to extend this latter claim much further by revealing the Afro-Indian pivot of the FGE and the vital agential roles that Africans and Indians (Hindu and Islamic) also performed, with the latter girded with structural power.

---

[149] Clarke (1997), Hobson (2004: 194–7) and Millar (2017).
[150] Zhao (2013: 6–8).
[151] Clarke (1997), Hobson (2004: ch. 9) and Zhao (2013: 8–12).
[152] Gaspar da Cruz cited in Millar (2017: 109).

3   The Afro-Indian Pivot (I)

Indian Structural Power and the Global Atlantic System

Introduction

While Chapter 2 advanced the claim that Chinese productive and mercantile agency constituted an important driver of the first global economy (FGE), the purpose here is to move beyond the Sinocentrism of various non-Eurocentric revisionist accounts within the California School.[1] For while there is no one country, region or people that was central to the FGE – indeed it was polycentric – nevertheless in certain key respects 'India', or at least key regions of it, played a vital role in creating and informally managing the global trading system. This was achieved through the structural power that Indian cotton textiles (ICTs) bequeathed to Indian merchants. Here, I focus on how Indian mercantile agency and structural power entwined with African agency to help produce and nurture the FGE.

For clarification purposes, it should be noted that the notion of 'India' conceived as a single entity did not exist at that time given that it comprised a conglomerate of states and regions following the decline of the Mughal Empire from the early-eighteenth century. Nevertheless, for convenience sake, I shall speak of 'India' and 'Indians' rather than 'South Asia' and 'South Asians' henceforth. And so as to prevent further confusion, it should be noted that Hindus and Muslims comprised important parts of the various Indian trading groups. Note too that I reserve my discussion of India's mode of production to Chapter 11, though I also consider its historical capitalism in Chapter 8. All in all, this is the first of the four chapters that consider the various dimensions of Indian global agency and structural power in the FGE.

Critically, while Indian merchants traded in a wide variety of goods, including horses, steel, tin, lead, copper, fruits, pepper and spices, rice, wheat, sappan wood, indigo, saltpetre, silk and silk textiles, ivory and African and Indian slaves, by far and away, their single most important

---

[1]   Most notably Frank (1998).

export item was that of ICTs. So important and extensive was the role of ICTs as a global commodity both in the formation and development of the FGE as well as in the subsequent rise of British industrialisation and the emergence of the second global economy (SGE), which I cannot cover in a single chapter, for in so many ways ICTs weave together much of the narrative of this book. A further key property of Indian structural power was derived from the fact that ICTs formed a 'universal currency'.[2] In particular, I argue that ICTs constituted a kind of global super-commodity chain as well as a promiscuous or hybrid, global super-production chain, insofar as these exports also enabled the production of many of the key globally traded commodities and raw materials. Thus, the Indian global cotton textile super-commodity chain morphed into a kind of promiscuous global commodity/production chain insofar as it triggered multiple production systems that generated key global trading commodities. Moreover, its global properties likely surpassed that of any global commodity chain or production chain that exists today.

In contrast to Eurocentrism's belief that the Africans and Indians were mere losers or 'peoples without history' during the so-called Vasco da Gama epoch of Afro-Asia, my analysis resuscitates the role of Indian and African agency in order to reveal how western India and East Africa had *entwined or entangled histories* before and during the so-called European era. Moreover, I take issue with both Janet Abu-Lughod's and Andre Gunder Frank's explicit marginalisation of Africa in enabling and promoting the global economy.[3] Finally, the larger theme that underpins my analysis is the inversion of the Eurocentric Big Bang theory/Expansion of the West narrative. For, British industrialisation did not precede but was born during the FGE, which in turn was enabled in a significant part by non-Western agents and processes in general, and the Afro-Indian pivot along with Indian structural power in particular. Accordingly, this chapter provides an important backdrop to the analysis of Chapters 9–11, 13 and 14.

The chapter proceeds through three sections. The first two sections provincialise the (in)famous Atlantic 'triangular' trading system. Rather than being a pure European creation, as Eurocentrics and critical Eurofetishists assume, there I reveal what I shall call the 'global Atlantic system'. The section 'Globalising the Atlantic System: Polycentric Foundations of the GSTS' tackles both Eurocentric and Sinocentric conceptions of the global silver trading system (GSTS) by

---

[2] Chaudhuri (2006: 16–17), Pomeranz and Topik (2006: 234), Prestholdt (2008), Davidson (2012), Riello (2013: 90), Machado (2014) and Kobayashi (2019).
[3] Abu-Lughod (1989) and Frank (1998: 67, 70).

revealing how it had polycentric rather than solely European or Chinese foundations. The section 'Discovering the "Global Atlantic System": The Entwining of the ICTTS, Black Slavery and the GSTS' follows on by revealing the key role that Indians performed in the FGE and how the Indian cotton textile trading system (ICTTS) fuelled, and was nourished by, the GSTS. I also reveal how ICTs, as the premier global super-commodity chain, enabled the production of other important global trading commodities. Finally, the section 'Provincialising the Atlantic Slave Trade: Unveiling the Heptagonal Slave Trade System in the Global Atlantic and Indian Ocean System' provincialises the Eurofetishist conception of the African slave trade that gives pride of place to the Europeans in the Atlantic system. This entails revealing the *heptagonal* slave trade systems that spanned the Atlantic and Indian Ocean systems. In the eastern hemisphere variant, the West Asian and Indian slave trades in Africans were prominent. Critically, because this heptagonal system was embedded fundamentally within the ICTTS which in turn was embedded within the GSTS, so the slave trade system had fundamentally global dimensions.

Globalising the Atlantic System: Polycentric Foundations of the GSTS

Certainly, the colonial integration of the Americas into the Afro-Eurasian economy was an important moment in the formation of the FGE, and the Europeans, of course, were vital in making this happen. In this important respect, the Europeans exhibited significant levels of global agency. And, of course, they were important in linking the Americas with Africa, India, West Asia, China, Southeast Asia and Europe, not least by exporting New World silver across the FGE and shipping Afro-Asian products back. But as I have explained elsewhere, the integration of the Americas was the final, rather than the first, piece of the global economic jigsaw puzzle, given that much of the integration of Afro-Eurasia had occurred already during the long era of Afro-Eurasian regionalisation (c. 600–1500) that was led by non-Western actors.[4] Accordingly, I view this period of Afro-Eurasian regionalisation as constituting the 'long primitive accumulation phase' of the historical capitalist FGE, linking Europe, Africa and Asia together into a system of growing economic interdependence that became fully global once the Americas had been brought into this system after 1492/1501. Moreover,

---

[4] Hobson (2004: ch. 2), Chaudhuri (1985) and Beaujard (2019).

despite the brilliance of Janet Abu-Lughod's seminal analysis in *Before European Hegemony*, where she argues that a global economy came into existence in the thirteenth century largely at the hands of the Muslims,[5] the fact is that there could have been no *global* economy before 1492 given that the Americas had not been linked into the Afro-Eurasian economy.[6] What she was really discussing in an extremely insightful way is what I am calling Afro-Eurasian regionalisation. Significant here is David Christian's point that

> The creation of a truly global exchange network in the sixteenth century decisively increased the scale, significance, and variety of informational and commercial exchanges. The coming together of the different world zones of the Holocene era marks a revolutionary moment in the history of humanity.... And the new level of creative synergy generated by linking the two largest world zones—Afro-Eurasia and the Americas—was and remains perhaps the most powerful single lever of change in the modern world.[7]

In particular, the convergence of American silver flooding into Asia's leading economies that enhanced the development of the latter provided a key driver of the FGE. But this occurred to an important extent as a function of the desire for ICTs.

Critical Eurofetishist and Eurocentric scholars highlight the Atlantic triangular trading system, which was not only created exclusively by the Europeans but was also *sui generis* in that it linked Europe, West Africa and the New World into a singular, self-contained economic circuit. In this and the next section, I effectively *globalise* the Atlantic system by revealing how it was embedded within the GSTS and the ICTTS that spanned the entirety of the Atlantic, Pacific and Indian Ocean systems. And, moreover, I take on both Eurocentrism and Sinocentrism that reify the role of the Europeans and the Chinese, respectively, by revealing the polycentric foundations of the GSTS, with Indians enjoying structural market power through their domination of global cotton textile markets. I shall begin by sketching the contours of the GSTS.

Binding the FGE with Silver Thread

Various prominent California School revisionists – most notably Andre Gunder Frank, Richard von Glahn, Kenneth Pomeranz, Robert Marks,

---

[5] Abu-Lughod (1989).
[6] See also Flynn and Giráldez (2006: 244).
[7] Christian (2004: 364–5).

as well as Dennis Flynn and Arturo Giráldez – have argued that a major integrationist boost to, if not the inception point of, the (first) global economy comprised the global movements of Spanish-American gold and especially silver.[8] The immediate launch pad moment came in 1571 when Manila was conquered by the Spanish, who then opened it up to the New World silver trade that kicked off in that same year. Thus, while the key mines in Potosí (Peru) and Zacetas (Mexico) were opened in 1545 and 1548, respectively, it was the deployment of the mercury amalgamation process at the very beginning of the 1570s that led to a proliferation of mined silver which, in turn, unleashed a tidal wave of silver across the FGE.[9] Initially, it was the Spanish who acted as the key global distributive agents. For having opened up the Pacific Route – or the 'Pacific Ocean silk road' – they transferred large quantities of silver to Manila, where they bought up large quantities of Chinese goods, especially silk textiles and porcelain as well as ICTs that they then exported back to the Americas.

It is precisely this transcontinental shipment of silver, as Flynn and Giráldez argue, that constituted the seminal moment in triggering global trade and globalisation. 'Global trade [and globalization] emerged [in 1571] when all heavily populated continents began to exchange products continuously—both with each other directly and indirectly via other continents—and on a scale that generated deep and lasting impacts on all trading partners'.[10] And they insist that prior to 1571, 'the world market was not yet fully coherent or complete; after that year it was'.[11] But the opening of the Pacific Route, vitally important though it was, turned out to be enhancing *global* trade that had begun seventy years earlier. For Afro-Eurasia was linked directly into the Americas after 1501, initially via the exporting of African slaves via the Atlantic 'Middle Passage' who, in turn, had been bought primarily with re-exported ICTs (as I explain later). Nevertheless, the arrival of Spanish-American silver after 1571 was clearly important in terms of boosting or intensifying not just global trade but also the Indian global cotton super-commodity chain and various other inter-linked global commodities, given that these were purchased largely with silver.

How, then, did bullion flows, most especially silver, bind the FGE together? Following the Spanish, New World silver was also distributed

---

[8] Flynn and Giráldez (1995a, 1995b, 2004, 2006, 2008), von Glahn (1996a), Frank (1998), Pomeranz (2000) and Marks (2002).
[9] Atwell (1982: 72) and Flynn and Giráldez (1995a).
[10] Flynn and Giráldez (2004: 83, 2006). See also de Vries (2003: 77) and Zhao (2013: 3–4).
[11] Flynn and Giráldez (2006: 235).

by the Portuguese, Dutch, French and English who began to re-export it to Asia via the 'Cape of Storms', as the Muslims had long called it but which was renamed the 'Cape of Good Hope' by the Iberians after 1498. Certainly, bullion comprised the majority of European exports to Asia. Indeed, 75 per cent of the English East India Company's (EEIC) total exports between 1660 and 1760 were in bullion, while the equivalent figure for the Dutch Vereenigde Oost-Indische Compagnie was 87 per cent (1660–1720).[12] Moreover, Kent Deng suggests that between 1699 and 1751, more than 90 per cent of British exports to China took the form of silver.[13] In addition, as I summarise later, New World silver was also transported either across the overland routes by Asian merchants from West Asia to India, having received these supplies from Europe given the latter's trade deficits with the Ottoman and Safavid empires, or via the Southern (sea) route from the Red Sea and the Persian Gulf, shipped primarily by the Muslims.[14] Finally, a significant stream of silver emanated from Japan, much of which went to India and especially China, although small streams of gold emanated from Africa and Southeast Asia which ended up in India, China and West Asia. All of which means, as Figure 3.1 reveals, that this deserves the appellation of the GSTS.

Although Figure 3.1 might well appear to my reader as bewilderingly complex, the way through it is to follow the money by tracing the numbers. There were sixteen silver passages that comprised a hexadecagonal system through which New World silver threaded the FGE together. Significantly, the hexadecagonal figure intersects with the twelve-sided (dodecagonal) ICTTS, as I explain later. Overall, the bullion trading system was multisourced, given that New World supplies comprised between 80 and 85 per cent of the global total between 1550 and 1800. But if we aggregate all of the silver (and gold) passages throughout the FGE, we end up with over twenty, with additional independent sources emanating from Africa, Southeast Asia and Japan, as noted earlier. Clearly, then, movements of silver and gold constituted the complex and intricate network of capillaries that helped supply the lifeblood of the FGE. Or, to run with my original metaphor, these manifold silver networks threaded the FGE together. But the key question now at hand is whether the GSTS was centred on China, as Sinocentric California School scholars argue, or whether it was dominated by British (and Dutch) agency, as Eurocentrics and Eurofetishists presume. My response

---

[12] Chaudhuri (2006: 512) and Frank (1998: 74).
[13] Deng (2008: 321).
[14] Barendse (2002: 219–20).

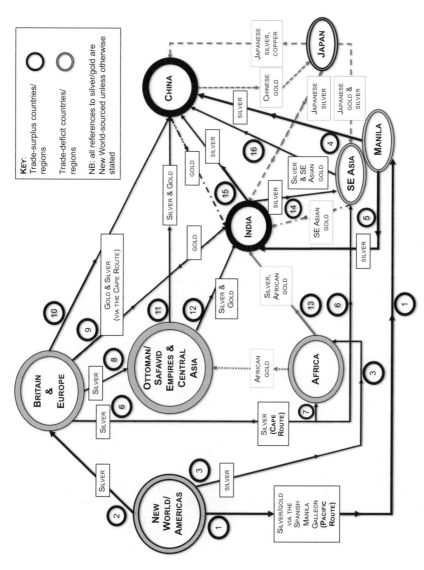

Figure 3.1 The global silver/gold trading system in the first global economy.

is that the error lies with the question itself, in part because the system was fundamentally polycentric and in part because one of the key roles that was performed by India has been eclipsed by Eurocentrism and Sinocentrism.

Sinocentric and Eurocentric Myths of China in the GSTS: Revealing the Agential Roles of Europeans, Indians and Chinese

This section provides a bridge between Chapter 2 and Chapters 4–6. My aim here is to ascertain the relative weighting of the agency to be accorded to the Chinese, Europeans and Indians within the GSTS. However, this necessarily entails a series of complex twists and turns, given the different vantage points of Eurocentrism and Sinocentrism. On the one hand, the European companies within East Asia exhibited very little agency vis-à-vis Chinese and Japanese *emperors* before the nineteenth century, as I explained in Chapter 2. But, on the other hand, as I also explained, while Chinese foreign trade was likely higher than that of Britain's in the eighteenth century, nevertheless the latter was still impressive. Which means that British traders were also, in aggregate, important global trading agents. However, against this is the core claim of the California School, which asserts that the British as well other rival East India Companies (EICs) dealt in *other* peoples' goods and it was only after 1750 that the British finally began trading their own home-made products in a relatively significant way. As such, these scholars insist that China was far more important to the GSTS as well as to the global trading system more generally, given that its production output sucked in silver from abroad. I shall argue that both Sinocentrism and Eurocentrism are problematic for their shared zero-sum or binary conception of global agency – either Europe has all of the global agency and China has none (as in Eurocentrism) or China has it all and Europe has none (as in Sinocentrism). Instead, I shall argue that Chinese, Indians and Europeans were all important agents within the GSTS.

Gunder Frank estimates that about 50 per cent of the world's silver ended up in China, which leads him to describe China as the world's 'silver sink', while Flynn and Giráldez echo this with their formulation of the 'Chinese silver suction pump'.[15] Others have even suggested a figure as high as 66 per cent.[16] This, in turn, underpins Gunder

---

[15] Frank (1998: 67, 115–17, 127–8, 143–9, 175–8, 185) and Flynn and Giráldez (2008: 377–8).
[16] Arrighi et al. (2003: 273).

Frank's Sinocentric conception of the global economy as well as Flynn and Giráldez's Sinocentric conception of the GSTS.[17] Key here is the revisionist claim that Chinese *demand* for bullion comprised an *active* force in underpinning Europe's role as a distributor of New World silver. One of the leading scholars of the California School, Kenneth Pomeranz, expressed this idea thus:

> the tendency to see silver as a residual store of value sent to China to pay for consumer goods has been reinforced by a long-standing tendency among Western scholars to see the West as the active (and desiring) agent in the knitting together of the world. But once we think about the dynamic created by changing the monetary base of perhaps as much as 40 per cent of the world's economy in this period ... it becomes hard not to see China's [and India's] silver demand as every bit as much an 'active' force in creating a global economy as was the West's demand for porcelain, tea, and so on.[18]

All of which culminates in Gunder Frank's claim that it was this strong demand for Asian products that reflects China's openness to the global economy and its primary role in the GSTS because silver flowed in as a function of China's trade surpluses with the rest of the world, particularly from Europe. Noteworthy here is that non-Eurocentric scholars often highlight the point that because China had little appetite for European goods, so the Europeans were forced to pay for Asian goods with Spanish-American silver (and gold).[19] But the key question here is whether China was as central to the GSTS as Frank, as well as Flynn and Giráldez, claim.

While it seems reasonable to claim that Chinese demand was a very important factor in driving global movements in silver both from the New World and Japan which in turn reflects China's openness to the FGE – as I explained in Chapter 2 – nevertheless, what *is* controversial is the claim that China sucked in *most* of the world's silver.[20] I argue that there are three core reasons why Gunder Frank's estimate is exaggerated. First, he reckons that some 89 per cent of silver that flowed from the New World to Manila then went on to China. But various Chinese specialists have shown that somewhere between 50 and 60 per cent went on to China.[21]

---

[17] Frank (1998: 111–17) and Flynn and Giráldez (1994, 1995b). See also Hamashita (1994) and von Glahn (1996a: 231–2).

[18] Pomeranz (2000: 161).

[19] Frank (1998: 74–5), Flynn and Giráldez (2008: 373). See also Chaudhuri (2006: 153–60).

[20] See also Hamashita (1994), von Glahn (1996a, 1996b), Arrighi et al. (2003: 273) and Pomeranz and Topik (2006: 91).

[21] See Qian (1985: 10). See also Quan as reported in Zhang Shizhi (2020: ch. 2).

Second, Frank claims that all of the silver that went from Europe to Asia in the seventeenth and eighteenth centuries ended up in China. But Prasannan Parthasarathi has shown persuasively that between 1600 and 1800 some 28,000 tons went to India *net* of the amounts that flowed on into China, which he reckons comprised 20 per cent of New World silver exports.[22] How plausible is Parthasarathi's estimate?

Parthasarathi's estimate boils down to an annual average of some 140 tons of silver and silver equivalents entering India between 1600 and 1800. Najaf Haider's detailed research on this topic estimates that 113 tons of silver entered Mughal India annually between the late-sixteenth to late-seventeenth centuries. But because this omits the amounts that were exported into South India, which comprised 15 per cent of the Mughal figure,[23] so his adjusted figure rises to 130 tons of silver imports per annum. Another specialist on the topic, Shireen Moovsi, argues that the amount of silver currency minted in the Mughal Empire in 1576–1705 was 152 tons per annum.[24] Given that the mints used only imported silver so this suggests that Parthasarathi's figure of 140 tons seems reasonable, lying mid-way between the Moovsi and Haider estimates. Thus, it seems plausible to suggest that some 20 per cent of New World silver ended up in India, and that China – according to the estimates of Zhang Shizhi and Peer Vries – absorbed perhaps around 30 per cent.[25] All of which means that India and China combined absorbed about 50 per cent of New World silver; a figure that coincides roughly with Jan de Vries's estimate of 47 per cent.[26] What then of Europe's role in the GSTS?

California School scholars tend to discount the Europeans as important global agents in the GSTS on the grounds that they acted, in effect, as 'passive exporters' of silver because this was the major means by which they could pay for their trade deficits with China, given that these were a function of Europe's productive weakness. At the other extreme, Eurocentrism views China and India as essentially 'passive exporters' in that they did not export their own products but relied on the Europeans to provide this service and who did very well out of it.[27] Accordingly, the logic of their argument is that in the absence of the EICs, there would have been no Asian trade. However, neither of these extremes is satisfactory. Indeed, Chapter 2 revealed this 'passive

---

[22] Parthasarathi (2011: 46–50).
[23] Ibid. (48–9).
[24] Moovsi (1987: 49).
[25] See Zhang (2020: ch. 2) and Vries (2015: 267).
[26] de Vries (2003: 80–1).
[27] Roberts (1985) and Vries (2015: 373–6).

exporter trope' in the Chinese context as a myth, as I also argue with respect to India in this and in Chapters 4–6. But by the same token, I argue that there were three core reasons why it is no less problematic to depict the Europeans as 'passive exporters'.

First, it is clear that the European discovery of New World silver and the creation of new sea routes – the Pacific and Cape – along which the Europeans carried directly the Spanish-American silver to Asia as well as Asian goods to Asia, Africa, Europe and the Americas were undoubtedly important in threading the FGE together (as I explain in Chapter 4). As the non-Eurocentric critic, Zhao Gang, argues,

[w]hereas Wallerstein's theory minimizes the part that the non-Western world played in global integration, revisionist [California School] theories have underestimated the historically unprecedented changes brought by the discovery of both the New World and new sea routes around familiar landmasses—both achievements of European navigators. To overlook those is to fail to grasp why crucial changes in China and other Asian states took place only after 1500.[28]

Second, in the process of forging the GSTS, the Europeans did much to stimulate the development of the FGE in general, as well as the Indian and Chinese economies in particular.[29] Indeed, 'the influx of silver led to more substantial monetization in both countries, offering more business in the handling and exchange of money to specialized communities. Among them were the Jains and Banias in India and the Shansi and Ningpo men in China.'[30] Within this context, it is a particular irony that in knocking out the Eurocentric 'Asian hoarding thesis', Gunder Frank offers as proof the infusion of New World silver into India and especially China, which did much to stimulate their economies.[31] Moreover, as Kirti Chaudhuri notes, 'the import of silver represented a rise in demand for output and an injection of extra income. The result must have been *ceteris paribus* a general expansion in the economy of those areas of India that were most actively concerned with foreign trade.'[32] Thus, this silver infusion also helped stimulate the global trading activities of the Chinese,[33] as well as the Indians, which in turn means that China was less autonomous than Sinocentric CS scholars would have us believe but was far more significant than Eurocentrism presumes (as was India).

---

[28] Zhao (2013: 4).
[29] Frank (1998: 158–64) and Zhao (2013: 3–4).
[30] Ray (1995: 464).
[31] Frank (1998: 153–64). See also Hui (1995: 53).
[32] Chaudhuri (2006: 159).
[33] Hui (1995: 54–5) and Flynn and Giráldez (1994).

Third, as numerous scholars have argued, one of the purposes of Europe's export of silver to China and India was to engage in global bullion 'arbitrage', given that silver was worth more relative to gold in China than it was in Europe.[34] This global silver recycling process is best described by Flynn and Giráldez thus:

> divergent bimetallic ratios imply that one could theoretically use an ounce of gold to buy say eleven ounces of silver in Amsterdam, transport the silver to China and exchange the eleven ounces there for about two ounces of gold. The two ounces of gold could be brought back to Europe and exchanged for twenty-two ounces of silver, which could again be transported back to China where its value was double again.[35]

Importantly, it was the Europeans who were responsible for, and motivated by, trading gold and silver from the New World with the (partial) intent of arbitraging profits in Asia, especially in China. Moreover, as Kirti Chaudhuri explains, 'the usual pattern of trade with the Far East [China] was to tranship some of the silver imported either from Europe or Mexico via the [Spanish-Manila] galleon on the China-bound ships and exchange it for gold or commodities in China which were then imported back to India and the proceeds used to purchase return cargo for Europe'.[36]

Accordingly, it would be reasonable to conclude that the Europeans exercised considerable global agency in arbitraging bullion in order to buy Asian commodities, even if this strategy was required in part because of the sustained problem of Europe's trade deficits. While I have argued that the British (as well as the Dutch) alongside the Chinese and Indians were all key agents within the GSTS, the next section considers the vital role that was played by ICTs. For I argue that the GSTS was entwined fundamentally with the ICTTS, which in turn was crucial in linking the Atlantic, Indian and Pacific Ocean production and trading systems together into one seamless web.

Discovering the 'Global Atlantic System': The Entwining of the ICTTS, Black Slavery and the GSTS

The familiar discussion of the Atlantic triangular trading system, as Eric Williams' seminal text *Capitalism and Slavery* explains,[37] focuses on how

---

[34] Atwell (1982), Flynn and Giráldez (1995a, 1995b), von Glahn (1996b: 432–6), Frank (1998: ch. 3) and Chaudhuri (2006: 153–80).

[35] Flynn and Giráldez (1995a: 75).

[36] Chaudhuri (2006: 182).

[37] Williams (1944/1964: ch. 3).

its commercial sinews stretched in the first instance between England and West Africa along which English ships sailed, having cleared London, Bristol and Liverpool laden with various manufactured and consumer goods that were then sold in Africa at a profit to buy African slaves. The second leg of the triangle saw the shipment of perhaps somewhere between 9.6 and 12.5 million slaves by all of the relevant European powers across the gruesome Atlantic 'Middle Passage' between 1501 and 1807;[38] though the latter figure comes down to around 10.5 million who actually arrived in the New World once we have 'factored in' the approximate 15 per cent death rate of the 'cargo' during the journey. Note, however, that Walter Rodney views the figure of ten million as such a gross underestimation that it functions as but a Eurocentric apology for the scale of European brutality.[39] Also noteworthy is that possibly four times as many slaves died on the land passage within Africa on their way to the coast than they did in the Middle Passage across the Atlantic on their way to the New World,[40] which might in aggregate have amounted to around six million deaths across the whole period. Nevertheless, according to John Wright, an average 15 per cent died on the land-based Middle Passage, which might have amounted to around two million.[41] So perhaps somewhere between two and six million slaves died *en route* within Africa. If so, then this clearly increases the numbers that were caught up in the slave trade system from the base figure of around ten million. Once landed in the Americas and the Caribbean, they were sold into slavery at a profit. And, having been put to work on the cotton, tobacco, coffee and sugar plantations, as well as in the sugar mills and the gold/silver mines, their produce was then shipped back to Britain on the final leg for a further profit that in turn helped fuel British industrialisation in numerous ways (as I explain in Chapters 8 and 9).[42] But the fundamental issue at stake concerns the means by which these slaves were purchased.

Indian Structural Power and the Promiscuous ICT Global Super-Commodity/Super-Production Chain (I): The Financial Cotton Roots of the African Slave Trade

In the familiar Eurocentric and Eurofetishist narratives, we receive a vision of 'cunning' Europeans selling *European* products – basic

---

[38] See Lovejoy (1989: 372–3) and Eltis (2019).
[39] Rodney (1972/2012: 96). See also Davidson (1992: 219–20).
[40] Klein (1999: 130).
[41] Wright (2007: 83).
[42] Williams (1944/1964: 51–2).

necessities and especially guns – to 'primitive and naïve' African slavers in exchange for slaves. For this underpins the points that the British were more advanced, powerful and ruthless on the one hand, while their products provided the key contribution to the 'first leg' of the triangle on the other. This, in turn, reflects the 'Eurocentric big bang' theoretical assumption that British industrial power was self-constituting and self-made and that the Atlantic system was built on a purely British and European foundation. The emphasis on guns is often advanced by critics who argue that the Europeans imposed a 'gun–slave cycle', wherein Africans were 'forced' to trade in slaves as a function of their avid desire for guns. This, in turn, required them to wage war within Africa, specifically to capture ever-more slaves in order to buy yet more guns to pursue ever-more wars in a kind of never-ending vicious cycle of warfare. And because Europeans supplied the weaponry, this is said to have exacerbated warfare within Africa.[43] There is certainly some truth to this, not least in terms of the role that warfare and slave capture played in promoting and reproducing centralised African warrior states.[44]

But the gun–slave dynamic was nowhere near the main driver, first because guns and gunpowder comprised only a small proportion of exports to Africa. And second, the fact is that most of the products that paid for the slaves came from the *non*-European world and were non-military in nature.[45] Of the total exports that the Europeans used to buy up African slaves in the seventeenth and eighteenth centuries, the following were most relevant: alcohol, especially American rum (12 and 10 per cent, respectively), various manufactured goods (12 and 10 per cent), guns and gunpowder (7 and 9 per cent), Swedish and English bar iron (2 and 5 per cent) and American tobacco (2 and 8 per cent).[46] Cowry shells from the Maldives were also used.[47] Interesting here is the point that in the eighteenth century just under a fifth of the products that were exported to Africa to purchase slaves were produced by the slaves in the New World. But by far and away, the most important item was cotton textiles, which comprised at least 50 per cent of slave purchases in these two centuries.[48] And, in turn, the most important component here was the large number and varieties of ICTs that were exported and re-exported by the West Asian Muslims and European Companies in

---

[43] See Davidson (1992: 222–3), Rodney (1972/2012: ch. 4) and Whatley (2017).
[44] Klein (1990).
[45] For more general critiques of the 'gun–slave cycle' theory, see Thornton (1998: chs. 3–4) and Northrup (2009: 96–105).
[46] See Klein (1999: 86–7) and Northrup (1998: 201).
[47] Frank (1998: 136–7) and Klein (1999: 111–14).
[48] Klein (2004: 218, 1999: 87–8) and cf. Northrup (2009: 86).

order to purchase African slaves.[49] Indian cotton textiles were already being re-exported from Europe to Africa in order to buy slaves as early as the sixteenth century;[50] though the Muslims were trading ICTs to Africa to purchase slaves (as well as gold and ivory) many centuries earlier (see Figure 3.2 below). Once again, the way through this figure is to trace the numbers.

Critical here, however, is the all-important eighteenth century, when the total numbers of slaves shipped from Africa to the New World by all Europeans escalated to around 6.5 million (having totalled 2.15 million in the two centuries after 1501). Moreover, those shipped by the British alone, net of deaths during transportation, comprised somewhere between 2.55 million and 2.9 million – having totalled only c. 430,000 between 1501 and 1700.[51] In this century, cotton textiles comprised some two-thirds of total British exports to West Africa,[52] the majority of which were re-exported ICTs. Indeed, these became the Europeans' principal medium of exchange for Black slaves in Africa, particularly for the English and the French – so much so that they became the 'linchpin in the Atlantic slave trade'.[53]

More specifically, in the first half of the eighteenth century some 90 per cent of cotton piece goods that the British exported to West Africa were Indian re-exports, while only 10 per cent were British made.[54] It is true that in the second half of the eighteenth century, British-made cotton textiles and linen exports to West Africa narrowed the gap significantly vis-à-vis ICT re-exports via the process of 're-export substitution',[55] but they still failed to close this deficit given that British products comprised 46 per cent and re-exported ICTs some 54 per cent of the total (1751–1807).[56] Moreover, this should not obscure the point that the size of the Indian re-export trade continued to increase considerably, not least because of the rising prices of the slaves, such

---

[49] For the role of ICTs in the West Asian slave trade, see especially Ray (2004: 22–4), Vernet (2009) and Davidson (2012: 4–12). Note that the Muslims also used cowry shells from the Maldives to buy African slaves; see Reader (1998: 386–90) and Klein (1999: 111–14).

[50] Parthasarathi (2011: 24–5).

[51] The lower figure is derived from *The Trans-Atlantic Slave Trade Data Base*, posted at: www.slavevoyages.org/assessment/estimates, while the upper figure comes from Inikori (2002: 237). Others estimate a mid-point figure of around 2.7m; e.g., Klein (1999: 208–10).

[52] Kriger (2009: 123).

[53] Parthasarathi (2011: 24). See also Wadsworth and de Lacy Mann (1931: 148–61), Kriger (2006) and Kobayashi (2019: ch. 3).

[54] Johnson (1990: 28–9, 54–5).

[55] Riello (2013: 147–51).

[56] Calculated from Inikori (2002: 444).

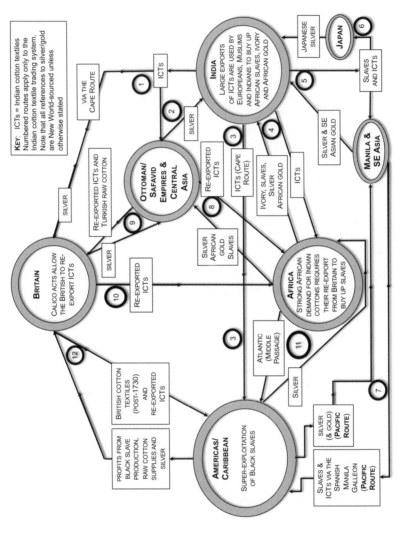

KEY: ICTs = Indian cotton textiles
Numbered routes apply only to the Indian cotton textile trading system. Note that all references to silver/gold are New World-sourced unless otherwise stated

INDIA LARGE EXPORTS OF ICTS ARE USED BY EUROPEANS, MUSLIMS AND INDIANS TO BUY UP AFRICAN SLAVES, IVORY AND AFRICAN GOLD

VIA THE CAPE ROUTE

ICTs

SILVER

1

2

JAPANESE SILVER

JAPAN

6

SLAVES AND ICTs

5

MANILA & SE ASIA

SILVER & SE ASIAN GOLD

RE-EXPORTED ICTS AND TURKISH RAW COTTON

OTTOMAN/ SAFAVID EMPIRES & CENTRAL ASIA

RE-EXPORTED ICTs

3

ICTs (CAPE ROUTE)

IVORY, SLAVES, SILVER AFRICAN GOLD

4

ICTs

SILVER

9

SILVER AFRICAN GOLD SLAVES

8

BRITAIN CALICO ACTS ALLOW THE BRITISH TO RE-EXPORT ICTS

SILVER

RE-EXPORTED ICTs

10

AFRICA STRONG AFRICAN DEMAND FOR INDIAN COTTONS REQUIRES THEIR RE-EXPORT FROM BRITAIN TO BUY UP SLAVES

ATLANTIC (MIDDLE PASSAGE)

3

11

SILVER

7

SILVER (& GOLD) (**PACIFIC ROUTE**)

12

BRITISH COTTON TEXTILES (POST-1730) AND RE-EXPORTED ICTs

AMERICAS/ CARIBBEAN SUPER-EXPLOITATION OF BLACK SLAVES

SLAVES & ICTs VIA THE SPANISH MANILA GALLEON (**PACIFIC ROUTE**)

PROFITS FROM BLACK SLAVE PRODUCTION, RAW COTTON SUPPLIES AND SILVER

Figure 3.2 Indian cotton textiles in the dodecagonal (twelve-sided) global 'super-commodity chain'.

that it was nearly four times larger in absolute/nominal terms and was just under three times higher in real terms in the second half of the eighteenth century compared with that of the first half. Calculated in real terms (i.e., as a proportion of British national income), annual ICT re-exports to Africa rose from roughly 0.7 per cent in 1699–1748 to 0.9 per cent in 1749–1789, before peaking at 1.9 per cent in 1790–1800.[57] As Kirti Chaudhuri concludes, '[t]he opening up of new markets and the rise of new production methods based on African slave labour, which created the famous triangular trade between Europe, West Africa, and America, provided the Indian cotton textiles with a sustained outlet for [more than] two centuries'.[58] And, while it is generally assumed that British cottons had superseded ICTs in West African markets in the first half of the nineteenth century,[59] Kazuo Kobayashi's archival research reveals that ICTs remained more popular with West African consumers right upto about 1850, though this should not obscure the considerable sales of ICTs that were undertaken by Kachchhi merchants in East Africa right into the twentieth century (see Chapter 13). For as Kobayashi notes, we also need to take into account the considerable amount of ICTs that were re-exported to West Africa by the French.[60]

But the story of the ICT-Atlantic slave trade nexus had an additional dimension because the standard Eurofetishist narrative focuses solely on the West African coast so it neglects the importance of the East African coast. Pedro Machado has quite brilliantly brought this largely hidden dimension to light.[61] In particular, Brazilian and Portuguese merchants sourced slaves from Mozambique and then shipped them back to the southern Atlantic. But this was only possible because of the critical role that was played initially by the Gujarati Vāniyā merchants from the 1750s through to about 1840, before their role was superseded by the Gujarati Kachchhis (as I discuss in Chapter 13). And here we encounter the important role of Indian structural power. In Mozambique, European slave merchants used New World Spanish silver dollars (*Piastres* and *Patacas*) to buy ICTs that were then used in exchange for African slaves, who in turn were shipped across the Atlantic to Brazil. And in turn, this was only possible because of the existence of a very robust silver market in Gujarat which, in turn, was derived from the structural power of ICT exports, given that it was these that sucked silver into India. Much of

---

[57] Figures in sterling are provided in Johnson (1990: 54–5) and Inikori (2002: 444).
[58] Chaudhuri (2006: 277).
[59] For example, Inikori (2002: esp. 444).
[60] Kobayashi (2019: ch. 2).
[61] Machado (2014: ch. 5).

the silver that was sent back to India ended up in Surat where the *sarrāfs* (bankers) used it to settle debts as well as to discount *hundīs* (bills of exchange). All of which, in turn, created more resources to finance yet more ICT trade in the Indian Ocean system. It is also noteworthy that the Portuguese re-exported African slaves from India, sending them to Manila whence they were shipped to the southern Atlantic aboard the Spanish Manila Galleon. And, in addition, the Portuguese exported ICTs from India directly to Brazil via the Cape and the Atlantic Ocean.[62] In sum, then, the global movement of ICTs enabled the construction of the famous 'Atlantic triangular trading system'.

It is also worth considering a further dimension of the dark side of the ICT trading system. For as Machado points, Indians purchased very large amounts of ivory with ICTs,[63] and, albeit to a lesser extent, African slaves (as I discuss in Chapter 4). Between 1800 and the 1830s, when the ivory trade had somewhat diminished in scale, Machado tells us that some 1,400 (metric) tons of tusks were exported to India in exchange for ICTs.[64] This would have required the slaughter of about 11,000 African elephants. Moreover, for the whole period in which the Vāniyā were present in Mozambique (c. 1750–1840), Machado reckons that somewhere between 26,000 and 31,000 elephants died to service the ivory trade from Africa to India – a truly grim death toll.[65] Furthermore, according to Prestholdt, the ivory trade took off again after about 1840, this time under the Kachchhis who had replaced the Vāniyās at that time as the principal merchants in the East African–Indian trade.[66] And, once again, ivory was purchased with ICTs. Of note too is that the Europeans became deeply involved in the East African ivory trade, exporting back to Europe some 280 (metric) tons in 1840 and as much as 800 (metric) tons in 1875.[67]

All of which means that Immanuel Wallerstein's well-known denial 'that the exchange of [Afro-Asian goods] … could have sustained so colossal an enterprise as the expansion of the Atlantic world'[68] needs to be rejected. For ICTs formed a vital component of the dual commercial and financial foundation of the African slave trade and the Atlantic system. And, in contrast to Wallerstein's assumption that it was only after 1750 that the hitherto, self-constituting and 'separate' Asian

---

[62] See also Datta (2008).
[63] Machado (2014: ch. 4).
[64] Ibid. (204).
[65] Ibid. (207).
[66] Prestholdt (2008: ch. 3) and Machado (2014: 268–76).
[67] Nicolini (2012: 123).
[68] Wallerstein (1974: 41–2).

economies began to be incorporated by the Europeans into an emergent global economy,[69] it is clear that the Pacific, Indian and Atlantic Ocean systems were woven together after 1500 in a significant way by ICT exports – in addition to the entwined role that was performed by the GSTS. It is for this reason that Giorgio Riello describes the Atlantic system as four sided or 'diamond shaped',[70] with India constituting the fourth pole.

But as Figure 3.2 shows and as I explained earlier, this was ultimately a twelve-sided (dodecagonal) ICTTS that intersected directly with the sixteen-sided New World component of the GSTS. Tracing the numbers in Figure 3.2, I begin by noting that ICTs were exported by the EEIC on the first leg back to Britain (via the Cape route) in exchange for New World silver. Indian and Asian merchants were key distributors of ICTs on the second leg to the Middle East/West Asia with New World silver flowing back in return. The third leg ran directly from Goa to Brazil on Portuguese ships, with Hindu merchants often aboard. For ICTs were in strong demand in Brazil, especially with slaves. The fourth leg saw ICTs exported by Indians directly to East Africa in exchange for African gold, New World silver as well as African slaves (ebony) and ivory. The fifth leg saw ICTs running from India to Southeast Asia with New World silver and Southeast Asian gold going back in return. The sixth leg saw ICTs running from India to Japan, with Japanese silver flowing back in return. The seventh leg ran from Manila to South America along which ICTs and re-exported African slaves were transported. The eighth leg saw ICTs re-exported from West Asia to Africa with African gold (alongside ebony and ivory) flowing back in return, while the ninth leg went from West Asia to Europe along which re-exported ICTs flowed in return for re-exported New World silver. Finally, the tenth through twelfth legs pick up the path of the familiar triangular trading system. Thus, on the tenth leg, the British and French re-exported ICTs to Africa in exchange for African slaves. These were then exported across to the Caribbean and the Americas on the eleventh leg via the Atlantic Middle Passage, before culminating in the twelfth leg wherein the British re-exported ICTs (and British cotton textiles after 1730) to the New World in exchange for slave-made raw cotton and silver, as well as numerous consumer products.

In light of all this, two summary points are noteworthy. First, I noted earlier that while China was an important driver of the GSTS, so too

---

[69] Wallerstein (1989: ch. 3).
[70] Riello (2013: 148).

was India. And here I note Parthasarathi's argument, which constitutes as good a summary of my overall claim as any:

> Claims that China absorbed the *bulk* of the silver that circulated in Asia are ... incorrect. Until the nineteenth century, the Indian subcontinent continued to be a major importer of not only silver but also gold, copper, cowries and badams. The Indian subcontinent held this position in global trade—and was therefore able to claim large quantities of bullion—because of an insatiable appetite for Indian cotton textiles in markets around the world. As a consequence, the subcontinent was awash in money and a highly commercialized economic order emerged from the late sixteenth century.[71]

For as I noted earlier, while China attracted in the region of 30 per cent of New World silver, India's pull was also significant, comprising about 20 per cent (net of the amounts that were re-exported to China).[72]

The second core upshot of this discussion is that while China attracted rather more New World Silver than did India, nevertheless the single most important trading product that lay at the centre of the GSTS was that of ICTs. It is for this reason that the GSTS and the ICTTS were mutually constitutive such that they cannot be disentangled. And it is this that reveals the structural power that Indian merchant capitalists accrued through their control of global markets as a result of the huge demand for ICTs. Ultimately, the key to Indian structural power derived from the fungibility of ICTs through their role as a universal currency, which means that their influence stemmed well beyond the dominance of cotton textile markets. And, it is in this light that I turn to consider how the ICT global super-commodity chain fed into a series of global production and commodity chains, which lay not merely at the centre of the FGE but also enabled the development of British industrialisation and the subsequent rise of the SGE (as I explain in Parts III–V of this book).

Indian Structural Power and the Promiscuous Role of the ICT Global 'Super-commodity/Super-production Chain' (II): Enabling Global Production

The prominent historian of Indian trade, Om Prakash, states that '[i]f there was one commodity that dominated the Indian Ocean trade through the ages well into the eighteenth century, it was Indian textiles'.[73] Beverly Lemire describes them as 'the first global consumer

---

[71] Parthasarathi (2011: 50), my emphasis.
[72] Ibid. (46–50).
[73] Prakash (2009: 160). See also Parthasarathi (2011: 26) and Riello (2013: 25).

commodity',[74] while David Washbrook describes India 'as the workshop of the world in cotton textiles'.[75] Although it is often supposed that Chinese exports of tea, silk, silk textiles and porcelain were dominant global commodities, the fact is that

Indian cotton textiles not only faced one of the most stable and continuous demands in Asian [as well as in African and European] foreign trade but were also finely adapted to suit the specialised tastes of different [Afro-Eurasian] markets. The adaptability of the Indian textile industry and its capacity for an astonishing product differentiation were the two factors most responsible for the creation of regional markets. In this respect it occupied an exceptional and unique place among Asian manufacturing industries.[76]

For Chinese silks as well as Middle Eastern products such as carpets, rugs and metal wares were less adapted to the specialised tastes found in different regional markets and, therefore, fared less well in comparison to ICTs. Most significant is the point that ICTs constituted a kind of promiscuous global 'super-commodity chain' insofar as they enabled the emergence of a series of other interconnected global commodity and global production chains via their role as a universal currency. How, then, did this play out?

The first key influence comprises the point that ICTs enabled the complex global movements of silver and gold, as I explained earlier, as well as those of tobacco, coffee, sugar, cacao, tea, rum and porcelain. During the eighteenth century, the importation of Chinese tea into Europe became increasingly important, rising from 1 per cent of total EIC imports to an average 15 per cent (1730–1760) and 30 per cent (1761–1834).[77] Moreover, tea comprised as much as 81 per cent of the EEIC's total imports from China (1760–1795).[78] In turn, Chinese tea was linked *indirectly* into the Atlantic system as the British imported massive amounts of sugar from the West Indies – from Barbados beginning in the 1640s and later on from Jamaica – in order to sweeten their Chinese tea (usually the cheap black variety known as *Bohea*). To quote from Kirti Chaudhuri once more:

the tea-drinking habit in Europe during the early years of the eighteenth century was an astonishingly rapid process in the assimilation of a new product. Its diffusion was easily comparable to the adoption of Indian cotton textiles in

[74] Lemire (2009: 226).
[75] Washbrook (2007: 87).
[76] Chaudhuri (2006: 205).
[77] Calculated from Bowen (2007) and Chaudhuri (2006: 538–9).
[78] Vries (2015: 371).

[seventeenth-century Europe], and the complementarity of tea and sugar probably explains the relative decline of pepper in household budgets. The greater availability of sugar supplies from the West Indian plantations and the decline in its cost provided the context in which the mass consumption of tea [in Europe] could become a reality.[79]

In essence, the importation of Chinese tea and West Indian sugar (in addition to Javanese sugar), as well as Caribbean (and Javanese and Yemeni Mocha) coffee, all of which was washed down by European consumers in ever-increasing amounts from Chinese porcelain and Chinese-imitated Dutch delftware, triggered a European 'consumer revolution' in the eighteenth century. All of which, in turn, fed into British industrialisation particularly via the 'consumer revolution' and its attendant 'industrious revolution' (as I note in Chapters 7 and 9).

The key point is that the movement of these various global commodities was to an important extent underpinned by the export of ICTs. Thus, New World commodities were produced through the super-exploitation of Black African slaves who, as we have seen, were purchased in Africa largely with re-exported ICTs, which in turn had been purchased with plundered Spanish-American silver. Which means that the peculiarly fungible nature of ICTs gave birth to the Caribbean and later the various North American global production chains that yielded these aforementioned raw materials and consumer products. And, all of which, in aggregate, fostered the deepening of the FGE.

An illustration of this deepening globalisation process that was induced by ICTs is that of the British insurance capitalists, much of whose business activity was conducted in selling insurance to cover the Black slave trade and the system of Black slave production in the Caribbean and the Americas (as I explain in Chapter 9). They were likely clothed in Indian cotton and frequented the Lloyds coffee house in London to conduct their business in insurance, where they smoked Caribbean tobacco and supped on Caribbean coffee that was sweetened with Caribbean or possibly Javanese sugar and which was often drunk out of Chinese porcelain. And then there was the Spalding Society (est. 1710), which met at the local coffee house and whose members included Sir Isaac Newton. It stipulated the following house rules: 'that the Chairman of the day should have the seat by the fire, and that there should be plenty of coffee [Caribbean or possibly Mochan/Javanese],

---

[79] Chaudhuri (2006: 385).

a pot of [Chinese] Bohea tea, "12 clean pipes and an Ounce of Best [Caribbean] Tobacco", a Latin Dictionary and Greek Lexicon, and a chamber pot [possibly made of Chinese porcelain or Dutch Delftware imitations of China]'.[80] In sum, then, as Sven Beckert puts it most succinctly: 'cotton from India, slaves from Africa, and sugar from the Caribbean moved across the planet in a complex commercial dance'.[81] The upshot of which, as Flynn and Giráldez note, is that '[b]y itself, the pedestrian act of drinking a cup of tea [or coffee] in Europe during the eighteenth century ... illustrates deep-seated connections that had long engulfed all of the world's heavily populated land masses'.[82] But the critical point is that it was the structural power of ICTs that made such interdependence possible.

Finally, it is noteworthy that ICT-derived structural power had a transformative impact on societies across the world, though this was a highly uneven process. The interesting point is that ICTs often *enhanced* domestic production in other countries, at least initially. Southeast Asia came to imitate them in order to develop its own indigenous 'Batik' industry,[83] while imitation also played out in the Ottoman Empire,[84] as it did in Africa.[85] That said, though, Indian structural power over time came to challenge rival producer countries across much of the world eventually hitting home perhaps hardest in Europe. Indian cotton textiles posed a fundamental challenge *and* opportunity to the British cotton industry, wherein British producers and inventors imitated Indian techniques and products that in turn led on to the industrialisation of this sector (as I explain in Chapter 10). All in all, as Riello explains, for much of the period of the FGE, the logic of trade was often complementary and supplementary rather than competitive.[86] And, most importantly, the FGE was a *non-hierarchical* system in contrast to the hierarchical nature of the SGE despite the presence of Indian structural power that was derived from ICT dominance of global markets before 1800. But there was yet another dimension to ICTs to consider, in that they enabled not just the Atlantic but also the Indian Ocean slave system.

---

[80] Cited from Uglow (2003: 5).
[81] Beckert (2015: 46).
[82] Flynn and Giráldez (2008: 379).
[83] Hall (1996: esp. 106–20).
[84] Gekas (2007) and Parthasarthi (2011: 115–25).
[85] Lovejoy (1983), Kriger (2005, 2006), Northrup (2009: 90), Klein (1999: 124) and cf. Machado (2014: 136–8). But see Rodney (1972/2012) and Inikori (2009).
[86] Riello (2013: 33).

Provincialising the Atlantic Slave Trade: Unveiling the Heptagonal Slave Trade System in the Global Atlantic and Indian Ocean Systems

We are, of course, accustomed to thinking of a *singular* slave trade in Black Africans and a *singular* triangular trading system, all of which is conflated in an axiomatic fashion with the Atlantic system that is said to be founded upon the binary of 'ruthless European hyper-agency versus African victimhood'. Such is one of the legacies of Eric Williams' aforementioned classic Marxist text,[87] as much as it is of Walter Rodney's equally classic (Eurofetishist) Marxist text, *How Europe Underdeveloped Africa*.[88] But, while the Atlantic slave trade was important in enabling British industrialisation in numerous ways, both directly and indirectly (as I explain in Chapters 8 and 9), there was also a vibrant trade in African slaves in the Indian Ocean;[89] all of which has gone largely un-noticed or, if it has been recognised by critical Eurofetishists, it has been whitewashed from our received picture of the African slave trade.

Indian Structural Power and the Promiscuous ICT
Global 'Super-commodity/Super-production Chain' (III):
The West Asian and Indian Slave Trade in Africans

The Atlantic slave trade was pre- and post-dated by the West Asian slave trade, wherein Africa was linked up with West Asia between the seventh and early twentieth centuries – though the Muslims had also been importing Black slaves during their time in Al-Andalusian Spain between 711 and 1492. In addition, it had a third incarnation in that it also extended to India as African slaves were imported either directly on ships or as re-exports from West Asia.[90] The Indian trade in Black slaves began in the eighth century with the initial transportation of Ethiopian slaves. This developed further during the Delhi Sultanate (1206–1526), when Abyssinian slaves were shipped to Northern India as well as to Ceylon. *Habshīs*, as they were called, were deployed in Bengal either as eunuchs or to perform military service in the last quarter of the fifteenth century. African slaves were also deployed in the Deccan Plateau in Central India as well as in Gujarat in north western India, where they were deployed in the army and navy.[91] This continued under Mughal

---

[87] Williams (1944/1964).
[88] Rodney (1972/2012).
[89] Campbell (2004).
[90] Machado (2014: ch. 5) and Vernet (2009: 48).
[91] Machado (2014: 213).

rule after 1526,[92] though slaves were also deployed in domestic service.[93] Nevertheless, it is also the case that the Portuguese and the British exported African slaves eastward to India, while the Dutch transported small numbers to Southeast Asia.[94] According to Richard Allen, around 0.5 million slaves were transported across the Indian Ocean by the Europeans between 1500 and 1850,[95] while Machado reckons that the Portuguese shipped on average 125–150 slaves per annum.[96]

Finally, there was a fourth incarnation – the internal trade in African slaves, which pre-dated the West Asian slave trade by about nine centuries. Nevertheless, the internal African slave system was less malign than the Atlantic system and, moreover, the slaves 'were often treated no differently from peasant cultivators, as indeed they were the functional equivalent of free tenants and hired workers in Europe'.[97] All of which means that when we talk about the slave trade in general, we cannot conflate it with the European-controlled Atlantic slave system.

While postcolonialists and Marxists focus on *the* Atlantic 'triangular trading system' in the western hemisphere that linked Europe with West Africa and the New World, nevertheless this found its proximate mirror image presence in the Indian Ocean triangular trading system of the eastern hemisphere which linked East Africa with West Asia and India. Note that I have omitted the Dutch deployment of African slaves in Southeast Asia from Figure 3.3, not so as to whitewash this trade but because the numbers were very small relative to those that were traded by the West Asian Muslims. Thus, as Figure 3.3 reveals, there was not one but two *triangular* Black slave systems. However, overall, there was a *heptagonal* African slave trade system given that there was a seventh side, along which African slaves were re-exported by the Portuguese from Goa to Manila whence they were transported on the Spanish Manila Galleon across the Pacific to the New World.[98] And, because these eastern and western systems were inter-linked as ICTs formed the primary means of payment for the purchase of African slaves, especially in the 1500–1800/1900 period, as I explained earlier, so the slave trade operated on a global scale. But even this heptagonal slave trade system is complicated further by the fact that there was an Indian slave trade

---

[92] Jayasuriya and Pankhurst (2003).
[93] Clarence-Smith (2013).
[94] Vernet (2009: 51) and Mbeki and van Rossum (2017).
[95] Allen (2010: 64).
[96] Machado (2014: 215).
[97] Thornton (1998: 87).
[98] Machado (2014: 214).

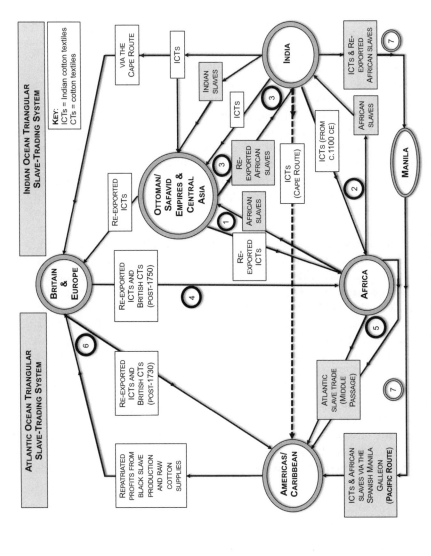

Figure 3.3 The seven-sided (heptagonal) African slave trade system.

in *Indians*,[99] who were exported to Central Asia and the Middle East (as I also note in Figure 3.3).

The situation, then, was much more complex than Eurofetishism's conflation of the slave trade with the Atlantic system.[100] Indeed, it is as if the critical Eurofetishists view the African slave trade with one eye shut. For the Atlantic system was neither *sui generis* and self-constituting, nor was it made solely by the British and other Europeans, given that it was embedded within this hybrid, heptagonal slave trade system in which Indians and Muslims played, albeit in different ways, very significant roles. Thus, Indians, armed with structural power, played a vital role in financing the slave trade, particularly through their export of ICTs, as explained earlier. Moreover, the slave trade system was embedded fundamentally within the twelve-sided dodecagonal ICTTS (see Figures 3.1 and 3.2). Certainly, Paul Gilroy's seminal postcolonial book, *The Black Atlantic*, provides a marvellous service in breaking down the monological construct of the Atlantic system by revealing how African, American and European/British cultures were melded together to produce something that transcended its individual constitutive components.[101] And this de-centring of the Atlantic system has been advanced most impressively by other postcolonial-inspired scholars.[102] But equally, we need to develop this much further by recognising that this was a 'Brown' as well as a 'Black' Atlantic, given the manifold roles that the Muslims and Indians performed within the slave trade in Africans.

However, for all my efforts to reveal the non-European incarnations of the trade in Black slaves, critical Eurofetishists would argue that I have taken a wrong turn in my postcolonial 'journey of re-discovery'. For they would seek to downplay these and, more preferably, to ignore them altogether. A notable example is found in the important book, *The World and Africa*, which was written by the prominent postcolonial Marxist, W. E. B. Du Bois, a good deal of which, I might add, I am in much sympathy with. Nevertheless, while he recognises the historical existence of the West Asian slave trade in his book, the reader learns very little about it – as is also the case in Rodney's and Davidson's books.[103] Du Bois downplays it in numerous ways, such as when he asserts that the West Asian slave trade 'did not transfer any large number

---

[99] Alam (1994: 207–8), Kolff (1990), Segal (2003: 71–6), Machado (2014: ch. 5) and Levi (2016: 102–15).
[100] Most notably, Williams (1944/1964) and Rodney (1972/2012).
[101] Gilroy (1993).
[102] Thornton (1998, 2012) and Benjamin (2009).
[103] Rodney (1972/2012) and Davidson (1992).

of persons';[104] or when he devotes a whole chapter to Asia (and Islam) in Africa wherein the West Asian slave trade receives a very conservative peppering throughout.[105] Most strangely of all, he asserts that 'Arab slave raiding was in the beginning, and largely to the end, a secondary result of the British and American ... slave trade and specifically was based on American demand for ivory'.[106] In this way he reduces the West Asian slave trade to its later incarnation that was centred upon Zanzibar and the rule of the Omani Sultanate in the nineteenth century, while simultaneously reducing this trade to the requirements of the Western capitalist system, as does Rodney.[107] Equally, Basil Davidson asserts that although the trans-Saharan slave trade to the east coast was small, 'the Indian Ocean or East coast trade in slaves was of even smaller significance up to the 1840s'.[108] All of which means that the West Asian slave trade that began in the seventh century is largely conjured into thin air, as if it never happened.

Apart from the fact that somewhere between one and two million Black slaves were channelled into Zanzibar between the 1770s and early-twentieth century, the immediate problem with this critical Eurofetishist erasure is that somewhere between eleven and fourteen million African slaves were traded by the Muslims between the seventh and twentieth centuries.[109] And significantly, these numbers were at least on a par with, if not larger than, the numbers that were traded by the Europeans in the Atlantic system, albeit the West Asian slave trade occurred over a much longer period of time – approximately four times longer. Increasingly, it is believed that the numbers that were traded in the Indian Ocean were probably higher than those that were shipped across the Atlantic Ocean.[110] Moreover, while many captured Africans died on the journey to the Atlantic coast, many also died on the land-based 'Middle Passage' across the Sahara or up the Nile Valley to the east coast before being transported to West Asia and India.[111] Furthermore, it is likely the case that in the 1500–c. 1900 period, some eighteen million slaves were exported from Africa, though 'only 11 million of them were shipped into

---

[104] Du Bois (1946/2015: 69).
[105] Ibid. (ch. 9).
[106] Ibid. (68).
[107] Rodney (1972/2012: 97).
[108] Davidson (1992: 219).
[109] For the lower figure, see Austen (1979: 66–8) and Lovejoy (1983: 24); for the upper figure, see Raymond Mauny cited in Segal (2003: 57) and Gordon (1989: 13).
[110] Larson (2007).
[111] Hunwick and Powell (2002: 67–81).

the Atlantic economy. These other [7 million] slaves were shipped into the Indian Ocean or across the Sahara to slave markets in the East'.[112]

Accordingly, this Eurofetishist erasure means that those eleven to fourteen million African men, women and children who were carried away by the Muslims between c. 700 and c. 1900 are swept under the carpet and thereby erased from our world historical memory. And while the numbers of Africans who were carried off by the Indians were indeed very much smaller, nevertheless, to erase them from our historical memory is no less lamentable. For example, in the 900–1100 period, Muslims imported some 1.74 million Black slaves across the trans-Saharan trade route to West Asia, while some 200,000 were subsequently re-exported to India.[113] All in all, I believe that there *is* one thing worse than the tragedy of the African slave trade in the West Asian and Indian contexts, and that is to turn around many decades after it finished and deny that it ever happened. Moreover, this silence becomes deafening when we confront the fact that the internal slave trade within Africa was also significant – so much so that by 1850 the numbers of slaves within Africa, possibly comprising ten million, surpassed those who resided in America;[114] notwithstanding the important point that the internal slave trade was far less repressive than the West Asian and, most especially the Atlantic, versions as I noted earlier.

The key question, of course, is why it is that three world-renowned experts on Africa, all of whom are genuinely concerned with the well-being of Africans, choose to largely whitewash these non-European variants of the slave trade. Or, put differently, why this 'anti-racist refusal' to recognise these non-Western processes and actors? The essential answer to this question is that critical Eurofetishists *choose* to ignore the roles of non-Western agency for fear of diluting the postcolonial prosecution's case against the West. Accordingly, almost all of the focus is aimed squarely at the Europeans and the Atlantic slave trade. In order to counter this, I turn in Chapter 4 to the thorny issue of *African agency* in addition to Indian and Islamic agencies – both within and without the African slave trade(s).

---

[112] Klein (1999: 129).
[113] Wink (1988: 37).
[114] Ibid.

4 The Afro-Indian Pivot (II)
Entangled Agencies and the Power of Africans,
Indians and West Asian Muslims

Introduction

Here, I advance the narrative that I began in the final section of Chapter 3 by factoring in the entwined roles of African, Indian and West Asian powers and agencies. I do this in two sections. The first considers this in the context of the slave trades, where I reveal African slaver agency/ power with respect to the Europeans. I undertake this as a means to counter the tendency of Eurocentrism and critical Eurofetishism to deny Africans both power and global agency – that is, the agency to have a constitutive or formative impact on the global economy. For here I interrogate the critical Eurofetishist preference to place the entire blame for the moral crime of Black slavery on the Europeans while portraying African slavers as but innocent victims of Western power who had no choice but to undertake this lamentable role and are, in the process, denied such agency and power. Thus, for my reader who is steeped in the critical Eurofetishist perspective, my analysis of Black slaver agency and power that not only made possible the Atlantic slave trade but also helped shape the first global economy (FGE) and second global economy (SGE) will very much constitute the core litmus test of my specific brand of non-Eurocentrism. And, here I take my cue from Maxine Berg who asserts the abiding problem here is that

[h]istorical structuralists such as Immanuel Wallerstein, Samir Amin and ... Giovanni Arrighi identified centre-periphery polarities, but instead of studying *interconnections* they focused on issues of domination and ascendancy by one part of the globe, the West, over the other, going back to the merchant capitalism of the fifteenth century.[1]

In turn, the second section extends the critique of critical Eurofetishism much further. There I develop the theme of African and Indian global

---

[1] Berg (2004: 89), my emphasis.

agencies by honing in on the relations between Gujarati Vāniyā merchants and the African 'prosumer' as well as the Swahili merchants on the East African coast, all of whom carried on their everyday commercial activities regardless of the presence of the Portuguese. And I also show how the Portuguese benefited from their entangled relations with the Vāniyā and the Bhātiyā merchant capitalists and financiers.

Islamic, Indian and African Agencies in the African Slave Trades

This section comprises two core themes, the first of which reveals the agency and power of African slavers within the slave trade, while the second considers the agency and power of Indians and West Asian Muslims in the Indian and West Asian slave trades.

African 'Slaver Agency and Power' in the African Slave Trades

In the first instance, the binary approach of Eurofetishism and Eurocentrism is deployed to explain how it was that the Europeans were able to purchase massive amounts of slaves at bargain-basement prices while also selling European products to the Africans at vastly inflated prices. For it is this 'bargain-basement' conception of slave sales, derived from the Eurofetishist binary of overwhelming, predatory Western market power and underwhelming African naivety and victimhood, that underpins the explanation of why the Europeans were able to purchase such large numbers of Black slaves in the vital eighteenth century. But neither the European merchants nor the African slavers conformed to this caricature.[2] For it was the long-established internal slave-market practices that reached back to the pre-Common Era and then forward in time to the West Asian slave trade after about 650 CE that equipped the African slavers with the ability to negotiate with the (belated arrival of the) Europeans from a position of equality and often strength.[3] Notable too is that they were able to resist the many European attempts at imposing monopoly conditions in order to maintain their own market autonomy,[4] and on occasion, the Africans 'actively coerced the Europeans into submission ... by seizing European ships that engaged in unsanctioned trade'.[5]

---

[2] See especially Northrup (2009: 54–82).
[3] Fage (1969) and Thornton (1998: ch. 3).
[4] Thornton (1998: ch. 2), Northrup (2009: ch. 3) and Klein (1999: 101, ch. 5).
[5] Anievas and Nişancioğlu (2015: 155).

The Europeans would much rather have established plantations in Africa instead of having to outsource them to the New World, not least because they would rather have plundered the slaves for free. But they were blocked from doing so by powerful African elites who had sufficient military power to keep the Europeans at bay. Moreover, the African ability to militarily block the Europeans from penetrating inland in order to capture slaves, 'where indigenous naval techniques proved considerably better suited to manoeuvring in, and hence protecting riverways',[6] meant that the Europeans had no choice but to rely on the African slavers to round up the slaves which they then had to pay for.[7] What's more, the Europeans had to fulfil numerous obligations to the African rulers, such as obtaining licenses as well as paying taxes, rents and charges in addition to providing gifts, just to gain access to these slave and consumer markets.[8] All of which means that the Africans confounded the desires of the Europeans such that the latter had no choice but to purchase slaves from the former and then ship them to the New World.

Not only were the Europeans forced to buy rather than plunder the African slaves but also equally 'confounding' is the fact that '[e]xperienced European traders harboured no doubts about [the] trading skills of the Africans ... Indeed, [the Europeans] regularly complained about the prices they had to pay for each slave or other [consumer] item[s]'.[9] For when measured in constant/deflated (i.e., real) prices, the price of slaves commanded by African slavers quintupled between 1700 and 1800,[10] notwithstanding the point that Europe's colossal *demand* for African slaves in this particular century also played a part. Not surprisingly, the Europeans found that they had no choice but to enter into 'partnership relations' with the African slavers, albeit as junior partners – or what David Northrup aptly refers to as 'joint African-European ventures'.[11]

Perhaps the core problem with Eurofetishism's agency-less vision of Black *slavers*-as-victims lies in the central, proactivist role that they played within the organisational foundation of the Atlantic slave trade as well as that of the Islamic, Indian and internal trades in African slaves. For they had developed a vast slave infrastructure over a period of seven, if not sixteen, centuries prior to the arrival of the Europeans.

---

[6] Ibid.
[7] See especially Klein (1999: ch. 4).
[8] Thornton (1998: 66–71) and Klein (1999: 103–4).
[9] Northrup (2009: 55).
[10] Klein (1999: 110).
[11] Northrup (2009: 60).

This comprised large numbers of porters and military armed convoys to guarantee safe passage of the slaves, who were rounded up mainly through warfare, raiding and kidnapping. The merchant slavers also 'had to be skilled in determining local market conditions and to be able to trade with the Europeans, along with using and obtaining credit from all their contacts, including the Europeans, all of which required long-term training and extensive knowledge'.[12] Critically, without this well-developed infrastructure in place, it would have been impossible for the Europeans to have accessed such large amounts of slaves precisely when they needed them most. All in all, '[m]ost of the early European slave trading with West Africa ... known as the "River of slaves" was simply an internal trade diverted to the Atlantic'.[13] In short, it was not the *cheapness* of the slaves that explains how the Europeans were able to ship such large numbers to the New World in the eighteenth century, but rather the massive and highly complex slave-based African infrastructure that was organised by powerful, market-savvy African slavers and elites that was crucial. Of particular importance too were the partnerships that Africans formed with various Indian merchants, especially the Vāniyā, between c. 1750 and 1840 and subsequently with the Kachchhis. For lying at the core of these relations was the exchange of slaves for Indian cotton textiles (ICTs).

Moreover, African slavers – the fishers of Black men, women and children – as well as the mass of African consumers (as I explain later) were both highly exacting in their cotton-textile consumer preferences (which, as we have seen, comprised the major items that they exchanged for the slaves) and were, once again, formidable market-price negotiators.[14] Indeed, they were able to

negotiate from a reasonable knowledge of international markets what items of European or ... Asian production most appealed to them.... In short, the [African slavers] were neither passive actors nor peoples innocent of the market economy, and were able to deal with the Europeans on the basis of equality. They were already well integrated into a market economy and responded to market incentives as well as any peoples of western Europe.[15]

---

[12] Klein (1999: 121). See also Machado (2014: ch. 5).
[13] Thornton (1998: 95–6, and 97, ch. 3). See also Reader (1998: ch. 28) and Klein (1999: ch. 5).
[14] Wadsworth and de Lacy Mann (1931: 150–1, 158–9), Machado (2009a, 2009b), Prestholdt (2008) and Kriger (2009: 124).
[15] Klein (1999: 107, 111).

Just as the African slavers had honed their market-negotiating skills over many centuries of slave trading with the Muslims, much the same point applies to their knowledge of ICTs, given that they had been buying these up for many centuries, from at least 1100 CE onwards.[16] Walter Rodney's Euro-structuralist/Eurofetishist approach insists that 'the European countries ... decided on the role to be played by the African economy.... As far as foreign trade was concerned, Africa was dependent on what Europeans were prepared to buy and sell.'[17] But, in fact, it turns out that the 'Africans negotiated the terms of trade by refusing all undesired goods, and the failure of British manufacturers to replicate the kinds of items in demand – certain Indian textiles, for instance – forced English merchants to depend [to their chagrin] on particular Indian [products]'.[18] For the 'inconvenient truth' that confronted the British is that the African slavers preferred the Indian fabrics over those produced in Lancashire. In short, then, the African slavers exerted considerable agency vis-à-vis the Europeans in the business of the slave trade.

Re-visioning Agency and Power in the African Slave Trade: Confronting Eurocentrism and the Eurofetishist 'Anti-racist Refusal'

In this section I challenge both Eurocentrism and Eurofetishism in the context of the African slave trade. I argue that Eurocentrics err by failing to recognise the horrors of the Atlantic slave trade (and how slaves played a vitally important role in enabling British industrialisation, which I consider in Chapter 9). While Eurocentric scholars absolve the Europeans of their moral responsibility for their crimes against the African slaves so Eurofetishists err by overplaying the role of the Europeans in the African slave trade while refusing to recognise the agency and power of the African, West Asian and Indian *slavers*.

However, it is precisely here where many anti-racist thinkers will object in the strongest possible terms to, if not be outraged by, my highlighting of the agency and power of the African *slavers* as well as the Muslims and Indians in all of this. And certainly, those readers of a Eurofetishist, anti-racist persuasion will likely view my focus as *flirting* dangerously, if not being complicit, with the arguments made by explicit white defenders of the West such as Ricardo Duchesne. For Duchesne highlights the 'Islamic' slave trade specifically as a means of absolving the moral shame

---

[16] Adenaike (2016) and Riello (2013: 139).
[17] Rodney (1972/2012: 76).
[18] Prestholdt (2008: 61).

and guilt of the Europeans in the tragic saga of the Atlantic slave trade.[19] My case is advanced in two stages, the first of which leads me to sketch some of the key differences between the Euro-Atlantic and the West Asian slave trades.

There is little doubting the point that the Black slave experience in the 'Atlantic system' at the hands of the Europeans was, to quote Orlando Patterson,[20] a tragic exercise in physical and 'social death' and echoed many of the hallmarks of the Jewish Holocaust under the Nazis (as I have argued elsewhere).[21] Indeed, it surely deserves the appellation of the 'African holocaust'. Nothing that I argue here should detract, either intentionally or *unintentionally*, from this point. The first key difference between the Atlantic and West Asian slave trades was that slaves were packed into European slave ships like sardines. Islamic dhows hosted much smaller numbers and gave them a larger personal space. And, while slaves in the New World had a life expectancy of a mere seven years, some African slaves became wealthy and powerful in the West Asian and Indian systems. Moreover, in contrast to the European conception of 'chattel slavery', many slaves in West Asia could look forward to freedom at some future point in time.[22] Women who became impregnated by their slave masters sometimes ended up becoming married to them through which they gained considerable power and wealth. Moreover, it is instructive to note that the 'Arabic word mamlūk means "possessed", or "slave", and the Mamlūk dynasty was a succession of Sultans who had been military slaves, translated to freedom by their very accession to rule'.[23] Eunuchs too could rise to positions of considerable power. And, more generally, slaves were used mainly in domestic service rather than solely as an expendable factor of production as they were in the Americas. This was reflected in the point that for every single enslaved male there were two females in the West Asian slave trade, which was the inverse of the Atlantic slave trade. Finally, slaves not only had certain rights under the Islamic law but also Islam viewed them as humans.[24] In general, it is fair to conclude that the West Asian slave trade/system was far less malign than its Atlantic counterpart.

---

[19] Duchesne (2016).
[20] Patterson (1982). See also Du Bois (1946/2015), Walvin (1992), Thornton (1998: 153–62), Fryer (1988) and Northrup (2009: 164–73). And for important first-hand experiences, see Equiano (1789/2003).
[21] Hobson (2004: ch. 8).
[22] See Gordon (1989: ch. 2).
[23] Segal (2003: 31).
[24] See especially Al-Djazairi (2017). For more general introductions, see Gordon (1989), Oliver (1999: ch. 10), Hunwick and Powell (2002), Segal (2003) and Wright (2007).

However, the second move in my response to the anti-racist refusal of Eurofetishism to recognise the power and agency of African slavers and Muslims in the West Asian slave trade points up the dark side of their involvement. Unlike the Europeans, West Asian Muslims and African slavers engaged in slave raids on villages, though many were captured as prisoners of war. But it wasn't just the African and West Asian slavers' vital role in rounding up the millions of slaves that is important here, but the manner in which it was achieved that reveals the slavers' ruthlessness and power. Tragically, as Murray Gordon notes in the context of the West Asian slave trade:

The great demand for concubines was reflected in the preponderance of girls and young women who fell victim to the slave traffickers. Africans who tracked down slaves for sale in Muslim markets paid special attention to catching these more desirables in their nets. In the predawn *razzias* [slave raids] on unsuspecting villages, it was not uncommon for the [African slavers], who often carried out these raids, to kill off as many of the men and older women and march off the young women [and girls] to the assembly points from where they would begin the long trek to the slave market.[25]

To the brutal conditions of capture can be added the point that many slaves died on the overland Middle Passage as was, of course, also the case vis-à-vis the journey to the west coast and thence across the Atlantic Ocean, as I noted in Chapter 3. In short, not all Africans were pure victims of European power, and it was not only the white man that many Africans feared. Indeed, as the famous Black slave, Ottobah Quobona Cugoano, confessed: 'I must own [up], to the shame … of my own countrymen, that I was first kidnapped and betrayed by some of my own complexion, who were the first cause of my exile and slavery.'[26]

Once captured, the slaves were then delivered to the east coast via the overland Middle Passage. Indeed, between one and two million were traded to Zanzibar between 1770 and the late-nineteenth century alone, with over half shipped abroad and the remainder being deployed to work in Zanzibar's clove plantations.[27] Note, *contra* Rodney, that the Zanzibari episode emerged *independently* of the Europeans (as I explain in Chapter 13). And, having been delivered to the West Asian slave markets, they were then sold off by the *nakkhas* – literally 'cattle dealers'.

---

[25] Gordon (1989: 80); see also Oliver (1999: 135).
[26] Cited in Perry (2009).
[27] Cf. Clarence-Smith (2013), Gordon (1989: 5), Fage (1995: 257) and Lovejoy (1983: 137).

Having been sold off in the West Asian slave markets, a small minority was put to work and faced the harshest routines. Some were deployed in Islamic sugar and cotton plantations – a model that the Europeans inherited and then adopted in the Caribbean and the Americas.[28] Some were deployed in gangs in agriculture and irrigation – most famously the 'Zanj' (Bantu) from the East African coast – as well as in mining, which also became a model that inspired the Europeans later on in the Americas. Then, there is the poignant case of the young African boys who were forced into deep-sea pearl diving and died either from drowning or shock.[29] And, of course, there were the countless young Black girls who were transported to West Asian slave markets before they were bought to work in the harem. Moreover, while many eunuchs rose to power, as noted above, the hidden tragedy here lies in the point that possibly only one in ten survived the castration operation.[30] While the account of the Atlantic slave trade is replete with stories of brutal punishment, equally this was not unique to the Europeans. Notable too is that the first major Black slave revolt did not occur in Haiti, as we are so often told by postcolonialists, but in Basra over nine centuries earlier – the infamous 'Zanj Rebellion' (869–883 CE) – when the Bantu slaves rose up against their harsh treatment in the draining of salt flats. What, then, of the African slavers?

The Eurofetishist conception of African slavers acting as dependent 'compradors' for the Europeans is problematic in the first instance because the former had been in the lucrative business of trading in slaves with their own elites before the Common Era as well as with the West Asian Muslims after about 650 CE, which occurred some seven to eight centuries before the arrival of the Portuguese on the west coast of Africa and their first extraction of slaves in 1441. Which means that they were not 'brought to life' by the requirements of the Europeans. Moreover, the African slavers viewed the slave trade as an opportunity to get rich, as they had done ever since the seventh century, if not before the Common Era when the internal African slave trade began.[31] Indeed, it was chiefs and wealthy elites who sold the slaves off to the Europeans, though it is also the case that small-scale traders played an important part.

But my core response to the Eurofetishist critique is that if we are to re-humanise the African people after their de-humanisation by scientific racism, we need to focus on their humanity, for better and for worse. For after all, to be human is to do good, sometimes to do bad and occasionally

---

[28] Mintz (1986).
[29] Gordon (1989: 50).
[30] Ibid. (95–6).
[31] Perry (2009).

to do evil. The irony here, then, is that to portray Africans and other non-Western peoples as naïve and innocent of all evil and power is reminiscent of the old 'noble savage' trope as much as it is of the old Eurocentric and scientific racist conception of African people as but children. And, in this vein, the deepest paradox emerges here in that whitewashing the African slavers of their moral crimes is ultimately to deny their humanity which, of course, is not to be conflated with 'humaneness'. For it was their avariciousness and ruthlessness that I am interrogating here – even though the African slavers cannot be held accountable for what the Muslims and especially the Europeans did to the slaves they bought, notwithstanding their complicity in all of this.

Thus, the irony here is that the flip side of the Eurofetishist propensity to blame only the Europeans for the slave trade is that it serves to get the Black slavers – as well as the Indians and West Asian Muslims – off the moral hook. Moreover, denying the African slavers power and agency leads into the Eurofetishist double standard, wherein many anti-racists have no trouble according agency (and power) to the white race within the brutal Atlantic slave trade, but cannot acknowledge this in the context of the African slavers or West Asian Muslims and Indians in the Black slave *trades*. Notably, this anti-racist refusal to recognise the non-Western dimensions of the slave trade or fear of muddying the waters of blame and thereby getting the Europeans off the moral hook comes at a large human cost. For as I noted in Chapter 3, Eurofetishist political expediency results in the elision, or the sweeping under the historical carpet, of the eleven to fourteen million Black Africans who were carried away in the West Asian slave trade – not to mention those millions who died on the Middle Passage to the east coast – as if this forced exodus never happened. And as I noted in Chapter 1, this leads into Eurofetishism's soft bigotry of low expectations vis-à-vis non-Western societies. For it would surely be lamentable to find that the only Black African slaves that mattered and who should be remembered were those who were carried away by the Europeans in the Atlantic slave trade. This is probably the prime historical casualty of Eurofetishism's political *modus operandi*.

Finally, and at long last, I turn to confront the (African) elephant in the room. For resounding ever louder in the mind of my Eurofetishist reader as the discussion has unfolded will undoubtedly, and quite rightly, be the question as to how on earth I can talk about African 'slaver agency' when the slave trade impinged negatively on Africa in all manner of ways.[32] But my definition of agency here refers to their contribution

[32] See especially Du Bois (1946/2015: ch. 3), Rodney (1972/2012: ch. 3), Davidson (1992: 220–1) and Nunn (2008).

to the FGE and SGE. Ultimately, my purpose in implicating the Black slavers – as well as the Muslims and Indians – derives in part from my desire to focus on instances of social injustice whomsoever commits them and wherever they do so. But, much more important is my desire to reveal how African slavers' agency and power formed an important component of the Afro-Indian *pivot* of the FGE. For it turns out that their actions, albeit unwittingly, were vital in drawing the Atlantic, Pacific and Indian Ocean systems together.

As I explained in Chapter 3, the slavers were interested principally in being paid in ICTs which, in turn, forced the Europeans and West Asians to buy them up in large amounts in order to purchase slaves. And it was in the Atlantic system where the slaves produced the goods that fed Britain's consumer revolution as well as the raw materials – especially raw cotton – that fuelled British industrialisation (as I explain in Chapter 9) as well as American development. Indeed, as Herbert Klein notes similarly vis-à-vis the United States, 'it was the African slaves who enabled this consumption [and industrial] revolution to occur. Without that labor most of America would never have developed at the pace that it did.'[33] Critically, in the absence of the African slavers, slaves and ICTs, the Atlantic system would have been fundamentally weakened, if not undermined altogether. All of which serves to challenge the Eurofetishist portrayal of the African people as passive, agency-less and relatively backward – i.e., a 'people without history' – such that their fate was determined wholly by the external impact of the all-powerful, hyper-agential West and the 'structural requirements' of Western capitalism.[34] In fact, to an important extent, the fate of the British industrial revolution as well as the FGE and SGE lay in the hands of the African slavers and slaves.

The Entangled Agencies of Indians and Africans

In this final section, I shall bring to the fore the 'global agency' of the mass of African consumers and merchants given that they also played a vital role in nurturing not just the FGE but also in laying down the

---

[33] Klein (1999: 102). See also Baptist (2016).

[34] Or, in the specific case of Walter Rodney and Basil Davidson, this can be modified to the idiom of the 'African people *stripped* of their history' after Europe's first contact in 1441. For Davidson (1992: chs. 1–4), Africa is depicted as a flourishing civilisation prior to the European arrival before the great leap backward began, while for Walter Rodney (1972/2012: ch. 2), the continent is viewed at only a slightly lower level of development to that of Europe's around 1500 before the rapacious process of 'under-development' became Africa's lot thereafter.

conditions that spurred on the British industrial revolution and the rise of the SGE (as I explain in Chapter 10). I shall deal with this in two sections, with the first focusing on the African 'prosumer' and the second dealing with the Swahili traders on the east coast.[35]

Revealing the Entangled Agencies of the 'African Prosumer' and ICT Producers/Merchants

While I have already established the point that the African slavers were highly discerning and discriminating in their consumer tastes, often rejecting British textiles in favour of Indian fabrics, the same point applies to the mass of African consumers.[36] For critical Eurofetishist and Eurocentric scholars alike miss the twin points that fashion tastes changed rapidly and varied considerably across Africa, on the one hand, and that Africans preferred to clothe themselves in sophisticated ICTs as well as those that they made themselves on the other. Thus, Europe was not exceptional with regard to its changing tastes in fashion and clearly Africa did not comprise a series of merely static and primitive market-less societies as Eurocentric scholars presume. Jeremy Prestholdt notes of a much later period that 'Joseph Thomson, who fit out a caravan for Lake Tanganyika in the 1870s, wrote that "fashion was as dominant among Central African tribes as among the belles of Paris or London".'[37] Moreover, the reality is that the British and Americans found, not infrequently, that having transported large amounts of British textiles to African markets, the local consumers rejected them, either for their inferiority or their incompatibility with changing African fashion tastes, leaving the British and Americans no choice but to return them to England or New England, respectively, invariably at a loss.[38] Speaking of the African consumers of textile clothing, one clearly frustrated contemporary European observer complained that 'at one moment they like this new fashion, at another moment that; and whatever appeals to them at a particular time they must have.... This is why so many [European] goods remain unsold and are sent back to Europe at a great loss.'[39]

Certainly, this would quite naturally have been perplexing for the British, given that their home cotton-textile consumer market

---

[35] For excellent introductions to Swahili culture and economic structure, see Middleton (1992) and Nicolini (2012: ch. 3).

[36] See Machado (2014: 131–6).

[37] Prestholdt (2008: 63).

[38] Ibid. (64).

[39] Wilhelm Johann Müller, cited in Thornton (1998: 52–3).

was remarkably unified as opposed to the highly fragmented nature of African consumer demand. Nevertheless, when the process of changing consumption/fashion tastes developed in Europe from the late-seventeenth century onwards, this is presented by Eurocentrism as a sign of 'modernity'. And, in any case, it wasn't the 'whimsical' or 'fickle' nature of the African consumer that was 'the problem' but that the British were not sufficiently organised to track these changing tastes and cater for them. For the proof of the pudding lies in the simple fact that the Indians were able to achieve this, as I explain below.

Critical Eurofetishism also buys into the Eurocentric trope of the 'primitive' African consumer, albeit from a different angle. Walter Rodney advances the dismissive claim that 'the majority of the [European] imports [into Africa] were of the worst quality even as consumer goods – cheap gin, cheap gunpowder, pots and kettles full of holes, beads and other assorted rubbish'.[40] But this is problematic for various reasons, not the least of which is that for the most part, the imports were not basic and crude necessities and consumer items. Rather, as John Thornton points out, 'Africa's trade with Europe was largely moved by prestige, fancy, changing taste, and a desire for variety—and such ... motivations were backed up by a relatively well developed productive economy and substantial purchasing power.'[41] Indeed, rather than exhibiting primitive consumption requirements, African consumer tastes were such that they sought the superior Indian textiles over the inferior ones that the British offered, much to the latter's chagrin. Thus, as Hebert Klein argues, '[t]hough some writers [most notably Walter Rodney] have suggested that Africans were seduced by shoddy goods and enthralled into permanent dependence on the trading of slaves, the history of ... imports everywhere [in Africa] shows unique local markets with constant changing tastes'.[42]

Not only does he ignore the importance of cotton textiles but Rodney's dismissal doubles down as a yet deeper critique of the African consumer, given the assumption that they were naïve and gullible and that, as such, they were easily manipulated by the cunning Europeans. Does he really believe that the Africans were so gullible as to buy 'pots and kettles full of holes' in exchange for the hard-earned capture and long and laborious transportation of slaves to market that involved numerous hazards and financial costs? The reality is that before 1650, if not later, Africa was like India as well as China to the extent that 'Europe offered nothing

---

[40] Rodney (1972/2012: 102).
[41] Thornton (1998: 45 and 52).
[42] Klein (1999: 115).

to Africa that Africa did not already produce'.[43] For example, African societies had long been in the business of cotton-textile production and iron production,[44] with the former stemming back to the first millennium CE and the latter beginning before the Common Era.

A second way in which the 'global developmental agency' of the African consumer/prosumer was manifested lies in the point that 'though often overlooked in the literature on cloth in the Indian Ocean, African demand was critical in sustaining high levels of weaver production in India', particularly in Jambusar in Gujarat up to the 1840s, in Kachchh from the 1840s and later in Bombay (as I explain in Chapter 13).[45] African demand also stimulated production in Salem in New England in the 1830s to about 1850 as well as in Lancashire, England.[46] This feeds into conceptualising the African as a 'prosumer', wherein African demand stimulated production in India – as well as in Britain and the United States – such that an 'elective affinity' existed between African consumers, on the one hand, and Indian, British and American producers on the other. This unsettles the standard 'productionist problematique' that dominates Marxist political economy, much as it destabilises the 'consumptionist problematique' of Smithian liberalism. Here, we need to recognise the global developmental agency of African 'prosumers' (which posits an elective affinity between production and consumption such that neither is privileged over the other).[47]

As signalled above, a significant part of the secret to Indian success lay in the fact that Indian weavers were highly responsive to the ever-changing fashion tastes of African consumers in different parts of the continent (as well as those in Europe and West Asia).[48] The Indians established a complex network across Afro-Asia, with African middlemen working in the African interior – the *Patamares* and the *Vashambadzi* – feeding information to the Vāniyā brokers, who then relayed it back to intermediaries in India who in turn relayed it back to the Gujarati weavers.[49] Note that the use of intermediaries in the final stage of the information relay process concerning African consumer demand was undertaken in order to protect the weavers from direct contact with merchants *and* brokers who might seek to harass or exploit them. In turn, the role of the African middlemen was indispensable as they knew

---

[43] Thornton (1998: 44).
[44] Du Bois (1946/2015: ch. 7), Oliver (1999: chs. 6 and 11) and Beaujard (2019).
[45] Machado (2009a: 170).
[46] Prestholdt (2008: ch. 3). See also Machado (2014) and Kobayashi (2019).
[47] Toffler (1980).
[48] Levi (2016), Goswami (2016) and Machado (2009a: 170–5, 2014: 141–9).
[49] Machado (2014: 36–44).

not only the best internal routes to ply but also the nature of the goods that local markets desired. As Machado notes:

Vashambadzi ... were lynchpins in African trade, leading caravans through lands where travel was often difficult because of the terrain or political circumstances, and where passing through a territory always required the payment of a gift to be permitted to do so. These African agents were organized, disciplined and assumed many of the physical risks of commercial life in eighteenth-century Zambesia.[50]

Not only were the Vashambadzi 'linchpins' in the trade into the African interior, given that caravan leaders played such a pivotal role in linking Indian (and American) cotton-textile producers with such consumers but they were also 'lynchpins in the system of global trade'.[51] And, much like the African slavers, so the caravan leaders developed large infrastructures that included hundreds or thousands of porters, all of which required specialised knowledge of local conditions and languages.[52] Of particular note is the point that these African merchants also employed local African artisans to finish off the ICTs to suit the local tastes of African consumers, given that these changed so rapidly.[53] This point, in turn, reveals the presence of the deep inter-continental connections and complex sinews that ran through the FGE as well as the entangled agential relations between Africans and Indians.

In sum, this 'elective affinity' between African prosumer agency and Indian commercial and productive agency – as well as the African prosumer and Britain's cotton industrialisation – is aptly referred to by Pedro Machado as 'direct reciprocities',[54] which recognises the twin-agential role that Africans and Indians performed in enabling the development of global trade. Equally as useful in this context is the notion of 'trans-regional dialogues' in a global perspective that is articulated by Kazuo Kobayashi.[55] All of which reflects my emphasis in this book on 'hybridities', 'entangled encounters/relations' and 'co-constitutive interactions/connections', which have been obscured by the Eurocentric propensity for 'essentialised differences' and what Jeremy Prestholdt aptly calls 'repressed mutuality'.[56]

[50] Ibid. (39).
[51] Prestholdt (2004: 764).
[52] Prestholdt (2008: 67–8).
[53] Prestholdt (2004: 765–7, 2008: 68–70).
[54] Machado (2009b: 57–8).
[55] Kobayashi (2019).
[56] Prestholdt (2008: 2).

Revealing the Entangled Agencies between Indian/Swahili
Merchants and Indian/Portuguese Merchants and Officials

Finally, I want to close this section by raising an important problem with the Eurofetishist approach, in which Africa is all-too-often reduced to its west coast given that this was the second pole of the so-called triangular trading system. And, in the process, Africa is often reduced to little more than the Atlantic slave trade under totalised European dominance. Typical here, once more, is the structural-Eurofunctionalist logic of dependency theory in which Rodney asserts that 'Europe allocated to Africa the role of supplier of human captives to be used as slaves in various parts of the world.'[57] Moreover, even in the few instances when the east coast is considered, it is usually obscured through its reduction to yet another European logic of domination. Thus, with the arrival of Vasco da Gama in Malindi (just north of Mombasa in Kenya) on the Swahili coast in 1498, it is often assumed that he launched, to paraphrase the well-known idiom advanced by the Indian nationalist writer K. M. Panikkar, the 'Vasco da Gama epoch of Africa'.[58] But right from the moment of their arrival in East Africa, it turns out that

[n]othing that Portuguese explorers had seen during sixty-five years of exploration of Africa's Atlantic coasts prepared them for the wealth and architectural magnificence of the trading cities of the Swahili [East African] coast. Astonishment mixed with avarice at the sight of their riches, and the deeply entrenched presence of Islam incited the crusading zeal that had been so prominent a part of Prince Henry's original undertakings.[59]

Far from triggering the 'Vasco da Gama epoch' of Africa, the Portuguese failed to dominate the trading world of East Africa. There were numerous reasons for this, one of which is that during the seventeenth and eighteenth centuries through most of the nineteenth, the West Asian Omanis maintained a sphere of influence that extended from the Persian Gulf down to the east coast of Africa in the western half of the Indian Ocean and to the west coast of India in the east. As Hung Ho-fung notes, '[t]he Portuguese, Dutch and the English could hardly break the trade monopoly of the Omanis, and were kept at bay by them'.[60] Certainly, there were many bouts of violence that the Portuguese initiated, though they were unable to maintain their position through military power, not

---

[57] Rodney (1972/2012: 77).
[58] Davidson (1992: 226).
[59] Northrup (1998: 194); see also Davidson (1992: 190).
[60] Hung (2000: 3).

least because of the superior power of the Omanis. Indeed, having been expelled by the Islamic Omanis in 1698, the Portuguese later renewed their effort to defeat the Muslims in 1729, but found that they had no choice but to finally flee for good from their original stronghold of Fort Jesus in Mombasa.[61] Instead, as I argue shortly, the Portuguese maintained their presence in large part through the enabling roles of the Vāniyā merchants from Diu and Daman in Gujarat.

A second reason why the Portuguese *economic* presence was limited lies in the point that the Swahili had substantial knowledge and penetrative reach into the African interior – something that had always eluded the Iberians.[62] Thus, when in the nineteenth century the northern Europeans arrived on the east coast, far from bringing Africa to economic life, they soon discovered that they could travel into the interior only 'with the help and guidance of established African merchants who were already in the business of long-distance trade'.[63] Even David Livingstone, the supposed pioneering explorer of the heart of Africa, was dependent on the hidden efforts, help and knowledge of those Africans with whom he travelled.[64] Moreover, not only did the Swahili enjoy a vibrant trading relationship with the Indians and West Asian Muslims, not least through their knowledge of Africa, but they could circumvent Portuguese attempts at imposing trade monopolies. And they traded far and wide, importing goods from China, India, Persia and Arabia via both land and sea (though this trade stems back to the early first millennium CE),[65] all of which energised African economies along the Swahili coast.[66]

No less pertinent is that the Portuguese interlopers would most likely have found out very quickly that the large trade, which stretched from Barawa (in present-day Somalia) to Inhumbane (south of Sofala in present-day Mozambique), was dependent upon ICTs,[67] not least because they comprised an informal currency that was exchanged for African products that included gold, slaves (ebony) and ivory.[68] Indeed, the 'early Portuguese remarked not only on the luxury of the … cotton … worn by the upper classes in the coastal towns, but also on the loin cloths worn by the slaves'.[69] Certainly, even a cursory reading of Da Gama's diary, *A Journal of The First Voyage of Vasco da Gama, 1497–1499*, which

[61] Sharman (2019: 51–5).
[62] Middleton (1992: ch. 2) and Machado (2009a: 176–7).
[63] Curtin (1984: 16).
[64] See Gappah (2019).
[65] Wink (1990: 45).
[66] Beaujard (2019: ch. 5).
[67] Machado (2009a: 165).
[68] Kriger (2006) and Kobayashi (2019: ch. 3).
[69] Segal (2003: 99).

was published by Ravenstein, is peppered with references to Africans wearing ICTs.[70] Still, this was hardly surprising given that Gujarati cotton textiles had been exported to East Africa from around the tenth century CE onwards.[71]

Certainly, the Portuguese would have noticed the strong connections that existed between the Vāniyā Gujarati traders and Swahili traders – though the former were later replaced by the Indian Kachchhis in the 1830s and 1840s with whom the Omani Sultanate had formed a very strong commercial alliance, first in Hadramaut and subsequently in Zanzibar (see Chapter 13).[72] Critically, these Afro–Indian relations operated alongside the Portuguese presence on the east coast of Africa.[73] In fact, what we find is a complex matrix of entwined agential relations between Vāniyā and Portuguese merchants, on the one hand, and between Vāniyā/Bhātiyā merchants and the Portuguese imperial state in both Mozambique and India on the other.

The economy of Mozambique rested on a bedrock of Indian Vāniyā-merchant finance and credit, upon which Portuguese merchants and the Portuguese state found that they had little choice but to depend.[74] The fact that the Vāniyā formed close relations with the *Patamares* and *Vashambadzi* gave the Indian merchants an effective access into the African interior and a knowledge base of the ever-changing fashion tastes of African consumers. Such were the benefits that ICT-derived structural power bequeathed the Indian merchants – a privilege that eluded the Portuguese as well as other Europeans.[75] The Vāniyā also formed entangled relations with the Portuguese imperial state in Daman and Diu in India, providing it with commercial and financial contributions 'in the absence of which, Portuguese imperial rule would have been greatly diminished'.[76] Moreover, the Bhātiyā merchants also played a key role in the trade that the Portuguese in Goa relied upon, particularly with respect to the importation of Brazilian tobacco and snuff. All in all, Russell-Wood only slightly exaggerates when he asserts that

In East Africa, the Portuguese intrusion was no obstacle to Arab and Swahili [as well as Indian] traders who continued freely to engage in commerce with the Red Sea, the Persian Gulf, and India. From the 1670s, Gujarati and Goan traders invested heavily in Mozambique and it was they, rather than the

---

[70] Ravenstein (2016).
[71] Kobayashi (2019).
[72] Dobbin (1996), Ray (1995) and Markovits (2000: ch. 1).
[73] Northrup (1998: 198) and Klein (1999: 56).
[74] Machado (2014: 63–6).
[75] Ibid. (131–2).
[76] Ibid. (270).

Portuguese, who reaped much of the financial reward.... When to this are added the commercial networks which extended to Indonesia and ... East Africa, and in which Indian textiles played a major role, it can be seen that such was the complementarity of supply and demand at different points on these commercial networks that a European component was [largely] superfluous.[77]

In any case, the reality was that the Portuguese found that they had little choice but to adapt to local conditions,[78] not least by working with Indian merchants.

In sum, then, when the subject of post-1500 Africa arises, Eurofetishism's first and often last instinct is to focus on the dramatic and gruesome headlines concerning the slave trade on the west coast that fed the Atlantic system. By contrast, my *first* instinct is to home in on the humdrum everyday economic agency of African, West Asian and Indian traders on the Swahili coast. For these merchants carried on in large part independently of European interference, though this should not discount the fact that the Portuguese were also entwined with Indian merchants. Moreover, it would be wrong to assume that East Africa was *sui generis*, as if it was isolated from the rest of the continent. For East African cities served as conduits for the diffusion of trade to southern and northern Africa.[79] Moreover, following the Islamic penetration of the continent beginning in the mid-seventh century, the eastern and western coasts became interlinked, both in the northern and sub-Saharan regions.[80] One such linkage was performed directly by the Muslims who were involved heavily in African slavery in both West and East Africa.[81] Significantly, the West Asian Muslims enjoyed their most profitable trade with West Africa, where gold, ivory and slaves were the key commodities that were purchased. And similarly strong connections were made between West Asia and East Africa, which were enabled by the pivotal role that was played by ICTs in general and the Vāniyā from about 1750 to 1840 and the Kachchhis thereafter in particular.[82] All of which refutes Wallerstein's claim that Africa was not part of the global economy before the mid-eighteenth century.[83] For not only was Africa integrated but it also formed alongside India, coupled with Indian structural power, the pivot of the FGE.

[77] Russell-Wood (1998: 135).
[78] Phillips and Sharman (2015: 145–9).
[79] Frank (1998: 73).
[80] Moseley (1992: 527) and Bovill (1933/2018).
[81] Lovejoy (2002).
[82] Prestholdt (2008: ch. 3).
[83] Wallerstein (1980: 17).

Conclusion

I want to conclude by addressing two core problems that lie at the heart of the Eurofetishist analysis, typified once more by Walter Rodney's work. First, and foremost, as I explained in the opening chapter, the ultimate problem with the critical Eurofetishist approach is that it buys, albeit unwittingly, into the binary ontology of Eurocentrism by separating out West from non-West and then awarding the former a monopoly of power and agency. Moreover, instead of elevating the West to the position of cultural and moral superiority as in orthodox Eurocentrism, Eurofetishism simply reverses the binary so as to indict the Western states as morally evil colonizers and to (re)present the non-Western peoples as morally superior, innocent victims. In the African context, the problem with this conception is brought poignantly to light by the non-Eurocentric Marxist scholars, Alex Anievas and Kerem Nişancıoğlu:

> World-systems approaches have often reinforced an essentially conservative view of African societies as passive [and agency-less].... For Walter Rodney, because Africa was at a 'lower level' of economic development than Europe, it was forced into a colonial relation in which African rulers gave up slaves in exchange for [basic] manufactured goods. [But] such approaches mistakenly project the 'modern' colonial relation retrospectively back to a time in which the power balance between Europe and Africa was much less clear cut.... Such explanations, whether benign [i.e., well-meaning] or not, therefore *tend to reinforce the naturalisation of black slavery*, by reproducing the idea that Africans were naturally prone to colonial subjugation and exceptionally suited to plantation work.[84]

Or as Quirk and Richardson state, this tendency 'has the effect of minimizing African agency and autonomy by relegating Africans to the role of pawns and passive victims at the hands of more dynamic and sophisticated Europeans'.[85] Critically, not only does Eurofetishism unintentionally naturalise African slavery but also, no less unwittingly, it naturalises and eternalises Western imperialism in Africa.

All of which leads directly into the second major problem concerning Walter Rodney's and Basil Davidson's claim that right from first contact in 1441,[86] European domination ensured that African 'dependency' was cast in stone for the next half millennium as the Portuguese initiated the so-called Vasco da Gama epoch of Africa. But European imperial domination did not occur until the end of the nineteenth century and

---

[84] Anievas and Nişancıoğlu (2015: 154–5), my emphasis.
[85] Quirk and Richardson (2014: 143).
[86] Rodney (1972/2012: 95–113) and Davidson (1992: ch. 5).

indigenous African iron and cotton production were not displaced by European imports before the mid-nineteenth century, which means that in so many respects, Rodney 'severely underestimates both the skill and the resilience of African craftspeople'.[87] Moreover, to reduce Africa to its relations with a fetishised Europe is problematic for its implied Eurocentrism given that there was far more to Africa than this relationship, as I have shown throughout this chapter. Thus, while Rodney, Davidson and others are correct to argue that the Atlantic slave trade depleted the supply of labour within Africa and caused damage in all manner of ways, as Nathan Nunn has also argued,[88] nevertheless this analysis should also be extended to the role of the West Asian slave trade. For undoubtedly, the forced exodus of millions of girls and women to West Asia would have impacted negatively on future African demographic rates – much more so than was the case in the Atlantic system given that twice as many girls and women relative to men were taken by the Muslims, while the reverse scenario occurred in the Atlantic slave trade.

Nevertheless, notwithstanding the undoubted harmful legacy of slave trading in those African countries that were most involved in it, the fact is that if Africa's present woes cannot be put down *solely* to the European (and West Asian) incursion much before 1884, then the argument that African *under-development* occurred from the fifteenth century onwards turns out to be a twentieth-century conception projected back in time in ahistorical fashion. For a key objective of my highlighting of African agency is to reveal Europe's precarious and fragile position in Africa before the late-nineteenth century, given that the Europeans were not all-powerful and nor were all Africans merely passive victims of European power. Clearly, then, a very great deal is at stake in Eurofetishism's dismissal of African agency. Finally, this chapter serves to set the scene for Chapters 9 and 10 by highlighting the global developmental agency of African slavers, slaves and consumers. But for the moment, the key question to be addressed is whether it was the Europeans who were the key agents that traded ICTs across the Indian Ocean, as Eurocentrism insists.

[87] Northrup (2009: 90).
[88] Nunn (2008).

5   Entangled Indo-European Agencies
The Implications of Indian Structural Power

Introduction

Having revealed in Chapters 3 and 4 how Indian cotton textiles (ICTs) helped weave together the Indian, Pacific and Atlantic Ocean systems into the first global economy (FGE), Eurocentric scholars would reply by arguing that even if this was true it was only because of the pro-active and primary trading role that was performed by the European East India Companies (EICs) in distributing those textiles. For as one critic of non-Eurocentric world history, Peer Vries puts it to me in private correspondence:

India produced cotton textiles [and raw cotton] that were brought to the rest of the world by British traders who earned a lot of money in selling them. So basically British producers were competing with British traders in Indian cotton. The Indians sat quietly at home and competed with no one in Europe or America.[1]

And, in turn, this feeds into the more general Eurocentric vision, typified in the words of John Roberts in his book, *The Triumph of the West*:

Why, after all, should food and raw materials [and Indian cotton textiles] from far-off places have been available to Europeans? The basic answer must be that Europeans willed it so, and they have had the physical, economic and psychological power to give their will effect. By many particular decisions, informally and formally, consciously and unconsciously, they created over two or three centuries world-wide economic interdependence ... By 1900 the system was as complete as it ever was to be; it is the only global economic system there has ever been.[2]

Interestingly, a Western-centric (i.e., Eurofetishist) position is found surprisingly often in critical approaches, to wit Sven Beckert's claim concerning the export of cotton textiles: by comparison with Britain,

---

[1] Peer Vries, private correspondence (August 2017). See also Vries (2002: 89–90).
[2] Roberts (1985: 272, 276).

'India and China ... had not even come close to ... global dominance ....
And yet, starting in the sixteenth century, armed European capitalists and
capital-rich European states reorganized the world's cotton industry.'[3]
Given the seminal role that ICTs played in weaving together the FGE,
there is much at stake in ascertaining who was largely responsible for
selling them across global markets.

This chapter comprises four sections. In the section 'Resuscitating
Indian Agency and Indian Structural Power in the Indian Ocean System',
I argue that Indian merchants likely carried significantly larger amounts
of ICTs to Indian Ocean markets than did the Europeans. This, in
turn, begs the question that if the EICs were supposed to have been so
dominant, then how were the Indians and Asians able to carry on their
trade? The section 'Indian Merchant Autonomy and the "Exit Option"'
argues that one reason for the success of Indian and Asian merchants
lay in the fact that they could deploy the 'exit strategy' in those cases
where the European Companies tried to monopolise trade. Moreover, if
the EICs were not as powerful as we have been told by Eurocentric and
Eurofetishist scholars, the section 'Incorporating the Europeans into
the Indian Ocean System through Indian Structural Power?' inverts the
standard claim that after 1750 Asia was incorporated into the European-
centred system by revealing how the quest for ICTs, in effect, led to the
incorporation of the Europeans into the Indian Ocean system. Even so,
this 'incorporation' was achieved through the entwining of Asian *and*
European agency. Which in turn begs the question as to how we might
best re-conceptualise Indo-European relations.

As I noted in Chapter 2, where I argued that the arrival of the
Europeans in East Asia can be summarised by the mantra that 'they
came, they saw, they kow-towed', in the section 'Partnership/Entangled
Relations and Competitive–Cooperation: The Core *Modus Operandi* of
Indo-European Relations' I argue that in the Indian context, 'they came,
they saw, they (competitively) cooperated'. All of which the Europeans
accepted because they had no choice but to do otherwise if they were to
gain from their trading presence in the Indian Ocean. In this respect,
Indian structural power formed the organisational matrix within
which the Europeans had to operate. I capture this through a focus on
'partnership relations', though interestingly, the EICs were generally
junior partners up to the early-eighteenth century but became equals
in various states within India during the late-eighteenth and nineteenth
centuries as the Mughal Empire declined.

---

[3] Beckert (2015: 54).

Resuscitating Indian Agency and Indian
Structural Power in the Indian Ocean System

As I explained in Chapters 3 and 4, ICTs constituted the key trading commodity throughout the Indian Ocean even before the belated arrival of the EICs. And, as I explained in Chapter 3, ICTs bequeathed a structural power to Indian merchants in part because they were in high demand to meet the clothing requirements of the Afro-Asians and in part because they constituted a universal means of payment – i.e., a universal currency – even after New World silver poured into the FGE (post-1571). It is true that the EICs began importing ICTs into Europe from the sixteenth century onwards, though they did not hold a monopoly of this import trade given that some of it came in via the overland routes, particularly as re-exports from the Ottoman Empire as well as into Russia courtesy of Indian Multānī merchants (as I note in Chapter 6). Certainly, though, the Europeans monopolised the sale of these textiles in the Americas. But the question is whether the Europeans became the dominant traders of ICTs in the all-important Indian Ocean system.

Uncovering the Hidden History of the Transcontinental
Indian and Asian Trade in ICTs

In fairness, so far as many historians rather than International Relations/ International Political Economy scholars and historical sociologists are concerned, the sole or exclusive focus on the monopoly trading role of the Europeans is not always a function of an *a prioristic* predilection to Eurocentrism or Eurofetishism. Many historians refuse to estimate the total size of the ICT export trade that was carried by Indians and other Asians on the grounds that there are *generally* no robust archival data in existence. Instead, they usually focus on the size of the import trade into Europe that was conducted by the EICs given that the latter had kept detailed records of this over a sustained period of time. And, in the process, the history of the transcontinental trade that was plied by the Indians and Asians is rendered invisible.

But for all the genuine efforts at promoting impartiality, this procedure can generate a circularity that forces our understanding of global trade back into a Eurocentric *cul-de-sac*, wherein the only significant global traders of Indian textiles were the Europeans because the only significant archival data that exist are that produced by the EICs for the Europeans on the European Company trade into Europe. Speaking of the tendency to fetishise the Company records, Prasannan Parthasarathi rightly points out that '[t]he abundance of European sources accounts in part for this [Eurocentric] bias', though he also notes that '[m]ore important than even source materials, however, is the deeply embedded assumption that Europe was the center of economic activity and, as such, the preeminent shaper of the global economy in the seventeenth and eighteenth centuries'.[4] And, for those historians who are not armed with a Eurocentric predisposition, this problem, if they will forgive the metaphor, is analogous to the proverbial drunken man who, having lost his car keys at the end of the evening, searches only the ground that is lit up directly beneath the street lamp. Accordingly, the activities of the Asians disappear in the long dark shadow that is cast behind the dazzling light of the activities of the EICs.

But in exploring the space within this shadow, various revisionist historians have asserted, albeit *en passant*, that Indian traders sold significant levels of textiles abroad, and a growing number argue that they sold much greater levels throughout the Indian Ocean than did the EICs.[5] As good as any summary statement of this literature is advanced by Pedro Machado:

> sufficient material has come to light ... to show that in the seventeenth and eighteenth centuries, particularly in the western reaches of the [Indian] ocean, the vast bulk of the trade in manufactures (especially in cotton textiles) was organized and carried by south Asian groups who were not deeply affected by European activity. Increasingly, historians have come to accept this conclusion.[6]

But equally, bar Machado – who provides estimates of the size of the Indian trade with East Africa as I explain shortly – they too stop short of providing estimates of total volumes on the not-unreasonable basis of the paucity of the data. Indeed, Ashin Das Gupta, one of India's greatest trade historians, openly laments that '[a] fact of life with which the student of India's medieval economy has learned to live is the absence of [trade] statistics'.[7] Cognisant of the extremely daunting and hazardous journey that guesstimating the size of the ICT trade entails, Parthasarathi notes that 'it is essential to have some sense of the place of Indian cotton cloth exports, both globally and within the sub-continent',[8] even though he too stops short of providing such guesstimates.

---

[4] Parthasarathi (2011: 116).
[5] For example, van Leur (1955: 212, 235), Perlin (1983: 55–6), Braudel (1992: 509), Maskiell (2002: 32), Balachandran and Subrahmanyam (2005: 29) and Chaudhury and Morineau (2007b).
[6] Machado (2009a: 175).
[7] Das Gupta (2001: 59).
[8] Parthasarathi (2005: 1).

In the present context, if we are to navigate beyond the Eurocentric and Eurofetishist frontier in order to gain an appreciation of both the importance of the Indian economy to the FGE, in general, and of the role that Indian and other Asian merchants played in distributing ICTs around the world relative to that performed by the Europeans in particular, we have no choice but to try and get 'some sense' of the relative trade volumes involved. For in the absence of such a guesstimate, the tendency will be to default to the Eurocentric position. However, it is important to note that I do not seek to come to definitive estimates of the relative shares of the trade conducted by the Europeans and the Asians, for this would indeed be impossible. Instead, I will provide exaggerated guesstimates and rough orders of magnitude of the European share relative to that of the possible Asian/Indian share of the ICT trade.

I begin by considering the ICT trade with Africa, which has the advantage of plausible data, thanks to the excellent archival work that has been undertaken by Pedro Machado. According to his findings, the long-distance Vāniyā Gujarati traders exported between three and five million yards of ICTs to East Africa annually by the mid-eighteenth century, though in some years this figure reached ten million.[9] Moreover, in the early 1600s, some 2.8 million yards were exported from Gujarat to the Zambezi Valley alone.[10] By comparison, in 1751/80 the British re-exported 0.7 million yards of ICTs per annum to Africa, which comprised between 14 and 23 per cent of the amount that the Indians exported independently into East Africa.[11] Moreover, this re-export trade at that time surpassed the sales of British-made 'fustians' – part-linen and part-cotton textiles – to Africa. Furthermore, even as late as 1763/80, fustian exports comprised between 6 and 10 per cent the size of the ICT exports that were sold by independent Indian merchant capitalists in East Africa.[12]

Because the data on trade in the wider Indian Ocean world beyond Africa are sparse, I can only make best guesstimates concerning the size of the European trade in ICTs. And if this side of the ledger is problematic so far as the EICs are concerned, it is even more so when we turn to consider the Indian and Asian trade in ICTs. Rather than clutter up the text with an extended discussion of the method and the data that I use, I shall merely report the findings here and refer my reader to Appendix 1 (pp. 456–460) and the accompanying footnotes.

---

[9] Machado (2009a: 167).
[10] Pearson (1998: 48).
[11] Re-export figure calculated from Wadsworth and de Lacy Mann (1931: 160).
[12] Calculated from Wadsworth and de Lacy Mann (1931: 138) and Chaudhuri (2006: 540–5).

Although my method is necessarily crude nevertheless, as noted, my concern is only with proximate relativities and orders of magnitude that simultaneously exaggerate the European share in order to effect the right direction of bias against my argument.

The following calculations are based on my guesstimate that average annual sales of ICTs that were conducted by Indian and Asian traders in the seventeenth and eighteenth centuries were approximately 100 million yards. My best guesstimates suggest that the amount of ICTs that were sold by Indians and other Asians relative to that of the British were higher by an approximate factor of thirty (in 1600–50), eighteen (in 1700), nine (in 1750) and four (in 1800).[13] As I also explain in Appendix 1, the British figure is certainly exaggerated. Regarding the overall European EIC share in the ICT trade, I calculate that the Indian and Asian share was higher by an approximate factor of thirteen (in 1600/50), six (in 1700), four (in 1750) and two (in 1800).[14] Critics will undoubtedly quibble with my crudely guesstimated proportion of the share that I have attributed to the Indians and other Asians. But the volume of ICTs that was exported by Indians and Asians, taking the average figure for the four 50-year guesstimates between 1650 and 1800, would have to be exaggerated by around fifteen times just to equate with the British share and about six times vis-à-vis the overall European share, all of which seems most unlikely.

This, in turn, folds into the larger question as to the overall size of Indian exports more generally. Again, records do not exist to make a firm calculation. The most conservative estimate of South Asia's foreign trade is produced by Tirthankar Roy, who claims that it comprised less than 3 per cent of gross domestic product (GDP) in 1750.[15] Running with the very crude estimates of Indian national income produced by Angus Maddison that I discuss in Chapter 11, I calculate that 3 per cent of Indian GDP around 1800 stood at about £28 million – a figure that is likely to be on the conservative side.[16] In 1795, British foreign trade comprised about £66 million, while China's foreign trade likely stood somewhere between £49 million and £72 million, though a more

---

[13] I have guesstimated the India and Asian share as follows: 89 million yards (1600/50), 97 million yards (1700), 101 million yards (1750) and 93 million yards (1800).
I guesstimated the British distribution of ICTs as follows: 3 million yards (1600/50), 6 million yards (1690/1710), 11 million yards (1745/55) and 24 million yards (1795/1805).

[14] I guesstimated the overall European trade in Indian cotton textiles as follows: 7 million yards (1600/50), 15 million yards (1690/1710), 27 million yards (1745/55) and 43 million yards (1795/1805).

[15] Roy (2013: 75–6).

[16] Maddison (2007: 379); cf. Parthasarathi (2005).

plausible figure is about £61 million.[17] On this basis, India's total foreign trade at the end of the eighteenth century might have been in the region of 40 per cent that of Britain's and around 45 per cent that of China's – notwithstanding the extremely fraught nature of the data that I am dealing with here. But as very crude ballpark figures, they suggest that India's foreign trade, though lower than Britain's and China's, was likely not inconsiderable. Moreover, given that most of India's foreign trade was in ICTs it is likely, therefore, that in aggregate they comprised the single most important global commodity. And given that Indians and Asians were the major exporters of ICTs, their role in the global trading system was, therefore, highly significant.

However, for all this, Eurocentric/Eurofetishist skeptics will remain unconvinced, given their adherence to the Caesarist vision of the EICs in the Indian Ocean – that 'they came, they saw, they conquered'. But as a wealth of historians have revealed, the reality is that the EICs gained only limited penetration of India's foreign trade markets, specifically in Gujarat, Bengal and the Coromandel and Malabar coasts. In Gujarat, Ashin Das Gupta argues that at the turn of the eighteenth century, around 12 per cent of the foreign trade of Surat (in Gujarat) was in European hands.[18] And in the important Gujarati cotton textile town of Ahmedabad, Giorgio Riello notes that 'the English, Dutch, French and Portuguese traders were just a small contingent within a wider [merchant] community formed by Jews, Arabs, Medes, Persians, Turks and [Tatars] trading not only in cotton textiles, but in silks and indigo'.[19] Riello also notes that the situation 'was no different in Bengal [which had become the largest textile producer in India by the late-seventeenth century] where the business community was dominated by Arabs, Parsees, Turks and Abyssinians, as well as Indian merchants from Chaul, Dabol and Goa'.[20] Of Bengali production, we have estimates of the amount of extra jobs that British exports enabled in the cotton industry ranging between 5 and 11 per cent,[21] neither of which was especially significant. Circumstantial evidence for this lies in the point that in the eighteenth century, '[t]he British noted with amazement that cloth merchants in Calcutta [in Bengal] gained even more silver from their internal Asian trade—with Persia, Central Asia, and Southeast Asia—than they did from trade with the Europeans'.[22] Then again, Sushil Chaudhury asserts

[17] Zhang Shizhi (2020: ch. 2).
[18] Das Gupta (2001: 193) and cf. Wink (1988: 65).
[19] Riello (2009b: 324–5).
[20] Ibid. (325).
[21] For the former, see Chaudhury (1995a); for the latter, see Prakash (1985: 242–4).
[22] Goldstone (2008: 128).

that in 1747 Asians exported two-thirds and the Europeans exported one-third of Coromandel's textile exports (in Southeast India).[23] But Prasannan Parthasarathi claims that for Southeast India *as a whole*, the British and Dutch trade in ICTs comprised between 5 and 11 per cent of the total production of the region.[24]

In short, the Europeans neither monopolised the ICT trade nor did they come anywhere near close to dominating it, playing at all times second fiddle to the Indian and Asian merchants. And, speaking of the Asian situation more generally, Jan de Vries notes that 'nearly every Asian product sent to Europe also enjoyed large markets with[in] Asia. European demand affected these industries at the margin, but it did not call them into being'.[25] Thus, the question now becomes why the so-called domineering Europeans were unable to monopolise the Indian Ocean trading system and how the Indians and Asians were able to carry on regardless of their presence. Here, I turn to one of the most fundamental properties of the FGE – the 'exit option'.

Indian Merchant Autonomy and the 'Exit Option'

Eurocentrism argues that one of the factors that made Europe unique and exceptional after 1500 was its competitive multistate system – or what Wallerstein calls the 'European world-economy' – as this armed capitalists with the 'exit option' that enabled them to move from one economy to another if conditions were not conducive in the originating, host country.[26] But this occludes the existence of the 'exit option' that had been available to African and Asian traders throughout the Indian Ocean system ever since the seventh century when Afro-Eurasian regionalisation emerged properly. Critically, they could take this option in the face of either potentially hostile rulers,[27] or European EIC efforts at monopolising Afro-Asian trade.

Despite the Europeans' hubristic claims of monopoly power, the mundane reality is that when confronted by the EICs, Indian and other Asian traders found ways of outflanking them. Taking the significant

---

[23] Chaudhury (1995b: 210).

[24] Parthasarathi (2005: 14). Here, it is important to appreciate that while I assume that about 8 per cent of aggregate Indian production was destined for export (see Appendix 1), these particular regions would have exported much higher percentages than this.

[25] de Vries (2010: 729).

[26] Wallerstein (1974: 348, ch. 3), North and Thomas (1973), Jones (1981), Giddens (1985), Collins (1985) and Vries (2015).

[27] McNeill (1982: 51–4) and Gordon (2008: 145).

trade in pepper as an example, it is true that the Portuguese established various strongholds along the Indian coast in the hope of monopolising this trade. But by the end of the sixteenth century, Indian rulers and merchants had succeeded in shifting the key trade routes northward in order to escape Portuguese control of Cochin, Quilon, Cranganore and Cannanore.[28] Moreover, the Moplah merchants of Cannanore gained the ascendancy to such an extent that they were even selling pepper to the Portuguese. And their trade 'was carried on with and without Portuguese *cartazes* [passports]'.[29]

In the early-seventeenth century, the Portuguese presence in Calicut in Malabar prompted a displacement of Asian trade, with new parallel trade routes emerging such that pepper was traded from Kanara (north of Malabar) as well as from Acheh in Southeast Asia. And the Portuguese managed to buy and ship a mere 10 per cent of the total amount of pepper produced in Malabar.[30] Of the Gujarati pepper trade, they took a mere 5 per cent. And when they took control of the Indian port of Diu in 1535, Gujarati traders soon started to collect massive amounts of pepper in the Bay of Bengal, whence this spice became traded throughout the Indian Ocean, thereby once again outflanking the Portuguese. One of the reasons for this is that the vast proportion of pepper was destined for Asian markets – especially those in India, China, Persia and the Ottoman Empire – and it was there that Asian spice prices were set. And more generally, as Sinnappah Arasaratnam notes,

studies of Gujarat, Goa, Malabar [Kerala], Hormuz and Malacca [show] that most of the trade carried on under Portuguese protection was Indian and that the Portuguese merely skimmed the surface of Indian Ocean trade.... Though the companies, from the outset, traded in competition with Asian merchants in the major markets, they never dominated those markets to the extent of driving Asian shippers out of the trade ... [Indeed] they never took any great proportion of the trade away from Asian merchants.[31]

All in all, the proof of all this lies in the simple fact that in the whole of the sixteenth century, Portuguese shipping comprised a mere 6 per cent of the total in the Indian Ocean.[32]

---

[28] Wink (1988: 58), Arasaratnam (1987: 104) and Meilink-Roelofsz (1962: 121, 171, 240, 243, 247).

[29] Arasaratnam (1987: 102).

[30] Meilink-Roelofsz (1962: 137–72), Curtin (1984: 144) and Balachandran and Subrahmanyam (2005: 29).

[31] Arasaratnam (1987: 124, 126). See also Balachandran and Subrahmanyam (2005: 29).

[32] van Leur (1955: 212).

Although the Dutch and English established a stronger position than the Portuguese in the Indian Ocean system, nevertheless they faced similar challenges and similar limits to their power. Thus, in the face of attempts at dominating trade by English East India Company (EEIC) and Vereenigde Oost-Indische Compagnie (VOC), the fact is that the Indian merchants

> were in their [element] and pulled out all the old arts of their trade to survive and eventually to beat this competition, certainly in respect of the trade westwards into Arabia and Persia.... In the Mughal-English conflict of the 1680s, Surat's trade to the Red Sea was greatly disrupted.... [But] even after a century of such operations, Surat's merchants' domination of the Red Sea and Persian Gulf markets was untouched by the [European] companies.[33]

Moreover, if the EICs disturbed the seaborne routes through military activities, then the Indians and Asians simply diverted their trade onto the overland caravan routes and continued unaffected – a typical case of the exit option.[34] As René Barendse notes, various Gujarati merchants often divided their trading wares between the overland and sea routes in order to diversify risk.[35] And, moreover, their linkage is borne out by the point that the price of goods carried on the sea routes fluctuated to a certain extent according to the amounts that were transported overland and *vice versa*.[36] In any case, before 1757, neither the Dutch nor the English could assert control through military power in India, and even after that date, the English struggled against various Indian states such as Mysore as well as the Maratha empire, such that their eventual victory was anything but a *fait accompli*,[37] as I explain in Chapter 12.

An important example of the limits of EIC power vis-à-vis Indian merchant competition concerns the VOC's efforts to dominate the Asian inter-country trade by exporting ICTs to Persia in the 1630s. Despite their best efforts to control this trade, the fact is that the VOC's market share was always much less than 10 per cent, with a profit margin of 4 per cent being well below the amount required just to break even. The key point though is that being dissatisfied with such low profits, the Dutch were astounded by their Gujarati rivals' capacity for competition. Why were the Indians able to outcompete the VOC in the cotton textile trade to Persia? Ultimately, the Company servants concluded, it was because the Indians operated at lower costs and that they had a far

---

[33] Arasaratnam (1987: 110).
[34] Dale (1994: 48) and cf. Riello (2013: 23).
[35] Barendse (2002: 245).
[36] Chaudhuri (1985: 172).
[37] Sharman (2019: ch. 2) and Yazdani (2017).

deeper knowledge of Persian market conditions.[38] In any case, in 1645–7, the VOC's trade volumes in ICTs with Persia averaged less than one million yards, which paled into insignificance when compared with the volumes that were carried to Persia by the Indians, Armenians and West Asian Muslims. Accordingly, by the early 1660s, the VOC terminated this trade between India and the Persian entrepôt of Bandar 'Abbas (which was a principal way station that received Indian textiles before they were transported onto Suez, Cairo and Constantinople).

In general, the Persians were able to control the EICs, circumstantial evidence for which lies in the point that Europe endured a trade deficit with Persia and paid for it in New World silver. Moreover, in the early-1600s, the VOC also began trading ICTs between India and Mocha in the Arabic Middle East, though this was even more short lived given the problem of superior Indian merchant competition and that the VOC decided against using force to create a monopoly trade for fear of Mughal state retaliation. And even as late as the second half of the eighteenth century, Asian merchants continued to control the trade with West Asia.[39]

The EEIC confronted similar limitations to its dream of imposing a trading monopoly, not least because Asian merchants operated at lower costs and undercut them throughout the Indian Ocean markets. Indeed, as early as 1681, the EEIC closed its trade with Bantam in Southeast Asia and from 'the number of complaints about the [challenging] markets and low prices of goods in Asian ports, we can in fact conclude that the European traders in the Indian Ocean were always on the verge of commercial ruin'.[40] So much so, of course, that the VOC was liquidated in 1799. In sum, the Europeans failed to take much trade away from the various Asian merchants,[41] with the latter continuing to dominate the trading sinews of the Indian Ocean either by outflanking the Europeans or simply by undercutting them on price in the case of head-on competition.

Incorporating the Europeans into the Indian Ocean System through Indian Structural Power?

All that has been argued thus far begs the question as to how we are to confront the familiar Eurocentric and Eurofetishist argument that the Europeans *incorporated* Afro-Asia into an expanding European capitalist world economy between 1500 and 1800. Most notably, Immanuel Wallerstein claims that it was after 1750 that the so-called

[38] Van Santen (1991: 88–9).
[39] Yazdani (2017: 430).
[40] Chaudhuri (2006: 212).
[41] Arasaratnam (1987: 124–6).

self-constituting and 'separate' Asian economies were incorporated by the Europeans into an emergent Western capitalist world economy.[42] But I argue that there is a sense in which it was the Asian producers and traders, especially those involved in ICTs, that in effect incorporated the Europeans into the Indian Ocean system and thence the FGE after 1500. This was achieved in large part by Indian structural power that was accrued through the production and sales of ICTs throughout Afro-Eurasia. Or, put more precisely, it was the structural power that ICTs bequeathed to Indian merchants that prompted the incorporation of the EICs into India and the wider Indian Ocean system.

This 'incorporation of Europe' argument begins with the point that the Europeans had very few goods to sell in order to buy Afro-Asian products. Thus, while a good deal of their financing of the Asian trade was derived from plundered American silver, as I explained in Chapter 3, nevertheless the EICs could only cover the shortfall by entering into the intra-Asian 'country trade'. And critically, they could only do this by gaining access to ICTs given that these comprised a universal currency throughout the Indian Ocean system. Moreover, the silver was used *inter alia* to buy ICTs, which were used to purchase other commodities that they then sold in Asia as well as in Europe and the Americas. Thus, when the Portuguese first arrived in Southeast Asia, girded with hubristic dreams of conquering the Asians and monopolising the spice trade, they were delivered a rude awakening. For it wasn't just that they encountered the strong presence of Gujaratis trading ICTs from the Coromandel coast that is key here.[43] More importantly, the Portuguese soon realised that the only way they could buy the spices that they were so anxious to acquire was to purchase ICTs from India, given that the Southeast Asians would accept nothing else in exchange.[44] For, this is precisely why the Portuguese wormed their way into India in the first place.

Much the same story applies to the EEIC and VOC.[45] As Sen notes:

[i]t was the example of the Indian and Arab merchants that taught the Portuguese, the Dutch and the English the importance of Indian textile goods in building up a profitable trade with Southeast Asia.... [T]he only reason for [initially] investing Dutch and English capital in textile goods in India was to acquire better purchasing power in Southeast Asia.[46]

---

[42] Wallerstein (1987, 1989: ch. 3).
[43] Levi (2016: 1) and Riello (2009b: 315).
[44] Hall (1996: 118), Pomeranz and Topik (2006: 233), Levi (2016: 1) and Riello (2009b: 315).
[45] Irwin and Brett (1970) and Chaudhuri (2006: 208–9).
[46] Sen (1962: 93, 94).

The VOC had intended simply to trade in Asian spices with Europe, but upon realising that the Southeast Asians would only accept ICTs in exchange, the Dutch set up trading factories on the Coromandel Coast as early as 1606 and 1610.[47] And, equipped with ICTs, they became deeply ensconced in the Asian inter-country trade. As early as 1612, Hendrik Brouwer, the future Governor-General of the East Indies, portrayed the East Indian Coromandel Coast as 'the left-arm of the Moluccas and the surrounding islands because without the textiles that come from [the Coromandel coast] the trade in the Moluccas will be dead'.[48] Thus, in 1619, Jan Pieterszoon Coen (Director of the VOC) stated that:

[Cotton] [p]iece goods from Gujarat we can barter for pepper and gold on the coast of Sumatra; rials [silver currency] and cottons from the coast [of Coromandel] for pepper in Bantam; sandalwood, pepper and rials we can barter for Chinese goods and Chinese gold; we can extract silver from Japan with Chinese goods; piece goods from the Coromandel coast in exchange for spices, other goods and gold from China; piece goods from Surat for spices ... one thing leads to another.[49]

In addition, the VOC's directors asserted later on in 1648 that 'the country trade and the profit from it are the soul of the Company which must be looked after carefully because if the soul decays, the entire body would be destroyed'.[50]

The EEIC followed suit by establishing numerous 'factories' in key cotton textile towns across India in order to source ICTs. Their first was set up as early as 1613 in Masulipatnam which is situated in Coromandel on the southeast coast and which was renowned for its Kalamkari block-printed ICTs. The company also established a factory in the early-seventeenth century in Surat, Gujarat in Northwest India, given its prominence as a major ICT-producing town. In 1639, the company purchased land in the south and in 1644 set up Fort St George, which became Madras (today's Chennai), specifically so as to gain access to ICTs.[51] The same logic underpinned the company's establishment of factories in Bengal, first at Hugli in 1651, second in Dhaka in 1668 and a third, Fort William in Calcutta, in 1696. The EEIC also established a factory in Bombay in 1665, once again to source ICTs. Thus, while our Western-centric imagination supposes that the British had developed a

---

[47] Davidson (2012: 8).
[48] Cited in Prakash (2007: 184).
[49] Cited in Anievas and Nişancioğlu (2015: 145).
[50] Prakash (2007: 182).
[51] Dobbin (1996: 136).

grand strategy to make India the 'Jewel in the Crown' from the outset, it turns out that they ended up in India as a function of the unplanned contingency of the need to access her superior ICTs.

All in all, then, the EICs became sucked or pulled into India in order to buy ICTs, some of which paid for African commodities – slaves, ivory and gold – and some of which paid for Asian commodities that they either imported into Europe or used in their dealings within the Asian country trade. In short, Indian structural power, which derived from the power of ICTs, was crucial in underpinning the Europeans' trading position within the Indian Ocean system. Tomé Pires famously remarked in his *Suma Oriental* that, 'whoever is lord of Malacca has his hands on the throat of Venice'.[52] Equally, we might conclude that the Indians had their hands on the throats of Java and Amsterdam. For while Eurocentrism and Eurofetishism imagine that Dutch colonial power was based in its autonomous stronghold in Java, it turns out that the VOC was only able to trade in the Indian Ocean system through its dependence on ICTs.

Rather than exercising imperial domination in the Indian Ocean, the reality was that the Europeans entered into 'partnership relations' with the Indians as a result of Indian structural power. The only instance in which European imperial domination played out before 1757, at the very earliest, is in the very marginal case of the VOC on the tiny spice islands in the Moluccas as well as in Ceylon. For there the company applied high levels of coercion in order to dominate the spice trade in Moluccan cloves, mace and nutmeg as well as Ceylonese cinnamon. But even then, the notion of Dutch autonomy is a myth given that they relied on the Chinese in Java (as I explained in Chapter 2) and that, more generally, the Europeans had no choice but to become incorporated and thereby become interdependent with the Africans and Asians if they wished to continue their trading presence in the Indian Ocean system.

It is important to note that the more general incorporation of the Europeans into the Afro-Asian economy was inherently uneven. We saw in Chapter 2 that the Dutch entered into a politically dependent relationship with the Chinese and Japanese emperors and that they were prepared to do so for the sake of maintaining trade. In India, they were sucked in through the impact of Indian structural power, where they formed competitive–cooperative relations with Indian agents. In West Asia, by contrast, the French and British were invited in.[53] And, far from imposing informal imperialism before the nineteenth century, the

[52] Pires cited in Abu-Lughod (1989: 291).
[53] Masters (1989: 75–6).

Europeans soon learned that it was the Ottomans who held the upper hand. For the Ottomans, like the Chinese, deployed a divide and rule strategy in their relations with the Europeans. Thus, in seeking to reduce the rival threat of the Venetians and the Russians, the Ottomans sought to play them off against the French and English.[54]

While Eurofetishism rightly focuses on the unequal treaties or 'capitulations' as well as 'extraterritoriality' that the British imposed on the Ottomans in the nineteenth century, it has, nevertheless, escaped notice among Eurocentrics and especially Eurofetishists that in the pre-1800 period the situation was precisely the reverse. Thus, the Ottomans granted capitulations (*imtiyazat*) to the British, awarding the EEIC legal trading status, extraterritoriality and freedom of movement. But the British were largely isolated there, although this was due to cultural differences rather than the result of intended government policy as it was in China. In effect, this general situation that the British endured marked the continuation of the dependent position that the Venetians had been prepared to tolerate in their relations with Egypt from 1291 to 1517 in order to gain access to the lucrative eastern trade that came in via the 'Southern (Red Sea) route'.[55]

This non-Western strategy of divide and rule was also performed by the Safavid Persian state, which used the EEIC as a means of counter-balancing its Ottoman rival. To this end, the Safavid ruler, Shah 'Abbas, was keen to attract European traders to Persia in the early-seventeenth century. In 1622, he granted permission to the EEIC to trade there because 'Abbas was keen for the British to export Persian silk to Europe by way of the Cape, given that this would avoid it being sent overland via his bitter rival, the Ottomans. He also sought to attract the British so as to gain the European military technology that he needed for his wars with the Ottomans.[56] The conclusion being that the presence of the Europeans in West Asia was far less the result of their 'dominant' coercive power and far more to do with them being invited in or 'incorporated' so as to serve the competing interests of the West Asian rulers while enhancing the Companies' trading opportunities.

The critique of my argument might be to deny that the Europeans were 'incorporated' into the Asian trading system precisely because they *chose* to join it and that they did so because it was profitable – a claim that is made by defenders of Eurocentrism such as Roberts and Vries as much as it would be by Eurofetishists. Certainly, it is the case that the

---

[54] Anievas and Nişancioğlu (2015: 113–17).
[55] Abu-Lughod (1989: 108) and Braudel (1992: 132).
[56] Pearson (1991: 100).

Europeans were not *actively forced* by the Asians into the Indian Ocean system as the 'incorporation thesis' implies – for they were indeed very keen to join the Indian Ocean trading system in order to enhance their commercial activities and profits. My point, rather, is that the Europeans had little choice but to become incorporated if they were to enhance their commercial profits since they lacked the military and logistical power to impose their monopolistic will.[57] Indeed, for the most part, they were highly dependent on the goodwill of Asian rulers and merchants and they had to operate both within the rules of the Asian system and according to the logic of Indian structural power. Accordingly, I concur with Andre Gunder Frank's assertion that

> there was no 'European world-economy' separate from an 'Indian-Ocean world-economy'. If anything, the latter 'incorporated' the former and not the other way around.... The only 'answer' is to understand that Europe and Asia ... had been part and parcel of the same single world-economy [i.e., the first global economy] since ages ago, and that it was their common participation in it that shaped their 'separate' fortunes.[58]

But certainly, the incorporation process benefited the Europeans. For, in the process of becoming incorporated, the Europeans were ever so gradually nurtured in strength within Afro-Asia and, much like a cuckoo that is nurtured to maturity in another bird's nest, they emerged in the late-nineteenth century to become the leading player in the region through informal and formal empire (as I note in Chapter 13).

In sum, then, it was the quest for ICTs that was the single most important driver of the various EICs' entry into the Asian inter-country trade. And that as such, this points to yet a further mechanism by which the structural power of ICTs wove together the Atlantic, Indian and Pacific Ocean systems ever more tightly into the FGE. However, this discussion of Indian structural power represents but the tip of a very large iceberg, the exploration of which I plumb later and in Parts III–V of this book. For the moment, the question that now arises is if the Europeans became incorporated into the Indian Ocean system, how, then, are we to understand Indo-European relations given the problematic Eurocentric and Eurofetishist assumption that it was the Europeans who held the whip-hand?

---

[57] Hobson (2004: 144–8) and Sharman (2019: ch. 2).
[58] Frank (1998: 335–6).

Partnership/Entangled Relations and Competitive–Cooperation: The Core *Modus Operandi* of Indo-European Relations

Rather than dominating the Indians, the Europeans found that they had no choice but to enter into 'partnership relations'. And these were based on entangled agencies. Two points are noteworthy: first, partnership relations did not imply friendship but were always competitive–cooperative in nature, such that they might also be called 'competitive partnerships' or 'competitive alliances'. And second, the Europeans often entered such relations as the junior partner. For in one sense this was, generally speaking, not a partnership between equals given that while the Asians could continue their trade whether the Europeans were present or not, the latter could not trade without the help of the former. Moreover, it was the Indians who enjoyed a position of strength as a result of their structural power that was derived from the hegemony of ICTs across the world. Accordingly, the Europeans found that they had little choice but to work within the rules and structure laid down by the Indians. That said, though, increasingly equal relations were struck up in the late-eighteenth century, as I explain later.

However, it is here where critical Eurofetishists and Indian nationalists join hands by asserting that Indian 'partners' were but 'compradors' and 'collaborators' who were dependent on serving the imperial interests of the EEIC and VOC at the expense of the 'Indian nation'. The negative political connotation of the term 'collaborator' as 'traitor' goes back, of course, to the collaboration between the French Vichy government and the Nazis. In this conception, then, the Indian partners lacked agency. But I concur with Tanja Bührer and her co-authors who argue that 'cooperation' rather than 'collaboration' is a more appropriate term because unlike the latter it allows conceptual space for the agency of the relevant Indian actors.[59] Here, I single out six instantiations of Indian agency which, in aggregate, problematise the Eurofetishist conception of European dominance and Indian compradors/collaborators in the seventeenth and eighteenth centuries.

First, the Eurofetishist conception rests on the problematic assumption that the Europeans dominated foreign trade such that all the Indians could do is to plug into the European mainstream and scramble for the crumbs that dropped off the 'imperial' table. But as we have seen

[59] Bührer *et al.* (2017).

already, before the mid-nineteenth century, it was more the other way round. As Tirthankar Roy concludes:

It is useful to remind ourselves just how dependent Indo-European trade was on Asian traders.... They functioned not only as agents ... for the Europeans inside India but also as the principal actors ... [dominating all] forms of caravan trade and the markets where caravan goods came to be sold [while] [r]iver-borne trade was [also] controlled by the Indians.[60]

It is true that the EEIC found to its considerable humiliation that it had to submit to the Mughal emperor as a 'slave' in order to gain a trading foothold in Gujarat.[61] But, it is also important to appreciate that with the decline of the Mughal Empire after 1707, the British began gradually to enjoy more equal relations with various Indian states and agents. Thus, as India devolved into a realm of competing states with the decline of the Mughal Empire, the EEIC developed stronger bargaining powers than it had during the period when Mughal rule was at its peak (1526–1707). As Kaveh Yazdani argues, some regions like Gujarat were more fragmented than ever before, which permitted the British to cooperate with certain segments of the nobility, merchants, chieftains and ethnic minorities (e.g., the Parsis). In the south, the EEIC also cooperated with a number of powerful landlords (*poligars* and *zamindars*) as well as various rulers as they went about defeating Mysore, as I explain in Chapter 12. Thus, it was not just in South India where the EEIC entered more equal relations, especially from the mid-eighteenth century on, but also in Northwest India (Gujarat) as well as, of course, in East India (Bengal).[62]

Second, the many Indians who formed the Indian trading networks, comprising firms, money changers and bankers, brokers, village chiefs and producers, were not brought to life by the advent of the 'dominant' British traders because these networks had developed a good number of centuries before the arrival of the EEIC (as I explained in Chapters 3 and 4, and see also the next section). Third, foreign merchants who operated in India had to employ a local broker who was viewed as a typical comprador by critical Eurofetishists and Indian nationalists. In Coromandel and Malabar, they were known as the *dubash*, while in Bengal, they were known as the *dadni*. But this comprador conception misses the point that brokers derived agency through the fact that they had local knowledge and command of the language as well as contacts

---

[60] Roy (2012: 97).
[61] Phillips and Sharman (2015: 149–56).
[62] Yazdani (2017: chs. 2 and 3).

with the producers and the bazaars, all of which the EICs lacked. Moreover, the brokers sometimes 'colluded with [their vast array of] ... under-contractors to cheat the companies on quality. Indeed, the brokers were under [constant] pressure to cheat their principals.'[63]

The brokers also gained a 'paradoxical' autonomy over the EICs via their role as *wakīls*, who were responsible to the local Mughal authorities. Because the Europeans trading in India borrowed money from Indian bankers, it was the brokers' role to inform the political authorities if the foreign merchants departed without paying their debts. As Ashin Das Gupta explains, one notable example concerns that of the Governor of Surat, Haider Quali Khan who, having learned of an English plot to blockade the port and knowing that they employed a Parsi broker, issued a threat to 'blow every Parsi in town from his guns' if the blockade went ahead.[64] Thus, Indian bankers and local authorities could wield power against the EICs through the *wakīls*.

Fourth, the fact is that the brokers and foreign merchants were mutually dependent on each other, though it is important to note that the broker had the choice of whom he worked for and if one group of merchants turned out to be disappointing he could withdraw his services and find another. As Ashin Das Gupta concludes, '[a] certain quality of freedom ... characterized the Mughal milieu, and the kind of dependency [that is associated] with the notion of a comprador cannot arise within it'.[65] What all this reflects, rather, is the notion of 'structural interdependence'.

Fifth, the EICs were dependent on the Indian *sarrāfs* or *shroffs* (bankers). The bankers performed a classic intermediary role that proved to be highly lucrative, converting silver bullion into coinage and deriving large profits from their monopoly in minting coinage and exchanging currency. Critical here was their role in ascertaining the exchange rate between the many different coins on the basis of their silver content, such that 'the greater the diversity of the coins, the more information and trust was needed in this exchange'.[66] Such was their expertise in this matter that Thomas Rolt, who was Chief of the Surat Factory, said of them that 'they are certainly the greatest masters of their art of any people in these parts of the world'.[67] Thus, because there were many such currency systems within India, their intermediary role proved to be as vital a

---

[63] Roy (2012: 100).
[64] Das Gupta (2001: 126).
[65] Ibid.
[66] Roy (2012: 98).
[67] Thomas Rolt cited in Chaudhuri (2006: 175).

service as it was lucrative. And, as information was not always sufficient and trust could break down, so Indian bankers would sometimes refuse to accept coins from a different region, leaving the Europeans high and dry in such instances. Similarly, because the bankers sometimes released coins that were debased, these would be refused in the bazaars, thereby once again leaving the EICs thoroughly frustrated. As one Company clerk lamented, EEIC business was controlled by 'base Banian brokers and zarofes [sarrāfs] ... of whome it is commonly spoken that they be Presidente and Cownsell and governe the [Companies'] affairs at their pleasure'.[68] For as Chaudhuri notes, '[t]he Company's servants had learnt from practical experience that the Indian shroffs [sarrāfs] ... apart from being skilled traders in precious metals, also wielded considerable financial powers'.[69] Indeed, the principal role played by the sarrāfs was to finance hundīs and provide credit for merchants, on which the Europeans often relied. As I explained in Chapter 4, the Portuguese were particularly reliant on this source of funds in Daman and Diu, as were the EEIC and VOC more generally.

Sixth, and finally, it is noteworthy that the most obvious sign of these partnership relations lies in the sharing of resources between the Indians and Europeans. Thus, rich Indians lent significant amounts of capital to the EICs. Indeed, not only were there some extremely rich Indians such as Mulla Abdul Ghafur, Shantidas Zaveri, Haji Mohammad Zahid Beg and Virji Vora,[70] but also their power and resources were such that even the VOC and EEIC became dependent on them for capital and were unable to gain leverage over them.[71] In fact, Virji was so powerful that '[t]he English records are replete with references to him reflecting the various attitudes of frustration, anger, and admiration for the man without whose assistance and cooperation the English could scarcely have found it easy to function in Surat'.[72]

A further example lay in the considerable intermingling of European and Asian traders to the advantage of both. For example, Asian merchants often had more goods on a Portuguese ship than did the Portuguese traders. One of the key reasons for this is that Indians believed it to be cheaper to cooperate with the Portuguese rather than waste money on arming their ships. That is, paying for a Cartaz (Portuguese passport)

---

[68] Boothby cited in Yazdani (2017: 408).
[69] Chaudhuri (2006: 175).
[70] See Yazdani (2017: 422–8).
[71] Gokhale (1979: ch. 7), Curtin (1984: 175), Marshall (1987: 287), Stein (1985: 6, 21), Van Santen (1991: 92), Braudel (1992: 489–90) and Dobbin (1996: chs. 4, 6).
[72] Gokhale (1979: 137).

was cheaper than arming their ships.[73] Also of note is that the Europeans learned that Indian ships were superior to their own not least because they were built of teak, which was more durable than the oak and pine of the European ships.[74] As with the Portuguese, so the Dutch and English intermingled with Asians in a variety of ways, not the least of which involved the mutual hiring of crews and even the hiring of whole vessels.[75]

Yet another example of the sharing of resources lies in the point, as indicated earlier vis-à-vis the brokers, that European vulnerability was to an important extent based on the lack of knowledge of local conditions as well as a chronic language deficiency. As Braudel explains:

In Kandahar … a Hindu merchant, taking the Spanish traveller for a Portuguese, offered his services because as he explained, 'the people of your nation do not speak the same language of these countries so you are sure to encounter difficulties unless you find someone to guide you'. Help, collaboration, collusion, coexistence, symbiosis—all these became necessary as time went by.[76]

Finally, the Dutch and English found that they had little choice but to cooperate and rely on the goodwill of Indian merchants and rulers.[77] Indeed, the VOC, which was the most significant of the EICs before 1800, found that even though Bengal supplied it with over a third of its total Asian cargo by 1700, the fact is that even there

the VOC did not have access to any significant special privileges in matters of trade, nor did it have any political power. The Company therefore operated within existing [Indian] power structures and did not create institutional changes; its only influence on the Bengal economy was through the increased demand for its goods.[78]

All of which, in sum, reveals that while the Portuguese, English and Dutch were dependent on numerous Indian agents, it was only through entwined or entangled competitive–cooperative relations that they could maintain their commercial presence in the Indian Ocean system. So in the light of all this, the issue now becomes that of ascertaining exactly who these Indian merchants were as well as where and how they operated so successfully.

---

[73] Curtin (1984: 144–8, 159–67).
[74] Yazdani (2017: 260) and Machado (2014: ch. 2).
[75] Marshall (1987: 280, 283, 287, 292–3).
[76] Braudel (1992: 489).
[77] Wolf (1982: 240).
[78] de Zwart (2016: 20).

6   Indian Merchant-Financial Capitalists
Navigating beyond the Western-centric Sea Frontier

Introduction

Despite all of the discussion thus far, the fact remains that the image of Europeans rather than Indians and Asians playing the key role in building the first global economy (FGE) after 1500 is so entrenched, both among laypersons and academics especially in International Political Economy (IPE) and International Relations (IR), that it is nearly impossible to imagine an alternative picture. As the notable historian Stephen Dale explains, 'the magnitude and influence of the Indian [trading networks] has remained virtually unknown in modern scholarship because of well-entrenched Eurocentric biases in historical studies on Eurasian commerce in the early modern era'.[1] Still, he also notes that part of this lacuna derives from the paucity of sources and data, which is why historians defer to the available English East India Company (EEIC) archival data, as I explained in Chapter 5. Equally, Claude Markovits, another important pioneer of this new research on Asian merchants, alludes to the Eurocentric and Eurofetishist illusion that frames the Western imagination when he asserts that for many decades 'the grand sweep of European imperialism in Asia during the 1750–1905 period ... exercised such a powerful pull on the mind of economic historians that it led them to overlook the dynamism shown by Asian commercial networks'.[2] Building on the previous four chapters, here I seek to reveal the dynamism of Asian commercial networks along the overland caravan routes.

A long-standing Eurocentric trope holds that after 1500 the overland caravan routes, which linked Mughal India with Persia, the Ottoman Empire, Central Asia, China and Russia, were akin to the proverbial oxbow lake that was increasingly isolated and bypassed by the mainstream of international trade that had been re-routed to the high seas by the

---

[1] Dale (1994: 3).
[2] Markovits (2000: 22).

all-powerful East India Companies (EICs). And to the extent that we might even begin to envisage Asians engaging in very long-distance trade on the overland routes at all, we conjure up the image of small-scale pedlars who bought cheap, tiny amounts of luxury-based trade that they packed into their backpacks before travelling to distant markets where they sold dear before returning home to sell a small amount of luxury foreign goods. At all times, it is assumed that they worked in the peripheral and shadowy recesses that were cast behind the bedazzling light of the superior modern trading activities and practices of the large-scale joint-stock EICs on the high seas. Note that while I began my discussion of the Indian *seaborne* trade in Chapters 3 and 4, I shall return to it more fully in Chapter 13.

Of course, I recognise that this Eurocentric conception has been challenged in many ways by historians over the past four decades, some of whom I draw upon here. But I interrogate this conception because such an image continues to grip the historical imagination of IPE and many IR scholars as well as historical sociologists. In navigating beyond the Eurocentric and Eurofetishist sea frontier we discover the presence of significant Indian merchant networks along the overland caravan routes that were far from constituting a 'backwater' to the European mainstream. Indeed, as I showed in Chapter 5, the inverse scenario was true. However, my task in this chapter is not merely to bring back to life the importance of the Indian and other Asian merchants who plied the overland caravan routes during the FGE. More importantly, I argue that these traders were not simply pre-modern, traditional merchants but that they engaged in modern capitalist activity.

In the era of the FGE there were two prominent Indian overland trading networks – those of the Multānīs and, after the mid-eighteenth century, the Shīkārpūris alongside the Multānīs (as I note in Chapter 13). Given that the Multānīs dominated the overland routes for much of the period of the FGE and given too that they were an exemplar of Indian business operations that reflected the practices of other key foreign trading groups (such as the Kachchhis, Vāniyās and Nattukottai Chettiars),[3] I shall focus on the Multānī practices and networks here. In this short chapter I consider various core interrelated issues that are dealt with in two sections. In the section 'The Rise and Development of the Overland Network of the "Multānī Nebular" after 1500' I consider where the Multānīs operated and how they expanded at the time when the EICs were supposed to have monopolised Asian trade. I also show

---

[3] See especially: Ray (1995: 525–6), Dobbin (1996: 143ff) and Goswami (2016).

how various regional rulers promoted the Multānīs' economic activities, which simultaneously undermines the familiar Eurocentric Oriental Despotism thesis. Finally, in the section 'Multānī Merchants as Small-Scale Pedlars or Large-Scale Commercial and Financial Capitalists?' I show how the conception of Multānīs as simple and traditional 'pedlars' fails to apply given that they were large-scale commercial and financial capitalists.

The Rise and Development of the Overland Network of the 'Multānī Nebular' after 1500

As noted above, although there was no single group of Indian merchants who plied the trans-regional overland trade, a significant proportion of them were concentrated in Northwest India – in Sindh (in present-day Pakistan) and in the Punjab – though this was hardly surprising given that this was the region that had direct access to the northern and western overland trade routes via the numerous passes.[4] The principal overland routes went through the Khyber and Bolān Passes, with Lahore, Multān, Kabul and Qandahar being the principal commercial entrepôts. In addition, the Gumal Pass went to Ghazni in Afghanistan while the Sanghar Pass, just north of Multān, went directly to Qandahar. There were also the Kashmiri routes that went directly north through Karakorum to Yarqand 'where the routes from Ladakh, Tibet, China and India were joined by those leading to Kashgar. From Kashgar the caravans proceeded to Samarqand and Bukhara'.[5] And from Samarqand, which was located in Transoxiana, the caravans joined the old Silk Route. For Samarqand constituted the key commercial entrepôt that was situated on the main route from India (via Kabul and Kashmir) to Persia and the Ottoman Empire in the west and to China in the east. However, it should be noted that Indian cotton textiles (ICTs) came from numerous parts of India before they were transported across the overland routes. For example, while Bengal accessed the northeastern overland routes that linked up directly with Tibet, Yunnan (in China) and Burma, it also linked indirectly with the overland trade to the west since Bengal exported ICTs to Gujarat whence some of them were then exported abroad.

The Multānīs, comprising Punjabi Khatrīs, came from the town of Multān, which was located in Northwest India in between Sindh

---

[4] For a full discussion of the overland routes, see Dale (1994: 49–55), Barendse (2002: 201–2) and Levi (2016: 97–101).
[5] Alam (1994: 203).

and the Punjab (lying in the eastern part of modern-day Pakistan). Although the town dates back to well before the Common Era, by the late first millennium it had become involved in trade with Persia and had become a significant cotton textile producer. The Hindu Khatrī community in Multān rose to prominence during the reign of the Delhi Sultanate (1206–1526), carrying on extensive trans-Himalayan trade and acting as agents and bankers to the Delhi nobility. The Multānī network developed much further during the sixteenth century when it 'branched out and established settlements in Central Asia, Safavid Persia, Muscovite Russia and the Ottoman Empire'.[6] According to Scott Levi there might have been about 35,000 such merchants dotted about throughout this vast region by the mid-seventeenth century, with the largest Multānī community abroad found in Isfahan in Persia (which housed between ten thousand and fifteen thousand at any one point in time).[7] And by the early eighteenth century the extensity of their reach was such that these merchants were dotted across the region – they resided in every major urban centre, regional town and across the rural areas in Afghanistan, Central Asia and beyond into Persia and parts of Russia.[8] It is for this reason that I talk of the *Multānī nebular*.

How, then, did the Multānīs expand at the time when the EICs were supposed to have monopolised Asian trade? There were two principal factors here, the first of which I discuss in this sub-section while I reserve the second for the next. First, the arrival of significant amounts of silver that the Portuguese and later the English and Dutch as well as the West Asian Muslims brought as a means of paying for Indian commodities was certainly important, helping to nourish the capital markets of all major Indian trading centres. Indeed, as Kirti Chaudhuri explains, 'in 1682 the supply of money in Surat was so plentiful that interest rates fell from the traditional 9 per cent to 6 per cent. There cannot be any question that the silver imported by the European Companies played an active and not a passive role';[9] a point that returns us to the argument made in Chapter 3. In turn, all of this was enabled by the initiation of an Indian silver currency in 1540 as well as the requirement that taxes be paid in silver which, in turn, spurred on production for the market. And all of which provided a very strong demand for foreign silver more generally.[10] Accordingly, the Indian and Chinese economies were

[6] Aslanian (2011: 221).
[7] Dale (1994: 66–7) and Levi (2016: 54, 145).
[8] Washbrook (2007: 97) and Levi (2016: 135–8).
[9] Chaudhuri (2006: 159).
[10] Haider (1996) and Moovsi (1987).

dependent upon the European delivery of silver and gold which in turn reflected the structural deficits that Europe endured vis-à-vis the key Asian economies in the three centuries before the 1820s.

Nevertheless, while these European silver flows intensified historical capitalism in India, it should also be noted that key Indian merchant capitalists such as the Kachchhis as well as the Multānīs had built up significant amounts of capital on their own account. Indeed, as early as the thirteenth century, Multānī firms owned a substantial amount of capital such that 'one might categorize the Multānīs ... as proto-portfolio capitalists, precursors to the Jagat Seth "world banker" banking house and the other great merchant houses of the seventeenth and eighteenth centuries'.[11] Of particular note is that considerable amounts of capital were raised in Hindu temples which financed inter-continental trade and long-term corporate investment.[12] Indeed, by the early-eighteenth century they raised some £4 million per annum, which was double the value of the total assets of the Vereenigde Oost-Indische Compagnie (VOC) and which was, according to Barendse, comparable to that of the Amsterdam bank.[13] And as Kaveh Yazdani notes, '[a]ccording to VOC documents the Gujarati temple-town of Vadnagar—where the wealthy Nagars resided—was the "clearing bank for the whole kingdom"'.[14] Accordingly, while Max Weber would dismiss their activities as lacking rationality (*Zweckrational*) because they were grounded in 'irrational' Islamic and Hindu religious principles, this obscures the co-constitutive relationship between their religious and economic activities. At this point a short diversion to consider the Kachchhis (from Kachchh in Gujarat) seems apposite.

Nowhere is the link between religion and historical capitalism clearer than in the Kachchhi Maths (Goswami monasteries). There were some forty such monasteries in Kachchh. By the end of the eighteenth century, these Maths had turned into banks, issuing credit notes through *hundīs* (bills of exchange).[15] Kachchhi monasteries resembled Armenian religious shrines that accumulated capital, which could be leveraged for trade. The capital was accumulated through donations and inheritances by religious people as well as from business profits, some of which were derived from the opium trade, banking and rents from landholdings.[16] Moreover, the head Math was known as the *Dnyanagar Nirmalgar*,

---

[11] Levi (2016: 34).
[12] Goswami (2016: 59–62).
[13] Barendse (2009: 726).
[14] Yazdani (2017: 419).
[15] Goswami (2016: 15).
[16] Ibid. (61).

which constituted the central bank and clearing house for all the other monasteries. And critically, '[t]he Maths' short- and long-term credit were both productive and remunerative; their banking set-up was deeply embedded within broader Indian Ocean networks'.[17] So much for the 'irrationality' of Asian religions!

Asian States as Commercially Repressive Oriental Despotisms?

Eurocentrics would intervene here by saying that all of this came to naught because of the repressive actions that were undertaken by the Oriental despotic states of the region, including the Mughal Empire. But the second reason for the flourishing of the Multānīs in the sixteenth century and, after the mid-eighteenth century, the Multānīs and Shīkārpūris, lay in the point that rulers in the region sought specifically to attract Indian capital and trade for the recognised stimulus that this provided their economies and treasuries. Foreign rulers also valued Indian merchants' services because lending cash money to local farmers to fund their agricultural activities, in turn, helped monetise these economies as well as furnishing the peasants with the liquid means to pay their taxes.[18] Moreover, Indians also acted as tax farmers for rulers across much of Eurasia and they advanced loans to rulers to finance their military campaigns in return for economic protection. This also means that such an arrangement was *not* unique to Europe, *contra* Eurocentrism. For as in Europe, Asian rulers knew that if they failed to pay back their loans or over-taxed trade, the merchants would exit and withdraw their services, as I discuss in the next chapter.

The establishment of the key states, Safavid Persia (1501–1722), the Mughal Empire (1526–1707/1858), the Uzbek Khanates – especially the Khanate of Bukhara (1533–1785) – as well as the Ottoman Empire (which had incorporated Egypt in 1517 where the all-important Cairo terminus to the Red Sea was located), provided a highly conducive environment for the extension of Indian foreign trade.[19] Stephen Dale claims that these states created a regional 'Pax Islamica' between the sixteenth and eighteenth centuries. However, although this claim is likely a step too far given that warfare was not infrequent – particularly between the Persians and Ottomans – nevertheless he *is* right to highlight their cooperation in matters of foreign trade.[20] This took various dimensions, the first of

---

[17] Ibid. (62).
[18] Levi (2016: 38–9, 53).
[19] Dale (1994: 30–41), Alam (1994), Das (2015) and Levi (2016: ch. 2).
[20] Dale (1994).

which is that they 'regularly [informed] each other of the details of the caravans to ensure appropriate protection in each other's territory',[21] and they also set up and paid for highway police (*Radhars*) to protect the Indian traders. As Gurcharan Das explains:

Akbar, the great Mughal, ruthlessly punished Afghan tribesmen who made a living by robbing caravans.... The Uzbek Khans of Bukhara created an official position in the administration, *Yasavul-i-Hinduwan*, 'Guardsmen of Hindus', whose job was to look after the welfare of Hindu traders, and help in collecting defaulted loans from among an intolerant Muslim majority. The Persian Safavid Empire ... equally protected Hindu merchants and their caravans.[22]

Second, these rulers built large caravanserais along the caravan routes where Indian and other Asian traders could rest up. Not only did some of the caravanserais develop into market places but also those that were located on the major trade routes often evolved into agricultural towns which had their own bazaars.[23] More generally, Dale notes that:

[t]he simultaneous pacification of trade routes and construction of roads and caravanserais throughout northern India, Iran as well as Turan [located in Central Asia on the north-eastern frontier of Persia] in the late sixteenth and seventeenth century established exceptionally favorable conditions for trade throughout the entire region.[24]

And third, these states ensured that tariffs on imports were kept extremely low – to a maximum of 5 per cent – precisely with the objective of attracting external trade. Given that low trade taxes coupled with laissez-faire and relatively free markets predominated, as I explain in the final section of Chapter 7, it would be fair to conclude that Smithian growth predominated in much of Asia.

Multānī Merchants as Small-Scale Pedlars or Large-Scale Commercial and Financial Capitalists?

The key issue surrounding the Multānī trading activities and business practices revolves around the Eurocentric claim that the Multānīs – and Asian merchants in general – were very small-scale 'pedlars', as was originally argued by Jakob van Leur and Niels Steensgaard.[25] But it was

[21] Alam (1994: 215).
[22] Das (2016: xvii).
[23] Dale (1994: 41).
[24] Dale (1994: 41); see also Levi (2016: chs. 2–4).
[25] van Leur (1955) and Steensgaard (1974).

Niels Steensgaard who developed this thesis furthest. Given the lack of source material – the Indians in particular were especially secretive about their trade, as I explain shortly – Steensgaard's analysis draws instead from a recently unearthed journal of the Armenian merchant, Hovannes, which recorded in fine detail his movements and trades between 1682 and 1693.[26] For Steensgaard views Hovannes as a typical small-scale pedlar.

But there is a perplexing problem here that needs confronting. Much of the trade that Hovannes conducted was indeed of a peddling variety insofar as he travelled with the goods that he sold. But as Philip Curtin explains, in specific relation to Hovannes' trading practices:

[w]here [Armenian] trade by sea a century or so earlier had been essentially a peddling trade, where the merchant had to travel with his goods, this was no longer required. Hovannes was able to send goods back and forth to his principals in New Julfa [the home base of the Armenian merchant community that was set up by Shah 'Abbās in Persia in 1606] without actually making the trip himself.[27]

In short, the separation of the capitalist creditor and the merchant agent that was the standard practice in much of Asia does not conform to the pedlar model. Moreover, like the Multānīs, the Armenians worked in family firms rather than as separate individuals; deployed *qirād* partnership contracts (which were similar to the *shah-gumāshtā* (creditor-agent)) partnership; used *hundīs* and other forms of bills of exchange; trust was in effect for them too 'the coin of the realm'; and they too were schooled in rigorous training that sought to inculcate an optimal level of economic rationality prior to becoming long-distance traders, and, moreover, they were able to outcompete the British and the Dutch, with the Europeans having limited success in penetrating Indian markets with their wares in part because the Armenians (and Indians) operated at lower costs.[28]

All of which reflects the points that the Armenians were *not* small-scale merchants, they were one of the most important long-distance trading communities in the FGE, and 'they developed into a trading [group that was] as sophisticated as … their western European competit[ors]'.[29] And, as I explain below, this also holds for the Multānīs, who constituted a more effective trading group than the Armenians, despite the highly

---

[26] See Steensgaard (1974: ch. 1).
[27] Curtin (1984: 196).
[28] Aslanian (2011: 221–3).
[29] Masters (1989: 83–4); see also Curtin (1984: 182–206).

impressive operations of the latter. This was in considerable part because the Multānīs were larger-scale merchants who had access to 'a much larger pool of agents from which to recruit' and, therefore, could expand to a far greater degree than did the Armenians.[30] All of which is bolstered much further as I now turn to build up a picture of the Multānī network by advancing six key rebuttals to the 'pedlar thesis'.

First, Steensgaard's confirmation of van Leur's thesis that Asian caravan traders engaged in high-value luxury goods is clearly incorrect. It is true that the Multānīs exported precious stones, though they also exported indigo, spices (and pepper), sugar, rice and Indian slaves.[31] But by far and away their major export item was that of everyday (coarse) cotton textiles, which were aimed at mass – rather than luxury – consumers. Second, Steensgaard claims that European trade with Asia was superior because European factors were uniquely able to marshal knowledge of consumer demand through regular contact with their principals.[32] But this claim is inverse to reality. For it misses the point that one of the most important reasons for the success of the Indian merchants is just how closely those who resided abroad were in contact with the home firm to which they relayed precise information on local market and shifting consumer preferences wherever they were based. And, as already noted, Indian traders did so well in part because Indian producers were highly adaptive and flexible enough to recalibrate production accordingly. Indeed, so important was this relaying of market information that the merchants' twin watchwords were 'trust' and 'secrecy'. Conversely, one of the reasons why the British had little success in selling their cotton textiles in Africa for much of the eighteenth century was precisely because they lacked precise information on the ever-changing African consumer tastes and demand (as I noted in Chapter 3).

Chhaya Goswami concludes that the Indian merchant firms 'lived up to Fernand Braudel's dictum: "to be well informed was even more important than to be well-trained." They were also early Braudel disciples in reportedly staying focused on secrecy, and on being first in line with new information.'[33] Significant too is the point made by David Washbrook: 'the degrees of "trust" generated in [Indian] family-, kinship- and caste-based community organisations may be superior to anything actually obtainable in the real world under the universal laws

---

[30] Aslanian (2011: 224).
[31] Alam (1994: 206) and Levi (2016: 89).
[32] Steensgaard (1974: 57–8). Nevertheless, van Leur argued consistently that the size of European trade was inferior to that of the Asian commerce.
[33] Goswami (2016: 171–2).

of [modern] capital—as, not least, the recent global financial crisis has demonstrated'.[34]

A third reason why the Multānīs could not be dismissed as mere pedlars is because they lived abroad on average for periods of seven or eight years. It is true that Steensgaard's analysis of Hovannes recognises that he resided abroad for over ten years. But the reason why the Multānīs stayed abroad for sustained periods is because the amount of textiles that they transported to the trans-regional markets was so large that if they sold them in one go the price would plummet. More important, though, is that the sale of textiles was merely the prelude for their subsequent lending activities, given that this furnished them with considerable amounts of capital. The Multānī *dallals* and *baqqals* lent money to local farmers, while rulers also gained loans from the Multānīs, as noted earlier. Given that the interest rate charged often exceeded 100 per cent and sometimes ranged from 200 to 300 per cent (annual percentage rate),[35] they were able to accumulate fortunes that were worth many times that of the initial sale of the Indian textiles. In essence, as Scott Levi notes, 'these were highly trained financial specialists who sought every opportunity to keep their capital profitably invested the full time they were abroad'.[36] In short, the Multānīs combined trade and lending for the sole purpose of maximising profits. Moreover, this objective was undertaken not simply to enhance the income of the merchant capitalist. Critically, on return to India, the profits were used initially to pay off the loan that the *gumāshtā* (the merchant) had been advanced by the firm's *shah* in the first instance, with the remaining capital often being used to set up the merchant's own business in India.

A fourth problem with the pedlar thesis is that the vastness of the scale of the Indian overland trade was such that the Multānīs were accompanied by Afghani *Powindahs* (Afghan Kuchis) who provided protection, as the former journeyed across the Afghan territory. The most famous of the *Powindahs* were the Lohānīs, the Nasīrīs and the Niyāzīs. Overall, this was a very well-organised operation. Moreover, the function of the *Powindahs* was not merely to protect the Indian caravans because a good number of them were traders in their own right. Indeed, they bought up Indian slaves and indigo to purchase horses and fruit which they then exported back to India.[37] Some of them even came to act as full-time traders who struck up legal agreements that were a variant

---

[34] Washbrook (2020: 147).
[35] Levi (2016: 73–4, 133).
[36] Ibid. (72).
[37] Ibid. (109).

of the Islamic *qirād/mudāraba* contract,[38] while also being involved in the marketing and merchandising of Indian goods. Their activities were also highly lucrative such that at the very beginning of the sixteenth century the Mughal ruler, Bābar, claimed that 'many Kabul merchants would not be satisfied with a 300 to 400 per cent profit'.[39]

A fifth problem, as I signalled earlier, is that the Multānīs were not lone individuals but were members of family-based firms that supported each other; as was frequently the case among other Indian groups. If such firms are decried as 'pre-modern' by Eurocentrism, it is notable that many of the British firms throughout the nineteenth century were no less family based, given that company existence was highly precarious and the spectre of bankruptcy often loomed large as a function of the problems associated with unlimited liability.[40] And, moreover, the contemporary Tata conglomerate, which is the single largest employer in the United Kingdom today 'is still a "family firm" whose high rate of accumulation remains protected by religiously-validated tax privileges: the majority of the stock in its principal "holding company" (Tata Sons) is owned either by family members and affines or else by a charitable trust'.[41] Striking too is the point that 95 per cent of U.S. firms that are listed in the Standard & Poor's 500 list are family based, while the figure in Germany today is 80 per cent.[42]

Indian family firms were able to optimise economic security not least because the Multānī and other merchant networks concentrated particularly on maintaining 'trust'. Part of the means by which trust was fostered within the Indian firms was by schooling family members through a long and intensive apprenticeship from a very young age. They were given intensive training in a range of key areas that comprised: accounting techniques, learning to distinguish the complex array of *hundīs* and their usages, methods to determine interest rates for different loans, legal matters both in relation to their own tradition and those found in foreign countries, and learning the secret codes that the commercial communities used when relaying information.[43] Cheating a customer by a single merchant would have had hugely damaging consequences for the firm as a whole as word would spread rapidly if this occurred even once. More importantly, the likes of Steensgaard draw a radical

---

[38] Dale (1994: 65–6).
[39] Cited in Levi (2016: 10).
[40] Arrighi *et al.* (2003: 287).
[41] Washbrook (2020: 147).
[42] Timberg (2014: 99).
[43] Levi (2016: 64).

contrast between the 'superior' formal organisational characteristics of the EEIC-as-joint-stock company compared with the 'inferior' informal, community-based nature of Indian family firms. But Tirthankar Roy notes that '[w]e should not overdraw the differences. [This] simplistic contrast between the informal community and the formal company can be misleading. It makes us overlook the strengths of the community ... and the weaknesses of the company form.'[44] And, as he goes on to explain, the EEIC was especially vulnerable to costly dispute resolution.[45]

Finally, a sixth problem lies in Steensgaard's claim that 'the ordinary entrepreneur operates on the pedlar level, and there is nothing in the sources to indicate the existence of comprehensive coordinated organizations—of an Armenian, Turkish or Persian [or Indian] version of a Fugger, Cranfield or Tripp... or the [English] East India Company'.[46] However, as Timberg notes of the 'Great (Indian) Firms' in the eighteenth and nineteenth centuries, they 'were comparable in many respects to the European (mainly often of Jewish origin) firms of families such as the Rothschilds, Mendelssohns ... Bleichroders, Warburgs'.[47] And, as should be apparent from the discussion thus far, Indian firms were founded on the basis of a 'comprehensive coordinated organisation'. Moreover, not only were there some extremely rich Indians such as Abdul Ghafur and Virji Vora,[48] upon whom the EICs were often dependent as I noted in Chapter 5, but also the key point as Chaudhury and Morineau conclude is that such was the power of some of these entrepreneurs that 'their varied and extensive operations ... can [indeed] be compared with the Medicis, Függers or Tripps of Europe'.[49] Equally of note is Dale's conclusion that the 'successful Multānī merchants of Isfahan and Astrakhan appear to have possessed the same entrepreneurial spirit and to have engaged in a similarly wide range of economic activities as Gino Luzatto's "great merchant" of the Italian Renaissance cities'.[50] Kaveh Yazdani adds to this by stating that the '[t]he mercantile classes of 17th and 18th century South Asia—including individual merchants, *sarrafs*, merchant conglomerations, firms, and families with large business networks—were one of the richest merchant communities in the whole world'.[51] And, as René Barendse concludes:

---

[44] Roy (2012: 120).
[45] Ibid. (121).
[46] Steensgaard (1974: 30).
[47] Timberg (2014: 32).
[48] See Yazdani (2017: 422–8).
[49] Chaudhury and Morineau (2007b: 3–4).
[50] Dale (1994: 134).
[51] Yazdani (2019: 5).

Those merchant houses of Amsterdam had nothing to teach their Indian counterparts in capitalist strategies; such as [occasionally] dumping to control the market ... or sophisticated financial techniques. The largest Indian firms—the Jagat Seth of Bengal, the Taravads of Surat and Delhi, the Dixit/Patvardans of Puna, the houses of Mulla Ali and Chellaby of Surat, or the Mhamas of Goa—were comparable to the greatest European multinational businesses of the period.[52]

Conclusion

This and the last four chapters reveal that the second step of the Eurocentric Big Bang theory, or the familiar 'expansion of the West' narrative, is flawed. For it is clear that the creation and development of the FGE owes much of its debt to the activities of the Indians/South Asians. Thus to fetishise the role of the European Companies in the Indian Ocean trading system is one giant leap too far for the history of global humankind. Indeed, before 1750/1800 the EICs found it impossible to police the spontaneous gaps that continuously sprung up in their imaginary 'monopolistic' trading-post empires. As we have seen, they failed to take any great proportion of the trade *away* from Asian merchants.[53] However, by the same token Rhoads Murphey goes too far when he claims that after 1500 'the more general shape of events of the succeeding centuries in mainland Asia, were essentially unaffected by the presence of the Europeans; it was as if they had never been there at all'.[54] Certainly, the Europeans played an important role, especially in the Americas, of course, as well as in their vital service in distributing New World silver around the FGE that nurtured trade and production in the Indian Ocean system. More accurate is Jason Sharman's conclusion that '[i]f not by dint of their modern powerful armies and navies, how, then, did Europeans dominate the Indian Ocean and Asia in the early modern period? The short answer is that they didn't, any more than Europeans dominated Africa before the late 1800s.'[55] But, the key point here is that the symbiotic relations that the Europeans struck up with the Asians enabled their mutual gain. Thus, while it would be wrong to confirm the Eurocentric- and Eurofetishist-reified conceptions of European power, equally it would be wrong to reify Asian trading power.

---

[52] Barendse (2009: 731–2).
[53] Arasaratnam (1987: 124–6).
[54] Murphey (1977: 13). Cf. Braudel (1992: 489, 496), Hodgson (1993: 99–100), Goldstone (2000: 181) and Das Gupta (2001: 79).
[55] Sharman (2019: 64).

Accordingly, we can problematise the generic defence made by Eurocentric scholars such as J. M. Roberts, David Landes, Niall Ferguson and the IR scholars Hedley Bull and Adam Watson: that the belief in Western domination of Asia after 1500 is not a product of Eurocentrism but merely reflects the *factual historical* record that is inherently Eurocentric. For in the light of this and the last four chapters, it turns out that such 'factual realism' morphs or degenerates into a form of Eurocentric confirmation bias, or what Anievas and Nişancioğlu usefully refer to as 'Eurocentric realism'.[56] For if the historical factual record *appears* to be centred on Western supremacy it is so only because 'Eurocentric facts' have been selected at the expense of the alternative ones that I have brought to light. All of which begs the question as to whether my claim that the FGE existed between 1500 and 1800 can stand up against two prominent Eurocentric critiques, which insist that a global economy did not emerge until after 1828 at the behest of the Europeans, if not until after 1945 under the auspices of the Pax Americana.

---

[56] Anievas and Nişancioğlu (2015: 93).

Part II

What Was Global about the First Global Economy, 1500–c. 1850?

7 Countering the Eurocentric Rejection of the First Global Economy (I)
Unveiling Global Structural Properties

Introduction

Chapters 2–6 foregrounded the agency of non-Western actors and Indian structural power together with the agential roles performed by the Europeans in the making of the first global economy (FGE). In this chapter, I want to step back from the details of those discussions to provide a robust justification for my claim that a global economy existed in the 1500–1850 period. Here, I reveal the many 'structural properties' of the FGE, though I reserve two of the most important of these for Chapters 8 and 14, which cover the presence of 'historical capitalism' and the 'Afro-Indian global cotton whip', respectively. Certainly, the vast majority of International Relations (IR) and International Political Economy (IPE) scholars would be sceptical, if not dismissive, of the presence of a global economy before 1850, if not before 1945. In order to justify my claim, this chapter interrogates the two most rigorous and comprehensive critiques, which deploy various threshold criteria that need to be met before we can declare the presence of globalisation and the global economy. The transformationalist critique that is advanced by David Held and his co-authors as well the neoclassical liberal-economic critique that is advanced by Kevin O'Rourke and Jeffrey Williamson deploy various threshold criteria, which lead them to reject the claim that globalisation and a global economy existed before 1828, if not before 1945. My critical defence deploys two key moves, the first of which lies in my claim that their defining criteria are situated in a series of historical arguments that emanate from a Eurocentric base. And, the second move emerges as a deep irony insofar as I redeploy their exact threshold criteria within a *non*-Eurocentric framework in order to prove the existence of a global economy between 1500 and 1850.

The chapter proceeds through three sections, the section 'Historical Globaloney? The Case against the Existence of a Global Economy before 1828/1945' provides a summary of the critiques that are advanced by the transformationalists, on the one hand, and O'Rourke and Williamson

(O&W) on the other. The sections 'The Ahistorical Eurocentric Temporal Binary (I): The Absence of Global Economic Flows/Processes before 1828/1945 and Their Presence Thereafter?' and 'Confronting the Ahistorical Eurocentric Temporal Binary (II): The Presence of Tariff Protectionism, Warfare and Irrational Institutions before 1828/1945 and Their Absence Thereafter?' debunk the two generic ahistorical Eurocentric temporal binaries that underpin their analyses. For these posit strict breaks between the pre- and post-1828 periods (O&W) and the pre- and post-1945 eras (the transformationalists). Thus, in the second section, I reveal the many continuities between the 1500/1850 and the post-1850 worlds with respect to global economic flows, while the third section reveals the many continuities with respect to the presence of warfare, freer trade and economically rational institutions.

Historical Globaloney? The Case against the Existence of a Global Economy before 1828/1945

Because I shall interrogate their many historical claims throughout this chapter, it is necessary to begin by providing a brief summary of the conceptual schemas that the two main sets of critics deploy in their efforts to disprove the existence of a global economy before the nineteenth, if not the mid-twentieth, century.

The 'Transformationalist' Critique

The most broad-ranging schema is advanced in the key book, *Global Transformations*, in which David Held and his various co-authors advance what they call a 'transformationalist' approach to globalisation. This operationalises four conceptual thresholds that must be deemed to be 'high' before a (thick) global economy and globalisation can be declared to properly exist. These comprise (1) 'extensity' or the degree to which global flows reach the majority of the world's population; (2) 'intensity' or the regularity of flows; (3) 'velocity' or the speed of flows; and (4) 'impact' propensity or the degree to which global flows lead to transformative change within societies.[1] And they advance five key historical reasons as to why a 'thick' global economy could *not* have existed before 1945.[2] First, they argue that the global economy only gradually came into existence under the auspices of European hyper-agency and structural power, wherein the phase between 1850 and 1945

---

[1] Held *et al.* (1999: 16–27).
[2] Ibid. (414–35).

is viewed, in effect, as one of Western-led *proto*-globalisation. Thus, they claim that 'the *impetus* to the formation of global processes, both in terms of extensity and intensity, was provided by the expansion of [the imperialist] European powers during ... the late nineteenth century'.[3]

Second, despite their recognition of the presence of intercontinental trade flows after 1500, these are nevertheless dismissed as relatively insignificant given that they lacked sufficient levels of 'extensity'. This is because such trade was based overwhelmingly on *luxury* goods that reached only the elites, who comprised but a small percentage of the world's population – 10 per cent at most. Put differently, only when mass-based consumer products are traded in sufficient volumes would they declare the existence of impactful and meaningful global trade. To this, they add the point that *global* credit/financial structures did not exist before 1945. And, moreover, because Europeans traded in *noncompeting* goods – i.e., products that they did not produce – so global trade *competition* was absent. Thus, while they view the *extensity* of trade as rising after 1500 through Europe's 'incorporation' of the Americas and later Asia, nevertheless it is deemed to have been too low to qualify as global. The remaining three objections follow in quick succession. Third, the *intensity* of trade flows was too low to qualify as global in scope because they were too sporadic. Fourth, the *velocity* of circulation was far too slow to qualify as globalisation given that trade was transported on camels, horses and oxen or very slow sailing ships and Islamic dhows. Fifth and finally, as a result of the deficiencies in extensity, intensity and velocity, trade flows had only a very limited *impact propensity* to invoke fundamental transformations of societies.[4]

O&W's Neoclassical Liberal-Economic Critique

The O&W approach dovetails considerably with the transformationalist framework in that it provides 'thresholds' of globalisation, even though it is both ostensibly narrower in focus and that it relies, unlike that of transformationalism, on *measurement* through data analysis. A further key difference lies in the dating of globalisation, given their claim that it was born in 1828 rather than in 1945. Curiously, at first blush, O&W claim that they are the *only* historians to offer a *definition* of globalisation.[5] For the irony here is that the very scholars with whom O&W entered into a debate, Dennis Flynn and Arturo Giráldez, assert that '[w]e have been

---

[3] Ibid. (41, 418–24), my emphasis.
[4] Ibid. (79, 153, 154, 161, 178, 417, 419–20, 423, 433).
[5] O'Rourke and Williamson (2004: 109).

disappointed ... to discover that few authors offer operational definitions of the term "globalization"'.[6] But what O&W mean by their claim is that the *only* viable definition of globalisation is one that entails a *measurable* conception of 'impact' and that this is absent in Flynn and Giráldez's definition. Moreover, as signalled in Chapter 6, O&W critique those who focus on the importance of transcontinental trade volumes as reflecting the presence of a global economy, as I have done in Chapters 2–5, by claiming that

> the worst way to gauge [global market integration] is to measure only the changing amount of trade taking place between ... markets, since those changes could be driven by supply and demand conditions within each trading region, the latter having nothing to do with changing transport costs, trade monopolies, war embargoes, tariffs or quotas—that is, having nothing to do with world market integration.[7]

Most importantly, they argue that the single sign of global economic integration is that of 'commodity price convergence' (CPC) across the world. Thus, they assert that 'the only irrefutable evidence that globalisation is taking place is a decline in the international dispersions of commodity prices or what might be called *commodity price convergence*'.[8] This is deemed important because it reveals the *transformative impact* of trade on societies. In essence, while they concur with Held *et al.* that impact is a core property of globalisation, nevertheless for O&W this is read off from the ability of changes in CPC to 'induce a reshuffling of [domestic] resources in order for trade to influence the things that really matter, like the scale of output, the distribution of income, absolute living standards or the quality of life'.[9] Or, put differently, 'only when trade displaces local production do you get the reshuffling of productive factors which leads to economy-wide distributional changes'.[10] Similar to the specific arguments made by the transformationalists, O&W claim that processes of global market integration did not exist between 1500 and 1828 because first, there was no significant reduction in 'transaction costs' given that trade barriers and state regulations of trade were high; second, transport costs did not fall; and third, international military conflicts were intense.[11] It was because of these factors that their

---

[6] Flynn and Giráldez (2006: 232).
[7] O'Rourke and Williamson (2004: 110).
[8] O'Rourke and Williamson (2002a: 26), my emphasis.
[9] Ibid.
[10] O'Rourke and Williamson (2004: 116).
[11] O'Rourke and Williamson (2002b: 426, 428, 2004: 109).

all-important criterion of global impact – CPC – is said to have been absent before 1828. Overall, then, it is this quantifiable definition of impact, realised through measuring CPC, that leads Jan de Vries to declare this as a 'hard' conception of globalisation as opposed to the 'soft' conception deployed by others, most notably Flynn and Giráldez, since the latter's does not lend itself to measurement.[12]

Finally, a further overlap with transformationalism is found in O&W's claim that before 1800 the intercontinental panoply of goods traded were *noncompeting luxuries* that were *monopoly* items.[13] This returns us to the points that such trade had *no impact propensity* because it did not displace or challenge domestic production structures in Europe, that there was *no trade competition* in evidence and that the prevalence of the trade in luxury goods affected at most only 10 per cent of the population. All of which means that however vibrant intercontinental trade was in this period – and they argue that it was not inconsiderable given that world trade grew by 1.06 per cent per annum between 1500 and 1800,[14] which translates into a 25-fold increase across the period[15] – nevertheless, it failed to impart significant *transformational impact* on societies that it touched. As they put it, '[t]here is plenty of evidence of a European intercontinental trade boom during the Age of Commerce, but there is very little evidence of declining trade barriers and commodity-price convergence between the continents.... The question is whether this trade boom was due to a process of market integration, or [merely] to demand and supply shifts in the various countries.'[16] And they conclude that 'globalisation has evolved since Columbus, but ... the most dramatic change by far took place in the nineteenth century.... Globalisation became economically meaningful [i.e., impactful] only with the dawn of the nineteenth century, and it came on in a rush.'[17]

The Ahistorical Eurocentric Temporal Binary (I): The Absence of *Global Economic* Flows/Processes before 1828/1945 and Their Presence Thereafter?

In this second long section, I problematise the economic arguments for the absence of a global economy before the nineteenth century. Here, the core problem lies in the imputation of an ahistorical Eurocentric

[12] de Vries (2010).
[13] O'Rourke and Williamson (2002b: 423; 2004: 115–16).
[14] O'Rourke and Williamson (2002b: 422, 2004: 110).
[15] See also de Vries (2010: 718).
[16] O'Rourke and Williamson (2002b: 428, 2004: 111).
[17] O'Rourke and Williamson (2004: 109).

temporal binary in which the pre- and post-1828 periods are presented as polar opposites. For in this binary conception, transcontinental trade in the pre-1828 era is (re)presented as more controlled/regulated, monopolistic, noncompetitive and luxury-based than it was so that the post-1828 or post-1945 era can be (re)presented as more laissez-faire, 'free trading' and competitive than it has been. In the process, this airbrushes out of the picture the significant continuities with the market-based, non-monopolistic and everyday-based trade between the pre- and post-1828 eras.

'CPC' in the FGE: Exaggerating the Trading Power of the East India Companies?

Typifying the economistic ontology of neoclassical analysis, the first major problem with the O&W approach is that it is highly reductive insofar as CPC is treated as the *only* measure of all things (economically) global. In their debate with the prominent global historians, Flynn and Giráldez – who, as I explained in Chapters 2 and 3, claim that after 1571 the global economy and globalisation came into existence – O&W assert that '[t]he central finding of our work is that there is very little evidence of world commodity price convergence in the three centuries after Columbus.... "[N]*owhere do Flynn and Giráldez challenge our evidence or our inference*"'.[18] However, there is one clear exception that Flynn and Giráldez advance that is all the more pertinent here because, by return favour, it remains unchallenged by O&W. This concerns the major case of global silver flows which, as Flynn and Giráldez have argued in many pieces, had undergone price convergence by 1700, which was followed by global price divergence thereafter until price convergence had emerged by 1750 – an argument that has been confirmed by others.[19] Nevertheless, on the issue of CPC vis-à-vis all the other key trading commodities, Flynn and Giráldez remain silent, even in their 2008 reply to O&W, defaulting instead to restating their 'non-measurable' definition of globalisation;[20] to wit globalisation emerged in 1571 when 'all heavily populated land masses began to exchange products ... in values [that were] sufficient to generate lasting impacts on all trading partners'.[21] But other scholars have emerged to challenge the O&W analysis of CPC.

---

[18] Ibid. (113), their emphasis.
[19] Flynn and Giráldez (1995a, 1995b, 2004, 2008); see also von Glahn (2003: 197, 200) and de Zwart (2016: 117).
[20] Flynn and Giráldez (2008: 368).
[21] Flynn and Giráldez (2006: 235 and 2008: 369).

Much as the definition of globalisation can pre-determine the dating of this phenomenon, the same is true concerning the various methods that exist to measure CPC. The one deployed by O&W looks simply at the 'mark-up ratios' between the initial purchasing price in Asia and the final selling price in Europe. But there are various problems with this approach, not least because it confines the analysis to measuring the price wedge between *two* different markets only. For if we want to understand CPC occurring across *many* markets rather than only two – which *should* be essential for any analysis of globalisation – then a better approach is the 'coefficient of variation' (CoV).[22] However, this procedure can reveal convergence as a function of a demand shock – something that does *not* constitute genuine globalisation according to O&W. Thus, to overcome this problem, a third procedure is available, that of measuring the 'standard deviation' across many markets.[23] Klas Rönnbäck's survey considers CPC through the prisms of the CoV and the SD, while Pim de Zwart's uses all three methods.

Surveying eleven key global commodities, Rönnbäck argues that nine of them demonstrate price convergence during the three centuries under review here.[24] However, he also points out that CPC is not a linear process that exhibits a general declining trend throughout the period owing to the effect of differential tariff rates across Europe. Rönnbäck concludes that 'O'Rourke [and Williamson are] correct insofar that such [protectionist] policies and wars often thwarted commodity market integration [but Rönnbäck's own] findings ... also [show that in spite] of this, the potential for market integration actually was realised in many intercontinental trades'.[25] His analysis has a further advantage over that of O&W's in that he considers CPC for the American-imported goods into Europe – something that O&W do not in fact do since they look only at the reduction in Asian/European transport costs.[26]

This analysis is advanced further by Pim de Zwart in his seminal book, *Globalization and the Colonial Origins of the Great Divergence*. The only limitation here, however, is that he ignores the Euro-American trade and focuses instead on the Asian/European trade that was conducted by the Vereenigde Oost-Indische Compagnie (VOC), specifically in Bengal, Ceylon and Java in South Asia and Southeast Asia as well as the Cape Colony in South Africa. The conclusion to his survey of sixteen globally

---

[22] Rönnbäck (2009: 100–1).
[23] For a full discussion of these methods, see Rönnbäck (2009: 98–107) and de Zwart (2016: 34–8).
[24] Rönnbäck (2009: 108).
[25] Ibid. (114).
[26] Ibid. (97).

traded goods is that between 1600 and 1800 there 'is sufficient evidence of price convergence, and thus the integration of Euro-Asian commodity markets, taking place'.[27] However, he is careful to break these commodities down into four categories, which reflect the market power of the VOC in different places. Thus, in the trade of the monopoly goods – cinnamon, mace and nutmeg – in which the VOC enjoyed significant market and political power in Ceylon and the Moluccas, there was no sign of CPC. But CPC occurred in the majority of Asian markets where the Dutch had to negotiate with stronger Asian merchants as well as with other European companies. Thus, CPC occurred in copper, pepper, porcelain, saltpetre, silk, sugar, tea, textiles, tin and cloves well before 1800.[28] More important still is the point that those products that exhibited convergence were also the ones that experienced the largest volumes, which leads de Zwart to conclude that *in aggregate* there is mostly convergence.[29]

In sum, then, the O&W analysis falls, albeit implicitly, into the Eurocentric trap of exaggerating the monopoly power of the East India Companies (EICs). For these alternative analyses suggest that the EICs were far less effective in inflating prices charged in Europe than O&W would have us believe, given the prevalence of global market competition and the Afro-Asian trading system. And a further problem, as I explain in the next section, is that even measuring 'mark-up ratios', 'CoV' and 'SD' misses the impact of smuggling, in which the informal prices of these goods were lower within European markets than the formal data suggest,[30] which means that the *actual* price wedge was much lower than O&W presume. Either way, though, it seems fair to conclude that the alternative analyses to that of O&W's 'mark-up ratios' point towards the likelihood of CPC during the FGE. But then again, even if CPC did occur, the key question is whether it is as important a measure of globalisation as O&W presume and whether, in turn, 'impact' can be derived from other forms of global economic flows.

The Eurocentric Myth of the Colonial 'Luxury' Goods Trade into Europe: 'CPC' as the Measure of All Things Global?

The second major claim made by transformationalists and O&W is that pre-nineteenth century intercontinental (colonial) trade was conducted merely in 'luxury goods'. But I argue here that these two

---

[27] de Zwart (2016: 195).
[28] Ibid. (45–51).
[29] Ibid. (49).
[30] On tea, see Nierstrasz (2015); on cotton textiles, see McCants (2008).

approaches buy into the myth of the 'luxury goods thesis'.[31] This is one of the most common arguments found in the wider literature. Critically, from the thirteenth century on, everyday mass products comprised at least 50 per cent of Afro-Eurasian trade,[32] which undermines this claim outright. Part of the reason for this is that ships required ballast that in general took the form of low-value, bulk goods – though as I explained in Chapters 5 and 6, cheap everyday Indian cotton textiles (ICTs) that were transported *overland* were also very important. But the more specific claim made by O&W is that in their trading relations with Asia and the Americas, the Europeans were involved primarily in three areas of 'luxury' goods: the Asian spice trade (pepper, mace, nutmeg, cinnamon and cloves); the Asian and American trade in 'drug-goods' (tea, coffee, sugar and tobacco);[33] and finally, the Asian cloth trade (raw silk, silk and cotton textiles), as well as Chinese porcelain. But here we confront five key problems.

First, it is noteworthy that from the early-1500s and up to the 1660s, pepper was by far the main commodity that was imported into Europe – though it should be noted that pepper imports began before then given that they were originally channelled from Asia into Europe via Egypt and thence Venice. Critically, pepper was a mass-based consumer product from the outset. However, between 1664 and 1699, black pepper comprised only 13 per cent of all Asian imports into Britain before dropping down to an average of 5 per cent for 1700/60,[34] as it was superseded by imported ICTs. Indeed, between 1660 and 1760, the latter comprised 65 per cent of all English EIC (EEIC) imports from Asia,[35] remaining as high as 42 per cent in 1761/99.[36] And, moreover, a similar set of trends played out vis-à-vis Dutch imports.

While Eurocentrism portrays ICT imports as luxury items, it was, however, the cheaper coarse variety that sparked off the 'Calico Craze' in Europe in the last third of the seventeenth century.[37] Beverly Lemire argues that everyday Indian calicoes were being widely adopted by the early-eighteenth century across all sectors of European society rather than only among the elites (see the next section).[38] While it is true that

---

[31] For example, Wallerstein (1974: 42, 333), Menard (1991: 229) and Wolf (1982: 32).
[32] Barendse (2002: 198–9), Chaudhuri (1985: ch. 9), Curtin (1984: 119–20, 134), Wink (1988: 44) and Frank (1998: 94–5).
[33] Mintz (1986).
[34] Calculated from Chaudhuri (2006: 529–30).
[35] Ibid. (540–5).
[36] Taken from Bowen (2007).
[37] Inikori (2002: 430–51), de Vries (2003: 65) and Lemire (2009).
[38] Lemire (1992: 56–76, 89–108). But see Riello (2009b: 344–5).

the 1701 and 1721/2 tariff acts (and excises) nearly doubled the price of Indian calicoes in Britain, with the latter Act prohibiting the selling of these textiles within Britain, nevertheless the rise of a vibrant smuggling trade ensured their continued importation and sale among all sectors of society (a point to which I return shortly). But such was the clamour of demand for ICTs within British society that this ban was repealed in 1774,[39] though tariffs were still applied thereafter. Overall, in the period between 1500 and 1850, the two major imports – pepper up to the mid-seventeenth century and ICTs after the 1670s – were largely everyday mass-based goods, not luxuries.[40]

Second, the assumption that the rest of the Asian and American imports were expensive luxuries is just as fraught. There is no doubting the point that most of them began as luxury items in this period, given their initial high price. But these items declined significantly in price during the following three centuries, thereby bringing them in the range of poorer, mass consumers.[41] Thus, coffee prices dropped substantially in Europe, from £1–37 per lb in 1710 to 45 pence per lb in 1800,[42] particularly as competing centres of production fed the European markets (as I explain in the next section). The first London coffee-house appeared in 1652 (which was set up by a Turkish merchant) and thence developed with remarkable rapidity in Britain and across Europe.[43] Once again, while it is true that tea was initially a luxury item, nevertheless the subsequent importation of the cheap variety of Chinese black tea known as *Bohea* came to meet the consumption needs of the poor by the early-eighteenth century.[44] Interestingly, the EEIC concluded that as early as 1705 'tea was an article of general consumption in England'.[45] Moreover, by 1750 *Bohea* comprised some 66 per cent of total tea consumption in England,[46] while by the 1790s about 7 per cent of household income went on purchasing it.[47] Indeed, by the end of the eighteenth century, annual tea sales provided 66 per cent of the population with half a pint of tea per day (much as is the case today).[48] In Holland too, its price in Amsterdam fell by 90 per cent between 1715/18 and 1785/9,[49] dropping

---

[39] McCants (2007: 460).
[40] But see Styles (2000: 136–40).
[41] Rönnbäck (2009: 108).
[42] Hersh and Voth (2009: 10).
[43] Mintz (1986: 111).
[44] Nierstrasz (2015); see also Mintz (1986: 110–19).
[45] Cited in Nierstrasz (2015: 263).
[46] McCants (2007: 443).
[47] Hersh and Voth (2009: 3).
[48] Cole (1958: 401–3).
[49] de Vries (2010: 721–2).

from £6–14 per lb to 70 pence.[50] The price of sugar also dropped drastically, from 33 pence per lb in 1600 to 8 pence by 1800, such that it too became a staple of poor households during the eighteenth century.[51] This, though, was hardly surprising given that sugar was in high demand in order to sweeten the tea that such households consumed.

Carole Shammas asserts that the 'grocery' products (i.e., Mintz's 'drug foods/goods') 'sugar, caffeine drinks [tea and coffee] and tobacco became objects of mass consumption long before 1800'.[52] In the late-seventeenth century, the *value* of groceries comprised 17 per cent of total European imports before rising to 33 per cent by the 1770s. And these sums are rendered all the more impressive by the fact that the price of these goods had fallen sharply. Shammas defines a mass-based good as one that is consumed by no less than 25 per cent of the population at least once daily. On this basis, she claims that in the 1650–1750 period, the following items had become mass-based consumer products: tobacco (1650s), sugar (before 1700) and tea (1720s).[53] To this we can add coffee, which was first imported into Europe by the VOC in the 1660s in very small quantities, before rising rapidly after 1690 such that by the late 1730s, 'tea and coffee accounted for nearly a quarter of all VOC sales in Amsterdam (24.9 per cent), second only to the category of silk and cotton textiles (28.3 per cent)'.[54] Anne McCants notes that by 1740, revenues derived from the sale of tea and coffee were 1,312 times higher than in 1669, leading her to conclude that coffee had become an everyday mass-consumer product in the Netherlands by the 1750s.[55]

Finally, it is generally thought that Chinese porcelain and Chinese and Indian silks were unequivocally luxury goods that were consumed only by the highest income groups. But this ignores the point that a major silk import into Europe was the Indian silk 'handkerchief' (which was a much larger item than that which is used today and was worn as a fashionable item of clothing back then). This was something that reached into the poorest households, as I explain in the fourth point below. Moreover, through her careful archival work on orphanage inventories, McCants shows that Chinese porcelain and (Dutch) delftware were bought by the poorest households.[56] Overall, she concludes that '[t]he consumption of tea, coffee, sugar, tobacco, porcelain, and silk and cotton

---

[50] Hersh and Voth (2009: 10); see also Cole (1958).
[51] Hersh and Voth (2009: 9).
[52] Shammas (1993: 178) and Hersh and Voth (2009).
[53] See also Shammas (1993); McCants (2007: 444) and Mintz (1986: ch. 3).
[54] McCants (2008: 176); see also Shammas (1993).
[55] McCants (2008: 178, 179).
[56] McCants (2007: 455–60).

textiles increased dramatically in western Europe beginning as early as the closing decades of the seventeenth century, only to accelerate through much of the eighteenth century'.[57]

All in all, Jan de Vries concludes that the luxury goods thesis, upon which the O&W and transformationalist critiques rest, is simply 'false'.[58] And this in turn reveals a third problem that reveals a vital slippage in the O&W logic upon which so much of their argument pivots. For having noted the decline in the prices of American and Asian products, de Vries asserts that CPC is *not* the most important measure of global integration. For as we have seen, while the cost of many though by no means all of these imports in the sixteenth century meant that they came mainly in reach of rich elite consumers, nevertheless thereafter commodity prices came down to such an extent that they came in range of the middling and lower-income consumers. Critically, he argues, it is not CPC that matters most here, but the decline in the price of the products. Thus 'if the price is right [for] the consumer, the issue of price convergence would have been distinctly of secondary consideration'.[59] Which means that the transformationalist/O&W assumption that Asian and American trade with Europe lacked sufficient extensity and impact because it served only rich consumers is incorrect. For by their definition, because trade served middle- and lower-income consumers, it must have been of sufficient 'extensity' and 'impact' to qualify as 'globalised'. This is reinforced further by McCants, who notes that '[w]e might even be tempted to believe that the consumer revolution [which was important to European economic development] would have been inconceivable without the stimulus provided by "luxuries" first trickling in and then streaming [as everyday consumer goods] into Europe from Asia [and the Americas]'.[60] All of which leads onto the fourth problem with the O&W luxury goods thesis.

For all the discussion thus far, O&W are likely to respond by arguing that the massive hikes in tariffs (as well as excise duties) on colonial imported goods that began in 1685 in Britain and France served to price these products out of the range of more modest and poor consumers. This is precisely why they argue that CPC can only occur once free trade arrives and why before 1828, particularly in Britain, these imports were luxuries that only the rich elites could afford. However, there is an elephant in the room in this whole discussion. For what all this misses

---

[57] Ibid. (460). See also de Vries (2008: ch. 4).
[58] de Vries (2010: 725, 2008: 154–64, 181–5).
[59] de Vries (2010: 722).
[60] McCants (2007: 438).

is that a good number of these colonial imports were smuggled into European countries, especially into Britain in order to avoid the tariffs (and excise duties) that the British state levied after 1684 in order to raise revenues to fund its extremely expensive imperial wars (as I explained in detail in Chapter 2, to which I return later as well as in Chapters 9 and 12). These heavily taxed items, including tobacco, chocolate, coffee, brandy and rum, silk and cotton textiles and, most especially, tea were also the most heavily smuggled items. But most importantly, we need to confront the Indian elephant in the room.

The hard test case for my argument lies in the import of ICTs as well as Indian silk textiles given that the former were prohibited between 1722 and 1774 and the latter were banned throughout the eighteenth century. I'll take each in turn. Clearly, as the 1784 House of Commons report that enquired into the whole issue of smuggling acknowledges, a large number of Indian cotton pieces were smuggled into Britain following the 1721/2 ban.[61] This took many forms, one of which was undertaken by the EEIC through a very wide variety of methods. Another avenue came from the European continent. Important here is that the Dutch state maintained free trade on Indian textile imports, which provided an opportunity for many opportunistic Dutchmen to smuggle these products into Britain, given that they could purchase them at much lower prices than could the British. But there were also various domestic avenues along which ICTs diffused to the masses. These included a very lively second-hand market in these goods, which were sold in dedicated retail shops within Britain, while another lay in outright theft which occurred on a widespread scale.[62] As a result, William Farrell concludes, 'cotton textiles entered the home market in significant numbers even after the [two] calico acts'.[63] While some scholars argue that '[t]here is little evidence that anyone wearing forbidden cloth was fined or prosecuted in England',[64] nevertheless Beverly Lemire points to some, albeit limited, evidence that prosecutions, imprisonment and fines were in fact levied.[65] Moreover, there were many instances of women wearing calicoes being attacked and on occasion killed by everyday people,[66] such was the febrile atmosphere that surrounded these imports given that they threatened the livelihood of British workers in the wool and silk industries.

[61] See Farrell (2016).
[62] Lemire (2011: ch. 3).
[63] Farrell (2016: 275); see also Kwass (2014: chs. 2 and 4).
[64] Riello (2013: 121).
[65] Lemire (2011: 58–62).
[66] Ibid. (ch. 3).

A similar story applies to the case of silk handkerchiefs which, as I noted earlier, were large products that were worn as fashion items. For they had become popular across *all* sectors of British society by the early-eighteenth century. Once again, they were bought either from second-hand retailers or were acquired through theft or via the black market that was supplied by smugglers.[67] Here, the 'leakage' that occurred from the EEIC ships that was smuggled into Britain was perhaps the chief avenue along which Indian silk handkerchiefs wended their way to all sectors of society. As Farrell concludes, '[t]he success of Indian handkerchiefs, and the role of the [English] East India Company in supplying them, supports the argument that new forms of consumption in Britain were created through Asian trade'.[68] Accordingly, it seems fair to say that the democratising genie of Asian silks and ICTs was now out of the bottle and no amount of prohibition or even random instances of everyday violence could put it back in.

However, smuggling was also pronounced vis-à-vis other colonial imports in the eighteenth century, most notably tea, rum, spices and tobacco. Perhaps around a third of the legal imports of tea and tobacco were smuggled in.[69] The main avenue for tobacco lay with the re-export trade, for having received the 'drawback' (the sum of the original customs duty) prior to re-export, the smugglers then managed to bring it back into England from Scotland, Dunkirk, Ostend, the Channel Islands and the Isle of Man.[70] Of note too is that tea was re-exported and, having already received the drawback, was then smuggled back into England from Denmark and Sweden or thence indirectly via Holland and France or Ireland.[71] And, to sum up this whole discussion, Susan North's claim is pertinent:

The complicity of the whole of British society in smuggling made the Collectors' task a losing battle as Customs staff found themselves pariahs in their own communities and were often forced to overlook … various frauds to avoid physical violence…. The British government began to rethink its attitude toward import taxes in the 1780s. Almost a century of attempts to prevent smuggling had failed thoroughly, while prohibition [of ICTs between 1721/2 and 1774 as well as silk textiles throughout the eighteenth century] and the escalation of duties served only to enhance the desirability of foreign goods.[72]

---

[67] Farrell (2016).
[68] Ibid. (293).
[69] Cf. Mui and Mui (1975), Cole (1958) and Nash (1982).
[70] Nash (1982: 361–2).
[71] Bowen (2002) and Mui and Mui (1975).
[72] North (2008: 101).

All of which means that whatever the official or formal picture looks like, smuggling enabled many of the colonial imports to enter poorer households.

The final upshot of this discussion confronts O&W's exclusive focus on the *formal* prices of these imports which, in turn, has crucial implications for the transformative impact of imported goods from Asia and the Americas. Of course, data do not exist on the informal prices that smugglers and thieves charged. But the upshot of this is that looking only at the formal prices of the goods sold in Britain serves to exaggerate the actual price wedge between British sales and European purchases of American and Asian products at source. And the conclusion is that these imports in the eighteenth century were neither luxuries nor were their prices out of reach of poorer consumers. Moreover, one dynamic that underpinned all of this is the role of *fashion*, which had now moved out of its previous monopoly preserve of the rich elites and into the heart of the middling and poor income groups. For in 1604, the enforcement of the old sumptuary laws – in which the old social hierarchy restricted fashionable wear to the rich elites – ended, thereby paving the way for the socially democratising role of cotton textiles as well as silk textiles, especially silk handkerchiefs. And this in turn followed Norbert Elias's model of the 'civilising process', wherein the lower-income orders imitated the fashionable practices of the upper classes.[73] All of which reveals that these imports, especially those of textiles, had a fundamentally transformative social impact on European society.[74] For they were an important component of the eighteenth century 'consumer revolution',[75] even if this kicked in much harder during the nineteenth century. Moreover, as I mention in Chapter 9, the 'prosumer argument' becomes pertinent here, in which women were motivated to enter the labour market in part so as to earn money in order to feed their new-found fashion desire in cotton textile clothing.[76]

All of which produces a fifth and final challenge to O&W's luxury goods thesis. For we can now see the problem with their claim that the global trade boom could be accounted for in the seventeenth and eighteenth centuries only by the rise in 'surplus income',[77] which refers to the increase in the incomes of the very rich. The issue here, then, is that the rising income of the middling and poorer groups was also

---

[73] Berg (2004: 99).
[74] de Vries (2008: ch. 4).
[75] McKendrick (1982).
[76] Lemire (2011: ch. 3) and de Vries (2008).
[77] O'Rourke and Williamson (2002b: 433–4, 2002a: 109).

important, albeit enabled by the roles of smuggling, theft and second-hand retail shops. Accordingly, this is something that O&W needed to factor into their model given that they bracketed out these lower-income groups by focusing only on changes in 'surplus income'. Thus, as Anne McCants rightly notes, O&W

> limit the potential stimulus from increased European import demand to be responsive only to increases in the incomes of the very rich, thereby ruling out *a priori* the possible importance of changes in taste broadly defined, or of increases in the incomes of other segments of the population. From this they draw the obvious implication that any changes in the standard of living of workers, and all others not counted among the landowners or the urban merchants who supplied them, 'would have had only a trivial impact on European import demand demand'.[78]

In short, the O&W model is tautological. For it is constructed in such a way that only the incomes of the rich are taken into account, which by definition rules out the possibility that these imported goods might have been bought up by mass consumers. And, in turn, this means, most problematically, that the notion that globalisation could have existed before 1828 is ruled out *tout court* from the outset in the O&W account.

The Eurocentric Myth of 'Noncompeting Monopoly' Imports into Europe: European Trade as the Measure of All Things Global?

The third major claim advanced by transformationalists, but most especially by O&W, is that these imported goods were *noncompeting*, insofar as none of these were produced in Europe, as much as European exports were noncompeting given that with the exception of (re-exported) silver, the rest were not produced in Afro-Asia. Accordingly, the critics' assumption is that the import (and export) trade in 'monopoly goods' signifies the point that there was a lack of market *competition* in transcontinental trade, which means that they imparted no impact propensity to invoke (as per O&W) 'the reshuffling of productive factors which leads to economy-wide distributional changes'.

The most immediate problem here is that ICTs, which were the major import item into Europe, clearly competed with domestic European textile producers, especially in Britain – which is precisely why they were targeted with very high tariffs and excises. But to the retort that ICTs were largely prohibited during much, if not all, of the eighteenth

---

[78] McCants (2007: 440).

century, I refer my reader back to the discussion of the previous section concerning their sale in Britain via smuggling and second-hand retail shops, as well as via theft. However, the critical point, as I explain in Chapter 10, is that it was the challenge of ICTs in terms of dominating global markets and threatening British domestic wool, silk and cotton producers that led the Lancashire producers and British inventors to undertake an intensive process of imitation which, in turn, promoted the transformation of the British economy into industrial capitalism. In the process, Britain underwent a fundamental shift in its comparative advantage away from wool into cotton textile production. And, as I also explain there, it was in part the context of global uneven and combined development, coupled with the Afro-Indian global cotton whip, which spurred on Britain's cotton-based industrialisation. Thus, if the impact of non-European imports is to be measured by their ability to promote the 'reshuffling of productive factors which [led] to economy-wide distributional changes', I can think of no other imported commodity in the last five hundred years that imparted such a transformative impact on Britain than ICTs. Moreover, as I argued in Chapters 3–6, ICTs were the key commodity that wove the FGE together and thereby contributed to the very process of global integration that O&W claim did not exist.

A further example is the importation of Chinese porcelain, given that this was imitated directly by the Dutch in their production of 'delftware',[79] notwithstanding various innovations that accompanied this imitation process and which led to the 'domestication' of these Asian products, not only in Europe but also across other parts of the world.[80] But, in turn, this propensity for imitation was a more generalised phenomenon in Britain, in which the British borrowed many non-European ideas, institutions and technologies, some of which I consider in Chapters 10 and 12 as well as elsewhere.[81] Which in turn means that looking for 'impact' only in terms of CPC is not the sole or even the major aspect of how the global economy shaped and reshaped societies in general and Britain in particular.

But the question now is whether the remaining imports were *noncompeting* and were, therefore, inconsequential both in terms of imparting impact on the European/British economies and contributing to the development of the FGE. The Eurocentric problem here is that the transformationalist/O&W lens is too narrowly calibrated on 'Europe at the centre'. And, as such, this means that it cannot pick up the *qualitative* point concerning the extremely high 'competitive impact' that everyday

---

[79] Finlay (1998), Styles (2000), de Zwart (2016: 61) and McCants (2007).
[80] Gerritsen and McDowall (2012).
[81] Hobson (2004: chs. 5–9).

ICTs as well as Chinese porcelain and Chinese and Indian silk textile imports imparted on British and Dutch producers. For when we widen our lens to survey the *global* scene, an altogether different picture emerges. Thus, while many, though by no means all, of the imports into Europe were indeed not produced there, they were, however, often produced in *competing* regions across the world.

Important here is that the price reductions that I discussed in the previous section were in part driven by global competition in most of these goods. Thus, the multiple centres of sugar production and exports from Taiwan, Java and the West Indies spurred on price reductions in Amsterdam and the convergence of global sugar prices.[82] Coffee too became subject to global competition. Being initially produced in Mocha in West Asia, subsequently the Dutch transplanted seedlings to Java which then became a major coffee producer. By the 1730s, some 75 per cent of coffee imports were sourced from Southeast Asia and only 25 per cent from Mocha. But then from the 1720s, coffee exports came on stream from French Réunion and especially from the West Indies such that by the 1750s, Asia supplied Europe with only a quarter of its coffee imports.[83] And, as have seen, porcelain was produced in China, of course, but later on in Japan, Holland and then Britain. Tea was produced mainly in China (with India only becoming a strong rival after the 1820s), which means that it was a monopoly good for most of the period of the FGE. Nevertheless, in the eighteenth century, competition between different European Companies operating in Guangzhou (Canton) became so fierce that it led to a considerable reduction in the price of the *Bohea* that was sold back in Europe,[84] as I noted earlier. What then of textiles?

Raw silk came from West Asia (Anatolia), as well as from India and China. Silk textiles too were produced in numerous areas within India, China and West Asia as well as in various European countries including Italy, France and Britain. Cotton textiles were produced in India of course, and also in China (with nankeens exported between 1760 and 1830), as well as in Southeast Asia, Africa, West Asia (especially in Anatolia), North Africa (Egypt) and in various European countries of course. And raw cotton was exported from Anatolia, Izmir and Thessaloniki (in the Ottoman Empire) as well as from India, the Americas and the West Indies. Indigo from Java competed with indigo produced in India and then later with West Indian indigo in the eighteenth century (note that indigo was a vital dye that was used on cotton textiles).

---

[82] de Zwart (2016: 65) and Rönnbäck (2009: 108–9).
[83] de Vries (2010: 721).
[84] Nierstrasz (2015).

Finally, although there were three monopoly spices – mace and nutmeg from the Moluccas and cinnamon from Ceylon – these, however, constitute the exception that proves the non-Eurocentric rule because they were marginal in volume after the 1660s and even before then the volumes of the everyday consumer product of pepper were larger. Thus, while spices and pepper comprised 75 per cent of Dutch trade in 1620, this figure declined to 33 per cent by 1670 and to 23 per cent by 1700;[85] though the proportion of the 'three' monopoly spices would be lower than this given that these figures include pepper.[86] Significantly, pepper was not a monopoly product as it was produced in significant amounts in Malabar (on the southwest coast of India) and in Southeast Asia (Java and Sumatra). Although the Dutch dominated the Southeast Asian pepper trade, nevertheless, like its Portuguese predecessor, the VOC was never able to dominate the Malabar pepper trade,[87] as I explained in Chapter 5. Noteworthy too is that when the VOC destroyed many clove trees in the Moluccas to force up the price in European markets in the mid-seventeenth century, merchants in various European countries turned to sourcing the cheaper substitute of clove-wood from Brazil.[88] Later on in the 1770s, the English and French smuggled out Moluccan clove seedlings and began clove production in East Africa and Southeast Asia. Although this competition only really kicked in during the early-nineteenth century, nevertheless as a consequence of these alternative sources of supply, the Dutch mark-up in clove prices declined from a factor of 25 in the mid-eighteenth century to 10 in 1800.[89] Which means, in fact, that there were only four monopoly items after the late-eighteenth century – mace, nutmeg, cinnamon and Chinese tea (though, as noted, the latter was rivalled by Indian tea from the 1820s onwards) – with the rest being produced in multiple competitive sites around the world.

All in all, something approximating global prices found its institutional place in Amsterdam as a result of global competition. As Glamann notes in relation to the commodity exchanges in Amsterdam:

yearly prices of colonial goods in this, the most important market place of northern Europe, mirror global trade conditions. This is a novel and momentous phenomenon seen in relation to the coastwise and more sporadic exchange of goods that typified earlier days. Now we see a regular flow of traffic through an

---

[85] Curtin (1984: 154).
[86] Unfortunately, I could find no discussion in the literature on the breakdown between pepper and spices in the VOC trade.
[87] de Zwart (2016: 68).
[88] Glamann (1958: 97–101).
[89] de Zwart (2016: 64).

immense network of trade routes that are linked together.... The beginnings of an international division of labour are established, or in the words of ... Dudley North, in 1691: 'The Whole World as to trade, is but one Nation or People, and therein Nations are as Persons'.[90]

Overall, then, the fact that most of the key products were not made in Europe is irrelevant given that they were produced in a *variety* of regions around the world and that they entered into competitive global and European markets. For we need to remind ourselves that the point of this whole exercise is to consider the wider global economy of which Europe was but a part, and whether competitive market relations existed in the world rather than solely within Europe.

In sum, the majority of the goods imported into Europe were bought in competitive Asian markets where European companies competed with each other, on the one hand, and with many more Asian merchants and different Asian producers on the other, all of which was discussed in Chapters 2–6. Thus, the existence of competing alternatives 'influenced the prices at which many Asian goods could be sold in Europe, limiting the "pricing [mark-up] power" of the trading companies [EICs]'.[91] In short, then, it turns out that the EICs 'were monopoly companies only in the sense that each one had exclusive access to its own national market';[92] though even there they faced competition from other European markets.[93] And this returns us to the point made above concerning the tendency of O&W to exaggerate the trading power of the EICs. That global competition existed and also affected price reductions led Pim de Zwart to conclude aptly:

it is therefore clear that, whether or not markets in Europe were perfectly integrated in the early modern period, the behaviour of prices for Asian commodities in Amsterdam—with the exception of [the three] monopoly spices—was influenced by prices in other cities, as well as the prices of similar goods brought into Amsterdam from elsewhere [i.e., Asia and the Americas].[94]

But to be clear, my argument here is not that changes in global supply and demand promoted CPC, but rather that the global trading commodities that entered Europe were competitive rather than noncompetitive.

---

[90] Glamann (1974: 451–2).
[91] de Vries (2010: 722).
[92] Ibid. (725).
[93] de Zwart (2016: 59).
[94] Ibid. (62).

The Twin Eurocentric Myths of Administered Prices and the European Company Trading Monopoly over the Market Laws of Supply/Demand

Given their (mistaken) assumption that trading goods were noncompetitive and monopolistic in nature, then logically transformationalists and O&W presume the absence of *competitive* laws of supply and demand in favour of a system of monopoly or administered prices. Here, one detects the whiff of the old Eurocentric trope of Oriental despotism and the Eurocentric/Eurofetishist premise of the monopolistic hyper-power of the EICs, wherein these various actors and states ensured that prices were controlled. But this is one of the greatest of all Eurofetishist/Eurocentric myths because it exaggerates the power of the EICs as much as it misreads the major Asian states. For the latter did much to promote the presence of competitive laws of supply and demand, as much as the EICs were largely unable to buck these laws, despite their very best efforts – as I explained in Chapters 2–6 and to which I return later.

As for the EICs, certainly, a hard test case for my argument is that of Melaka, given that it was allegedly dominated by the Portuguese after 1511 and the Dutch after 1641, both of whom are thought to have monopolised Asian trade. But even here it turns out that the Portuguese and Dutch were unable to dominate much Southeast Asian trade because *ad lib* (i.e., monopolistic) price-fixing proved impossible to maintain. Phillip Curtin describes one of the vital commercial institutions that emerged in Asia – a system of 'collective price bargaining' – which occurred between merchants and their hosts. He cites the discussion by the famous sixteenth century Portuguese apothecary, Tomé Pires, who described this system in terms of the example of Melaka in the early-sixteenth century, 'the final price agreed was "done orderly, so that they did not favour the merchant from the [incoming] ship, nor did he go away displeased; for the law and the prices in Malacca were well-known"'.[95] And, as Curtin also notes, '[w]hen price fixing was attempted by Portuguese merchants [in Melaka], the incoming [Asian] ship usually did a side-deal—this proved the rule in these situations'.[96] While this system was something less than 'perfect competition', given that the owner of the imported merchandise bargained with a limited number of local merchants (between ten and twenty), nevertheless it stopped well short of an 'administered' or imposed 'monopoly' price system. In sum, Luis Thomaz notes of the Melakan trade practice that '[f]or

---

[95] Pires cited in Curtin (1984: 133).
[96] Curtin (1984: 134).

the most part prices were fixed by the [proximate] laws of supply and demand'.[97] And this is reinforced by the fact that customs tariffs were kept purposefully low in Melaka, possibly to a maximum of 5 per cent; a point I return to in the next section.

Most significantly, as noted earlier, the Melakan case reflects the wider situation in the Indian Ocean trading system around 1500. But thereafter, competitive laws of supply and demand became more fully autonomous. For a key reason why the Europeans were unable to dominate Asian trade was precisely due to the presence of proximate global prices, which were informed by competitive laws of supply and demand – a point which, once again, reflects the robustness of the FGE. Indeed, as John Wills notes, 'Europeans traded in ports and markets ruled by Asians, where they could not exclude or distort the competition of Asians and other Europeans and prices were set [mainly] by market forces,'[98] all of which I discussed in Chapters 2–5.

The core Eurocentric problem with characterising European trade as based on monopolies is that it exaggerates the role played by the EICs in the Indian Ocean system. For this not only conjures away the element of competition that the Europeans faced from Asian traders but equally, it whitewashes the fact that in the game of competition it was the Asians who generally won out. This is reinforced by the point that there were times when the laws of supply and demand were broken by strong Asian agents such as Virji Vora and Abdul Ghafur, who sometimes dumped large amounts of a particular product on Indian markets in order to undermine the selling price that the Europeans would receive for their sales of the relevant product. Nevertheless, these were largely the exception to the non-Eurocentric rule that the 'bulk of Asian products or markets were never subject to [a sustained] monopoly, or controlled in any other way'.[99] Accordingly, if the presence of commodity competition and competitive laws of supply and demand are the sign of a global economy, then the period of 1500–1850 would seem to confirm its presence – a point that I return to at the end of the next section. But all of this is obscured by transformationalists and O&W because they buy into the twin Eurocentric myths of Oriental despotic states and the EICs' monopoly of trade.

In turn, this means that transformationalists and O&W have been looking in the wrong place for signs of a global economy in the 1500–1850 period. For the rest of the world was even more integrated into

---

[97] Thomaz (1993: 72).
[98] Wills (1993: 134).
[99] Van Santen (1991: 88).

the global economy than was Europe – which means, once again, that treating European trade as *the* measure of globalisation occludes this wider picture. All in all, using the very threshold criteria that are offered by transformationalists and O&W, I have demonstrated in this first section that Europe's external links were not only sufficiently extensive and intensive but that global linkages and flows imparted significant transformative impact upon European and non-European societies in manifold ways. Moreover, I have also made the case for a broader conception of 'impact' to O&W's highly delimited one of CPC.

Confronting the Ahistorical Eurocentric Temporal Binary (II): The Presence of Tariff Protectionism, Warfare and Irrational Institutions before 1828/1945 and Their Absence Thereafter?

Having dealt with the numerous issues that surround the specific *nature* of the commodity trade into Europe from Asia and the Americas, I now turn to consider the second part of the transformationalist and O&W critiques. This concerns their arguments about how various institutional and technological factors promoted (thick) economic globalisation only after 1828 (O&W) or after 1945 (transformationalism). For O&W, the fact is that CPC is merely a symptom of a larger portfolio of independent variables that are responsible for global integration, all of which function to reduce 'transaction costs'. As noted in the first section, O&W argue that between 1500 and 1828 government regulations, especially tariffs on imports as well as transport costs, remained far too high to enable global economic integration – a problem compounded by the disruption that was caused by the prevalence of inter-state imperial wars. But in the nineteenth century, they argue, all this changed almost over-night in world-historical terms, with the emergence of first, the 'Hundred Years' Peace' after 1815; second, significant trade liberalisation after 1828 and third, the lowering of oceanic transport costs. For these, in aggregate, enabled a unique world-historical jump into globalisation.

By critically interrogating these claims I aim to show, much as I did in the last section, that a non-Eurocentric approach can reveal how economic globalisation emerged after 1500 rather than after 1828/1945. And I reinforce this claim by pointing to various factors that significantly enabled the reduction in transaction costs which, curiously, are ignored both by transformationalists and O&W. Once again, the core problem lies in the imputation of an ahistorical Eurocentric temporal binary in which the pre- and post-1828 periods are presented as polar opposites. For in this binary conception, the pre-1828 era is (re)presented as more state-regulated and violent than it was while the post-1828 period is (re)presented as more laissez-faire and peaceful than it has been.

The Eurocentric Myth of Tariff Protectionism before 1828 and Free Trade Thereafter

The first main argument advanced by O&W is that it was the sudden onset of trade liberalisation after 1828 in Britain and thence the rapid shift to 'free trade' in Europe that promoted global economic integration in the nineteenth century. However, I argue that the notion of a great trade regime divide that separated the protectionist era before 1828 from its free trade successor is a Eurocentric myth for a number of reasons, not the least of which is that this occludes the situation in the non-Western world. While very high tariffs on imports existed in Europe between 1685 and 1860, it is the low levels of tariffs that existed across much of the non-Western world that catches the eye. Still, this is not to say that there was an absence of trade regulations and restrictions in play, which in the second half of the eighteenth century included not least Japan's restrictions on the outflow of specie, China's regulations that restricted European traders to Guangzhou and Mysore's mercantilism under Haidar Ali and Tipu Sultan. But as I argued in Chapter 2, average tariffs on foreign imports into China after 1684 were about 6 per cent. Moreover, average tariffs on all Indian imports into Central Asia, Safavid Persia and the Ottoman Empire were in the range of 3–5 per cent – much as average tariffs on imports into the Mughal Empire were kept at similar rates.[100] More generally, the Ottoman state ensured that taxes on all trade were kept to a minimum, relying instead on land taxes to fund the central state,[101] as was the case in Mughal India and China. But what of the trading hubs beyond the major Asian states?

In the Asian port cities/emporia such as Aden, Hormuz, Calicut, Melaka, Acheh, Bantam and Makassar, to name but a few, tariffs were kept very low as part of an explicit strategy to attract foreign trade. Rulers there were keenly aware of the 'exit threat' that merchants could invoke if trade was over-taxed,[102] though this also held for the rulers of the Central Asian Uzbek Khanates, Safavid Persia, the Ottoman Empire and Mughal India.[103] As William McNeill puts it,

---

[100] See also Yazdani (2017: 487) and Pearson (1991: 56, 97).
[101] Parthasarathi (2011: 131–3).
[102] Pearson (1991: 70–1).
[103] Wink (1988: 57).

[Asian] [r]ulers ... were simply unable to dominate behavior ... [M]erchants made themselves useful to rulers and subjects alike and could now safeguard themselves against confiscatory taxation and robbery by finding refuge in one or another port of call along the caravan routes and seaways, where local rulers had learned not to overtax the trade upon which their income and power had come to depend.[104]

Michael Pearson rightly notes of the Asian rulers in the many port cities that the 'crucial element in the encouragement [of trade] was the very existence of free[r] markets, which were precisely not embedded in any political system but rather operated free from political interference'.[105] And Chaudhuri claims that '[t]he Indian Ocean emporia ... were markets in every sense'.[106]

More generally, notwithstanding important forms of regulation and restrictions, numerous scholars have claimed that freer trade – with an approximate average tariff of 5 per cent – was the norm in the Asian world between 1500 and 1850.[107] Such a trading posture complements the point I made earlier concerning the presence of competitive laws of supply and demand across Asia. All of which, in sum, dismantles the standard Eurocentric conception of the major Asian states as but Oriental despotisms that taxed trade and merchants out of existence. But it is equally noteworthy that before 1789 – the year when the newly formed United States of America turned to very low levels of protectionism, mainly to raise federal government tax revenues[108] – the (North) Atlantic system was also based largely on low levels of tariffs. Curiously, though, the deep irony here is that Williamson is well aware of the picture that I have presented here. For as he put it elsewhere with his co-author, David Clingingsmith, while Britain protected local textile producers nevertheless 'Parliament kept the [North] Atlantic economy as a competitive free trade zone. [Moreover] the large Indian Ocean market was also a free trade zone, and India had dominated this for centuries'.[109]

But the deepest irony here is that it was Europe, not Afro-Asia, which turned to protectionism during the FGE. As I explained in Chapter 2, Britain moved increasingly to very high levels of protectionism after 1684. Having levied an average tariff rate of a mere 5 per cent before 1684, which was likely in line with the Asian norm, thereafter it escalated upwards.[110]

[104] McNeill (1982: 53–4).
[105] Pearson (1991: 74).
[106] Chaudhuri (1985: 224).
[107] Balachandran and Subrahmanyam (2005: 30) and de Zwart (2016: 74).
[108] Hobson (1997: 150–1).
[109] Clingingsmith and Williamson (2005: 212, n. 5).
[110] Davis (1966).

In the long British industrialisation phase (1700–1850), average tariffs were probably around six times the levels that were levied in Asia and some eight times higher in the first half of the nineteenth century. Thus, the first problem with the O&W argument is that it universalises the European experience when it turned out to be the provincial protectionist exception. This, of course, does not change the point that integrating Europe into the FGE was to an extent muted by the effects of European tariff protectionism according to O&W logic, though its effects should not be overplayed given that trade continued to enter Europe from Asia and the Americas both legally and illegally. But by O&W logic, the fact that much of the rest of the world engaged in freer trade means that integration must, at least to a certain extent, have been promoted there. Accordingly, when we provincialise the European trade regime rather than universalise it, so the wider global integrative process comes to the fore. And, this in turn, dissolves O&W's Eurocentric temporal binary construct of a protectionist world before 1828 and a freer trading one thereafter.

Drilling down further, we encounter a second major problem with the O&W argument, which concerns the general claim that Europe moved to free trade after 1828. Here, the Eurocentric temporal binary raises its head once more. Ironically, this claim is reinforced by IR/IPE hegemonic stability theorists who assert that it was Britain that guided Europe into free trade.[111] But Europe only started to move towards free trade as late as 1860 following the Cobden-Chevalier Treaty of that year. And, moreover, the era of so-called European free trade was remarkable only for its brevity, lasting about two decades before the continent reverted back to moderate protectionism. Furthermore, this was not a free but a *freer* trade interlude (where tariffs on all imports averaged about 8 per cent), sandwiched as it was between an era of extremely high levels of European protectionism before then and one of moderate protectionism thereafter (of about 11 per cent). And, far from driving the European shift to freer trade, it is notable that Britain did very little to promote it.[112]

But surely, as received wisdom tells us, even if the British state did little to promote freer trade in Europe, it is undeniable that it progressively liberalised its own trade regime after 1825 such that by 1846, it had achieved free trade.[113] Here, we confront the third major problem with the O&W argument. For the fact is that while average British tariff rates (i.e., average tariff rates on *all* imports) had risen to very high levels during the late-seventeenth and eighteenth centuries, nevertheless rather

---

[111] Krasner (1976) and Gilpin (1981: 135, 1987).
[112] Hobson (1997: 200–1) and Lacher and Germann (2012).
[113] O'Rourke and Williamson (2002a: 40).

than trending down thereafter in a long-term liberalisation trajectory that culminated in the Repeal of the Corn Laws in 1846, it turns out that after the 1790s British tariff rates 'became so much more severe in weight and effect ... that they constituted virtually a new [ultra-protectionist] system'.[114] Thus, while average British tariff rates stood as high as 25 per cent in 1715–95,[115] they jumped to a very substantial 40 per cent in 1796/1845. More specifically, tariffs stood at an average rate of 44 per cent (1811/20) having been 37 per cent (1801/10), before rising again to a colossal 50 per cent (1821/30).[116] It is true that rates came down in the 1830s, but the assumption that they went into free fall thereafter remains problematic. For they were still as high as 33 per cent in 1841/5 on the very eve of the repeal of the Corn Laws (1846) – a figure that was about 70 per cent higher than the famous American Smoot-Hawley Tariff of 1930,[117] which is generally reckoned to be one of the most protectionist acts ever passed. And, as I noted in Chapter 2, they were also higher than the average tariff rate of the Tsarist Russian state during its industrialisation phase (1880–1913), which is generally reckoned to be the most protectionist of the European industrialisers.[118] Moreover, while O&W support their trade liberalisation argument by stating that as early as 1825 some 1,100 tariff acts were repealed, this misses the point that as late as 1840, tariffs were placed on no less than 1,146 items.[119] Of note, too, is that the Repeal of the Corn Laws in 1846 might well not have occurred had it not been for the contingency of the Irish potato famine.

In sum, while O&W utilise the neoclassical Heckscher-Ohlin model of trade regime change, which utilises a 'factors of production' analysis, I argue that bar the cases of corn/grain, cotton textile and iron imports where production and class factors were highly important, the major driver behind Britain's deepening protectionist trade regime between 1685 and 1846 was the need for tax revenues to fund the state's imperial wars (as I explain in Chapter 9 as well as in Chapter 2).

This leads onto the fourth problem, which in one important respect is germane to the O&W argument, that even 1846 did not quite mark the turning point of British free trade. Average British tariffs still stood at a substantial 20 per cent in 1846/60 (which approximates with the American Smoot-Hawley Tariff Act of June 1930), remained

---

[114] Imlah (1958: 115).
[115] Calculated from O'Brien (1988: 9).
[116] Calculated from Imlah (1958: 121).
[117] See US Department of Commerce (1975: 888). Note that the US figure is average tariffs on *all* imports, which is the correct procedure for measuring tariff rates.
[118] Gerschenkron (1962).
[119] Imlah (1958: 148) and Davis (1966: 310–11).

moderately significant at 10 per cent in 1861/80 and only dropped to a low of 6 per cent as late as 1881/1913.[120] In fairness, though, these were pure *revenue tariffs* that were applied mainly to colonial imports such that they had no *protectionist* rationale since these items were not produced in Britain. But while this might appear to confirm the O&W thesis, nevertheless the paradox is that these rates undermine their argument about global integration, given that these high tariffs were levied on everyday consumption products and would, therefore, have impacted negatively on working-class consumption. Recall that for both transformationalists and O&W, only when *all* classes within society benefit from the consumption of imported goods can the presence of global economic integration be confirmed. And the main paradox here is that Britain constitutes the best-case scenario for the O&W and transformationalist thesis, given that most other European countries moved back to moderate protectionism after about 1880.

So where does all this leave us with respect to O&W's key claim that an autarkic model applies to the 1565–1828 period while an open economic model applies to the 1828–1936 era?[121] The fact is that freer trade only emerged properly in the West in the 1980s and even then there remained all manner of barriers to agricultural imports. Accordingly, the temporal binary that the O&W construct with respect to protectionism before 1828 and free trade thereafter should be reframed as one of ultra-high European protectionism before 1828 and moderate-to-high protectionism from the 1880s up to the 1980s, as much as low tariffs were the norm in Asia between 1500 and 1900. This is significant because it unsettles a major component of their argument. Recall that for O&W, reduced trade barriers comprise a key causal property of global integration, whereas *trade linkages* between regions do not. This means, as I mentioned earlier, that while Europe developed relatively strong trading linkages with Asia and the Americas but remained protectionist, so by O&W logic Europe should have remained *outside* of the global economy throughout the nineteenth century and even up to the 1980s. It also means, given their exaggerated focus on European trade, that globalisation more generally could not have occurred in the nineteenth century. Given that this was clearly not the case, then 'impactful trade linkages' that I have described in this and Chapters 2–5 might be a more appropriate indicator of global economic integration than is the (relative) absence of trade barriers.

---

[120] Calculated from the data in Imlah (1958), O'Brien (1991) and Mitchell (2011).
[121] O'Rourke and Williamson (2002a: 40–4).

The Eurocentric Myth of Imperial Warfare before 1815 and Peace Thereafter

To recall, the second core aspect of the O&W thesis concerning the non-integration of Asian/American trade with Europe before 1828 and its integration thereafter is explained by the predominance of pronounced international military conflict before 1815 while peace ensued thereafter up to 1914. Once again, the problem with the Eurocentric temporal binary construction becomes apparent. For the reality is that imperial wars did not recede after 1815 but if anything intensified in geographical scope. Thus, the British state was involved in wars in Abyssinia (Ethiopia), Afghanistan, Argentina, the Ashanti Empire (Ghana), Brazil, Burma, Canada, Ceylon, China, Egypt, Jamaica, Japan, New Zealand, Nigeria, North America, the Ottoman Empire, the Persian Gulf, South Africa, Zulu Kingdom and Zanzibar. And none of this includes the numerous wars that the EEIC in India was involved in. True, the leading imperial power, Britain, spent very much lower amounts on such wars after 1815, as did all other European imperial powers. But this was in significant part because the British were able to rely on the Indian army to fight many of them on their behalf.[122] And, no less important is the point that it was the Indian taxpayer that financed the Indian army. Accordingly, we should ask what Britain's military burden might have been had the Indian army not been used as the vanguard of British imperial expansion. For this gives us an insight into the reality of imperial military spending in the wider world beyond Europe.

On the basis of a very crude back-of-the-envelope set of calculations, I reckon that Britain's military burden could have risen from 3.1 per cent of national income in 1870–1913 to possibly somewhere around 8 or 9 per cent.[123] And this could have increased the total burden that

---

[122] Washbrook (1990: 480–1) and Yazdani (2017: 566–7).

[123] I made the above calculations on the following basis. In 1859, the Indian government spent as much as half of that spent by the British government on military expenditures for home defence (Richards 2012: 427) and Mitchell (2011: 588). And by 1876, the figures might have been on an approximate par. Extrapolating these figures out, I calculate that the British military burden (D1) of 3.1 per cent of national income (1870–1913) could have risen to around 5 or 6 per cent had the British army taken on the role that the Indian army performed on behalf of the British empire. Note that D1 refers to ordinary and extraordinary military spending. However, given that Indian troops were paid far less than those in the British army so this differential also needs to be factored in. If British soldiers had been paid the same amount as their Russian counterparts, this would have reduced British military spending by as much as 40 per cent – i.e., by 1.3 per cent of national income, 1903–13 (Hobson 1993: 488–93). And Indian wages were likely even lower than Russian. Accordingly, if we factor this in by increasing the British burden by say 50 per cent (instead of 40 per cent), this would take the final British burden up from 5 or 6 per cent to somewhere around 8 or 9 per cent of national income.

the average British taxpayer would have shouldered to somewhere in the region of an extra 60–75 per cent – clearly a large sum. By way of comparison, this was possibly higher than Britain's (D1) military burden of 7.5 per cent in its long industrialisation phase (1715–1850). And notably, Britain's was by far and away the most militarised industrialisation undertaken in Europe, given that D1 was twice as high as the average burden of the European great powers during their industrialisation phases.[124] Moreover, this figure was likely slightly higher than Britain's average military burden (D1) for 1914–80, which, of course, included two world wars, as I explain in Chapter 9.

The wider point, though, is not simply that the Indian army and taxpayer shouldered the burden of Britain's military expansion across Asia but, more generally, that the price of relative peace in Europe between 1815 and 1914 was paid for either directly or indirectly by the non-Western peoples. That is, Europe's imperial wars were outsourced to the non-Western world. Thus, the appearance of peace after 1815 can be maintained only through a narrow lens that is focused solely on Europe. In this way, a Eurocentric sleight of hand ensures that Europe's imperial wars in the non-Western world are conjured away into thin air. And precisely the same point applies to the post-1945 Cold War era, given that the price of maintaining peace between the United States and USSR within the West was the similar outsourcing of wars into the Third World. Thus, the Eurocentric slippage in the O&W approach entails their move to universalise the intra-Western experience of peace between 1815 and 1914 as well as after 1945, such that it fails to see the *continuity* in global imperial/neo-imperial warfare throughout both periods. All of which means that if peace was not a global good throughout the 1500–2000 period, then by O&W logic there could have been no global integration in the nineteenth or twentieth centuries. My simple point is that international peace *cannot* be a key factor in the promotion of globalisation and the global economy. For, in the wider world beyond Europe, imperial warfare was a constant throughout the nineteenth century at the very time that O&W claim that globalisation came into existence.

Problematising the Issue of Transport Costs and the Eurocentric Assumption of Asia's 'Irrational' Economic Institutions

Finally, O&W's third causal variable that supposedly led to global integration after 1828 is the reduction in transport costs. It is certainly true that they declined significantly in this period when compared

---

[124] Hobson (1993).

with the previous era. But once again we encounter the whiff of yet another ahistorical Eurocentric temporal binary. For what O&W look for – following Russell Menard – is the specific sign of a 'transport revolution' based on technological changes such as the one that occurred after 1869 when iron steamships, telegraphs and the opening of the Suez Canal radically undermined the 'tyranny of distance'. When viewed through this lens, the pre-1830 period is indeed bereft of such a revolution. But equally, we find that transport costs *did* come down in the seventeenth and eighteenth centuries, even if this was largely a function of improvements in the packing of goods, as well as ships taking shorter routes, coupled with the reduction in crew sizes.[125]

Paradoxically, I point to the arguments made by Russell Menard to support my case here. For the above-mentioned factors led to tobacco transport costs from the American colonies dropping from 3d per lb in 1620 to less than half a penny per lb in 1750.[126] Equally, Menard charts a significant drop in freight charges for American rice imports in the eighteenth century, though he also notes that transport costs in sugar remained stable throughout the period.[127] Moreover, he claims that other goods from the Americas also enjoyed declines in their transportation costs such that from the 1480s to the 1620s, the general freight index fell at a considerable annual rate of 1.2 per cent per annum. But these disappear from view in the O&W argument because they did not occur as a direct function of a *transport revolution*. Surely what matters, however, is the fact of declining transport costs whatever their source or cause might be? Certainly, the much more significant decline in transport costs in the late-nineteenth century brought on by the transport revolution led to an *intensification* of global integration, but it did not create the global economy. For this merely reflects the point that the second global economy (SGE), which emerged in the second half of the nineteenth century, enjoyed higher extensity, intensity and velocity than did the FGE. Or as Pim de Zwart puts it, 'the entering of a new phase of globalization [in the nineteenth century], as revolutionary as it might seem, does not alter the reality of the globalization that came before'.[128]

However, what is particularly surprising here is that one would fully anticipate neoclassical economists such as O&W to consider how *transaction costs* were reduced by *institutional* innovations. Such an argument was originally made famous by Douglass North,[129] and more

---

[125] Glamann (1974: 452–3).
[126] Menard (1991: 254).
[127] Ibid. (264–9).
[128] de Zwart (2016: 197).
[129] North (1991) and North and Thomas (1973).

recently by Daron Acemoglu.[130] It is true that there were no centralised global institutions during the FGE as there have been during the SGE. But I argue that they did not have to exist given that numerous shared economic institutions were present across the world after 1500. That rational economic institutions are thought to have been absent in Afro-Asia before the nineteenth century merely reflects the Eurocentrism of the transformationalist and O&W approaches. For as I show in Chapter 8, there was a wide array of rational economic institutions throughout the non-Western world that supported global trade as well as enabling the production upon which this rested. According to Kirti Chaudhuri, the vast array of small ports and caravan emporia constituted

the valve that regulated the flow of trans-regional trade in Eurasia. It supplied commercial services in all forms: brokers able to enter into contracts guaranteeing deliveries of trade goods at a future date, markets supplying them on the spot, and bankers who smoothed out payments through the mechanism of credit and bills of exchange. Local mints, dockyards, and shipping—and in the case of caravan towns, transport animals and their forage and stabling—all these essential components of the overall machinery were brought together in the urban centres.[131]

All of which reveals that there were sufficiently rational economic institutions throughout the FGE to enable the reduction of 'transaction costs', thereby enabling global integration.

Conclusion

The *modus operandi* of this chapter has been to demonstrate the globality of the FGE by using the very same criteria that transformationalists and O&W deploy to reject its existence. Such a paradoxical finding occurs through the transposition of their criteria into a non-Eurocentric historical–sociological framework. Moreover, I argue that the final definition of globalisation that transformationalism settles upon – bar the category of high velocity – can be applied equally to the era of the FGE; to wit, globalisation constitutes

a process (or set of processes) which embodies a transformation in the spatial organization of social relations and transactions—assessed in terms of their extensity, intensity ... and impact—generating transcontinental or interregional flows and networks of activity, interaction, and the exercise of power.[132]

---

[130] Acemoglu et al. (2005).
[131] Chaudhuri (1985: 181).
[132] Held et al. (1999: 16).

And, while high levels of velocity of global flows were indeed missing before the 1870s, their presence thereafter reflects merely the intensification, rather than the inception point, of globalisation.

This, in turn, means that I also endorse the definition of globalisation that is advanced by Flynn and Giráldez: '[g]lobalization began when all heavily populated land masses initiated sustained interaction [i.e., significant *intensity*] – both directly with each other and indirectly via other land masses – in a manner that deeply and permanently linked them [i.e., significant *extensity*]'.[133] And this definition is completed when they argue that *global* trade, which they take as a core dimension of globalisation, emerged when 'all heavily populated land masses began to exchange products continuously [and they] did so in values sufficient to generate lasting impacts on all trading partners [i.e., high impact propensity]'.[134] All of which speaks directly to transformationalism's conceptual thresholds of extensity, intensity and impact propensity though not, of course, velocity.

There is also the generic problem of Eurocentrism that underpins the frameworks of O&W and transformationalism. For locating globalisation's origins to the nineteenth century or after 1945/73 reflects an inherent Eurocentrism because these were the periods when the West was either emerging as dominant or was clearly dominant. As such, they buy into the claim that only the West was sufficiently powerful to create a global economy. But, as I have argued in Chapters 2–6, non-Western actors in aggregate constituted a significant driving force of the FGE after 1500. And, moreover, the creation of the SGE was to an important, though by no means complete, extent enabled by non-Western influences and pressures. The ultimate significance of Asia and the Atlantic in the FGE was that, in effect, they constituted if not the womb within which Europe's later global-industrial hegemony gestated throughout this period, then at least the midwives in the birth of modern European capitalism. Which, in turn, points up significant impact propensity that satisfies the core litmus test for the presence of the FGE – all of which is revealed in Parts III through V, given that they focus in part on the global context within which modern Western capitalism and the SGE were born.

---

[133] Flynn and Giráldez (2008: 369, and see 2006: 235).
[134] Flynn and Giráldez (2006: 235).

8 Countering the Eurocentric Rejection of the First Global Economy (II)
Unveiling Global Historical Capitalism

Introduction

While the arguments of Chapter 7 might persuade some sceptics of the presence of a global economy before the arrival of modern capitalism in the nineteenth century, they will not persuade many a Marxist reader. For most Marxists, a global economy can only be said to exist once modern industrial capitalism had emerged in Europe and later in the United States, and only once it had diffused outwards to culturally and economically convert the world according to the isomorphic Western property of capitalist social relations of production. Accordingly, a '*global* economy' exhibiting commercial relations resting on an agrarian production base is simply a non-sequitur. And, in any case, commercial capitalism is deemed by most neo-Marxists to be ontologically secondary and residual to – i.e., it is produced and determined solely by – capitalist social relations of production such that it is relegated to the rump 'sphere of circulation'. Yet a further reason why Marxists insist that modern capitalism is the vital pre-requisite for globalisation and a global economy is that only the capitalist mode of production (MOP) can impart a 'globally impactful' process via the 'capitalist whip of external necessity'. For orthodox and fundamentalist Marxists, no such global whip existed before about 1850, given the absence of modern global industrial capitalism. In sum, then, what preceded 1850 was, at best, only weakly global commercial linkages that, by definition, were not properly capitalist given that supposedly only agrarian relations of production existed. All of which culminates in the conclusion that a global economy could not have existed before the mid-nineteenth century.

My reply to this orthodox Marxist dismissal of the first global economy (FGE) is undertaken in two stages. First, this chapter argues that orthodox neo-Marxists have largely failed to recognise the existence of global 'historical capitalism' between 1500 and 1850. And the irony here is that I draw *inter alia* on a string of neo-Marxists as well as Karl Marx to make my case. Second, in Chapter 14, I summarise a key structural property of the FGE, that of the global Afro-Indian cotton whip that was linked to Indian structural power. Most importantly, because in what follows I argue that the FGE and its historical capitalist base were underpinned to a certain extent by modern capitalist properties, this early global economy likely meets the Marxist threshold criterion to qualify as 'global'. Certainly, it dispenses with the likely Marxist dismissal that before 1800 the world was founded on an agrarian productive base and a thinly spread set of global commercial trading relations. And here, I pay particular, albeit not exclusive, attention to the hybrid historical capitalist MOP within which the principal global commodities were produced.

This chapter is divided into four sections, the section 'Navigating the Conceptual Maze of Fundamentalist Marxism (I): Defining Modern Capitalism' undertakes some conceptual brush-clearing work vis-à-vis various conceptual problems that I have with 'fundamentalist Marxism' – specifically its heavily reductive conception of capitalism and the MOP. The section 'Navigating the Conceptual Maze of Fundamentalist Marxism (II): Defining Historical Capitalism' conceptualises historical capitalism, while the section 'The First Layer of Historical Capitalism: Part-Modern/Part Agrarian Social Relations of Production and Pre-industrial Technologies' focuses on how the principal global trading commodities were produced within the historical capitalist MOP. The section 'The Second Layer of Global Historical Capitalism: Modern Rational Capitalist Economic Institutions' reveals the rational commercial and financial institutions of historical capitalism, in the absence of which global trade could not have existed. And finally, I conclude the chapter with a very brief summary of global trade, which reprises much of the analysis of Chapters 2 through 7 in order to complete my analysis of global historical capitalism.

Navigating the Conceptual Maze of Fundamentalist Marxism (I): Defining Modern Capitalism

My task in what follows is not to undermine the Marxist analysis of capitalism but rather to produce a more sophisticated conception that draws on various modern scholars, who include Jairus Banaji, Maxime Rodinson, Fernand Braudel, Alex Anievas and Kerem Nişancioğlu, Sébastien Rioux, Genevieve LeBaron, Peter Verovšek and others, while also drawing on Karl Marx.

Confronting the 'Fundamentalist Marxist'
Reductive Conception of the Capitalist MOP

While the advantage of orthodox 'fundamentalist Marxism' is that it has a very clearly defined and precise conception of capitalism and the global economy, paradoxically this strength reflects one of its greatest weaknesses (in addition to its Eurocentrism). As I explain further in Chapter 10, my issue with the fundamentalist neo-Marxist approach – most especially that of Political Marxism – lies not in its reductive 'base-superstructure model' as is the complaint of neo-Weberians,[1] but in its quadruply reductive conception of the MOP. For the essential definition of modern capitalism, according to Political Marxists reduces down to the social relations of production which in turn are defined purely as free wage labour versus capital. While I shall interrogate this narrow definition of the social relations of production in the next section, here I want to stand back and advance my alternative complex definition of capitalism. In essence, my conception of *capitalisms* (historical and modern) has four key components:

1. Forces of production: technologies;
2. Hybrid social relations of production;
3. Rational economic institutions;
4. Global trade.

In what follows, I shall consider three of these points, leaving the second for the next section.

The first occlusion of modern fundamentalist Marxism lies in its downplaying, if not eradication, of the role that mechanised technologies play as a causal factor in defining and making possible modern industrial capitalism. Indeed, it seems like a very long time ago now, back when I was an undergraduate student in fact, when Gerry Cohen's defence of Marx appeared, in which he focuses on the important role that technologies/forces of production play in modern capitalism.[2] Since then, the 'forces of production' appear to have quietly blipped off the neo-Marxist conceptual radar scanner. However, technologies – or the *means/forces* of production – are not only key defining components of the MOP but they were also as important for Karl Marx as were the *relations* of production. Indeed, in his famous 1859 'Preface to the Critique of Political Economy', Marx even went so far as to assert that technologies

---

[1]   Giddens (1985) and Mann (1986).
[2]   Cohen (1980).

are the motor of development to which social relations follow and adapt,[3] as he also argued in *The Communist Manifesto*.[4]

A further occlusion of fundamentalist Marxism lies in the presence of a plethora of rational economic and legal institutions that are essential for the development of capitalism and global trade, which will be discussed more later. My reader might detect a Weberian influence here. But, in fact, I side with Fernand Braudel as well as Maxime Rodinson, who place much emphasis on the role of rational capitalist economic institutions in *historical* as well as modern capitalism. For Weber, rational economic institutions were created solely within Europe and are germane only to modern capitalism. But I argue that many of the key rational economic institutions were pioneered by Indians and West Asian Muslims (a good number of which might well have been copied or borrowed by the Italians after about 1000 CE). Moreover, these rational institutions were designed not only to support global trade but also to enable lending and credit. And here, it is notable that global historical capitalism did not simply rest on a thin commercialism and small-scale merchant pedlars operating across the non-Western world. Indian foreign merchants, for example, likely earned more income by lending money to producers and states than they did from trading in Indian goods. In East Africa, they financed mortgages that Africans and Portuguese took out on landed property, while in Central Asia, they advanced credit for local agricultural production, the yields from which they sold in the market place.

A further occlusion is that of global trade, which was as important to historical capitalism as it is to modern capitalism. Here, I anticipate the fundamentalist Marxist response that I am merely straying into a kind of defunct 'neo-Smithian Marxism' given my highlighting (*inter alia*) of global trade, as Robert Brenner would no doubt argue. But it is important to appreciate that my claims are not only consistent with those made by Braudel, Rodinson and Banaji, but they are also, I believe, very much in the spirit of Karl Marx's approach. Thus, while most neo-Marxists have generally dismissed the causal significance of *world* or *global* trade in the rise of British industrial capitalism – as, most ironically, did Wallerstein[5] – no less ironically, Marx argued *for it*. As he put it in the first volume of *Capital*:

[t]he production of commodities, their circulation, and that more developed form of their circulation called commerce, these form the historical ground-work from which [capital] rises. The modern history of capital dates from the

---

[3] Marx (1859/1977: 389) and Cohen (1980). See also Davidson (2012).
[4] Marx and Engels (1848/1977: 85).
[5] On this, see Hobson (2012: 236–42).

creation in the 16th century of a world-embracing commerce and a world-embracing market.[6]

Or, as the unorthodox neo-Marxist International Relations/International Political Economy scholar, Burak Tansel, puts it more pithily, 'the world market itself forms the basis for [the capitalist] mode of production'.[7]

Nevertheless, at this point, the likely fundamentalist Marxist defence would be to quote Marx's well-known claim that merchant capital's place in 'proto-industrialisation' did *not* lead on into modern industrial capitalism in Britain. This pivots on the well-known passage in *Capital*, Volume III, where Marx confronts the 'proto-industrialisation thesis' by arguing that where

the [proto-industrial] merchant establishes direct sway over production himself.... however much this serves historically as a stepping stone—witness the English 17th-century clothier, who brings the weavers, independent as they are, under his control by selling the [raw material] to them and buying their cloth—it cannot by itself contribute to the overthrow of the old [feudal] mode of production, but tends rather to preserve and retain it as its precondition.[8]

It is true that Alex Anievas and Kerem Nişancioğlu have unearthed the claim made by Marx in the first volume of *Capital* where he argued that there *is* a relationship between merchant capitalist proto-industrialisation and the rise of industrial capitalism.[9] But this is not the precise issue at stake here, notwithstanding the point that I see no link between proto-industrialisation and the rise of modern capitalism, either in Britain or in India and China, where proto-industrialisation had existed at least since the seventeenth century (as I explain in Chapter 11). All I am seeking to establish here is the point that Marx viewed *world trade* as playing an important constitutive role both in the making of modern industrial capitalism and its ongoing *modus operandi*, much as I also see it as a fundamental component of global historical capitalism.

As implied earlier, my hunch is that the seminal Political Marxist interventions by Robert Brenner had a lot to do with the re-tracking of modern neo-Marxist theory onto this one-dimensional plane that I am interrogating here. For he, like Maurice Dobb before him,[10] effectively hollowed out the Marxist conception of the MOP, leaving only the

---

[6] Marx (1867/1954: 145).
[7] Tansel (2015b: 85).
[8] Marx (1867/1959: 334).
[9] Anievas and Nişancioğlu (2015: 171).
[10] Dobb (1959).

social relations of production, which are market dependent as the single defining property.[11] Accordingly, the analysis of the domestic economy, and by implication the global economy, devolves into a violently reductive class fetishism. And, in the process, we enter into a binary conception in which trade is relegated to the ontologically 'inferior' non-capitalist 'sphere of circulation' as much as the forces of production are deemed to be 'epiphenomenal' – i.e., determined solely by class relations – given that only the relations of production qualify as *the* meaningful criterion of capitalism. Here, I concur with Leonardo Marques' neo-Marxist point:

[i]nstead of the violent abstractions that separate different spheres of capitalism in order to elect one of them as the defining feature of the system, one should search for 'production, distribution, exchange, and consumption as a unified field of relational concepts linked by the commodity form'.[12]

Or, as the French Marxist, Maxime Rodinson, puts it equally forcefully when advancing his eclectic conception of capitalism, 'it would be too easy to adopt one particular definition [i.e., the social relations of production], as so many dogmatic [fundamentalist] Marxists have done, and settle the matter on the basis of this definition'.[13]

Confronting the 'Fundamentalist Marxist' Reductive Conception of Capitalist Social Relations of Production

Here, I turn to perhaps the most controversial part of the argument, which asks how we might best conceptualise capitalist social relations of production. If Political Marxism defines capitalism solely in terms of the social relations of production as I explained earlier, it then doubles down in its reductive modality by defining these relations as based purely on free wage labour (and capital). Interestingly, this definition dovetails with that advanced by Adam Smith, who views unfree labour as incommensurable with modern capitalist relations not least because it is highly inefficient, on the one hand, and anti-liberal on the other.[14] In an important recent article, Sébastien Rioux, Genevieve LeBaron and Peter Verovšek point out that unfree labour (forced labour and slave labour) have deepened and become more extensive across the global economy in recent decades.[15] If we run with Adam Smith's and Political Marxism's

---

[11] Brenner (1977, 1982).
[12] Marques (2020: 75), citing Dale Tomich.
[13] Rodinson (2007: 33).
[14] Smith (1776/1937: 364–5).
[15] Rioux *et al* (2019). See also LeBaron and Ayers (2013) and Rioux (2013).

definition of capitalism as based on free wage labour, then clearly the opposite tendency *should* be occurring. Indeed, Adam Smith and other liberals as well as numerous Marxists believe that unfree/forced labour is a feature of pre-modern production practices and that it is destined to die out as capitalism develops.[16] Thus, for Political Marxists as well as neo-Smithian liberals, the contemporary extension of unfree labour can only be explained through reference to *ad hoc*, exogenous factors such as the individual greed of particular capitalists, none of which are thought to be linked to the *structure* of capitalism. As Rioux *et al.* argue, this renders Political Marxism's definition as essentially 'neo-Smithian'.[17]

Interestingly, the paradox here is that Brenner and Wood follow on in the footsteps of Maurice Dobb, who had hollowed out Marx's conception of the MOP to leave only the social relations in place, before these were distilled down even further to leave us with the pure 'essence' of free wage labour (and capital).[18] This, in turn, reveals the paradox that this position, which effectively boils off the role of unfree labour in the reductive distillation process, turns the tables on Brenner's claim that Wallerstein's approach represents a 'neo-Smithian Marxism'.[19]

Still, my intention here is not to get lost in the labyrinth of Marxism's internecine conceptual struggles, but rather to establish the key point that it is simply too reductive and theoretically inadequate to define modern capitalist social relations of production as resting on a monolithic free wage labour base. For in '[p]rivileging theoretical clarity over historical complexities, the neo-Smithian [Marxist] tradition is limited by the explanatory power of its concept of capitalism'.[20] Once we allow for a more complex and hybrid conception of the social relations of production that incorporates free and unfree labour, a much more complex universe of capitalism(s) opens up in both its contemporary and historical incarnations. Nevertheless, while this leads a string of Marxists to claim that the exploitation of slave labour in the Caribbean colonies took on a modern capitalist form,[21] I argue against this claim because of the specific nature of the Caribbean's forces of production where no technological accumulation process existed, as I explain in

---

[16] Smith (1776/1937), Schumpeter (1943/2010), Dobb (1959) and Anderson (1974).
[17] Rioux *et al.* (2019: 14).
[18] Dobb (1959).
[19] Brenner (1977). And see Rioux *et al.* (2019: 14).
[20] Rioux *et al.* (2019: 13).
[21] Williams (1944/1964), Mintz (1986), McMichael (1991), Tomich (2004), Eley (2007), Blackburn (2010), Rioux (2013), Anievas and Nişancioğlu (2015), Rioux *et al.* (2019) and Marques (2020).

detail later. And so to my definition of modern capitalism that I laid out at the end of Chapter 1.

I define modern capitalism as a global system wherein *mechanised* productive technologies that are subjected to constant upgrading (technological accumulation) are deployed within a *hybrid* set of social relations, which comprise part unfree and part free wage labour that produce for the domestic and global market and where global trade is supported by rational economic institutions. And here it is important to note one of the key ramifications of this definition. For modern capitalism per se could *not* have existed *before* British industrialisation because mechanised productive technologies and the process of technological accumulation did not exist. To presume that modern capitalism existed in Europe after 1500 can only be sustained on the basis of a highly reductive definition. But equally, I suggest that we can conceive of (historical) capitalism before modern capitalism, as I now explain.

Navigating the Conceptual Maze of Fundamentalist Marxism (II): Defining Historical Capitalism

The notion of 'historical capitalism' has been advanced by the innovative and eclectic Marxist historian, Jairus Banaji, in his ground-breaking book *Theory as History*.[22] Moreover, there are all manner of cues that resonate in the extensive works of Fernand Braudel, even if these lack the kind of conceptual precision that I need here. All in all, I shall take some interpretive license by developing these ideas with some help from those scholars whom I cited earlier.

I define historical capitalism as a global system in which *non-mechanised* productive technologies, which are *not* subjected to constant upgrading, are deployed within a complex, *hybrid* portfolio of social relations that comprises partly unfree labour, partly free wage labour, partly wage labour (which is not fully dispossessed from the land) and partly agrarian/household labour, all of which produce to varying extents for domestic and global markets and where global trade is supported by rational (modern) economic institutions. Critically, I view historical capitalism as representing an *intermediate* phase of historical development that existed between the pre-modern/agrarian and modern capitalist modes of production.

The immediate problem is that fundamentalist Marxism's reductive and rigid schematic of successive modes of production serves to cover

---

[22] Banaji (2010).

up this interstitial global social formation given its complex, hybrid properties. For this global formation can be reduced neither to modern capitalism nor to feudalism. Accordingly, to assume that there is a neat point of demarcation between modern capitalist and pre-modern forms of social relations/modes of production cannot explain this complex interstitial global social formation that resided within an 'in-between space'. Moreover, given that this formation lasted for at least 400 years, it could not be dismissed as but a mere temporary historical aberration. And nor should we view the long phase of global historical capitalism as existing along a teleological, evolutionary continuum that leads ineluctably into modern capitalism. For I believe that this complex social formation would likely have lasted much longer had it not been for the radical discontinuity that the British *industrial* transformation injected into global economic history. As such, I concur with Andre Gunder Frank's assertion that

there was no unilinear 'progression' from one 'mode' of production to another; but all manner of relations of production were and remain widely intermingled even within any one 'society', not to mention world society as a whole. Many different relations of production have 'delivered' products that have been competitive on the world market.[23]

All of which means that the 'fundamentalist' neo-Marxist conception of the successive unfolding of monoglot-like modes of production is too unwieldy and clunky to capture this long intermediate phase.

This conception feeds into the analysis of historical capitalism that is advanced by Banaji, while also complementing Paul Sweezy's original analysis of the transition from feudalism to capitalism. Thus, Burak Tansel notes Banaji's important point that treating free wage labour as the cardinal property of modern capitalism is problematic because the capitalist exploitation of labour can also take various other modalities, which include chattel slavery, sharecropping, coerced/forced labour and slave labour in the colonies.[24] Moreover, Sweezy originally pointed out that the production for market exchange is compatible with all sorts of social relations of production, including slavery, serfdom, independent self-employed and free wage labour.[25] Which means that singling out the social relations of production in general or reducing these down to one single element such as landed peasants/serfs or free wage labour as

---

[23] Frank (1998: 331).
[24] Banaji (2010: 359), LeBaron and Ayers (2013), Rioux *et al.* (2019) and Tansel (2015b: 83).
[25] Sweezy in Sweezy and Dobb (1950: 134–57).

the exclusive, all-determining component of the MOP and the wider economy cannot deal with such complexities.

Nevertheless, it would be wrong to assume that I side with Sweezy and Frank against Dobb in the famous 'transition debate'. I take issue with Frank's follow-up claim to the above-cited quote, which asserts in highly dismissive fashion – or 'bourgeois' fashion in orthodox Marxist terminology:

> the moment we recognize [the primacy of world trade], the whole discussion about 'modes of production' more than pales into insignificance and irrelevance: it becomes instead no more than a distraction from the real issue, which is the holistic analysis of the whole that all these [Marxist] discussions are so intent on avoiding.[26]

This, it seems to me, is to bend the conceptual stick too far the other way and thereby returns us into the equally reductive *cul-de-sac* of neo-Smithian Marxism. For reducing the MOP to world trade is as problematic as reducing the latter to the former. To be more specific, I argue that global trade was a vital component of global historical capitalism as were the relations of production, part of which were modern capitalist. And, moreover, global trade played a vitally important, albeit, *indirect* role in the transition to modern capitalism in Britain – 'indirect', that is, because global trade did not stimulate a corresponding industrialisation of the two leading economies, China and India, as I explain in Chapters 11 and 12.

Here, it is important to respond to the fundamentalist Marxist rejection of this claim, which is perhaps no more clearly articulated than in the Political Marxist work of Ellen Meiksins Wood's *The Origin of Capitalism*.[27] And here, I concur precisely with Banaji's poignant critique, which singles out various pertinent core claims that she makes.[28] Overall, she claims that before the advent of modern capitalism long-distance trade was divorced from production, that it did not entail competition and that it was non-capitalist. In certain respects, this returns us to the neo-classical economic critique of the FGE that is advanced by Kevin O'Rourke and Jeffrey Williamson. And, as I argued in Chapter 7, competition in the global trading system as much as production for exchange value in factories and workshops were a common place. As Banaji rightly points out, 'Wood's is a world without mining,

[26] Frank (1998: 332).
[27] Wood (2002).
[28] Banaji (2018: 145).

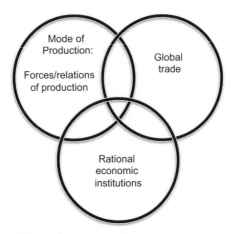

Figure 8.1 The overlapping relations of the three primary
components of global historical capitalism.

shipbuilding, textiles, domestic industry, putting-out networks, sugar
plantations etc'.[29] Indeed, not only did all this exist and much more to
boot, but the production of global commodities was undertaken in part
under modern capitalist social relations, all of which is explained in
considerable detail in the next section.

What is needed is an analytical 'via media' that tacks between
factoring in *historical* global trade and rational economic institutions,
along with combined amalgams of the social relations of production
that are part modern (free wage labour and forced labour) and part pre-
modern (peasant households) when understanding historical capitalism.
Rather than viewing *pre-modern* global trade and part modern capitalist
relations of production as mutually exclusive entities, it seems to me
that there are all manner of connections that link them together. To
this end, Figure 8.1 depicts the relationship between the three primary
categorical components that, although having a certain amount of
ontological autonomy in their own right, nevertheless, overlap given
that they mutually shape one another. And, by way of summary, my
overall position feeds directly into the unorthodox neo-Marxist analysis
of Anievas and Nişancioğlu when they assert that 'it might appear to
make more sense to talk about *capitalisms* rather than capitalism ...
[T]he history of capitalism is a multiple, polyvalent one, irreducible to
any singular process or social relation'.[30]

---

[29] Ibid. (145–6).
[30] Anievas and Nişancioğlu (2015: 9) and see also Yazdani and Menon (2020).

Finally, it is noteworthy that one of the key messages that comes through in Marx's exceptionally impressive analysis in *The Eighteenth Brumaire of Louis Bonaparte* – which is also in my view the most articulate of all of his writings – is that when he analysed social historical events he revealed a world of complex social realities that require a more nuanced approach when analysing 'concrete social determinations'.[31] Thus, Marx's generic conceptual schema of modes of production as laid out in *The German Ideology*[32] is probably best understood as one of *ideal types* that in practice cannot be mapped on precisely to a given social formation in history. A key mistake that Marxist fundamentalism makes is treating these ideal types as inflexible, monoglot-like categories that can be used as a neat template to be overlaid on any society across time and space to reveal its essential properties. For in the process, historical capitalism disappears from view, given that this template cannot map on to this complex social formation. Accordingly, when trying to unveil global historical capitalism, the fundamentalist Marxist method is akin to bashing a square conceptual peg into a round social hole. For the world in all of its greys demands more complex analysis, and certainly, Marx, as he demonstrated in *The Eighteenth Brumaire*, was entirely up for this task.

Conceptualising the Three-Layered Architecture of the 'Historical Capitalist' FGE

Figure 8.2 provides the basic schematic of the historical capitalism of the FGE. Here, I want to dispel the potential misinterpretation that this conception comprises an *economic* 'base-superstructure model', wherein the MOP comprises the causal base, while economic institutions and world trade are demoted ontologically to the residual sphere of the *economic* superstructure. For as explained already, production for global exchange value can lead to modern capitalist as well as agrarian social relations as much as *vice versa*. Which means that there *is* a relationship between social relations of production and world trade, but that it is not unidirectional and reductive, for it is more contingent and pluralist than a fundamentalist Marxist approach allows for. This is why Figure 8.2 displays down arrows running from the global historical capitalist whip at the top to the MOP at the bottom as much as there are up arrows from the bottom. In what follows, I consider the first two layers in detail before

---

[31] Marx (1852/2009).
[32] Marx and Engels (1846/2011).

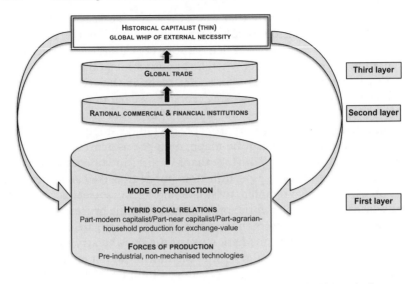

Figure 8.2 The three-layered architecture of global historical capitalism.

providing a very brief summary of the third layer in the conclusion to this chapter given that this has been covered in great detail in Chapters 2–7.

The First Layer of Historical Capitalism: Part Modern/Part Agrarian Social Relations of Production and Pre-industrial Technologies

Here, I shall consider the majority of the principal global trading commodities of the FGE, revealing how they were produced under either modern capitalist social relations or under hybrid relations that also comprised pre-modern agrarian forms in addition to the deployment of *pre-industrial* technologies. However, sceptics of historical globalisation, as we saw in Chapter 7, would discount the following discussion of trading commodities as meeting the globalisation threshold on the grounds that most were 'luxuries', such that they had only limited reach into mass consumer markets around the world and that, accordingly, such trade lacked sufficient global extensity and intensity. But as I also explained in detail in Chapter 7, the principal global trading commodities were largely everyday items that reached into middle-income and lower-income households around the world – a situation that applies even in the case of Chinese porcelain as well as Chinese and Indian silk and cotton textiles. All of which, to reiterate my claim made in Chapter 7, means that global trade had sufficient intensity and extensity to qualify as 'global'.

New World Slave Production: Raw Cotton, Tobacco, Sugar, Cacao, Coffee, Rum and Indigo

Although the production of commodities and raw materials in the Caribbean was undertaken by slaves, I argue that the system was based ultimately on historical rather than modern capitalism, though it certainly drew extremely close to the latter. I argue this not because unfree labour rather than free wage labour was deployed, but rather because there was no systematic mechanised technological accumulation process in play within the Caribbean *until* British industrialisation emerged, as I explain shortly. But for this one difference, it is the similarities between Caribbean and Lancashire cotton textile production that stand out.

Certainly, the slaves produced for the world market and faced rates of super-exploitation with the resulting profits going in part into capital accumulation and investment within the British (rather than the Caribbean) economy; a point I return to shortly. Notable here is Banaji's discussion of Marx's position:

> Marx wrote that in the English colonies which produced tobacco, cotton, sugar, the colonists acted 'like people, who, driven by motives of bourgeois production, wanted to produce commodities ...' He described these plantations as enterprises of 'commercial speculation' in which 'a capitalist mode of production exists, if only in a formal sense ... The business in which slaves are used is conducted by capitalists'. He described the exploitation of slave-labour as a 'factor in a calculated and calculating system', driven by the compulsion to produce 'surplus value'.[33]

Also of relevance here is the unorthodox neo-Marxist claim of Anievas and Nişancioğlu:

> market competition compelled [Caribbean] plantations to operate according to distinctly capitalist rules of reproduction ... [and] where profit maximisation was the cardinal aim.... What is more, as slave plantations were so thoroughly integrated into the world market, the evidence reveals a sharp convergence of average rates of profits and standardised methods of procedure, as we would expect from enterprises operating on a fully capitalist market.[34]

---

[33] Banaji (2010: 67).
[34] Anievas and Nişancioğlu (2015: 161).

And, to return to Banaji, he adds that 'the building of an Atlantic economy was not just a "pre-condition" for the growth of capitalism in Europe or Eurasia *but embodied the embrace of capital through its own forms of capital accumulation'*.[35] Notable too is the neo-Marxist, Leonardo Marques, who in following Philip McMichael, is interested in how slavery 'was part of the total ensemble of global relations that formed the capitalist world-economy between the sixteenth and the nineteenth centuries. It is a history of slavery in capitalism.'[36] And, last but not least, Geoff Eley reinforces this by asserting that Atlantic slavery produced 'the first modern proletariat of large-scale, highly organized, and integrated capitalist production'.[37]

Although most orthodox neo-Marxists, alongside liberals, paradoxically discount the role of the Atlantic colonies in spurring on British capitalist industrialisation, as I explain in Chapter 9, it bears noting that Marx himself rejected this viewpoint. As he argued, 'world trade is the necessary condition of large-scale machine industry [in Britain].... [and] [New World] slavery is an economic category of the highest importance';[38] to which he added the point that 'the veiled slavery of the wage-workers in Europe needed, for its pedestal, slavery pure and simple in the new world'.[39] And, then of course, there is the well-known and highly significant claim that Marx makes in Chapter 31 of the first volume of *Capital*, where he states, not unsarcastically, that

[t]he discovery of gold and silver in America, the extirpation, enslavement and entombment in mines of the aboriginal population of that continent ... signalised the rosy dawn of the era of capitalist production. These idyllic proceeding are the chief momenta of primitive accumulation.... [Such] force is the midwife of every old society pregnant with a new one.[40]

If ever there was a better case in which workers were violently expropriated from the land – as in the 'primitive accumulation of capital' – to work for the advantage of an employer, the African slaves who were shipped to the New World would be it (as I explained in Chapter 4). Just as free wage labour has its labour power commodified, slaves have their whole person commodified. And, as I explained earlier, both forms of labours are compatible with modern capitalism. Moreover, the linkages

---

[35] Banaji (2018: 149), emphasis in the original.
[36] Marques (2020) and McMichael (1991).
[37] Eley (2007: 165).
[38] Marx (1846/1975: 95).
[39] Marx (1867/1954: 711).
[40] Ibid. (703).

deepen when we examine the modality of production in the Caribbean sugar mills, given that it was near identical to that experienced in the Lancashire cotton mills.

In the context of the Atlantic sugar mills and plantations, echoing the thrust of the 'Williams thesis', Sidney Mintz expresses his central claim thus:

[t]he specialization by skill and jobs, and the division of labor by age, gender, and condition into crews, shifts, and 'gangs', together with the stress upon punctuality and discipline, are features associated more with industry than agriculture.... [T]he sugar-cane plantation is gradually winning recognition as an unusual combination of agricultural and industrial forms, and I believe it was probably the closest thing to industry that was typical of the seventeenth century.[41]

Indeed, Mintz views the Caribbean sugar mills as a likely precursor to, or even the model for, Britain's industrial factories. Interestingly, this feeds into Timothy Mitchell's important claim that 'many forms of social organization and cultural production that, since [Michel Foucault's] *Discipline and Punish*, we have come to consider as important, such as wage-labour and the factory system, in the emergence of European modernity were first developed well beyond the Northern Europe of Michel Foucault's analyses'.[42]

The highly disciplinary and exploitative conditions endured by the African slaves mirrored – as well as pre-empted – those suffered by mainly women and children working in the 'dark satanic' English cotton mills well over a century later. Speaking of the Caribbean situation, the contemporary commentator, W. L. Mathieson, tells us that

[d]uring the sugar cane harvest the mills operated unceasingly, and the labor requirements were horrendous ... The only break in the working week was from Saturday night till Monday morning. Otherwise, the twenty-five men and women in [this particular] factory worked continuously in shifts lasting all day and part of the night, or the whole of every second or third night.[43]

Likewise, the English cotton workers, of whom a not-insignificant proportion were children under the age of 10, were kept in the mill round the clock, working anywhere between eleven and sixteen hours per day for six days a week with only Sundays off. And, incidentally,

---

[41] Mintz (1986: 47, 48).
[42] Mitchell (2000: 3).
[43] Mathieson cited in Mintz (1986: 49).

while the British state banned child labour through various Factory Acts in the nineteenth century, the practice continued regardless given that the toothless inspectorate, which comprised a mere four inspectors for the whole of the north of England, meant that mill owners found all manner of ingenious ways of concealing the children when the inspectors turned up. The most notable example of which is that having been tipped off by other mill owners concerning the impending arrival of an inspector, the rest hid the children in 'privies' that looked like unceremonious coffins.

Close parallels also become apparent in terms of the nature of the working environment. Indeed, four of the common defining features were the sheer heat, noise, danger and intensity of work patterns. The Barbadian colonist, Thomas Tryon, described the working conditions of the sugar mills thus:

Tis to live in a perpetual Noise and Hurry.... Since the Climate is so hot, and the labor so constant, that the Servants [i.e., slaves] night and day stand in great Boyling Houses, where there are six or seven large Coppers or Furnaces kept perpetually Boyling; and from which heavy Ladles and Scummers they skim off the excrementitious parts of the Canes, till it comes to its perfection and cleanness.[44]

And, of course, the sheer heat, noise and work intensity that workers endured in the Lancashire cotton mills has been well documented.[45]

As for the problem of the presence of constant physical danger, Mathieson described this in the context of the Caribbean sugar mills thus: '[t]hose who fed the mill were liable, especially when tired or half-asleep, to have their fingers caught between the rollers. A hatchet was kept in readiness to sever the arm, which in such cases was always drawn in; and this no doubt explains the number of maimed watchmen'.[46] Friedrich Engels, in his seminal book, *The Condition of the Working-Class in England in 1844*, lists in graphic succinctness various workplace tragedies that unfolded in the Lancashire mills in a mere six-week period:

[b]etween June 12th and August 3rd, 1843, the *Manchester Guardian* reported the following serious accidents ... June 12th, a boy died in Manchester of lockjaw, caused by his hand being crushed between wheels. June 16th, a youth died in Saddleworth seized by a wheel and carried away with it; died, utterly mangled.... July 24th, a girl in Oldham died, carried around fifty times by a strap; no bone unbroken.[47]

[44] Thomas Tryon cited in Mintz (1986: 47–8).
[45] Gaskell (1833) and Engels (1952).
[46] Mathieson cited in Mintz (1986: 50).
[47] Engels (1952: 165).

And, as he explains on the same page, 'whoever is seized by the strap [which is attached to the motor of the cotton machines] is carried up with lightning speed, thrown against the ceiling above and floor below with such force that there is rarely a whole bone left in the body, and death follows instantly'.[48] In sum, not only were there parallel work conditions but equally the surplus value that was extracted from both sets of labourers was extremely high and, moreover, both industries were geared for the world market that produced super-normal profits for their owners.

Regarding its modern features, management was frequently separated from ownership and financial investment in the Caribbean sugar industry – a sure sign of modern business practice. Richard Drayton goes so far as to argue that the Caribbean sugar complex was 'at the cutting edge of capitalist civilization' on the basis of its large workforce, its high degree of specialisation and the domination of time discipline in addition to its capital and technological intensiveness as well as its production for the world market.[49] Relevant too is James Pritchard's observation that

[i]n view of the labour, discipline, and organisation of work, the interchangeability of labour units, time-consciousness owing to the crop's rapid perishability, the separation of production from consumption and [of] the slaves from their tools [as well as the optimal extraction of surplus value], [Caribbean] sugar manufacture was the most industrialised form of human enterprise [before the British industrial revolution].[50]

All of which reinforces Mintz's argument that the Caribbean sugar mills constituted a model for, or at the least were a precursor to, the later Lancashire mills and factories.

The discussion thus far suggests that Caribbean slave production conformed to modern capitalism. This is largely because the profits that were extracted from the slaves were used in part for investment within the British economy, thereby helping to stimulate the Lancashire cotton-based industrial revolution.[51] Certainly, Caribbean slave production constitutes the litmus test for my differentiation of historical from modern capitalism. While I argue in Chapter 9 that Caribbean production was instrumental to British industrialisation, nevertheless I argue that the former was an instantiation of historical capitalism

---

[48] Ibid. (165, 149–67). See also Gaskell (1833: 202–9, 244–66).
[49] Drayton (2002: 102).
[50] James Pritchard cited in Crowley (2016: 404).
[51] See also Rioux (2013).

rather than modern capitalism. Thus, while forced labour and surplus value extraction for investment are components of modern capitalism, the key point as I signalled earlier, is that there was no mechanised technological accumulation process in Caribbean production before British industrialisation.

Here, I draw on the excellent work found in Stuart Schwartz's important edited volume, in which he notes that the Caribbean sugar mills did not operate on a process of mechanised technological renewal but more on non-mechanised technological stasis. And thus by inference, of course, technology was *not* used as a means of replacing labour so as to drive down costs of production as would become the case in modern (Western) capitalism.[52] Put differently, in the Caribbean before 1750, there was no rising 'organic composition of capital' in play. Critically, it is significant to note in this context that technological improvements were only made to the standard wooden vertical three-roller cane crusher *after* 1750, when it was converted into an iron machine before it was subsequently converted into a *horizontal* (fully mechanised) crusher that was harnessed to the steam engine.[53] And, no less critically, these technologies were produced in, and imported from, industrialising Britain.

All of which confirms the point that I am making here, because all of these technological improvements came as a *result* of the British industrial revolution rather than the other way around, even though the latter was partly created by Black slavery. Accordingly, Caribbean production ultimately reflected *historical* capitalism rather than modern capitalism. And, as Schwartz also points out, Eric Williams said of the sugar plantations that they combined 'the sins of feudalism and capitalism without the virtues of either',[54] a reference that Sidney Mintz also made.[55] Still, as I explained earlier, but for this one difference, the organisation of the Caribbean sugar mills and Lancashire cotton mills was otherwise near identical. Which means that the analytical line separating modern capitalism from historical capitalism can at times be wafer thin.

The Dutch Spice Trade: Mace, Nutmeg, Cinnamon, Sugar and Cloves

The trio of mace, nutmeg and cloves was grown in the Banda Islands (in the Moluccas), while cinnamon was grown in Ceylon – all of which was conducted under Dutch imperial control. Much the same kind of historical

---

[52] Schwartz (2004b).
[53] Mazumdar (1998: 340–6).
[54] Williams cited in Schwartz (2004b: 5).
[55] Mintz (1986: 60).

capitalist logic that I have described in the case of the New World applied to the production of these four spices, given that the Dutch Vereenigde Oost-Indische Compagnie (VOC) relied on imported slave labour. For in the aftermath of the Dutch genocide of the Banda population, the VOC drafted in slaves who were subjected to extremely high rates of exploitation – a practice that mirrored New World production.[56] Moreover, it is also interesting to note that in Zanzibar after 1840, the centre of global clove production, African slaves were exploited under the colonial rule of the Omani Sultanate.[57] All of which reinforces my claim concerning the presence of historical capitalism in the production of these important global commodities. What then of Javanese sugar production?

I noted in Chapter 2 that the Dutch were aided in sugar production by Chinese residents who had emigrated to Java before the former's arrival. I also noted that before the Dutch massacre of the Chinese in 1740, some seventy-eight out of a total eighty-four owners of the sugar factories were Chinese. And, I noted too that after that particular massacre, the Chinese remained the majority owners, given that the Dutch had no choice but to court more Chinese to operate the factories given the former's dependence on the latter.[58] As is well known, Javanese sugar was a key global trading commodity, with the key point being that these Chinese factories employed wage labourers. According to Nagaoka Shinjiro, each sugar factory had more than 200 waged employees. They called the factory a 'company', and the Chinese communities that developed there were based on these 'companies' and 'factories'. Such dynamics could be witnessed in other Chinese industries in Southeast Asia, such as the tin and gold mining industries in Kalimantan Island (Borneo) – otherwise known as the Langfang Republic – between 1777 and 1784. Nevertheless, as Roger Knight rightly points out, these factories deployed only crude pre-industrial technologies,[59] which is why I refer to them as historical capitalist factories – part modern and part pre-industrial.

Key Chinese Global Trading Products: Porcelain, Silk and Cotton Textiles, Tea and Sugar[60]

Chinese Tea While Chinese porcelain and silk textiles had a very long trading lineage, tea became popular in Europe in the

---

[56] Anievas and Nişancıoğlu (2015: 238–40).
[57] Cooper (1977: 156–70).
[58] Shinjiro (1960/1983: 107).
[59] Knight (2014: esp. 63–92).
[60] All Chinese texts and archival information discussed and cited below have been supplied and translated by Zhang Shizhi, to whom I am most grateful.

eighteenth and nineteenth centuries, especially the cheap *Bohea* variety (as I explained in Chapter 7). It is commonly assumed that Chinese tea was an agricultural product that had no relationship to capitalist production. Peer Vries, for example, asserts that while tea was grown on plantations in India and Ceylon, it was grown on small family plots in China.[61] But there is evidence to suggest that Chinese peasants either planted tea and sold it to the factories and tea merchants or that they worked in tea factories as wage labourers. According to Zhang Shizhi, the historical records and the secondary Chinese-speaking literature reveal that tea in China was also produced by free wage labourers who worked in factory conditions. He notes that tea production developed significantly during the Ming (1368–1644) and especially the Qing (1644–1911) periods. In particular, Fujian province was the centre of tea production, where the popular brand of *Bohea* was produced. As Hung Ho-fung explains, '[t]he mountainous Fujian province was ... a major tea-producing region in eighteenth century China. Tea leaves were collected by wholesale merchants from Guangzhou (Canton). Tea processing workshops were set up in the market towns or cities in the vicinity of tea-growing villages. The processed tea was then transported to Guangzhou and sold to the Hongs [Co-Hong], and in turn sold to the EIC [for shipment to Britain].'[62]

It is unclear in the Chinese-speaking literature how early the tea factories were established, though it seems fair to say that they were a going concern since at least the mid-eighteenth century.[63] One archival quote reveals that tea factories employing wage labour had emerged in 1762:

In 1762, *Shi* rents a tea mountain from the landlord, *Liang Shengqi*, for a tea business in Jiangxi province. *Shi* builds up a tea factory and hires *Deng* and *Zhou* to work. They make an agreement concerning the duration and payment of work. Work duration runs from April to July, and payment is four taels [just over £1] per person.[64]

Zhuang Guotu argues that during this period, these tea workers were free wage labourers and that the emergence of an employment relationship and a division of labour made an important contribution to the further development of tea production in China.[65] Of note too is that there

---

[61] Vries (2013: 176).
[62] Hung (2001: 496); see also Zeng (1993).
[63] Peng (1982: 19).
[64] Taken from the Jianyang Gazetteer, cited in Zhuang (1999: 153).
[65] Zhuang (1999: 153).

are various passages in the historical records, which reveal that very significant amounts of tea production occurred during the Qing period.

Most tea factories are built in the remote mountainous areas ... In Ouning county, the number of tea factories [was] more than one thousand. Each factory has tea workers from dozens to hundreds, and the total number of tea workers in this county is more than ten thousand.[66]

Significantly, Zhuang suggests that Ouning county was not even the main region for tea production in Fujian, with the number of workers and tea factories being even larger in other places such as Chongan county.[67]

Moving forward in time, we find that in 1838, the size of the *Bohea* tea export trade out of Guangdong was 300,000 picul (9,000 tons), which comprised approximately 75 per cent of total Chinese tea exports in that year,[68] though Fujianese production remained important. Zhang Shizhi notes from Li's research that prior to 1840 on the eve of the first Opium War, tea production was highly commercialised and specialised.[69] The tea-processing industry emerged during this period in Guangdong where merchants invested and built tea factories and reprocessed tea, which was purchased from other areas before the re-processed tea was sold onto foreign traders. A contemporary foreign merchant observed and recorded the situation in a typical tea factory thus:

In tea production factories in Henan island [Guangdong province], women and children are busy picking the yellow and brown leaves from black tea ... Approximately, each [wage] worker can gain 60 copper coins [per day] doing this job ... These factories are capacious two floors buildings. On the lower floor, there are various tools and different kinds of tea. On the upper floor, hundreds of women and children are doing picking and sorting works.[70]

Li concludes that the division and specialisation in tea production were highly developed. For production required five or six types of specialised work, which was coupled with other upstream and downstream works.

Thus, there is a strong case for revising the standard Eurocentric and traditional Chinese view that tea production was simply a pre-modern agricultural activity that was undertaken within the Chinese household. For Chinese tea production in this period was based to a significant

---

[66] Jiang cited in Peng (1982: 19). See also Zhuang (1999: 148).
[67] Zhuang (1999: 148).
[68] Zeng (1993: 54).
[69] Li (1983: 411–13).
[70] Qi, cited in Li (1983: 412).

extent on a historical capitalist factory system that employed part-time and full-time wage workers. And, production was undertaken for exchange value given that it was destined for domestic and international markets. Critically, though, there is no sign of profits being reinvested in upgrading technologies of production or in deploying mechanised technologies. What then of the complementary product, sugar?

Chinese Sugar Production According to the research of Mazumdar as well as Xu and Wu, sugar production in China developed significantly during the Ming and Qing periods (1368–1911),[71] and it was an important export product throughout the period of the FGE.[72] The key centres of production were in Taiwan (Formosa) as well as in Fujian, Guangdong and Guangxi provinces. When the Dutch colonised Taiwan, they stimulated local sugar production and exported most of it to Persia and western Europe. Sugar exports increased from 113 tons to 514 tons in 1662, with the latter figure comprising about 50 per cent of total Chinese production. After the Qing state expelled the VOC from Taiwan in 1684, sugar production expanded at an exponential rate. By 1697, average annual production had jumped to 30,000 tons and then to 52,000 tons by 1799. But what of the social relations of sugar production?

In the early eighteenth century, Huang Shujing collected information on sugar production in his book *Taihai Shicha Lu*, in which he recorded that

In March, it is easy to seed sugarcane because of rainy days during the spring....
[B]efore October, the owner of a sugar workshop needs to install all production equipment and hire workers ... [T]hese included 2 sugar producers, 2 boiling workers, 2 squeezing workers, 2 cattle governors, 7 reaping workers, 1 food-gathering worker (cattle food), 1 guard (cattle guard). Total payment for these workers is 60–70 taels per month [£20–£23].[73]

Chen Xuewen argues that this paragraph reveals two significant pieces of information.[74] First, it is clear that the division of labour had emerged in sugar production in Taiwan. Interestingly, Xu and Wu estimate that the total value of sugar production in this particular workshop/factory was at least 2,000 taels (c. £670) per annum, which suggests that production

[71] Mazumdar (1998) and Xu and Wu (2003).
[72] Mazumdar (1998: ch. 2).
[73] Huang Shujing, *Taihai Shicha Lu*, Vol. 3, p. 10, cited in Zhang (2020: ch. 3).
[74] Chen (1991: 33).

levels were impressive.[75] Second, whether these people were specialised and skilled workers or just casual labourers remains unclear, though overall, this approximated to modern capitalist relations.

Notable too is the sugar industry on mainland China during the Qing dynasty. According to Xian and Tan, mainland sugar production in Guangdong developed significantly in the Qing period, with large amounts of commercial capital and loans being invested in the industry. As some investors became owners of sugar 'workshops' and 'factories', so they transformed the household sugarcane and sugar producers as well as farmers into wage workers within these work places. One particular archival finding records that 'during the Qianlong period (1736–1799), a merchant (Yang) built a sugar workshop and hired numerous workers who were paid a weekly wage'.[76] This phenomenon emerged extensively in Guangdong at that time, all of which suggests the presence of modern capitalist social relations. But ultimately, it is the absence of mechanised technologies and a technological accumulation drive that renders the Chinese sugar industry an example of historical capitalism rather than modern capitalism.

Chinese Silk Textiles   Chinese factories for cotton spinning and weaving emerged first in the 1880s (with the exception being the deployment of handlooms in large state-owned workshops/factories that had produced luxury cotton textiles for the royal household and court for centuries previously). However, factory production and wage labour as well as unfree labour were by no means alien to the Chinese textile industry before the late-nineteenth century. Unlike in the cotton sector, silk spinning and weaving were more complex and capital intensive given that silk looms were expensive, which is why silk factories and workshops developed from an earlier stage. The large and highly sophisticated, complex silk weaving looms required two or three workers, which is more labour than an individual household could spare (see Chapter 11).

Given the need to house these 'machines' under one roof, so factory production became a commonplace. Indeed, from the earliest times, these operated in both the private and public sectors. Although Chinese silk production stems back well before the Common Era, it seems that silk factories emerged in the Yuan period (1279–1368), with Chao Kang noting that 'an unambiguous case of a private [silk] factory was first cited by a Yuan writer sometime between 1356 and 1367'.[77] Such factories

---

[75] Xu and Wu (2003: 366).
[76] Xian and Tan (1994: 94).
[77] Chao (1977: 29).

then developed subsequently in the Ming period, particularly in large cities in the Lower Yangtze valley where thousands of workers were employed.[78] Notable too is that silk factory workers were paid a daily wage. The growth in the size of factories was such that the subsequent Qing government finally issued an anti-trust law, which specified a maximum of 100 looms per factory, not so as to stymy the industry but to prevent particular producers from dominating the market. And, when the edict was revoked at the end of the seventeenth century, silk factories expanded to incorporate as many as 500–600 looms (which compared in size with many of Lancashire's cotton mills in the nineteenth century). The state-owned factories, known as the Weaving Bureaus, which relied heavily on *corvée* labour (forced labour), dominated for most of the Ming era and part of the Qing. But by 1711, the abolition of the forced labour system was finally completed, after which wage labour predominated.[79]

Still, it would be wrong to convey the impression that silk textiles were produced only in factories for there was also a significant rural silk handicraft sector. As Xu Yingnan notes, speaking of the late-nineteenth century:

Although the most advanced handicraft methods long predated [nineteenth-century] steam filatures, mechanized reeling was still so capital and labor intensive that costs were often higher than hand-reeling. The generally superior uniformity and strength of [factory-made] filature silk meant that [it] rightly displaced hand-reeled silk in export markets where uniformity was important for use with mechanical looms. However, in markets ... such as the domestic Chinese market, where uniformity and quality was less important, weavers continued to hunger for the lower cost hand reeled silks and in the process insuring the survival of handicraft until the Second World War.[80]

Interestingly, as I explain in Chapter 13, much the same logic applied in the cotton textile industry after the 1880s (as was also the case in India). All in all, the Chinese silk industry was a complex amalgam of the rural household production system and the factory/workshop, which combined part-time and full-time waged workers as well as rural peasants after 1711. And, in turn, this points up the presence of modern and pre-modern capitalist social relations of production together with, albeit highly sophisticated, *non-mechanised* pre-industrial textile technologies under historical capitalism.

---

[78] Ibid. (29–30).
[79] Zhang (2020: ch. 3).
[80] Xu (2011: 27).

Chinese Cotton Textiles (Nankeens)   During the FGE, Chinese cotton textiles or 'Nankeens' became significant export products between 1760 and about 1830. Interestingly, there is some confusion as to their origin, with various writers assuming that they were called this because they were produced principally in Nanjing (in Jiangsu province in the Yangtze River Delta), which was Anglicised to 'Nanking' by the British. In fact, though, they were produced in Suzhou and Songjiang in Jiangnan province.[81]

As I explain in detail in Chapter 11, cotton-spinning and weaving were undertaken within the Chinese (and Indian) pre-industrial household, while printing, dyeing, calendaring and finishing were conducted in small- and large-scale workshops and factories that employed either temporary wage labour or permanent free wage labour. There I refer to the cotton industry as based on historical capitalism – part modern capitalist and part rural agrarian – while non-mechanised technologies of production predominated. Nevertheless, even the rural industry was an example of Chinese (and Indian) historical capitalism because production was undertaken in part not only for use value but also for exchange value. And many peasants relied on the market for purchasing raw materials even in those instances where production for use value was predominant. As I also note in Chapter 11, a significant portion of cotton textile production was undertaken in Jiangnan in the Lower Yangtze Delta in the eighteenth and nineteenth centuries, the output of which, incredible though it might seem, surpassed total Indian output before the 1920s and British output before the 1850s. All of which, in sum, means that cotton textile exports from China (and India) were founded on hybrid social relations that were partly modern capitalist and partly agrarian household based, which, in turn, utilised non-mechanised technologies, thereby once more pointing up the presence of historical capitalism.

Chinese Porcelain   Finally, Chinese porcelain was, of course, a well-known global commodity, especially during the era of the FGE. It was exported to Central Asia and the Islamic Middle East, Africa, Europe, Korea, Japan and the Philippines and thence to the New World aboard the Spanish-Manila Galleon.[82] Although porcelain was produced right across China, its main production sites were found in Longquan, where green 'celadon' was produced, before it was superseded during the FGE by the production of blue and white porcelain in the city of

---

[81] Chao (1977: 50) and Fan (2016: 105–6).
[82] Kerr and Wood (2004), Finlay (2010) and Zhao (2013).

Jingdezhen (though notably the blue and white style was derived from Islamic West Asia and Jingdezhen potters began producing it in the early-fourteenth century).[83] Notably, Jingdezhen was known as 'The Town of Year-Round Thunder and Lightning' on the basis of the constant flares from the fire-kilns and the sound of thousands of pestles.[84] As Robert Finlay notes:

> By the sixteenth century, the changes that had begun in the late Yuan period had made Jingdezhen the largest industrial operation in the world, with over 1,000 kilns, 70,000 workers, and a production process that anticipated modern methods of assembly-line manufacture. A sophisticated division of labor made possible improvement of quality along with a great increase in production.[85]

And, according to Maxine Berg,

> [t]he porcelain city Jingdezhen was rebuilt in the later seventeenth century, and its factories and workshops were reorganized and increased in size and productivity. Factories were departmentalized even down to a high degree of division of labour in the decorating studios.... The city was said to have a million people, eight hundred kilns and three to four thousand factories.[86]

Moreover, to the highly sophisticated division of labour, I add the point that the largest kilns, known as 'dragon kilns', were 55 metres long and 9 metres wide.

Certainly the arrival of the East India Companies (EICs) provided a boost in demand for Chinese porcelain, all of which was promoted further by the influx of New World silver after 1571. Trading around a million pieces at the end of the seventeenth century, the VOC upped its game by importing forty-three million pieces from the beginning of the eighteenth century to the start of the nineteenth. Moreover, a further thirty million pieces were shipped to Europe by other EICs, including the English, French, Swedish and Danish.[87] And it is possible that Chinese annual output by the mid-eighteenth century was in the region of sixty million pieces.[88]

The traditional account holds that the Jingdezhen factories were basically state owned and were not proto-capitalist.[89] But a number

---

[83] Finlay (1998: 152–7).
[84] Hsu (1988: 140).
[85] Finlay (1998: 156).
[86] Berg (2004: 118).
[87] Finlay (1998: 168).
[88] Gerritsen (2020: 312).
[89] See, for example, Xing (2000).

of prominent revisionists have challenged the traditional Chinese understanding. Robert Finlay notes that 'the *imperial* kilns represented no more than a fraction of those in Jingdezhen',[90] while Anne Gerritsen claims that in the Qing period the total output of the imperial kilns was less than 1 per cent of total Jingdezhen production.[91] Moreover, Albert Feuerwerker tells us that '[e]ven in the silk and porcelain industries, in which the Imperial Silkworks at Suzhou, Hangzhou, and Nanjing, and the Imperial Pottery at Jingdezhen figured so prominently, the great majority of the manufacturing establishments and trading firms were privately owned'.[92] Still, according to Kent Deng, because many of the workers owned plots of land in the rural areas from which they derived an income, so they were not landless free wage workers. Certainly, in the state-owned factories and workshops, a significant proportion of workers were 'battalions' (soldiers) as well as *corvée* labourers who worked to pay off tax obligations. But after 1711, there was a transition from *corvée* and battalion labour to free wage labour, which leads Gerritsen in the context of porcelain production in Jingdezhen to conclude that '[t]he centrality of labour, especially waged labour, in the rise of [Chinese historical] capitalism is clear'.[93] All in all, the presence of near-assembly line production, industrial-sized kilns, a very highly developed division of labour and the presence of free wage labour in the Qing period, together with mass production for the market – local, national and global – means that this industry was based in part on modern capitalist lines.

And to conclude this long section more generally, the vast majority of global trading commodities were produced under partly modern capitalist social relations, often in conjunction with pre-industrial agrarian social relations, which thereby satisfies the first criterion of historical capitalism in the FGE. Moreover, while some of the technologies were remarkably sophisticated, they were, nevertheless, non-mechanised and therefore pre-industrial or historical capitalist.[94]

The Second Layer of Global Historical Capitalism: Modern Rational Capitalist Economic Institutions

The second layer of global capitalism, historical and modern, comprises rational economic institutions in the absence of which global trade would

---

[90] Finlay (2010: 23), my emphasis.
[91] Gerritsen (2020: 311–12).
[92] Feuerwerker (1984: 305).
[93] Gerritsen (2020: 314) and Hsu (1988: 138–9).
[94] Note that at least before 1400, the Chinese deployed mechanised technologies in their iron industry as well as in the abortive ramie textile industry.

have been impossible. I discuss these precisely because the presence of *rational* institutions is thought to be typical of modern capitalism, as Max Weber originally argued.[95] Here, I concur with Fernand Braudel, Maxime Rodinson, Janet Abu-Lughod and Marshall Hodgson, who emphasise the presence of all manner of rational economic institutions in the non-Western world well before the nineteenth century.[96] Thus, because these were a key component of global historical capitalism, this provides a further defence of my claim that a global economy existed between 1500 and about 1850. To provide a flavour of these, I shall focus on Indian/South Asian and Islamic commercial and financial institutions, not least because they were predominant throughout the Indian Ocean system (while I reserve a discussion of China's rational economic institutions for Chapter 11). And here, we enter the world of the trans-regional 'bazaar economy'.

Rational Islamic Economic Institutions

While I have, regrettably, focused far less on Islamic countries in this book than ideally I would have liked, it is notable that Islam likely formed the most extensive trans-continental trading network in the world well before 1000 CE,[97] all of which was made possible by its penchant for rational economic institutions that were utilised by capitalists and near-capitalists. And it is notable that the Muslims were engaging in very long distance trade at the time when 'Europe' was mired in the Dark Ages. Indeed, as I have argued elsewhere, the Muslims were the primary economic agents in the process of Afro-Eurasian regionalisation, weaving together Africa, Asia and Europe into a growing interdependence between c. 650 through to 1500.[98] And Mecca, the so-called home of the backward, economically irrational Islamic religion was, in fact, one of the key economic centres of the trans-continental Islamic economic trading network.

Nevertheless, at this point, Eurocentric logic intervenes in one of its most perverse instantiations by insisting that one of the principal reasons for the so-called impossibility of rational Islamic economic institutions and hence the 'absence' of Islamic trade lies in Islam's prohibition of usury or lending at interest (known as *riba*) – notwithstanding the double

[95] Weber (1922/1978).
[96] Abu-Lughod (1989), Braudel (1992), Hodgson (1993) and Rodinson (2007).
[97] For example, Hodgson (1993), Rodinson (2007: ch. 3), Chaudhuri (1985), Wink (1988, 1990), Abu-Lughod (1989), Bentley (1996), Hobson (2004: ch. 2), Koehler (2014), Finlay (2010: ch. 5) and Beaujard (2019).
[98] Hobson (2004: ch. 2).

standard wherein Eurocentrism conveniently brushes over the fact that the Catholic Church no less prohibited usury. But no matter. The key point is that this Eurocentric dismissal is problematic in every respect, for the irony is that Muslim traders found all manner of ingenious ways to circumvent the ban on usury, not least by creating various rational institutions that supported long-distance trade.[99] As Abraham Udovitch explains:

> The restrictions in the area of trade and exchange, as well as in other areas of life, placed certain areas of [mercantile] practice on an inevitable collision course with [Islamic] legal theory. This situation gave rise to a special branch of legal writings, the *hiyal* (legal devices) literature, in which the lawyers attempted to narrow down the area in which actions would be in violation of the law by making them conform to the law formally while in reality circumventing it.[100]

Of the three forms of *hiyal*, it was those of the Hanafī School – Shaybānī and al-Khassāf – that applied to commercial practice. Thus, for example, to circumvent the religious ban on usury, payment was frequently delayed by several months; or arrangements were made that entailed a higher price if credit rather than cash was extended in order to conceal the interest paid; or again, *qirād* investments were deployed which allowed for a return on the capital advanced that exceeded the original amount that was offered. All of these provided the same needs as interest-bearing loans through which the investor received a profitable return while also providing a flow of capital to the trader.[101] And, in any case, as Benedikt Koehler points out, the ban on usury applied to lending but *not* to investment on the grounds that lenders should be paid 'irrespective [of] whether the borrower has made a profit, whereas an investor ... shares the risk of the undertaking'.[102]

Critically, Islamic bankers – known as *hawāladars* and *sarrāfs* – were a commonplace feature of Islamic trade and production. The *hawāladars*, operating in the 'bazaars', were a vital conduit for intercontinental trade in that they transferred funds from one place to another;[103] much as they still do today. Moreover, the paradox here is that in the Western imagination, the Asian bazaar represents an ideal typical modality of 'traditional' commercial practices, supposedly populated by small-scale pedlars and poor peasant consumers, all of whom engaged in face-to-face

---

[99] See especially Rodinson (2007: 65–78).
[100] Udovitch (1970: 11).
[101] Goitein (1967: 197–9) and Udovitch (1970: 80).
[102] Koehler (2014: 125).
[103] Ibid. (111–12) and Thompson (2011: ch. 4).

haggling and barter amidst truly chaotic scenes. But it turns out that the bazaar embodied modern capitalist practices, including 'indigenous money markets which finance, through promissory notes, bills of exchange (suftajas and hundis) and other institutions, the wholesale and forward trade over the longer distances'.[104] According to Thomas Timberg, the key actors within the trans-regional bazaar were Baghdadi Jews, Gujarati Hindus and Muslims, Armenians, Greeks, Iranians, Chinese and Portuguese.[105] To this can be added the development of *funduqs* across the Indian Ocean system, which were centres of trade that were frequented by foreign merchants.[106] The *funduqs* were founded on legal provisions and mercantile transactions were taxed at low rates. Such institutions were similar to the caravanserais that were constructed along the overland routes that traversed Central Asia across to West Asia (which I discussed in Chapter 6).

But to return to the discussion of the Islamic bankers, it is significant to note that they issued credit notes – the 'demand note' or bill of exchange at a distant location (*suftaja*) and the 'order to pay' (*hawāla*), which was identical to a modern cheque: '[a]t the upper left corner was the amount to be paid (in numbers), and in the lower left corner was the date and then the name of the payer'.[107] Individual investors as well as banks also entered into *qirād* or *mudāraba* partnerships – which may very well have provided the model for the later Italian *commenda* partnership or *Collegantzia*.[108] The *qirād* or *mudāraba* partnership is an arrangement, whereby an investor supplies capital to an agent (often a trader) who uses this to conduct trade, the profits from which are shared by an agreed amount between the two (plus the return of principal to the investor which is, in reality, interest on the original capital).[109] Typically, the investor puts up the majority of the capital (say 75 per cent) and the trader the remaining 25 per cent, with the profits derived from trade being shared equally. In essence, this institution linked the holder of capital, who sought to put it to productive ends but did not have the means to realise this, with the trader who lacked sufficient capital but had the means to trade. *Qirāds* were taken out to finance either long-distance trade or industrial production (*mufāwada*).[110] Nevertheless, this

[104] Ray (1995: 452).
[105] Timberg (2014: 19).
[106] Koehler (2014: 129–33).
[107] Abu-Lughod (1989: 223).
[108] Udovitch (1962), Goody (1996: 58), Markovits (2000: ch. 5) and Hobson (2004: 119–20).
[109] Koehler (2014: 123–8).
[110] Goitein (1967: 362–7) and Udovitch (1970: ch. 6).

should hardly come as a revelation for, after all, the Prophet Muhammad had been a *qirād* trader who had married a rich woman from the *Qurayshi* tribe – a tribe that had prospered both from the caravan trade and banking.[111]

All in all, Maxime Rodinson's summary seems most apposite here: that 'the merchants of the Muslim Empire conformed perfectly to Weber's criteria for capitalistic activity. They seized any and every opportunity for profit, and calculated their outlays, their encashments and their profits in money terms.'[112] Noteworthy too is that this point was made originally by Abd al-Rahmān Ibn Khaldūn in his seminal text, *The Muqaddimah*. Interestingly, this was written back in the fourteenth century, and it pre-empted many of the claims that we associate with the Scottish political economist, Adam Smith.[113]

Rational Indian/South Asian Economic Institutions (Part Islamic and Part Non-Islamic)

Paralleling these Islamic economic institutions were numerous developments that emerged in India in order to support trans-continental Afro-Eurasian trade. As René Barendse points out, if we are speaking of the Gujarati merchants, then '[t]here seems to be no reason to call [them] capitalists if one thinks about [fixed-capital] investments in production.... [But] the term capitalist makes perfect sense if thinking about sophisticated institutions for credit and insurance, rational bookkeeping, or ways to manipulate the market'.[114] As I noted earlier, finance capitalists are as important a feature of modern capitalism as they were of historical capitalism. Moreover, the *Banjāras*, who were long-distance traders operating *within* India, were supported by the *Banias* who comprised various groups – the *dallāls* (brokers), *baqqals* (wholesalers) and the *sarrāfs* (bankers and money changers).[115] Note that the term *sarrāf* was often Anglicised to *shroff*. The *dallāls* purchased large amounts of low-cost bulk goods from farmers, mainly cotton and grains, and then sent them on to wholesale merchants in regional markets. The *baqqals* were not only wholesalers who dealt specifically in the grain trade but the *dallāls* and *baqqals* also provided loans to farmers for the purchase of seeds and livestock, for which they received part of the final harvest

---

[111] Rodinson (2007: 29–30).
[112] Ibid. (59–60).
[113] Ibn Khaldūn (1377/1958).
[114] Barendse (2002: 180).
[115] For a fuller discussion, see Gokhale (1979: ch. 6), Mehta (1991: ch. 3) and Habib (1960, 1990).

that was then transported to, and sold in, wholesale markets.[116] As I explained in Chapter 6, the *Banias* had access to very large resources and capital and were able to finance long-distance trans-continental trade at much higher levels than even the Dutch and English EICs achieved in the seventeenth and eighteenth centuries.[117] Moreover, the *Banias* in India extended to and linked up with *Bania* firms across the Indian Ocean system, which included the Persian Gulf, Yemen, East Africa and Zanzibar as well as Central Asia and Southeast Asia.[118] And, particularly significant in the light of one of Max Weber's key defining criteria of modern capitalism, many *Banias* utilised double-entry bookkeeping.

The Indian *sarrāfs* engaged in deposit banking and lending out deposits, mainly to merchants, at higher rates of interest, which constitutes a feature of modern banking finance.[119] The Ahmadabad *sarrāfs* were particularly important in this respect. A key instrument here was the Indian bill of exchange, the *hundī*, which was close to the Islamic *suftaja* or *hawāla*. Interestingly, the *hundī* precedes the *hawāla* by several centuries, reaching back to the early years of the first millennium CE.[120] Its function was straightforward: '[r]ather than risk transporting large amounts of cash, merchants and others deposited their money with a *sarrāf* or banker and received an order, or a *hundī*, upon the banking firm for that amount in another place'.[121] The *hundī* was extremely secure. As Scott Levi explains, *hundīs*

were fully saleable instruments, meaning firms could buy and sell them, and use them as a negotiable medium for transmitting large amounts of wealth among multiple financial houses across great distances. They were also fully secure meaning that were it lost or stolen, the holder did not suffer a financial loss. Rather the agent who issued it could confirm the existence of the hundi and its value, and the holder would eventually be paid in full.[122]

And the *hundī* had in common with Indian cotton textiles (ICTs) a reach that covered the entirety of the Indian Ocean system.[123]

Jains comprised the leading bankers from the eleventh century onwards, and certainly, by the seventeenth century, the Jain and Bania

---

[116] Levi (2016: 38).
[117] Goody (1996: 128).
[118] Barendse (2002: 181), Ray (1995), Dobbin (1996), Markovits (2000) and Levi (2016).
[119] For further information on Indian credit, see Barendse (2002: 182–7).
[120] Thompson (2011: 96–7).
[121] Parthasarathi (2011: 63).
[122] Levi (2016: 37).
[123] Das Gupta (2001); see also Levi (2016: 36–8).

bankers had created an unprecedented credit network. Indeed, this linked India south-eastwards through the Straits of Melaka to Bantam, Acheh and the Philippines as well as westward to Basra, Hormuz and Mokha, thereby serving the Mughal, Safavid and Ottoman empires.[124] As Rajat Kanta Ray notes, by the seventeenth century, the *hundī* network, which had been set up originally to transfer funds from one place to another in order to support long-distance trade, comprised a

highly centralised financial device for raising credit for long distance trade on the bankers at Surat and Agra. A merchant short of ready cash could raise money at every major commercial centre in India and at any foreign port of the Indian Ocean with a well-established Gujarati financial and mercantile presence, by drawing a hundi on the Bania bankers of Surat at rates that varied from place to place.[125]

Moreover, the *sarrāfs* discounted *hundīs* to cover interest, the cost of insurance and the transmission of money,[126] thereby making profits in the process. The wealthiest *sarrāfs* were known as Seths, the most famous of which was the Marwari Jagat Seth banking house of the seventeenth and eighteenth centuries.

The Islamic *qirād/mudāraba* institution found its proximate equivalence in the Indian partnership institution known as the *shah-gumāshtā* (creditor-agent). This too stipulated that the shah provides the capital to finance the activities of the agent who then travels abroad to engage in Afro-Eurasian trade. This, like the *qirād* partnership, enabled a regular supply of very large amounts of capital that financed long-distance trade.[127] While I discussed the Multānī traders in detail in Chapter 6, here it is relevant to note that

The Multanis' trade had little in common with the standard peddler model of buying cheap, transporting far and selling dear, and doing the same on the return journey. Rather, these were highly trained financial specialists who sought every opportunity to keep their capital profitably invested the full time that they were abroad. As soon as they retrieved capital from a sale, the Multanis were busy at work reinvesting it in other ventures. It was not uncommon for a Multani who had sold his initial capital investment to choose to completely leave behind the buying and selling of merchandise in favour of the highly profitable moneylending trade.[128]

---

[124] Ray (1995: 462).
[125] Ibid.
[126] Machado (2014: 66).
[127] Markovits (2000: 157–64).
[128] Levi (2016: 72–3).

In short, the Multānīs were commercial and financial capitalists who combined trade and lending for the sole purpose of maximising profits. And, as I also noted in Chapter 6, the significant trans-continental economic diasporas, including the Armenians – to which I would add the Jews – utilised these or similar commercial and financial institutions. All in all, Fernand Braudel's important claim seems pertinent:

> We ... can challenge the traditional [Eurocentric] image ... of Asiatic traders as high-class pedlars hawking about in their small packs tiny quantities of valuable [luxury] merchandise—spices, pepper, pearls, perfumes, drugs and diamonds. The reality is rather different. Everywhere, from Egypt to Japan, we shall find genuine capitalists, wholesalers, the rentiers of trade, and their thousands of auxiliaries—the commission agents, brokers, money-changers and bankers. As for the techniques, possibilities or guarantees of exchange, any of these groups of merchants would stand comparison with its western equivalent.[129]

Finally, it is important to note the existence of various rational *trans-regional* institutions that overlaid these Indian and West Asian institutions which, in turn, enabled both Afro-Eurasian regionalisation between c. 600 and c. 1500 and the development of the FGE between c. 1500 and 1850. Kirti Chaudhuri explains that all foreign merchants who traded at any one of the Indian Ocean trading emporia could rely on the provision and existence of four key commercial and legal services.[130] First, provisioning a ship required 'spot' or forward markets that specified clear price indicators as well as continuity of supply. In order to minimise risk vis-à-vis price volatility, long-distance merchants often operated through a broker, with whom they left a list of goods that they wanted, which the broker subsequently purchased and then shipped in the coming trading season – a practice that 'was essentially a form of forward commodity dealing which avoided the speculative effects of rapid market changes'.[131] Second, monetary institutions and bankers were needed to provide credit, as I explained earlier. Third, means to settle accounts and recover debt existed, alongside the required levels of trust as well as recourse to legal courts. And fourth, a market for shipping space was necessary because those merchants who chose to trade luxury, high-value goods by sea sought to spread the risk by distributing them on numerous ships to hedge against shipwreck or hijacking by pirates. Critically, Chaudhuri argues that all of these services would most likely have emerged after the eighth century CE,

[129] Braudel (1992: 486).
[130] Chaudhuri (1985: 197–200).
[131] Ibid. (198).

thereby reinforcing my point that the requisite trans-continental rational institutions certainly existed alongside the aforementioned diasporic and regional-specific institutions during the FGE, as well as during the era of Afro-Eurasian regionalisation that preceded it.

Conclusion

As Figure 8.2 illustrates, my third layer of historical capitalism comprises global trade. But because this has been discussed in detail in Chapters 2–7, I shall not repeat those findings here. Suffice it to say that I have traced throughout Part I of this book the processes by which global trade played an integrationist role within the FGE. Chapters 3–5 paid special attention to the Indian global super-commodity and super-production chain that fed the 'dodecagonal' (twelve-sided) ICT trading system. This system wove all parts of the world together and ran in tandem with the integrationist role that was performed by the sixteen-sided global Atlantic silver/gold trading system. And in turn, as I also explained, all of this nurtured in various ways the diffusion of other global commodities such as Chinese porcelain and tea, cotton textiles (Nankeens) and silk textiles. In addition, ICT exports enabled Caribbean slave production that generated raw cotton, tobacco, sugar, cacao, coffee, rum and indigo, given that ICTs played such an important role in financing the purchase of the African slaves in the first place. The same point applies in the case of those slaves who were shipped to North America where, after about 1793, they produced the raw cotton in the southern part of the United States that fuelled the British industrial revolution (as I explain in Chapter 9). And because ICT production entailed hybrid social relations in India (as I explain in Chapter 11), this provides a vital cue for a link between global trade and historical capitalist production. All in all, what I have described in Part I is how Indian structural power played a key role in creating and nurturing the FGE. In turn, its significance is developed much further in Parts III–V of this book, where I consider how the Afro-Indian global cotton whip of necessity played an important role in enabling the rise of British industrialisation and subsequently the SGE.

Here, I want to highlight one final problem with the fundamentalist Marxist definition of capitalism, wherein its reductive conception omits other economic components of historical capitalism. In particular, financial capitalists played a vitally important role in enabling global trade and production in the FGE as much as they do today. And this, in turn, points up the important role that was performed by rational economic institutions more generally, without which neither production nor global trade could exist. Accordingly, because historical capitalism has partly modern properties, this means that it cannot be dismissed as antithetical to the status of 'globality', as is the wont of fundamentalist Marxism.

I want to close this chapter by answering a series of key questions. First, was historical capitalism a pre-modern phenomenon? No, because parts of it embodied modern capitalist dimensions, most notably some of the financial aspects of historical capitalism, the many rational economic institutions as well as the partly modern capitalist social relations of production within which many of the FGE's trading commodities were produced. Second, was this a 'transitory' mode that is situated between pure feudal and pure modern capitalist modes such that it would flow inevitably into the latter? No, because there was nothing at the domestic or global levels pushing either China or India to initiate a mechanisation of cotton textile or iron/steel production as I explain in Chapters 11 and 12. Nor was this likely, even had global and international pressures been of sufficient intensity given significant ecological constraints to industrialisation in both raw cotton and coal in China and India. In any case, itinerant merchant capitalists were 'satificers' who saw no need to replace the household form of cotton textile production with centralised factories given that they derived large profits from it and that domestic sociopolitical factors were geared to maintaining historical capitalism in these two countries. Third, could the modern global capitalist economy have emerged in the absence of historical global capitalism? Possibly, though cotton textile industrialisation in Britain would almost certainly not have occurred in the absence of Indian structural power and the Afro-Indian cotton whip that was central to the FGE. And, given the centrality of cotton textiles to Britain's industrialisation that in turn comprised an important component of the SGE, so the emergence of these two economic phenomena would have been muted at the very least. Thus, it is to a consideration of the partly global economic origins of Britain's transition into modern industrial capitalism that Part III of this book is framed which, in turn, is advanced further in Part IV, which considers why Britain industrialised and why China and India did not.

Part III

Empire and the First Global Economy in the Making of Modern Industrial Capitalism, 1500–1800

The Global Atlantic Production
Driver and the Imperial Primitive
Accumulation of British Capital

Introduction

This is the first of two chapters that, in aggregate, reveal how the first global economy (FGE) in tandem with British late-developer agency helped promote Britain's transition into modern industrial capitalism. Here, I advance the argument that the Atlantic colonies, the global Atlantic system and the system of Black slave production provided important causal inputs, either directly (via economic drivers) or indirectly (via fiscal-military drivers), into the British industrial great transformation. Nevertheless, two points are of note, the first of which is that I do *not* conflate the Atlantic contribution with empire. For the African input was partially 'non-imperial' given that Africa was only properly colonised by the Europeans after 1884 – though this point is more relevant to the argument of Chapter 10 where I consider the Atlantic consumption driver. And, moreover, North America became independent after 1776 just *prior* to the time when it became the key supplier of raw cotton to Britain. In addition, I also highlight various other non-Western inputs, where the latter were *not* linked to empire – most of which I consider in Chapter 10.

I argue that external global factors, imperial and non-imperial, provide a necessary but ultimately insufficient base for an explanation of industrialisation because British domestic agential factors were also important. For the fact is that there were plenty of other imperial states that included France, Spain, Portugal, Holland and China, though none of these made the initial transformation into industrialisation. Thus, it wasn't simply the fact of empire that was important but the way that it was managed by British agency that also needs to be factored in. Moreover, I place British agency in the context of global 'uneven and combined development' (UCD) – a framework that builds on the important historical–sociological analysis that is advanced by Alex Anievas, Kerem Nişancioğlu and others.[1] Here, I add to their analysis of UCD

---

[1] Anievas and Nişancioğlu (2015), Matin (2013) and Rosenberg (2006, 2008).

by considering it in the context of the rise of British industrialisation. This takes on further significance because orthodox neo-Marxists assert that UCD – via British imperialism and Western globalisation – cuts in only *after* British industrialisation, not before. In this way, integrating the process of global UCD as *prior* to, and constitutive of, British industrialisation leads to an inversion of the Eurocentric Big Bang theory (BBT). This also enables me to transcend the propensity for 'analytical bifurcation',[2] in which Eurocentric analyses relate industrialisation by bracketing out external and imperial processes in favour of focusing solely on internal/domestic causal factors in accordance with the 'logic of immanence'.

Typically, here is Ellen Meiksins Wood's Political Marxist dismissal that 'we cannot go very far in explaining the rise of capitalism by invoking the contribution of imperialism to "primitive accumulation" or, indeed, by attributing to it any decisive role in the *origin* of capitalism'.[3] Thus, by focusing exclusively on class struggles *within* Britain, all non-Western influences and imperial stimulants are cut out altogether. Such a position is also embraced by the 'father' of Political Marxism, Robert Brenner.[4] Three particular ironies emerge here, the first being that Brenner's posthumous mentor, Karl Marx, saw in the Western colonial-Atlantic system an important vehicle that helped deliver the primitive accumulation of British capitalism,[5] as I explained in Chapter 8. A second and particularly acute irony here is that Brenner turns out to be guilty of the very 'neo-Smithian Marxism' that he accuses Immanuel Wallerstein of succumbing to.[6] For Smith was insistent that imperialism did nothing to promote the overall economic development of the metropole.[7] Finally, the third irony is that for all the much-touted differences, it turns out that Brenner's and Wallerstein's theories share in common a strikingly similar Eurocentric approach given their subscription to the BBT and the logic of immanence.[8] Fortunately, however, there is a small band of pioneering non-Eurocentric neo-Marxist-inspired scholars, including Eric Williams, Andre Gunder Frank, James Blaut, Robin Blackburn

[2] Go (2016: 89–92, 104–10).
[3] Wood (2002: 148).
[4] Brenner (1977: 67).
[5] Marx (1867/1954: chs. 31 and 33).
[6] Brenner (1977).
[7] On this, see Hobson (2012: ch. 2).
[8] On Wallerstein's and Brenner's Eurocentrism, see: Frank (1998: 29–31), Hobson (2012: 236–40), Bhambra (2007: 4–5, ch. 6, 2014: 50–7, 68–70), Tansel (2015a) and Anievas and Nişancıoğlu (2015: ch. 2).

and, not least, Alex Anievas and Kerem Nişancıoğlu, who provide important alternatives that factor in the role of Atlantic imperialism.[9]

All in all, my inversion of the BBT is reflected in Gurminder Bhambra's claim that 'modernity does not itself produce a [globally] connected world, but is itself a product of [already global] interconnections',[10] and that 'colonial expansion preceded [modern] capitalist relations, given that the latter were created and maintained through colonial [economic and military] violence'.[11] Moreover, notwithstanding the unfortunate elision of the role of the Indian Ocean system given its strong links with the Atlantic system, Daron Acemoglu and his co-authors posit a strong linkage between the American/Caribbean colonies and the development of Europe, to wit: 'it appears that the rise of Europe between 1500 and 1850 is largely the rise of Atlantic Europe [in the global Atlantic system], and is quite different in nature from the European growth that took place before 1500'.[12]

This chapter proceeds through four sections. In the section 'The "Global Atlantic/Black Slave Production Driver" of British Industrialisation (I): Supplying Raw Cotton to Lancashire', I focus on the key role that Black slaves played in supplying Lancashire with cheap and high-quality raw cotton, all of which is framed within the conception of the 'global Atlantic system' that I described in Chapter 3. The section 'The Global Atlantic/Black Slave Production Driver (II): The Aggregate Caribbean Input into British Industrialisation' seeks to quantify the aggregate input that Caribbean slave production imparted on British industrialisation, all of which advances further the argument that was made originally by Eric Williams. The section 'The Imperial-Military Driver of British Industrialisation: The Imperial-Military Debt Multiplier' focuses on another key global Atlantic driver of British industrialisation – specifically, the 'imperial-military debt multiplier'. There I quantify the amounts that this generated in terms of promoting investment in the British economy. And finally, in the section 'The Imperial-Military and Global Atlantic Drivers of British Industrialisation: Financial Institutions and the Iron and Steel Revolution', I consider the positive qualitative impact that imperial warfare and Atlantic markets made on Britain's iron industrialisation, while the conclusion aggregates all of the various colonial-related inputs into industrialisation in order to come to a final reckoning on the benefits of empire.

---

[9] Williams (1944/1964), Blaut (1993), Frank (1998), Blackburn (2010) and Anievas and Nişancıoğlu (2015); see also Eley (2007).
[10] Bhambra (2014: 142).
[11] Ibid. (56).
[12] Acemoglu et al. (2005: 546–7).

The 'Global Atlantic/Black Slave Production Driver' of British Industrialisation (I): Supplying Raw Cotton to Lancashire

As I explained in detail in Chapter 3, the Atlantic triangular trading system was in reality embedded within both the sixteen-sided (hexadecagonal) New World-sourced global silver trading system and the twelve-sided (dodecagonal) Indian cotton textile trading system (ICTTS). Relevant here are the African consumers/prosumers and African slaves in the Caribbean and the Americas (see Figure 9.1 below). And, as with the figures posted in the earlier chapters, the way through this one is to follow the numbers.

As Figure 9.1 shows, for the first three centuries after 1500, the global Atlantic system was underpinned by the ICTTS. Thus, the global Atlantic began as a means by which the British (and French) re-exported Indian cotton textiles (ICTs) to Africa in order to purchase slaves who were then exported to the Caribbean where, *inter alia*, they produced the raw cotton that was exported to Lancashire. But during the eighteenth and early-nineteenth centuries, the Afro-Indian global cotton whip of necessity prompted the British to industrialise their cotton textile sector in part through a raft of heavy protectionist measures, such that by the 1820s, the system had been transformed into one that was finally dominated by British-made cotton textiles (as I explain in Chapter 10). But my key focus in this section is on the New World system of slave production as well as the export of raw cotton that fed the Lancashire cotton mills.

In addition to the various quotes from Karl Marx's work that I cited in Chapter 9 concerning the causal input of the Atlantic colonies to British industrialisation, here I note that Marx was not far off the mark when he asserted that

Without slavery, no cotton; without cotton, no modern industry; the colonies have created world trade [or, more accurately, they fed into the trading system of the first global economy]; world trade is the necessary condition of large-scale machine industry [in Britain].... Thus slavery is an economic category of the highest importance.[13]

The morphing of the global dodecagonal ICTTS into one that was dominated by British cotton textiles in the nineteenth century owed a considerable debt to Black slave producers of raw cotton, initially in

[13] Marx (1846/1975: 95). See also the various relevant quotes by Marx in Chapter 8.

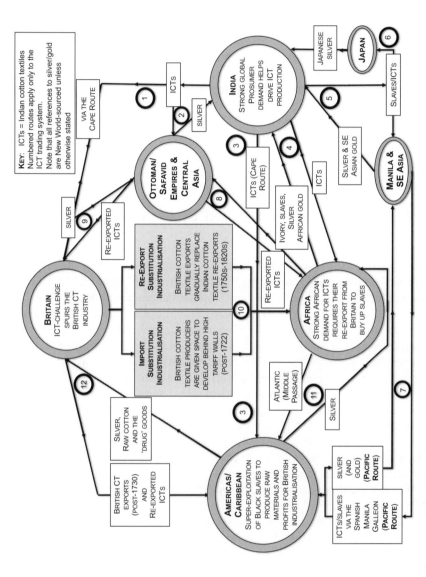

Figure 9.1 The 'Global Atlantic production driver' of Britain's cotton industrialisation.

the Caribbean and subsequently, before and after about 1793, in the United States – though it should be noted that Ottoman sources were also important in the eighteenth century.[14] Raw cotton production began in Barbados in the 1620s and later on in Jamaica in 1670. However, by the 1770s, Caribbean cotton became increasingly expensive, not least because the relatively limited output could not meet the rapidly growing British demand. And, this came at a time when a large price-gap opened up between Caribbean raw cotton and Indian raw cotton. For by the 1790s, Indian raw cotton was about 20 per cent the cost of the Caribbean product,[15] which naturally enhanced India's global competitiveness relative to Britain's. Added to this was the impact of the Haitian revolution in 1791 (which occurred some nine centuries after the first major African slave rebellion in Basra). Thus, the year before 1791, Saint Domingue had supplied just under a quarter of Britain's cotton imports, whereas some four years later, it had dropped to just under 5 per cent.[16]

But at precisely this time serendipity intervened. Ironically, through no intention of the British – in fact quite the opposite – North American raw cotton came on line to service Lancashire's rapidly growing appetite. And, while it was highly fortuitous that vast amounts were delivered in the first half of the nineteenth century, it was no less highly ironic given that it was only with the *end* of the British empire that the United States gained the freedom to produce raw cotton for export. For under British rule, North America had been largely prohibited from growing raw cotton as it was seen as a competitor to British wool exports. Nevertheless, behind the picture of the bright sunny uplands that Lancashire basked in lay the hidden dark side of the Native 'Indian' tragedy. For the development of cotton plantations led to the clearing of vast areas of land for cultivation, which entailed the purging of Native Indians, most notably the Cherokees following the Indian Removal Act in 1830.[17] In this way, the industrialisation of cotton production within Britain rested on the pedestal of the forced dispossession of the Native Indians from their lands in the United States.

There were three principal reasons why this primitive accumulation by Native dispossession was entirely serendipitous for the Lancashire cotton manufacturers. First, a new 'long-staple' seed was developed that was known as 'Upland cotton' (*Gossypium hirsutum*), which was used alongside

---

[14] Wadsworth and de Lacy Mann (1931: 183–5).
[15] Broadberry and Gupta (2009).
[16] Beckert (2015: 96).
[17] Riello (2013: 203–9).

the long-staple Sea Island variety (*Gossypium barbadense*).[18] Moreover, after the 1820s, the Americans began growing the Mexican variety of *G. hirsutum*, which increased the yield and improved productivity. Critically, these varieties of long staple were far better suited to the new machines that the British invented in the 1760s through the 1780s than was the short-staple Caribbean variety. To be clear, though, long-staple Sea Island cotton *was* grown alongside short-staple varieties in the Caribbean, but the amounts produced of the former were woefully inadequate to meet Britain's escalating industrial demand, as Williams originally noted.[19]

As I note in Chapter 10, these long-staple varieties enabled yarn that was of sufficient tensile strength for the warp that was required for Britain's new power looms, on the one hand, and the production of medium- and high-count yarn that yielded more sophisticated cotton textiles on the other. The short staple could not have performed these functions as it lacked sufficient tensile strength. And it is on this simple point that so much hangs. For as I explain in Chapter 11, one of the many likely reasons why the Chinese and Indians chose *not* to industrialise their cotton sector is because they grew only the short-staple cotton variety – probably the shortest of any cotton in the world. Or, put differently, had the Indians and Chinese tried to initiate industrialisation, it would have been severely limited by the inferior, short-staple raw cotton that they relied upon. It was, therefore, highly serendipitous for Lancashire that the new long-staple American cotton varieties came on stream at the very same time that Arkwright's water frame (1769), Crompton's mule (1779) and Cartwright's power loom (1785) were bedding in within the British mills.

The second major piece of good luck that accrued to the Lancashire manufacturers was Eli Whitney's famous invention of a new cotton gin, otherwise known as a 'cotton saw'. This was required for removing the seeds from the cotton, the effect of which was to increase ginning output by a factor of 50. 'Only then did the American dream of massive planting of Upland cotton in the southern states and exporting it to England become a reality.'[20] Third, and finally, the organisation of Black slaves on the North American plantations also proved highly serendipitous for Lancashire. In particular, between 1800 and 1860, there was a fourfold increase in the amount of cotton picked. Some scholars put this down

---

[18] Ibid. (258).
[19] Williams (1944/1964: 70).
[20] Chao (1977: 76).

to the role of slave gang-labour,[21] which had first been developed by the British on the sugar plantations in the Caribbean. One contemporary observer explained that the gangs 'moved across the fields in parallel lines, with a considerable degree of precision and underlined the near military organization of such a regime of labour'.[22] Indeed, even before 1860, the planters were involved in experimenting in the scientific management of slave labour to effect higher productivity. Riello explains that the work regime was one that was based on the 'maximum efficiency principle', in which the most efficient slaves were placed at the front of the line while all the others had to keep with up with their pace of work. And, *contra* Adam Smith,[23] it turns out that when compared with farms run on free-wage labour, the gang system was able to produce up to 40 per cent more.[24]

The effect of these three serendipitous developments was a radical reduction in the costs of raw cotton such that its price fell by 64 per cent between 1796/1800 and 1846/50, thereby providing a further boost to Lancashire's ascendance to *near* global cotton-supremacy in the nineteenth century.[25] For it is notable that Lancashire's output failed to exceed that of China's during the nineteenth century, as I explain in Chapter 13. As early as the 1820s, the price of raw cotton that was supplied to Lancashire was only a fraction higher than the cost of Indian raw cotton,[26] though thereafter further price reductions played in Britain's favour as these enhanced Lancashire's competitiveness vis-à-vis Indian exports and re-exports. Thus, as Caribbean cotton supplies tailed off at the end of the eighteenth century and increasingly large North American supplies came on stream, so the great divergence between the two suppliers took off in favour of the United States after 1805, such that by the 1820s, the United States supplied some 75 per cent of Britain's raw cotton needs.[27] Accordingly, without these supplies of high-quality raw cotton that were sent to Britain, it would have been extremely difficult for Lancashire to have sustained such high levels of either domestic manufactures or exports.[28] Thus, the Atlantic's plentiful supplies were critical to Lancashire's success,[29] such that between 85 and

---

[21] Fogel (1989).
[22] Frederick Law Olmstead cited in Riello (2013: 258).
[23] Smith (1776/1937: 364–5).
[24] Riello (2013: 258) and Metzer (1975).
[25] Blackburn (2010: 555) and Inikori (2002: 368).
[26] Broadberry and Gupta (2009).
[27] Inikori (2002: ch. 8).
[28] Pomeranz (2000: 54–5, 276–8).
[29] Farnie (1979: 82–3).

98 per cent of Britain's raw cotton imports in 1784/1856 came from the Americas and the Caribbean.[30] And it was this that 'supplied the means by which [British manufacturers could] overcome [the] formidable Indian competition'.[31] All of which, in sum, was as serendipitous for Lancashire as it was tragic for the Native American Indians and the imported Black slaves.

While initially the Atlantic system of slave production was significantly, though not exclusively, financed by ICTs, this position had changed in Britain's favour by the 1820s. For by then, British-made cotton textile exports finally took the lead over re-exported ICTs to meet African and American consumer needs. Thus, while in the first half of the eighteenth century, British-made cotton textile exports to Africa were a mere 10 per cent that of re-exported Indian calicoes (as I explained in Chapter 3), thereafter they traded places such that by the 1830s, ICT *re-exports* to Africa were a mere 9 per cent that of British-made textile exports and a mere 4 per cent by the 1840s.[32] Even so, as I explain in Chapter 13, Indian merchants continued to sell ICTs independently in East Africa.

However, because this North American input into British industrialisation did not comprise a pure 'imperial' component given that the United States had become fully independent just prior to its move into raw cotton production, so some scholars have argued that the Atlantic *colonies* were *not* responsible for stimulating the British industrial revolution.[33] But this argument occludes the more significant point that the lowest common denominator of the Caribbean and North American supplies before and after 1793 lay in the mass exploitation of Black slaves in the provision of Britain's raw cotton requirements. Thus, to paraphrase Malachy Postlethwayt's well-known claim with respect to British trade, we might conclude that Britain's industrialisation was, albeit in part, 'a magnificent superstructure of [Atlantic] commerce and [British] naval power on an African foundation'.[34] And it is notable that even after the US Emancipation Act in 1865, Black forced-prison labour remained important on the Southern cotton plantations.[35]

[30] Inikori (2002: 372–4).
[31] Blackburn (2010: 555).
[32] Calculated from the data in Inikori (2002: 444).
[33] For example, Vries (2013: 262).
[34] Postlethwayt cited in Williams (1944/1964: 52).
[35] LeBaron (2012).

*A Counterfactual Thought Experiment: Would Britain's Cotton
Industrialisation Have Happened in the Absence of Black Slavery?*

Here, it is worth engaging in a counterfactual thought experiment. It is clear that in the eighteenth century, huge numbers of Black slaves were shipped from Africa to the Caribbean and the Americas. The scale of this trade can be gauged by the fact that while the British population in 1800 was around ten million,[36] the British alone transported from Africa to the Americas between 2.55 and 2.9 million slaves during the eighteenth century, as I noted in Chapter 3. But in the absence of the trade in African slaves, or even allowing for much-reduced numbers, the history of Britain's presence in the Caribbean and North America would have been very different, of course, but critically it would have likely impacted negatively on Lancashire's fortunes.

Not very long after the fateful year of 1492, it became clear that the Europeans were unable to rely on the indigenous Indian population in the Americas to work on the plantations, sugar mills and mines because many of them had been wiped out either by European diseases – up to 90 per cent in some regions – or by European guns.[37] The solution to plugging the indigenous labour-gap was, of course, the importation of African slaves, who had the added advantage of being resistant to European diseases. But had a much-reduced trade in African slaves transpired, then it is possible that the gap would have remained unplugged. And it is unlikely that the Europeans would have been able to make good this deficit either by exporting British labourers or using Chinese and Indian indentured labour as they tried to do after 1833 – the year the British abolished slavery. It is also notable that in the whole of the Americas, Black African labour was highly significant given that the share of *all* export commodities produced by African slaves comprised just over 50 per cent in the sixteenth century, before rising to 69 per cent in the seventeenth century and to just over 80 per cent in the eighteenth century.[38]

But surely, it might be replied, the British could have sourced their raw cotton from elsewhere, most notably from India or Egypt, and thereby avoided their reliance on Black slaves. After all, didn't India become a major supplier to Lancashire after 1861? But as I explained earlier, the new British cotton machines – the water frame/mule/power loom – worked much better with 'long-staple' raw cotton. Which means

---

[36] Flynn and Giráldez (2008: 380).
[37] Crosby (1972: ch. 2). Or as James Blaut (1993: 184) notes, it seems fairer to say that the 'Americans were not conquered: they were infected'.
[38] Inikori (2002: 196–7).

that Indian supplies were not a realistic long-term alternative given that its cotton was a weak, short-staple variety and, as numerous Britons complained, it also suffered various other problems such as being 'ill prepared, ill-cleaned, and even adulterated with foreign substances such as mud, leaves, and stones'.[39] This is why the British shifted away from Indian raw cotton supplies very rapidly after 1865, having relied on them for only four years as a means of making good the deficit in US cotton supplies that had occurred during the US Civil War (known as the 'Lancashire cotton famine'). As I also explain in Chapter 13, despite the familiar postcolonial and Marxist claim that Britain de-industrialised India's cotton textile industry and then turned India into a raw cotton supplier for Lancashire in the second half of the nineteenth century, the reality is that the British manufacturers were far more interested in the much higher quality, long-staple Egyptian cotton. However, while Egyptian production levels were maintained during the 1870s after US supplies had been restored, the fact is that Egypt could never have constituted a viable alternative to American supplies given that it could not match the sheer scale of the latter. And, as noted, nor could India have constituted a long-term alternative prospect given that the attempts to introduce long-staple American cotton through the 'cotton improvement programme' (1865–75) failed.[40] Interestingly, though, Egypt constituted the exceptional counterfactual that proves the slave-rule: for its production of raw cotton was achieved through deploying Black slaves (and Turkish *corvée* labour) between 1860 and 1877, with 25–30,000 Black slaves imported each year from Africa via the West Asian slave trade to work on the Egyptian cotton plantations.[41] All of which means that Lancashire's fortunes would have taken a major hit in the absence of the Black slave production of raw cotton.

The final prong of my counterfactual thought experiment lies in the point that a much smaller slave trade to the New World might have reduced the *desire* on the part of British cotton inventors and producers to supersede the very strong African demand for ICTs during the eighteenth century. For, as noted, ICTs were the key currency of exchange for purchasing slaves and it was this, in particular, that drove British inventors to mechanise production in Lancashire so as to overcome Britain's hitherto dependence on using re-exported ICTs to purchase slaves in Africa (as I explain in Chapter 10). Which means that in the absence of the Atlantic slave system, British manufacturers might

[39] Earle (1926: 527).
[40] Earle (1926) and Harnetty (1970).
[41] Baer (1967) and Cuno (2009).

never have chosen to industrialise the cotton industry in the first place. Nevertheless, we need to qualify this claim. For, British manufacturers were *also* driven by wresting Indian structural power that could then be reinforced by imperial state power, having learned of the mass-scale global markets for ICTs during their Afro-Indian apprenticeship (as I also explain in Chapter 10).

However, while the supply of Caribbean cotton had its heyday in the second half of the eighteenth century, it is important to recognise that the West Indies produced large amounts of sugar and also supplied an array of other consumer 'drug goods' that included rum, tobacco and coffee. And it is this bigger picture that I now want to quantify in order to consider the *aggregate* Atlantic colonial input into British industrialisation.

The Global Atlantic/Black Slave Production Driver (II): The *Aggregate* Caribbean Input into British Industrialisation

This section seeks to develop and quantify the twin claims that were advanced by Karl Marx, the first of which is contained in an 1846 letter to Pavel Vasilyevich Annenkov:

Freedom and slavery constitute an antagonism.... We are not dealing with the indirect slavery, the slavery of the [English] proletariat, but with direct slavery, the slavery of the black races in Surinam, in Brazil, in the Southern States of North America. *Direct slavery is as much of the pivot of our industrialism today as machinery, credit, etc.*[42]

And the second claim is advanced in Chapter 31 of the first volume of *Capital*, where Marx asserts that '[t]he colonies secured a market for the budding manufactures, and, through the monopoly of the market, an increased accumulation. The treasures captured outside Europe by undisguised looting, enslavement, and murder, floated back to the mother country and were there turned into capital.'[43] These insightful cues were then developed into a full-blown account of the Atlantic origins of British industrialisation in Eric Williams's classic text, *Capitalism and Slavery*.[44] The following discussion advances further the 'Williams thesis' to show that the Caribbean colonies in general and slave-based

---

[42] Marx (1846/1975: 95), my emphasis.
[43] Marx (1867/1954: 705).
[44] Williams (1944/1964).

production profits in particular were of a sufficient scale to have made a significant contribution to the formation and development of British industrialisation.[45] I begin by quantifying the overall 'Atlantic (Black slave) production driver' of British industrialisation.

Quantifying the Black Slave Contribution to the Imperial Primitive Accumulation of British Capitalism

The debate on the economic benefits of Black slavery, which takes as its cue the *Williams thesis*, has often been reduced to the question of the profits that were derived from the *slave trade*. Critics, especially of a liberal persuasion, deride this potential contribution to British industrialisation.[46] Perhaps most well-known is Roger Anstey's argument that between 1761 and 1807, slave trade profits averaged a mere £115,000 per annum which, he claims, would have increased total investment in the British economy by an inconsequential 0.11 per cent of national income per annum. Dismissing these profits as but 'small ratios' led him to conclude that such contributions are 'derisory enough for the myth of the vital importance of the slave trade in financing the British industrial revolution to be demolished'.[47] Although higher figures have been produced,[48] the fact remains that focusing solely on the profits from the *slave trade* obscures the much larger profits that were derived from slave-based colonial *production and its related trading profits*. And it is this wider slave-based context that I focus upon here.

Table 9.1 provides an overview of various calculations that I have made in order to estimate the economic benefits of all related Atlantic slave production and trade that helped drive British industrial investment. So as not to clutter up the text, I have tapped the details and sources into Appendix 2 (pp. 461–463). And note that I also include a figure for what I call the imperial-military debt multiplier, which I consider in the next section.

Column 2 reveals the amounts that were available from the profits derived from slave-based production and trade, which I estimate at providing between 18 and about 20 per cent of investment in the British economy. Critically, then, *contra* Anstey's dismissal of these as but inconsequential 'small ratios', my figure points to a significant,

---

[45] See also the discussions in Engerman and Genovese (1975), Solow and Engerman (1987), Solow (1991) and Inikori and Engerman (1992).
[46] Engerman (1972) and Thomas (1968).
[47] Anstey (1975: 24).
[48] Engerman (1972: 440) and Esteban (2001: 60).

Table 9.1 *Atlantic-sourced profits and revenues in Britain's industrialisation as percentage of British domestic investment (gross fixed capital formation)*

1	2	3	4	5
Years	Aggregate slave-based profits	Imperial-military debt multiplier	Total (Cols 2 + 3)	Col. 4 as percentage of total fixed investment in iron and cotton industries + related transport infrastructure
1770	18	19	37	64
1760–1820	c. 20	31*	51	136
1760–1820	c. 20	18**	38	80

Notes: For sources and explanation of all calculations see Appendix 2.
*Annual average of *all* of Britain's imperial-related wars.
**Calculation includes *all* of Britain's imperial wars but includes only 25 per cent of the expenditures on the French wars (1793–1815) on the basis that empire was not the key motivating factor.

though certainly not a massive-ratios argument.[49] And these could have financed up to 53 per cent of total (fixed capital) investment in the two leading industries, cotton and iron and the related infrastructural supports (1760–1820). Accordingly, this in turn raises the question as to the likelihood of these colonial-derived profits finding their way into these industries. Here, I shall focus on the cotton industry.

While we will probably never know the precise domestic avenues along which these colonial profits wended their way into financing the British economy, we do know that the linchpin of the 'triangular trading' and Caribbean colonial production system was the city of Liverpool. Numerous British economic historians, in seeking to understand why the majority of the cotton mills were located in Lancashire (which centred on Manchester and its surrounding areas), cite factors such as access to cheap coal, relatively low wages, low land values, clear access to water power and so on,[50] all of which were clearly important. But it seems particularly curious that they tend to overlook the proximity of the Lancashire cotton industry to the port of Liverpool, which in turn was connected directly to the West African ports where slaves were purchased and where significant consumer markets existed. And, of

[49] Cf. Solow (1985: 105).
[50] Crafts and Wolf (2012) and Allen (2009).

course, Liverpool was linked directly to the cotton-producing plantations and cotton textile markets of the Americas/Caribbean on the final leg.[51] Indeed, as Eric Williams originally noted, the 'growth of Manchester was intimately associated with the growth of Liverpool, its outlet to the sea and the world market [via the so-called triangular trading system]. The capital accumulated by Liverpool from the slave trade [as well as profits derived from slave-production and related trade] poured into the hinterland to fertilize the energies of Manchester.'[52] Moreover, many of the Caribbean's absentee landlords resided in Liverpool and its surrounding areas.

There was certainly a considerable overlap of Atlantic and Lancashire cotton interests that converged in Liverpool. Riello notes the examples of Sir William Fazackerly and Samuel Touchet, both of whom were cotton manufacturers and members of the Company of Merchants Trading to Africa. Touchet was a Liverpool trader who was involved in the trade to Africa and the West Indies, while also being a cotton check manufacturer in Manchester. Notable too is that he was one of the main financial backers of Lewis Paul and John Wyatt's first (albeit failed) attempt to construct a cotton spinning machine.[53] To these names, Eric Williams adds that of the Hibberts, who owned sugar plantations in Jamaica and who also supplied cotton checks and imitation calicoes to the Royal African Company for the purchase of Black slaves.[54] Moreover, Robin Blackburn notes that of the twenty key merchants involved in the Atlantic slave trade, a good number resided in Lancashire.[55] A particularly notable cotton manufacturer was Samuel Greg, who had deep roots in the colonies and within the process that Sven Beckert calls 'war capitalism'.[56] Part of the money that financed Greg's cotton mill (Quarry Bank Mill on the edge of Manchester) was derived from the profits of his sugar plantation in the Caribbean. As Beckert explains,

Greg's uncles Robert and Nathaniel Hyde ... [who] also provided much of the capital for the building of Quarry Bank Mill, were also textile manufacturers, West Indian plantation owners, and merchants. Greg's wife, Hannah Lightbody, was born into a family involved in the slave trade, while his sister-in-law's family had moved from the slave trade into the export of cloth into Africa.[57]

---

[51] See especially, Beckert (2015: 212–24).
[52] Williams (1944/1964: 68); cf. Wadsworth and de Lacy Mann (1931: 211).
[53] Riello (2013: 152).
[54] Williams (1944/1964: 70–1, 88–9).
[55] Blackburn (2010: 547–50).
[56] Beckert (2015).
[57] Ibid. (60).

Accordingly, it is not implausible to hypothesise that a significant amount of the reinvestable profits that were derived from the Atlantic world could have been channelled into the Lancashire cotton mills, particularly by those who were investing in the cotton plantations in the Americas that in turn supplied the raw cotton for Lancashire. But in any case, we do know that the Manchester cotton manufacturers were deeply embedded in selling their wares most especially to Africa, such that the Black 'prosumer' that I discussed in Chapter 4 played a key role in the technological industrialisation of the British cotton sector. All of which is captured in the global Atlantic consumption driver that I discuss in Chapter 10. For the moment, though, I want to consider a further role that the Atlantic colonies played, albeit *indirectly*, in stimulating British modernisation.

The Imperial-Military Driver of British Industrialisation: The Imperial-Military Debt Multiplier

Here, I turn to factor in the imperial geo-fiscal input into British industrialisation. Specifically, I quantify the amounts of money that the 'imperial-military debt multiplier' fed back into the British economy. This reflects my generic claim that *imperial* warfare had all manner of positive, knock-on effects for British economic growth. In the process, this reveals another blind spot of much of neo-Marxism and neo-Weberianism. While Marxists and neo-Weberians place much emphasis on the role that warfare played in driving European capitalism forward, nevertheless these approaches sequester or quarantine British warfare from the political economy of empire and capitalist development. This emerges from their shared base-line assumption that it was largely the impact of *intra*-European geopolitical competition, which was a function of the 'anarchic' European inter-state system, that drove the rise of European capitalism.[58] By contrast, I argue that while warfare was indeed very important to the rise of British industrialisation and that most of it was indeed conducted between European states, nevertheless it was the *imperial context* that was vital in the British case.[59] Seen in this light, then, Marxists and neo-Weberians default once again to the Eurocentric manoeuvre of 'analytical bifurcation' by splitting the British

---

[58] A smattering of this literature comprises Wallerstein (1974), Anderson (1974), Tilly (1990), Brenner (1977, 1982), Giddens (1985), Collins (1985), Ferguson (2011) and Vries (2013, 2015).

[59] See especially, Satia (2018).

state into two halves and then focusing only on the European context to the exclusion of the imperial.

The imperial-military debt multiplier refers to the process whereby the credit that was raised in the City of London to pay for the extraordinary military expenditures in Britain's imperial wars received substantial interest payments from the state, part of which was then invested back into the economy. And this is fundamentally entwined with Britain's 'forced industrialisation' insofar as the moneys that paid the interest via the regressive tax system were redistributed mainly from low-income groups to the rich investor class in the city which then invested part of it within the British economy.

However, before I quantify this particular contribution, it is important to note a further liberal counterfactual, which emerges as a legacy of Adam Smith's argument:[60] that imperial-military spending served only to *undermine* domestic economic development as it diverted taxpayers' money into 'wasteful outlets', in the absence of which they could have been ploughed into more productive investment at home.[61] One of the leading proponents of the liberal counterfactual, Jeffrey Williamson, puts it thus:

Why was British growth so slow in the six decades before the 1820s? One answer might be that the conventional dating of the industrial revolution is simply wrong. Another answer, however, is more plausible: that Britain tried to do two things at once—industrialize and fight expensive wars, and she simply did not have the resources to do both.[62]

And he goes on to argue that annual British growth rates could have been a not inconsiderable 30 per cent higher (or 0.6 per cent per annum) between 1761 and 1820 in the absence of these wars.[63] It was for this reason that when calculating the profits that were derived from the Caribbean sugar islands, the well-known critic of the 'Williams thesis', Robert Thomas, *deducted* the *whole* amount that was spent on the prosecution of the imperial-military defence of these colonies. Thus, congruent with Williamson's logic, Thomas argues that 'for the year 1773 the income of Englishmen would have been at least £0.6m higher had the West Indies not been a part of the empire. It appears ... that

---

[60] Smith (1776/1937: 580–3, 592–3).
[61] See most notably, Vries (2013: 261–2), McCloskey (2010), Mokyr (2009), Williamson (1984), Engerman (1972: 442) and Thomas (1968: 34).
[62] Williamson (1984: 689).
[63] Ibid. (702); see also Mokyr (2009) and McCloskey (2010).

Adam Smith was correct, at least with respect to the sugar colonies – they were "mere loss instead of profit".[64]

One problem with the liberal counterfactual is that it rests on a simple binary, which comprises a zero-sum relationship between imperial-military spending and domestic economic growth – i.e., that you can't have both at the same time. But the argument of this section is that there existed a positive-sum relationship between the two such that imperial-military spending *spurred on* industrialisation. Here, I shall focus on how the 'imperial-military debt multiplier' imparted *indirect* benefits to the British economy. But first, it is necessary to consider the size of imperial-military spending.

Quantifying the Real Cost of Britain's Imperial-Military Spending

The first thing to note about the long eighteenth century (1688–1815) is that the many wars in which Britain was engaged were influenced heavily and often exclusively by imperial concerns. Indeed, this period has been labelled 'the second hundred years war' given that Britain and France engaged in warfare in order to win the twin-prize of empire and world trade domination.[65] It is certainly true that some of these, such as the War of the Austrian Succession and especially the Napoleonic Wars, were fought principally by the numerous combatants over the European balance of power. But the fact is that even in these instances, colonial issues were highly significant so far as Britain was concerned. Thus, as Julian Go explains, during the War of the Spanish Succession Britain 'feared that a Bourbon prince on the Spanish throne would enable the French to dominate the Spanish Indies, which would in turn threaten Britain's holdings and trade'.[66] Accordingly, the British engaged in battles in the West Indies and North America. And, following the end of the war, they gained the naval bases of Gibraltar and Minorca, Nova Scotia, Newfoundland and the Hudson Bay territories. Part of the War of the Austrian Succession was also fought in North America. Moreover, a large component of the Napoleonic Wars so far as Britain was concerned was the battle over the Atlantic colonies and trade.[67] For with the opening up of the imperial world, overwhelmingly in the Atlantic, a competitive struggle over empire and trade erupted not infrequently into military conflict between the key European imperial powers, of which Britain was the major and most consistent combatant.

[64] Thomas (1968: 38). See also Vries (2013: 261).
[65] Sheridan (1969: 13).
[66] Go (2011: 35).
[67] Blackburn (2010: 568–72).

Table 9.2 *The costs of Britain's major imperial and imperial-related wars, 1689–1815*

Major wars	Dates	D1	D2
Nine Years' War (and King William's War)	1689–97	10.9	11.7
War of the Spanish Succession (& Queen Anne's War)	1702–13	9.5	12.5
War of the Austrian Succession and the War of Jenkins' Ear	1740–48	9.6	13.3
Seven Years' War	1756–63	14.6	19.1
War of American Independence	1776–84	12.5	18.5
Revolutionary Wars/Napoleonic Wars	1793–1815	16.1	24.5

Source and Notes:
Military expenditures: Mitchell (2011: 578–80, 587–90).
National income: This is explained in Weiss and Hobson (1995: 130).
D1 = Total ordinary plus extra-ordinary military spending as a percentage of national income.
D2 = D1 plus interest payments on extraordinary military spending (financed out of the national debt) as a percentage of national income.

Indeed, according to the data provided by Julian Go, in the 1706–59 period, Britain added only four colonial territories though the territorial accumulation process escalated thereafter with forty-three added in 1760–1814, with the largest number being accrued during the wars with France between 1793 and 1815.[68]

Table 9.2 reveals the *real* costs of Britain's major imperial wars. Clearly, these costs were historically unprecedented. While in the first half of the eighteenth century, the *real* military burden – i.e., military expenditures expressed as a percentage of national income – was about three times that of the 1860–1913 period, the second half expended just under six times more. To give a clearer idea of just how exceptional these expenditures were, I calculate that the British imperial-military burden (D1) was about twice as high as those that were experienced by France, Germany, Italy and Russia during their industrialisation phases. Moreover, the figure for D2 was about three times those of France, Germany and Italy and about twice that of Russia in their respective industrialisation phase.[69] Finally, I calculate that between 1914 and 1980 (which included two world wars, of course), British D1 was 7.8 per cent and D2 was 12 per cent, which compared with 7.5 per cent (D1) and 13.5 per cent (D2)

---

[68] Go (2011: 31).
[69] For a full discussion of the complex calculations that produce these ratios, see Hobson (1997: 284–90).

for the 1715–1850 period. Notable too, as I explained in Chapter 2, is that Britain's spending (D2) was thirteen times larger than China's in 1760–1815.

Quantifying the Economic Benefits of Britain's Imperial-Military Spending

As noted, in financing these sustained and highly expensive imperial-based wars between 1689 and 1815, the British state had to resort to loans that were supplied by the City of London. The imperial-military debt multiplier rested on an effective programme of 'forced savings', which constituted an 'indirect' version of the Tsarist (and Soviet) state's strategy of 'forced savings' and 'forced industrialisation'.[70] The logic of this is that in the absence of a strong bourgeoisie in Russia in the second half of the nineteenth century, the state stepped in as a substitute because its autocratic nature enabled it to tax the lower orders very harshly through high and regressive taxes, with the proceeds being invested by the state in the economy so as to force through industrialisation.[71]

In the British version of this strategy, the state also effected a highly *authoritarian* 'forced industrialisation', albeit in an *indirect* way, insofar as it taxed the lower orders harshly through highly regressive indirect taxes, with the proceeds being redistributed to the rich financial class through interest payments on the national debt. And subsequently, these profits were then invested in the domestic economy by the City of London finance-capitalists rather than the state (hence 'indirect' state intervention), thereby helping drive industrialisation and economic growth. Moreover, I argue below that the British strategy was in some ways more pronounced than Tsarist Russia's and, as I have argued elsewhere, it was certainly far more effective given that Tsarist autocracy achieved only a *partial* industrialisation.[72] However, for those readers who assume that the British state was democratic during its industrialisation phase, Peer Vries is correct to assert that it

would really be too naïve and simplistic to explain the strength of Great Britain's state solely via representation and inclusion. Just as often, if not more often, it

---

[70] Gerschenkron (1962: 17, 20, 119–42) and von Laue (1963); cf. Trotsky (1906/2010: 42–51).

[71] Note that for Trotsky (1906/2010), Tsarism's forced industrialisation was driven by a military rationale whereas for Gerschenkron it was motivated primarily for the economic purpose of catching up with Britain. But see the latter's ambiguous thoughts concerning possible military impulses (Gerschenkron 1962: 360–1).

[72] Weiss and Hobson (1995: ch. 4) and Hobson (1997: chs. 3–4).

was based on non-representation and exclusion. Public debt ... was a vehicle for redistribution of wealth, making the wealthy even more wealthy.[73]

Critically, the working classes, from whom the majority of the money went to paying the interest on the national debt, had no say in any of this given that they only became enfranchised well after the main industrialisation phase (1700–1846).[74]

As in the last section, here I shall report various findings, the sources and calculations of which are reported in Appendix 2. Here, I refer my reader back to Table 9.1. In 1770, the amount that was available for reinvestment in the British economy via the imperial-debt military multiplier comprised some *19 per cent of gross fixed capital formation (GFCF)*. Nevertheless, there is strong evidence to suggest that the City of London did *not* finance *fixed capital* investment in manufacturing. Does this mean that such funds did not find their way into financing British industrialisation? Postan originally argued that investment in industry was largely self-financed – though informal credit structures were also relevant.[75] But towards the end of the eighteenth century, country banks and the City of London began financing manufacturing's *working* rather than fixed capital.[76] How, then, does this relate to the financing of the cotton industry? It is generally accepted that the cotton industry could finance its fixed capital requirement – machinery, buildings, etc. – out of its operating profits, though some of this was certainly financed out of the profits of Atlantic slave production, especially when setting up a cotton mill in the first place, as I argued earlier. But what proved much more onerous was financing 'circulating' (or 'working') capital, which funded the cost of raw materials as well as the marketing and selling of the finished products in foreign markets.[77] And this is reckoned to have been much higher than the cost of fixed capital investment – perhaps by as much as 300 per cent.[78]

Critically, as both Hudson and Inikori point out, the financial institutions, of which the City of London was especially important, provided much of the funds for circulating capital.[79] Thus, if the cost of circulating capital in the cotton industry in 1770 was about

---

[73] Vries (2015: 233).
[74] Universal male suffrage was only won in 1918 and universal suffrage (including all women) in 1928.
[75] Postan (1935).
[76] Shapiro (1967).
[77] Blackburn (2010: 532).
[78] Chapman (1972/2006: ch. 3).
[79] Inikori (2002: 315, 316–17) and Hudson (1986).

£1.2 million, then the £0.8 million that the city derived from interest payments from war-related credit that was available for reinvestment could have financed around two-thirds of this figure for circulating capital – though, of course, by no means would all of this have gone into such a venture, not least because the London and regional banks were also important sources.[80] But with the help of the city and the country banks that were also nourished by the profits of financing Atlantic slave production and trade (as I explain later), so this freed up the cotton manufacturers to finance their fixed capital, either out of their operating profits or out of those that were derived from Atlantic slave production and trade. Put differently, had the Lancashire entrepreneurs been forced to rely on self-financing their circulating capital, they would not have had the resources to invest in the fixed capital of their cotton mills. And, as Inikori explains, 'the financial institutions ... made indirect contributions to the funding of fixed capital investment in manufacturing' and that this constituted a critical function in the process of industrial investment.[81] But what of the 'forced savings' argument that I raised earlier? Here, we need to know how much of the money that went from the city came out of the pockets of the poor. I now move to the second calculation as signalled above.

In order to pay the City of London creditors for advancing the massive loans to prosecute Britain's sustained imperial wars, the state sought to raise most of the funds by taxing the poor. To this end, regressive indirect taxes – i.e., customs and excise – were increased to an average 66 per cent of total central government taxes between 1715 and 1850, a move that began in 1685.[82] Moreover, the real burden of these particular taxes stood at an annual average of 9.5 per cent of national income in this period, which was higher than the equivalent tax burden that was extracted by any other European central government in its industrialisation phase, including Tsarist Russia (8 per cent) and Wilhelmine Germany (2.5 per cent). Thus, the highly regressive nature of British taxes hit the lower income groups more punitively than any other equivalent social group in Europe.[83] Notable here is that while in Britain the growth of taxes on the low-income groups outstripped the growth in their earnings in the eighteenth century

[80] Chapman (1972/2006: ch. 3).
[81] Inikori (2002: 316–17).
[82] For excellent discussions of the social factors that were at work behind this fiscal regime, see Mathias and O'Brien (1976), O'Brien (1988) and Ashworth (2017: ch. 5).
[83] Mathias and O'Brien (1976: 616–21), O'Brien (1989: 345–56), Williamson (1984: 699–700), Beckett and Turner (1990: 391–6) and Hobson (1997: chs. 2 and 4).

and first half of the nineteenth century,[84] the Russian peasantry's income outstripped its tax burden during the Tsarist industrialisation phase.[85] And, as I explained in Chapter 2, relative to the average poor British taxpayer, the Chinese peasants fared even better, indeed far better.

I calculate that in 1770, about 2.5 per cent of national income was redistributed from the poor to the rich investors in the City of London. And this figure rises to around 2.9 per cent of national income in 1770 when we include the middle classes. Certainly, this was a significant amount, bearing in mind that in 1770, the state spent 3.9 per cent of national income on warfare (D1). Accordingly, there is strong evidence to support my claim that Britain underwent a forced savings and forced industrialisation in the eighteenth century.

But a third calculation needs to be made so far as the imperial-debt multiplier is concerned because the year 1770 is unrepresentative. For if we consider it in the wider context of the all-important 1760–1820 period, the figure available for reinvestment rises from 19 per cent in 1770 *to an average 31 per cent of GFCF*, which comprised 2.0 per cent of national income. And when aggregated with the amounts of Atlantic profits that were available for investment, which I estimated at about 20 per cent of GFCF in the previous section, then aggregating these figures brings us to about *50 per cent of GFCF*. Moreover, the imperial-military debt multiplier was in operation up to about 1850, given that the accumulated national debt stood at a colossal 180 per cent of national income in 1815.[86] This means that interest payments remained very high right up to the mid-nineteenth century – comprising an average 7.6 per cent of national income in 1815–50 – which translated into an amount to reinvest that comprised *23 per cent of GFCF* or 2.1 per cent of national income. In addition, the amounts that were redistributed from the poor to the rich city financiers through 'forced savings' comprised as much as 4.5 per cent of national income in 1815–50 and 5.3 per cent of national income from the working and middle classes combined. Note that in real terms, this was about double that of the already high figure for 1770. And, bearing in mind that Britain spent an average 4.4 per cent of national income on military expenditures in 1815–50, so the sums that

---

[84] Beckett and Turner (1990: 388–91).

[85] Crisp (1991: 257–8).

[86] Despite its striking size, this figure is, however, less than the standard one that is usually provided (i.e., somewhere between 226 and 260 per cent of national income in 1815), which is derived from the relevant source in the British Parliamentary Papers. But due to an error in the reporting technique, I recalculated the figure by aggregating the accumulated central government deficits for each year.

were redistributed were very high by historical standards. All of which provides yet further evidence of Britain's 'forced industrialisation'.[87]

However, one final calculation needs to be made. For it might be objected that the hugely expensive Napoleonic Wars revolved principally around the balance of power *within* Europe rather than around imperial concerns, which means that I have exaggerated the fiscal-military benefits of empire in my calculations earlier.[88] But as I also noted, an important component during the Napoleonic Wars *so far as Britain* was concerned, which is the sole focus here, lay in the control of the Atlantic colonies. If we assume that only 25 per cent of the military spending during the Revolutionary and Napoleonic Wars was imperial-related, then I calculate that the final average figure that could have been reinvested between 1761 and 1815 comes down from around 31 to *18 per cent of GFCF*, and 20 per cent for the 1760–1850 period. All of which means that when aggregated with the reinvested profits from the Caribbean colonies, which I guesstimated at around 20 per cent of GFCF in 1760–1820, this still comprises a very substantial *38 per cent of GFCF*. Accordingly, the amounts that were generated by *all* Atlantic colonial sources for reinvestment in the British economy stood somewhere between 38 and 51 per cent of GFCF. In the light of this significant figure, I conclude that the colonies played a very important role in driving British industrialisation.

To close this complex discussion, it is useful to consider Peer Vries's counterfactual critique of the argument that the British state's policy of 'imperial-military Keynesianism' spurred on economic growth under conditions of a 'Keynesian depression'. To this end, he asserts that 'I fail to see how taking money from fairly ordinary consumers and then transferring them to the military as such can create a substantial amount of extra *demand* and growth.'[89] But the basis of my argument is precisely that forced savings served to undermine *aggregate demand* in order to *enhance investment and economic growth*.[90] For the fiscal exploitation of the poor consumers, who were *non*-savers, provided money for the City of London to invest in the economy – a point I return to in the conclusion later. Moreover, it would be problematic to assume that military spending inherently retarded economic development while domestic civilian spending would necessarily have had the polar opposite effect.

[87] Only after 1850 did interest payments drop off significantly to an average of 2.6 per cent of national income (1850–1913), which was a third of their previous size (1815–50).

[88] See the discussions in Holsti (1991: 86–7).

[89] Vries (2015: 213).

[90] See also Crafts (1987: 247) and O'Brien (1989: 376–7).

And certainly, it is questionable as to whether investment rates would have been boosted by higher civilian spending to a greater extent than they were via the imperial-military debt multiplier – though I return to this issue in the conclusion at the end of this chapter.

More generally, the final upshot of this discussion is that while many economic historians are correct to assume that the British state, unlike Tsarist autocracy, did not intervene by investing *directly* in the economy, they miss the point that it was in part through the state's imperial fiscal-militarism that the conditions for private investors to invest substantial amounts in the economy were promoted, all of which might not have happened to the same extent in the absence of these wars.[91] Even so, this is not the sole economic input that military spending stimulated. For there is an additional series of qualitative benefits that imperial-military spending provided for the British economy.

The Imperial-Military and Global Atlantic Drivers of British Industrialisation: Financial Institutions and the Iron and Steel Revolution

A second major reason why military spending should *not* be deducted from the profits derived from slavery concerns the various spin-off effects that slavery and imperial warfare imparted on the rise of Britain's core financial institutions and the industrialisation of the iron and steel industry – an argument that I develop further in a comparison with China in Chapter 12. The first two sections consider the industrialisation of the British iron and steel sector, while the latter two consider the core financial institutions.

Imperial-Military Origins of Britain's Iron and Steel Revolution

Here, I focus on the numerous economic spin-offs that high military demand imparted beyond those that were derived from the imperial-military debt multiplier. Drawing on the data in Mitchell,[92] I calculate that the state's investment in military ordnance averaged £1 million per annum between 1770 and 1800. This was approximately equivalent to the whole of the sum that was invested in the fixed capital stock of the iron and cotton industries together with the construction of canals, docks and harbours. Moreover, the costs of investing in new

---

[91] Cf. John (1955: 340–1), McNeill (1982: 210–11), O'Brien (1989: 354–5, 1991: 22–3), Beckett and Turner (1990: 387) and Rodger (2010: 9–11).
[92] Mitchell (2011: 579–80).

naval ships dwarfed the amounts that went into the iron and cotton industries. In the first half of the eighteenth century, the entire capital investment that went into the naval fleet was five times that of the total fixed capital cost of the 243 mills in the West Riding woollen industry.[93] Furthermore, the imperial state's promotion of the navy had forward and backward linkages to the economy. The former stimulated the shipbuilding industry that in turn stimulated coal-mining, chemical production, iron-making and engineering. And, the latter took the form of the Royal Navy guaranteeing imperial trade routes while providing a secure environment within which the City of London's financiers could conduct their business.[94]

Of course, as noted in the last section, the conventional liberal counterfactual emphasises the *opportunity costs* of such military spending, arguing that the money spent on war could have been more profitably invested directly in the economy. But the military-strategic demand for iron and cotton – where the latter was used for military uniforms and the former for weapons and naval-related requirements – was no less economically strategic for industrialisation. Critically, given the presence of a Keynesian depression, albeit one that was in part stimulated by the state's extremely high regressive taxes to pay for its imperial wars, it is unlikely that the money would have gone automatically into private investment, even if it would have stimulated further the eighteenth-century 'consumer revolution'. However, in response to Vries's criticism of this form of argument,[95] my claim here is merely that these military spin-off effects were important, but were certainly not the sole source of technological and institutional innovation (as Chapter 10 testifies). Here, in the interests of space, I present a few notable examples.

Demand for iron weapons via military ordnance played a considerable role in nurturing the development of the iron-manufacturing sector.[96] As Eric Hobsbawm notes, 'war was pretty certainly the greatest consumer of iron, and firms like Wilkinson, the Walkers and the Carron Works owed the size of their undertakings partly to government contracts for cannon, while the South Wales iron industry depended on battle'.[97] Interestingly, the famous 'carronade' weapon, which had played a decisive role in Britain's defeats of the French in the late-eighteenth and early-nineteenth centuries, was based on 'a highly improved cast iron,

---

[93] Brewer (1989: 34); see also Rodger (2010: 13–16).
[94] Brewer (1989) and O'Brien (1989, 1991).
[95] Vries (2015: 316).
[96] Ashworth (2017: 168–72), McNeill (1982: 211–12), Sen (1984) and Mumford (1934).
[97] Hobsbawm (1969: 34) and Inikori (2002: 453).

which was first applied to guns at the famous Carron works (from which carronade derived its name)'.[98] Moreover, these unprecedented levels of military demand helped stimulate numerous industrial–technological innovations. The inventions of Abraham Darby's highly important 'coke-smelted iron process' in 1709 (following the imperial conflict of King William's War and during the imperial conflict of Queen Anne's War), James Watt's steam engine in 1776 (following the imperial conflict of the Seven Years' War) and Henry Cort's 'puddling process' in 1784 (following the imperial conflicts of the War of American Independence and the Anglo-Dutch War) were all stimulated, albeit in part, to meet the on-going war-time demand for iron.[99]

Henry Cort began as a naval agent who was 'anxious to improve the quality of the British product', justifying the patent for his puddling process that produced wrought iron with coking coal by arguing that this invention could enhance the supply of iron to the Royal Navy. He obtained a contract with the navy in 1782 and was delivering it wrought iron by 1784.[100] And the equally famous Bessemer Converter for advanced steel production was invented in part as a means to reduce the cost of steel for military ordnance.[101] As Bessemer noted in his memoirs, having spoken with Napoleon III concerning the need to produce steel in order to improve upon iron artillery, he recorded that this conversation 'was the spark which kindled one of the greatest revolutions that the present century has to record, for during my solitary ride in a cab that night from Vincennes to Paris, I made up my mind to try what I could to improve the quality of iron [actually steel] in the manufacture of guns'.[102] Notable too is that Henry Maudslay, who was a pioneer of machine tools, began his career in the Woolwich Arsenal though he maintained contracts with the Navy subsequently.[103] Relevant too is that behind James Watt's steam engine was John Wilkinson's cannon-boring machine which enabled the boring of an air-tight cylinder.[104] Moreover, the moneys gained from the West Indian colonial trade helped, albeit in part, to finance the Boulton and Watt firm.[105]

---

[98] Wertime (1961: 171).
[99] Mumford (1934: 163), McNeill (1982: 175, 177) and Sen (1984: 104–11).
[100] Smiles (1863: 114). Note too that the important reverbatory furnace was adopted in the seventeenth century to meet imperial-military demand (John, 1955: 330).
[101] Mumford (1934: 91) and Sen (1984: 73).
[102] Henry Bessemer cited in Wagner (2008: 361–2).
[103] Hobsbawm (1969: 34).
[104] Smiles (1863: 90) and McNeill (1982: 212).
[105] Lord (1923: 113).

Perhaps the most significant point here is that Britain's iron industrialisation was the result of a 'state-driven expansion ... and experimentation with industrial organization.... Growing state demand had turned greater Birmingham [the centre of the iron industry] into a government factory by the end of the [eighteenth] century. The entire Midlands metallurgical world became invested in mass production for war.'[106] Though warfare was clearly not the only driver of the British iron industry, it was undoubtedly important, as indeed it had been ever since the fifteenth century.[107] And one reason why war was not the only driver is because the Atlantic markets were also important.

The Global Atlantic Driver of Britain's Iron and Steel Revolution

Important here is not simply that Atlantic demand for cotton textiles helped drive Britain's cotton industrialisation – as I explain in Chapter 10 – but that the cotton industry provided crucial backward linkages to, and thereby stimulated the industrialisation of, the iron sector.[108] In addition to the large amounts of machinery that the cotton mills required, there was also a whole series of infrastructures that was needed for the associated export and import trade, including docks, harbours and warehouses as well as roads, canals and railways. Accordingly, many iron foundries grew up in and around Manchester to supply the cotton mills. Also important were the ships, especially for the slave trade, as well as those that delivered cotton textiles and other export products to Africa and the Americas in particular. These, of course, required large amounts of iron for items such as anchors, chains, shackles, bolts, nails and ballast.[109] There was also the export trade in guns to Africa which became relatively significant after about 1750 and which helped stimulate Birmingham's iron manufacturers.[110] Guns were also used on board slave ships with the Carron works, in particular, doing a roaring trade in meeting this demand during the Napoleonic Wars when British merchant shipping came under attack in the Atlantic.

All in all, the scale of this market was likely very large with Inikori claiming that it was possibly as large, if not larger, than that which supplied government military contracts.[111] Either way, a leading scholar on British trade, Ralph Davis, concludes that the 'expansion of the

---

[106] Satia (2018: 5).
[107] Wertime (1961: ch. 2).
[108] This paragraph relies on Inikori (2002: 451–72).
[109] Williams (1944/1964: 84).
[110] Ibid. (82).
[111] Inikori (2002: 459).

American market for iron- and brass-ware was on so great a scale that it must have contributed very significantly to the eighteenth-century development of those industries in England'.[112]

Imperial-Military Origins of Britain's Core Financial Institutions

Imperial wars also stimulated the creation of a range of Britain's core financial institutions. Here, I endorse Marx's original argument that imperialism and imperial wars were the 'forcing house' for British public credit, such that '[t]he public debt becomes one of the most powerful levers of primitive accumulation.... [I]t has given rise to joint-stock companies, to dealings in negotiable effects of all kinds, and to agiotage, in a word to stock-exchange gambling and the modern bankocracy'.[113] All of which brings us back to the role of the British state once more. Of course, it is often claimed that the continental industrialisers of Tsarist Russia, Germany and Austria–Hungary were examples of how state intervention spurred on late-industrialisation.[114] And Germany's industrialisation, in particular, is thought to have been promoted significantly by the banking system. While all this was successful in the case of Germany, nevertheless it was far less successful in Austria–Hungary and even less so in Tsarist Russia. But while British industrialisation is supposed to be the celebrated instance of how a 'laissez faire posture' can promote industrialisation,[115] it turns out that the state adopted a highly interventionist role (as I also argue in Chapters 10 and 11). And, moreover, the *quality* of its intervention was vital in driving the economy forward in contrast to the clumsier *modus operandi* of the Tsarist Russian state (as noted earlier).

It was specifically during the imperial conflict of King William's War that the British state initiated the 'financial revolution', which saw the creation of the Bank of England in 1694 and the establishment of the national debt in order to organise loans for Britain's rising levels of imperial-military spending, which could not be financed out of taxes alone.[116] Moreover, it was during the Napoleonic Wars, which were in part about imperial interests so far as Britain was concerned, that the state established the London Stock Exchange in 1802 in order to rationalise the

---

[112] Davis cited in Inikori (2002: 457).
[113] Marx (1867/1959: 706).
[114] Gerschenkron (1962).
[115] Deane (1965), Landes (1998), Mokyr (2009) and McCloskey (2010).
[116] Dickson (1967: 9–12), Brewer (1989: 207–8), Inikori (2002: 321–2) and Vries (2015: 318–19).

selling of government war-time bonds;[117] a development that had major knock-on effects for stimulating the growth of Britain's regional banks. Overall, Britain's imperial wars helped cement the pivotal 'City/Bank of England/Treasury nexus'.[118] Thus, while Douglass North, a world-leading liberal scholar on state–economy relations, correctly recognises the important role that warfare played in establishing and nurturing Britain's financial institutions,[119] nevertheless he fails to recognise the vital role that the *imperial* context played in underpinning this.

Atlantic Black Slave Production and the Imperial Primitive Accumulation of British Finance Capital

However, we cannot leave this account here because the system of Black slavery also contributed to the rise and development of Britain's core financial institutions in general and finance capital in particular. Because trade and production in the Atlantic system was highly risky and challenging on account of the distances and long time lags involved, so a banking system came into operation to meet these demands. As Inikori explains, '[w]hat made credit an important requirement in British trade in the seventeenth and eighteenth centuries was [its] expansion beyond Europe [owing to the large distances involved in the Atlantic system].... This called for a large amount of capital investment in trade that was beyond the resources of the traders.'[120] More specifically, the long distances involved required companies to place agents abroad who could oversee the buying and selling of Atlantic goods and who could ensure the remittance of all slave debts. Particularly important was the need for bills of exchange in the seventeenth and eighteenth centuries. These served to reduce transaction costs significantly because first, they minimised risks in the face of dangers such as robbery in the Atlantic Ocean[121] and second, because they minimised the need to hold large amounts of cash and precious metals that could be freed up for investment rather than lying idle for long periods.

While the Bank of England was set up to meet the state's requirements for desperately needed military loans (as I explained earlier), nevertheless the other core function that it performed was in the issuing of bank notes as a means to settle bills of exchange within the Atlantic slave-based

---

[117] O'Brien (1989: 349–50, 1991: 29).
[118] Dickson (1967: 9–12) and Brewer (1989: 207–8).
[119] North (1991: 33).
[120] Inikori (2002: 322).
[121] Price (1991: 283).

system. Bill discounting too became a vital function of the city, with private banks also springing up to perform this role, all of which led to the establishment of the London Clearing House. The private and country banks were especially valued because they had a quicker system of dealing with protested bills. Note that discounting occurs when the bill-holder wants to sell it off before it matures in order to obtain funds quickly, in which case the bank advances him the cash less the interest on the outstanding amount. In addition, company bonds promoted investment opportunities for the various credit institutions, with the English East India Company, the South Sea Company and the Royal African Company offering the majority of such outlets. For these Atlantic-based companies 'provided an immense contribution to the size of the market for credit in London'.[122]

A key driver of the rise and development of Britain's financial services comprised the massive amounts of funds that slave traders and slave employers required. Very large sums were needed to set up a plantation, for purchasing slaves both in Africa and the Caribbean/Americas as well as for financing the trade in slave-produced goods – all of which could only be done through access to large amounts of credit. Speaking of the banks, Inikori notes that '[t]he discounting of bills of exchange received for the slaves sold in the New World was their main source of credit'. And these credit instruments furnished Liverpool, London and Bristol with an immense amount of business. Moreover, as Inikori goes on to point out, '[i]t is important to note that the [regional] banks that grew up ... in the second half of the eighteenth century, particularly in Lancashire, were primarily, if not entirely, bill-discounting banks'.[123] Notable too, as Eric Williams originally pointed out, is that various British banks – Barclays and Lloyds in particular – grew up on the profits of the American and West Indian colonies that were in turn guaranteed by the Royal Navy.[124]

A further vital service that underpinned the Atlantic system was the marine insurance market, which also fed into the bills of exchange market. This was required to insure the 'cargo' of the slave ships as well as that of the ordinary trading vessels plying the Atlantic Ocean. And it was also used to insure the bills of exchange.[125] Lloyds Coffee House lay at the centre of this market and grew up initially to meet this

---

[122] Inikori (2002: 321).
[123] Ibid. (336).
[124] Williams (1944/1964: 98–102); also Inikori (2002: ch. 7).
[125] Price (1991: 289–90).

demand.[126] As risks increased, especially during the eighteenth century when Atlantic commerce and the trans-Atlantic slave trade grew rapidly, so insurance cover became increasingly required. This in turn increased the size of the credit market and the development of specialist insurance services such as underwriters and brokers. By the 1790s, some 63 per cent of the total insurance market was absorbed by the slave trade alone.[127] This greatly enhanced the development of the London insurance market with Lloyds lying at its centre. And of particular note here is Inikori's claim that the annual dealings in *all* mercantile instruments associated with the slave trade and Atlantic trade and production were greater in value than the dealings in government securities that were taken out to finance Britain's imperial wars;[128] a point I return to in the conclusion.

In sum, then, Britain's imperial wars in the long eighteenth century – many of which were fought over the American colonies in one way or another – along with the profits of colonial slave-production and the Atlantic trade and the associated profits that were derived from British credit and insurance institutions constituted the fiery crucible within which the London capital market, the Bank of England and the national economy more generally were born. All of which reinforces Marx's claim cited earlier wherein the colonial system and its associated maritime trade and imperial wars constituted the 'forcing house' for British public credit. In the light of all this, then, I conclude that ultimately the 'liberal counterfactual' that dismisses all of this *tout court* performs, in effect, the intellectual service of laundering or censoring the dark side of British industrialisation, thereby airbrushing out of history the manifold roles of empire and the super-exploitation of Black slaves in stimulating British industrialisation.

By Way of Conclusion: Towards a Final Reckoning of the Benefits of the Atlantic Colonies

Before I bring together the various quantitative calculations of this chapter, it is important to consolidate the discussion of agency that has been advanced in the book thus far. For the Atlantic was, in fact, a 'global Atlantic system' from 1500 onwards because it was underpinned by the twelve-sided (dodecagonal) ICTTS that in turn was embedded in the hexadecagonal (sixteen-sided) New World-based global silver trading system. This means that Britain's Atlantic colonies were propped up by

---

[126] Williams (1944/1964: 104–5).
[127] Inikori (2002: 361).
[128] Ibid.

the global agency of Indian textile producers and merchants alongside African prosumers and Black African slavers (all of which was explained in Chapters 3–5). And, moreover, Black slave production, much of which was financed out of the sale of re-exported ICTs, was important to the successful development of the British economy, as I have argued in this chapter. But we also need to factor in British developmental and global agency, first of all because it was the British who exported the slaves from Africa and set up the New World production system. And, moreover, the imperial-related benefits were not wholly exogenous to Britain for it is the specific *domestic responses* to the challenges of imperial militarism and Black slavery that also mattered.

Notable here is that Britain developed the most efficient fiscal bureaucracy of any state in Europe, or indeed of the world (as I discussed in Chapter 2), and it was this that enabled it to extract high levels of excise taxes which, alongside very high tariff revenues, underpinned the 'forced savings' mechanism. Moreover, the state oversaw the creation of the national debt, the Bank of England and the Stock Exchange as well as the demand that it generated through loans for imperial warfare. For these fostered the development of the City of London throughout the eighteenth century and first half of the nineteenth century. Critically, none of this occurred in Britain's great imperial rival, France, which had a far less efficient fiscal bureaucracy that was incapable of raising such large amounts of taxation.[129] Thus, it was constitutional (albeit socially authoritarian) Britain rather than absolutist France that was able to promote an (indirect) forced industrialisation and an effective fiscal base to prosecute its expensive imperial wars. And, as I explain in Chapter 12, the same argument applies to the comparison between Britain and China (see also Chapter 2). How, then, might we come to a final, albeit proximate, reckoning of the benefits of the empire to Britain's industrialisation?

Here, I shall aggregate the quantitative calculations that I have made throughout this chapter into one final estimate. As I explain in Appendix 2, I estimate that somewhere in the region of 4.5–5.0 per cent of the national income was channelled back into investment in the British economy via the various imperial routes. But this begs the question as to the actual impact this had on British economic growth. As I explained earlier, Jeffrey Williamson argues that Britain's economic growth rate in this period would have been about 30 per cent higher in the *absence* of the Napoleonic Wars. That is, the annual growth rate of the national income

---

[129] Mathias and O'Brien (1976).

was depressed by 0.6 per cent per annum. However, my analysis suggests that the many economic aspects of Britain's Atlantic colonies, coupled with the costs of defending them, served to *raise* British economic growth by about 0.6 per cent per annum. Note that I calculated this figure following the exact same method that Williamson deployed.[130] And because this figure comprises just under a third of British national income growth (1760–1820), which averaged about 2.0 per cent per annum,[131] so this confirms that colonial-related activities provided a significant boost to industrialisation.

However, these refer to the amounts that were siphoned off from the Atlantic-derived profits and related activities. Which means that the *total* amount of economic activity that was generated by these imperial-related activities in the critical industrialisation phase (1760–1820) comprised around 15 per cent of the national income.[132] This figure deserves the label of 'enormous ratios' to quote from Barbara Solow. Interestingly, she deployed this phrase in the context of the impact of the profits from the Atlantic *slave-trade*, which she reckons were equivalent to a mere 8 per cent of total investment and 0.54 per cent of national income.[133] But for all this, the liberal counterfactual to my claim would be to ask why we should focus on the 15 per cent imperial-derived figure when the sources of the remaining *non*-imperial inputs to national income (i.e., 85 per cent) were clearly far more significant.[134] I offer two replies.

First, it is true that this figure of 15 per cent of the national income does not allow me to conclude that imperial-derived profits and related activities can *fully* account for Britain's industrialisation. But apart from the fact that this is a very considerable sum whichever way we look at it, this figure still does not capture *all* of the inputs that the Atlantic- and imperial-related activities imparted on British industrialisation. How, for example, do we measure the spin-off effects that imperial wars and the profits from African slave production and commerce imparted on the *technological* development of the iron and steel industries, none of which I have sought to quantify? Or again, how do we measure the impact of the

---

[130] See the notes to Table 4 in Williamson (1984: 701).

[131] I have run with the growth rate figure from Deane and Cole (1969), which is higher than the data provided in more recent revisions – e.g., Crafts (1987). This serves to affect the right direction of bias against my claim.

[132] I calculated this figure by noting that the average savings rate for the rich investor class was around 30 per cent across this whole period, so that I multiply the figure of 4.5 per cent by 3.3 to derive the final figure of about 15 per cent.

[133] Solow (1985: 106, 105). And even this figure is a considerable over-estimation given that the amount that would have been *available for reinvestment* would have been between a quarter and a third of this.

[134] See, for example, McCloskey (2010: 222, 229) and Vries (2013: 261–2).

global Atlantic consumption driver as it spurred on the vitally important technological revolution in the cotton industry (which is the subject of Chapter 10)? And, last but not least, how do we measure the boost that the consumer/industrious revolution imparted on the British industrial revolution, given that the former was spurred on by the slave-produced 'drug goods' in the Caribbean?[135] For as Richard Drayton points out, 'the ... "industrious revolutions" at the [imperial] centre depended on coerced latifundial labour at the [peripheral] frontiers, and the consequences of both continue'.[136] All of which means that the figure of 15 per cent of the national income *understates* considerably the likely impact of the colonies as well as the non-imperial parts of the Atlantic system. Which, in turn, means that this figure constitutes a minimum threshold.

My second reply to the liberal counterfactual critique lies in the inescapable fact that Britain industrialised in part because of the colonies and the related imperial-military spin-off effects for the national economy.[137] Should this not receive the acknowledgement that it deserves rather than being dismissed on the basis of an imaginary counterfactual 'optimal' scenario that is grounded in liberal 'assumptions' as to what might have happened in the absence of what in fact transpired? And, in the process, my argument in this chapter leads to an inversion of the Eurocentric BBT, given that the Atlantic empire preceded, and was constitutive of, British industrialisation.

It is worth noting one final critique which asserts that imperialism was largely irrelevant to the fortunes of industrialisation given that most European countries achieved this in the *absence* of empire.[138] But the political economy and fiscal-militarism of the British empire, alongside global economic forces, played an important role in promoting the country's core industrial technologies, which were then emulated subsequently by the late(r)-developing continental economies to promote their industrialisations. In this way, then, Europe's continental economies benefited indirectly from the technological spin-offs from Britain's empire, whether they were imperial powers or not. To close, though, it is important to note that perhaps the *key* factor that spurred on the vital technological innovations of Britain's cotton industry was the aforementioned global Atlantic *consumption driver* to a consideration of which I now turn.

---

[135] McKendrick *et al.* (1982), Brewer and Porter (1993) and de Vries (2008).
[136] Drayton (2002: 103).
[137] Ashworth (2017: 117).
[138] For example, McCloskey (2010: 223–4) and O'Brien (1982).

10   The Global Atlantic Consumption Driver and British Late-Developmental Agency in Global Uneven and Combined Development

Introduction

While I devoted four pages in chapter 9 in my book *The Eastern Origins of Western Civilisation* to the argument that the British borrowed numerous Chinese ideas and technologies in order to industrialise their iron/steel and cotton textile sectors, here I develop this much further and in new non-Sinocentric directions. For much of my focus will be on Indian- and African-prosumer agency alongside Afro-Indian challenges and influences in stimulating Britain's cotton industrialisation. Accordingly, I build on the analysis of Chapter 9, but this time by focusing on the global Atlantic *consumption* driver. A further corrective to my earlier Sinocentric analysis is that I factor in British late-developmental *agency* in the context of global uneven and combined development (UCD). For British agency received all-too-short-thrift in my 2004 book – a problem that constitutes a major blind spot of much of the California School more generally, as I explained in Chapter 1. All of which leads me, once more, to invert the Eurocentric Big Bang theory (BBT)/Expansion of the West narrative by revealing how the first global economy (FGE) and the global context of UCD played important roles in driving Britain's transition. Note that I hone in on the cotton and iron/steel sectors because they constituted the key twin-pillars of British industrialisation. And I focus on the origins of capitalist industrialisation because it forms the primary economic base of the second global economy.

The prominent California School revisionist, Kenneth Pomeranz, argues in his pioneering and agenda-setting book, *The Great Divergence*, that *the* critical development underpinning the 'great divergence' – by which he means the industrial overtaking of China by Britain – was the invention of the steam engine in addition to British industry's close proximity to cheap coal supplies (as well as the benefits of New World raw cotton supplies). This constitutes a very important and necessary argument but which ultimately comprises an insufficient account of what was really the *second* 'great cotton divergence' and the *second* 'great iron and steel divergence' – given that India and China had led and pioneered cotton production for half a millennium and iron/steel production for up to two millennia. Certainly, the steam engine helps account for the huge quantities of iron/steel and cotton textiles that the British pumped out following the 1820s and 1830s, respectively, though this served to clinch rather than create the second great divergence. For I argue that the industrialisation of these sectors was based on a whole series of crucially important *prior* developments both within Britain in particular and in the global context in general. What we need to know, therefore, is what drove this industrialisation process in the first place before the steam engine finally entered the British cotton mills as well as the iron and steel factories. And this in turn leads me into the kind of postcolonial 'actor network theory' that Julian Go advocates,[1] through which I reveal the complex network of lines and interconnections that integrate Western and non-Western actors across the Eurocentric frontier.

Here, the story is based in part around Indian structural power, which was derived from the fact that Indian cotton textiles (ICTs) both dominated global markets and comprised a universal currency that could be exchanged for all commodities in the global trading system. In particular, because ICTs were in such high demand with African consumers or prosumers, so the Europeans and West Asians had to buy them first, often with New World silver, in order to purchase African slaves and ivory in particular (as I explained in Chapters 3 and 4). And it was this structural power that ICTs afforded Indian merchants which, in turn, effectively forced the Europeans to negotiate and competitively cooperate with the Indians ever since the East India Companies first arrived in the Indian Ocean system, as I explained in Chapter 5. Moreover, it was precisely Indian structural power that pushed the British to find ways of competing with ICTs especially in Africa, the ultimate solution to which was the mechanisation of the cotton industry and the concomitant industrialisation of the British economy. In this way, the British came to finally usurp India's structural power during the nineteenth century.

The argument of this chapter unfolds in five sections. First, I focus on the role of the British state-as-late-developer that engaged in significant levels of intervention in the face of UCD, wherein protectionism and import-substitution industrialisation (ISI), coupled with re-export substitution industrialisation (RSI), created an important space for the development of Britain's cotton (and iron) sector. In the section '"Global

---

[1] Go (2016: 131–9).

Atlantic Consumption Driver" of Britain's Cotton Industrialisation', I focus on Atlantic and especially African consumer demand for ICTs. In the sections 'The "Afro-Indian Global Cotton Whip of Necessity" (I): The Global Atlantic Consumption Driver in the Mechanisation of Cotton Printing, Dyeing and Finishing' and 'The "Afro-Indian Global Cotton Whip of Necessity" (II): The Global Atlantic Consumption Driver in the Mechanisation of Cotton Spinning and Weaving' I focus on Britain's 'Afro-Indian apprenticeship' and how the 'Afro-Indian cotton whip of necessity' – via the global Atlantic consumption driver – drove British technological innovations in printing, dyeing and finishing and, later on, in cotton spinning and weaving. Important here is the associated presence of global UCD, given that the British combined or emulated Indian textiles and some of their production methods. And finally, the section 'How did the British Industrialise the Iron and Steel Sectors? British Late-Developmental Agency under Global UCD' considers the other main pillar of the British industrial revolution – iron and steel – where I situate the British achievement in the twin contexts of the long global iron/steel cumulation and global UCD. There I argue that British inventors looked to Indian and possibly Chinese technologies and techniques for inspiration when mechanising the iron and steel sectors, though British developmental agency was also crucial. Overall, this chapter's argument complements that of Chapter 9, given that the global Atlantic system constituted *one* of the drivers of the British iron and steel revolution and the core driver of the cotton industrial revolution.

The British Late-Developmental State and the Global Atlantic Consumption Driver of Industrialisation

I begin here by considering the important interventionist role of the British state, which sets the scene for the technological-innovation process that underpinned Britain's cotton industrialisation and which, in turn, was driven by Atlantic consumer demand challenges. Britain, of course, has traditionally been viewed as the archetypal case of a successful 'laissez-faire industrialisation' in the extensive literature on the topic.[2] This is often assumed to have been tied in with Britain's 'first mover advantage', as Alexander Gerschenkron as well as Leon Trotsky famously argued,[3] given that only *late developers* require interventionist states in order to catch up. But in cotton and iron, Britain was a late

---

[2] For example, Landes (1969, 1998), Mokyr (2009), McCloskey (2010); and Ferguson (2011).

[3] Gerschenkron (1962) and Trotsky (1906/2010: 42–51).

developer and the second great divergence was in part enabled by strong state interventionism, as is consistent with the theory of 'late development' that is linked to the process of UCD. While a good deal of British state intervention in the economy was an unintended or indirect consequence of its imperial fiscal militarism, as I explained in detail in Chapter 9, nevertheless there was also a significant element of *direct* interventionism that took the form of 'infant industry protection' for the pivotal cotton textile and iron sectors.[4] Crucial here was the economic threat of the more advanced ICTs that were imported by the English East India Company (EEIC) under conditions of UCD. As I explained in Part I of this book, this particular threat took the form of the 'Calico Craze' that emerged in the 1670s, as British consumers took very rapidly to ICTs.

Nevertheless, as a significant aside, it is important to recognise that Indian textile imports were not, in effect, *sui generis*, because they had to be 'domesticated' to suit the consumption requirements of the British population. To this end, the agency of the EEIC was very important in that it repackaged and merchandised these textiles in order to sell them in Britain.[5] Or, put simply, the Calico Craze was in part constructed by the EEIC. For as Maxine Berg notes, it was the subjective perception of *taste* that had to be constructed first in order to sell ICTs to British consumers. And this 'domestication' of the Indian product or its 'indigenisation' within British society[6] entailed 'product innovation' and the merchandising of clothing by the EEIC.[7] For one of the ironies to emerge here is that the 'exotic' designs that festooned the Indian textiles within the imagination of British consumers were, in fact, the product of a Western construct that was invented by the EEIC. Thus, while the EEIC began marketing ICTs in England from 1643 on, by the 1660s it was also placing highly specific orders for cotton clothing to the Indian producers, which included the specifications of print designs.[8] Still, this merely reflected the centuries-long practice in which Indian merchants relayed information on changing African and Asian consumer preferences back to the weavers in India, who then continuously adapted production to meet these needs (as I discussed in Part I of the book). As cotton became highly desirable and fashionable

---

[4] Wadsworth and de Lacy Mann (1931: 118, 144), O'Brien (1989: 364, 1991: 27–8), Inikori (2002: 149–55), Chang (2002: ch. 2), Ashworth (2017), Parthasarathi (2011: 125–31), Beckert (2015: 47) and Vries (2013, 2015).

[5] Styles (2000).

[6] See, respectively, Prestholdt (2008) and Berg (2009: 395).

[7] Styles (2000) and Berg (2009).

[8] Irwin and Brett (1970), Chapman (1972/2006: 15) and Styles (2000).

among British consumers, especially women of all classes, so it initiated a democratising effect in the clothing industry via the circumvention of the old sumptuary laws (as I noted in Chapter 7).[9] For as Beverly Lemire rightly notes, cotton indeed *became* 'fashion's favourite'.[10]

The British State's Unique Shift to Protectionism: Combining ISI with Export-Oriented Industrialisation and RSI

The domestic consumer clamour for ICTs (the 'Calico Craze') was such that by the 1690s British wool and silk interests clamoured equally strongly for protection against the superior textile imports that were threatening their livelihoods.[11] As David Washbrook notes, even as late as 1750, 'so terrified [was] Western Europe [by India's economic] power that [European states] put up tariff barriers against it'.[12] In order to meet and contain the Indian calico import threat, the British state resorted to hiking tariffs. But because tariffs on ICT imports were more about protecting the wool and silk industries, given that the cotton industry only emerged properly in the 1710s, so describing the state's protection of the cotton industry as being entirely congruent with the theory of late development needs to be qualified.

In 1685, a duty of 17.5 per cent was applied to ICTs, which was then raised to 27.5 per cent in 1690, before Indian *printed* calicoes and muslins (made of fine yarn) were prohibited in 1701. Nevertheless, the importation of *plain* white Indian cloth was still permitted, and indeed it flooded in to meet the burgeoning British consumer demand. And, it was allowed in so long as it was printed on by British printers who could then sell it either at home or abroad, thereby helping spur on the cotton cloth printing industry. In the wake of the 1701 Act, British-printed Indian-made calicoes enjoyed a rapidly growing demand among British consumers such that the amounts produced for the home market rose to seven million yards in 1717 and ten million in 1718/20.[13] As Edward Baines originally pointed out,

Calico printing could not for a long time have succeeded in England, if parliament had not prohibited the introduction of the cheap and beautiful prints of India, Persia, and China, which was done in 1700.... This Act was intended

---

[9] Parthasarathi (2011: 37).

[10] Lemire (1990, 2009, 2011: ch. 3).

[11] Parthasarathi (2011: 125–31), Chaudhuri (2006: 278–9, 294) and Inikori (2002: 431–3).

[12] Washbrook (2007: 87–8).

[13] Chaudhuri (2006: 296–7); cf. Inikori (2002: 432).

to protect the English woollen and silk manufactures from the competition of Indian goods, but it also had the effect of stimulating and greatly increasing the infant trade of printing: for the English had then become accustomed to the use of printed [Indian] calicoes and chintzes, and the taste for these articles could only be gratified, after the prohibition of the Indian prints, by printing in this country the plain Indian calicoes, which were still admitted under a duty.[14]

But as these printed Indian cottons displaced British wool and silk markets, this sparked a further round of complaints from such producers, which led parliament to enact a further piece of tariff legislation in 1721. As a result, tariffs on Indian calico imports together with high excise taxes came to an aggregate tax rate as high as 82 per cent *ad valorem* (and the excises were only repealed as late as 1831). And a further follow-up piece of legislation on 25th December 1722 produced a final position in which Indian calicoes could be imported so long as they were subsequently re-exported but that no plain white Indian calicoes could be printed on by British printers and sold in the home market. Accordingly, ISI began in earnest in 1722, given that the home market was effectively closed to ICTs between then and 1774 – notwithstanding the important qualification that British consumers acquired ICTs through smuggling, as I explained in Chapter 7. Even so, in 1787 a very high tariff was placed on Indian (Dhakan) muslin imports. All of which means that British producers had no choice but to develop their own textiles to sell at home and export abroad.

Clearly, this was no ordinary ISI strategy, given the common assumption that it implies a *de-linking* from the international trading system. For its ingenuity was that it ran in tandem with a specific export-oriented industrialisation strategy, which pre-empted those that were implemented by the state-led industrialisations in East Asia after World War II.[15] And what mattered in particular was the development of RSI,[16] wherein domestic cotton textile producers were allowed to import Indian cloth so long as they re-exported it. And if they re-exported it, they were able to draw back the cost of the import tariff. Re-exporting ICTs was necessary in order to buy up African slaves, who were needed to produce the raw cotton in the Caribbean that would supply Lancashire's needs. But the critical point is that the 1721 and 1722 Acts spurred on British producers to develop their own cotton clothing industry, which would eventually match and surpass the Indian product in global markets.

---

[14] Baines (1835/1966: 259).
[15] Chang (2002: 22).
[16] Inikori (2002: chs. 2 and 9, and especially 149–55) and Riello (2013: 147–51).

In the first instance, this led Lancashire to substitute its own products for the re-exported Indian calicoes in the African and American markets (i.e., *RSI*).[17] And, during their 'Afro-Indian apprenticeship' the British learned of the wider global demand for ICTs beyond Africa at which they aimed their sights (as I explain later). In essence, superseding India's iron grip on Afro-Asian cotton textile markets became, in effect, the key driver of the British cotton industry. All in all, the interventionist actions of the British state reflected an important element of British late-developmental agency in the context of UCD.

Countering the Liberal Counterfactual through Counterfactual History

But the liberal-inspired critique of any argument that points to the global or imperial or the state-interventionist origins of British capitalism always defaults to various counterfactual (opportunity cost) scenarios that, if followed, would *a priori* have produced more optimal outcomes. In this way, any global non-European demand-driven impetus for, or state-interventionist foundations of, British industrialisation that I identify here are magically conjured into thin air as if they never happened (as I explained in the conclusion of Chapter 9). Thus, my claim that Atlantic consumer/prosumer demand constituted an important driver of British industrialisation is rejected by the liberal counterfactual, which asserts that promoting domestic investment and demand coupled with a free trade policy would have produced more optimal economic outcomes. And so we return to the spirit of David Ricardo's logic,[18] wherein the British would have been better off by specialising in their area of 'comparative advantage' – producing woollen textiles – and then importing ICTs on a free trade basis.

In response I posit my own counterfactual to this liberal counterfactual. For had Britain chosen the so-called optimal path of free trade, then there would likely have been no cotton-based industrialisation given that the industry would have been overwhelmed by superior Indian imports. Moreover, defaulting to British wool production would have been problematic because woollen textiles had only limited popularity within global markets such that the unimpeded imports of Indian cottons would have devastated the domestic wool industry. In any case, because there was no major global woollen competitor, as there was for cotton textiles, so there would have been no need to industrialise the

---

[17] Parthasarathi (2011: 94).
[18] Ricardo (1819: ch. 6).

wool sector. Moreover, the woollen industry was known for its highly conservative nature.[19] And even had there been an industrialisation of the wool sector, the fact remains that it would have been outcompeted by ICTs given their superior popularity both at home and throughout the world.

All in all, then, thanks to the role of infant industry protection via import-substitution industrialisation (ISI), British producers gained the space they needed to develop their own cotton textile industry and, as history would later testify, cotton became the king of the future, wool the past. In short, it was state interventionism through ISI and RSI that helped promote the shift of Britain's 'comparative advantage' away from sub-optimal woollen textiles and into optimal cotton textiles.[20] Or, put differently, had Britain shifted to freer trade after 1684 rather than in 1846, British producers would have continued to misallocate resources to what had become in the global context its area of comparative *disadvantage* – woollen textiles – to the possible cost of either forfeiting industrialisation altogether or, at best, mitigating its development.

Interestingly, it was the Ottoman state that conformed much more closely to Adam Smith's maxim that '[i]f a foreign country can supply us with a commodity cheaper than we can make it, better buy it of them with the fruits of our own industry, employed in a way that we have some advantage'.[21] For as Parthasarathi puts it:

[t]he lack of protection for manufacturing reflected an Ottoman economic philosophy that was radically different to the [statism] of seventeenth and eighteenth century Britain ... [and that reminiscent of Adam Smith's thought the] goal of the state was to ensure abundant supplies of essential commodities at reasonable prices with little concern for where the goods were produced.[22]

At first, the importation of ICTs served to propel the Ottoman cotton industry forward as it sought to produce imitations. But the state's lack of protection for the domestic cotton textile industry that had once been a key producer ultimately proved disastrous for the Ottoman economy, given that superior British competition in the nineteenth century delivered the *coup de grâce*.[23]

---

[19] Grinin and Korotayev (2015: 67).
[20] Wadsworth and de Lacy Mann (1931: 144), Inikori (2002: 484), Chang (2002: ch. 2), Parthasarathi (2011: 125–31) and Riello (2013: 147).
[21] Smith (1776/1937: 424).
[22] Parthasarathi (2011: 131).
[23] Gekas (2007).

However, I do not argue that ISI and RSI alone guaranteed British success because other states deployed protectionist policies to far less successful effect. Thus, while the French response to imported Indian calicoes was an outright ban that was enacted in 1686,[24] this served to retard rather than advance the development of the French cotton industry.[25] Rather, my point here is articulated nicely by Bennet Bronson, who argues that what mattered most was that behind these high tariff walls, British inventors and producers

> seem not to have succumbed to the ... tendency to relax into old and inefficient ways [but instead] initiated a major, long-term program of research and development. They made intensive studies of Indian weaving, cloth-printing, and dyeing methods. Slowly and then with increasing speed they began to learn.... By 1785, after two decades of remarkable innovation, they had made most of the key inventions of the Industrial Revolution.[26]

Thus, the actions of British capitalists and investors constituted a further dimension of the British developmental agency that needs to be factored into the explanation of industrialisation.

But to my claim that the imperial markets of North America and the Caribbean were important drivers of British production before 1776/83, the liberal counterfactual that was first advanced by Adam Smith rears its head once more. For one of his chief criticisms of colonialism is that 'monopoly trade' with the colonies is inherently sub-optimal and that free trade with continental Europe would have required more efficient production at home to meet that demand, which in turn would have led to a more robust industrialisation.[27] But the problem here is that these Atlantic markets spurred on Britain's cotton industrialisation during the eighteenth century at the very same time that European demand fell away, not least because of the application of very high continental tariffs.[28] And a final problem with the liberal counterfactual critique is that once the major spinning technological innovations came on stream in the 1770s and 1780s, it soon became apparent that even the optimal size of British domestic demand was inadequate to absorb the rapidly growing size of British cotton textile production, as I explain in the next section.

[24] Parthasarathi (2011: 133).
[25] Ashworth (2017: 100).
[26] Bronson (1982/3: 4–5).
[27] Smith (1776/1937: 563; see also 558–60, 561–2, 564–79).
[28] Davis (1962) and Inikori (2002: 447–9).

The 'Global Atlantic Consumption Driver' of Britain's Cotton Industrialisation

As we have seen, conventional Eurocentrism brackets out the global and Atlantic contexts, given that it envisages Britain's cotton industrialisation as a wholly internal or domestically generated affair that was based largely on the invention of numerous spinning and weaving technologies, all of which accords with the Eurocentric logic of immanence – i.e., the first step of the Eurocentric BBT/Expansion of the West narrative. And it is assumed that these inventions generated vast amounts of textiles that subsequently *created* markets around the world. Put simply, Britain's productive capacity is generally assumed to have come first, global markets second. But the immediate problem is that Afro-Asian markets, which were based on high demand for ICTs, had been in existence many centuries before the British set out to develop a cotton industry (as I explained in Chapters 3–6); something that they learned of during their Afro-Indian apprenticeship and their encounter with the Afro-Asian world more generally. Most critically, it was those global markets that found the British, not the other way round. As Beverley Lemire asserts,

the iconic [i.e., Eurocentric] history of Western industrial triumph should not obscure the productive genesis of Indian manufacturers and the profoundly important role they played in supplying consumers across the world. Indian merchants cultivated global [and/or Afro-Asian] markets for centuries. Indian fabrics set the standard against which [the British successors] were measured.[29]

Or as Prasannan Parthasarathi argues, the principal challenge facing the Europeans 'was not to *create* demand, for that already existed in abundance, but to reach Oriental standards'.[30] Most poignantly, Riello puts this core point nicely: '[c]otton did not become a global commodity because its production was mechanised and industrialised [in Britain]; on the contrary, it became mechanised and industrialised thanks to the fact that it was [already] a global commodity'.[31] Accordingly, this means that we need to invert the Eurocentric BBT by noting that global market demand came first and Britain's cotton industrialisation followed in its wake.

It is noteworthy, however, that the situation vis-à-vis the New World was slightly different, as the Indians had not independently exported their wares there. Instead, the Europeans re-exported ICTs to the Americas

[29] Lemire (2009: 226).
[30] Parthasarathi (2011: 90), my emphasis.
[31] Riello (2013: 149).

either aboard the Spanish Manila Galleon after 1571 or from Europe – especially from Cadiz in the first instance – though the Portuguese also exported ICTs from India to Brazil via the Cape Route, as I noted in Chapter 4. But even when the British exported their own cotton textiles to the Americas after 1730 they were, once again, competing with re-exported ICTs that were in high demand among African slaves.

All of which means that when factoring in the global context we need to recognise the productive and mercantile agency of Indians as it entwined with the agency of African and Afro-Caribbean 'prosumers', whose demand for such textiles spurred on not only Indian production (as I explained in Chapters 3 and 4), but also American cotton production and the British industrial revolution. The key argument here is that the 'global Atlantic consumption/prosumption driver' stimulated the numerous technological innovations that resulted in the industrialisation of the British cotton sector. In this way, my argument takes as its starting point Eric Williams' original claim that '[t]he first stimulus to the growth of Cottonopolis came from the African and West Indian markets'.[32]

The Specificities of the Global Atlantic Consumption Driver

Here, I reveal the 'global Atlantic consumption driver' of Britain's cotton textile industrialisation, which folds into Britain's 'RSI' as well as Britain's Afro-Indian apprenticeship as I consider in the next section. And, in turn, this forms the backdrop to the mechanisation of the British cotton sector as I explain in the following two sections. In the process, as I explained in Chapter 3, it becomes clear that this was not a pure 'White Atlantic' that was made by the Europeans, nor was it solely a 'Black Atlantic' as postcolonialists sometimes presume. Instead, it was a Black and Brown Atlantic or, better still, a 'global Atlantic' system (see Figure 10.1). For ICTs played *the* vital role in the European purchase of African slaves.

By 1760, one-third of British textile production was exported, and by the 1770s this figure had jumped to near 40 per cent.[33] However, it was not simply the case of exporting British products that mattered here, but rather the point that only by imitating Indian calicoes could they hope to meet the tastes of the sophisticated African prosumer as well as the British prosumer at home. Cotton checks were the leading branch in Britain and they were also the most favoured item among African consumers, leading Inikori to conclude that '[s]ince ... the [British]

---

[32] Williams (1944/1964: 68, 68–73).
[33] Inikori (2002: 435).

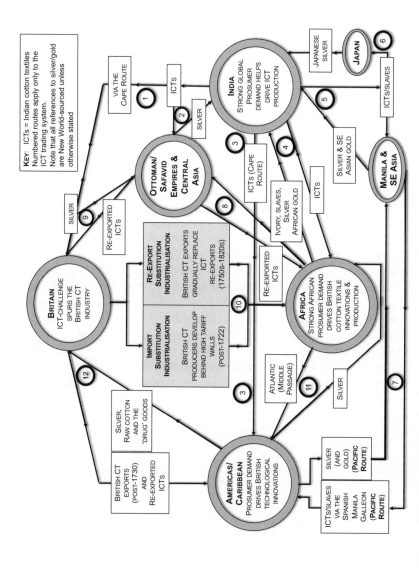

Figure 10.1 The 'Global Atlantic consumption driver' of Britain's cotton industrialisation.

export sector of the cotton industry was founded upon the export of cotton checks, the inference can be drawn that the initial development of the export sector was a function of demand by Africans'.[34] Between 1750 and 1802 Africa took the lion's share of these exports with those sold to African slaves in the New World plantations coming in second. Or as Stanley Chapman pointed out, '[i]t was the carefully cultivated domestic and overseas market, rather than superior technology, that was the key to British achievement in the cotton industry until after the middle of the eighteenth century'.[35]

Critically, these Atlantic markets took the majority of the *rising increment* of total British cotton textile exports during the eighteenth century, probably around 70 per cent.[36] Moreover, while in 1700 the Atlantic markets took 15 per cent of the share of *total* British exports, by 1770 they took 70 per cent of a much larger volume of exports.[37] Equally, while total British industrial exports rose by over 150 per cent in these 70 years, domestic demand rose by a mere 14 per cent.[38] Indeed, Deane and Cole claim that 'eighteenth-century trade expansion was almost entirely due to the growth of colonial [Atlantic] trade', and that 'the existence of exploitable international markets [especially the Atlantic system] was probably crucial in initiating the process of industrialization and the growth in real incomes which was associated with it'.[39] And, as I noted in Chapter 9, given that European demand declined in the eighteenth century, the Atlantic markets came to Lancashire's rescue, in addition to the fact that they spurred on technological innovations back in Britain. Thus in 1750, some 60 per cent of Britain's cloth exports went to Africa, while by 1769 this had risen to nearly 75 per cent of Lancashire's output.[40]

But re-asserting the traditional liberal-internalist view, Colin White dismisses the role of external market drivers of domestic development when he asserts that we need to

focus attention on the internal rather than the external economy.... The general case is that the external sector represents a market which is small relative to the internal market ... even in the most favourable cases, the contribution of the external sector does not seem decisive, being at best, only supportive.[41]

[34] Ibid. (437).
[35] Chapman (1972/2006: 16).
[36] Deane and Cole (1969: 185) and Inikori (2002: 149, 450).
[37] Blackburn (2010: 518–27).
[38] Deane and Cole (1969: 78).
[39] Ibid. (34, 312, also 281). See also: Inikori (2002), Du Bois (1946/2015), Williams (1944/1964) and Rodney (1972/2012).
[40] Parthasarathi (2011: 134).
[41] White (2011: 234–5).

The problem here, though, is that while in 1760 domestic demand for cotton textiles comprised 67 per cent and foreign demand 33 per cent, thereafter – as Britain's cotton industrialisation developed – British textile production escalated rapidly such that these ratios swiftly came to trade places. Thus, by 1800, British cotton textile exports comprised 61 per cent and domestic consumption 39 per cent.[42] Put simply, as signalled in the last section, domestic demand was inadequate to absorb the vast quantities of cotton textiles that Arkwright's water frame, Crompton's mule and Cartwright's power loom were pumping out in the British cotton mills by the late-eighteenth century.

Overall, by the early-nineteenth century the Lancashire textile industry was far more closely linked to the Atlantic world than it was with the rest of the national economy.[43] And while the Atlantic market share declined in the nineteenth century, particularly as Asian markets came on stream and Europe's market share recovered, nevertheless 'exports to the rest of Europe did not contribute much to the demand pressure that culminated in the mechanization of weaving [via the application of the steam engine] in the 1830s. This came from the Atlantic markets, to which was added the fast-growing markets of Asia from the 1830s.'[44] The critical point, though, is that these Atlantic markets, combined with the competitive pressures of ICTs, drove British producers and inventors to industrialise the cotton sector, such that they eventually succeeded in replacing the dodecagonal Indian cotton textile trading system with one that was dominated by British cotton textiles, as I explain in the next two sections.

The 'Afro-Indian Global Cotton Whip of Necessity' (I): The Global Atlantic Consumption Driver in the Mechanisation of Cotton Printing, Dyeing and Finishing

Here, I build on the insights of Eric Williams and Joseph Inikori, which assert that Atlantic market demand for cotton textiles was decisive in driving forward Lancashire's industrialisation. I argue that African consumer preference for Indian cotton clothing drove the British to technologically innovate in order to match and ultimately defeat the Indian competition, the result of which was the British industrial revolution. However, I need to preface that discussion by considering

---

[42] Deane and Cole (1969: 187) and Inikori (2002: 436).
[43] Farnie (1979: 56–61) and Inikori (2002: 436).
[44] Inikori (2002: 448).

Britain's 'Indian apprenticeship' that enabled the invention of various technological innovations back in Britain.

Britain's 'Indian Apprenticeship' in Dyeing, Printing and Finishing

Interestingly, back in 1777 Bishop Abbé Raynal claimed that

> If Saxony and other countries of Europe make up fine China, if Valencia manufactures Pekins superior to those of China; if Switzerland imitates the muslins and worked calicoes of Bengal; if England and France print linens with great elegance; if so many stuffs, formerly unknown in our climates, now employ our best artists, are we not indebted to India for all these advantages?[45]

For as Prasannan Parthasarathi and Giorgio Riello both argue, Britain's 'apprenticeship' in Africa was preceded by the EEIC's apprenticeship in India, which began at the start of the seventeenth century, with a similar process playing out vis-à-vis the Dutch Vereenigde Oost-Indische Compagnie (VOC).[46]

Ironically, the origins of this apprenticeship turned out to be serendipitous and contingent. For the European interlopers, bristling with hubristic self-conceptions of imperial power and glory, had not anticipated that upon arrival in the Indian Ocean they would, in effect, find that they had little choice but to sign up to an Indian apprenticeship under Indian cotton masters, and so quickly at that. As I explained in Chapter 5, both the EEIC and the VOC – as had the Portuguese before them – learned almost immediately upon their arrival in the Indian Ocean that the key currency that was accepted throughout the region's economies, apart from the plundered American gold and silver, was ICTs. For it is this that explains why both companies wormed their way into India in the first place and why they, albeit to varying degrees, became ensconced in the Asian inter-country trade. It was this process that comprised the 200-year British apprenticeship in cotton textile production (c. 1600–1800). Moreover, this apprenticeship constitutes an important component of the process of UCD, in which the British borrowed and learned from the more advanced Indian ideas and techniques.

However, many historians have discounted the possibility of 'British learning' from India on the grounds that Indians were notoriously

---

[45] Raynal (1777: 295).
[46] Parthasarathi (2011: ch. 4) and Riello (2013: ch. 5).

secretive about their cotton textile production and market techniques (as I discussed in Chapter 6), which is one reason why they did not codify their knowledge. Not surprisingly, therefore, this means that there is not always a sufficient paper trail of archival relics available, which comprises the cardinal criterion of the proof of transmission so far as many historians are concerned. Indeed, it was this lack of codified Indian knowledge that caused Dr Helenius Scott to express considerable frustration in his own writings, though he managed to send a sample of Indian dyes back to England for further research in 1792. However, while the Europeans had shown very little interest in Indian civilisation before 1500, this situation changed thereafter and then escalated rapidly after about 1650 when 'for the first time since the European "discovery" of the Orient [India], its products began to attract widespread admiration not just for their richness and rarity but for the technological [or technical] skills they embodied'.[47]

Notable here is the point that the Jesuits, who are usually thought to have been significant for sending information on Chinese civilisation back to Europe, also undertook a systematic operation in India to get large numbers of Indian texts translated and dispatched back to Europe. Matteo Ricci, for example, looked specifically to Indian astronomy texts to assist with the Gregorian calendar reform in Europe. There was also considerable interest in Indian mathematics,[48] in which the Indians had led the way for over a millennium – though much of their knowledge had been relayed indirectly to Europe via the West Asian Muslims during the European Renaissance.[49] Soon, growing numbers of Europeans, especially Britons, travelled to India with the express intent of learning its secrets. And, most importantly, alongside that of Indian wootz steel was British interest in Indian cotton printing, dyeing and finishing.

There is no doubt that Indian dyeing, printing and finishing techniques were well in advance of what the British had developed. In particular, over the centuries the Indians had developed 'resists', which were used during the dyeing process in order to confine colours to precise patterns. Moreover, they used mordants in order to fix and thereby make permanent the applied colours so that they could be washed repeatedly without fading.[50] In the British context, all of this appeared as wholly revolutionary and not surprisingly, therefore, attracted a great deal

---

[47] Bronson (1986: 27).
[48] Bala (2006), Joseph (1992) and Raju (2007).
[49] Hobson (2004: 173–83), Goody (2004), Ghazanfar (2006), Al-Rodhan (2012) and Al-Hassani (2015).
[50] Baber (1996: 61), Bronson (1982/3: 3) and Mukund (1992: 2059–60).

of interest. Thus, as Dr Helenius Scott wrote in a letter to Sir Joseph Banks (President of the Royal Society), 'I have for several years past been attentive to the methods used by the [Indians] for dyeing their cotton cloths and I think I have discovered the singular circumstance by which they are enabled to give that permanency of colour which is so admired.'[51]

There were numerous transmission paths or avenues across which Indian knowledge of printing, dyeing and finishing diffused to the West through which the Europeans learned of these Indian techniques.[52] One such avenue was the publication of numerous texts that were written by European sojourners in India during the late-seventeenth through eighteenth century. These included those written by Jean Baptiste Tavernier (1667),[53] Georges Roques (c. 1680), Nicolas de Beaulieu (c. 1734),[54] and, much later on, Edward Baines (1835).[55] Bennet Bronson suggests that overall it was likely that those Britons who stayed at home and read such books perhaps learned the most about Indian technologies.[56]

A second important avenue of knowledge transmission was via the Armenians, who had in turn brought back this knowledge from their time in India. For knowledge of all this diffused out from India and arrived in Safavid Persia and the Ottoman Empire around the sixteenth century, where it was maintained avidly by the Armenians. A number of early European calico printers acquired technical assistance from dyers and printers from the eastern Mediterranean, where cotton production had emerged via learning from India. Moreover, the quest to use 'Madder' or 'Turkey Red' was learned about in France via the knowledge that was passed on by the Armenian, Johann Althen.[57] Important too was Jean-Claude Flachat, who was the first to set up a European Turkey Red dye works, whence the practice diffused across Europe and to Britain in particular.[58] Moreover, printing in Britain was nurtured initially by French Hugenot immigrants, who likely learned of this practice from the Armenian printers.[59] And, of course, observing such practices first hand was possibly more instructive than reading about them in books.

---

[51] Scott (1790–1801/1983: 264–5).
[52] Wadsworth and de Lacy Mann (1931: 124–8), Parthasarathi (2011: 90–5) and Riello (2013: ch. 8).
[53] Tavernier (1667/1889).
[54] Riello (2013: 167).
[55] Baines (1835/1966: ch. 12).
[56] Bronson (1986: 28).
[57] Parthasarathi (2011: 91).
[58] Riello (2013: 178–9).
[59] Ashworth (2017: 157).

Ultimately, the discovery of India's use of mordants was a revolutionary finding that was readily adopted by British printers.[60]

Having discussed Britain's Indian apprenticeship, I now want to combine this with a consideration of the 'Afro-Indian cotton whip of necessity' and how Atlantic consumer demand for ICTs spurred on technological innovations in printing, dyeing and finishing as well as the mechanisation of cotton spinning. All in all, as we shall now see, the '[l]arge and expanding [Atlantic] markets fostered cost-reducing and quality-raising innovations: it pushed up the productive capacity of the industry and served as an "apprenticeship" for the successful engagement of England'.[61] Which means that African prosumer demand formed an elective affinity with the development of the British cotton industry. And as Parthasarathi notes, it was in significant part within 'the markets of West Africa [that] British cotton manufacturers served their apprenticeship under Indian masters'.[62]

The key problem that the British confronted was that the English 'fustians' (cotton–linen hybrids) were inferior to the ICTs because the latter hosted vibrant colours that retained their brilliance after repeated washing. It was this that in significant part appealed to everyday African consumers as well as to rich African elites and African slavers who wore them as status or prestige items – much to the chagrin of the British manufacturers![63] Moreover, the pure cotton fabrics were also more comfortable than the stiffer British fustians that could neither host brilliant colours nor could they be washed. This is in large part why the whole process of imitating Indian techniques of printing, dyeing and finishing became a major factor in Britain's subsequent cotton industrialisation. However, it would be wrong to assume that Britain's industrialisation was simply the product of a *pure* diffusion of Indian knowledge, not least because the British exhibited significant agency in terms of industrialising the cotton sector. How, then, did this play out?

The Afro-Indian Global Cotton Whip of Necessity:
Mechanising Cotton Printing, Dyeing and Finishing

The conventional account of Britain's cotton-technological industrialisation focuses almost exclusively on the numerous spinning

---

[60] Chapman (1972/2006: 11).
[61] Riello (2013: 150).
[62] Parthasarathi (2011: 134).
[63] Wadsworth and de Lacy Mann (1931: 151), Thornton (1998: 50–2), Northrup (2009: ch. 4), Machado (2009a, 2009b, 2014: 135–6), Riello (2009a: 266–7) and Parthasarathi (2011: 92–5).

and weaving technologies that were invented by 'The Few'. That is, those few pioneers who invented the various technologies that enabled industrial-scale cotton spinning and weaving and upon whom the standard trope that every British schoolchild effectively learns: 'never in the field of technology was so much owed by so many to so few'. This heroic narrative of sacrifice is reinforced further by the fact that Richard Arkwright was the only cotton-spinning inventor to prosper from the moneys that his invention produced.[64] As Sven Beckert notes,

[f]ear of mob violence drove [John] Kay and [James] Hargreaves away from the places that they had made their inventions. Neither translated their inventions into wealth; after losing their efforts to defend their patents, they lived modestly. When Hargreaves died in Nottingham in 1778, he owned little more than a prize from the Society for the Encouragement of Arts and Manufacturers, and his children were destitute.[65]

To which, added Richard Arkwright, Hargreaves' 'invention was cruelly wrested from him [via invasion of his patent]; and he died in obscurity and great distress'.[66] The fate of Samuel Crompton, the world-famous inventor of the mule, was no better and he too died a poor man. But, at the risk of adding insult to injury, this heroic narrative of the invention of the various cotton-spinning machines constituted neither the whole process of Britain's cotton industrialisation nor did it mark its inception, given that these spinning technologies came towards the *end* of the process. For the initial thrust was based on developing techniques in painting and especially printing, dyeing and finishing through the use of mordants, by emulating Indian methods so as to compete with ICTs in the Atlantic markets, most especially in Africa.[67] And here I turn to consider the British agential input wherein Indian processes were adapted to higher industrial ends.

The first point of note here is that in contrast to the small Indian printing workshops, the British developed large industrial-scale printing factories that employed hundreds of workers. This was vital because it enabled a more capital-intensive system of printing. And, as I note in Chapter 11, the primitive accumulation of capital that Marxists emphasise was certainly an important factor here. Perhaps the key point is that the English population preferred different designs to those that Indian calico imports sported. For as John Irwin originally noted, 'Europe was

---

[64] Baines (1835/1966: ch. 9).
[65] Beckert (2015: 68).
[66] Arkwright cited in Baines (1835/1966: 161).
[67] Mukund (1992), Parthasarathi (2011: chs. 2 and 4) and Riello (2013: 176).

attracted to Indian decorative textiles on account of their cheapness and technical excellence (especially their fast and brilliant designs), not their *qualities* of design'.[68] In particular, the Indians preferred white patterns on a blue background, whereas the English preferred blue patterns on a white background. As Riello explains, printing on a blue background was more straightforward wherein '[t]he Indian technique for the production of "blue cloth" was a so-called indigo resist-dyeing process [that was] based on tepid indigo fermentation at 115 degrees Farenheit'.[69] But this was unsuitable for achieving a 'blue on white design' because this required waxing most of the cloth given that waxing protected those parts of the cloth that the printer did not want to dye. To this end, the British invented a new process which used cold vats that dissolved the blue indigo dye into iron sulphate. This had the added advantage of overcoming the problem with the Indian process, in which the hot fermentation of indigo sometimes damaged those parts that were waxed. Again, as Riello explains, British wax printing was a labour-saving process – or a 'labour-substituting' process as I explain later – in contrast to the Indian labour-intensive process of painting (batik) wax onto the cloth.

The British also discovered a method for printing indigo, rather than dyeing it, which required the use of quicklime, potash and orpiment. 'This technique, called "English blue" … allowed printing in several colours, something that was immediately recognised as an advantage over Indian producers' who could dye but not print several colours at the same time.[70] Nevertheless, it took the whole of the eighteenth century before the British could match the quality of the Indian dyes.[71] Even so, as late as the early-nineteenth century, the contemporary, Benjamin Heyne, reported that Europeans could still learn much from the Coromandel dyeing practices.[72] For various reasons, the process of bleaching cotton textiles was a particular challenge, though the British finally resolved it through the cheap method of using chlorine.[73]

A further improvement that the British made was to apply science and scientific principles to dyeing and printing. Bronson notes that although the Indians had developed to a high level 'their dyeing and finishing techniques … equally, they did not apply scientific methods to developing what for them had always been an empirical practice that was handed

[68] Irwin (1959: 57).
[69] Riello (2013: 176).
[70] Ibid. (178).
[71] Ashworth (2017: 161).
[72] Heyne in Yazdani (2017: 186).
[73] Ashworth (2017: 163).

down from generation to generation'.[74] Indeed, it is generally recognised that it was the British rather than the Indians who applied modern chemistry to the dyeing, printing and finishing processes. Thus, for example, they sought to develop precise and systematic measurements and procedures concerning the fastness of colour.[75] Moreover, unlike the Indians, the British sought to codify all of this knowledge and to develop it further by applying scientific principles.[76] More generally, the application of science had the added advantage of creating shared knowledge pools of 'open technique' that European producers could utilise – a theme that I return to in Chapter 11.

A further challenge was to speed up the printing process, which was labour intensive in India, for this was the only way that the British could compete with the Indian products. Nevertheless, it is noteworthy that in addition to the labour-intensive process of painting designs, the Indians also used woodblock printing as well as wood-and-metal block printing that were much quicker. Initially, the British too resorted to woodblock printing, but to speed this up, they turned to technological innovation. In 1743 a key innovation was the creation of a three-colour wooden roller printing system, which was replaced in 1754 by copper plates. These were larger than the Indian woodblocks so that they could effect a speeding up of the printing process. And this was improved further in 1783 with the invention of engraved cylinders by Thomas Bell in Preston (Lancashire), which enabled 6-colour prints and high-quality roller printing. All of which led to a revolutionary jump in printing on cotton textiles.[77] Thus, while it took an Indian painter 14 days to paint a 7-metre-long calico, later on in 1851 British machine printing could produce some 5,600–14,000 yards per day.[78] Moreover, British roller printing was at least 20 times more productive than Indian woodblock printing. And while in 1750 Britain produced 0.5 million yards of printed cloth, this had risen to 10 million by 1796 and 86 million by 1830.[79]

All in all, ICT exports and African consumers' preference for them in aggregate constituted the 'whip of external necessity' to which the British responded in late-developer fashion via the process of UCD. For behind the great British tariff wall, domestic producers emulated

---

[74] Bronson (1982/1983) (no page given).
[75] Riello (2013: 182–3).
[76] Mukund (1992) and Chaudhuri (2006: 275–6).
[77] Chapman and Chassagne (1981) and Berg (2009: 409–11).
[78] Riello (2013: 179–81).
[79] Broadberry et al. (2015). However, it should be noted that roller printing was very expensive, hence block printing continued throughout the nineteenth century; Ashworth (2017: 160).

or 'combined' Indian printing, dyeing and finishing techniques so as to develop the British cotton industry. Indeed, as Michelle Maskiell notes, '[w]ith the help of early-eighteenth century legal restrictions on the importation of Indian cotton textiles into England and the copying of Indian cloth-dying technology, British manufacturers invested some of the capital gained from their colonies to produce textiles that substituted for imported Indian cottons'.[80] Or, as Sven Beckert notes:

Just as was the case with the [Chinese] spinning wheel and the horizontal treadle loom in the centuries prior, Asia from the sixteenth through the eighteenth century remained the most important source of cotton manufacturing and, especially, printing technology. As European domination of the global networks of cotton quickened, so too did the pace of European assimilation of [Asian] cotton technology.[81]

Nevertheless, the assimilation process was filtered through British developmental agency to enable the great industrial leap forward.

Ultimately, though, what eluded Lancashire's producers was the production of a *pure* cotton, which was the optimal medium for hosting vibrant prints that were durable and washable. For, in the absence of a pure cotton fabric, all the impressive and revolutionary advances in printing, dyeing and finishing would have come to little. Accordingly, the race was on to produce a *pure cotton* yarn, the outcome of which was the full industrialisation of the cotton textile sector.

The 'Afro-Indian Global Cotton Whip of Necessity' (II): The Global Atlantic Consumption Driver in the Mechanisation of Cotton Spinning and Weaving

Within economic history there are two sets of debates concerning the motivations for the invention of the famous spinning and weaving technologies in the industrialisation of the British cotton sector. The first pits two opposing approaches that are both founded on a 'challenge and response model'. The traditional and dominant conception focuses on a process that is entirely endogenous to Britain (as in the Eurocentric logic of immanence). This hones in on the uneven process of technological development in spinning and weaving, where the emphasis is on the need to maintain parities or an equilibrium between the speed of the two textile processes. That is, bottlenecks in either the spinning or the

---

[80] Maskiell (2002: 36).
[81] Beckert (2015: 50).

weaving processes are ironed out over time by subsequent technological innovations until the optimal production frontier is reached.[82] Thus, while initially it took five spinners to produce sufficient yarn for one weaver, after the introduction of John Kay's flying shuttle for the loom in 1733 the imbalance grew yet wider, thereby necessitating machines to increase the speed of spinning, the result of which saw the invention of Hargreaves' spinning jenny (1767) and Arkwright's water frame (1769). All of which means that in bracketing out external or global pressures/ drivers so this view accords with David Landes' notion of Britain's 'self-generated' technological change;[83] or, the Eurocentric 'logic of immanence'. By contrast, the exogenous model factors in external challenges, which were generated by superior ICT competition that in turn spurred on technological advancements in British cotton spinning and weaving;[84] an approach that points up the global dimension of 'other-generated change'.

However, within this global-oriented framework there are, in turn, two approaches for explaining the introduction of new spinning and weaving technologies. Here, the dominant approach is advanced by what Riello refers to as the 'quantitativists',[85] which includes a good number of non-Eurocentric revisionists as well as many Eurocentric scholars. This position asserts that these technological innovations were motivated by the need to drive down the costs of production – specifically the cost of labour, given that Indian wages were between 40 and 85 per cent lower than British rates. Thus, increases in productivity so as to compete more effectively with the cheaper ICTs are thought to have spurred on the technological innovations.[86] Accordingly, the core challenge for the Lancashire manufacturers was to cut the costs of production in order to overcome the wage gap by introducing labour-saving technologies. On the other side of this debate are the 'qualitatitivists', who argue that technological innovations were required so as to improve the *quality* of the yarn in order to produce pure cotton textiles that, in turn, could compete with the ICTs in global markets. This was necessary because only a pure cotton medium could host the permanent and bright colours that so attracted consumers around the world to ICTs, as I explained

---

[82] For example, Deane (1965: 88–90), Landes (1969: 84), Hobsbawm (1969: 42–3) and Kindleberger (1996: 132).

[83] Landes (1969: 39).

[84] For an excellent discussion of these two positions, see Parthasarathi (2011: 98–114).

[85] Riello (2013: 214–16).

[86] Cf. Elvin (1973), Wolf (1982: 270–1), Frank (1998: 286–94, 300–14), Chaudhuri (2006: 273), Broadberry and Gupta (2009), Allen (2009) and Beckert (2015: 64–5).

earlier. And, recall that the printing, dyeing and finishing techniques *preceded* the new spinning and weaving technologies.

While I certainly do not dismiss the traditional *endogenous* challenge and response model given that it clearly has some resonance, nevertheless I emphasise the importance of the *exogenous* challenge and response model in the guise of the 'Afro-Indian cotton whip of necessity'. And I also argue that the debate between the quantitativists and qualitativists is something of a non-debate, given that they both point to equally important global drivers of Britain's technological innovations. However, while I seek to relativise the British industrial revolution within the wider global context, I do not seek to relativise it out of existence as do some California School scholars, given my point that British developmental agency was also very important. I shall begin with the way in which the British met the 'qualitative challenge' before considering their solution to the 'quantitative challenge', the outcome of which was Britain's full cotton industrialisation.

Britain's Labour-Substitution Industrialisation (I): The Race to Produce Better Quality Cotton Yarn to Match that of India's

The challenge confronting British producers in the 1750s was that they were unable to produce a pure cotton cloth that could host the vibrant dyes and prints. Thus, while British innovations caught up with Indian printing quality and then enabled the second great divergence in printing techniques by the 1780s in Britain's favour, the fact is that even by the mid-eighteenth century Lancashire was still producing a cotton–linen hybrid product. These 'fustians' or 'Manchester cottons', which were generally known as Indian *chintzes* given that these replicated the special finish that was applied by the Indians were, however, vastly inferior to the Indian pure cotton textiles.[87]

The first major challenge confronting British cotton manufacturers was the relatively low skill levels of British spinners. Riello points out that '[t]he difficulty of creating cotton yarn of sufficient tensile strength was caused by the fact that it had to be of a constant thickness, something that Europeans did not seem to be able to achieve as easily as the Indians'.[88] What was required was a strong enough yarn that could act as the *warp* thread (which had to be strong because it was stretched between two points lengthwise and acted as the base through which the weaker *weft* was threaded between the warp in a horizontal fashion). It was precisely

---

[87] Berg (2009: 405); see also Parthasarathi (2011: 94, 96–7) and Riello (2013: 152).
[88] Riello (2013: 225).

because English spinners, unlike their Chinese and Indian counterparts, were insufficiently skilled to produce the warp that the weavers were forced to use inferior linen for the warp right up to the 1760s, while cotton was used for the weft (hence the fustian hybrid of linen and cotton).[89] Given the need to close the gap with Indian exports, so the race was on to invent machinery in order to substitute for the low-skilled British spinners. For new machines were invented to produce *pure* cotton textiles that could host the vibrant and permanent prints, which had been developed through the British revolution in printing, dyeing and finishing. This is why I argue that the new machines were designed to be *labour substituting* rather than labour saving. And, more generally, this constituted the first dimension of Britain's 'labour-substitution cotton industrialisation'.

Here, we encounter the turn to technologies to produce *higher quality* yarn at lower cost round about the 1760s, specifically to match the quality of the Indian product. Only then could Lancashire begin to compete with the Indian products in the Americas and especially Africa.[90] Thus, as Maxine Berg argues, 'during the period of the industry's crucial technological and organizational change inventors, manufacturers and merchants prioritized the *quality* of their products.... The challenge for early British cotton manufacturers was [that] of a newly fashionable and high-quality product from India.'[91] Indeed, it seems that '[q]uality considerations ... figured prominently in Robert Kay's enumeration of the benefits expected to accrue from his father's [flying] shuttle [i.e., John Kay's]. The greater quantity of yarn carried on the shuttle would necessitate fewer piercings, while the more direct path taken across the warp would ensure a more even weave.'[92] Moreover, Wyatt and Paul's machine (1738) was designed primarily 'to control the quality of yarn rather than to raise the number of spindles'.[93] Richard Arkwright's water frame (1769) constituted the really revolutionary breakthrough because it could produce a pure and stronger cotton thread that could act as the warp. Its strength was especially important because the tension required for the warp in a power loom was higher than that which was required for handlooms. And, as Chapman and Chassagne note, '[i]t was textile printing that provided the primary stimulus for Arkwright's enterprise'.[94] This logic also underpinned the invention of Samuel Crompton's mule

[89] Chao (1977: 67).
[90] Parthasarathi (2011: 97–8).
[91] Berg (2009: 391), my emphasis.
[92] Griffiths et al (2008: 636–7).
[93] Chao (1977: 65).
[94] Chapman and Chassagne (1981: 38).

(1779), called as such because it was a hybrid of the water frame and spinning jenny and designed specifically to compete with the highest quality Indian yarn (known as 'muslin'). Not only did it enable mass manufacturing but also the quality of the yarn was greatly improved. So successful was this advance that by the 1780s the production of high-count yarn came to match the quality of the lower grade Indian yarns, though it likely remained inferior to the Dhakan fine cotton muslin right up to the end of the nineteenth century. Interestingly, it was only in the late-nineteenth century that the Dhakan weavers switched to the imported British yarn, not because it was superior but because it was cheaper.[95]

As a result of this rush of inventions, British weavers in the mills no longer needed to rely on linen for the warp, thereby paving the way for the replacement of the sub-optimal fustian hybrids with an optimal pure cotton-based textile. And, as I explained in Chapter 9, all of this was enhanced much further once the superior, long-staple American cotton varieties came on stream – initially the Upland variety and after the 1820s the Mexican strain. All of which, in aggregate, enabled the production of high-count yarn that was of sufficient strength to act as the warp for the newly developed power loom which, in turn, could produce textiles that could compete with the Indian product.[96] Thus, by the 1770s the dream of printing vibrant and fast colours on pure cotton finally became a reality.

Significantly, these inventions – especially the mule – were recognised at the time as the means by which all of this could be realised. As Maxine Berg explains, '[t]he 1812 Committee on Crompton's petition claimed that "in the invention of the mule may be found one of the chief causes of the transference of the seat of an industry to the Western from the Eastern world, where it had been situated from time immemorial"'. To which she adds the assertion advanced in *The Memoir of Samuel Crompton* that the famous textile manufacturer, Samuel Oldknow, 'took new ground by copying some of the fabrics imported from India, which at that time supplied this kingdom with all the finer fabrics, and which the mule-spun yarn alone could imitate'. And finally, she cites a group of merchants who told the Lords of the Council for Trade that 'the object they [the inventors] grasped was great indeed—to establish a Manufacture in Britain that should rival in some measure the Fabrics of Bengall [sic]'.[97]

---

[95] Mukund (1992: 2058).
[96] Parthasarathi (2011: 98).
[97] Berg (2009: 405, 407).

Britain's Labour-Substitution Industrialisation (II): The
Race to Produce Higher Quantities of Cotton Textiles
to Defeat India's Domination of Global Markets

It would, however, be problematic to argue that quantity considerations – the need to increase productivity – were irrelevant, for they were in fact extremely important, though not for the conventional reasons posited by the quantitativists. The popular claim made by quantitativists – Eurocentric and non-Eurocentric alike – which concerns the need to increase productivity in the face of the 'wage gap' between Indian and British cotton workers, is problematic for at least three reasons. First, Stanley Chapman originally pointed out that the problem many cotton mill owners confronted was not replacing labour with machines but that of acquiring workers to work the machines in the first place. Especially in the rural areas where the mills were located largely before the 1830s, there was something of an aversion to working under highly supervised and disciplined factory conditions. Moreover, even in the second half of the eighteenth century, skilled workers were much in demand in the cotton industry. Thus, in order to attract labour, mill owners sought to *raise* wages.[98] Accordingly, higher wages, at least initially, tended to *follow* the inception of new machinery rather than precede it. And this, in turn, suggests that a 'high-wage labour-saving' rationality was *not* the key factor that spurred on the inventions for spinning. Kenneth Pomeranz chimes in here by asserting that '[i]f the makers of the Industrial Revolution were primarily economizing on expensive labor, they were unaware of it'.[99] Moreover, he cites Christine MacLeod's conclusion that is based on an examination of eighteenth-century English patentees. For she claims that most innovators cited the reason for their work to be motivated by saving on capital and improving the final product rather than saving on labour. To this end, she reports that below 4 per cent of the inventors cited saving on labour as their goal.[100] Second, Kirti Chaudhuri and Prasannan Parthasarathi have challenged the common wage-differential explanation directly by arguing that *real* wages were on an approximate par in India and Britain in the eighteenth century.[101] But I want to argue that there was a third, complementary rationale here.

Having learned of the vast scale of global markets in cotton textiles during their Afro-Indian apprenticeship from the early-seventeenth century onwards, the British manufacturers set about to muscle in on the

[98] Chapman (1972/2006: ch. 5).
[99] Pomeranz (2000: 52).
[100] MacLeod (1988: 158–81).
[101] Chaudhuri (1974) and Parthasarathi (2011: 37–46).

global trading action. In this respect, the key hurdle that stood in their way was not high wages but the *small pool* of available British workers. Thus, what has been missed by qualitativists and quantitativists alike is that even had the British spinners' skills deficit in spinning a pure cotton warp been entirely eradicated and even had wage-cost differentials been completely eroded, the British manufacturers would still have been massively outcompeted by India, given the sheer scale of its workforce and output levels. Even as late as 1833 the number of British workers employed in the 1,200 cotton mills stood at roughly 220,000,[102] which compared with 6.3 million Indian cotton workers in 1800.[103] Thus India's cotton textile producers comprised 66 per cent of the whole of the British population. Notable too is that in China, there might have been about twenty-five or twenty-six million spinner- and weaver-adult equivalents in total.[104] This figure seems plausible given that China produced about four times the output of India in 1750 and that there were perhaps around six million Indian producers (on the basis that productivity levels were about equal).[105]

Sven Beckert argues that the colossal numbers of Indian and Chinese spinners were reflected by the fact that 'Chinese spinners and weavers processed about 420 times as much cotton in 1750 as their counterparts in Britain in 1800, and the numbers for India were similar';[106] though this certainly exaggerates the Indian achievement relative to China's (as noted). Either way, though, the unequivocally colossal size of the Chinese and Indian workforces succeeded in massively out-producing Britain's even as late as the 1830s in the case of India and the 1880s viz. China – i.e., well into Britain's cotton industrialisation.

---

[102] Chapman (1972/2006: 60). Note that while Farnie (1979: 24) produces estimates of 242,000 in 1801 rising to 427,000 in 1831, this figure includes the many handloom weavers who were still operating.

[103] Twomey (1983: 54).

[104] Li (1998) produces the figure of 3.5 million adult equivalents for the Lower Yangtze Delta alone (which was the single most important cotton textile region), though Pomeranz (2000: 332) argues that this would be very much on the conservative side. Xu and Wu (2003: 313) estimate that 45 per cent of the total population was involved in cotton cloth production in 1840, which comprised approximately 34.2 million households. Given that 1.5 people in each household are counted as producers of cotton textiles (children and elders are treated as 0.5 of an adult equivalent), so this works out at a total labour force of 51.3 million. However, given that the average working days devoted to production comprised about 50 per cent of the year (Xu 1992: 215–16), so this works out at a final figure of around 25 or 26 million (adult-equivalent) producers. My thanks to Zhang Shizhi for these calculations. See also Zhang (2020: ch. 3).

[105] For the similar levels of Chinese and Indian productivity, see Riello (2013: 75–6).

[106] Beckert (2015: 80).

Thus, the challenge was to create not so much labour-saving but *labour-substituting* technologies in order to produce the vast quantities of pure cotton textiles that the British required if they were to have any hope of meeting the Indian challenge, let alone defeating it. This Atlantic and colonial-market driver, then, constituted a key rationale for the invention of the spinning jenny and the water frame and, most especially, the mule. Overall, an important rationale for the invention of new spinning (and weaving) machines was to instigate a labour-substitution industrialisation. And in the process, Britain moved rapidly into the modern industrial-capitalist mode of production.

Although the spinning jenny and the water frame were very important, it was ultimately the mule that fundamentally revolutionised spinning output by multiplying the number of spindles used. Further adaptations culminated in Richard Roberts' 'self-acting mule' in 1825, which came to hold as many as 1,320 spindles. The net upshot of all these inventions was a revolutionary increase in the productivity of cotton textile output. Thus, to produce 100 lbs of 80 count yarn it took Crompton's mule 2,000 'woman' hours in 1780, 1,000 hours for the 100 spindle mule, 300 hours for the power-assisted mule in 1795 and a mere 135 hours for the self-acting mule in 1825.[107] In the space of just four to five decades, productivity had increased 370 times. Moreover, these revolutionary advancements in spinning were reinforced by advances in mechanised weaving. Notable here was the revised version of Edmund Cartwright's power loom, which was first built in 1785 but would only become fully automated by the early-1840s courtesy of Bullough and Kenworthy.[108] And finally, when the power of the steam engine was harnessed from the 1830s so the second great cotton textile divergence took off between Britain and India after about 1840 – though as I explain in Chapter 13, Indians and Chinese remained important producers nonetheless, with the latter exceeding Britain's industrial output for the vast majority of the nineteenth century. What then of the second core pillar of the British industrial revolution – the iron and steel sector?

How did the British Industrialise the Iron and Steel Sectors? British Late-Developmental Agency under Global UCD

Here, I focus on the *second* great iron and steel divergence, which needs to be situated within the very *longue durée* of the global iron and steel

---

[107] Broadberry and Gupta (2009: 298).
[108] Griffiths *et al.* (2008) and Parthasarathi (2011: 95).

cumulation. For India and China had led the *first* great divergence vis-à-vis Britain and Europe. I advance two specific arguments concerning the industrialisation of the iron and steel sectors. First, I continue the theme of British late-developmental agency in the global context of UCD which, in turn, bleeds into the second core argument that considers the extent to which the British undertook a Chinese and Indian apprenticeship in iron and steel production.

The Long Global Iron Cumulation, c. 512 BCE to 1850 CE: From the Early Developers of China and India to Britain-as-Late-Developer

The Chinese began producing iron around 512 BCE and steel in the second century BCE,[109] while Indian wootz steel production was a clear going concern from the mid-first millennium CE.[110] The origins of the term 'wootz' are unclear. Interestingly, Shashi Tharoor argues that it was a 'corruption of the Kannada word "ukku", mistranscribed in English as "wook" and mangled into "wootz"'.[111] So far as the Chinese were concerned, they were producing wrought and cast iron *before* the Common Era. Moreover, during the Song dynasty (960–1279) they produced about 125,000 tons of iron in 1078, the scale of which is brought into relief by the fact that seven centuries later the British were producing only 76,000 tons in 1788.[112] And, although various experts have sought to downgrade this Chinese iron output figure, none has challenged China's massive lead.[113] Thus, it could not be argued that the British were *inherently* superior in their iron- and steel-based technological prowess because the Indians and Chinese had pioneered the way during the previous two millennia. And moreover, I suggest that the British built upon at least some of these earlier developments. Paradoxically in this context, I countenance against 'relativising' the British achievement out of the picture, for Britons exhibited considerable developmental agency in revolutionising iron and steel production, taking the earlier Chinese and Indian developments to radically new heights during the nineteenth century.

While it is often thought that Chinese iron production tailed off after 1400, it seems fairer to say that iron production continued, albeit at very

---

[109] Needham (1964) and Wagner (2008: 83–4).
[110] Bronson (1986).
[111] Tharoor (2017: 32).
[112] Hartwell (1966: 32–3).
[113] For example, Golas (1999: 169–70, esp. n. 495).

much lower rates of growth than before 1078. Thus, moving forward in time we find that by the early-twentieth century China produced some 170,000 tons of 'native iron'.[114] Also of note is that in eighteenth-century India some 10,000 iron and steel furnaces in aggregate produced about 200,000 tons – though Dharampal argues that even as late as 1840 Indian iron and steel was as good in quality as well as cheaper than the British product.[115] Either way, though, the fact is that by 1820 the British produced 400,000 tons of iron and a staggering 6 million tons by 1870,[116] thereby clinching the second great (iron) divergence. One of the key questions here is whether the British achieved this *ex nihilo* or whether they learned from the early developers of India and China. And, if the latter, so this begs the question as to whether Britain was a 'passive developer' – merely borrowing from others – or whether Britons borrowed but then added to them through developmental agency. In my 2004 book, I argued for the former case whereas here I argue for the latter.

Traditional Eurocentric accounts hold that a key innovation was Abraham Darby I's famous discovery of coking coal in 1709, which acted as a fuel substitute for wood/charcoal in the context of the problem of massive deforestation.[117] Moreover, this innovation served to reduce significantly the cost of iron as well as boost production, given that it enabled the construction of much larger furnaces that could utilise a more powerful blast at higher temperatures and had the added benefit of combusting contaminating material. Note too that coke is a purer form of coal given that the roasting process removes impurities such as sulphur and that the resulting product is almost pure carbon. However, it is more accurate to say that while this was an extremely important development in the British context, it could not be described as 'pioneering' because it obscures the fact that the Chinese had been deploying *coke* in blast furnaces up to two millennia earlier.[118]

Although it is the case that for much of the time before the fourteenth century the deployment of coal rather than coke in the blast furnace was ordinarily sufficient, this was largely because the Chinese had learned very early on to add limestone in order to overcome the problem of sulphur contamination from coal. Peter Golas argues that '[i]t now seems beyond doubt that coal was used as a fuel both for industrial and

---

[114] Xing (2000: 418).
[115] Dharampal (1983: 213–51).
[116] Fry and Willis (2015: 38, 45).
[117] Deane (1965: 129), Landes (1969: 95) and Braudel (1992: 553–5).
[118] Wertime (1961: 49), Hartwell (1966: 55–7) and Wagner (2008: 318).

household purposes no later than the final years of the Han [206 BCE to 220 CE] and possibly considerably earlier'.[119] Furthermore, China enjoyed plentiful supplies of coal in the northern zone of the country, particularly in Shensi. And, most critically, it was during the Song dynasty (960–1279) when coal was used on a sustained basis in blast furnaces – predominantly in the north – specifically as a means of solving the problem of massive deforestation.[120] Thus, the Chinese pre-empted Abraham Darby I's 'seminal invention' in the same context by some seven centuries. Moreover, during the Song period the Chinese developed large coal-fuelled furnaces (6–9 metres tall) that were used in Sichuan and which were sometimes deployed in large-scale factories.[121] Significantly, these required large amounts of capital and labour, with some factories employing up to 1,000 free-wage labourers.[122] Moreover, mining and smelting at Li-kuo chien in Northern Kiangsu saw as many as 3,600 wage labourers employed by iron masters, with the latter providing the capital and owning the ore deposits to supply 36 smelting plants. This, to an extent, approximated with the modern conception of a capitalist complex,[123] though certainly the constant need to upgrade technologies was not a core feature as it would become in fully modern (especially Western) conceptions of capitalism.

Also of note is that Abraham Darby II helped pioneer the use of steam engines to pump water into higher pools, which then supplied twenty-four foot water wheels that supposedly operated the 'largest pair of bellows' ever to have been made.[124] Clearly, the Chinese did not invent the steam engine – notwithstanding Joseph Needham's suggestion that the Chinese double-acting piston bellows shared certain principles in common with the later steam engine, and that it remains a matter of conjecture as to whether these informed through a direct process of emulation and adaptation the efforts of James Watt.[125] Either way, though, while the Briton, John Smeaton, is credited with inventing the water-powered bellows for iron production in the early-1760s, it turns out that this innovation was pioneered in China some eighteen centuries earlier in order to raise the temperature of the blast furnace – a vital

---

[119] Golas (1999: 193); see also Needham (1964: 19).
[120] Hartwell (1966: 54), Golas (1999: 195–6), Wagner (2008: 3–4) and Parthasarathi (2011: 162–4).
[121] Wagner (2008: ch. 2).
[122] Hartwell (1966: 45–8) and Wagner (2008: 305–11).
[123] Hartwell (1966: 44–51).
[124] Roepke (1956: 21).
[125] On this see Needham (1970: 136–202), Needham et al. (1986: 544–68) and Pomeranz (2000: 61–2). But see Deng (2004).

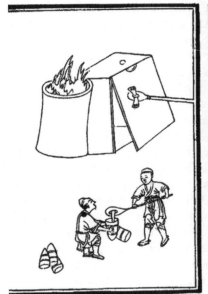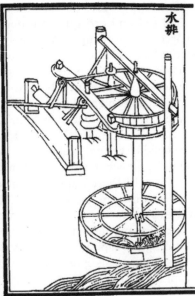

Figure 10.2 Chinese water-powered hydraulic blowing engine for metallurgy (illustration from Wáng Zhēn, *Nong Shu*, 1313).

innovation that was required when using coke and coal as fuel.[126] More specifically, the Chinese invented the double cylinder bellows as early as the fourth century BCE, the double-acting single-cylinder bellows in the second century BCE, all of which culminated in Tu Shih's mechanised water-powered bellows in 31 CE (see Figure 10.2).[127]

Nevertheless, there is no doubting the fact that the steam engine was considerably superior to the Chinese bellows and blowing engines and that it was vital in enabling the generation of massive amounts of iron and steel upon which the second great divergence in iron/steel – as well as the second great divergence in cotton textile – production was clinched during the nineteenth century. And the invention of the steam engine can only be adequately explained by highlighting the role of science and British developmental agency more generally, which I consider in Chapter 11.

A further famous innovation that underpinned the British iron revolution is that of Henry Cort's 'puddling process' in 1784 (where 'puddle' means 'to stir about'), which converted cast iron into wrought iron. This revolutionised production beyond the achievements of the

[126] Needham (1964: 47).
[127] Ibid. (1970: 119).

Figure 10.3 Cort's iron puddling process (post-1784) and the Ancient Chinese puddling process (c. first century CE). Note on the right-hand side of the bottom diagram is a picture of the double-acting box bellows. Picture taken from Song Yingxing's *Tiangong Kaiwu* (1637/2017).

earlier bloomery process. However, wrought iron had long been produced in China in what Donald Wagner calls a 'puddling furnace', into which the important flux, silica, was added. Silica is vital because it converts those rocky elements of iron ore into slag, which otherwise would not melt in the furnace. Critically, Wagner claims that 'the operation of the Sichuan chaolu [puddling furnace] had many characteristics in common with the "puddling" process patented by Henry Cort in 1784'.[128] And, as the diagrams in Figure 10.3 illustrate, both processes required the stirring of the iron so as to help separate out the impurities while lowering the carbon content of the cast iron – i.e., decarburisation – in order to produce wrought iron. Nevertheless, the difference was that British technological agency led to an improvement of the Chinese

[128] Wagner (2008: 30, and see 30–4).

process through the use of much larger puddling beds, the development of roller bars to produce rolled iron, and the generation of much larger quantities all round.

It is also interesting to note here that the invention of malleable cast iron is usually attributed to Prince Rupert and was patented in 1760, though it only became important in Britain in the nineteenth century. Nevertheless, the Chinese were producing cast iron from at least the third century BCE,[129] which was used in everyday tools and items, far too numerous to list here.[130]

Finally, by way of an addendum, in classic late-developer fashion the British state levied very high tariffs on iron,[131] increasing them five-fold in the first half of the eighteenth century alone. This late-developer state strategy enabled an iron-based ISI for it gave British entrepreneurs, inventors and 'iron producers the space in which they could experiment and innovate, especially with the use of coal in place of charcoal in smelting and refining'.[132] Again, as with the cotton industry, the British state also engaged in an export-promotion policy, in which domestic producers who exported their products would gain a rebate on the tariffed raw materials that they imported.[133]

The Long Global Steel Cumulation, c. Second Century BCE to 1850 CE: From the Early Developers of China and India to Britain-as-Late-Developer

A very similar story applies in the case of the second great steel divergence. For, the great technological spurt of the 1850s enabled Britain to produce about 1.3 million tons of steel by the late-nineteenth century, whereas Chinese and Indian production would have been less than 100,000 tons each. In brief, the story runs as follows. Up until 1740, the British produced steel by immersing wrought iron bars in charcoal that were heated for up to a week, thereby enabling the carbon to enter the iron – i.e., the 'carburisation of wrought iron'. But this 'cementation process' was identical to that which the Chinese had developed around the fifth century CE.[134] And while a significant step forward was taken by Benjamin Huntsman in 1740 through the development of 'crucible cast steel', in which steel was melted in small crucibles, this process

---

[129] Ibid. (167, 359–61).
[130] For a full list, see Hobson (2004: 52).
[131] Davis (1966: 315–16) and Brewer (1989: 166).
[132] Parthasarathi (2011: 169).
[133] O'Brien (1989: 364; 1991: 27–8).
[134] Needham (1964: 9–11) and Wagner (2008: 66–8).

mirrors that which was pioneered originally in ancient China and was reminiscent of Indian wootz steel production.[135] Not surprisingly, the problem here is that this produced only small amounts of steel, as was the case in China and India.

However, the great leap forward in British steel production came in the 1850s, when both the Siemens-Martin co-fusion and the Bessemer process were invented. And it was only when Thomas Gilchrist discovered that adding a limestone flux to counter the negative effects of phosphorus did a stronger, less brittle steel finally become a reality.[136] But again, as noted above, this flux had been used by the Chinese for over 2,000 years. And, moreover, the co-fusion process was a higher adaptation of the Chinese 'perfusion process' that was invented around the sixth century CE, in which wrought and cast iron billets were piled up and heated together to equalise the amount of carbon content between the two metals – or the 'decarburisation of cast iron', given that steel's carbon content lay in between that of wrought and cast iron.[137] Nevertheless, the Siemens-Martin process represented a technological great leap forward given that it completely melted the steel and that it produced enormous quantities at that. And it was this that clinched the second great divergence in steel production in the second half of the nineteenth century.

Whether these British inventions in iron and steel were made entirely independently of the earlier Chinese ones remains an open and indeed fraught question, to which I return later. What is undeniable, however, was the presence of considerable British interest in Indian wootz (crucible) steel, given that since the mid-first millennium it had been the most prized in the world. It was distinguishable by its watery surface pattern and the famous wootz-based 'Damascus sword' was prized for its razor-like sharpness. Note that the term 'Damascus' steel should not be confused with the Syrian city but derives from the term 'damascene', meaning 'watery pattern'.

A long line of illustrious British experts worked with wootz in order to discover its secrets. They read like a list of the 'who's who' of the world of steel, including George Pearson, David Mushet, Robert Mushet, Michael Faraday and James Stodart, John Holland, Josiah Heath, Henry Wilkinson and Henry Bessemer.[138] Interestingly, in his 1864 book on

---

[135] Wagner (2008: 261–4) and Srinivasan and Ranganathan (2014: 3, 39).
[136] Fry and Willis (2015: 102).
[137] Needham (1964: 10–11, 26–31, 1970: 109), Wagner (2008: 255–67) and Lox (2009: 377).
[138] Pearson (1795), Mushet (1805, 1840/2011), Stodart (1818), Faraday (1819), Stodart and Faraday (1822), Holland (1833) and Wilkinson (1837, 1841: 196–237).

metallurgy, John Percy, having discussed David Mushet's 'seminal' work on steel concluded wryly: '[i]t is curious that Mushet's process, so far as [it] relates to the use of malleable iron in the production of cast-steel, should in principle, and I may add in practice too, be identical with that by which the Hindoos have from ancient times prepared their wootz. I can not discover any essential difference between the two.'[139] Moreover, Nikhiles Guha, when discussing the superiority of wootz production over European steel methods claims that '[t]he credit for converting malleable iron into cast-steel by fusing it in a closed crucible in contact with iron was earned by [David] Mushet in 1800, who patented it. This was very similar to the process in Mysore [in south-west India].'[140] To which we can add James Stodart, who famously asserted that '[t]he experience of twenty-five years fully confirms the sanguine opinion then given, Wootz, when properly treated, proving vastly superior to the best cast-steel of Europe ... is invaluable for surgical instruments, where mediocrity is not, at least'.[141] Then again, the significant contemporary, M. H. C. Landrin, asserted that '[t]he way Wootz steel is made in Asia ... brings to mind that the modern metallurgists, when they invented blast furnaces, have but imitated the processes of ... Golconda [where the best Indian steel was produced].[142] Last but not least, Srinivasan and Ranganathan note that '[w]hile it is ironic that Benjamin Huntsman in Sheffield in 1740 is credited with developing the process of crucible steel production, it is quite likely that he took his cue from some of the processes of crucible steel making in India described by the European travellers of the 17th and early 18th centuries'.[143] And there is a string of other notable metallurgists who made similar remarks.[144] All in all, it would be reasonable to conclude that the role of carbon in steel was discovered in part as a result of enquiries into wootz.

By Way of Conclusion: Emulating China and India in the Global Context of UCD?

Here, I want to conclude this chapter by considering the global context within which British industrialisation was embedded. So far as Britain's cotton revolution is concerned, Giorgio Riello claims that

---

[139] Percy (1864: 776–8, 778).
[140] Guha cited in Yazdani (2017: 194).
[141] Stodart (1818: 570–1).
[142] Landrin (1868: 41).
[143] Srinivasan and Ranganathan (2014: 3).
[144] See the discussion in Yazdani (2017: 192–3).

What seems to be often forgotten is that Europe did not suddenly acquire the skills, knowledge and 'outlook' to produce and sell cotton textiles and that even when they did, they were not the simple result of technological innovation [*ex nihilo*]. It was a long process of learning that started back in the 1500s that eventually led … to Europe becoming one of the world's leading cotton manufacturing areas.[145]

To which William Ashworth adds that '*imitative innovation* was promoted as a way of overcoming Asian supremacy and, crucially [it was] conducted behind a wall of prohibitions and tariffs'.[146] Bennet Bronson notes that '[t]he Indian calico makers are acknowledged by the very well informed [Edward] Baines … to have played a major role in stimulating the great [technical] innovations of the late-eighteenth century that ushered in the [British] industrial revolution'.[147] And finally, while Sen is right to say that '[t]he poor Indian weavers shaped the course of world history by unconsciously laying the foundation of [the] British and Dutch colonial empire',[148] this might be adapted to say that the poor Indian weavers (and spinners) shaped the course of world history by unconsciously laying the foundation of Britain's cotton industrialisation. But what of Britain's iron and steel revolution?

While it is likely that British inventors learned much from Indian wootz steel, the larger question is whether they also borrowed ideas and techniques from China. This is a fraught question because there is no archival paper trail that can confirm this question one way or another. And it is largely because of this that historians have defaulted to the Eurocentric proposition that Britons came up with all of the inventions independently. The immediate problem that we confront here, though, is that

if we hope to find explicit acknowledgement of such [Chinese] influence in their [British inventors'] works we shall be [mostly] disappointed: Western writers and inventors plagiarised each others' ideas shamelessly … [and] we may be sure that they had no scruples in passing off their own, ideas that had come from the other side of the world.[149]

Paradoxically, John Styles notes that

great efforts were made by private entrepreneurs, the state and patriotic societies to establish in England what had previously been exclusively foreign forms of manufacturing. More often than not the initial intention was simply to make

---

[145] Riello (2009b: 310).
[146] Ashworth (2017: 103), my emphasis.
[147] Bronson (1986: 27).
[148] Sen (1962: 92).
[149] Bray (1984: 571).

English copies of foreign products. Copying and imitation had few negative connotations at this period; originality, in its uncompromising modern sense, was not necessarily prized.[150]

All of which means that while there is accepted evidence that the British learned from various Indian cotton textile and steel production processes, we cannot say for sure that Chinese iron and steel processes were in some way emulated by the British inventors. But we can, however, plausibly conjecture that there might well have been a trace that has gone largely un-recognised.

Refining the proof of transmission theory, Arun Bala has argued that we can reasonably infer transmission of early technologies and processes in those situations where a particular culture (in this case Britain) becomes interested in understanding earlier inventions (in this case Chinese), and when the non-Western inventions soon after that interest is displayed become adopted as well as adapted to higher ends (as in Britain's industrial era).[151] For at precisely the same time that British inventors were looking to advance the iron industry, we find that British and other Europeans and especially many Enlightenment philosophers became not only extremely interested in all things Chinese between about 1650 and 1780,[152] but that a veritable wave of books and pamphlets on Chinese civilisation flooded into Britain and Europe to meet this interest. And, we know that they were read very widely.[153] Moreover, it was precisely at this time that various Chinese technologies were brought over to Europe that in turn helped promote the British agricultural revolution – most notably the rotary winnowing machine and the all important curved iron mouldboard plough.[154]

None of this, of course, proves that British iron and steel inventors borrowed Chinese ideas and techniques. But what we *can* say definitively is that the British were *not* working from a historical *tabula rasa*, given the existence of the long global iron and steel cumulation that stems back some two millennia to the pioneering developments that unfolded in India and China. Thus, it turns out that very much later on the British found themselves plying similar iron and steel paths to those that had been trailblazed by the Indians and Chinese. Nevertheless, even if the key British iron and steel inventors had emulated the Chinese within the global context of UCD, it is equally clear that they adapted them

---

[150] Styles (2000: 130–1).
[151] Bala (2006: 50).
[152] Bray (1984: 569) and Clarke (1997).
[153] Needham (1970: 174), Lach and Kley (1993: 1890) and Clarke (1997).
[154] Bray (1984: 366–79, 553–5, 558–9, 581–3).

to much higher ends to make the breakthrough into industrialisation. Accordingly, I reject the claim that industrialisation was 'born in a global womb', given the importance of British late-developmental agency. But, I think it reasonable to argue, at the very least, that the FGE constituted the midwife in the birth of Britain's industrialisation. No less significant in this context is that despite the presence of historical capitalism in China and India, neither of these countries made a spontaneous breakthrough into industrial capitalism, as Chapters 11 and 12 explain.

Part IV

The Second Great Divergence, 1600–1800: Differing 'Developmental Architectures' in Global Contexts

11 Why Britain Initiated a Cotton Industrialisation and Why India and China Did Not

Introduction

This is the first of the two chapters that in aggregate consider what Kenneth Pomeranz calls the 'great divergence', though as noted already I prefer to call it the *second* great divergence. The first great divergence in cotton production began in the first millennium CE and took off in thirteenth-century India and China. And the first great divergence in iron production goes back to the early fifth century BCE in China, while the first great divergence in steel production emerges in the second century BCE in China.[1] Certainly, by the mid-first millennium, the first great iron and steel divergence had been achieved by India and China. I shall deal with the 'second' great divergence in the cotton textile industry in this chapter while reserving the analysis of the second great divergence in iron and steel for the next.

Here, as in Chapter 12, I confront one of the thorniest issues in historical sociology and global economic history: that of the 'Needham problem' or the 'Needham question'. This boils down to asking 'why China (and to an extent India), which had been a pioneer of technological development for over two millennia failed to industrialize, whereas Britain, which had been a laggard for several millennia, succeeded?'[2] Despite the essentially *non*-Eurocentric underpinnings of the monumental 'Needham enterprise' of scholarship that has developed over the last seven decades, his own solution turned out to be surprisingly Eurocentric. For Joseph Needham focused on the bureaucratic-hydraulic nature of the (Oriental despotic) Chinese state that emerged as a function of maintaining centralised irrigation systems as well as the presence of an anti-merchant culture. And in Europe, by contrast, aristocratic feudalism turned out to be more conducive to the rise of capitalism not least because of the presence of numerous social conflicts within Europe that enabled 'powers and

---

[1] Needham (1964).
[2] Needham (1969: 16).

liberties' to thrive.[3] Nevertheless, many non-Eurocentrics would argue that the question forced a Eurocentric answer in the first place, given that it supposedly requires us to single out 'rational presences' in Britain and their 'absence' in China.[4] But in this and Chapter 12, I propose a solution to the Needham problem that avoids falling back into the Eurocentric trap.

While I shall consider some 'surprising resemblances' between India/China and Britain, I shall also hone in on their *differing* 'developmental architectures', all of which is done through a comparative analysis of Britain and China/India (see Figure 11.1 and Figure 12.1). It is important to note that while the California School produces highly significant insights on the surprising resemblances of Chinese and British economic institutions as well as considering global trade and the (second) great divergence, nevertheless, it is striking just how little it tells us about the ways in which production is carried out. Here, I want to respond to my potential neo-Marxist critic in this chapter by factoring in class relations and the mode of production in explaining how and why Britain broke through into modern capitalism and why China and India did not. Simultaneously, this enables me to fill in one of the most striking lacunae in much of California School scholarship. However, while this is certainly part of my focus, nevertheless, mine is much wider than one that highlights *only* class relations. I prefer the more complex conception of a 'developmental architecture', which factors in state–society relations and the modes of production, empire, warfare, taxation and epistemic construction. And, as I explained in Chapter 8, my conception of the mode of production is more eclectic than the reductive approach that is advanced by orthodox, fundamentalist Marxists.

I also place these three countries in their respective global and regional contexts specifically by considering pressure differentials and opportunities that emanated from the first global economy (FGE) and the three respective regional inter-state systems within which China, India and Britain were embedded. To which I also borrow but extend further Pomeranz's argument concerning differences in ecological fortunes – in cotton in this chapter, and coal in Chapter 12. Note that while I shall consider India in this chapter, nevertheless, I do so mainly within the confines of my analysis of modes of production and class analysis, though I shall focus on the Indian state of Mysore in detail for the post-1750 period in Chapter 12.

---

[3] Ibid. (211).
[4] Bray (1999: 162–8) and cf. Hobson (2004: 295–300).

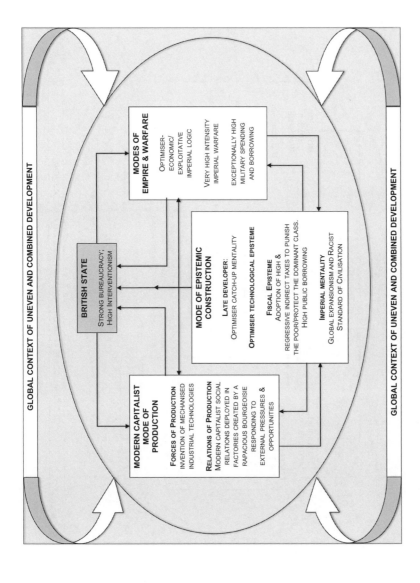

Figure 11.1 British and Chinese 'developmental architectures' in the global context of uneven development.

GLOBAL CONTEXT OF UNEVEN AND COMBINED DEVELOPMENT

GLOBAL CONTEXT OF UNEVEN AND COMBINED DEVELOPMENT

MODES OF EMPIRE & WARFARE

Optimiser-Economic/Exploitative Imperial Logic

Very high intensity imperial warfare

Exceptionally high military spending and borrowing

BRITISH STATE

Strong Bureaucracy; High Interventionism

MODE OF EPISTEMIC CONSTRUCTION

Late Developer: Optimiser catch-up mentality

Optimiser Technological Episteme

Fiscal Episteme
Adoption of high & regressive indirect taxes to punish the poor/protect the dominant class. High public borrowing

Imperial Mentality
Global expansionism and Racist Standard of Civilisation

MODERN CAPITALIST MODE OF PRODUCTION

Forces of Production
Invention of mechanised industrial technologies

Relations of Production
Modern capitalist social relations deployed in factories created by a rapacious bourgeoisie responding to external pressures & opportunities

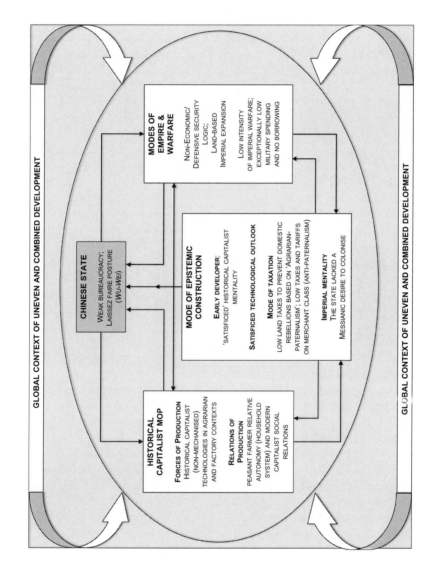

Figure 11.1 *(cont.)*

However, while I deploy a comparative historical sociological analysis, nevertheless Gurminder Bhambra notes perceptively that the problem with the *comparative method* is that it tends to bracket out the manifold interconnections that exist between countries – in this case Britain, China and India.[5] Thus, while I seek to bring domestic factors and differences 'back in', given that much of the California School kicks them back out in favour of a focus on 'surprising resemblances' between China and Britain,[6] nevertheless I argue that these domestic characteristics vary *in part* because of differing international and global contexts and forces – hence my *multi-spatial* conception of a developmental architecture.

In essence, my solution to the 'Needham problem' is two-fold: first, neither China nor India was on a trajectory into a cotton-based industrialisation owing to the nature and the structure of their developmental architectures and most especially the nature of their systems of production and class relations. Second, there was neither a desire nor a need to industrialise, in part because there was an absence of international geopolitical, imperial economic and global economic pressures pushing them to do so, and in part because these societies were, in effect, 'historical capitalist satisficers'. For, as I noted in Chapter 8, there is nothing intrinsic to proto-industrialisation and historical capitalism that leads inevitably into modern industrial capitalism (see also Chapter 14). And, while I focus on the role of the FGE in this chapter, I turn to consider international geopolitical, imperial and fiscal factors in the next, where I analyse the differing propensities for an iron and steel industrialisation.

By contrast, Britain became an 'industrial capitalist optimiser' partly in response to a series of very considerable external pressures that were largely global economic and imperial geopolitical in nature and in part because of the specificity of the structure of British state–society relations and a particular set of class relations that produced super-hierarchical production systems. As I also noted in Chapters 9 and 10, it is not simply the presence of strong external pressures that accounts for why Britain industrialised first, given that many of these existed in the case of other European great powers, most notably France. Rather, it is the *specific manner* of the response and the nature of the social structures that also count, which points to the important role of British developmental agency that is generally ignored by the California School. All of which, in turn, leads back to an inversion of the Eurocentric Big

---

[5] Bhambra (2014).
[6] One clear exception here that brings domestic factors in – specifically the role of the scientific revolution in Britain – is Goldstone (2000, 2002, 2008).

Bang theory given my claim that globalisation and the FGE came first and British industrialisation followed.

This chapter proceeds through four sections. The first two challenge the standard Eurocentric belief that China was lacking the rational institutions and rational culture that are pre-requisites for capitalist industrialisation. Thus, in the section 'An Absence of Firms, Property Rights and Rational Economic Institutions in China?', I consider some of the core dimensions of China's 'historical capitalism', focusing in particular on the surprising similarities or resemblances between Britain and China with regards to economic institutions, property rights and entrepreneurship – all of which dovetails with the logic of the California School. I then turn in the section 'An Absence of Chinese (and Indian) Technological Creativity in the Cotton Industry?' to consider China's capacity for technological innovation, noting that the Chinese had led the world for some two millennia and that it was not for lack of such an inherent capacity that China did not industrialise, though it *is* the case that technological innovation tailed off in the Qing era (1644–1911). There I argue that the Chinese might have converted their water-powered/mechanised big spinning frame for ramie into a cotton machine to thereby bring about a cotton-based industrialisation but chose not to because of the nature of the household system of production and the ecological challenge of its weak raw cotton. Moreover, paralleling the Chinese situation, its inferior short-staple raw cotton also made mechanisation far less likely in India, which reinforced the economic sovereignty of the Indian household system of cotton textile production.

To the Eurocentric reply that this renders the Asian household production system a blockage to modern capitalism, the section 'Why Neither India nor China Underwent a Cotton Industrialisation: Differing Class Relations and Modes of Production under UCD' considers three reasons why neither the Chinese nor the Indians undertook an industrialisation of their cotton sectors, which are linked to class–society and state–society relations as well as these countries' position at the apex of global cotton textile production. Finally, the section 'Why Britain Underwent a Cotton-based Industrialisation: British Cotton Capitalists as "Industrial Optimisers"' considers the industrialisation of the British cotton sector, arguing that a much more hierarchical set of class relations existed alongside a partly bourgeois-based and partly aristocratic-based state within the context of global uneven development. For, Britain's un-competitive cotton sector in the face of India's dominance of global markets necessitated the mechanisation of the industry in order to enhance bourgeois profit rates (as I explained in Chapter 10).

An Absence of Firms, Property Rights and Rational Economic Institutions in China?

Eurocentrism discounts the possibility of industrialisation occurring in China and India before Britain because of a presumed 'absence' of Asian firms, rational economic institutions and property rights. Here, I shall focus on China's historical capitalism to consider this critical issue, given that I revealed the many rational economic institutions that existed in India in the final section of Chapter 8. And here, I concur with the California School's focus on a series of 'surprising resemblances' between Britain and China.

The Eurocentric claim here is usually tied in with the Oriental despotism thesis insofar as the presence of formal legal institutions are associated intimately with the modern Western, economically rational liberal state. But even in the context of European trade, it has become increasingly recognised that *informal* institutions were important.[7] And, on the basis of numerous archival findings, various revisionists have shown that significant *informal* institutions existed within China to support commerce, contracts and property rights.[8] Indeed, the prolific size of China's internal commerce, which, according to Adam Smith,[9] was as large as the whole of intra-European trade, means logically that contracts and property rights of some kind must have existed. Indeed, Peter Perdue argues that the reality was largely commensurate with the European situation, given that

ordinary Chinese ... were not simply victims of a mythical oriental despotism, denied of legal guarantees and subject to the whims of an autocratic state; they lived in a growing commercial-agrarian society governed by a complex mixture of legal provisions and informal procedures not so different from early-modern Europe.[10]

And far from constituting an obstructive or economically invasive state, the Qing was interested in the stability of business practice and erred, if anything, too much towards a laissez-faire posture. As Madeleine Zelin notes, 'Qing economic policies were relatively benign, limiting neither the movement of capital and workers, nor the entrepreneurial energies of merchants and manufacturers ... [T]he Qing tax system as a whole

---

[7] Greif (2006).
[8] Rosenthal and Bin Wong (2011: ch. 3) and Perdue (2004).
[9] Smith (1776/1937: 645). See also Rosenthal and Bin Wong (2011: 79, 93) and Millar (2017: 109).
[10] Perdue (2004: 56).

was relatively benign in its extraction of profits from manufacturing and commerce',[11] a point I confirmed at the end of Chapter 2.

Various scholars have revealed the role of written contracts in agriculture as well as equity in businesses. Rosenthal and Bin Wong point out that the unearthing of large amounts of historical private contracts in the last three decades reveal, in aggregate, that the presence of private property in land was a fact of life across much of Qing China.[12] And, moreover, these contracts and titles were often enforced by county magistrates. Zelin's intensive study of the salt industry in Zigong in Sichuan that emerged in the early Qing era is especially instructive. She reveals how merchants mobilised capital, developed new technologies, captured markets and constructed corporate business organisations. In particular, she argues that the

success of Zigong's investors in transforming their industry from one of handicraft workshops to large-scale industrial firms ... belies long-held beliefs that social structure, the absence of modern banking, and [Confucian] cultural bias against business precluded industrial investment and development in China.[13]

The case of Chinese banking is also instructive. Elvin highlights the emergence of the (northern) Shansi banks in the eighteenth century as a prominent example of a large-scale economic organisation,[14] though this should not obscure the 'native banks' in the south (*Ch'ien chuang*) and the many southern 'money shops' that handled New World silver imports. Moreover, local money shops in the south 'began commercial credit operations by consigning silver shoes, needed for larger mercantile transactions, against a delayed payment in copper [the domestic currency]'.[15] And Bin Wong notes that 'native banks' (*zhangju, piaohao* and *qianzhuang*) took deposits and made loans – a sure sign of modern banking practice. 'The first *zhangju* appears to have been established in Zhangjiaku in 1736 by a Shanxi merchant who committed 40,000 taels [£13,000] of capital.... [The *piaohao*] dealt in inter-regional remittances to facilitate the transactions of the Shanxi merchants, who were located in the northern half of [China] as well as in the Jiangnan region [in the south]'.[16] And finally, the *qianzhuang* were common in Jiangnan.

---

[11] Zelin (2005: xv).
[12] Rosenthal and Bin Wong (2011: ch. 3).
[13] Zelin (2005: xv).
[14] Elvin (1973: 296–7).
[15] Ray (1995: 463).
[16] Bin Wong (2002: 451–2). See also Rosenthal and Bin Wong (2011: ch. 5).

More generally, Kenneth Pomeranz points out the existence of Chinese family-based firms over many centuries and that many of them not only raised significant sums of capital and share capital according to joint stock principles but that they also achieved vertical integration. Moreover, some employed between 3,000 to 5,000 workers, which 'made them some of the largest firms in the pre-industrial world and certainly suggests that they could raise enough money to manage any preindustrial or early industrial process'.[17] I also noted in Chapters 6 and 8 that there were numerous Indian *bania* family firms that operated on a large trans-continental scale. Moreover, they were girded by commercial partnerships and a range of other rational-commercial institutions including double-entry bookkeeping, the commercial partnership (*shah-gumāshtā*) and, not least, the use of various bills of exchange (*hundīs*). I noted too that very substantial amounts of capital were raised in Hindu temples, the size of which were comparable to those raised by the Amsterdam bank.[18] And, last but not least, not only were Indian interest rates on loans comparable to those in Britain in the sixteenth and seventeenth centuries but also insurance rates on trade were very low, thereby revealing the relative security of the trade routes.[19] Nevertheless, all of this goes under the Eurocentric radar screen because many of these institutions were largely 'informal' in nature in comparison to Europe's alleged formal institutions. But to reiterate, the irony here is that many economic institutions that supported trade in Europe were informal in nature, as Avner Greif has shown.

All of which means that historical capitalism existed in the Qing era as well as in India during the FGE. For as I explained in Chapter 8, historical capitalism existed in China and India on the grounds that prolific trade was supported by rational institutions and that the key trading commodities were produced according to hybrid social relations – part modern capitalist and part agrarian.

An Absence of Chinese (and Indian) Technological Creativity in the Cotton Industry?

Eurocentric thinkers would respond to the claims made thus far by arguing that even if this was all true, the fact remains that the Chinese and Indians were incapable of technological innovation, which is why they maintained a pre-industrial cotton-based system of household production. Because it was China that was the more technologically

---

[17] Pomeranz (2000: 168).
[18] Barendse (2009: 726) and Yazdani (2017: 419).
[19] Habib (1960: 10–12).

innovative of these two societies, so I shall focus on it here. I argue that there was indeed a relationship between historical capitalist Chinese cotton spinning/weaving technologies and the household system, though it was the latter that largely gave rise to the former rather than the other way round (as in the Eurocentric position).

The Striking but Abortive Industrial Potential of the Chinese Big Spinning Frame for Ramie

In his seminal book, *The Pattern of the Chinese Past*, Mark Elvin pointed out that the Chinese had developed the 'big spinning frame for ramie' as early as the thirteenth century, though it was used for spinning hemp and ramie (a bast plant) rather than cotton and fell out of use probably within a century. Figure 11.2 reproduces the picture that was originally published in Wáng Zhēn's famous 1313 encyclopedia *Nong Shu* (*Treatise on Agriculture*), as well as Song Yingxing's equally famous 1637 encyclopedia *Tiangong Kaiwu* (*Exploitation of the Work of Nature*). Critically, this machine was fully mechanised, given that it was driven by water power and, moreover, it bore certain features in common with Richard Arkwright's water frame.

In his famous encyclopedia, *Nong Shu*, Wáng Zhēn claimed that the thirteenth-century big spinning frame for ramie spun 130 lbs in 24 hours.[20] However, this level of output is truly staggering given that it was seven times greater than Richard Roberts' self-acting mule (1825). This figure, seems implausible, but unfortunately it is all we have to go on. Nevertheless, even if the true figure was only a sixth of Wáng's estimate, this would still have been extraordinarily impressive. Which means, as Mark Elvin claims, that had this been converted into a cotton spinning machine, it is possible that China could 'have had a true industrial revolution in the production of textiles over four hundred years before the West'.[21] Critically, as Dieter Kuhn points out,

Chinese textile technicians had invented all the essential parts of a spinning device [similar to the water frame and the spinning jenny] for industrial use as early as the thirteenth century.... Indeed in terms of mechanical structure, even the spinning jenny, which was never easy to operate, did not match the quality of the big spinning frame for ramie.[22]

---

[20] Wáng Zhēn (1313: ch. 22), cited in Kuhn (1988: 228), Chao (1977: 59) and Elvin (1973: 195).

[21] Elvin (1973: 198, 194). See also Mokyr (1990: 212–13, 218–19).

[22] Kuhn (1988: 224). See also Kuhn (1988: 225–36) and Elvin (1973: 194–9) for a full description of the ramie frame. More generally, see Chao (1977: 56–68) and Zurndorfer (2009: 51).

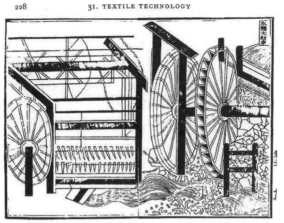

228   31. TEXTILE TECHNOLOGY

Fig. 148. Water-powered multiple spinning-frame for ramie (*shui-chuan ta-fang-chhe*), +1313. *NS* (+1530)

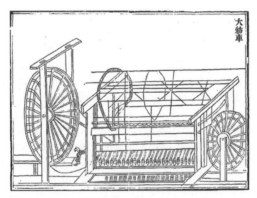

Figure 11.2 The Chinese water-powered big spinning frame for ramie. (Wáng Zhēn's *Nong Shu* (*Treatise on Agriculture*), 1313, reprinted in Kuhn (1988: 227, 228).) See also the illustrations in Elvin (1973: 196) and Kuhn (1988: 230).

Although the Chinese big spinning frame for ramie was very much like Arkwright's water frame, a key adaptation was required before it could be applied to cotton spinning – specifically, the addition of a draw bar.[23] For the Chinese frame did not utilise a draw bar because ramie requires twisting, whereas cotton has to be drawn out. However, not only would it have been easy to add a draw bar in a technical sense but it was also something that the Chinese could have done had they chosen to, given

[23] Chao (1977: ch. 3) and Kuhn (1988: 224).

that they were aware of the principle, as I explain shortly. Although there is a broad consensus that this machine was not converted to spinning cotton before the twentieth century, Li Bozhong claims that it had been converted during the eighteenth century.[24] But for his one-line claim, I have found no other reference to its existence before World War II. Thus, the critical question is why the ramie frame was not converted into a cotton machine before the twentieth century.

Following his aforementioned counterfactual claim further, Elvin goes on to argue that

[n]one of these [changes] was out of the reach of Chinese skill in the fourteenth century. None of them was ever made, and perhaps in consequence the [Chinese] machine gradually fell out of use and finally disappeared altogether. We are compelled to conclude that, at least in the case of textiles, the basic obstacle in the way of further technological progress in China after this time was *not* a better scientific knowledge given China's scientific precocity. Rather it must have lain in a weakening of those economic and intellectual forces which make for invention and innovation.[25]

But as I explain later, the rate of Chinese inventions continued apace down to about 1700. And, moreover, while the machine did indeed fall out of use, it was because ramie fell out of fashion after the fourteenth century as the popularity of cotton textiles rapidly superseded it.[26] While it is true that the ramie frame *was* converted into a cotton spinning machine, nevertheless, this came much later in 1937/45 during World War II.[27] So the issue at stake is whether converting the machine for cotton spinning to enable industrialisation was beyond the technological capacity of the Chinese before the twentieth century.

Problematic here is Joel Mokyr's summary dismissal – that 'it seems hard to believe that such a relatively simple device [the draw bar] never occurred to some ingenious Chinese. But if it did, there is no sign of it.'[28] For the fact is that a draw bar *did* occur to the Chinese, though it was used when spinning with five spindles when the five rovings were drawn out with a *hand-held* drawbar – since spinners, of course, do not have six fingers.[29] Why, then, was it not fitted to the water-powered big spinning frame? Chao Kang provides a different take to that of Mokyr, which provides a fascinating twist on Elvin's argument:

[24] Li (2009: 389).
[25] Elvin (1973: 199).
[26] Kuhn (1988: 236).
[27] Chao (1977: 69) and Kuhn (1988: 224, 236).
[28] Mokyr (1990: 221).
[29] See the pictures of the hand-held draw bar in Kuhn (1988: 222) and Chao (1977: 68).

Based on this comparison one can easily conclude that the Chinese big spinning wheel [for ramie] could have been converted into a spinning jenny [or a water-frame] simply by adding ... a draw bar. The technical problem in making such a transmission is simple. [It is, therefore] inconceivable that over a long period of 600 years no one in China came up with the idea of the drawbar.[30]

And, having noted the existence of the hand-held draw bar, Chao goes on to assert that

every key element that constituted the spinning jenny is proven to have been present [minus the *mechanised* draw bar] in China [around four centuries] before 1637. The unavoidable conclusion would then be that the big multi-spindle [ramie] spinning machine had been rejected by the Chinese cotton industry on grounds *other than technical difficulties*.[31]

While Chao Kang and Dieter Kuhn argue that these 'non-technical difficulties' were related to the exigencies of the household production system (as I explain shortly), we also need to factor in the larger global economic context (as I explain in a later section), as well as the very low-quality of indigenous Chinese raw cotton, to a consideration of which I now turn.

Why the Big Spinning Frame for Ramie Was Not Converted into a Cotton Frame (I): Ecological Challenges

The first reason why the big spinning ramie frame was likely not converted for mechanised cotton spinning lies in a significant piece of ecological misfortune – specifically, China's low-quality raw cotton. Chinese cotton was a short-staple variety, being much shorter than the American Upland variety as well as that of Egyptian and Sea Island cotton. Moreover, while Sea Island cotton averaged 300 twists per inch and Indian short-staple cotton averaged 150 twists, Chinese cotton averaged a paltry 66. Note that the greater the number of twists attained, the higher the quality of the yarn. Added to these two deficiencies is that Chinese cotton had a low elasticity.[32] All of which, in aggregate, means that Chinese raw cotton was weak and was not well suited for mechanised spinning machines and power looms. By contrast, as I explained in Chapter 9, the British were extremely fortunate in that at the very time when the mechanised technologies of the water frame,

---

[30] Chao (1977: 67).
[31] Ibid. (68), my emphases.
[32] Ibid. (24).

mule and power loom were bedding into Lancashire's cotton mills, the long-staple American Upland cotton variety came on stream rapidly after 1793 as did the American-grown Mexican variety after 1820. This was fortunate given that the machines required strong raw cotton that had high tensile strength (as I discussed in Chapters 9 and 10).

However, it might be argued that because imported Indian raw cotton came on stream in China in the second half of the eighteenth century,[33] so this might have appeared in the nick of time to prompt the mechanisation and industrialisation of Chinese cotton spinning and weaving. But, as noted earlier, the problem here is that Indian cotton was also a short-staple variety and was very low in tensile strength. Indeed, Chao points out that Indian cotton – bar the exceptional Dhakan variety – was 'slightly inferior to that of certain Chinese varieties produced in the Yangtze valley; but it was good enough for hand spinning, which could produce only a low count [crude or coarse] yarn anyway'.[34] And this in turn points up the very high levels of skills that the Indian spinners attained given the challenge of creating the warp with such short-staple cotton. Moreover, while the Chinese began mechanised cotton textile production in the 1880s, the factories could produce only the very lowest count (i.e., coarse) yarn. But to produce moderate- to high-quality yarn – from twenty-count yarn upwards – they came to rely on imported American long-staple raw cotton as early as 1898, though subsequent improvements were made to Chinese cotton through the use of seed selection following the initiative of the Chinese Cotton Improvement Commission that was established in 1919.[35] Interestingly, by the early 1970s, China had returned to being the world's leading producer of cotton at the same time that the Chinese began importing significant amounts of the superior American cotton. By contrast, the British were able to produce up to one hundred-count yarn with the imported American cotton from the early-nineteenth century. Finally, the deficiencies of Chinese raw cotton helps explain the puzzle as to why it was that peasants banded together to spin ramie with the water-powered (i.e., mechanised) big spinning frame back in the thirteenth century but resorted to non-mechanised cotton spinning within the individual household. All of which means that the household system of production was not so much a blockage to mechanised cotton spinning because the former existed in part as a function of the weakness of China's domestic raw cotton.

[33] Bowen (2009).
[34] Chao (1977: 103).
[35] Ibid. (24–7, 261–2).

Why the Big Spinning Frame for Ramie Was
Not Converted into a Cotton Frame (II): The
Nature of the Household Production System

A second reason why the ramie frame was not converted, as Chao Kang and Dieter Kuhn have argued, is that within the household production system – as was the case in the British putting-out cotton sector – low-cost technological considerations were paramount, alongside the need to deploy individual spinners and weavers rather than teams of workers.[36] Accordingly, converting the big spinning frame for cotton spinning was likely rejected because it was simply too expensive for individual households to buy, on the one hand, and because had it been adapted it would have required three operatives, which was a luxury that no single Chinese household could afford on the other. This also explains why the Chinese chose *not* to utilise the large cotton-ginning machine shortly after its invention in the thirteenth century, for they could not spare three people in a single family to work it.

This is reinforced by the point that perhaps as much as 75 per cent of silk textile production, especially that of high-grade silk, was undertaken in large workshops and factories precisely because it required both higher levels of capital-intensive (albeit non-mechanised) machines and two or three workers to operate a silk loom. Accordingly, one could ask why factory-based cotton production could not have replaced the cotton-based household system of production. As I explained earlier, so fundamental was the Chinese household system of cotton spinning and weaving that making the final technological innovations that were required for full mechanisation was deemed both *undesirable* and unnecessary given the colossal scale of Chinese cotton textile production. Moreover, the sanctity of this system was enshrined in government policy on the basis that it was deemed a vital institution for maintaining rural stability. This was a core prerogative of the Qing dynasty, even though this state-based policy began back in the Yuan period in the thirteenth and fourteenth centuries. And as also noted earlier, factory production for cotton textiles did occur, as I noted with respect to Songjiang in the Lower Yangtze Delta, but for dyeing, finishing and calendaring rather than for cotton spinning and weaving. The exception that proves this rule is the spinning and weaving of high-quality cotton textiles in government-owned factories, for these could only be produced over very long periods of time given the weakness of China's raw cotton.[37]

---

[36] Ibid. (ch. 3) and Kuhn (1988: 225, 235–6). See also Mazumdar (1998: 187–8).
[37] Zurndorfer (2009: 54) and Beckert (2015: 19).

But to summarise these claims, it is worth noting that a similar set of factors played out in the Indian context, all of which countenanced against the need to mechanise cotton spinning and weaving. In India, what spinners and weavers lacked in terms of sophisticated technologies, which were undoubtedly cruder than the Chinese models, they made up for in their exceptional skills, especially in spinning. Because this underpinned India's phenomenal output levels and given that Indian cotton textiles (ICTs) enjoyed a massive domestic market and simultaneously dominated Afro-Eurasian markets – as I explained in Chapters 3–5 – so industrial–technological development was neither required nor desired. Moreover, the highly skilled Dhakan spinners rejected using anything but the crudest spinning technologies to produce the finest Indian muslin, given that more advanced spinning wheels could not produce the required high-count yarn.[38] Instead, the 'threads for Dacca Muslins continued to be spun with needle-like bamboo rotated on pieces of hollow shells long after the spinning wheel was adopted [elsewhere in India] for spinning coarser [i.e, cheaper and cruder] fabrics'.[39] And, as in China, India's prevailing household production system demanded low-cost considerations such that technological innovation was not desirable – notwithstanding the point that the Indian system was not entirely devoid of innovations.[40]

The Eurocentric reply would assert that this household system constituted a fundamental blockage to industrialisation. But it seems more appropriate to view it as a rational and optimal historical capitalist production unit in the dual context of the challenge of a weak short-staple raw cotton together with the vast scale and skill of the industrious labour force, which not only supplied the large internal market and underpinned India's domination of global markets but also granted Indian merchants with a structural power to organise and shape the FGE. In the light of all this, the relevant mantra would be 'why fix something that ain't broken?'

Did the Chinese Lack Technological Creativity in General?

Finally, there is the issue of technological creativity more generally. This is necessarily a highly fraught issue that takes us on a series of complex twists and turns. One of the drivers of the British industrial revolution was undoubtedly the rise of a new *mechanistic worldview*,[41] or

---

[38] Mukund (1992: 2058).
[39] Baber (1996: 58).
[40] Ibid. (62).
[41] Jacob (1997), Mokyr (1990, 2002, 2009) and Goldstone (2002, 2008: chs. 7–8 and 162–72).

what Goldstone usefully calls a 'culture of innovation',[42] which found its explicit manifestation in numerous Learned societies that were linked to the industrial enlightenment. Typical here was the Lunar Society, whose members comprised the likes of Matthew Boulton, Josiah Wedgwood, Joseph Priestley and James Watt, and whose motto was, in Wedgwood's phrases, to 'surprise the world with wonders' and 'to make such *machines* of the *Men* as cannot Err' – or, in the words of Priestley, 'to bring paradise on earth' through technological innovation.[43] However, while Peer Vries cites various lists of inventions, which suggest that the British were far more inventive than the Chinese,[44] nevertheless this is tempered when placed in the context of the long global technological cumulation. For as Joseph Needham and his colleagues have shown, Chinese technological innovation led not only Britain but the world for several millennia;[45] a point I return to later.

It is noteworthy that there were Learned societies in China as well as many published encylopedias – most famously of all, Wáng Zhēn's *Nong Shu* (1313) and Song Yingxing's *Tiangong Kaiwu* (1637/2017) – all of which, of course, benefited from China's strong print culture.[46] However, David Landes would refute this on the basis that printing never 'exploded' in China.[47] But as I explained in chapter 8 of my book, *The Eastern Origins of Western Civilisation*,[48] it is noteworthy that the first movable type printing press was invented in China by Pi Shêng around 1040, while the world's first movable metal-type printing press was invented in Korea in 1403 – a full half-century before Gutenberg's far more famous invention. Critically, the fact is that even by the end of the fifteenth century, China probably published more books than all other countries combined. Notable too is that even as early as 978 CE, one of the Chinese libraries contained 80,000 volumes – though at that time this was surpassed by the holdings of some of the major Islamic libraries that held up to 400,000 volumes.[49] This early achievement was made possible by Chinese block printing, which was invented at the beginning of the ninth century, with the earliest extant printed book dated to 868. And from about 950 onwards, printing took off in China, boosted further after 1040 with Pi Shêng's invention.

---

[42] Goldstone (2008: 134–5).
[43] See Uglow (2003) and Finlay (2010: 291).
[44] Vries (2013: 308–10); see also Mokyr (1990: 224).
[45] A good introduction to this massive corpus of work is Needham (1970).
[46] I am grateful to Kaveh Yazdani for this cue.
[47] Landes (1998: 51).
[48] Hobson (2004: 183–6).
[49] Goldstone (2008: 141–2).

But to return to the narrative above, it is especially notable that a good number of the *key* 'British inventions' that Vries lists were, in fact, pioneered by the Chinese many centuries, if not millennia, earlier – to wit: coke-smelted iron, iron smelting with anthracite, wrought iron puddling, the steel cementation process and crucible steel process (to which I would add the use of various fluxes such as limestone and silica), the double-cylinder bellows, double-acting single-cylinder bellows and the water-powered bellows in iron production, development of drainage in mines (to which I would add long drill bits for the drilling of deep mines up to 4,800 feet), seed drills, threshing machines, curved iron mouldboard ploughs, the water-powered spinning frame (for ramie) and cotton gins – many of which much later on became fundamental components of the British iron/steel and agricultural revolutions. Moreover, a good number of these were either borrowed directly from China or they were very possibly copied from Chinese manuals that flooded into Europe between 1650 and 1800 (as I suggested in Chapter 10).

Mark Elvin's widely accepted claim that China entered a 'high-level equilibrium trap' after the fourteenth century elides the point that the number of innovations that emerged in China between 1300 and 1700 kept pace with the numbers achieved in the 900–1300 period. Equally, though, in the critical 1700–1900 period, there was a marked drop off in the number of new Chinese innovations,[50] at the very same time that British innovations began to escalate. Thus, the second technological divergence opens up in the eighteenth century, with British industry developing in a febrile inventive atmosphere that constituted a kind of technological hothouse, thereby enabling Britain to finally undergo the great leap forward into industrialisation through mechanisation between c. 1700 and 1850. And while some of this was the result of the emulation or combination of earlier non-Western technologies – as I explained in Chapter 10 – it is certainly clear that these were advanced to higher industrial ends through British developmental agency.

However, in yet another twist, Lin Justin's reiteration of one of Needham's arguments is notable: that 'China fell behind the West in modern times because China did not make the shift from the experience-based process of invention to the experiment cum science-based innovation, while Europe did so through the scientific revolution in the seventeenth century'.[51] Much the same point applies to India despite the fact that Indians had been advancing scientific knowledge

---

[50] Ibid. (122).
[51] Lin (1995: 276).

many centuries before Europe.[52] But while such an explanation certainly makes some sense in various critical areas, most notably in the case of Watt's development of the atmospheric steam engine,[53] it fares less well in others. As has been argued many times over by British economic historians, none of the British inventors of the key cotton spinning and weaving technologies had much, if any, scientific knowledge. What mattered in Britain was the Enlightenment's 'culture of (technological) innovation', as Goldstone as well as Margaret Jacob and Joel Mokyr have argued.[54] And here, we encounter a critical difference in that the 'diffuse benefits' of circulating knowledge in Britain where many people could gain collectively contrasted strikingly with India, where secrecy was the order of the day, as I explained in Part I of this book.[55] Overall, the marked drop off in the rate of new Chinese innovations after 1700 came at precisely the same time that Britain's great leap forward in both the circulation of knowledge and its mechanistic world view took off. But, in turn, we also need to consider whether class relations, state–society relations and modes of production also made a critical difference.

Why Neither India nor China Underwent a Cotton Industrialisation: Differing Class Relations and Modes of Production under UCD

In the 1980s, a group of scholars made the case that in the cotton sector, British industrialisation was preceded by a 'proto-industrial' phase in the form of the 'putting-out system' and the family 'mode of production' or what I have referred to as the household system of production. Textiles were not only produced for subsistence or use value but also for market exchange value via the putting-out system. Franklin Mendels characterises the putting-out system as a form of 'proto-industrialisation' – or what has been called 'industrialisation before industrialisation'.[56] Although many scholars have read this literature as embodying an evolutionary teleology in which proto-industrialisation evolves naturally and inevitably into industrialisation,[57] it would be fairer to say that such advocates of the proto-industrialisation thesis also emphasise the importance of international imperial politico-economic causal factors, as I note shortly. In this and the next section, I develop a comparative analysis

---

[52] See Parthasarathi (2011: ch. 7), Bala (2006), Raju (2007) and Yazdani (2017).
[53] Goldstone (2008: 155–60).
[54] Jacob (1997) and Mokyr (2002, 2009).
[55] My thanks to Andrew Linklater for this particular formulation.
[56] Mendels (1972) and Kreidte et al. (1981).
[57] Perlin (1983).

that differentiates the British from the Indian and Chinese cotton textile sectors. I argue that what led to a cotton-based industrialisation in the former as opposed to the latter two economies were two factors: first, a specific set of class relations and second, differing global economic pressures under conditions of uneven and combined development.

Indian and Chinese Cotton Merchant Capitalists as 'Historical Capitalist Satisficers'

Eurocentrism presumes that the Indian and Chinese economies were founded almost entirely on basic subsistence agriculture as a function of Oriental despotism. Certainly, Marx's conception of the Asiatic mode of production (AMP) buys into this.[58] But the plot thickens, however, when we factor in Frank Perlin's claim that a proto-capitalist (cotton) system existed in India,[59] to which we could also add the case of China. And Perlin is at pains to reveal the similar economic systems that characterised pre-industrial Europe and India, although he is highly critical of the teleological conception of proto-capitalism/proto-industrialisation. His claim is reinforced further by historical revisionists who demonstrate how much of rural India was linked into the commercial market system that, in turn, was linked into the global trading system.[60] My argument here is that despite these *historical capitalist* parallels concerning proto-industrialisation and commercial impetus, neither of these Asian economies would have evolved into modern industrial capitalism for reasons that are inverse to the British situation. For as I explain in Chapters 8 and 14, there is no necessary or inevitable path that runs from historical to modern capitalism. In this respect, I agree with Marx's claim that the British putting-out system did *not* constitute a path that led on into modern industrial capitalism,[61] though I do so for reasons that he did not consider. And one of these is that proto-industrialisation did not evolve into modern industrial capitalism in China and India.

The opening point to consider is that of the 'class relations' that existed in China and India. Of particular note is that Indian and Chinese cotton spinners and weavers largely owned and controlled the means of production,[62] a point I return to later. Moreover, this household production system was part of a larger historical capitalist system in which dyeing,

---

[58] Marx (1969). See also the brilliant critiques in Anderson (1974: 462–549) and O'Leary (1989).
[59] Perlin (1983). See also Mukund (1992).
[60] For example, Grover (1994).
[61] Marx (1867/1959: 334).
[62] Dutt (1916: 518) and Deng (2012a: 35).

printing, calendaring and finishing were often undertaken in Indian and Chinese urban factories and workshops that employed full- or part-time free wage labour (as I discussed in Chapter 8). The only exception to this lay with the small number of state-owned factories in China where luxury cotton textiles were spun and woven, as I explained in the last section.

In the Indian context, Romesh Dutt asserts that '[l]and in India belongs primarily to small cultivators who have their hereditary rights in their holdings; the landlord, where he exists, cannot eject them so long as they pay their rents'.[63] Moreover, while Tapan Raychaudhuri asserts that 'wage employment [in factories] was by and large confined to [the] European Companies',[64] this misses the point that 'the usage of hired labour in urban manufactures was known to India long before the European Companies began their activities. In the sixteenth–eighteenth centuries hired assistants were employed by the artisans [well-off weavers].... Wages for the hired labourers were generally low but nevertheless the supply of free hands exceeded the demand.'[65] Furthermore, *Karkhanas* (factories/workshops) were established by the rulers of the Delhi Sultanate (1206–1526), which employed large numbers of artisans and craftsmen. And some well-off artisans set up *Karkhanas* in the late-nineteenth century that used handlooms and power looms in which either free wage labour or family members were employed (as I discuss in Chapter 13). All in all, as Shireen Moovsi argues, '[m]oney wage payments can thus be regarded as largely the rule in seventeenth-century Indian towns and markets, and in imperial and aristocratic establishments. "Commodified labour" was thus practically universal'.[66]

Thus, viewing the cotton industry as based upon a purely household system ignores the complex division of labour and multiple forms of social relations and production environments that existed within this sector, some of which were modern capitalist and some were agrarian, household based. Moreover, we encounter a highly developed division of labour across space, such that 'cloth woven in Ahmadabad was bleached in Broach and printed in Sironj with the help of dyes from Sarkhej and wooden blocks supplied by Pattan.'[67] And, while cotton textile spinning and weaving took place in the Indian household, this was often embedded within a village setting, where whole Indian villages concentrated in the production of a single, highly specialised type of cotton textile.

---

[63] Dutt (1916: 518).
[64] Raychaudhuri (1982: 287).
[65] Vanina (2004: 103). See also Mehta (1991: 121) and Yazdani (2019: 9–10).
[66] Moovsi (2011: 246). Also de Zwart (2016: 184–5).
[67] Vanina (2004: 8).

Not only did many Chinese and ICT producers own the means of production, but they also had more autonomy vis-à-vis the itinerant merchant capitalists relative to their counterparts in Britain;[68] though clearly, the autonomy of those Indian peasants who performed unfree labour via debt obligations was greatly weakened.[69] In Indian villages, itinerant merchants had to negotiate with village intermediaries rather than dealing directly with the individual producers. This is also true for the Indian brokers who relayed information on the changing fashion tastes of foreign consumers,[70] as I noted in Chapter 4. All of which served to strengthen the hand of the Indian producers and reflected their relative independence from the itinerant merchant capitalists and brokers when compared with their equivalents in Britain.[71] Conversely, the European merchant putter-out

> often employed agents and middlemen whose position and authority varied greatly on local conditions. They could be mere employees who carried out orders and received fixed commissions; or they could be quite independent businessmen. But the subordinacy and weakness of the mass of producers was increased rather than reduced by this system, since these middlemen often reduced their incomes even further.[72]

The itinerant Indian merchant capitalists advanced *cash* sums that provided the working capital for the *dādanī* (putting-out) system,[73] as opposed to the situation in Britain and Europe where the raw materials were advanced by the merchant capitalist in exchange for the final product on the basis of fixed piece rates.[74] This alone weakened the British peasants compared with their Indian counterparts.[75] For, unlike Chinese and Indian merchants, the British sought to muscle in on the production process. Nevertheless, Kaveh Yazdani notes that there were some cases where raw materials were advanced instead of cash and, moreover, he claims that in Mysore at the beginning of the nineteenth century, the *dadani* system was 'more similar to the English putting out system than [is commonly recognised]'.[76] Be that as it may, in India '[t]he contractual arrangement could be flexible, and it seems that little leeway

[68] Riello (2013: 61–70). But see Beckert (2015: 20).
[69] Vanina (2004: 91–3) and Anievas and Nişancioğlu (2015: 241).
[70] Machado (2014: 143, 146).
[71] Parthasarathi (2011: 40).
[72] Schlumbohm (1981: 103).
[73] Chaudhuri (2006: 253–6).
[74] Washbrook (2020).
[75] Beckert (2015: ch. 2).
[76] Yazdani (2017: 190).

existed for merchants to enforce contracts, with the result [being] that the weaver could sell his product to someone else and return the advance'.[77] Thus, in his intensive study of Gujarat – a key regional centre of ICT production – Yazdani points out that 'some Gujarati producers worked for several purchasers and possessed a certain degree of manoeuvrability in negotiating prices which increased their bargaining power'.[78] While weavers sometimes refused to honour agreements, often returning the cash advance if a higher offer was tendered from another broker, 'there are examples where weavers failed to return advances and placed brokers and merchants in awkward positions without much chance for redress'.[79] For this reason, the English East India Company sought to advance raw materials that were coupled with the imposition of strict conditions as a means of closing down the relative autonomy of the Indian weavers.[80]

Indian weaver and spinner autonomy was boosted yet further by the fact that producers could sell their products in 'free' markets, as was the case in China – a point that also refutes Marx's AMP conception of autarkic Indian and Chinese villages as, for that matter, did the presence of itinerant long-distance merchants. Finally, the printers, dyers and finishers were also independent of the Indian merchant capitalists. All of which means that this 'centrifugal system' of cotton spinning and weaving, as Giorgio Riello argues, countenanced against centripetal and concentrated factory-based production.[81] Thus, it was not that factories were an alien concept to the Indians and Chinese – quite the contrary. But it was the specific nature and structure of Chinese and Indian class relations as well as state–society relations that precluded the deployment of factories for the spinning and weaving of cotton textiles, at least before the mid-nineteenth century. For by then, wage workers were deployed in the new mills and the *Karkhanas* (small-scale workshops), as I explain in Chapter 13.

While the proto-industrial putting-out system also existed in China and was significant, nevertheless many peasants worked outside of it. It is the case that proto-industrialisation existed in Songjiang (Sungchiang) – a district of Shanghai in Jiangnan province in the Lower Yangtze Delta which constituted the country's single most important cotton textile producing zone,[82] a point that I return to shortly. But the majority of cotton textile production – probably about 80 per cent – was undertaken in rural Chinese households, many of which were not even part of the

[77] Riello (2013: 63).
[78] Yazdani (2017: 365).
[79] Machado (2014: 146) and Yazdani (2019: 12).
[80] Dutt (1906).
[81] Riello (2013: 63–8).
[82] Li (1998).

putting-out system and those that were tended to be more autonomous from merchant capitalists than were their British counterparts. And, in further contrast to the British situation but like that of the Indian, when Chinese merchants were involved, they advanced cash rather than raw materials and did not seek to influence the pace of production.[83] As Peer Vries notes, '[t]he system of domestic industry that prevailed in Qing China can be best characterised as a Kaufsystem, which means that "centralised" coordination, financing and capital accumulation were much less important than in the [European] putting-out system'.[84] Then, again, there were many peasants who produced for exchange value. And, finally, there were a good number of Chinese peasants who produced predominantly for use value, although they also often bought and sold cloth and textiles in local markets independently of the putting-out merchants.[85] Perhaps around 20 per cent of such production was destined for the market in this way.[86] Overall, by 1840 at least 53 per cent of cotton textile production was sold in Chinese markets.[87] This, then, comprises another prong of China's historical capitalism.

However, given the higher levels of autonomy that Indian and Chinese peasants attained relative to their British counterparts, so it might be argued that there was all the more reason for Asian merchant capitalists to morph into industrial capitalists in order to circumvent the levels of autonomy that the cotton textile producers enjoyed within the household production system. But there are numerous *production*-related reasons why neither India nor China evolved into a full cotton-based industrialisation, three of which are noteworthy. First, Indian spinners and weavers moved around the country periodically in response to shocks as well as to opportunities. As David Washbrook explains, retreating floods in the deltas of Bengal and South India left rich silt deposits that offered opportunities for cotton production, much as localised droughts that occurred in the absence of monsoon rains also stimulated 'exit'. Then again, given that India comprised a self-contained South Asian inter-state system in the eighteenth and nineteenth centuries, so peasants would move to other states should taxes become oppressive in one or when other states sought to attract them through tax incentives.[88] The same 'exit logic' applies in those cases where localised political

---

[83] Zurndorfer (2009: 59).
[84] Vries (2013: 217).
[85] Chao (1977: ch. 2).
[86] I am grateful to Kent Deng for providing this advice (personal communication, 21/09/2018).
[87] Xu and Wu (2003: 331) and Zurndorfer (2009: 61).
[88] Washbrook (2007: 93–5).

turbulence occurred. High mobility, then, worked against a fixed-factory, centripetal system in India.

Second, a complex and specialised division of labour had developed in India over a period of many centuries which, as I noted earlier, led to a highly decentralised or 'centrifugal' system that, once again, tended to countenance against the possibility or *need* for centralised/centripetal, concentrated factory production in cotton textile spinning and weaving.[89] Much the same point applies to China. This second factor bleeds into the third wherein the Indian and Chinese putting-out cotton industry, which began well before the arrival of the Europeans, worked extremely effectively both in terms of production output and producing profit for the itinerant merchant capitalists. For the Chinese and Indian cotton industries led the world and, in strict contrast to Britain, they did not face more advanced competitors within the global economy. Both Asian countries were central to the long global cotton cumulation right up into the nineteenth century. And in both cases, large-scale itinerant merchants enjoyed large profits and had access to capital and massive internal markets to sell in, all of which was aided by the impressive transportation facilities that were provided by long-distance merchants.

In India, the *Banjāras* (long-distance internal traders) utilised large stocks of bullocks and oxen, which were crucial 'vehicles' for transporting cotton textiles to markets throughout the country.[90] According to Irfan Habib, as early as the seventeenth century, there may have been some 400,000 *Banjāras* and some 9 million oxen that carried goods in the region of 821 million metric tons per annum. The enormity of this feat is brought into relief by the point that the *Banjāras* carried a third the volume of goods that were carried by the railways some two centuries later in 1882.[91] And in China, we find that Jiangnan province in the Lower Yangtze Delta – where Songjiang and Suzhou (sometimes dubbed the 'Venice of the East') were located – was not only 'criss-crossed by a series of canals and narrow waterways which facilitated communication and marketing',[92] but this region was also linked directly to the north of the country by the Grand Canal. Noteworthy too is that Jiangnan's cotton textile output levels were colossal, with various authorities claiming that they varied between 1.3 billion and 1.7 billion yards in 1620,[93] rising to somewhere around 2 billion yards in the mid-eighteenth century.[94]

[89] See Riello (2013: 66–7).
[90] Grover (1994) and Washbrook (1988: 66, 2007: 97).
[91] Habib (1990: 376–7).
[92] Zurndorfer (2009: 49).
[93] See, respectively, Li (2000: 39–40) and Xu and Wu (2003: 170–3).
[94] Pomeranz (2000: 330).

The staggering size of which is brought into relief by the fact that these amounts were approximately equivalent to, if not higher than, the *whole* of Indian average annual national output throughout the nineteenth century on the one hand and surpassed total British production right up to the early-1850s on the other.

However, the Eurocentric reply might well be that the household system was predominant because there was a lack of capital in China and that it was this particular social formation that constituted a blockage to industrialisation. But the most important large-scale itinerant merchants (*keshang*) invested very significant amounts of working capital to buy up cotton cloth from households, particularly in the all-important Songjiang district. Most well known were the merchants from Huizhou and Anhui provinces though the Shaanxi merchants were the most powerful. The *keshang* were able to borrow money from credit markets,[95] and individuals invested a minimum of 10,000 silver taels (c. £3,000) to buy up 50,000 bolts of cotton cloth at any one time, which comprised a very substantial 2 million yards.[96] The size of this is brought into relief by the point that this was more or less equivalent to the entire annual amount that was imported into Britain by the English East India Company in the mid-seventeenth century. Also of comparative note is that the average cost of fixed capital for a British cotton mill was £5,000 in 1805,[97] though Samuel Greg (of Styall Mill fame) laid out £3,000 back in the 1780s.

If this Chinese figure of 2 million yards for an individual *keshang* merchant sounds fantastic, then it should be kept in mind that it likely comprised less than 0.05 per cent of total Chinese cotton textile output in 1750. And, in any case, Chinese historical records point out that occasionally the largest *keshang* might have used between 100,000 and 200,000 taels (£30–60,000) to buy up cotton textiles at any one time.[98] These figures translate to between 20 and 40 million yards, which would have comprised 0.5 per cent of total Chinese output. Their staggering size is brought into relief by the fact that forty million yards was about four times larger than the total annual average of ICTs that *all* of the European companies imported from India to Europe in the 1750s. And this by one *keshang* merchant!

While initially the Chinese merchant putters out employed intermediaries (*Ya Hang*), nevertheless subsequently they did away with them during the Qing era and then set up the *Bu Zhuang* in order to enhance their

---

[95] Bin Wong (2002: 451–2) and Rosenthal and Bin Wong (2011: ch. 5).
[96] Zurndorfer (2009: 59).
[97] Rodger (2010: 10).
[98] Fan (2016: 120). See also Zhang (2020: ch. 3).

profits further. These were cloth houses, which were built with additional processing workshops such as dyeing houses. The merchants recruited handicraftsman locally to reprocess cotton cloth, before selling this on to other regions. Suzhou in Jiangnan in the Lower Yangtze was the central market for the transaction of cotton products in the mid-Qing period, where roughly 20,000 people were employed in cotton industry workshops[99] and where 'factories hiring up to several hundred waged workers were not uncommon … [So much so that class] conflicts between workers and factory owners became an emergent pattern of urban life'.[100] Moreover, large-scale companies (*buhao*) came to play a vital role in developing the cotton textile industry in Songjiang in the eighteenth and nineteenth centuries.[101] And finally, there were various itinerant merchants (*pu-chuang* and *pu-huang*) who operated on a local scale.[102]

All in all, as Chao Kang points out, '[s]o far as financing is concerned, the commercial capital that had been directed to support processing factories like dyeing and calendaring shops should [have been] able to support spinning and weaving mills too. It is equally implausible to contend that no handicraft mills had been established due to the lack of entrepreneurship, for the experience in the silk industry was readily imitable.'[103] And, it is also notable that factories as well as small- and large-scale workshops were not uncommon in China, as I explained in Chapter 8. All of which points up the presence of historical capitalism in the Chinese cotton textile industry.

Overall, it seems fair to say that the Chinese and Indian economies were not lacking in capital,[104] and it is clear that Chinese and Indian itinerant cotton merchant capitalists lacked neither capital nor entrepreneurship.[105] Indeed, Mark Elvin claims not only that there were large concentrations of capital in merchants' hands, but that for most of the last millennium the Chinese economy fizzed with entrepreneurial activity.[106] It might be replied, however, that the famous Shaanxi merchants comprised a mere 3,000 members who, in constituting a mere 0.001 per cent of the total population, were insufficient to drive a cotton-based industrial revolution.[107] But the total number of industrial entrepreneurs in the

---

[99] Fan (1990: 160–79).
[100] Hung (2001: 495–6).
[101] Li (1998, 2009) and Zhang (2020: ch. 3).
[102] Chao (1977: 51–2) and Zhang (2020: ch. 3).
[103] Chao (1977: 32).
[104] Lippit (1987: 240–1) and Pomeranz (2000: 180, ch. 4).
[105] Dobbin (1996: chs. 2–3).
[106] Elvin (1973: ch. 12 and 286–9, 299–301).
[107] As Professor Kent Deng told me (private correspondence, 04/01/2019).

British cotton industry in the late-eighteenth century would have been far smaller given that there were only 900 mills in 1800 and about 1,200 around 1830. Moreover, because the number of British entrepreneurs comprised about the same proportion of the British population, so this Chinese figure appears to be more than sufficient to have launched industrialisation had it been so desired. Thus, given the fact of large economic profits that were generated from the vast scale of Chinese cotton textile output, it seems more accurate to say that the Chinese merchants *chose not* to mechanise spinning and weaving. For achieving such an outcome was *potentially* possible had it been so desired, given the precedence of the water-powered big spinning frame for ramie of the thirteenth century that I discussed earlier.

Thus, Chinese and Indian merchants were 'historical capitalist satisficers', given that they had *no need or desire* to mechanise cotton textile production in order to boost production. And, moreover, merchant relations with peasant producers were far less direct and coercive than were those that obtained in Britain, as I explain in the next section. But what also mattered greatly was the specific global economic context within which India and China were embedded. For while ICTs dominated global export markets, and China enjoyed a colossal domestic market that guaranteed massive sales, so there was simply no need to increase production through labour-substituting technologies as there was in Britain. Chinese cotton industry merchants made huge profits and saw no need to change the system.[108] Moreover, the colossal size of the Indian and Chinese workforces made household production a rational option. But the question that now arises is whether the primitive accumulation of capital and the need to undergo enforced peasant dispossession was possible in China and India. My argument is that it was extremely unlikely, on the one hand, and that it was neither technically necessary nor desirable on the other. I shall take the case of China to illustrate my case.

Was the Primitive Accumulation of Capital Necessary and Possible in China?

In China, we confront a notable difference to the situation in Britain (with the latter the subject of the next section). Kent Deng notes that '[u]ntil 1949 in some vast regions such as the Guanzhong Plain in Shaanxi, landlords were non-existent. One cannot even use class struggle to explain why that region was so desirable for Mao to establish

---

[108] Zhang (2020: ch. 3).

his permanent base for his "class war".'[109] Moreover, he argues that '[u]ntil the end of the Qing, about 70 per cent of China's farmers were freeholders. Of the remaining 30 percent, landlords constituted no more than 3 per cent and tenants 27 per cent.'[110] Ironically, Deng's attack on the notion of class struggle as a proxy for his critique of Marxism works, albeit entirely unwittingly, to reinforce Karl Marx's argument about China's AMP in tandem with Oriental despotism, which places agrarian communal production and the lack of coercive dominant/subordinate class relations as a key property. For it is clear on Deng's figures that many peasants enjoyed a relative if not complete social autonomy vis-à-vis landlords, which clearly exceeded that of their British counterparts and that made a generalised primitive accumulation of capital far less likely. In turn, though, I argue that such a process was unlikely to have occurred in China for a series of reasons that are linked to the specific nature of Chinese state–society relations.

As I explained in Chapter 2, in stark contrast to the British state, the Qing embodied an 'agrarian paternalist posture',[111] such that it was embedded in the peasantry in order to maintain domestic order.[112] Accordingly, peasant proprietorial rights were far stronger than they were in Britain. However, when it came to state/merchant class relations, the Qing adopted an anti-paternalist 'managed laissez-faire' commercial posture.[113] For not only did the move to freer trade require considerable state intervention, as I noted in Chapter 2, but the Qing also intervened in other areas. In particular, the state intervened and assumed production in a range of areas and industries that included mining, metal manufacturing, silk factory production and *luxury* cotton textile factory production, porcelain, grain distribution, shipbuilding as well as the exchange of salt vouchers for grain shipments that went to provisioning the troops that were located in the north west.[114] Interestingly, the Qing state's heavy regulations that were applied to the copper trade with Japan after the 1680s reinforces my general claim because this was the source of China's copper-based domestic currency.[115] Overall, the state did not seek to supplant private markets but only intervened in those areas where either the market failed or where there were specific requirements of the imperial court or where individual merchants sought to distort

[109] Deng (2012a: 102).
[110] Ibid. (35).
[111] Vries (2010: 746, 2013: 361).
[112] Bin Wong (1997).
[113] See Zhang (2020).
[114] Bin Wong (2002: 456).
[115] Dunstan (1992).

market prices to the disadvantage of consumers,[116] much, though not all, of which echoes Adam Smith's liberal prescriptions. Noteworthy too, is that state-owned industries were dwarfed by the private sector.

Given the twin points that there was no prevailing Chinese dominant agrarian class that desired to enclose much of the land, as much as the merchant class did not desire to create spinning and weaving factories since it enjoyed excellent profits from the putting-out system, so there was no domestic class driver of primitive accumulation. And, even had both groups desired this, it is highly unlikely that the Chinese state would have obliged by initiating a coercive policy of enforced peasant dispossession, given that it was socially embedded in the peasantry. Indeed, as Harriet Zurndorfer notes, 'whatever potential cotton cloth fabrication may have had toward mass manufacture, [Chinese] government policy encouraged its production to remain integral to household production'.[117] Noteworthy too, as I noted earlier, is that this tradition stems back to the earlier Yuan and Ming periods (1279–1644), wherein the state played a key role in spreading the practice of cotton textile production across the country.[118] And, moreover, because of the Yuan dynasty's insistence that Chinese people should wear cotton clothing, so this constituted a major stimulus to the widespread diffusion of cotton textile production across the country. In short, the state and the rural cotton sector formed an embedded social complex from the inception point of Chinese cotton production. All of which means that while the primitive accumulation of capital was promoted by the British state in cahoots with the landlords and cotton masters against the peasants, precisely the inverse scenario played out in China. But this, in turn, prompts the question as to whether a widespread enforced peasant dispossession was a necessary pre-requisite for Chinese industrialisation, as neo-Marxists presume, much as whether state–society relations constituted a blockage to Chinese industrial capitalism as Karl Marx originally believed.

The logic of Marx's argument in the European context concerns the need to displace the peasants from the land so that they would move to the towns to work in the factories as landless, free wage labourers. But while this was certainly necessary in the British context, it misses the point that China had long hosted vastly superior levels of urbanisation going back to the Song Dynasty (960–1279) at the very same time that

[116] Zhang (2020: ch. 3).
[117] Zurndorfer (2009: 57).
[118] Ibid. (44–9), Chao (1977: 19–22), Riello (2013: 68) and Zhang (2020: ch. 3).

the Chinese cotton sector was beginning to emerge as a key 'industry'.[119] Goldstone points out that in 1500, four of the largest top cities in the world were located in China, which in aggregate hosted some 1.2 million people. And, in 1800, three Chinese cities were in the world's top ten, comprising in aggregate some 2.3 million people.[120] Critically, William Skinner provides a rough figure of some twenty-one million people living in urban conurbations throughout China in 1843.[121] Note too that during the Mughal era, Indian urban centres hosted in aggregate around twenty-two million people, though there were possibly twenty-seven million in 1801.[122] Moreover, in these urban centres, 'money wages were universally in vogue for both skilled and unskilled labour and in domestic service',[123] as I noted earlier.

Recall from Chapter 10 that the size of the British cotton mill workforce in 1833 was a mere 220,000, which comprised less than 0.05 per cent of China's population. This means that to a significant extent, the need to initiate a widespread primitive accumulation of capital in China was unnecessary, for the numbers already resident in the towns and cities that could have worked in cotton spinning and weaving factories, especially in the all-important Lower Yangtze region dwarfed the amounts that were mobilised in Britain's industrialisation. And the same situation applies to India. Moreover, as was noted earlier, there were around 20,000 full-time and part-time waged workers employed in cotton finishing factories in Suzhou in the Lower Yangtze alone.[124] Notable too is that in the Ming and Qing eras, the expansion in the scale of cities and towns in Jiangnan in the Lower Yangtze absorbed a part of the surplus rural population, wherein migrations from the countryside fuelled the workforce in the cotton finishing and silk textile industries.[125]

Interestingly, Peer Vries dismisses the importance of factory workers in Qing China by asserting that they would likely have comprised a mere 5 per cent of the workforce.[126] But against this are two figures: first, that around twenty million resided in towns which, as noted, could have supplied a far larger workforce than existed in Britain. And second, 5 per cent of the workforce would have constituted a minimum of 7.5 million workers in 1800, which compared with a figure of about 1.5

[119] Elvin (1973: 175–6) and Skinner (1977).
[120] Goldstone (2008: 84).
[121] Skinner (1977).
[122] Broadberry et al. (2015: 67).
[123] Moovsi (2011: 246).
[124] Zhang (2020: ch. 3).
[125] Wu (2004: 108–110).
[126] Vries (2013: 218).

million in Britain across the *whole* of the industrial sector.[127] In sum, then, had there been a will for industrialisation in China, I suggest that the household system of production did not constitute a fundamental blockage.

Why Britain Underwent a Cotton-based Industrialisation: British Cotton Capitalists as 'Industrial Optimisers'

As noted earlier, we find that in the British putting-out system – in strong contrast to the situation in China and India – the merchant capitalist enjoyed a much more direct and controlling relationship with the cotton spinners and weavers that were located in their homes and who became, as Marx originally argued, wage labourers.[128] Giorgio Riello notes how, in strong contrast to the Indian and Chinese situations, European merchant capitalists erected a deeply hierarchical relationship with the household producers while also undertaking a direct role within the finishing stages (dyeing, printing, pressing, calendaring and packing). As Riello also notes, echoing the eminent economic historian Sidney Pollard, the English merchants were not only (proto)capitalist but they were also bureaucratic and managerial.[129] And, as I noted earlier, in further contrast to the Indian and Chinese putting-out systems, the English merchant capitalists supplied the spinners and weavers with the raw materials, thereby entering directly into the production process. It is true that sometimes Indian merchants advanced raw materials, to the weavers and spinners, though such instances were exceptional. Moreover, occasionally Chinese merchants advanced the raw materials, though this was undertaken in the exceptional circumstance in which they supplied more sophisticated long-staple cotton. Jürgen Schlumbohm explains that the British putter-out came to own the means of production and thus had the power 'to decide whether, what, how, and how much should be produced'.[130] And, moreover, investing in the means of production meant that the merchant capitalist raised the rate of exploitation of the producer. This, however, was a necessary but ultimately insufficient step to industrialisation.

As noted earlier, Karl Marx, with not atypical insight, was correct to argue that proto-industrialisation did *not* naturally evolve into industrial

---

[127] British figure from Broadberry *et al.* (2013).
[128] Banaji (2018: 156–7).
[129] Riello (2013: 67).
[130] Schlumbohm (1981: 103).

capitalism in Britain;[131] notwithstanding the qualification he made in the first volume of *Capital*, as I noted in Chapter 8. I advance three reasons why this was so. First, *contra* Mendels and Chapman,[132] it is going too far to assert that the profits that the merchant capitalists had accumulated during proto-industrialisation laid the foundation for machine-based cotton factory production. For we know that the cotton manufacturers borrowed from banks as well as from the City of London, as I noted in Chapter 9. And while I also noted there that much of the City's funds were used to finance 'working' rather than fixed capital, nevertheless, this freed up the entrepreneurs' capital for fixed capital investment. As I also noted there, it is possible that many merchants derived substantial sums from their role in Black Atlantic slavery. Second, not all of the merchant-turned industrialists were connected to the putting-out textile system. For example,

John Smalley, [Richard] Arkwright's first partner, was a 'liquor merchant and painter', and Arkwright himself had been a barber, perukemaker [wig-maker], hair merchant, and publican. Examples can be found of cotton manufacturers who had been grocers, salesmen, horse-dealers, and excise officers, and others who can only be identified as innkeepers' sons and bankers' sons.[133]

Third, at least within continental Europe, some of the proto-industrial regions did not evolve into industrial capitalism,[134] though in fairness Kriedte concedes this point.[135] So, if there was no internal driver within 'proto-capitalism' that would lead on to industrial capitalism what, then, accounted for the transition?

Particularly important was the *global context of uneven development* within which the British putting-out system was embedded. Mendels and Kriedte argue that the reason why proto-industrialisation was superseded by full industrialisation in Britain was because the peasants in the putting-out industry generated *insufficient* levels of cotton textile output, given that they also engaged in agricultural activities. Nevertheless, many Chinese and Indian cotton textile producers also engaged in agricultural activities, though this was not a problem given the sheer scale of their workforce that collectively produced colossal amounts of output. Indeed, India's output was larger than Britain's before the 1840s – i.e., well into Britain's cotton industrialisation – while

---

[131] Marx (1867/1959: esp. 334–5).
[132] Mendels (1972: 244) and Chapman (1972/2006: 11).
[133] Shapiro (1967: 176).
[134] Riello (2013: 64–5).
[135] Kriedte (1981a: 135).

China's outpaced Britain's throughout most of the nineteenth century and was only superseded in the early-twentieth century.

As I explained in Chapter 10, the tiny size of the British cotton textile workforce, which might have comprised a maximum of 4 per cent of India's and a mere 1.5 per cent of China's, was simply incapable of matching Indian and Chinese output. And, as I also noted, British spinners – unlike their Indian and Chinese counterparts – were not skilled enough to manually create the warp. It was partly for this reason that the new spinning technologies of the water frame and mule were invented. These, in turn, necessitated factory production since these machines could not have been deployed in households – unlike the spinning jenny, though this was the exception that proves the rule given that it was incapable of creating the warp and was used only for making the weft. Still, while there were factories in China, some of which were much larger than anything that the British developed,[136] these did not match the centripetal concentration and high degree of technological mechanisation and discipline of labour that was the hallmark of the British factories. And nor were mass cotton textiles produced in them.

In turn, because of the *small-scale* production output of British household weavers and spinners, it was vital that the primitive accumulation of capital through rural peasant dispossession be initiated in Britain. In this way, a landless proletariat was created that supplied the labour force for the cotton mills – as well as for the iron and steel factories. British state–society relations within a wider international/ global context were particularly important in this regard. In Britain, the state was socially embedded within the nobility and the mercantile/ industrial/financial classes. The latter were prized for the economic and military benefits that they provided, particularly given the voracious demand that imperial wars imposed (as I explain in Chapters 9 and 12). Accordingly, forcing the peasantry off the land to go and work for the bourgeoisie in the towns harmonised with the nobility's desire to privatise and enclose the common lands. And the part aristocratic/part bourgeois state was happy to oblige both classes.

To this end, the British Parliament played an important and supporting role in facilitating noble strategies of enclosure so as to complement the needs of the cotton textile manufacturers, as was originally pointed out by Marx.[137] Not uncoincidentally, the rate of enclosure increased substantially during the eighteenth and early-nineteenth centuries when imperial wars together with industrial requirements were biting hard.

[136] de Zwart (2016: 184) and Beckert (2015: 19).
[137] Marx (1867/1954: 671–95).

All in all, between 1727 and 1845, Parliament passed 1,385 Acts of Enclosure which, in total, enclosed some 1.77 million acres or 2,760 square miles that covered an area equivalent to 20 times the size of modern-day Sheffield.[138] Critically, the majority of these enclosures occurred in the north of England where the cotton industrialisation (as well as the iron/steel industrialisation) process took off.

But this whole process was, in turn, pushed forward by the impact of the global economic environment that the British confronted. As Schlumbohm notes, for 'England, which was politically and militarily the most successful country, the "virtual monopoly among European powers of overseas colonies" established during the phase of proto-industrialization was one of the central preconditions that [carried] proto-industrialization beyond itself into the Industrial Revolution'.[139] As I explained in Chapter 10, critical here was the 'Atlantic consumption driver' of Britain's industrialisation. For the central argument that I made there is that British merchant capitalists were highly aware of the very significant size of the Atlantic markets that were dominated by ICTs – so much so that they became very keen to tap into them in order to compete and eventually dominate them in the future.

Typical here was Samuel Greg, who in 1783 set up his famous cotton mill (Quarry Bank Mill in Styall that is located on the outskirts of Manchester). As Sven Beckert points out, Greg 'knew first hand that the market for cotton fabrics ... along the coast of Africa, and in the Americas—was rapidly expanding',[140] not least because he owned slaves on the island of Dominica and exported his cloth to the West Indies and elsewhere.[141] Accordingly, because the putting-out industry constrained British output – in striking contrast to the situation in India and especially China – so technological innovation was required in order to boost production to meet the buoyant Atlantic demand. For this demand took the lion's share of the increment of Britain's foreign trade in the eighteenth century, as I explained in Chapters 9 and 10. All of which necessitated the creation of concentrated arenas of factory production in which, as E. P. Thompson and Friedrich Engels inform us,[142] harsh discipline as well as violence and coercion – physical and sexual – alongside the more humdrum process of the dull compulsion of capitalist social relations were the core *modus operandi*.

---

[138] Figures calculated from Mooers (1991: 167) and Deane and Cole (1969: 272).
[139] Schlumbohm (1981: 131); see also Kriedte (1981b: 35–6).
[140] Beckert (2015: 62).
[141] Ibid. (2015: 56–63).
[142] Engels (1952) and Thompson (1965).

Here, it is particularly important to note that it was the extremely hierarchical structure of dominant/subordinate class relations that promoted the centripetal system of super-concentrated factory production. For the situation regarding the more independent position of peasant producers in China and India was an important factor in the maintenance of their centrifugal and non-mechanised cotton textile production systems.[143] And even within the part-mechanised *Karkhanas* of the post-1870 period, Indian workers did not face the kind of harsh disciplinary environment that the English workers confronted (as I explain in Chapter 13).[144] Of note too is that Chinese and Indian producers retained historical capitalist technologies. The British, by contrast, moved quite rapidly to fully mechanised industrial technologies. Although initially these were 'labour-substituting' technologies rather than 'labour-saving' technologies in nature (as I explained in Chapter 10), nevertheless in the twentieth century, the ever-increasing resort to technology to reduce labour costs via the rising organic composition of capital came to mark a vital component of modern Western capitalism.

By contrast, in significant part because of the huge size of their populations, India and China undertook what Kaoru Sugihara refers to as an 'industrious' revolution in which technologies were to an important extent 'labour augmenting' (to use Tirthankar Roy's phrase), as I discuss in Chapter 13. Note that the British 'industrious revolution' was very different and refers to labourers taking on more work to pay for the new consumer products. Mechanising the cotton textile industry was not necessary on technical grounds given the skill of Chinese and Indian spinners. And nor was it likely given firstly that it would undermine the state–society relationship and the foundation of both China's and India's historical capitalist developmental architectures; and secondly, because merchant capitalists did not desire it. It was these factors rather than any 'deficit' in India's and especially China's technological ability that mattered most. And, from my earlier discussion, I believe that the Chinese could have converted the water-powered big spinning frame for ramie into a cotton spinning machine had they so desired. The fact that they achieved this during World War II provides some testimony to this. Finally, I have chosen to defer the conclusion of this chapter until the end of the next, given that Chapter 12 completes my account of the second great divergence by explaining why Britain industrialised its iron and steel sector and why China and India did not.

[143] Riello (2013: 63–8).
[144] Haynes (2012).

12 Why Britain Initiated an Iron and Steel Industrialisation and Why India (Mysore) and China Did Not

Introduction

Alongside the cotton industry, the iron and steel industry constituted the other main pillar of the British industrial revolution. Here, I seek to advance a comparative analysis to explain why Britain underwent an iron and steel industrialisation and why China and India did not. Note that my focus here is on the Indian state of Mysore, given that of all the Indian states in the eighteenth century this had the most potential to undertake an iron and steel industrialisation. Eurocentrism insists that only Britain had the sufficiently rational institutions to make this transition. The revisionist/non-Eurocentric California School, in swinging ontologically eastward, generally seeks to eradicate the 'great rationality divide' between East and West by focusing on 'surprising resemblances' alongside an appeal to either 'contingency' (serendipity or bad luck) or changes in the global economy as the bases of their explanations. While surprising resemblances should not be discounted, nevertheless I focus far more on the many 'surprising differences' in this chapter. While I highlight some surprising differences in global and international imperial/geopolitical contexts as well as some highly surprising resemblances, all of these constitute necessary but ultimately insufficient factors in my explanation, given that differing *domestic* factors and properties also play a very important role. For as I explained in the penultimate section of Chapter 1, without some kind of a focus on the domestic properties of state–society relations, we are in effect robbed of an *explanation* of the second great divergence. Certainly, one of the more significant 'surprising differences' concerns the superior strength and effectiveness of the British state compared with the Qing and the Mysorean Sultanate. This chapter follows the schematic in Figures 11.1 (Britain versus China) and 12.1 (Britain versus Mysore).

Given that the introduction to Chapter 11 sets the scene for this one, I shall simply summarise the five sections that comprise this chapter. The section 'China versus Britain (I): Contingent Ecological Differentials

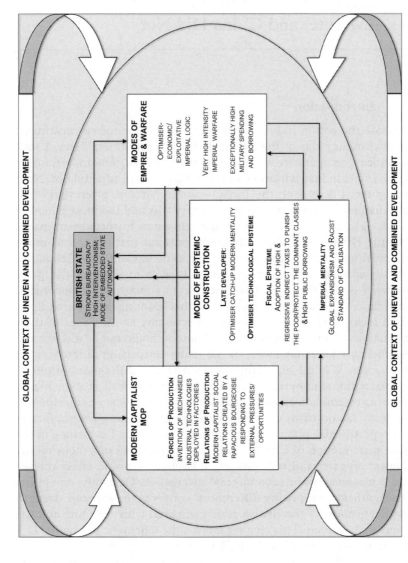

Figure 12.1 British and Mysorean 'developmental architectures' in the global context of uneven development.

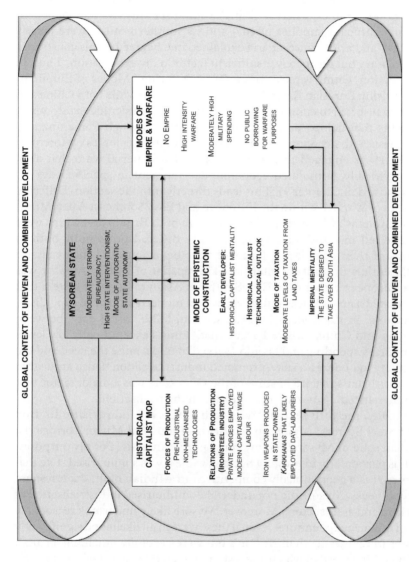

Figure 12.1 (*cont.*)

between Northern England and Southern China' develops Kenneth Pomeranz's well-known argument that Britain industrialised its iron and steel sectors because it had easy access to cheap coal and that it invented the steam engine in order to pump the water out of its deep and flooded mines, whereas China's southern industries did not benefit from significant supplies of coal and its southern mines were largely shallow and arid. However, as I explained in Chapter 10, this constitutes a necessary but ultimately insufficient factor in my explanation. Thus, in the section 'China versus Britain (II): "Differing" Modes of Empire or 'Surprising Eurasian Resemblances'?', I argue that while both China and Britain resorted to empire, only the latter's provided significant economic benefits that helped promote industrialisation (though Pomeranz also emphasises the economic benefits of the Atlantic colonies). Moreover, Britain was engaged in massively expensive imperial wars that also, paradoxically, stimulated economic development in specific ways (as I explained in Chapter 9). This leads directly into the section 'Differing Modes of Warfare within the European and East/Southeast Asian Multi-state Systems', which argues that although both Britain and China were embedded in multi-state systems, these differed profoundly both in terms of their constituent forms of state behaviour and their massive differentials in military intensity. The upshot of which is that it was the European rather than East/Southeast Asian multi-state system that generated a geopolitical-military driver of modern industrial capitalism. And this, in turn, feeds into the section, 'The "fiscal gap" between Britain and China', where I argue that China's exceptionally low levels of military spending and taxation served to undermine the need and the capacity to undergo a state-promoted industrialisation. I also argue that the overly laissez-faire posture of the Qing state was a major factor that countenanced *against* an iron and steel industrialisation.

Finally, the fifth section 'Why India Did Not Industrialise Its Iron and Steel Sectors: Mysore in the British Industrial Mirror', brings the Indian state of Mysore into my comparative analysis. For my purposes, this is particularly interesting because while it was a militarised state that was part of a geopolitically competitive intra-Indian multi-state system, nevertheless, Mysore did not undertake a militarised industrialisation of its iron and steel sectors. Moreover, Mysore likely undertook reasonably high military expenditures, even if these were in all likelihood significantly lower in real terms than Britain's but were certainly much higher than Qing China's. All of which suggests a much narrower set of differentials between Britain and Mysore when compared with those between Britain and China, notwithstanding the point that Mysore failed to develop an empire given Tipu Sultan's thwarted ambitions. Instead, I turn to an alternative framework in which differing state–society relations as well as differentials in the modes of state interventionism, coupled with a different *form* or socio-geopolitical *logic* that underpinned the competitive Indian multi-state system, together with certain ecological limits concerning the challenge of Indian coal, comprised the main differences in explaining the second great divergence between Britain and Mysore.

China versus Britain (I): Contingent Ecological Differentials between Northern England and Southern China

If, as I explained in Chapter 10, the Chinese had been so far in advance of the British in iron and steel production and it was only in the nineteenth century when the latter finally overtook the former, it begs the obvious question why the Chinese did not instigate an iron and steel industrialisation. For the Chinese were producing iron using coal and coke along with fluxes and mechanised bellows as early as the start of the first millennium CE, all of which saw China producing more iron in 1078 than Britain did in 1788. However, it is often assumed that after the fourteenth century, the Chinese iron and steel industry faded away, thereby paving the way for Britain to rise to the fore some five centuries later. But Kenneth Pomeranz provides a fascinating twist to this old argument. He argues that there was, in effect, an 'abortive revival' of the Chinese industry after 1420 as it relocated to the south, with new production centres emerging in Guangdong, Fujian, Yunnan, and Hunan.[1] This industrial shift occurred as a function of the challenges and catastrophes that had struck the north between c. 1100 and 1400, which included the Mongol invasions as well as floods and plagues. But such a shift proved to be fatal for the prospects of a full Chinese iron and steel industrialisation.

Pomeranz argues that charcoal rather than coal was used in iron production in the south not least because the major coal supplies were located in the north and that these were completely out of reach – with only 1.8 per cent of coal supplies being located in the south. He also argues that although there were coal mines in Xuzhou and Suxian in Jiangsu that were potentially within reach of the Lower Yangtze Delta, the problem here is that coal producers in the eighteenth century were poor and unemployed people who dug small, shallow mines. He

[1] See Pomeranz (2000: 62–8).

concludes that the problem confronting China was not the lack of a technological-innovative capacity but a very poor distribution of coal mines which, he argues, is brought into sharp relief by the fact that the British iron and steel industry enjoyed excellent access to cheap coal. Accordingly, the British were able to industrialise their iron and steel sector given that coal was a vital pre-requisite, whereas China's reliance on charcoal after 1400 was not conducive to industrialisation.

However, given the presence of China's deep northern mines that might have supplied the requisite coal to the southern producers via the Grand Canal, the question arises as to why more efforts were not made to link up with them – specifically by building canals in the north to link these mines with the south via the Grand Canal. Moreover, there is precedent here in that cotton textile producers in the Lower Yangtze relied on raw cotton supplies from the north. And, after all, the Chinese were past masters in canal building, having constructed over 50,000 km during the Song dynasty (960–1279) alone, which compared with Britain's 6,000 km in the heyday of canal construction (1750–1858). It was the largely-un-heard-of Qiao Weiyue who invented the pound-lock in 984, almost 800 years before the more well-known Briton, James Brindley, claimed to have invented it.[2] But Pomeranz argues that the problem might have been technically unsolvable at that time, given that coal sites in the north were cut off from Jiangnan because they were blocked by mountains such that 'without modern construction equipment and motor vehicles, no financing mechanism could have solved the transport problem'.[3] A further claim here is that while coal was used in northern iron and steel production, the shift to production to the south that was based on wood/charcoal after 1400 robbed China of the potential to invent a steam engine.

However, drawing on the pioneering work of Peter Golas,[4] Prasannan Parthasarathi notes that coal continued to be used in northern iron and steel production after 1400, albeit on a smaller scale, but most critically, that some 150,000 tons of coal were transported from Hunan to Hankou and thence to Nanjing and Shanghai in the south via the Yangtze River. And, moreover, by the nineteenth century, Chinese coal output might have been in the region of two million tons.[5] All of which leads him to question Pomeranz's argument. But these figures pale by comparison with the situation in Britain. By 1855, Britain produced about sixty-two

[2] Needham *et al.* (1971: 300–6, 344–78) and Tang (2018: 134–9).
[3] Pomeranz (2000: 184).
[4] Golas (1999: 186–201).
[5] Ibid. (196–7) and Parthasarathi (2011: 159–60, 162–4).

million tons of coal,[6] which was about thirty times that of China's output. Indeed, this is all the more impressive given that at that time Britain had a population of 21 million whereas China's was in the region of 430 million. And this means that two million tons would have struggled to accommodate the heating requirements of the Chinese population, given that it works out at a mere eleven lbs of coal per person, thereby leaving little to fuel an iron and steel industrialisation. Interestingly, Parthasarathi makes the plausible argument that the British state was an important factor in enabling coal mining in various ways, whereas the Chinese state did far less.[7] Which returns us to the notion of a more laissez-faire Chinese state in contrast to the more interventionist and activist British state that I considered in Chapter 2. All of which points up the role of domestic agential-developmental factors that underpinned Britain's industrialisation which I discussed in Chapters 9 and 10. But the role of British developmental agency does not end with the activist role of the state.

Pomeranz's core argument, which runs on from Britain's easy access to cheap coal, lies in his claim that the energy-power of British coal supported the 'all-important' steam engine that in turn underpinned the iron/steel (as well as cotton textile) industrial revolution – an argument that is supported by another California School scholar, Jack Goldstone.[8] Pomeranz rightly argues that the steam engine was invented as the result of ecological contingency or serendipity – specifically to pump the water out of Britain's deep and flooded coal mines. And he argues that China, by contrast, suffered ecological misfortune in that its coal mines (in the south) were shallow and arid and, therefore, did not require the invention of the steam engine – hence why no industrialisation transpired.[9]

However, saying that the British *needed* to find a way of pumping water out of the mines can lead into problematic ecological-functionalist analysis. For while necessity might be the mother of invention, this cannot explain *how* and *which* child was born. Notable here is that many of China's *northern* mines were equally as deep and flooded as those found in northern England.[10] Critically, both countries found solutions to this challenge but they did so in different ways. For the Chinese invented the hydraulic bellows pump and the square pallet chain pump. In short, same mother, different children. And, because the British

---

[6] Deane and Cole (1969: 216); cf. Mitchell (2011: 247).
[7] Parthasarathi (2011: 162–8).
[8] Goldstone (2008: 129–32).
[9] Pomeranz (2000: 59–68).
[10] Hartwell (1966: 48) and Golas (1999: 186, 285–7, 336–51, 429–35).

invention turned out to be far more propitious for industrialisation, so we need to factor in significant developmental agency to British inventors rather than ending our analysis with the ecological fact of flooded mines and leaving it at that. Moreover, Margaret Jacob, Toby Huff and Jack Goldstone add to this by rightly pointing out that the rise of science was important in the pioneering developments that were made by James Watt,[11] thereby highlighting a further dimension of British developmental agency.

All in all, while ecological contingency played an important role in explaining the second great divergence in iron and steel production, so British developmental agency in its various dimensions also needs to be factored in. More generally, the much bigger question arises as to the wider socio-political factors that pushed the British, as opposed to the Chinese, to initiate an iron and steel industrialisation. Here, I return to my discussion of the differences in developmental architectures (see Figure 11.1 in Chapter 11). These comprise differentials in military pressures and modes of empire, warfare and taxation. Here, I build in particular on the framework that I set up in Chapter 2, which I deployed to explain why Britain moved to high protectionism after 1684 at the same time that China moved to freer trade.

China versus Britain (II): 'Differing' Modes of Empire or 'Surprising Eurasian Resemblances'?

Commensurate with neorealist international relations (IR) logic, the prominent scholars of Chinese great power politics, Peter Perdue and Wang Yuan-kang, argue that Qing China and the European great powers exhibited 'surprising resemblances' insofar as they all engaged in imperialism, war and state-building.[12] And the 'cultural realist', Alistair Iain Johnston, implies as much.[13] As such, this bears something of a resemblance with the approach of the California School, as Perdue notes.[14] True, the British and Chinese empires deployed similar modalities of colonial rule, including 'indirect rule', 'divide and rule' and, at the extreme, genocide. For the Qing saw to the destruction of the Zunghar Mongols with somewhere between 600,000 and 1 million

---

[11] Goldstone (2008: 132–4), Jacob (1997), Mokyr (1990, 2002) and Huff (2011: ch. 8).
[12] Perdue (2005: ch. 15, 2015) and Wang (2011).
[13] Johnston (1995).
[14] Perdue (2005: 536–42).

being either wiped out or displaced.[15] As I explain later, it is certainly the case that military conflicts between China and its northern and western neighbours comprised a constant problem before they were imperially incorporated by the Qing during the late-seventeenth and eighteenth centuries. Moreover, one might extend this 'isomorphic vision' of 'surprising resemblances' to include the construction of similar hierarchical conceptions of the world.

Certainly, the British and Chinese constructed 'three-worlds conceptions' that were based on their respective *standards of civilisation*. The Sinic standard of civilisation placed China at the centre as the 'Middle Kingdom' on the basis of its civilised Confucian culture, while the 'Other' was divided into two key inferior zones. The 'second world' (or region) comprised the 'inner zone of manifest civility', which contained those tribute states that were most Confucianised and which were in closest proximity to China – specifically, Korea, Vietnam, Japan and the Ryūkyūs (present-day Okinawa). Placed within the 'outer zone' were the many Southeast Asian tribute states that were less Confucianised than those within the inner zone. And beyond this was the 'third world' or 'zone of savagery', which comprised the nomadic societies on China's northern and western frontiers. These included the Jurchens, Manchus and numerous Mongolian tribes such as the Tatars and Zhungars as well as the tribal conglomerate of the Oirats – the Choros, Dorbets, Khoids and Torghuts. The received wisdom holds that the Chinese and British worldviews were highly similar, given that the Chinese conception appears on first blush to be reminiscent of the British standard of civilisation – not to mention their shared conceptions of scientific racism at the very end of the nineteenth century.[16] For in a similar manner, this elevated Britain to the top of the 'civilised centre' with the rest of the world divided into the inner 'civilised' zone (the first world of Western Europe), the second world of 'barbarism' (Oriental despotisms in China, India and the Middle East) and the third world of 'savagery' (anarchic societies in Africa, the Americas, Polynesia and Australasia).[17]

But on closer inspection, this isomorphic vision obscures numerous critical differences that are relevant for my discussion of the Chinese and British imperial projects. First, China's 'worldview' was not really

[15] Perdue (2005: ch. 9, 2017: 10), Lorge (2008: 166–7) and Phillips (2017). Note that 20 per cent of the male population were killed, 40 per cent died from smallpox and 20 per cent fled to Russia and the Kazakh region.

[16] Dikötter (1997); cf. Jacques (2012: 308–17).

[17] See Hobson (2004: ch. 10).

global given that in practice it extended only to the immediate region. China was interested in neither Europe nor the Americas, given that they were so far away – notwithstanding the point that once the 'barbaric' European East India Companies arrived in China, they were treated with some suspicion such that they were constrained in their freedom of movement within the country after 1757 (as also occurred to the Dutch within the Japanese tribute system after 1639), as I explained in Chapter 2.

Second, the construction of the Other entailed different meanings within the Chinese and British 'worldviews'. For the Chinese preferred to cooperate with the Mongol 'savages' and not infrequently treated them as equals,[18] whereas most paradoxically, the 'barbaric' states in the 'inner zone of manifest civility' were treated unequally in status. Indeed, states *outside* of the tribute system such as Tujue and Tufan often enjoyed 'status-equality' with China.[19] Thus, during the Han (206 BCE to 220 CE), Sui (581–618) and T'ang (618–907) dynasties, the Chinese established 'brotherly relations' – i.e., equal relations – with their powerful (savage) northern and western nomadic and semi-nomadic neighbours.[20] A particularly notable example here comprised the policy of *Heqin* (peace and friendship) that the Han dynasty struck with its 'barbarian' northern rival, the Xiongnu, to which the Chinese paid annual tribute for some time.[21]

Third, and most importantly, the 'savage Other' construct only became operationalised when the Mongols chose to attack China. Outside of these times, the Chinese state *generally* viewed the *Hua* (the Sinic peoples) and the *Yi* (non-Sinics) in broadly inclusivist terms.[22] Thus, when the Mongols and other nomadic and semi-nomadic peoples cooperated with China, so an inclusivist conception of the *yi* predominated but when the *yi*, especially the Mongols, initiated hostilities with China, so they were 'othered' as aggressive savages.[23] As Zhang Feng notes, '[w]henever relationships with them turned problematic, Chinese officials began to attribute "the (bad) nature of the yi and di" (*yi di zhixing*) as the fundamental cause'.[24] By contrast, if a country was deemed to be 'savage' in the British construction of the world, not only was cooperation ruled out *tout court* but it was also deemed ripe for imperialism wherever it

[18] Zhang (2009: 555–6, 560–1), Zhang and Buzan (2012: 22) and Perdue (2015: 1006).
[19] Zhang and Buzan (2012: 22).
[20] Zhang (2009: 555–6).
[21] Zhou (2011: 148).
[22] Zhang and Buzan (2012: 22) and Zhang (2015: 210).
[23] Zhou (2011: 153).
[24] Zhang (2015: 211); see also Perdue (2005: ch. 15).

was located – as the Africans and the American- and Australasian-Aborigines found out to their shock. So what are the ramifications of these differing worldviews for the Chinese and British modes of empire?

Critically, while both Britain and China began their imperial projects in the seventeenth century, the logics of imperial expansion or their modes of empire differed fundamentally. First, in clear contrast to the British, the Chinese lacked a Messianic purpose to colonise and culturally convert the world to its standard of civilisation. And while Britain undertook a major sea-based imperial-economic and cultural expansion to all corners of the world, China's far more limited imperial expansion was land-based and was undertaken for defensive-military purposes. In essence, the nomadic regions were incorporated into a greater China so as to put an end to the consistent provocations and attacks that the Middle Kingdom had long suffered on its northern and western frontiers at the hands of the nomadic invaders.[25] Notable too is that China had been conquered and ruled by neighbouring nomadic peoples at various points in time, most notably by the (Manchurian) Jurchen Jin dynasty during the Northern Song period (1127–1234), and by the Mongol-Yuan dynasty (1279–1368). And, of course, having invaded and taken over the Chinese state in 1644, the new Manchu Qing rulers knew only too well the perils and challenges of the north-eastern frontier that connected China with Manchuria!

All in all, China's land-based imperial thrust necessarily problematises President Xi Jinping's claim – so reminiscent of President George W. Bush's various public denials of American imperialism – that 'China was long one of the most powerful countries in the world. Yet it never engaged in colonialism or aggression. The pursuit of peaceful development represents the peace-loving cultural tradition of the Chinese nation over the past several thousand years.'[26] But given that China near-tripled in size between 1683 and 1760, what word other than 'empire' could capture this?

While a racial epistemic logic was important in driving British imperialism – far more so than was the case with China – so too was an emergent capitalist logic. The critical difference between these modes of imperial expansion is that the British exploitative-economic and 'civilising' logics contrasted strikingly with China's security-based rationale that imparted few, if any, economic benefits.[27] Peer Vries cites

---

[25] Perdue (2005), Vries (2015: 397) and Arrighi (2007: 317–21).
[26] President Xi Jinping speech at the Korber Foundation, Germany (March 2014), cited in Zhao Suisheng (2015: 962).
[27] Perdue (2005: 328, 334–6) and Vries (2015: 397–401).

various authorities to this effect, to wit: Joseph Fletcher's claim that '[n]o great [economic] revenues flowed to Peking from Inner Asian dependencies. Indeed there was nothing the Qing wanted from them but peace,'[28] while Sabine Dabringhaus asserts that '[t]he search for wealth, for gains in trade, or the wish to convert unbelievers did not play any role'.[29] Indeed, the Chinese lacked the desire to explore, control and exploit other peoples for economic profit, and nor did they construct slave plantations for economic production in the colonised territories.[30] In short, as Bin Wong notes, 'we do not seem to find a European kind of desire for expansion based on the wedding of profit and power'.[31] In essence, the Chinese position was almost the exact inverse of Britain's colonial project, for rather than extracting economic resources *from* the new imperial territories the Qing state sought to allocate resources *to* them.[32] No such security logic underpinned British imperialism given that no non-Western people sought to invade, let alone takeover, Britain.

One possible response to my claim might well be that the *imperial* extraction of economic tribute was a fundamental part of the Chinese tribute system (CTS). However, as I explained in Chapter 2, this assertion misunderstands the nature and function of tribute, given not only that it was symbolic rather than economic in nature,[33] but also that symbolism entailed and indeed required an *economic loss* for the Chinese state. And, as I also explained there, the Chinese state was so badly out of pocket from the tribute trade as well as the official trade that this system was brought to a *de facto* close in 1684.[34] Accordingly, because the colonies helped stimulate both the emergence of British industrialisation – as I explained in Chapter 9 – as well as its expansion in the nineteenth century, so the absence of an equivalent imperial-economic enabler constitutes a further reason why the Chinese did not industrialise.[35]

Differing Modes of Warfare within the European and East/Southeast Asian Multi-state Systems

One factor that I highlighted in Chapter 9, which concerns the pressures that drove Britain's iron and steel industrialisation, was

---

[28] Fletcher cited in Vries (2015: 397).
[29] Sabine Dabringhaus cited in Vries (2015: 398).
[30] Vries (2015: 86, 361, 399, 400).
[31] Bin Wong (2002: 455).
[32] Bin Wong (1997: 148).
[33] Martin-Fox (2003: 76).
[34] Zhao (2013: 110–11) and Arrighi (2007: 324–5).
[35] See also Bin Wong (2002).

the twin-demand that imperial warfare and the Atlantic slave system imposed. Notwithstanding the bracketing out or the whitewashing of the imperial and slave-based dimensions through the Eurocentric method of 'analytical bifurcation',[36] numerous scholars claim that Britain was part of an anarchic European multi-state system in which geopolitical competition between the great powers was a key driver of their constituent economies.[37] Specifically, they refer to the 'industrialisation of war' and the 'militarisation of industry'.[38] In this context, the most common Eurocentric move is to draw a key comparison with China on the grounds that because it was an isolated 'world-empire' and was *not* part of a multi-state system or an international society of states, so there was no such competitive-geopolitical logic driving the development of the Chinese economy – hence its 'failure' to break through into modern industrial capitalism.[39] While *imperialist* geopolitics forms an important part of the causal story that I narrate here, nevertheless I endorse it for reasons that are very different from those that are proffered by Eurocentrism.

First of all, as noted in Chapter 2, China was very much part of a multi-state system that reached from Russia in the north and west to Indonesia in the southeast.[40] And, within the inner zone of the CTS, it is possible to argue that there was a 'thick' international society of states (where shared Confucian cultural norms were deeply embedded), while in the outer zone there was a 'thin' international society (where there was a mixture of cultural norms). However, some scholars would respond by insisting that no such international system/international society existed because the region was governed by the 'imperial-hierarchical' CTS, which meant that there were no sovereign states in existence. Ironically, it is here where the Eurocentric and Sinocentric conceptions of East/Southeast Asia converge, for both exaggerate the coherence and centrality of the hierarchical CTS within the region. Thus, one of the core properties of the CTS was that the so-called vassal states enjoyed *de facto* sovereignty given that they were largely free to conduct their own domestic and foreign policy.[41] Space, unfortunately, precludes

---

[36] But see McNeill (1982: 143) and Arrighi (2007).
[37] For example, North and Thomas (1973), Wallerstein (1974), Jones (1981), Gilpin (1981), Giddens (1985), Collins (1985), Mann (1986), Tilly (1990), Landes (1998) and Arrighi (2007: 266–74).
[38] Trotsky (1906/2010: 42–51), Mumford (1934), John (1955), McNeill (1982), Sen (1984), and Rodger (2010).
[39] For example, Wallerstein (1974) and Jones (1981).
[40] See also Goldstone (2008: 100–2).
[41] Kang (2010: 37, 54) and Zhang and Buzan (2012: 15, 27); cf. Arrighi *et al.* (2003: 269–70).

a full justification of this claim, but in essence the notion of Chinese hierarchy applies only to *status*- rather than *political*-inequality. That is, although the vassal states sent envoys to the Chinese capital to grant external legitimacy to the Chinese state and its domestic Confucian hierarchical-social relations – specifically the five key sets of relationships within China: 'those between husband and wife; father and son; older and younger brother; friend and friend; and sovereign [emperor] and [minister]' – [42] they were, nevertheless, happy to do so not only for the economic benefits that this granted them (as I explained in Chapter 2) but also because the conferral of legitimacy was a two-way reciprocal process. For equally, the Chinese emperor's approval of a new vassal-state ruler enhanced the latter's legitimacy domestically.

In general, not only were the 'vassal states' largely free to conduct domestic and foreign policy according to their own interests,[43] but they also 'had their own non-Chinese views of their relationship to China and accepted Chinese views only in part, [sometimes] superficially or tacitly, as a matter of expedience'.[44] Strikingly, it was not uncommon to find that many Chinese emperors felt that their proclaimed cultural superiority was based more on myth than reality.[45] And to add yet further complexity here, it is important to note that there was room for considerable vassal-state agency vis-à-vis China within the CTS which, once again, gives the lie to the Sinocentric conception of the hierarchical CTS.[46] Problematic here is the analogous theory of heliocentrism, that in Sinocentrism (and Eurocentrism) the vassal states are likened to satellites that simply revolve around the all-powerful gravitational pull that was issued by China at the centre. But this centripetal conception needs to be tempered by one that recognises centrifugal forces, wherein the vassals enjoyed considerable agency vis-à-vis China.[47] Indeed, they engaged in competitive–cooperation with China and exercised much influence over it. Moreover, there was a strong element of interdependence between China and its vassals rather than one of mere vassal dependence. Thus, Song Nianshen is correct to argue that China did not unilaterally create the mode of inter-state connections in pre-modern East Asia: '[r]ather, the "system", if there was indeed such a thing, was an institutional

---

[42] Zhang and Buzan (2012: 13).
[43] Song (2012: 163–4) and Zhang (2009: 570, 563).
[44] Zhang and Buzan (2012: 31) and Bin Wong (1997: 89).
[45] Zhang (2009: 556–7).
[46] Zhou (2011), Song (2012) and Zhang (2015).
[47] Suzuki (2007).

mechanism mutually constructed by both the central and peripheral regimes'.[48]

However, this mode of interdependence should not be conflated with a purely cooperative one given that competitive–cooperation between China and its 'vassal states' was important. As Zhou Fangyin notes, 'we cannot simply assume that the tributary system represents the Middle Kingdom's use of hard power to force demands on its neighbours in the periphery'.[49] For the assumption is that China did all the coercing and initiated military conflict while being solely responsible for governing the regional order. But as Zhou Fangyin argues, some of these conflicts were the consequence of border harassment and were initiated by the vassals rather than China. He also asserts that these were undertaken in order to extract more benefits from China, though Song Nianshen argues that there were many more factors that informed such actions.[50] Either way, whatever the motivating factors were, the key point is that China's default position was generally to *ignore* these vassal-invoked hostilities rather than engage them militarily. Still, the problem with such a conciliatory stance is that it was interpreted as a sign of Chinese weakness that in turn served merely to embolden the vassals to up the ante yet further; all of which eventually prompted China's deployment of occasional punitive expeditions as a last resort so as to pacify such incursions in the hope of deterring future acts of vassal-state aggression.

Finally, there was yet another layer of complexity that problematises the conflation of the region with a singular Chinese hierarchical centre. For, as I explained in Chapter 2, the region was far more complex than the CTS given that it comprised numerous overlapping 'international' hierarchical systems that criss-crossed it. Thus, the region was divided *vertically*, albeit in a harmonious, hierarchical fashion between the CTS and various sub-tribute systems. For example, while Vietnam was a vassal of China, it also had Laos as its own vassal while China's number one vassal, Korea, had Tsushima as its vassal. And all such vassals also paid homage to the Chinese emperor (hence the 'harmonious' conception of hierarchy). But the region was also divided *horizontally* in either a competitive or competitive–cooperative fashion. This included the Japanese 'tribute system' after 1603 and the, albeit brief, Zheng ('piratical') tribute system, as well as the various Mandala systems in Southeast Asia, most notably that of the Majapahits. The Mandalas

---

[48] Song (2012: 155).
[49] Zhou (2011: 150).
[50] Song (2012: 163–4).

were similar to the CTS, but they were not derivative of it because they originated from the ancient Indian tradition associated with Kautilya.[51]

The main reason why there was no geopolitical-competitive driver underpinning China's economy was not the lack of a multi-state system, but rather that states within the CTS *chose* to 'under-balance' or *bandwagon* with, rather than balance against, China.[52] Still, the term 'bandwagon' is not perfect here because it implies that China gained disproportionately from such a relationship when in fact all states benefited equally, albeit in different ways. Most significantly, the striking aspect of the regional order that was linked to the CTS was its predominantly peaceful relations.[53] Critically, when we compare the military conflict ratio – i.e., the number of conflicts divided by the total number of years – it is clear that China's very low figure contrasted strikingly with that of Britain's and the European great powers'. David Kang covers the Ming and most of the Qing eras – specifically 1368–1841 (i.e., 473 years) – and argues that China was involved in only three key wars in the inner tribute system: the invasion of Vietnam twice (1407–28 and 1788–9) and China's protection of Korea against Japan in the Imjin War (1592–8).[54] By contrast, he notes that England fought France alone over forty-six times between 1300 and 1850.

Focusing specifically on the key Qing period (1644–1839), Robert Kelly speaks of a 'Confucian Long Peace' within the inner zone of the CTS, which contrasts with that of sustained conflict in Christendom. Thus, Qing China's peace ratio of 99.5 in 1644–1839 contrasts strikingly with Latin Christendom's ratio of 39 per cent (based on 92 wars in 1648–1789).[55] That is, China was engaged in war within the inner tribute system for only 0.5 per cent of the time, whereas the figure for Europe was 61 per cent. In sum, such evidence suggests that despite the protestations of the likes of Peter Perdue, Geoff Wade and Wang Yuan-kang,[56] the CTS was striking for its surprisingly peaceful relations, especially when compared with the situation in the European states system.[57] All of which prompted Giovanni Arrighi to speak of a 'five hundred year' East Asian peace.[58] Accordingly, there is a case to argue

---

[51] See Grey (2001), Dellios (1996) and Manggala (2013).

[52] Kang (2010: ch. 5). The term 'under-balancing' comes from Kelly (2012: 419).

[53] Shambaugh (2004/5: 95).

[54] However, Kang (2010: 90–1) also argues that during the Ming, there were a further eight minor Sinic 'incidents' (which occurred between two or more states, comprising China, Korea, Vietnam and Japan) and one in the Qing era (1644–1841).

[55] Kelly (2012).

[56] Wade (2004), Perdue (2005: 548) and Wang (2011).

[57] Kang (2010: chs. 1 and 5) and Kelly (2012).

[58] Arrighi (2007: 316).

that it was the more sophisticated nature of the East Asian multi-state system and the social norms within which it was embedded, which stood in striking contrast to the cruder, militaristic and highly competitive nature of the European system, that needs to be taken into account. All of which suggests that the general lack of (serious) geopolitical competition entailed the absence of a geopolitical driver of a potential Chinese iron and steel industrialisation. However, we cannot leave the analysis here.

As I noted in Chapter 2, it would be problematic to conclude that 'China does not have a significant history of coercive statecraft'.[59] For while this is true with respect to its tribute system, nevertheless it was engaged in frequent conflicts with the nomadic societies on its northern and western borders. According to Kang, these comprised 75 per cent of all military engagements between 1368 and 1841 and as much as 90 per cent in the Qing period.[60] And Perdue points out that according to the Chinese Academy of Military Science, China was involved in 3,756 wars between 770 BCE and 1912 CE (or 1.4 wars per annum).[61] Nevertheless, these Sino-nomadic relations disappear in front of the eyes of Eurocentric IR scholars because these particular societies generally did not develop more formal state structures and are therefore perceived not to have been part of a (formal) multi-state system. Upon such fictions has the myth of Chinese political isolation been founded and indeed maintained for several centuries of Western scholarship. Either way, though, does this point contradict my claim that there was no geopolitical-competitive driver to spur on a potential Chinese iron and steel industrialisation?

The key point by way of reply is that the 'wars' with the nomadic societies comprised largely skirmishes and small-scale raids. According to Kent Deng, there were only ten major nomadic invasions between 1125 and 1644.[62] Most significantly, because highly mobile, light horses with their riders equipped with bows and arrows constituted the core *modus operandi* of Mongol warfare, so meeting this challenge required no major drive to develop more sophisticated industrialised modes of warfare. Moreover, even China's '[e]arly firearms were ineffective against steppe and desert nomads'.[63] Interestingly, Kenneth Chase traces innovations in military weaponry to periods of disunity,[64] with the period when China was divided by the Song dynasty in the south

---

[59] Shambaugh (2004/5: 95).
[60] Kang (2010: 91).
[61] Perdue (2015: 1004–5).
[62] Deng (2012b: 340).
[63] Chase (2008: 3) and Lorge (2008).
[64] Chase (2008: 32).

and the Jurchen Jin dynasty in the north (1127–1279) being especially notable, given that this is when the Chinese military revolution really kicked in. It is true that China was involved in wars in the creation of the Ming. But, as Chase notes,

[a]fter 1368 [the year of the Ming dynasty's birth], the theater of war shifted from the valleys of south China to the dusty plains of north China and the steppe and desert of Mongolia. The kind of warfare ... with ships battling for control of rivers and infantry besieging walled cities, largely disappeared from China after 1368. How firearms might have developed in China if ships and infantry had continued to dominate warfare can only be imagined.[65]

Thus, to paraphrase the final sentence of this quote, how iron and steel might have developed in China if ships and infantry had continued to dominate warfare can only be imagined.

Accordingly, the counterfactual that emerges here is that had there been significant geopolitical competition between the 'vassal states' in the CTS, given that they were more advanced polities than those of the nomadic societies, then this might have triggered some sort of Chinese drive into a militarised iron and steel industrialisation (notwithstanding the significant ecological limits after about 1400 that I discussed earlier). However, there is one exception here that proves this rule – that of Zungharia, which was located on China's north-west frontier. For while the Zunghar rulers developed iron-production factories for armaments alongside agriculture,[66] this proves the rule because by 1760, Zungharia had been completely destroyed by China's genocidal policy, with its territory thereafter incorporated into the new Chinese province of Xinjiang. The paradox here is that the window of any potential geopolitical competition that might have spurred an industrialisation of the Chinese iron and steel sector was slammed shut on the very eve of Britain's iron industrialisation. Thus, if the multi-state system within which China was embedded lacked anything it was that of an *arms-race* driver. Accordingly, it would be safe to say that China was not involved in the *peculiar form* of geopolitical competition that prevailed in Europe and which helped promote a militarised industrialisation in Britain. All of which yields a further profound paradox.

Just as the Chinese had pioneered all manner of iron and steel production methods, as I explained in Chapter 10, so they had also led the world in military technologies. Most notably, the Chinese initiated

---

[65] Ibid. (35).
[66] Perdue (2017: 2, 11).

the first significant military revolution (c. 850–c. 1300), inventing gunpowder (c. 850), the first metal-barrelled gun firing a metal bullet (c. 1275) and the first cannon (known as the 'eruptor') around 1290 – though since Needham made this latter dating others have suggested the much earlier date of the early-twelfth century.[67] Moreover, it is likely no coincidence that the first English cannon in 1327 was identical to the Chinese eruptor.[68] The Chinese also invented various other military technologies such as rockets and multiple rocket launchers, mines, bombs, grenades and flame-throwers.[69] To which we can add the Song dynasty's creation of a massive navy in 1132 in order to defend against the Jurchens who had taken over the northern half of China. With a well-armed fleet of some 20,500 ships,[70] this Chinese fleet, had it so desired, could have taken out any single European power and probably the entirety of Europe's combined naval power at the time.

But, after the thirteenth century and especially the fourteenth century, China did not follow up on these innovations so that gradually, having borrowed the military technologies that the Chinese had pioneered,[71] the Europeans caught up and then came to occupy the leading edge by the late-sixteenth century.[72] Nevertheless, it took a long time before the difference was felt, given that the Chinese emulated European developments in military technology after the fourteenth century in what amounted to a reversal of the previous modality of East–West transmissions and Europe's emulation of Chinese military technologies.[73] Thus, although Chinese military power had no problems holding the European East India Companies at bay even as late as the eighteenth century, nevertheless the military-technological tectonic plates were shifting gradually beneath the surface such that China was finally caught by surprise by the British in the First Opium War in 1839–42;[74] though the waning of the Qing state during the nineteenth century also played an important part.[75]

All of which means that in the critical period (1550–1900), when European military power developed significantly, though most

[67] Chase (2008: 32).
[68] Needham et al. (1986: 572–9) and Hobson (2004: 186–8).
[69] Needham et al. (1986), Hobson (2004: 58–61), Chase (2008: esp. ch. 2) and Lorge (2008: ch. 1).
[70] Deng (1997: 70).
[71] Needham et al. (1986: 49, 47–50, 77, 455–65, 570–9), Hobson (2004: 186–8), Chase (2008: ch. 3) and Lorge (2008: ch. 1).
[72] Chase (2008: ch.3) and Lorge (2008: ch. 3).
[73] Chase (2008: 145–50).
[74] Goldstone (2008: 165).
[75] Sharman (2019: 141–2).

especially in the nineteenth century, China's previous leading-edge military-innovative capacity was lost owing to a lack of high-intensity geopolitical pressures. Accordingly, borrowing from Victoria Hui's seminal comparative analysis of ancient Chinese Warring States and early-modern Europe,[76] which in turn borrows from Charles Tilly,[77] I argue that Britain underwent a 'capital-coercive path' of state- and modern industrial-capitalist-formation. For the exceptionally high costs of war required the British state to form a very close relationship with the capitalist class. But Qing China enacted much less expensive wars such that undertaking the capital-coercive path was not chosen.[78] As Giovanni Arrighi concluded, 'the synergy typical of the European developmental path between militarism, industrialism and capitalism, which propelled, and was in turn sustained by, ceaseless overseas territorial expansion [for economic ends], was absent in East Asia'.[79] The deepest paradox here is that it was Europe's warring states as opposed to East/Southeast Asia's relatively peaceful tribute states that goes a considerable way to explaining the second great divergence in iron and steel production.

Finally, I showed in Chapter 2 how Britain's real military burden dwarfed that of China's in the long eighteenth century. But the immediate liberal response would be to argue that such high levels of military spending would have either undermined or at least constrained British industrialisation (which I critiqued in detail in Chapter 9), as much as China's super-low military burden should have been highly propitious. However, I concur with the claims made in this context by Peer Vries, who notes that the 'impact of war in terms of stimulating China's economy would have been so marginal, particularly by comparison with Britain, that it is pointless even to consider it'.[80] And, as he put it elsewhere: '[t]o the extent that a thing like "military Keynesianism" actually existed, the chances of finding examples of it in Western Europe must have been substantial. In China, that lacked all characteristics of a fiscal-military state à la Britain, they definitely were absent.'[81] For as I argued earlier as well as in Chapter 9, Britain's super-high imperial-military spending underpinned, in numerous ways, a state-enabled industrialisation.

[76] Hui (2005: 207–11).
[77] Tilly (1990).
[78] See also Arrighi (2007: ch. 11).
[79] Arrighi (2007: 335).
[80] Vries (2015: 314).
[81] Vries (2013: 375).

The 'Fiscal Gap' between Britain and China

As I also explained in Chapter 2, Britain's taxes dwarfed those of China's both in real terms as well as in per capita terms in the long eighteenth century (1688–1815). Once again, to my liberal reader, these arguments would appear to provide the perfect rationale as to why China should have industrialised and why Britain, which should have been crippled by fiscal-imperial overstretch, should have remained a pre-industrial economy. But rather than being propitious for industrialisation, the reality is that the cost of Kangxi's decision to freeze the land tax in 1712 was the decline of the Qing state in the nineteenth century.[82] And, this also had negative knock-on effects on local government finance.[83] The all-important Chinese direct per capita land-tax burden, which comprised about 75 per cent of central government revenues, halved in real terms between 1620 and 1770 and halved again between 1753 and 1908.[84] And while British taxes also declined significantly in real terms in the nineteenth century as the cost of warfare and interest payments on the national debt declined dramatically, especially after 1850, nevertheless we find that the gap in per capita taxation in that period widened considerably such that the British burden was 6,230 per cent that of the Chinese in 1800/99 (324 grams of silver versus 5.2, respectively).[85]

Despite the Eurocentric image of a heavily bureaucratised Chinese Oriental despotism and the British light-touch night-watchman state, it turns out that Britain's exceptionally high spending was only possible because of the strength of its fiscal bureaucracy, which was certainly the strongest and most centralised in Europe,[86] if not in the world. By comparison, China's bureaucracy was striking only for its weakness. In the late-eighteenth century, the number of British fiscal officials relative to the size of the population was 1:1,300,[87] whereas the relevant figure for the Qing state was a mere 1:250,000.[88] Moreover, running with Kent Deng's figure yields a ratio of as little as 1:1,000,000.[89] Thus, Deng is surely right to conclude that the Qing state declined in the nineteenth century as a result of its small, cheap and low-density bureaucracy

[82] Hung (2001: 502–5).
[83] Zelin (1984: especially 307–8).
[84] Feuerwerker (1984: 306–7).
[85] Calculated from Bin Ma (2013: 489).
[86] Brewer (1989: 127), Mann (1986) and Weiss and Hobson (1995: chs. 2–4).
[87] Weiss and Hobson (1995: 45).
[88] Vries (2015: 143).
[89] Deng (2012a: ch. 3).

that was committed to Confucian principles of good governance,[90] as I explained in Chapter 2. And, as Albert Feuerwerker asserts, '[t]he consequence[s] of a light fiscal hand, which in turn was partly due to an inflexible tax system, were thus not always desirable ones for the state or for the economy. But the pervasive support for light taxation in traditional China, which based itself on aspects of the dominant Neo-Confucian ideology, must itself not be taken lightly.'[91]

Overall, China's super-low tax and spending regime certainly promoted 'Smithian growth' that is consistent with historical capitalism right through the seventeenth and eighteenth centuries.[92] But critically, it did not enable 'Schumpeterian growth', which requires new social structures that are in part promoted by the state.[93] For while the Chinese state was well placed to enable historical capitalism, it was largely inadequate to the task of promoting modern capitalism and nor was it interested in doing so. Here, I concur with Dwight Perkins' argument that China's low taxes and expenditures cut off the option either of a Chinese state-led modernisation or a state-enabled industrialisation.[94] Or, to quote Albert Feuerwerker once more: '[t]oward *modern* economic growth ... the Chinese state contributed little if anything, in contrast to the history of early modern Europe'.[95] Indeed, the comparison here is precisely with Britain, which underwent a state-enabled industrialisation as I explained in Chapters 9 and 10.

Why India Did Not Industrialise Its Iron and Steel Sectors: Mysore in the British Industrial Mirror

While I have argued that China and Britain constituted polar opposite cases with respect to the key criteria that I have selected here, nevertheless, the addition of Mysore under the Islamic Sultanate between 1761 and 1799 complicates but also enriches my comparative analysis in fascinating ways. In essence, this is because the Mysorean sultanate, unlike the Qing but very much like Britain, was heavily embroiled in warfare within a multi-state system and looked to develop the iron and steel industry through a state-led programme in order to strengthen its military base. As signalled earlier, I consider Mysore here because of all the Indian states in the eighteenth century it was the most likely

---

[90] Ibid. See also Zelin (1984: 307–8).
[91] Feuerwerker (1984: 308).
[92] Rosenthal and Bin Wong (2011: 205).
[93] Schumpeter (1943/2010).
[94] Perkins (1967: 487–8).
[95] Feuerwerker (1984: 322), my emphasis.

candidate to break through into an iron and steel industrial revolution. Such a comparison is also compelling because before 1792 Mysore and Britain were similar sized countries while after 1792 Mysore and England were about the same size, much as Mysore and Britain had similar sized populations before 1792, while after that date, the populations of Mysore and England were not significantly different.[96] Here, I shall go through the same criteria that informed my comparison of China and Britain.

The Indian Multi-State System in the European Mirror

Eurocentric scholars tend to conflate 'India' – or more accurately 'South Asia' given that 'India' only came into existence in 1947 – with the Mughal Empire between 1526 and 1858. And because they view it as an 'Oriental despotism', or a 'world-empire' in Wallerstein's terminology, so they assume that India was a single state system. But this misses the point that after 1707, with the ensuing decline of the Mughal state that was brought about to a significant extent by the military challenge that was imparted by the Marathas via the Mughal–Maratha wars (1680–1707) as well as various subsequent invasions, most especially those of Nādir Shāh (the Persian ruler), India had devolved into a fully multi-state system by the mid-eighteenth century. The immediate issue at hand, therefore, concerns the nature of that system.

I argued above that Qing China was embedded in a large multi-state system within East/Southeast Asia. And I also argued that this was a relatively peaceful one given the general lack of geopolitical competition between the vassal states and China – bar that between the Qing and the nomadic invaders. For as I noted, the constituent (vassal) states' predominant foreign security policy was one of 'bandwagoning'. By contrast, between 1761 and 1799, Mysore under the new Islamic Sultanate that had replaced the Hindu Wodeyar dynasty (1399–1761) found itself embedded within a geopolitically competitive Indian multi-state system that shared certain similarities with that of its European counterpart. Nevertheless, there was a key factor that ultimately differentiated them. In Europe, states ganged up, or balanced against, a would-be-imperial power that sought to take over the European state system. The imperial aspirants, the Habsburgs and Napoleon Bonaparte (and much later on Adolf Hitler of course), failed because of this balancing mechanism. However, while such an outcome is in line with standard Waltzian

---

[96] Yazdani (2017: 118–20).

neorealist- and English School IR theory-logic,[97] neither of these theories can capture the situation that the Mysorean Sultanate confronted.

India at this time was in the process of being colonised by the English East India Company (EEIC). The EEIC had, of course, taken over Bengal after Robert Clive's victory at the Battle of Plassey in 1757. And, in 1765, the Company extracted taxes from Bengal in order to support its subsequent imperial-military campaigns in India. Kaveh Yazdani points out that

[f]rom the late 1760s up to the 1790s Mysore was Britain's greatest enemy in Asia and seriously threatened the Company's pursuit of colonial expansion. As a matter of fact, in the late eighteenth century, the Mysorean and Maratha armies were more or less on a par with their British counterparts on the ground, not in the least because they recruited a considerable number of European military experts, mercenaries and sepoys.[98]

Washbrook notes that Mysore (as well as the Peshwa's Maratha Confederacy and Ranjit Singh's Punjab) 'gave the English East India Company a real fright'.[99] And Pradeep Barua notes that the EEIC's campaigns against Mysore 'marked the start of a more deliberate or coordinated strategy towards empire in India. Here the British acted on a strategic long term goal to completely eliminate in India both French influence and potential Indian threats to their presence.'[100] Moreover, the fall of Mysore to the British in 1799 constituted 'one of the most important catalysts in launching the British East India Company ... decisively on the road to the total conquest of the Indian sub-continent'.[101] Furthermore, the clash between the EEIC and Mysore was ultimately a battle between two imperial aspirants, given that Tipu Sultan was keen to expand across the sub-continent.[102] And significantly, Mysore's army was likely the best in India, if not in Asia.[103] But the key point here is that both Waltzian neorealism and the English School of IR would predict that the constituent Indian states should have ganged up and balanced against the EEIC.

However, it turns out that the other powerful rulers in the region – the Nizam of Hyderabad, the Carnatic state and the Maratha Confederacy – ganged up against Mysore by siding actively with the British imperialists.

[97] Most notably, Waltz (1979), Mearsheimer (2001) and Bull (1977).
[98] Yazdani (2020: 37).
[99] Washbrook (2020: 138).
[100] Barua (2011: 27).
[101] Ibid. (22). See also Hasan (1971).
[102] Macdougall (2011: 299–300).
[103] Yazdani (2020).

The EEIC was also aided by the Bibi of Cannanore, the Rajas of Coorg, Cochin and Tanjore, some Malabar chiefs and the Nawab of Awadh. To these can be added a host of non-state actors including many *Banjāras* (long-distance traders within India), various merchants as well as numerous Mysorean *poligars* (local potentates) who had been alienated by the Sultans' – especially Tipu's – state-formation programme. Moreover, had Mysore, Hyderabad and the Marathas joined forces along with the combined navies of the Marathas and Sidis in order to balance against the EEIC, they would most likely have been able to defeat it.[104] In such an event, the full British take-over of India during the ensuing century would most likely have been stopped in its tracks, the profound consequences of which would have been not merely the continuation of the Mysorean sultanate after 1799 but also the maintenance of Indian autonomy and the absence of the Raj. Still, Mysore was hardly an innocent victim of its fellow Indian states' aggression given that Tipu Sultan's imperial ambitions did much to provoke them. And, moreover, alienating local Mysorean potentates also helped undermined his cause. Either way, though, it seems fair to conclude that the Indian state system operated differently to that of Europe's as well as that of the East and Southeast Asian multi-state system. In this respect, it bears something of a resemblance to China's ancient warring states system in which one state, the Qin, managed to take out the other six one by one to create a Qin-based 'empire', given that the other states failed to balance against it.

Of course, it might be replied that the balance of power mechanism did not so much 'fail' to cut in within the ancient Chinese Warring States system but that it was over-ridden by the dominant Qin state's 'divide and conquer' strategy.[105] By analogy, the same logic might be applied here in the case of the EEIC in late-eighteenth-century India. But the autonomous actions of the so-called Indian collaborators, who had their own axes to grind against the Mysorean sultans, especially Tipu Sultan, were particularly important, none of which can be explained away as but a function of Britain's supreme, imperial hyper-agency and power. For we should keep in mind David Washbrook's poignant point that

painful though it has been for a historiography heavily influenced by twentieth-century [Indian] nationalism to accept, there now seems preponderant evidence that the Company's achievement of state power in most of South Asia [including Mysore] was accomplished through, and on the back of, these groups, who not infrequently 'subverted' the regimes of their sometime rulers.... Colonialism

---

[104] Yazdani (2019: 8, 17).
[105] Hui (2005: ch. 2).

had a set of 'indigenous' origins [which were] no less part of the social history of capitalism than those deriving from Europe. In a certain sense, [British] colonialism was [as much] the logical outcome of South Asia's own history of … development [as it was of British initiative and agency].[106]

Indeed, the fact is that in the late-eighteenth century, if not throughout the nineteenth, the British were not sufficiently powerful to create an empire by themselves and had to rely on all manner of non-Western agents and Indian processes to achieve what otherwise would have been far beyond their grasp. Most ironically, it was their use of Indian troops (*sepoys*) together with expropriated Indian taxes that made up for the crucial deficit in British fiscal resources and military manpower that played such an important role in colonising India.[107] One final difference with the European state system is that Indian inter-state wars were, according to Yazdani, 'less pronounced than in Europe and arguably played a significant role in *retarding* similar military and socio-economic developments'.[108] For prior to the late-eighteenth century, these conflicts were based predominantly on light cavalry warfare.

However, the immediate point to establish here is that both of Mysore's sultans – Haidar 'Ali Khan Bahadur (r. 1761–82), and his successor son, Tipu Sultan Fath 'Ali Khan (r. 1782–99) – prioritised the need to prosecute warfare in order to defend themselves against the EEIC in the four Anglo-Mysore Wars (1767/9, 1780/4, 1790/2, 1798/9). To this end, they pursued many policies that were reminiscent of Britain's and were radically different from those of Qing China's – which is why adding Mysore into the mix enriches my comparative analysis.[109] But there were also many subtle differences that de-mystify these seemingly 'surprising resemblances'. The first task is to ascertain the intensity of Mysore's fiscal-militarism in relation to Britain's.

The Military-Expenditure Gap between Mysore and Britain

In Chapter 2, I explained how there was a colossal fiscal military-expenditure gap between Qing China and Britain during the eighteenth century, while I also explained earlier how this helped spur Britain's industrialisation of its iron and steel sectors as much as it *failed* to prompt a similar Chinese response. What then of the British–Mysore

---

[106] Washbrook (1988: 76).
[107] Roy (2011: 213–14).
[108] Yazdani (2019: 14), my emphasis.
[109] For details, see Yazdani (2017: 115–20).

comparison? Yazdani reckons that before 1792, Mysore's state revenues would not have exceeded £3 million p.a. (per annum) and might have been around £1 million p.a. in 1792/9.[110] I will assume that very roughly £2 million p.a. was spent on war in 1761/1792 and very approximately £0.6 million p.a. in 1792/9, which averages out at about £1.7 million p.a. for the whole period – notwithstanding the point that these are crude estimates given the paucity of available data. How does this compare with Britain in the 1761–99 period? As was the case in Chapter 2, here I make two calculations for British military expenditures: D1, which comprises ordinary and extraordinary military expenditures, and D2, which comprises D1 plus interest payments made on the national debt that were incurred for extraordinary military spending. For 1761–99, I calculate that British D1 spending was £11 million p.a. and D2 was £19 million. Which means that British D1 was over six times higher than Mysore's, while D2 was eleven times higher. Still, as I also explained in Chapter 2, we need to understand what per capita spending levels were in addition to ascertaining the comparative 'real' military burdens.

With respect to per capita spending, I note that the size of the British (as opposed to the English) population in this period was around ten million whereas, according to Yazdani, the Mysorean population was about six million.[111] Thus on a per capita basis, Mysorean military spending was about £0–30 while the British figure was about £1–10 (D1) and about £1–90 (D2). Seen in this light, British per capita spending was higher by approximately three or four times (D1) and six times (D2). While this is still a very significant gap, it is clearly far smaller than that between Britain and Qing China. Nevertheless, as I discussed in Chapter 2, the critical figure is the 'real' military burden, which comprises military spending as a percentage of national income. Unfortunately, however, national income data for Mysore do not exist in this period. Instead, I shall make a series of extremely crude back-of-the-envelope estimates to get some sort of sense of the military burden differential.

Various scholars claim that by the 1790s, Mysorean tax revenues comprised 40 per cent of gross output.[112] But there are two principal problems here. First, while I often see such figures quoted for the Mughal Empire, in addition to Mysore, these reflect the proportions that were extracted after 1945 by European states that had very much higher levels of infrastructural power – or bureaucratic power/reach – than were available to pre-modern states. And I remain highly suspicious

[110] Yazdani (2017: 227–9).
[111] Ibid. (118).
[112] See the discussion in Yazdani (2017: 228, and n. 487).

that such claims in the case of India are made by supporters of the Eurocentric Oriental despotic state thesis (though I concede that this is by no means always the case). Second, if this calculation of taxes as constituting around 40 per cent of output is correct, then this suggests that Mysore's total economic output comprised a mere £2.5 million in the 1790s. This is as implausibly low as much as the calculation of government revenues as a proportion of output is absurdly high. And so to my crude back-of-the-envelope guesstimates.

Angus Maddison's figures of national income, albeit extremely crude, tell us that total Indian national income in 1700 was eight times larger than Britain's and was three times higher in 1820. British national income in 1700 was about £50 million and by 1820 it stood at around £316 million. This suggests that Indian national output in 1700 was in the region of perhaps £400 million and was in the ballpark area of £950 million in 1820. The total Indian population around 1800 was about 200 million. Assuming that national income was spread evenly across India, though Mysore was one of the richer economies, and given that the latter had a population of around 6 million, so this apportions out at about £30 million of national output for Mysore in 1800.

Running with this extremely crude guesstimate suggests that Mysore's total tax burden in the 1790s was about 9 per cent of national income (rather than 40 per cent), while the real *military* burden was around 5 or 6 per cent of national income. This compares with the British real military burden of 10 per cent (D1) and 17 per cent (D2) for 1761–99. Even so, on these crude figures Mysore's military burden was significant – broadly equivalent to that of Tsarist Russia's (1860–1913), which comprised the highest burden in Europe at that time.[113] On this very crude reckoning, Mysore's military burden comprised around half that of Britain's D1 and around a third that of Britain's D2 burden. Which leads me to conclude that the British military burden was in all likelihood considerably higher than Mysore's, though I feel wholly confident in concluding that the differential was much smaller than that between Britain and Qing China.

Nevertheless, if we run with the notion that Mysore's military spending was pronounced, though not colossal as was Britain's, so this leads us into altogether different territory to that which I explored in the Qing–British comparison. Given that Mysore did not industrialise, so this means that high military expenditures are clearly not in themselves a cause of industrial modernisation. What matters most are the policies

[113] Hobson (1993).

and activities that accompany such spending, as I argued in Chapter 9. Here, my point is that British state policies and its 'embedded autonomy' posture vis-à-vis capitalists and capitalism was an important factor in enabling British industrialisation. By contrast, Mysore's autocratic 'disembedded state autonomy' posture and its overly top-down policies proved to be far less propitious for industrialisation, even though they aided historical capitalism to a certain extent.

Differing Modes of State Intervention: Mysorean 'Autocratic-Patrimonial Disembedded State Autonomy' versus British State 'Embedded Autonomy'

In certain respects, Haidar 'Ali and Tipu Sultan implemented state-centralisation strategies that were reminiscent of those that were undertaken in Europe. As Yazdani puts it, 'it was Haidar 'Ali who seriously tackled and Tipu Sultan who accelerated the process of subduing, removing, disarming, expelling and confiscating local potentates and hereditary intermediaries such as *deshmukhs*, *poligars*, *gaudas* or *patels* to collect taxes directly from the peasants via [central] government functionaries'.[114] Nevertheless, under Haidar 'Ali, this did not constitute a total assault on those potentates (which approximated with their European noble counterparts), given that only those who resisted his centralising powers and requests for higher funds were extirpated. It was Tipu Sultan who sought to destroy this intermediate layer of societal interests and replace them with central-state tax officials.[115] To this end, *poligars* and *zamindars* were decimated and hereditary title was terminated as their roles were superseded by central-state functionaries. Even so, some *poligar*s resisted this assault and they took their final revenge on Tipu when they sided with the British in the fourth and final Anglo–Mysore War which culminated both in his death in 1799 and the subsequent British imperial take-over of Mysore.[116]

All of which marked a radical departure in the history of state-formation within South India wherein Mysore moved onto the path of 'military fiscalism' that was also unfolding within Europe.[117] This marked a reversal of the previous centrifugal forces in favour of centripetal state-formation in a manner that at first sight appears similar to the European

---

[114] Yazdani (2017: 138–9).
[115] Washbrook (1988: 69) and Stein (1985: 401–2).
[116] Yazdani (2017).
[117] Stein (1985: 392–3, 401, 411).

situation that was so brilliantly analysed by Norbert Elias.[118] Moreover, as in Europe, this process was undertaken in order to extract higher revenues for military spending. And this, in turn, suggests that a key prerequisite of capitalist modernisation was in place in Mysore. Finally, it is also noteworthy that Mysore was likely the first Indian state to establish a standing army along European lines, as much as the state emphasised the importance of drilling the infantry as well as equipping them with flintlock rifles, as was also occurring under European modernisation.[119]

But the surprising resemblances, important though some of them were, obscure some equally surprising differences. For the process of Mysorean Sultanate state-formation was nested within a specific mode of top-down, coercive state interventionism that characterised state–economy relations and the process of political centralisation. Of course, as I explained in detail in Chapters 9 and 10, the standard notion that Britain industrialised through a minimalist night-watchman laissez-faire state, which would point up immediate differences with Mysore, is belied by my claim that the British state was heavily interventionist in manifold ways, thereby suggesting 'convergent processes' and 'surprising resemblances' with Mysore. However, it is important to understand that modes of state interventionism vary and that British state interventionism was very different to that of Mysore. I argue that the interventionist British state pursued a strategy of 'embedded autonomy' which, in essence, worked with and through both the capitalist and aristocratic classes.[120] That is, while the British state usurped the local fiscal, military and political power base of the feudal nobles and aristocrats, nevertheless it sought to accommodate their interests for fear of alienating them. By contrast, Tipu, in particular, pursued a reckless autocratic-patrimonial strategy of top-down coercive-disembedded state autonomy that often worked against merchant and 'aristocratic' social interests. And, with little or no compensating social-accommodationist strategy in place so he ended up alienating many of these economic interest groups and socio-political intermediaries, which would later blow back in his face and fatally at that, as I noted earlier. The autocratic nature of the state is well reflected by what Yazdani refers to as Tipu's 'state of terror' that was established to control society. As he explains, Tipu ordered the placement of 'spies throughout the whole fort and town, in the bazaar

---

[118] Elias (1939/1994). And see the equally brilliant analysis in Linklater (2016).
[119] Yazdani (2017: 242, 248).
[120] For such a discussion of the British state's embedded autonomy in historical context, see Weiss and Hobson (1995: chs. 2–4). For the British state's continuing strong relationship with the aristocracy, see especially Haldén (2020).

and over the houses of the principal officers and thus gain intelligence
of every person who goes to the dwelling of another and of what people
say'.[121]

It is certainly true that the notion of a *pre-modern* autocratic state,
as much as a pre-modern Oriental despotism, is based more on fiction
than fact – as was suggested above concerning the level of taxes as a
proportion of economic output that the Sultanate extracted. But as
David Washbrook notes,

[p]art of the development of [Mysorean] 'military fiscalism' involved rulers
laying 'Sultanist' claims to the possession of all resources in their domains
and, while they could rarely realize an administrative control over resources
held in their name by scions of the new classes, they could occasionally resume
or confiscate them. Particularly in the context of military crises, merchant
capital and erstwhile 'personal' wealth not infrequently found itself at risk of
confiscation.[122]

This, then, marks a core difference between the British and Mysorean
states, with the paradox being that the British state's embedded autonomy
posture reflected a much stronger mode of state power that turned out to
be economically, fiscally and militarily more effective than Mysore's top-
down autocratic mode of state power. How, then, did this play out in the
economic realm in general and in the iron and steel sectors in particular?

Mercantilist State-Formation and the 'Over-the-Top-Down' Regulation of the Mysorean Economy

In classic mercantilist style, Haidar 'Ali and Tipu Sultan sought to
develop the economy and the state through an intertwined process. The
development of the iron and steel industry in particular, together with the
creation of a centralised state bureaucracy, were undertaken ultimately
to enhance the military capacity of the state. This particular form of
state intervention was codified in a document entitled 'the Mysorean
Revenue Regulations'. At first blush, this suggests yet another 'surprising
resemblance' between Britain and Mysore, which appears to dovetail
with the classic theory of mercantilism that is usually thought to apply to
the European context after 1685. Moreover, while both were mercantilist
states, nevertheless, both sought to promote trading relations abroad (as I
explained in earlier chapters, viz. Britain). Thus, the Sultans established

[121] Yazdani (2017: 225).
[122] Washbrook (1988: 75).

some thirty trading houses (*Kothis*) within Mysore as well as setting up some in foreign countries, including in the Persian Gulf (Muscat, Hormuz and Jeddah), in addition to creating various *Kothis* within India such as in Kachchh. Under the Mysorean Sultanate, the economy was subordinated completely to the immediate military demands of the state and, above all, the state undertook a nationalisation programme that differed profoundly to the British mercantilist approach.[123] Of course, it is certainly true that the British state also utilised the economy to enhance its (imperial) fiscal-military power base (as I argued in Chapter 9). But this superficial similarity elides the point that the British state nurtured the economy and allowed considerable autonomy for private capitalist interests rather than seeking to control or by-pass them directly through *Etatization* and nationalisation.[124] In short, owning the means of production was simply not part of the British state's repertoire of interventionism.

In Chapter 9, I highlighted, *inter alia*, the importance of the Bank of England in the state–war–economy nexus. Tipu also set up a central bank while bankers from Gujarat moved into Mysore to carry on their financial activities there. And finance was also procured for trade and investment through temples, as I noted in Part I of this book. However, while from 1694, the British state organised a massive loan-programme through the Bank of England that also brought the City of London into play so as to finance its imperial wars, Mysore had no public debt to draw upon. It seems that Mysore's central bank was designed to principally help the poor and possibly provide, albeit limited, investment capital for merchants, though we know too little to say any more about this.[125] What we can say, however, is that the Mysorean central bank fell prey to overly statist mercantilist logic in that 'the venture contradicted the capitalist logic of banking and capital accumulation [such that] it had little to do with a central bank in the true sense of the term and is therefore a rather misleading denomination'.[126] This significant comparison aptly reflects these differing modes of state intervention and their relationship to the economy.

Although Mysorean state intervention was designed to control the economy in order to enhance its military power base primarily to fight the EEIC, an important paradox emerges here in that such a strategy

[123] Yazdani (2017, 2019, 2020).
[124] Weiss and Hobson (1995).
[125] I am grateful to Kaveh Yazdani for this information in private correspondence (13/9/2019).
[126] Yazdani (2017: 182).

unleashed a kind of 'push-me-pull-you' process. Thus, state intervention nurtured but simultaneously undermined economic development. The most obvious example of this economically contradictory process lay in Tipu's strategy of cutting off supply lines to the EEIC, which entailed the wholesale ravaging of large swathes of the country, from Belur to Seringapatam, through a scorched-earth policy.[127] Moreover, in deploying his navy to blockade the British, Tipu prohibited the export of numerous products for fear that they would end up in British hands. Similarly, he blocked merchant exports to parts of India, again so as to prevent them from getting into the hands of the EEIC. And, last but not least, Tipu attempted to restrict his own local merchants by establishing state monopolies, again in order to restrict those merchants who traded with the British enemy. As Tipu himself explained: 'I prohibited the export of linen from my states by the Carnatic route because I know that the English are doing considerable business with it and I do not want to contribute to their profits.'[128] In pursuing this line of thinking he sought to become the country's 'principal merchant' in addition to his desire to increase profits to feed the military machine.[129] All of which served to undermine the organic development of an indigenous and autonomous merchant class. For the twin paradox of all this was not simply the reduction of economic gains within Mysore that served to hinder modernisation, but equally that it was a partial factor that enticed the British to invade Mysore.

This economic monopolisation strategy was schizoid or internally contradictory in various other ways. While Tipu's key economic concern was to develop the iron and steel sectors in order to supply his weapons industry, the latter was governed by a nationalisation programme. Before 1792, he established ten state-owned weapons factories (*Karkhanas*), though these were reduced to seven following his defeat in the Third Anglo–Mysore War in 1792.[130] The 'Regulations' stipulated the priority that Tipu placed on the development of the iron and steel industry for the purpose of making weapons including cannon, firearms and rockets – with the latter being a technology that Mysore excelled in, so much so that Sir William Congreve used them as a model to develop British rockets between 1801 and 1805.[131] But how was weapons production carried out?

[127] Ibid. (172–3).
[128] Tipu cited in Yazdani (2017: 177).
[129] Ibid., 170–84.
[130] Yazdani (2020: 23).
[131] Roy (2005) and Yazdani (2017: 251–4, 2020).

Yazdani describes the social relations of production as caught up within a 'transitional' economic mode, in that it combined semi-industrial and pre-industrial elements. While very little is known about the social relations of production within the state-owned *Karkhanas*, nevertheless it seems likely that day-wage labourers were employed on a significant basis.[132] And, as I noted in Chapter 11, there were many such labourers in India who were available to work in factories. Tipu also utilised forced labour in the guise of European artisans within these *Karkhanas*, often having been caught as prisoners of war. Finally, despite the sophistication of some of the technologies of weapons production, the fact is that these remained in a pre-industrial stage. This is perhaps no more clearly illustrated than in what was the most sophisticated technological tool of weapons production – a boring machine that bore 130 musket barrels simultaneously – given that it was powered not by steam or water but by two bullocks.[133]

The iron and steel sector was, however, dominated by privately owned forges.[134] These might be thought of as proto-industrial, though it is unlikely that such forges were on a path into modernity. They employed wage labour, but the workers did not meet the strict, fundamentalist Marxist criterion of 'free-wage labour' since they still relied on agricultural employment. However, as I explained in Chapter 8, I do not view free-wage labour as the sole defining criterion of either capitalist social relations of production or modern capitalism *per se*. Moreover, somewhere between 66 and 80 per cent of the profits that were gained through the exploitation of wage labour went directly into the pockets of the entrepreneurs, which is suggestive of a modernising capitalist component. However, while Yazdani describes this as a 'transitional' mode of production given that profits were not reinvested in fixed capital,[135] perhaps a better label would be 'intermediate'. For it is my view that Mysore was not on a spontaneous path into industrial modernity but was lodged within historical capitalism. This was in part because there was no technological accumulation process in play. But, in addition, it is especially noteworthy that wrought iron rather than cast iron was produced in Mysore, owing in part to the nature of the furnaces. And here the key issue revolves around the question as to why the furnaces were insufficient to stimulate an industrialisation drive in iron and steel.

---

[132] I thank Kaveh Yazdani for this information in private correspondence (13/9/2019).
[133] Yazdani (2020: 24).
[134] Yazdani (2017: 212).
[135] I am grateful to Kaveh Yazdani for advice on these matters.

Ecological Limits to a Mysorean (or Indian) Iron and Steel Industrialisation

As I noted in Chapter 10, although the quality of Indian (wootz) steel was well in advance of Europe's in this period and remained so well into the nineteenth century,[136] nevertheless, Indian iron technologies of production lagged behind those of Britain from as early as the sixteenth century. Eugenia Vanina claims that the Indian blast furnaces were similar to the old medieval European *stückofen*,[137] though the more exceptional *Kathiawar* furnace found in Northwest India was more like the later European reverbatory furnace, even if this might well have been an imported borrowing.[138] Still, the importance of this furnace should not be overplayed, for as Yazdani points out, the *Kathiawar* furnace produced only around 17 tons per annum and, moreover, the total number of such furnaces in India/South Asia produced in the region of a paltry 100 tons per annum.[139] The most important problem lay in the point that Indian furnaces used charcoal rather than coal as an energy source. For this single fact plays a very important role in explaining why India in general and Mysore in particular did not, and indeed were most unlikely to, undergo an iron and steel industrialisation. A further complementary problem lay in the fact that the Indians did not deploy fluxes, unlike the Chinese and British, so that a great deal of iron was wasted in the furnace.

Following Pomeranz, I noted earlier how iron and steel production in southern China in the post-1400 period was constrained by poor access to coal. For the major coal deposits were located in the north, while southern coal mines were insufficient to generate significant amounts of fuel to power the dominant southern blast furnaces on an industrialised basis. Much the same problem blighted the Mysorean iron and steel sector. For Mysore, located in the south-west, was far away from the coal deposits in the north-east in Bengal.[140] But there was a further problem here. For while some of it was fairly high grade, particularly that which was sourced from Burdwan (130 miles from Calcutta in Bengal),[141] the fact is that much of India's coal suffered numerous defects such that it was incapable of supporting a generalised indigenous iron

---

[136] Indeed, not only was cast steel produced in Mysore but it is likely that this was copied by the British steel expert, David Mushet, as I suggested in Chapter 10.

[137] Vanina (2004: 44–5)

[138] Biswas (1999: 296).

[139] Yazdani (2017: 471)

[140] Cf. Roy (2012: 194).

[141] Parthasarathi (2011: 231).

and steel industrial revolution.[142] This was complemented by the fact that abundant wood supplies in Mysore meant that the quest for coal as an energy source was not pursued in any serious way, notwithstanding Tipu's abortive attempt to obtain samples of coal from the Ottoman Empire and to harness coal for iron and steel production.[143] In any case, Indian furnaces were insufficient to use coke or coal, not least because they did not use a mechanised bellows system.[144]

Certainly, it wasn't that the Indians were incapable of producing high-quality iron and steel. For as I explained in Chapter 10, Europeans were highly impressed by its quality, especially that of wootz steel, which had become famous throughout the world from as early as the second half of the first millennium CE. The problem, however, is that without coal, a full industrialisation is not possible. Moreover, the less-effective charcoal fuel had become very expensive in India during the nineteenth century, not least because of the very high costs of transporting it, thereby leading to a considerably less competitive product relative to British iron.[145] And this, in aggregate, constrained iron production in the nineteenth century when the shortage of wood hit home. For the deployment of coal or coke together with mechanised bellows that fuelled iron and steel production in Britain, as well as in Ancient China before the Ming dynasty, did not spontaneously emerge across India and, accordingly, its furnaces remained small with overall output levels remaining extremely low by modern standards.

Evidence for all this is borne out by the point that Mysorean iron forges produced between 5 and 8.5 tons per annum, which compared with 350–400 tons for an average British blast furnace as early as 1603.[146] As I noted in Chapter 10, there were perhaps 10,000 furnaces throughout India in the late-eighteenth century that produced at most some 200,000 tons (of iron and steel combined).[147] This approximated with the level of British pig-iron output in 1800. But the 'second great divergence' in iron production emerges in the 1820s and takes off thereafter. By 1850, Britain pumped out ten times the amount of iron produced in the whole of India and by 1885 British output exceeded eight million

---

[142] Singh (2006: 366–75).

[143] Parthasarathi (2011: 208) and Yazdani (2017: 290–1).

[144] Biswas (1999: 298–300). Still, Biswas also notes that mechanised bellows were used in the far north-western part of the sub-continent on the border with China, so it remains a perplexing conundrum as to why these were not universalised.

[145] Roy (2009).

[146] Ibid., and Yazdani (2017: 197).

[147] Biswas (1999: 301).

tons.[148] Strikingly, this latter figure comprised some forty times that of total Indian output in 1850 – though this *understates* the gap in 1885 given that Indian iron and steel production declined in the nineteenth century. Moreover, in the late-eighteenth century, Mysore produced between 4,500 tons and 7,200 tons,[149] which comprised at most 4 per cent of British output in 1800 and a mere 0.1 per cent of British output in 1885. Given that Mysore was roughly the same size as Britain before 1792 and was roughly equivalent to the size of England between 1793 and 1799, so these output differentials are all the more striking. All in all, as Arun Biswas argues,

the Indian persistence of charcoal furnaces, the non-use of mineral fuels, the non-use of flux, the non-availability of mechanized bellows, and the non-development of high-grade refractories represented different aspect of a complex phenomenon resulting in stagnation and atrophy of [the Indian iron and steel sector during the nineteenth century].[150]

And here I note that the later British imperial policies of 'malign neglect' and 'containment' served merely to add insult to injury (as I explain in Chapter 13).

Socio-epistemic Limits to the Industrialisation of the Iron and Steel Sectors

When comparing Britain and Mysore, 'the great gap', Yazdani argues, 'was in the fields of mechanical engineering, coal mining, and Newtonian science'.[151] These 'knowledge deficits' in India were especially unfortunate given that they were important pre-requisites for Britain's iron and steel industrialisation. Indeed, in Chapter 12, I emphasised the importance of the rise of a 'mechanical outlook' within Britain that developed rapidly in the post-1700 period at the very time that China's millennial, if not two millennial, lead in this regard tailed off. Equally of importance was the role of 'circulating knowledge' in Britain, which was promoted by printed works and all manner of societies such as the Lunar Society and, of course, the Royal Society. This environment enabled the exchange of ideas that generated reciprocal and diffuse knowledge from which many people could benefit, much as I suspect did the influx of

---

[148] Deane and Cole (1969: 225).
[149] Yazdani (2020: 20).
[150] Biswas (1999: 299).
[151] Yazdani (2019: 14–15).

pamphlets and books on Indian and Chinese production processes (as I explained in Chapter 10).

Yazdani insists that no such organisations existed in India, which included the non-existence of institutions of higher learning and the absence of the printing press – despite Tipu's efforts to introduce it – though there was a limited degree of circulation of useful knowledge.[152] Certainly, he is rightly at pains to point out that India was not 'lacking' in advanced knowledge more generally, for it had long led the world in mathematics, for example, many centuries before Europe finally caught up.[153] A different view, however, is advanced by Prasannan Parthasarathi, who argues that there was an exchange of sophisticated knowledge in India and that Europe was not unique in this respect.[154] But the key issue at stake concerns the exchange of advanced technological ideas as well as scientific ideas, coupled with sophisticated knowledge of engineering, all of which helped promote the industrialisation of the iron and steel sectors in Britain. And it seems that in this particular respect, Britain was far more richly endowed than was India. So where does this all leave us regarding the prospects of Mysorean industrialisation?

Ultimately, Asok Sen might well be close to the truth when he argues that Tipu's heavily regulationist and overly top-down control of the economy served to scupper the long-term potential of the economy to move into industrial modernity.[155] Nevertheless, Yazdani argues that given the premature termination of Mysorean autonomy at the hands of the imperial EEIC in 1799, it is impossible to rule out some kind of a transition had the EEIC never intervened. Moreover, he takes issue with Kate Brittlebank's denunciation of Tipu as but a voice of 'premodern tradition'.[156] While overall it seems fair to say that Tipu was not a moderniser in the pure sense, nevertheless some of his policies such as his army and state bureaucratic reforms certainly had some modernising elements. And the social relations of production in the iron forges and in the weapons factories contained elements of modern capitalism. Here, I concur with Yazdani's conclusion that Tipu's efforts can neither 'be exclusively understood in terms of tradition nor do they reflect the minds of modern rulers. They manifest a historical juncture that was neither dominantly traditional nor modern, but resided in a transitory phase'[157] or what I have called an 'intermediate' phase. For I

[152] Ibid. (15–16, 2017: 279–85).
[153] Joseph (1992), Bala (2006) and Raju (2007).
[154] Parthasarathi (2011: 213–19).
[155] Sen (1977: 95).
[156] Brittlebank (1982).
[157] Yazdani (2017: 287).

believe that ultimately, this 'intermediate historical capitalist' phase had no modern industrial telos driving it. Thus, for reasons that I explained in Chapter 10, Indian producers and merchants were historical capitalist optimisers who saw no need for fully mechanised production. In sum, then, I conclude that Mysore was certainly not an Oriental despotism and nor was it a traditional state, for it brought in all manner of modernising reforms, even if ultimately these were insufficient to enable a *spontaneous* South Indian industrialisation of the iron and steel sectors.

Conclusion

Here, I want to conclude this and Chapter 12 together. I have argued that neither India nor China was on a path that would culminate with industrialisation. All of which returns us to the thorny Eurocentric proposition that only in Britain were there sufficiently rational institutions to propel the economy over the line into modern-capitalist industrialisation, which leads to the conclusion that Britain was a success story as much as India and China were failures. But this framing is problematic for its exclusively internalist ontology that focuses *only* on the British logic of immanence and internal Asian blockages. The California School seeks to transcend this generic Eurocentric conception of the 'great rationality divide' by focusing instead on the 'surprising resemblances' between Europe and the leading Asian economies and emphasising contingencies or changes in the global economy as the core causal variables. But black-boxing social domestic properties in this way, it seems to me, is to bend the ontological stick too far in the opposite direction, thereby leaving us with no way of providing a proper *explanation* of why only Britain industrialised.

Thus, although I have specified numerous and significant 'surprising resemblances', nevertheless I have also focused on some 'surprising differences'. One clear difference lay with the nature of the state, wherein Britain's interventionist mode of 'embedded state autonomy' resided mid-point along a continuum, where at one extreme stood the overly laissez-faire Qing state (notwithstanding those times when it intervened to overcome market failures), while at the other lay Mysore's overly top-down interventionist posture. Moreover, unlike in Britain, the harnessing of mechanised technologies to cotton and iron/steel production was not undertaken in either China or India. And there were also differences regarding the circulation of useful knowledge and a mechanistic worldview. But, by the same token, focusing *only* on internal differences returns us into the Eurocentric *cul-de-sac*, as many of the California School scholars would argue. Invoking my complex conception of a 'developmental architecture', I have argued that domestic properties were also shaped to an extent by global-economic and international-geopolitical processes. Neither Indian nor Chinese entrepreneurs and merchant capitalists saw any need to centralise cotton textile production within concentrated factories that deployed labour-substituting mechanised spinning and weaving technologies. For the fact is that China and India led the global economy in terms of cotton textile production output. By contrast, confronting the challenge of uneven and combined development meant that British cotton textile producers could not hope to compete with China's production levels and India's dominance of global cotton textile markets without initiating modern-capitalist forces and relations of production.

Similarly, one important factor that led to the second great divergence in iron and steel production lay with Britain's geopolitical-imperialism which, in such an intensely geopolitically competitive European multi-state system, helped prompt the drive into an iron/steel industrialisation. By contrast, although China developed an empire, it faced no imperialist competitors in East/Southeast Asia and the majority of conflicts that it did engage in did not require an intensive development of iron weapons after 1368. And nor did the Qing gain economically from its empire. Mysore, by contrast, faced the strong imperial-military threat of the EEIC in the context of an Indian multi-state system – one in which the 'balance of power mechanism' failed to cut it in on Mysore's behalf. And nor did the Sultanate's economic policies promote the development of mechanised iron and steel production, not to mention the point that its policies stifled the indigenous merchant class and the private sphere of the economy more generally. Accordingly, no *spontaneous* industrialisation occurred and nor was it likely to have, even in the absence of the British imperial challenge. And, unlike Britain, Mysore had no colonies from which it could derive economic benefits. Finally, I have argued that Mysore's and China's lack of access to sufficient amounts of high-quality, cheap coal constituted a clear limitation to a potential iron/steel industrialisation, much as Chinese and Indian raw cotton was too weak to enable a robust cotton-based industrialisation.

Thus, while there were important *domestic* differences that need to be considered when explaining the second great divergence in which industrial Britain overtook historical capitalist China and India, we also need to factor in the different geo-economic, geopolitical and imperial contexts. While I have considered the EEIC's role in undermining Mysore by 1800, one of the key questions now at hand is whether British imperialism crushed the economic lifeblood out of the Indian sub-continent during the nineteenth century.

Part V

Rehabilitating and Provincialising Western Imperialism: Afro-Asians inside and outside the Shadow of Empire

13 Multicultural Origins of the Second (Modern Capitalist) Global Economy
Unveiling the 'Multicultural Contact Zone', c. 1850–c. 1940

Introduction

By the mid-nineteenth century, the industrialisation of the cotton sector enabled Britain to finally wrest structural power away from India's cotton producers and merchant capitalists. For by then, Lancashire had superseded India's domination of global cotton textile markets. As I explained in Chapter 10, Indian merchant capitalists' creation of markets throughout Afro-Asia before and during the first global economy (FGE) turned out to be a boon for the British. For they were spared the massive task of setting them up in the first place and were able to muscle their way in simply by undercutting Indian exports through their cheaper Indian imitations that were machine made in Lancashire. And, having established their formal empire in India in 1858, Britain's newly won structural economic power was converted into imperial power through which they sought to press home their advantage not only in India but across the non-Western world. This wider process, of course, comprised both formal and informal imperialism, where the latter was based on the imposition of 'unequal (trade) treaties'. And, more generally, the creation of modern industrial capitalism in Britain and subsequently in Europe was clearly a very important factor in the transition from the first to the second global economy (SGE). Moreover, the polycentric nature of the FGE that had been underwritten by Indian global structural power was transformed into a hierarchical formation in the SGE, with European empires standing atop and the non-Western polities strewn out below them.

My purpose in this chapter is not to undermine the point that the European empires became dominant in the nineteenth century in Afro-Asia and nor is it to deny the point that they did much harm to many non-Western economies and peoples. Certainly, we need to rehabilitate the dark side of the British Empire in the face of Eurocentric apologies and implausible rationalisations of it as a benign civilising mission. However, to an extent we also need to provincialise empire in the face

395

of Eurofetishism's portrayal of the imperial expansion of the West as a 'totalising project' that exorcises the spirit of non-Western agency *tout court* and thereby (re)presents non-Western peoples and societies as but helpless and passive victims. For the deployment of Western imperial power through coercion and exploitation constitutes the potent outer layer of a large onion, the deeper layers of which form the hidden dimensions of entangled Afro-Eurasian synergistic agencies and humdrum non-Western everyday acts, which existed throughout the nineteenth and into the twentieth century. While significant amounts have, of course, been written on Western imperialism, nevertheless, the problem is that the inner layers have been obscured by the pungence of the debate that surrounds the outer layer. For, although well meaning, nevertheless portraying the Indian people as helpless and largely devoid of agency means that Eurofetishist and Indian nationalist accounts run the very real risk of *naturalising* the British Empire and underestimating Indian resilience. Thus, the paradox here is that revealing these deeper layers of Indian agency while simultaneously provincialising Western empire serves to de-naturalise British imperialism.

Here, we confront the paradox of the emergence of the SGE during the nineteenth century. For, on the one hand, the emerging dominance of the West in Afro-Asia saw the creation of a thicker and more coercive imperial global whip of modern capitalist necessity that simultaneously witnessed the ramping up of global inequality. But, on the other hand, Eurofetishism obscures the many agential roles that were performed by the Omani Arabs and, most especially, by the Indians and Chinese in the making of the SGE. And, moreover, the Western expansionist thrust turned out to be far more uneven than either Eurocentrism or Eurofetishism recognises. Notable too is the more general point that the rise of the SGE in the nineteenth century followed and was made possible by the FGE which also witnessed many instantiations of non-Western agency that combined with Western agency. Above all, without such non-Western agency it is possible that not only might the imperial West have struggled to expand across much of Afro-Asia during the nineteenth century but, equally, that the rise of the SGE may not have been a foregone conclusion.

The argument develops through three sections. In the section 'British Imperialism and the "Discontinuous Continuity" of Indian and Chinese Cotton Textile Production', I qualify the Eurofetishist 'de-industrialisation thesis' by revealing how in the critical area of cotton textile production, Indian and Chinese artisans exhibited continuing agency and considerable resilience such that they were able to maintain their production output in the face of British imports and imperial policy. The sections 'The "Multicultural Contact Zone": Entangled Agential Relations in the Making of Western Empire and the SGE' and 'The Emergence of the SGE as the Symbiotic Convergence of the European CWE and the Asian Bazaar System' advance the theme of entwined non-Western and Western agencies by revealing the various Asian 'push *and* pull factors' that need to be considered alongside the Western-generated 'push processes', all of which crystallised in what I shall call the 'multicultural contact zone' within which the SGE was produced.

British Imperialism and the 'Discontinuous Continuity' of Indian and Chinese Cotton Textile Production

Here, I turn to consider the well-known Eurofetishist and Indian nationalist argument, which asserts that China and India were *de-industrialised* through unfair means via British imperial policy. Overall, the de-industrialisation thesis covers numerous sectors of these non-Western economies, though the iron/steel and cotton textiles (CTs) constituted the stand-outs. My argument is that the thesis needs both refinement and some considerable qualification in the context of Indian and Chinese cotton textile (ICT) production in particular. That is, the thesis tends to overstate the power of the British imperialists as much as it understates the agency and resilience of the Indian and Chinese cotton textile producers. Or, put differently, despite all of the damage that the British undeniably caused, nevertheless we should not conflate their *desire* to bring Indian and Chinese textile producers to heel with the *reality* of the outcomes on the ground. However, I want to preface what follows by considering very briefly the Eurofetishist and Indian nationalist claim that British imperialism de-industrialised the Indian iron and steel industry.

As I explained in Chapter 10, the 'first great divergence' in iron and steel production occurred very roughly between 500 BCE and 500 CE when India and China came to lead the world. Thus, the question becomes: Was the *second* great divergence in iron and steel production, wherein British output levels came to dwarf those of India and China during the nineteenth century, achieved through the imperial de-industrialisation of these Asian industries?[1] That is, was this divergence achieved through unfair imperial means? My argument is that during the nineteenth century, though not before, the British implemented a dual-colonial strategy of

---

[1] For example, Tharoor (2017: 32–5).

'malign neglect' and 'containment' with respect to the Indian iron and steel industries. The first strategy was less the result of *coercive* imperial policies and more a 'strategy of buying British'. In Chapter 9, I explained that Britain's imperial militarism stimulated the industrialisation of her iron and steel sectors. But because the building up of the Indian army in the nineteenth century was achieved by importing British iron and steel weapons, so this served to advance British industrialisation at the cost of a potential Indian iron and steel industrialisation. Precisely, the same logic applied to the massive Indian railway-building programme, where British metal was imported to supply the rails.[2] One can only imagine the boon that such demand could have imparted for India's iron and steel sector were it not for this imperial strategy.

The 'imperial containment' strategy was the flip side of 'malign neglect', wherein the British ensured that permission to set up factory production sites in India, as well as granting financial assistance to iron and steel entrepreneurs, went to Britons rather than Indians. Of the many examples that could be produced here, Arun Biswas reports the case in which '[t]he proposal of Mr Inder Narain Sharma for large-scale production of iron in Birbhum in 1774 was turned down, whereas a few British entrepreneurs were granted the necessary permissions'.[3] Indeed, hostile or biased British imperial state policy did much to prevent a potential Indian iron and steel revolution from emerging in the nineteenth century. But while there is much truth in the de-industrialisation thesis in this specific context, nevertheless it needs qualifying. For although British imperialism caused all manner of problems and imparted no benefits at all, as I argued in detail in Chapter 12, it seems most unlikely that either Mysore in particular or India more generally was on a path into a spontaneous iron and steel industrialisation, even had the English East India Company (EEIC) been absent. What then of the all-important ICT industry?

The Indian nationalist and Eurofetishist position on the impact of British CT exports to India (and China) is aptly summed up by Karl Marx, in unlikely cahoots with Lord Bentinck: 'the English cotton machinery produced an acute effect in India. The Governor General [Lord Bentinck] reported 1834–35: "The misery hardly finds a parallel in the history of commerce. The bones of the cotton-weavers are bleaching the plains of India."'[4] In this vision, the cruel and terminal fate of the Indian handloom weaver was sealed by the teleology of Western

[2] Parthasarathi (2011: 251–8).
[3] Biswas (1999: 301).
[4] Marx (1867/1954: 406).

industrial capitalism, delivered through the perfidious and brutal hand of the British Empire. Reflecting the logic of the de-industrialisation thesis, Shashi Tharoor in his important recent book *Inglorious Empire* sets up a zero-sum game approach wherein any arguments that dent the British 'fatal impact' thesis are presumed to be mere apologies for empire. But we do not need to 'let the British off the moral hook' to query some of these critical claims.

My argument is that despite the various recidivist, imperial-retardive and economic containment efforts made by the British to *destroy* the ICT sector these, nevertheless, failed. Two of the principal reasons for this failure lay first of all in the point that there were simply far too many cotton textile producers that were too widely dispersed (as was also the case in China), such that they were able to escape through the interstices of Britain's clumsy imperial net. And second, such producers were far more resilient than the Eurofetishists have recognised. By contrast, the British imperial policy of 'containment/malign neglect' vis-à-vis the Indian iron and steel industries was made possible because aspiring Indian entrepreneurs had no choice but to gain permission directly from the Raj to set up a factory.

More generally, none of what follows is intended to whitewash the many cruel and economically damaging depradations that the British Raj inflicted on India, some of which I touch upon later. My point is simply that Eurofetishism's zero-sum conception is problematic for its whitewashing of the many entangled Western and non-Western agential relations that not only made the Raj possible in the first place but that also allowed the Indians to counter many of its specific negative effects in the ICT sector. Relevant here is Rhoads Murphey's reference to the story that someone related who was interviewing rural Indians in the 1950s. The interviewer asked '"[d]o you think things are better for you now, or were they better under the British"' to which a frequent, though not majority, reply was '"Who are the British"?'[5] But by the same token, none of this is to embrace some kind of liberal-voluntaristic conception of Indian agency in which artisans could do simply as they pleased. For the fact is that they operated under certain conditions of constraint that were laid down by British imperial policy.

Certainly, imperialism gave the British an unfair advantage in one particular respect vis-à-vis the ICT sector. For at the very time that British imports were beginning to flood into India in the 1850s, the British Raj ensured that India's external tariffs were maintained at

---

[5] Murphey (1977: 27).

roughly 5 per cent *ad valorem* (1859–82). Moreover, at the very peak of British imports in the 1880s, tariffs were lowered to zero (1882–94). And even after 1894, tariffs on cotton imports were kept at extremely low levels while Indian producers were punished with an excise tax.[6] The racist double standard here is that while the British had erected very high tariff walls around their home market to block out ICT imports in their critical industrialisation phase during the eighteenth century, thereby enabling their infant cotton industry the space to develop, nevertheless the very same privilege was denied to India in the late-nineteenth century at precisely the time when British CT imports were flooding in. All of which was very much in tune with what Friedrich List originally referred to as the (imperial) free trading strategy in which the leading state 'kicks away the ladder by which he has climbed up'.[7]

Critically, as I explain later, had India been able to limit or prohibit the importation of British yarn and textiles in the second half of the nineteenth century, then the ICT sector might have expanded considerably. However, this is a very different point to the claim made by Indian nationalists and Eurofetishists, who insist that British imperial policy undermined and broke the ICT industry through the imposition of free(r) trade on CT imports into India. The question, then, is whether Romesh Dutt is right to conclude that '[i]n India the Manufacturing Power of the people was stamped out by protection against her industries [in eighteenth-century Britain], and then free trade was forced on her [in the late-nineteenth century] so as to prevent a revival'?[8]

The (Discontinuous) Continuity of Indian Handloom Weaving

Trade data on the ICT sector for the nineteenth century are often presented in order to reveal the massive displacement of Indian domestic production as the trickle of British imports turned into a tsunami after 1850. Jeffrey Williamson reports the 'unequivocal' trade data thus:

By 1833 [India] had become a net importer, amounting to 5 per cent of the domestic market. Between 1800 and 1833, this amounted to a fall of 11 to 12 percentage points ... By 1877, the foreign import share of the domestic textile market had risen to between 58 and 65 per cent. Over three-quarters of a century the foreign import share of the domestic market rose, and the domestic producers' share fell by the huge factor of between 64 and 72 percentage points.[9]

---

[6] Dutt (1916: 336–52, 537–44).
[7] List (1841/1885: 368).
[8] Dutt (1906: 302).
[9] Williamson (2011: 76–7).

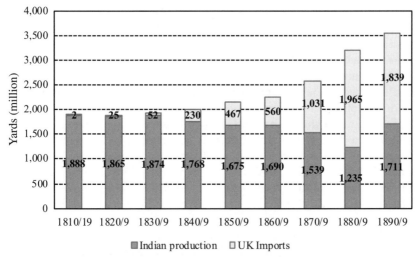

Figure 13.1 Indian cotton textile consumption: Domestic production relative to British machine-made textile imports in the nineteenth century. (Derived from Broadberry and Gupta (2009: 285)).
Notes: Curiously in a later article, they produce a very different set of data (Broadberry *et al.* 2015: 66). Significantly, though, the ratios between domestic Indian production to British imports remain broadly similar, thereby retaining the integrity of their 2009 data that are presented here. Interestingly, their 2015 figures suggest an even steeper increase in domestic demand for cotton textiles across the nineteenth century than their earlier 2009 data suggest.

Likewise, Romesh Dutt conflates the rise in British imports with a decline in Indian ICT production.[10] The problem, though, is that there is a trick of the light here given that British imports only marginally displaced Indian domestic production. For the nationalist illusion rests on a presumed zero-sum contest between levels of imports and domestic output, which is belied by the fact that domestic demand *increased* significantly throughout the nineteenth century.[11]

Figure 13.1 reveals that British CT exports certainly encroached on the Indian economy in the second half of the nineteenth century. But it also reveals that such imports did *not* significantly displace aggregate indigenous production because Indian domestic demand near doubled across the whole of the nineteenth century. Thus, total Indian output levels remained steady down to the 1830s, dropped marginally by around

[10] Dutt (1916: 344–5)
[11] Twomey (1983: 46).

5 per cent in the 1840s and by around 10 per cent in the 1850s and 1860s, before declining more significantly by about 20 per cent in the 1870s and 35 per cent in the 1880s, after which they underwent a very significant recovery (as I explain later). Accordingly, with the exceptional interlude of the 1870s and 1880s, it seems fair to say that Indian handloom production levels more-or-less held up during the nineteenth century even if there were different regional experiences in play.

To return to the point made above concerning Britain's imperial attempt to 'kick away the ladder', it is certainly fair to say that had India been able to protect its domestic market against British imports, as the British had done vis-à-vis ICT imports in the eighteenth century, then ICT production might well have doubled in size in order to have met this demand. But the critical difference here is that while Indian nationalists such as Jawaharlal Nehru and Romesh Dutt assert that it was the British colonial policy of denying India the benefits of tariff protectionism and its harmful effects on the ICT sector that caused India's de-industrialisation,[12] my claim is that British imports coupled with the hostile (freer trading) colonial state policy did much to prevent the *expansion* of the ICT sector but that they did not *de-industrialise* it. And, in any case, as I explained in Chapter 11, that India was *not* on a spontaneous path into cotton industrialisation before the eighteenth/ nineteenth centuries renders the notion of 'de-industrialisation' a misnomer.

We can shed more light on all of this by drawing on Douglas Haynes's superb study of the Bombay Presidency, which comprised one of the most significant CT producing regions in India (covering Gujarat, much of Maharashtra state, north western Karnataka state and Sindh Province). The essential account that Haynes produces reveals how artisanal CT production held up largely as a function of the artisans' ability to adapt to the new local and global economic conditions of the post-1850 period – a condition that others claim existed across India.[13] There is no doubting the point that Indian *hand-spun* yarn declined dramatically in the nineteenth century throughout the sub-continent – a point that Eurofetishists make much of. But, once again, this was no zero-sum game because many Indian spinners simply shifted into weaving, which is one reason why handloom weaving production continued. It is true that Indian cotton mill production developed after 1850, as I explain in the next section, and that it escalated rapidly thereafter such that by

---

[12] Nehru (1947: 247–53) and Dutt (1916: 40–4, 518, 537–44).
[13] For example, Roy (2012: 193–4) and Washbrook (2020).

1914, there were 271 mills in place that employed 260,000 workers.[14] And this was hardly a trivial sum given that it was more than the whole of the English cotton mill workforce in 1833. But to presume that the cotton mills displaced handloom weavers is, once again, to fall into the trap of zero-sum analysis. For it turns out that the mills did not displace but in fact *promoted* handloom weaving, given that the former produced cheaper yarn that helped spur on the latter.[15] Thus, Haynes notes that 'the growth of the textile mill industry in Bombay itself was no doubt highly dependent on the demand generated by western Indian weavers'.[16] Moreover, even the famous Dhakan weavers in Bengal who produced the finest Muslin switched to buying British yarn because it was cheaper despite the fact that Dhakan yarn remained superior in quality.[17]

Haynes places particular emphasis on the development of the *Karkhanas* – small workshops with a limited number of looms – though these had been around for many centuries previously, as I noted in Chapter 11. However, there are continuities and discontinuities in play here given that more well-off artisanal weavers often scaled up to become workshop owners (*Karkhandars*), who deployed cheap power looms that were imported from Britain and were deployed *alongside* traditional looms, the aggregate effect of which was an increase in productivity and output. These *Karkhanas* were located in the towns and became the backbone of what Haynes calls 'small town capitalism', in which production was tied in with the activities of merchant capitalists that were driven by market demand. And, while it is the case that wage labour was employed in the *Karkhanas*, nevertheless to conflate them with a pure Western model would be problematic. For they continued to rely considerably on craft skills and, most importantly, many of these were family-based firms that above all

retained the loose system of labour discipline that had been associated with [traditional] artisanal manufacture [i.e., handloom weaving]. Workers kept a great deal of control over their time and their pace of work.... In other words, many characteristics of artisanal [production] remained, despite the fact the *Karkhandars* had introduced electric power [to drive the power looms].[18]

This, of course, contrasted markedly with the working environment that labourers faced in the British mills, as I explained in Chapters 8 and 10.

[14] Roy (2012: 190).
[15] Twomey (1983: 47).
[16] Haynes (2012: 49).
[17] Mukund (1992: 2058).
[18] Haynes (2012: 263).

Critically, as noted earlier, the new *Karkhanas* developed *in tandem* with the Indian mills, which in turn undermines the assumption that Western imperialism simply wiped out indigenous Indian production systems.[19] After the 1850s, the ICT production system was highly mixed, based in part on partially mechanised *Karkhanas*, in part on fully mechanised mills and in large part on the traditional household system of production. Of particular note here is that the British domestic market for CTs was largely unified, whereas in India, by contrast, it was highly fragmented and segmented.[20] This benefited Indian artisans because they could specialise in textiles that the mills did not produce. Moreover, total Indian domestic demand increased between 40 and 50 per cent between the late 1890s and early 1920s while handloom production increased to meet this.[21] No less importantly, the increase in Indian factory production tended to displace imports rather than indigenous handloom weavers.[22]

Finally, it is noteworthy that the 'small town capitalism' that Haynes associates with the *Karkhanas* was *never* wiped out by Western capitalism. Strikingly, the 'informal economy' employed as much as 88 per cent of the Indian workforce even at the end of the twentieth century,[23] at the very time when the return of India as a member of the BRICS was biting. All of which means that the impact of the Western capitalist global economy on India was never a one-way ticket to Westernisation but was, and indeed continues to be, mediated by Indian agents within local contexts and traditions through which they carved out and continue to carve out a relatively autonomous space.

As a brief addendum, it is noteworthy that a similar story played out in the Madras Presidency in south India. Ian Wendt has shown powerfully how the number of handloom weavers also held up there throughout the second half of the nineteenth century. He also notes similarly that while mechanisation entered the CT production process, nevertheless, 'the diffusion of mechanised processes for cotton cleaning, spinning, warping, weaving and dyeing was partial, halting and gradual'.[24] And, while the process of mechanisation stepped up several gears at the end of the nineteenth century, this applied mainly to cotton cleaning, spinning and dyeing which, as such, did *not* displace handloom weaving.

[19] Ibid. (93).
[20] Ibid. (110–18).
[21] Ibid. (97).
[22] Ibid. (109).
[23] See also Wendt (2009) and Haynes (2012: 303–13).
[24] Wendt (2009: 211).

Accordingly, when Tharoor claims that in the absence of the British empire, the Indian handloom weavers 'would surely have been able to hold on to a niche market, as they do to this day',[25] he is half right. For what this claim misses is that this situation applied equally to the second half of the nineteenth century, not just the twentieth. On the basis of the truly dire claims concerning the fate of the handloom weavers that are produced in the Eurofetishist and Indian nationalist literatures, we would fully expect to see a massive decline in the numbers of such producers. But if there were around six million handloom weavers in 1800,[26] there were about ten million in 1900.[27] And, against the assumption that the cotton mill manufacturing industry replaced the handloom weavers in subsequent decades, it turns out that there were still some ten million handloom weavers in 1935.[28] Moreover, as Tirthankar Roy explains, in utilising some of the new European technologies such as the flying shuttle, the Jacquard loom, the dobby and the drop box – in what amounted to a reversal of the earlier East–West transmission of techniques and processes during the FGE – so '[b]etween 1900 and 1930, the volume of hand-loom cloth production [increased], even as the number of workers and looms did not change'.[29] Evidence not only for the continuity of handloom weavers but for their *predominance* vis-à-vis cotton mill manufacturing is revealed by the report of a government officer, which stated in 1935 that '[f]or every worker employed in cotton mills there are five employed in handloom weaving'.[30]

While Tharoor concedes that Indian producers and manufacturers began to recapture the domestic market after World War I, it is important to appreciate that this was achieved through the process of entangled agencies in which Indians borrowed various European technologies and then adapted them to suit their own indigenous practices – hence why I refer to the 'discontinuous continuity' of Indian production. For what this points to is a *partial* merging of historical capitalist ICT production with modern capitalist processes through what Kaoru Sugihara refers to as the Asian 'industrious revolution' – a point that I return to in the final section of this chapter.[31] And, although it is certainly the case that the EEIC had muscled in on the weaver production process within the household system of production in the eighteenth century

[25] Tharoor (2017: 8).
[26] Washbrook (1990: 489) and Twomey (1983).
[27] Roy (2012: 193).
[28] Ibid. (194).
[29] Ibid.
[30] Haynes (2012: 2).
[31] Sugihara (2003).

by purposefully removing Indian intermediaries in order to exploit the weavers, the fact remains that despite the very best of their retardive efforts, Indian handloom production continued on apace.

Here, it is useful to confront the inevitable postcolonial/Marxist reply that relies on Paul Bairoch's data on shares of world manufacturing output (WMO). These show how India traded places with Britain such that in 1750, the Indian share of WMO comprised 25 per cent and a mere 2 per cent in 1900, while Britain went from 2 per cent in 1750 to 23 per cent in 1880.[32] Interestingly, though, while Eurofetishists and Indian nationalists often deploy these data to confirm their picture of Britain's imperial economic rape of India, Bairoch himself does not advance such a conclusion. For elsewhere, he rejects the argument that imperialism undermined the economies of the colonies as much as it failed to enhance the British economy.[33] Which means that there is nothing intrinsic to these data that clinches the de-industrialisation thesis. Certainly, Bairoch recognises that before the late-nineteenth century, the majority of manufacturing output in the 'third world' was based on CT production, and this is clearly the case with respect to India.

There are two key problems with using Bairoch's data to support the cotton de-industrialisation thesis, the first of which is that in 1750, when India supposedly enjoyed 25 per cent and China 33 per cent of WMO, the fact is that the latter produced four times India's output of ICTs. Given that it is likely that the Chinese figure for WMO is an upper-bound estimate, so it would seem fair to say that the Indian figure is significantly over-estimated. If so, then the massive decline of India's share of WMO through the nineteenth century would have been less precipitous than Bairoch's data suggest. But second, even if we reject this claim, the key point is that these aforementioned figures represent *relative* shares of WMO. Which means that the massive decline in India's share of WMO appears as a trick of the light that Eurofetishist scholars have been fooled by. For all that was really happening was that Britain, as well as Europe and the United States, enjoyed a massive increase in their shares of WMO as they underwent industrialisation such that India's share declined *relatively* rather than absolutely. Indeed, the fact remains that aggregate ICT output levels remained fairly steady in the nineteenth century, bar the drop in the 1870s and 1880s, before undertaking an upward trajectory thereafter.

[32] Bairoch (1982: 275, 296).
[33] Bairoch (1993: chs. 6–7).

Certainly, the *second* great divergence in CT production output between Britain and India began in the 1840s. Moreover, by 1810/19, British exports had overtaken the approximately 100 million yards that the Indians likely exported on an annual basis in the seventeenth and eighteenth centuries (see Appendix 1). Beaming forward in time to 1870, British textile exports comprised 3.3 billion yards worldwide and reached 6 billion by 1900 before peaking at about 7 billion on the eve of the World War I,[34] all of which dwarfed India's exports even at their pre-nineteenth century peak. Nevertheless, ICT exports recovered significantly in the first half of the twentieth century and overtook Britain's in the 1950s.[35] Accordingly, we can discern a *third* great divergence that takes us back to the future of the FGE. This began as early as 1933 when Japan became the world's largest cotton textile producer and was consolidated when India became a leading global producer in the 1950s with China following on in the 1970s.[36] All of which, by return favour, secured the de-industrialisation, or more accurately the termination, of the British cotton manufacturing sector by the 1980s. For by then, India and China had returned to their leading global positions in CT production that they had enjoyed both during and even before the FGE. And to conclude this discussion, I argue that Indian handloom cotton weavers disappear from our view of India in the post-1800 era not so much because of the fatal impact of British cotton textile imports in cahoots with British imperialism, but largely as a function of the blind spot that marks the vision of Eurofetishism and Indian nationalism.

The Myth of Britain's Conversion of India into a Raw Cotton Supplier for Lancashire

As noted earlier, a further core component of the cotton textile de-industrialisation thesis is that British imperialism ensured that India was converted and demoted from its prime position as the world's leading CT exporter into a mere peripheral raw cotton supplier for Lancashire.[37] Such a claim reflects the famous boast proclaimed by the EEIC in 1840: that it had 'succeeded in converting India from a manufacturing country into a country exporting raw materials'.[38]

---

[34] Mitchell (2011: 356).
[35] Robson (1957: 358).
[36] Riello (2013: 294).
[37] For example, Dutt (1906).
[38] Cited in Wallerstein (1989: 150).

It is certainly true that from roughly the 1820s on various organisations in Britain were established, most notably the (Manchester) Cotton Supply Association (est. 1860) – prophetically as it turned out – to enquire into potential alternative suppliers of raw cotton. For worries developed within Britain concerning Lancashire's over-dependence on US supplies and what might happen should this flow be interrupted in the future. Certainly, India was considered to be a potential alternative supplier, with Frenise Logan claiming that 'India was "the cotton hope" of Britain'.[39] These associations turned out to be as timely as they were prophetic given the crisis of the 'Lancashire cotton famine', which exploded onto the scene between 1861 and 1865 as a result of the drying up of US raw cotton supplies during the Civil War.[40] It is also true that during this four-year period, India produced the majority of raw cotton supplies for Lancashire to the tune of about 55 per cent,[41] while Egypt supplied 12 per cent by 1865, having supplied a mere 3 per cent in 1861.[42] However, this constituted the temporal exception that proves the rule of the myth of India as a raw cotton supplier to Lancashire. Thus, by the 1870s, with the resumption of cheap US cotton supplies, Lancashire moved rapidly away from its temporary reliance on Indian raw cotton. And by 1875, Britain's hopes of converting India into its raw cotton supplier had faded away. But why did this happen given that we are so often told that the inverse was the case?

As I explained in Chapter 9, Indian raw cotton was a short-staple variety that rendered it unsuitable for the British machines since these required strong, high-tensile long-staple cotton. And, while numerous remedial attempts were made to grow long-staple Upland cotton in India, especially between 1865 and 1875, nevertheless for various reasons that included the nature of the climate and the soil, these efforts failed.[43] Instead, as I also explained in Chapter 9, the British were more interested in sourcing the long-staple Egyptian cotton in the absence of US supplies. However, there is a twist in the story in that what made raw cotton production an attractive proposition to Indian producers in 1861 was the tripling of its price, given the shortage of world supplies following the inception of the US Civil War.[44] Not surprisingly, the entirely rational response that many Indians made – for they were neither stupid nor irrational – was to undertake a partial shift out of agricultural and into

[39] Logan (1958: 473).
[40] Earle (1926), Logan (1958) and Harnetty (1970).
[41] Logan (1958: 475–6).
[42] Earle (1926: 535).
[43] Ibid., Harnetty (1970) and Riello (2013: 259–62).
[44] Logan (1958) and Harnetty (1970).

raw cotton production. But the sting in the tail is that their resulting enhanced prosperity saw the British Raj increase taxes accordingly, such that when the reduction in prices cut in after 1865, this left many peasant producers suffering real economic hardship in trying to meet the inflated taxes.[45] And, to add insult to injury, a good proportion of these taxes went into financing British imperial expansion across Asia that was undertaken by the Indian army. All in all, then, the claim that in the second half of the nineteenth century, India had been converted into a raw cotton supplier for Lancashire is simply a myth. A truer proposition is that India became a key supplier to China in the last third of the nineteenth century, having displaced British exports in 1880.[46]

But the Eurofetishist/Indian nationalist response, typified by Shashi Tharoor's rhetorical question, asks '[l]eft to itself, why wouldn't existing Indian industry have modernized, as industry in other non-colonized countries did?'[47] And, he goes on to argue on the same page that it is 'preposterous' to claim that India 'failed' to modernise as a result of some sort of 'native deficiency'. I agree entirely with the nationalist assumption that India was not a backward economy prior to the British rule. As I explained in Chapter 11, India was in essence a 'historical capitalist satisficer' that had reached optimal levels of cotton textile production and that before the 1840s, it had led the world along with China. Accordingly, there was no need to break through to industrial modernity, notwithstanding the very significant ecological limits that constrained the possibility of such a process. And, it seems that its specific 'developmental architecture' was primed for historical capitalism.

To the Eurofetishist reply that I have, albeit inadvertently, let the British imperialists off the moral hook for their numerous crimes against the Indian people, merely returns us to the deficiencies of binary, zero-sum thinking. For it is perfectly possible to highlight Indian resilience and agency while simultaneously recognising British exploitation and coercion. The key point is that '[i]t is a one-sided and largely ahistorical view of colonial India that notes only collapse, decay, and the fossilization of society into a museum of relics. There were also processes of reconstruction, change, and development that reflected a South Asian as well as a British genius.'[48] Alas, the ability to celebrate those genuine Indian achievements is the inevitable casualty of the fatalist perspective of Eurofetishism, which brushes these sites of Indian agency under the historical carpet in its

---

[45] Dutt (1916).
[46] Chao (1977: 93–4) and Bowen (2009).
[47] Tharoor (2017: 34). See also Dutt (1906, 1916).
[48] Washbrook (1990: 489).

one-eyed obsession with prosecuting British brutality and exploitation in the postcolonial academic court of social justice.

Certainly, there were countless examples of British economic exploitation and brutality, not the least of which was the firing of 400 Indians out of cannon as punishment for the 1857 'mutiny', not to mention the 'late-Victorian holocausts' in which somewhere between 12 and 29 million Indians died through British policy-induced famines.[49] Nor do I recognise Niall Ferguson's claim that Victorian India was booming, thanks to the role of British capital and empire.[50] Relevant here is the famous 'drain theory' that Indian nationalists highlight. Dadabhai Naoroji (who was, most ironically, a loyal supporter of the British empire) originally estimated the drain that was extracted from India through numerous forms of British charges at an annual average of £13 million between 1835 and 1872.[51] Subsequently, the theory has been either supported or critiqued for its exaggerated nature.[52]

But Naoroji might well have severely underestimated the more *invisible* side of the 'drain process'. Returning to my discussion of the amounts that the British extracted from the Indian taxpayer to fund the Indian army that acted as the vanguard of Britain's imperial expansion in Asia, I estimate this in the region of an annual average of between £50 million and £90 million (1870–1913). Moreover, as I explained in Chapter 7, it is possible that British taxes would had to have been increased by between 60 and 75 per cent had the Indian army not been available at the expense of the Indian taxpayer.[53] As Pradeep Barua notes, the '[Indian] military resources and revenues at [Britain's] disposal ensured that the wars in India [and beyond] would not traumatize British public opinion and the British taxpayer'.[54] Tragically, however, a 'financial number' cannot be put on the costs of the sacrificed Indian lives. Perhaps worse still is that Britons do not commemorate or honour those fallen Indian lives when they wear the red poppy each year – given that this symbol commemorates only fallen white men – which, if nothing else, serves as an annual reminder of their egregious failure to remember.

And yet, in the face of all these imperial predations – human, political, financial, fiscal and economic – the deepest irony emerges in the point that India's CT producers turned out to be far more impressive, resilient and adaptive than the nationalists and their Eurofetishist academic

[49] Davis (2001).
[50] Ferguson (2002).
[51] Naoroji (1901: 34).
[52] See the discussions in Cuenca Esteban (2001: 66–9) and Washbrook (2020).
[53] See Footnote 123, p. 195.
[54] Barua (2011: 40).

brethren have presumed. Indeed, as Arun Biswas tells us, the fact is that 'the indomitable [Indian] artisans ... exhibited gallant and persistent craftsmanship. Their vitality [that was] sustained through centuries ... could not be extinguished by ... British colonialism'.[55]

The De-industrialisation of China's Cotton Textile Sector?

Given China's lead in CT production in the last millennium, I want to consider the de-industrialisation thesis in the Chinese context. My claim is *not* that Western intervention did *no* damage to China's economy and society but rather that British policies and imports failed to 'de-industrialise' the Chinese ICT sector. The most striking problem with the de-industrialisation thesis is not simply how *little* impact British cotton yarn and textile exports imparted, but how Chinese production levels remained strikingly high throughout the nineteenth century even in the face of an approximate 20 per cent drop in the last third. Given the lack of systematic and official data on Chinese production levels for the nineteenth century, I shall marshal various pieces of information that are available in the secondary source literature.

As explained already, British CT output and exports only became significant in the 1830s. But, despite all the talk of the 'great divergence' – or what I have called the *second* great divergence – in cotton production between Britain and India that began in the 1840s, it is likely that at *no* point in the nineteenth century did the British out produce the Chinese. Indeed, the second great cotton textile divergence between Britain and China emerged only in the early-twentieth century which means that China led Britain for about 95 per cent of the time in the last millennium. The data on raw cotton production that are presented in Pomeranz's seminal book translates into Chinese CT production of around 6 billion yards in 1750,[56] while 70 years later, the British produced a mere 0.4 billion. For 1840, Wu and Xu suggest a figure of around 4.4 billion yards in China,[57] though Zhang Shizhi estimates a minimal figure of about 5 billion yards.[58] Either way, though, both these estimates considerably

---

[55] Biswas (1999: 309–10).
[56] Pomeranz (2000: 330–6).
[57] Wu and Xu (2003: 330–1).
[58] Zhang (2020: ch. 3). He assumes an average cotton output in Hubei province at 30 catties per mu (33 lbs) during the early Qianlong reign (Wu and Xu 2003: 210) which, according to Pomeranz (2000: 330), is lower than the average 39 lbs per mu in Jiangnan – China's most productive region. And, on the basis that the area under cotton cultivation was no larger than 5 per cent of the total agricultural output before 1840 (Wu and Xu 2003: 211), this works out at approximately 1.2 billion lbs – or about 5 billion yards – nationwide for 1840.

outpaced Britain's output of 1.8 billion yards in 1840. By 1870/80, the Chinese figure stood at about 7.5 billion yards, which clearly surpassed the British figure of 5.3 billion in 1880. Finally, by 1900, both countries produced about six billion yards apiece. Although British production output peaked at around ten billion yards in 1913,[59] China regained the lead in the 1950s, and by the 1970s it had returned to its place as the world's premier producer of CTs, which it had enjoyed before 1900. All of which means that we need to talk about the 'return' rather than the 'rise' of China today,[60] as I explain in Chapter 14.

Given the sheer size of China's CT output throughout the nineteenth century, it is hardly surprising to learn that the country's experience in the face of British imports replicated in so many ways that of India's. Thus, Chinese handloom weavers in the household system of production more or less *maintained* their high levels of output during the nineteenth century though also, not unlike the Indian situation, there was something like a 20 per cent decline in the late-nineteenth century. One difference with India's experience, however, was that even as late as 1871–80, British-finished CT imports comprised only about 14 per cent of total Chinese production.[61] One reason for the vitality of China's output is that Chinese preferred wearing their own home-made CT outfits, which they found more durable as they were stronger (i.e., cruder and coarser) than the finer Lancashire product, while also being cheaper and warmer in winter.[62] But what of imported foreign yarn?

In 1831, foreign imports of *machine-made* yarn comprised a mere 0.1 per cent of total Chinese finished textile output.[63] Initially, many handloom weavers relied on the short-staple, low-count Indian (coarse) yarn imports with which they maintained their production of heavier cotton piece goods than the British were able to produce.[64] And, given that by 1880 India was China's key foreign supplier of yarn, so the British de-industrialisation thesis in this particular context cannot apply thereafter. Significantly, as with the Indian case, so there is a similar paradoxical trick of the light here. For as in India,[65] although China's domestic *spinning* contracted in the late-nineteenth century as foreign machine-made yarn entered the country, this was because Chinese producers turned to buying up the cheaper foreign yarn in order to

[59] Robson (1957: 358) and Mitchell (2011: 355).
[60] See also Zhang (2020).
[61] Feuerwerker (1970).
[62] Murphey (1974: 27).
[63] Xu (1988: 34).
[64] Chao (1977: ch. 7).
[65] Morris (1963: 612).

weave their finished product. Indeed, imported foreign machine-spun yarn escalated after about 1870 to meet this growing demand. The combination of foreign machine-made yarn for the warp and Chinese hand-spun yarn for the weft 'made [for] an even better cloth to compete with foreign piece goods'.[66] And critically, the slowness of Chinese hand-spinning relative to handloom weaving created natural bottlenecks that were solved by the use of foreign-manufactured yarn. Thus, the penetration of foreign-spun yarn into China cannot be associated with Chinese de-industrialisation because these yarn imports *enabled* Chinese handicraft weavers to expand production from the very late-nineteenth century onwards.[67] More significantly, while the Chinese established their own mechanised cotton mills in the 1880s,[68] handloom weaving nevertheless continued apace. And, most significantly, by 1936, imports of machine-made yarn comprised a mere 1 per cent that of Chinese machine-made yarn, which leads Xu Xinwu to conclude that 'it is clear that *domestic* machine-spun yarn had [by then] a far greater capacity than did imported yarn to displace native [handicraft-spun] yarn'.[69]

Once again, like the Indian producers, the Chinese handloom weavers also used various Western technologies, which included the flying shuttle, the Jacquard loom and, more uniquely, iron-gear looms that sped up the production process considerably while producing better quality cloth. And, this in turn created a larger surplus that became available for export.[70] Thus, while exports of hand-woven cloth (Nankeens) had dried up by the late 1830s, nevertheless exports began to recover from the 1850s before they surpassed the earlier 1821/5 peak during World War I.[71] And, once again mirroring the Indian situation, we find that in Hopei by the 1930s some 80 per cent of total cloth production was undertaken by handloom weavers, this time by using Chinese machine-spun yarn along with foot treadles and Jacquard looms.[72] All of which reveals 'surprising parallels' with Anglo–Indian relations, though not for the reasons advanced by Eurofetishism. For these parallels comprised entangled agential relations and interconnections that bound Europe and China together as Chinese producers combined traditional historical capitalist and modern industrial capitalist processes. Thus, not only did domestic handicraft weaving hold its own in the face of foreign

---

[66] Feuerwerker (1970: 348).
[67] Arrighi *et al.* (2003: 294) and Chao (1977: 186).
[68] Chao (1977: ch. 5).
[69] Xu (1988: 37), my emphasis.
[70] Chao (1977: 177–85).
[71] Ibid. (82).
[72] Murphey (1974: 29).

competition,[73] but the assumption that Lancashire's cotton yarn and textile exports conquered China's domestic markets does not hold up to scrutiny. Fitting here is Feuerwerker's conclusion:

[t]he simplistic indictment of 'foreign competition' by some contemporary Chinese [and some Western] historians for having progressively 'crushed' and 'exploited' [China's] domestic rural handicraft industry from the mid-nineteenth century onward is belied by the [fact that by the mid-1930s some] 73 per cent of cloth [when measured in linear yards] was woven by [Chinese] handicraft methods.[74]

Still, none of this is to say that Britain's informal imperial intervention was innocent or benign and did no harm to the Chinese economy, though this can be easily exaggerated.[75] Rather, my claim is simply that the Eurofetishist de-industrialisation thesis fails to apply to the all-important Chinese CT sector. And while this and the last section in aggregate make the case for the resilience and continuing agency of Chinese and ICT handloom weavers and producers, I now wish to expand this point by considering how Western and non-Western agency met and combined in the 'multicultural contact zone' to produce the SGE.

The 'Multicultural Contact Zone': Entangled Agential Relations in the Making of Western Empire and the SGE

Eurofetishist analyses of the imperial expansion of the (second) global economy work within the Eurocentric Big Bang theory/Expansion of the West narrative, painting a melodramatic picture of an irresistible and devastating Western capitalist tsunami rolling outwards from the European metropolitan core to flood the old structures of the backward Asian economies in the periphery. And, having destroyed them, so Western imperialism proceeded to regenerate them up to the standard of Western capitalist civilisation, thereby finally bringing the non-West out of its so-called regressive isolation and into the modern Western-made global economy in which they would be ruthlessly exploited.

But my claim here is that behind these melodramatic headlines of European hyper-agency and coercive power lies a hidden, humdrum picture in which these non-Western economies had long been integrated into the earlier FGE while, equally, Western and non-Western agents continued to entwine in the 'multicultural contact zone' to produce the

---

[73] Feuerwerker (1970: 374).
[74] Ibid. (377).
[75] Frank (2015: 269–75).

SGE, much as they had done vis-à-vis the FGE (as I explained in Part I of this book). That is, the production and development of the SGE was based on mutually constitutive interactions between Western and non-Western agencies, though these were not so much collaborative as 'competitive–cooperative' in nature. In particular, as we have seen throughout this book, the Western thrust did not enter a vacuum or virginal space in the Indian Ocean, but interfaced with the pre-existing non-Western transcontinental 'bazaar economy' that was based on 'historical capitalism' (which I described in detail in Chapter 8).

To the extent that non-Western actors and agency enter the peripheral vision of the Eurofetishist lens, which is focused resolutely on the Western capitalist origins of the (second) global economy, they do so as mere 'compradors' or 'collaborators', who were destined merely to service the needs of the European imperialists from whom they derived 'traitorous' side payments. However, as I discussed in detail in Chapter 5, viewing Asians as compradors and traitors to their nations via their complicity with European imperialism whitewashes both their economic agency and the interdependence of European and Asian agents. This was as true of the period when the Europeans first arrived – as I explained in detail in Chapter 5 – as it was during the nineteenth century at the time when the West was allegedly 'stamping its dominance' through its creation of the modern SGE. As I also explained there, from the early-seventeenth century onwards, the Europeans became incorporated or pulled into the FGE as a function of non-Western trading logics and Indian structural power. And, from then on, the Companies were nurtured in all manner of ways. Equally, to an important extent, this process underpinned the creation and development of the SGE during the nineteenth century, as the Asians once again helped *pull* the Europeans deeper into Afro-Asia. How, then, did all this play out? Here, I focus on various Asian financial, mercantile and industrial capitalists, though I shall hone in on some of the most significant ones to illustrate my case.

Entangled Parsi–British Agencies, 1661–1940

Eurofetishism would likely view the Parsi as the exemplar of an Indian comprador, given that the Parsis provided all manner of services to the English imperialists. But as I explained in Chapter 5, the English and other Europeans found that one of the chief obstacles that they confronted in India was their lack of knowledge of the place, which is one reason why they had to rely on all manner of non-Western and Indian 'intermediaries', without whom they would ultimately have been unable to sustain their presence there. Moreover, describing the Parsis as but compradors/collaborators who were economically 'brought to life' by the English imperialists misses the point that they had prospered in their own right long before the arrival of the Europeans. The Parsis arrived in India between the eighth and tenth centuries, and their knowledge, language and contact with the interior of India that they had acquired over some six or seven centuries gave them a massive head-start on the British, upon whom the latter had little choice but to rely when the EEIC arrived much later. The Dutch and Portuguese also relied on Parsis, though the Vereenigde Oost-Indische Compagnie (VOC) in Malabar (on the southwest coast of India) employed Jews as their chief brokers.

Important here is the point made by Michael Pearson, who explains that there were numerous types of brokers. There were particularistic brokers who dealt in specialised commodities within a specific country, but there were also 'general brokers' who were important in enabling foreign trade in the Indian Ocean. Critically, the British and other Europeans found that they had to rely on these general brokers when dealing with trade across the Indian Ocean and the particularistic brokers when trading within India. The aforementioned language skills constituted a vital advantage that the indigenous brokers held over the Europeans given that 'linguistically-incompetent people were easy to cheat'.[76] Pearson goes so far as to claim that in many ways it was the non-Western brokers who wove together the Indian Ocean 'world economy'.[77] From their stronghold in Gujarat, the Parsis developed a strong and symbiotic relationship with the British following the EEIC's settlement in Bombay in 1665. As Dobbin notes, '[n]early all the European agency houses especially after 1813 had Parsi guarantee-brokers who guaranteed the solvency of the constituents and advanced considerable sums of money to enable them to continue to trade'.[78]

A further problem with the Eurofetishist 'comprador/collaborator thesis' is that it obscures the point that the Parsis could provide numerous services to the European imperialists only because they traded on their own account and created their own firms independently of the Europeans, as indeed they had long done prior to the arrival of the British. One notable example comprises the Parsis' role in the Indian opium trade to China. This is interesting because postcolonial and Marxist scholars often highlight the imperial policy of exporting Indian opium to China as the principal means by which the British

---

[76] Pearson (1988: 462).
[77] Ibid. (472).
[78] Dobbin (1996: 84).

overcame their historic trade deficit with the 'Middle Kingdom',[79] an argument that I also made in my 2004 book.[80] While there is a good deal of truth to this claim, nevertheless, nowhere in these discussions is a consideration of the relatively autonomous role that was played by Indians and Chinese who are, instead, simply conjured into thin air through a Eurofetishist sleight of hand.

By the 1850s some 50 per cent of the opium trade was conducted by the British and 25 per cent by Indians, with the rest likely being undertaken by Chinese.[81] Sindh, for one, benefited from the conflict between the EEIC and Indian capitalists over the opium trade. For when the British sought to monopolise it, the Indians fought back by re-routing it through Sindh (in present-day Pakistan). This province became key to the Malwa opium trade, with some 2,400 camels transporting opium to China in 1838 alone. Still, it was not Sindhis but Gujaratis and Marwaris who were the key opium traders and financiers, respectively, on this northern route.[82] While efforts by the EEIC to stop this initially came to nothing, eventually they annexed Sindh in 1839. But this did not mark the end of the Indian role in the opium trade.

The Parsis became significantly involved in the opium trade as much as they became *modern* industrial capitalists in their own right. While one of the greatest Marwari banking firms of the nineteenth century, Tarachand Ghanshymadas, built its fortune in opium,[83] it was ultimately the Parsis who were probably the key mediators between Indian producers of opium and British merchants. A key Parsi, Jamsetjee Jeejeebhoy, worked closely with the British firm, Jardine Matheson, in the Malwa opium trade and he became very rich in the process.[84] It would be impossible to characterise the Parsis as pedlars because they were large-scale traders. And, Parsi families had major economic interests within China whence they gained enormous amounts of wealth.[85] Moreover, they branched out into banking and manufacturing in the nineteenth century and in the process became modern capitalists, as did the Marwaris. For example, one-third of the shareholders of the European-dominated Bank of Bombay were Parsis. Equally as important was their shift into investing capital in modern capitalist cotton mills.

---

[79] For example, Arrighi *et al.* (2003: 291–3) and Frank (2015: 116–23).
[80] Hobson (2004: 273).
[81] Dobbin (1996: 85).
[82] Markovits (2000: 39–43).
[83] Ray (1995: 500) and cf. Timberg (2014: ch. 3).
[84] Subramanian (2016: ch. 3).
[85] Dobbin (1996: ch. 4).

Certainly, the benefits worked both ways to each other's mutual benefit – hence 'entangled agential relations' – insofar as Indians in general and Parsis in particular utilised British machinery to advance their own economic interests. For example, the Indian cotton mill industry, which had borrowed key British industrial technologies, spawned the development of an Indian industrial entrepreneurial class by the late-nineteenth century. Notable here is the Parsi, Kavasji Davar, who in 1854 set up through shareholder agreement the joint stock company in Bombay – the Bombay Spinning and Weaving Company – which was the very first indigenous ICT factory that was worked by steam engines. Davar was followed rapidly in 1854 by Manakjs Petit, who set up the Oriental Spinning and Weaving Company.[86]

But the most famous of the Parsi industrialists was Jamshedji Tata, who set up a cotton mill in 1869 in Nagpur, which he followed up with the establishment of the Empress Mills in 1877. Tata then set up the Swadeshi mills, which competed directly with British manufacturers, spinning and weaving a much finer yarn that proved very successful abroad, particularly in Chinese markets. His adaptive innovation of deploying ring spindles was especially important. And, as I noted earlier, Indian yarn exports to China outcompeted those from Britain from about 1880. Overall, Tata's name is today, of course, synonymous with iron and especially steel. For shortly after his death in 1904, his sons set up a company called Tata Iron and Steel Co, with the rest, as they say, being modern history, the recent climax of which saw the company take over the British steel company, Corus, in 2006.

In sum, it is here where we encounter the British contribution to this relationship in that the Indian entrepreneurs imported machinery to India that was then deployed in the Indian cotton mills, though these in turn played an important role in ICT production that could resist the negative impact of British textile imports into India. In this clear respect, it was the synergies that were most important, all of which are obscured behind Eurofetishism's melodramatic binary headlines of British coercive imperial domination versus Indian passivity and dependency.

*The Kachchh–Oman–Zanzibar–East Africa Axis of the
Indian Ocean Trading System, c. 1840–c. 1900/39*

Another key trading network that flourished in the FGE and well into the SGE was that of the Kachchhis, Omani Arabs and East Africans.

---

[86] Ibid. (88–9).

The Kachchhis came from the district of Kachchh (often referred to as Kutch), which is located in north-west Gujarat and lies about 150 miles south of Hyderabad in Sindh (not to be confused with Hyderabad in South India). By the beginning of the nineteenth century, much of the international trade from East Africa and West Asia had shifted from Surat to the Gulf of Kachchh. But this thrust, in turn, reaches back to the mid-sixteenth century when the Jadeja (Rajput) dynasty sought proactively to promote Kachchhi trade in order to derive tax revenues from it. In addition, the dynasty set up infrastructures such as shipbuilding and ports – most notably Mandvi – while also co-opting financiers into the court. The Kachchhi firms comprised a number of mercantile communities, comprising Hindu Bhātiyās, Shaivaite Goswamis, Bhanushalis and Lohanas as well as the three Muslim groups: Khojas, Bohras and Memons. Like the Multānīs, they prized their honesty and integrity above all else – a point that was commented upon in the VOC records.[87] Moreover, like the Multānīs that I described in Chapter 6, the Kachchhis engaged in money lending as much as trade, while also acting as true capitalist bankers given that they accepted deposits.

Kachchhi trading activities extended far and wide, ranging from Mandvi, Bombay and Karachi across to Muscat – situated in Oman in Hadramaut (present-day Yemen) at the mouth of the Persian Gulf – as well as southwest to the economically strategic island of Zanzibar and Southeast Africa more generally. It is true that the Americans and British also played an increasing role in the East African trade, but overall, it seems that Arabs and Kachchhis were the major traders in the western Indian Ocean. One of the factors that enabled the Kachchhi comparative trading advantage was that the Mandvi merchants possessed deep knowledge of the local African and West Asian markets, as was the case with the Hindu Gujarati Vāniyā merchants before them, as we saw in Chapter 4. While the Kachchhis had arrived in East Africa in the late-eighteenth century, they only came to displace the economic primacy of the Vāniyā after 1840, largely as a function of the Omani–Kachchhi alliance in Zanzibar that took off after that date (though as I explain later, this did not spell the end of the overseas trading activities of the Vāniyā).

The decline of the Safavid Persian Empire in the eighteenth century saw the emergence of Oman in Hadramaut. The Sultan of Oman, Hamad bin Seyyid (1785–92), began by reducing import duties from

[87] Ibid. (12).

9 to 6.5 per cent. By the late-eighteenth century, Muscat was a vital entrepôt among the Persian Gulf, the Red Sea and India. Critically, under the leadership of Sulṭān bin Aḥmad Saʿīd Āl Bū Saʿīdī, Omani-Arabic traders developed a division of labour with the Kachchhis, wherein the former managed the shipping and freighting, while the latter dealt in sales, storage, purchasing and finance.[88] Kachchhis exported to Mandvi numerous African and Arabic products and took in the reverse direction all manner of raw materials and products including grain, iron and steel, pearls and above all ICTs to Muscat. By the early-nineteenth century, there was a resident Kachchhi community of some 4,000 in Muscat.[89] Bania merchant communities settled not only in Muscat but also in Bahrein, Sharjah and Kuwait where they were able to compete successfully with Jewish and Armenian merchants in the Persian Gulf trade. About three or four Bania firms controlled the whole of the cotton yarn and piece-good trade, which comprised British as well as Japanese and Indian-made products.[90] Moreover, the sultan oversaw the construction of some fifty ships between 1790 and 1803, which travelled to: Bengal, where the Arabic traders bought muslin (fine Indian cotton yarn) and finished ICTs; Bombay and Malabar to buy timber and pepper, as well as Mauritius, where they bought coffee and cotton.

As the interior of Africa was increasingly opened up, the Omani state sought to centralise the 'whole foreign trade of Africa from eastern Zaire to the Indian Ocean as their entrepot'.[91] The major exports to Zanzibar were ICTs which, even by 1811, were of better quality than the Manchester product and were about half the cost. The Kachchhis enabled the Omani-Arabic merchants to buy African ivory and Black slaves in exchange for ICTs. The Indians then became heavily involved in the caravan trade into the interior of Africa. As signalled earlier, a particularly important feature of the Indian Ocean system became the Omani–Kachchhi–Zanzibari–East African axis that emerged in 1840 when Sulṭān bin Saʿīd Āl Bū Saʿīdī relocated the capital of Oman to Zanzibar.[92] Critically, he actively encouraged the Kachchhis to settle there with whom, *inter alia*, he was keen to foster trade in Africa and throughout the Indian Ocean. For the Omanis had long been reliant on the Indians for shipping and banking purposes.[93]

---

[88] Ibid. (77–9).
[89] Cooper (1977: 32) and Goswami (2016: 77–9, 84).
[90] Ray (1995: 540, 554).
[91] Dobbin (1996: 114).
[92] Machado (2009a: 178).
[93] Cooper (1977: 32).

In Southeast Africa, the Kachchhis were also brokers for the European traders, buying and selling American CTs (*merekani*). Indeed, the Europeans and Americans were so reliant on the Indian *bania* for help and advice that they often sought partnerships with the Kachchhis – as was the case with respect to Vāniyā/Portuguese relations in both India (Diu and Daman) and Mozambique (as noted in Chapter 4). This occurred because Indian merchants had developed a long-established infrastructure that enabled trading, brokering and the transferring of money throughout the Indian Ocean within the trans-regional 'bazaar economy'. So significant was the Kachchhi role in all of this that the British consul in Zanzibar, Colonel Rigby, complained that the Indians 'may be said almost entirely to monopolize the trade of Zanzibar, as although there are European and other merchants settled there, they are supplied with produce for export, and their imports are nearly all purchased by Indians'.[94] It is true that between the mid-1830s and the 1850s American machine-made CTs (*merekani*), which came from New England – specifically Salem in Massachusetts – comprised just over 50 per cent of the textile imports of East Africa.[95] But the crisis in textile production that accompanied the US Civil War (1861–5) undermined the American trade to East Africa such that the Kachchhis regained their leading role in selling ICTs there.[96] Indeed, by 1888, the Indian share was 30 per cent higher than the American was at its peak.

A similar problem confronted the British right across East Africa, with the British official, Thomas Metcalf, communicating the following to the Manchester Chamber of commerce: 'cotton of Indian manufacture [has] seriously interfered with our goods.... [T]he comparatively flimsy material which the rising manufacturing industry of India is now producing can be sold at little more than half the cost of the heavier and more durable fabrics of Manchester and Massachusetts'.[97] This alone was a considerable achievement given that British textiles were generally made of a relatively high count yarn. The irony here, though, is that this was *in part* made possible by the borrowing of Western technologies. Thus, once the Indians had developed their own mechanised textile mills by utilising British technologies after the mid-nineteenth century, so this enhanced their share of the East African markets vis-à-vis the English and Americans.

---

[94] Goswami (2016: 181).
[95] Ibid. (159–64, 175–6).
[96] Prestholdt (2008: 72–8) and Machado (2014: 272).
[97] Goswami (2016: 168).

Not surprisingly, Western merchants were keen to overcome their reliance on the Kachchhis. But while the former benefited in many ways through their entangled connections with the Gujarati merchants, nevertheless they were unable to overcome this interdependence even with the onset of European imperialism in Africa. In particular, Indian structural power was still a crucial factor that shaped Western actions and trading activities in the Western Indian Ocean. For example, the Kachchhi dominance of the exchange markets in East Africa enhanced their bargaining power while also hurting that of the French and British in particular. As Chhaya Goswami explains, the Kachchhis favoured American gold and the Indian rupee. As a result, they traded sterling and the Franc at a discount to their official rates. The French consul complained about this practice, but 'found himself helpless when Ibji Shivji ... declined to consent to a decision that overvalued the 5 franc piece'.[98] Even the Omani Sultan in Zanzibar could not push through this reform. The British were equally put out, particularly in 1873/4 when the value of sterling against the gold dollar resulted in heavy losses in remittances to and from Britain. The only way round this problem was for the British to get their specie in rupees from Bombay, with the resulting irony being that '[t]he Consul ended up on the side of a stronger rupee and a weaker English sovereign'.[99] Overall, the Indians dominated the financial infrastructure that comprised drafts, loans and mortgages, all of which the Arabs and Westerners relied upon. And given the financial acumen of Arabic *sarrāfs* – an institution that stems back to the seventh and eighth centuries – it was surprising that even they relied on the Kachchhi financial agents, which in turn enhanced the power of the Gujaratis. Thus, while Arabs and Swahilis and some Europeans were the main owners of the plantations, nevertheless about 80 per cent of them were mortgaged to Kachchhis, as had been the case previously under the economic primacy of the Vāniyā since 1750.

As signalled above, even the Europeans' imperial ambitions relied to an important extent on their interdependence with the Kachchhis. Following the 1884 Berlin Conference in which Africa was carved up by the various European colonial powers, the British were granted the protectorate of East Africa. But to develop these lands, the British depended on Indian capital, trade and services. Thus, for example, when the British claimed their East African Protectorate in 1895 and sought to build a railway that would stretch from Uganda to the east coast, Indians played a vital role. But while the Eurofetishist and Eurocentric

[98] Ibid. (183).
[99] Ibid. (184).

imagination conjures up teams of Indian indentured labourers being put to work in building the railways for their British capitalist masters, this misses the point that Indians were the key contractors. For Kachchhi businessmen were heavily involved in the railway and construction business in Uganda and Kenya. Moreover, Ismailis (the generic term for Kachchhis) were vital in developing the Ugandan cotton industry from 1903 onwards. Cotton emerged rapidly to comprise the largest component in Uganda's export trade by 1907 with the Bombay mills providing a strong outlet for Ugandan cotton.[100] Not only did Indian capitalists invest capital in the Ugandan cotton industry but ginners also moved from India to set up ginnery businesses there, such that by 1925, Indians owned 100 out of a total 114 ginneries.

In general, Gujarati businessmen played numerous key roles in East Africa during most of the twentieth century, particularly in Mozambique, Kenya, Tanzania and Uganda, until they were forced to leave in the 1970s under ignominious circumstances, most notoriously those associated with President Idi Amin of Uganda. Nevertheless, President Yoweri Museveni later rescinded Idi Amin's act and invited the Indians back into Uganda at the end of the twentieth century precisely so as to help rebuild the country. All in all, then, the story of the British colonial takeover of East Africa 'would have been a difficult enterprise without the willing participation of certain communities from western India' and 'successive British government enquiries concluded that Indians were essential to the making of East Africa and its economic development would have been impossible in their absence'.[101]

Finally, it is noteworthy that the Gujaratis were not only important to European imperialism in East Africa but also their alliance with the Omani sultanate in Zanzibar enabled the Kachchhis to engage in the dark side of the East African trade, much as the Vāniyā had done before them. For they derived substantial profits from ebony (the Black slave trade) and ivory. Moreover, these two 'dark' trades were complementary. Unlike the Europeans who were confined mainly to coastal trading regions, the Kachchhis ventured inland in their trading activities, as noted earlier. There they exchanged ICTs for ivory. But in turn, the ivory trade went hand-in-hand with the slave trade. Thus '[a]lmost every caravan that came from the interior had thousands of [African] porters, who were then disposed of as slaves. In financing the ivory trade, the Kachchhis were perforce financing the slave trade too.'[102] In this

---

[100] Dobbin (1996: 122) and Markovits (2000: 16).
[101] Dobbin (1996: 109, 119).
[102] Goswami (2016: 141).

respect, once again, they continued the role that had been undertaken previously by the Vāniyās (as I explained in Chapter 4). Moreover, the proliferation of the African slave trade on the east coast of Africa during the nineteenth century revolved around Zanzibar.[103] Strikingly, as I also noted in Chapter 4, somewhere between one and two million slaves were traded to Zanzibar between 1770 and the late-nineteenth century, with just under half of them being deployed in the Zanzibari clove plantations with the remainder being subsequently shipped abroad predominantly to West Asia.

When Zanzibar went into decline in the late-nineteenth century, the Gujaratis then relocated into inland Africa. There, they continued to sell ICTs, carrying their trade into Tanganyka, Kenya, Mozambique and Uganda as noted earlier. Their success ultimately boiled down to their ability, which the Europeans lacked, of financing trade (as I explained in Part I of this book). So while they were able to carve out their own autonomous spheres of trading influence in East Africa, they also acted together with the Europeans in other parts, given that the latter depended on them for their financial and marketing services within the bazaar economy.

The Nattukottai Chettiars, Sindworkies, Vāniyās, Multānīs and Shīkārpūris Inside and Outside the Shadow of the British Empire

While I have chosen to highlight the important role that was played by the Parsis and, most especially, the Kachchhis in the nineteenth and twentieth centuries within the Indian Ocean system, it would create a misplaced impression if we left the discussion at that. For there was also in play a series of other Indian foreign trading groups, who included the seaborne traders – the Sindworkies, Nattukottai Chettiars (NCs) and the Vāniyās – as well as the Multānīs and Shīkārpūris who plied the overland caravan routes. Space considerations preclude a full discussion, but a few summary points are in order.

Particularly important were the NCs from South India. Note that the term 'chettiar' means large-scale merchant and/or banker. Like the Multānīs, they were not brought to life by the arrival of the Europeans as their commercial activities began back in the eleventh century through the raising of capital from Indian temples.[104] Accordingly, to borrow Dobbin's useful phrase, the NCs were 'pre-adapted' to maximising their economic opportunities when the Europeans arrived in India. And,

[103] Nicolini (2012: ch. 5).
[104] Dobbin (1996: 133).

much like the Parsis, they were heavily involved in the opium trade, playing a key financial role in the Malay Straits in close association with the Oriental Bank (est. 1846), the Chartered Mercantile Bank (est. 1854) and the Chartered Bank of India, Australia and China (est. 1861). Of note here is that the NCs were the key channel for the financing of the Chinese opium syndicates (see later). Although their role within the Indian banking system was significant, nevertheless in the second half of the nineteenth century, they exploited new financial niches in Southeast Asia.

One such venture that was initiated by the NCs was in providing credit to Southeast Asians from their new base in the Lower Irrawaddy Delta in Burma. The NCs were especially important in the development of the Burmese rice industry, which became the world's leading rice exporter. The British also moved into Burma, specifically to develop rice production for export back to Europe. For, with the opening of the Suez Canal in 1869, it finally became possible and profitable to export Burmese rice to Britain – given that before then food cargoes were shipped via the Cape and the six-month journey often meant that these rotted. This led to an increase in Indian and British rice mills in Burma from 52 in 1890 to 613 by 1930. George Orwell argued that Burma was exploited and thereby under-developed by the British.[105] But without the 'Chetty' money and the administrative apparatus that the NCs provided, the British would never have been able to undertake this vast enterprise in the Delta.[106]

In addition to the NCs, the Sindworkies from Hyderabad in Sindh became an important trading community during the nineteenth century. They began selling 'curios' in India around 1840, which were 'exotic' Oriental products that included silk textiles. But between 1890 and 1940, they established branches throughout the world as they sold their wares to global consumers.[107] The Sindworkies were complemented by the Vāniyās. For when they were displaced from East Africa around 1840 by the Kachchhis, the Vāniyās relocated to the southern ports of the Red Sea, where they invested in the ivory, gold and pearl trades. Moreover, they rose to prominence in providing banking and credit to the merchants in the region. In contrast to the Eurocentric vision of European and American merchants dominating the Indian Ocean in the nineteenth century and consigning Asian merchants to the backwater of history, the fact is that 'rather than representing a transformative moment

---

[105] Orwell (1929).
[106] Dobbin (1996: 139). See also Ray (1995: 529).
[107] Markovits (2000: ch. 4).

in the history of the ocean's inter-regional exchange and commerce, the imposition of colonial rule and the demands of industrial capitalism did not fatally undermine these networks and their exchange economies'.[108]

The impression created thus far is that Indian merchant capitalists were largely seaborne foreign traders. At the end of Chapter 6, I noted that the Multānīs fled from their home town to Shīkārpūr, following Nādir Shāh's invasion of Multān in 1747. And there they teamed up with the Shīkārpūris in order to continue plying the overland caravan routes from the mid-eighteenth century right through into the twentieth. Because I discussed the Multānīs in detail in Chapter 6, here, I shall make a few points concerning the Shīkārpūris. They began by helping to finance the Afghani Durrani state as well as Afghani agriculture and artisanal production. But following the collapse of the Durrani state, the Shīkārpūris turned to financing the caravan trade between North India and Central Asia. Later still, they redeployed their energies into financing commercial agriculture in Bukhara and, above all, in the Ferghana valley in Central Asia, which ran through Kyrgyzstan, Uzbekistan and Tajikistan. Despite facing hostility from the Soviet Bolshevik state, the Shīkārpūris managed to maintain and indeed enhance their economic activities more generally. Moreover, they also increased their business in Afghanistan and Persia as well as in Xinjiang (in Northwest China, which had been held previously by the Zunghar Mongols before their extermination by the Qing army in the late-1750s). And, finally, in the twentieth century, they relocated from Shīkārpūr to Bombay, where they became the leading indigenous bankers in India, not least by taking on the Gujaratis and Marwaris on their own ground.[109]

Competitive–Cooperation and Entangled Chinese and Western Agencies

Last, but not least, I turn to consider some of the ways in which Chinese and Western agency became entangled in the nineteenth century. In Chapter 2, I explained how the Dutch VOC in Java was entangled with resident Chinese producers, merchants and tax farmers. But the Dutch were still reliant on Chinese financiers/traders during the nineteenth century, with the latter trading heavily in Indonesian products to Singapore and making the latter a rich entrepôt. Rajat Kanta Ray cites the US trade Consul's remark that was made at the beginning of the twentieth century: that it 'is this trade in Dutch East Indian

---

[108] Machado (2014: 273).
[109] See especially Markovits (2000: ch. 3).

products ... carried on by the Chinese that has built up Singapore into one of the greatest primary markets of the world'.[110] And Ray goes on to point out that the Chinese also set up 'money shops' in Singapore that increasingly displaced the itinerant remittance agents – a process that was completed after 1886 when the business became concentrated in about 250 Chinese remittance banks that transmitted the moneys via telegraph. By the beginning of the twentieth century, Chinese private banks morphed into joint stock banks, with the establishment of Kwong Yik Bank in 1903 that was the first of its kind in Singapore. Moreover, a group of Chinese investors set up the Sze Hai Tong Bank in 1906 that had branches in Bangkok and Hong Kong. Of note too was the establishment of the Chinese Chamber of Commerce in 1906 as well as three Chinese corporations of unprecedented size: the Eastern United Assurance Corporation (an insurance company), the Ho Hong Bank (1917) and the Chinese Commercial Bank (1912). Overall, the Chinese were fully capable of not only meeting but also working with British financial capital. More generally, though, the Chinese were primary in the Java–Singapore–Siam–China axis of trade.

So strong were the Chinese and Bugi (Indonesian) mercantile networks that even the British could not penetrate them. Instead, the British had to rely on the Chinese to negotiate with the Bugis and other Asian traders. Although the advent of the steamship undermined the trading power of the Bugis, the resilience of the Chinese enabled them to maintain their trading power in the Java–Singapore–Siam–China trading axis, given the extensity of their commercial networks, coupled with their own deployment of steamships.[111] Indeed, the Chinese traders and finance capitalists proved adept at navigating the modern Western business channels so that they could compete on their own terms with the Europeans and Americans. The Nanyang (Southeast Asian) Chinese enterprises of the early-twentieth century – the Ho Hong Combine in Singapore and the Oei Tiong Ham enterprise of Semarang in Java – managed to successfully straddle the Chinese and Western business worlds of commerce. Then in 1917, the Ho Hong Bank was established in Malaya, which provided banking services that could compete with the Western banks. It had worldwide connections that reached from Shanghai and Hong Kong to London and New York. Overall, before 1941, the vast majority of capital in Southeast Asia was Chinese, from which the English merchants benefited.[112]

---

[110] Cited in Ray (1995: 503).
[111] Ray (1995: 502–21).
[112] Ibid. (512–21).

If, according to Eurofetishists, the British monopolised the opium trade, how then are to explain that they found it difficult to penetrate the Chinese opium syndicates? As noted earlier, perhaps around 25 per cent of the opium trade was in Chinese hands. In the eighteenth century and especially nineteenth century, local Chinese merchants were able to effectively dominate provincial Chinese opium markets. And, moreover, there developed the Chinese opium guild. So successful was this guild that in 1879 and 1880, two Westerners tried to sue it, viewing it as a 'conspiracy against trade', but what in reality amounted to a conspiracy against the Western aspiration to gain trading dominance of China. The British complained that 'not a single one of us can trade independently and the trading is no good at all so long as this underground system exists'.[113] Moreover, the Chinese opium syndicates operated internationally, with 'the most significant of the new nineteenth century Nanyang Chinese partnerships [being] the opium syndicates. They emerged across the Malay Straits around 1889.'[114] Note that Nanyang comprised the southern border region of China and reached down into Southeast Asia. Ray singles out in particular the Penang opium and liquor farm syndicate (1907–9) that was formed by sixteen prominent Chinese businessmen and which paid the government $135,000 a month, while retailing the imported opium through no less than 145 licensed sub-farms.[115] Thus, to answer my question posed earlier, the British struggled to penetrate the Chinese opium syndicates because the latter were too powerful and autonomous.

The Emergence of the SGE as the Symbiotic Convergence of the European CWE and the Asian Bazaar System

In this section, I want to stand back to consider the bigger picture concerning the co-production of the SGE by Western and non-Western agents that I began in the last section. As we have seen throughout this book, Eurofetishism operationalises a binary, zero-sum game framework, which climaxes in the assumption that the expansion of the Western capitalist world economy (CWE) created the (second) global economy by forcibly 'incorporating' Afro-Asia through coercive capitalist imperialism. Put in the terms that I have discussed in this book, in the Eurofetishist vision, Western expansion – in what amounts

---

[113] Kasaba (1993: 235).
[114] Ray (1995: 531–2, 516–17).
[115] Ibid. (516–17).

to a strategy of *Drang nach Osten* – came at the direct cost of the Afro-Asian economies and peoples. However, this all obscures the process by which the Western CWE and the trans-regional Indian Ocean bazaar system converged within the multicultural contact zone to thereby create the SGE, rather than the two fronting off in a Manichaean battle to the death.[116]

While Eurocentrism is likely to dismiss the bazaar economy as but a 'traditional' and 'uncivilised' socioeconomic formation, the fact is that it contained elements of historical and modern capitalism as I explained in Chapter 8. Indeed, as Part I of this book has shown, the bazaar economy was based not simply on capitalist financial networks but was embedded fundamentally in extensive trading networks and hybrid production networks – so much so that Western capitalists were keen to accommodate it. Thus, the meeting of the Western capitalist system and the Asian bazaar economy should not be viewed as an instance of Western 'gesellschaft' triumphing over Asian 'gemeinschaft'.[117] For as Rajat Kanta Ray points out, Indians and Chinese in particular

were private bankers, wholesale merchants and commissioning agents who had been independently engaged in mobilizing and employing capital through time-tested Asian techniques and channels, which not only proved perfectly capable of yielding large returns in the new colonial context[s], but which the Western corporations found sophisticated enough to utilize for their own operations on terms profitable to themselves and to their Asian counterparts.[118]

Moreover, Christine Dobbin adds to this picture when she notes that between 1850 and 1940,

[w]ith centrality given to the conjoint communities themselves, we see expanding Western commerce and shipping in our period resting on a bedrock of Indian and Chinese money, commercial expertise and diaspor[ic] connections: Indian and Chinese firms both collaborating and competing with Western companies.... These Asian communities were conjoint to an even deeper extent; they not only helped to finance European economic endeavours in new markets flung across Asia, but they developed marketing networks, supplying credit for indigenous producers and traders and investing in local processing industries, so establishing essential links between [Europe and Asia].[119]

---

[116] See especially Washbrook (1990: 502) and Ray (1995: 552–3).
[117] Ray (1995: 551–2).
[118] Ibid. (553) and also Markovits (2000: 22).
[119] Dobbin (1996: 198, 199).

The binary vision of Eurofetishism also obscures the ways in which an effective division of labour was struck between Europeans and Asians across the globe in the nineteenth and twentieth centuries. Notably, numerous Asian groups expanded through synergistic practices that were conducted with European capital, though others migrated to the lower latitudes as the Europeans expanded into the 'tropical zone' – a process that marked not separate but inter-related expansions.[120] Thus, although European capitalist imperialism sometimes superseded the activities of Asian merchants and producers, nevertheless, the latter were sufficiently flexible enough to adapt and redeploy their activities into new areas and regions. And, in any case, intra-Asian trade still surpassed West–East trade throughout the nineteenth century.[121]

It is no coincidence that Eurofetishism finds its strongest expression in world systems theory. Having been forcibly 'incorporated' into the CWE, India is viewed as suffering 'dependency' in the formal-colonial 'periphery', while China faced a not-dissimilar fate in the informal-colonial 'semi-periphery'. But this necessarily buys into the trope of Asian passivity along with the whitewashing of Asian agency that is coupled with a fetishised conception of Western hyper-agency and structural imperial power. By contrast, revealing the interconnections between Western and non-Western agency brings to the fore the multicultural origins of imperialism and the SGE. For, as David Washbrook points out most aptly:

[t]he British Empire, and the world capitalist system which it did so much to expand, rested heavily on the intermediation of agencies constituted outside the core. Without those agencies, the forces of world capitalism would have been either much weaker, or else of a very different kind, than they were—and the history of the world would have been of a very different order.... It was precisely because the British did not have to invent, and therefore pay for, any of this that these intermediary agencies were so useful: the British harnessed their dynamic potential and rode them to a new world empire. It was an empire that, in critical ways, was as much Indian as British and contributed a strong Indian component to the world capitalist system it helped to develop.[122]

One notable example of such synergistic complementarities returns us to our discussion of ICTs. For while the Eurocentric and Eurofetishist literatures are replete with the claim that global markets were established through the onslaught of British-manufactured CTs, this misses the fact

---

[120] Ray (1995: 454–5, 553).
[121] Frank (2015: 276–80).
[122] Washbrook (1990: 490).

that the British did not create these markets *ex nihilo*. As I explained in Part I of this book, these markets had been created many centuries earlier by the Indians and Asians. Indeed, such markets did not spring out of nowhere but took centuries to develop. Thus, all the British were doing were superseding the ready-made ICT-dominated global markets, for as Giorgio Riello puts it nicely, '[p]art of the success of Western [cotton textile] producers lay ... in their capacity to use [pre] existing networks of exchange that allowed for the sale of their products worldwide'.[123] Nevertheless, this 'supersession' of Asia by the West was never complete and it was extremely short lived by world historical standards (as I explained in the first section of this chapter). In short, the reductive Eurofetishist ontology of the core/semi-periphery/periphery model means that it is unable to envisage or see the existence of the multicultural contact zone, which leads it to whitewash the many ways in which the Asians shaped and enabled European economic expansion as much as *vice versa*.

A final problem with the Eurofetishist conception of the 'European incorporation of Afro-Asia' lies in the point that Asians did not simply replicate Western economic practices. I discussed this in relation to the Chinese and Indian cotton textile industries in the first section of this chapter. More generally, the assertion that Giovanni Arrighi and his co-authors make with respect to East Asia's relationship to the modern Western capitalist thrust in the nineteenth century serves as a useful conclusion for my analysis of Asia, beyond the confines of China and Japan. Thus, with the European thrust, they argue,

the historical heritage of the East Asian system did not vanish in a generalized convergence toward Western practices ... There was convergence but through a process of hybridization that preserved and eventually revived important features of the East Asian system. And this hybridization was vital in revitalizing the region ... After 1945 rapid East Asian economic integration and expansion could occur only through the mobilization and revival of forms of business organization that resembled more closely the informally integrated networks of Chinese enterprises than the vertically integrated and bureaucratically managed structures of US enterprise.[124]

Kaoru Sugihara has argued persuasively that Asian countries did not replicate the Western industrial revolution, but funnelled it through their own brand of modern capitalism that he terms the 'Asian industrious

---

[123] Riello (2013: 266), my emphasis.
[124] Arrighi *et al.* (2003: 318–19).

revolution'.[125] This enabled them to utilise very large numbers of workers in line with their huge populations such that their capitalist technologies were designed not to be 'labour substituting', as was the case in the West, but to be 'labour intensive',[126] or, in Tirthankar Roy's phrase, 'labour augmenting'.[127] Accordingly, the Asian and the earlier European industrious revolutions should not be conflated. And, to reiterate from above, lest it be thought that this hybrid system comprised in part some kind of 'traditional' hangover, it should be borne in mind that Japan, China and India all overtook American and British cotton textile output in the middle-third of the twentieth century. Not only does this mean that 'tradition' and 'modernity' are not antithetical but also that 'they often co-exist happily [and] that tradition may prove in some cases to contain highly effective vehicles or instruments of change. Many traditional Asian institutions and forms proved surprisingly resilient or have been capable of adapting to meet new pressures without losing their essential character'.[128] In short, *contra* Eurofetishism, the fates of China and India cannot be simply read off from the imperial actions of the British or the logic of the Western-based CWE.

But what now remains to be answered are the twin questions as to how we can understand the transition from the first to the second global economy and whether there are significant continuities between these two social formations.

---

[125] Sugihara (2003).
[126] Chandavarkar (1994: ch. 7).
[127] Roy (2004: 3242).
[128] Murphey (1977: 29).

14 Varieties of Global Economy
From Historical to Modern Capitalism, c. 1500–2020

Introduction

The purpose of this chapter is not to summarise in slavish fashion all of the arguments of this book but rather to situate them within an analysis of the nature of, and the relations between, the two global economies that I have identified. In Chapter 8, I rebutted the common, orthodox Marxist claim that a global economy could *not* have existed before 1850 given the alleged prevalence of agrarian and pre-capitalist social relations of production alongside a 'thin merchant capitalism'. There, I argued that the first global economy (FGE) and the global trading system rested on a *historical capitalist* base that contained complex, hybrid forms of social relations, of which significant elements took modern capitalist forms. But, as I also noted in that chapter, this still does not answer the neo-Marxist insistence that the structural property of a global whip of external necessity was absent before 1850, thereby rendering the existence of the FGE null and void. Thus, for orthodox Marxists, the 'global whip', in conjunction with the presence of uneven and combined development (UCD), is a proxy for what transformationalists refer to as 'impact propensity'. And, given that these processes constitute vital defining characteristics of a global economy, so their presence needs to be confirmed if I am to maintain my claim that the FGE existed between 1500 and 1850.

The section 'Re-visioning the Global Whip of External Necessity beyond the Eurocentric Conception' executes two key tasks. The first task reveals both the Eurocentrism of the orthodox Marxist approach and, as a rebuttal to this, the presence of the Afro-Indian global cotton whip under conditions of UCD within the global historical capitalist FGE. This discussion also enables me to summarise the role of Indian structural power that derived from India's domination of global cotton textile markets. Second, I consider the differences between the historical capitalist and the modern capitalist global whips, revealing that the former was not only thinner than, but was qualitatively different to, the latter. For there I avoid the ahistorical trap of extrapolating back in time the specific properties of the modern capitalist whip. All of which, *in toto*, completes my defence of the existence of the FGE that I began in Chapters 7 and 8. And, in turn, revealing the different nature and intensities of the two respective whips simultaneously highlights the varieties of global economy that have existed in the last half-millennium.

The section 'Unveiling the Continuities between the First and Second Global Economies: Eleven Temporal Capillaries' challenges the prevailing ahistorical assumption in IPE and International Relations (IR), not to mention many other disciplines, that *transnationalism* within a properly global economy emerged only after 1945/79, given the highly problematic belief that mercantilist *internationalisation* prevailed before then. I challenge this ahistorical temporal binary conception by revealing a significant number of important continuities between the two global economies. However, as with my conception of the global whip of external necessity, I reject the claim that the global economy/globalisation has taken a single isomorphic form in the last 500 years. For this would, in turn, be a fundamentally ahistorical move, given that it would entail an extrapolation of the present contours of the modern capitalist global economy back to 1500. Indeed, as I argue in the first section, the FGE had different organisational properties to those of the second. Moreover, in the process, I reveal the much deeper historical origins of the second global economy (SGE) than have been recognised hitherto.

Re-visioning the Global Whip of External Necessity beyond the Eurocentric-Marxist Conception

This section, in effect, considers the dynamics of globalisation and the issue of global systemic economic change and transformation. This is undertaken by interrogating the neo-Marxist claim that a key factor underpinning the rise of the modern global economy lies with the emergence of the modern global capitalist whip of external necessity, which, in turn, promotes the *uniquely* modern capitalist phenomenon of UCD.

Historicising and Countering the Eurocentric Conception of the Global Whip of External Necessity

The insistence that a global whip of external necessity appears only with modern capitalism is captured neatly by the neo-Marxist IR scholar, Sam Ashman, who claims that UCD is not a theory of the initial or first transition to capitalism, but of 'late' capitalist development—that is, of development which occurs in the context, and perhaps also as a consequence, of capitalism's pre-existence elsewhere. Once capital exists in one small corner of north-western Europe, development for all others is immediately transformed [via the external modern capitalist whip of necessity].[1]

However, while it is certainly true that Britain's capitalist industrialisation was important in shaping the SGE, nevertheless, the dismissal of global factors in stimulating the 'first (i.e., British) transition' to industrial capitalism necessarily leads us back into the two-stage Eurocentric/Eurofetishist Big Bang theory. For it presumes the exceptional, endogenous British 'logic of immanence' in the rise of industrialisation (i.e., the first step) and its subsequent expansion through imperial globalisation to thereby re-make the world along capitalist lines (i.e., the second step). More significant in this context is my claim that the Afro-Indian global cotton whip was important in stimulating the British industrial transformation.

In a series of pioneering articles, Justin Rosenberg has advanced the original and provocative claim that UCD and external whips of necessity have existed not only before the nineteenth century but also throughout *all* of human history.[2] However, Sam Ashman and Neil Davidson have argued that this entails a *transhistoricised* conception of world history such that we should confine the twin processes of UCD and the external global whip of necessity to the period of *modern* global capitalism.[3] Given that Rosenberg is a leading proponent of global historical sociology (GHS), such a criticism is particularly stinging as it threatens the historical sociological integrity of his approach.

Importantly, since his early, albeit tentative, forays into the historical dimension of UCD and the external whip of necessity,[4] Alex Anievas, along with his co-author Kerem Nişancioğlu, developed this into a full-blown theoretical and empirical narrative in their superb 2015 book. There they reveal numerous historical episodes of external whips which, they claim, existed during the eras of what I refer to as Afro-Eurasian regionalisation (c. 600–1500) and the FGE (c. 1500–1850).[5] Nevertheless, as I noted in Chapter 1, the numerous external whips that they unveil in the pre-1850 era tend to be largely regional in nature, whereas the key one that I highlight for the 1500–1850 era is global in

[1] Ashman (2010: 184, 194). And see Davidson (2009: 18).
[2] For example, Rosenberg (2006, 2008).
[3] Ashman (2010) and Davidson (2009).
[4] Allinson and Anievas (2010).
[5] Anievas and Niancioğlu (2015).

nature. Though these regional whips are in my view extremely important for understanding the rise of the West, nevertheless, it is the presence of a *global* whip that is vital here, given that this is required to seal my argument concerning the existence of the FGE. But, as with the aforementioned criticism of Rosenberg's approach, so the challenge for mine is to produce a properly *historicised* conception of both UCD and the global whip of external necessity, in the absence of which the integrity of my own GHS approach is equally in jeopardy.

Impact Propensity via the 'Afro-Indian Global Cotton Whip of External Necessity' and UCD: A Key Property of Global Historical Capitalism

Having identified the Afro-Indian global cotton whip in Part I of this book, the issue now at stake lies in ascertaining how it served to bind and weave together the FGE. First of all, as I explained in Chapters 3 and 5, the key to global trade lay with the acquisition of Indian cotton textiles (ICTs), partly because they were so popular to wear but above all because they constituted a key means of universal exchange. It was for this reason that the Europeans sought to locate themselves within India so as to gain access to ICTs. As I also explained, the export of ICTs, partly by Europeans but above all by Indians and Asians, led to the creation of a twelve-sided (dodecagonal) ICT trading system that penetrated all continents after about 1500/71. Moreover, this ICT trading system was embedded within, and helped breathe life into, the global bullion trading system. The latter hinged on the sixteen-sided New World global silver trading system that also helped bind or thread the FGE together. In particular, with perhaps about 20 per cent of New World silver being sucked into India between 1600 and 1800 largely to finance non-Indians' purchases of ICTs, this, in turn, helped monetise and capitalise the Indian economy, which thereby enabled further investment in production that generated additional ICT exports across the world.

In this way, the supply of New World silver and the production and export of ICTs formed an entwined productive, financial and commercial global loop, thereby reflecting the global scope and significance of ICTs and the Afro-Indian cotton whip within the context of global UCD. All of which, in turn, reflects the importance of Indian structural power as a key process or property of the FGE, given that this mode of power organised and shaped the global trading system. But the critical question revolves around the way in which the Afro-Indian global cotton whip enabled the shift from global historical to modern global capitalism and thence the transition from the first to the second global economy.

As I explained in Chapters 3, 4, 9 and 10, the British had to rely principally *on re-exporting ICTs* to Africa in order to buy up slaves. For these slaves became important producers of raw cotton both in the Caribbean and later in the southern United States that supplied Lancashire's mills. Britain's dependence on acquiring ICTs reflected Indian structural power. Challenging India's cotton textile dominance, therefore, meant challenging Indian structural power in the FGE. As Figure 14.1 reveals, this objective spurred on the Lancashire cotton producers to mechanise the industry in order to produce very large quantities of high-quality cotton textiles that could *substitute for Indian textile re-exports*, none of which would have been possible under the prevailing inferior conditions of British handloom-weaver production. To this end, British inventors came up with the spinning jenny (1767), the water frame (1769), the mule (1779) and the power loom (1785), though these followed and complemented the invention of printing machines, most especially the wooden three-roller printer (1743) that was later perfected with the invention of the engraved metal-cylinder six-roller printing machine (1783). Initially, the spinning and weaving machines were driven by water power though this was superseded by steam power in the 1830s, which thereby enhanced massively the quantity of output. Only in this way could the British hope to compete and eventually outcompete ICTs in the Atlantic markets and, subsequently, across the many global markets that the Indians and Asians had created many centuries earlier. In short, responding to the Afro-Indian global cotton whip saw the British industrialise their cotton textile sector. How, then, might we conceptualise the Afro-Indian global cotton whip in relation to the modern British capitalist-imperial global whip that succeeded it?

Figure 14.2 presents the conceptual overview of the historical capitalist FGE and its succession by the modern-capitalist SGE under conditions of UCD and the impact of the Afro-Indian global cotton whip. The up-arrow on the far left-hand side is dashed in order to connote the point that the transition from the FGE to the SGE was more contingent than inevitable. This is largely because the Afro-Indian global cotton whip was qualitatively different from that of the modern global capitalist whip that was wielded by imperial Britain from c. 1850 to c. 1945 and subsequently by the liberal-imperial United States. Specifically, I describe the Afro-Indian cotton whip as 'thin'. For while the British were certainly responding to it under conditions of UCD when they mechanised their cotton industry, there was nothing inevitable about this particular response. For no other country or region responded to ICT imports in this way. So far as Britain and indeed other Western

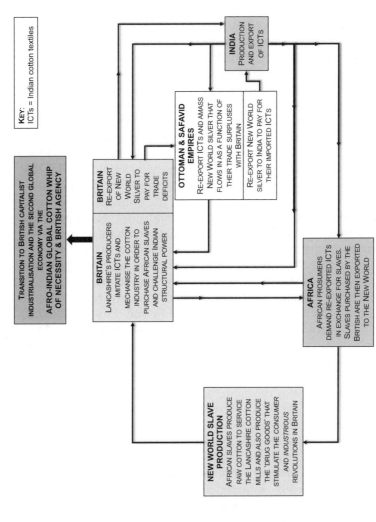

Figure 14.1 A simplified schematic of the Afro-Indian global cotton whip of necessity as a driver of Britain's cotton industrialisation.

Notes: I have not filled in all of the regions and countries that were affected by ICT exports. For the full image, see Figure 3.2 in Chapter 3.

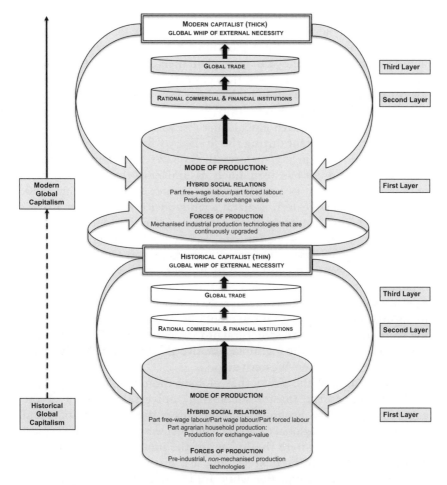

Figure 14.2 The three-layered architecture of historical global and modern global capitalism.

states were concerned, there was no other method that was available or indeed conceivable that could have met the Indian competition.

However, while the British had no choice but to invent these machines in order to compete with ICTs, this was nevertheless achieved through a remarkable degree of creative and inventive human agency. For this needs to be highlighted rather than ignored or downplayed. And, in any case, to ignore this element of Western agency simply leads us into the trap of Oriental fetishism. Which means that the transition from historical to modern capitalism, as much as that from the FGE to the SGE, was not inevitable but was more contingent. In short, the Afro-Indian global cotton whip opened up a space for the subsequent invention of numerous technologies, though only by factoring in British late-developmental agency can we explain their emergence. Overall, the upshot of this discussion is that the very process of UCD under global historical capitalism was itself highly 'uneven' – which is why I describe the Afro-Indian global whip as 'thin'.

By contrast, the modern global capitalist whip of necessity has been thicker and more potent during the SGE, by which I mean that UCD has been more 'even' in its transformative effects when compared with its predecessor, even if it has been much less universal than Eurofetishists have assumed. Thus, as I explained in Chapter 13, since about 1850, Western and non-Western societal agents borrowed the new British cotton machines together with the steam engine in order to enhance production in their own countries and regions, though handloom weaving remained a very important component in China and India well into the twentieth century. Which means that while the modern capitalist global whip has indeed been thicker than its historical capitalist predecessor, it would be wrong to reify or fetishise it within a Western totalising narrative. For to do so would be to exaggerate the power of the West and the Western structural properties of the SGE as much as it would underestimate the manifold adaptive and agential roles that have been performed by non-Western actors.

Relevant here is the point that globalisation scholars often view neoliberalism as the master-socialising, universal ideology of the contemporary global economy. Indeed, this is thought to be part and parcel of the modern global capitalist whip of necessity. Although critical scholars often exaggerate the impact of the modern global capitalist whip, as I explain in the next section, it *is* distinct from the previous Afro-Indian global whip. For while Indian structural power and the Afro-Indian global whip created structural processes within which global actors worked, nevertheless, this particular whip did not serve as a vehicle that sought to promote the imperial cultural conversion of societies along Afro-Indian civilisational norms.

Moreover, the associated process of UCD also needs to be properly historicised. Thus, under the SGE, non-Western societies have found themselves in positions of disadvantage relative to Britain first and the United States subsequently. Accordingly, the need to shift towards modern capitalism became important and indeed necessary, even if this has been done in different ways by different countries at different intensities. In the context of the FGE, by contrast, all countries around the world were behind both India and China, particularly with respect to cotton textile/yarn production as well as iron and steel production. But, as noted, this did not promote the response of industrialisation across the world to compete with them, for this was undertaken only by British developmental agents in the first instance. Accordingly, we can trans-historicise neither the external whip of necessity nor the associated process of UCD, since these change over time given that they exhibit both different forms and intensities and have existed at different levels – regional and global. But nor, by the same token, can we assume that the global whip of necessity is unique only to the post-1850 period, as is the wont of orthodox Marxists. All of which is brought together in Figure 14.3.

To reinforce my argument, it is worth considering various counterfactuals that my analysis throws up. Critically, we need to ask whether Britain's cotton-based industrialisation would have occurred in the absence of the Afro-Indian global cotton whip of necessity. The answer would likely be in the negative. More specifically, in the absence of the challenge of ICT exports, the British would most probably not have undergone a cotton-based industrialisation. For the woollen interests would have remained the key clothing producers in Britain. And, given that wool did not enjoy sufficient demand, domestically or globally, so mechanising the production process would *not* have happened – and nor

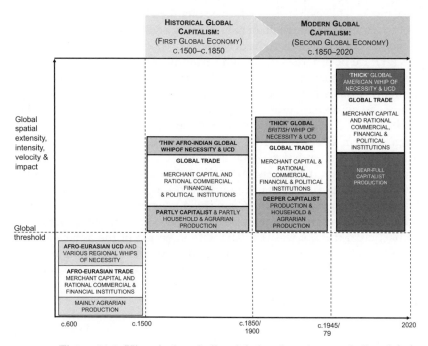

Figure 14.3 Historical capitalist global and modern capitalist global economies.

for that matter was mechanisation needed for the construction of the woollen warp as it was for the cotton warp in Britain. But in any case, as I noted in Chapter 10, the industry was known for its conservative nature, which means that radical technological change was highly unlikely to have occurred.[6] Moreover, given that the industrial mechanisation of the cotton industry was the most important driver of Britain's industrialisation more generally, so the absence of the former would have imparted a significant blow to the fortunes of the latter. Perhaps most intriguing of all is the point that if no ICTs had been re-exported to Africa, then the British would have had to have found something else with which to buy the slaves that they so desperately sought, though what this might have been remains a puzzle since no other British product was in sufficient demand in Africa. Certainly, neither wool nor iron and steel, including the production of weapons, would have filled the gap. And, in any case, an absence of African demand for ICTs in exchange for slaves might have had the effect of cutting off the tap-root of the cotton industrialisation process that Lancashire undertook.

On the other hand, the iron and steel revolution would most likely have occurred and the steam engine would also have been invented given that this was developed in order to drain water out of the flooded British coal mines. However, this needs to be qualified by the point that had the British Empire and its high demand for iron and later on steel for warfare purposes not existed, then the drive to industrialise iron/steel production would have been reduced, though certainly not eradicated. And, given that the British Empire, to a surprisingly important extent, was enabled in many ways by the role of ICTs, so in the absence of the global cotton whip, the existence of the empire might have been compromised. For as I explained earlier, Britain's Caribbean slave colonies that were so important in the seventeenth and eighteenth centuries rested on an ICT financial foundation. And, as I explained in Chapters 5 and 13, the English East India Company (EEIC)'s move into India during the seventeenth century was far more the result of the need to gain access to ICTs as a function of Afro-Asian trading logics in general and Indian structural power together with the Afro-Indian global whip of necessity in particular, than it was the deliberate intention of the 'official mind'. All of which is to say that global factors, in this case the empire, in conjunction with the Afro-Indian cotton whip under global UCD, played an important role in stimulating Britain's drive into a cotton and iron/steel industrialisation.

[6] Grinin and Korotayev (2015: 67).

Unveiling the Continuities between the First and Second Global Economies: Revealing Eleven Temporal Capillaries

As noted earlier, modern theories of globalisation and the global economy, particularly in IR and IPE, assume a 'great (ahistorical) temporal divide' between the pre- and post-1945 worlds. Typically, it is assumed that before 1945, the world was governed by *internationalisation* that comprised interconnections between nation states while after that date global *transnationalisation* predominated wherein transnational flows cut across sovereign state borders. Such a conception gives pride of place to *discontinuous* world historical change and development. But the problem here is that this takes us back to the ahistorical Eurocentric temporal binary that I discussed in Chapter 7, wherein the pre-1945 era is portrayed as less global than it was so that the post-1945/79 era can be (re)presented as even more global than it is. Partly so as to reveal the *significance* of the FGE, I seek here to transcend this temporal binary by highlighting all manner of continuities between these two global economies, while simultaneously qualifying the notion that the SGE has been *sui generis* and entirely unique.

To capture these continuities, Figure 14.4 reveals eleven 'temporal capillaries' that have run through both global economies and have thereby bound them together in hitherto unanticipated ways. Moreover, in a few cases, some of these even reach back into the era of Afro-Eurasian regionalisation (c. 600–c. 1500). But, as I explained earlier, this should not be taken to imply that the two global economies took homologous forms, not least because we would then have to talk about a singular global economy in the last 500 years.

To reinforce my claim that there were two global economies rather than one, I want to preface my analysis by highlighting various important discontinuities. By far and away, the key difference concerns the distribution of power. For the FGE lacked a hierarchical centre such that the distribution of power was polycentric.[7] Thus, although China and India were the two leading 'national' economies of the FGE, nevertheless, the roles of Europe, Africa, the Americas, Japan and the Islamic Middle East were also important, albeit to varying degrees. And none of these dominated the global economy. Moreover, while I have emphasised the significance of Indian structural power throughout this book, this did not entail the construction of a hierarchical global system, even though it enabled Indian merchant/finance capitalists to effectively

---

[7] See also Riello (2013) and Frank (1998).

organise financial, productive and commercial infrastructures that others, including the Europeans, relied on so that they too could engage in the FGE. By contrast, the architecture of the SGE has seen power skewed through a Western hierarchical formation, first under the European empires after 1492 in the Americas and subsequently in Afro-Asia after the mid-nineteenth century, before the United States took over the mantle of liberal-imperial hegemon after 1945. Nevertheless, with the current return of India and especially China, we are now witnessing a reversion towards the polycentrism of the FGE, a process that has been dubbed by Grinin and Korotayev as 'the great convergence'.[8]

A second key difference constitutes, in effect, a 'discontinuous continuity'. Here, I have in mind the point that the FGE was based on historical capitalism (as I explained in Chapter 8), whereas the SGE has rested on modern capitalism. A third key difference that globalisation scholars so often point to concerns the presence of international and global institutions/regimes. While much emphasis is accorded by IPE scholars to the UN institutions, typically the World Bank and the IMF, globalisation scholars also note that international institution-building began in the nineteenth century, with the International Telecommunication Union (1865), the Universal Postal Union (1874) and the European freer trade regime (1860–c. 80) usually being singled out. The consensus is that international and global institutions have been a feature of what I refer to as the SGE, and, no less significantly, these are generally presumed to be Western creations. Although my hunch is that many important modern institutions and regimes have also been partially shaped by non-Western actors,[9] most of which has gone underneath the Eurocentric radar, nevertheless no such global institutions existed in the FGE.

A fourth key difference concerns the velocity of global flows, which has, of course, sped up massively during the SGE, beginning with the transportation revolution that is associated with the opening of the Suez Canal in 1869 and the innovations of steam ships and telegraphs in the 1870s, all of which culminated with aeroplanes and the internet during the twentieth century. It is also clear that the rapidity of global flows can have equally sudden and rapid transformative impacts on global society and its constituent national societies.

The fifth key difference involves perhaps the ultimate 'globalisation paradox'. Apart from the near-universal consensus that globalisation

[8] Grinin and Korotayev (2015).
[9] See Lauren (1996) and Helleiner (2014).

is Westernisation, the second most common trope found in modern globalisation theory is the claim that the post-1945 era is radically distinct from the 1648–1945 era because the latter was dominated by 'internationalisation and the sovereign state', while the former saw the predominance of 'transnationalisation and the decline of the sovereign state'.[10] But the acute irony or paradox here is that the institutional matrix of sovereignty has *deepened* or *broadened* as the SGE has developed. Thus, if globalisation refers to 'the onset of the borderless world', as Kenichi Ohmae famously argued,[11] then the period of the FGE and that of Afro-Eurasian regionalisation between 600 and 1850 would be a far better candidate, given that rigid borders were generally not a feature and that all manner of political functions operated across boundaries. For example, Indians often served as tax collectors in many Asian states.[12]

What has made the sovereign state the pre-eminent political form today has been the numerous waves of decolonisation that have swept through the SGE. For non-Western agency succeeded in washing away the formal imperial systems that had emerged during the FGE, in which the metropolitan countries enjoyed (imperial) sovereignty while their colonies were strewn out below in a procession of gradated or partial sovereignties.[13] Although the sovereign state emerged during the FGE within Europe while non-sovereign political units predominated under European empires, nevertheless during the SGE decolonisation ensured that such colonised non-sovereign political units became transformed into sovereign states. Accordingly, I agree entirely with globalisation scholars that with respect to the presence of the sovereign state the post-1945 era was radically distinct from the previous era, but I do so for precisely the inverse reason that they advance. And so to the continuities.

Uncovering Eleven Temporal Capillaries Spanning the First and Second Global Economies

Here, I shall single out eleven temporal capillaries that have an interstitial quality in that they have run through both global economies. I shall consider these capillaries in descending order as they are presented in Figure 14.4.

---

[10] For example, Burton (1972), Camilleri and Falk (1993) and Strange (1996).
[11] Ohmae (1990).
[12] Pomeranz and Topik (2006: 32–5).
[13] Crawford (2002), Hobson and Sharman (2005), Bowden (2009), Phillips and Sharman (2015), Reus-Smit (2013), Acharya (2018: ch. 3), Gopal (2019) and Mathieu (2020).

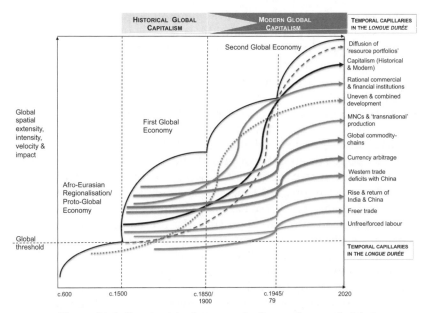

Figure 14.4 Continuities between the first and second global economies.

First, Eurocentric analyses assume that a unique feature of the modern global economy is the significant diffusion of 'resource portfolios' – ideas, institutions and technologies – specifically from west to east. But as I have argued at various points in this volume, and in much more detail in my 2004 book, many resource portfolios flowed across from the non-West to the West during the FGE. Moreover, while in this book, I have sought to factor Western (late-developmental) agency into the explanation of Britain's transition to capitalist industrialisation – unlike in my 2004 book – nevertheless, I argue that Britain did not modernise *ex nihilo* as the product of a purely endogenous journey, but was enabled *in part* by its emulation and higher adaptation of non-Western resource portfolios. And while it is true that diffusions from west to east have predominated during the SGE, nevertheless, the generic phenomenon of global diffusion remains a constant across the two global economies.

Relevant here is the point that globalisation scholars on both the left and right view neoliberalism as the master-socialising, universal ideology of the contemporary global economy.[14] Indeed, this is thought to be part

---

[14] Harvey (1991), Friedman (1999, 2005) and Wolf (2005).

and parcel of the modern global capitalist whip of necessity. But while it is true that there was no equivalent universal ideology in the FGE, nevertheless, this should not be taken to imply that ideologies and ideas did not move around the world in impactful ways. For no country lived in splendid ideological isolation, and religions such as Christianity, Islam and Buddhism flowed across boundaries to re-make societies throughout the world.[15] Moreover, all manner of ideas on science, astronomy, mathematics, geography, philosophy and many other intellectual areas flowed to Europe from the Islamic Middle East and North Africa as well as from India and China that helped propel the Renaissance and European Scientific Revolution.[16]

But while neoliberalism is the key *global* ideology of the SGE, the problem is that many analyses, Eurocentric and Eurofetishist alike, associate it with a totalising Western homogenisation process.[17] And this necessarily obscures the continuity of non-Western agency. Numerous non-Eurocentric scholars have qualified or challenged this totalising Eurocentric/Eurofetishist narrative by considering how Western and non-Western cultural forces generate 'heterogeneous dialogues',[18] which produce a 'cultural melange' that reflects a global 'transculturalism'.[19] And others have rightly focused on how Western ideas are refracted through non-Western cultural filters to produce hybrid outcomes in different countries through processes of 'domestication', 'glocalisation' or (subversive) 'mimicry',[20] as also occurred during the FGE. Equally, Indian and Chinese cotton industrialisations after the mid-nineteenth century 'domesticated' Western industrial processes within their indigenous production systems and cultures, as I argued in Chapter 13. All of which challenges the notion of a totalising global 'civilising process',[21] while also pointing up continuing elements of non-Western agency.

One particular notable example here is that of IMF structural adjustment programs, which are said to culturally convert third world economies according to the Western standard of neoliberal civilisation. Though undoubtedly containing elements of truth, nevertheless, the assumption that the West completely guts non-Western cultures and socially re-engineers them along pure neoliberal lines leads us into

---

[15] For a particularly sophisticated discussion, see Bayly (2002).
[16] Goonatilake (1998), Hobson (2004: ch. 8), Goody (2004), Bala (2006), Ghazanfar (2006), Raju (2007), Al-Rodhan (2012) and Al-Hassani (2015).
[17] For example, Harvey (1991) and Krishna (2009).
[18] Appadurai (1996).
[19] See, respectively, Pieterse (2020) and Kraidy (2005).
[20] See, respectively, Prestholdt (2008), Acharya (2018) and Bhabha (1994).
[21] Linklater (2020: ch. 5).

the Eurofetishist trap. For this presumes that the West imprisons non-Western states and cultures within a neoliberal-imperial *iron cage*. A better analogy would be to view this as a neoliberal-imperial *net*, given that non-Western states sometimes find various ways of escaping through its gaps and holes.[22]

Given that the next three capillaries were described in the first two sections of this chapter, so I shall move through them very quickly. Thus, a second inter-related temporal capillary is that of capitalism, though this takes the form of *historical* capitalism before c. 1850 and *modern* capitalism increasingly thereafter. But it is also clear that the modern capitalist global economy is much deeper and more intense than was its historical capitalist predecessor. A third key temporal capillary is that of rational commercial and financial institutions, which comprise the second layer of historical and modern global capitalism, as I explained in Chapter 8. And, a fourth key temporal capillary is that of the external whip of necessity alongside UCD. For while these exhibit certain differences in the first and second global economies as I explained in the last section, nevertheless, these vital features are not entirely unique to the SGE. All of which means, to cite Pim de Zwart once again, that 'the entering of a new phase of globalization [in the nineteenth and twentieth centuries], as revolutionary as it might seem, does not alter the reality of the global economy that came before'.[23]

A fifth temporal capillary comprises the multinational corporation (MNC) and transnational production. Presentist IPE scholars view the latter as unique to the post-1979 era and the former as a post-1945 phenomenon.[24] While there is certainly some pertinence to this discontinuity, nevertheless, there were some preliminary signs of these phenomena during the FGE. The European East India Companies (EICs) are relevant here insofar as they were precursors to the modern MNC.[25] Notable too is the production of ICTs that the Companies sourced in India. Four processes are relevant here.

First, the EICs were joint stock companies that exported foreign direct investment and, moreover, they enjoyed limited liability. Second, during the eighteenth century the EEIC issued specific design orders for the Indian textile producers to meet so that it could import ICTs to British consumers. And, later, the company dealt directly with the Indian producers given that before then it was dependent on Indian

---

[22] Broome (2010) and Seabrooke (2010).
[23] de Zwart (2016: 197).
[24] Gereffi *et al.* (2005).
[25] Held *et al.* (1999: 238–9) and Robins (2012).

intermediaries and agents. After 1722, the British were allowed to import plain Indian textiles into Britain so long as they were printed on and then re-exported for sales abroad rather than at home. But as I explained in Chapter 6, Indian family firms were also early proto-global companies, exporting trading products abroad, predominantly ICTs. Subsequently, they financed foreign production – often agricultural – through extending loans, from which they derived large profits that were later remitted back to India and invested in new firms. Moreover, these merchants had access to large pools of capital funds that were as large as those that the biggest banks in Europe could provide (as I also explained in Chapter 6). Indian cotton textile producers were relayed consumer information from abroad that was used to tailor their production not only for markets in England but also for those that were peppered throughout the Indian Ocean system. In Africa, indigenous intermediaries – the *Patamares* and the *Vashambadzi*, for example – fed this information to the resident Indians who then relayed this to producers back in India via intermediaries. But, in addition, local African producers often re-worked the imported ICTs to suit the changing tastes of consumers in local African markets. Though clearly different to the transnational production systems that we find today, nevertheless, all of this constituted a crude but early form of such production. That is, the ICT trading system constituted an early and extensive global production chain.

A sixth temporal capillary comprises the existence of global-commodity chains. Though certainly an important feature of the late SGE, there are signs of such a phenomenon occurring during the FGE. Chapters 3 and 4 discussed in detail what I have called the global 'super-commodity ICT chain'. By the mid-eighteenth century, this extended to all parts of the world that covered the twelve-sided (dodecagonal) ICT trading system. It involved Indian as well as Asian and European merchants transporting ICTs across the world. Moreover, this was no ordinary commodity chain. For it was unique in that its core property was one of exceptionally high fungibility, given that other trading groups used ICTs as a currency of exchange that was deployed to a wide variety of commercial and productive ends. All in all, no global-commodity chain of such qualitative magnitude and transformative significance exists to rival it today. For not only did it weave the FGE together but it also played a vital role in stimulating Britain's transition to industrial capitalism, which in turn has been a vital component of the SGE.

The next three temporal capillaries relate most especially to India and China. The seventh capillary refers to the trade deficits that the United States has endured, first with Japan in the 1970s and 1980s – though these have continued since then but have gone un-noticed – as well as with West Asia and subsequently with China, especially from around 2000. But this, in turn, is not unique to the late SGE because it fast-tracks us back to the future of the FGE when European countries suffered structural trade deficits with India, China and West Asia. Moreover, this seventh capillary overlaps with the eighth, which concerns the contemporary outflow of US dollars in the form of treasury bonds to China (as well as to Japan and West Asia), given that this finds its approximate equivalent in the outflow of American silver to pay Europe's trade-creditor countries during the FGE – specifically, China as well as India and Islamic West Asia once again. Poignantly, this silver took the form of various dollar denominations such as Spanish Rix dollars and Portuguese Piastres and Pacatas. And while it is certainly true that currency speculation and currency arbitrage trading is a prominent feature of the modern SGE, back during the FGE, this occurred through the global silver recycling process, as I explained in Chapter 3. This was certainly a global process back then, not least because silver was extracted from Latin America and then shipped across to Europe, China, Islamic West Asia, Southeast Asia, Africa and India before some of the gold was shipped back to Europe or to India. All of which was embedded in the sixteen-sided global Atlantic silver system. But the process was somewhat less extensive and far less intensive than it is today, even though it was extremely important in binding the FGE together.

The ninth temporal capillary refers to the importance of China to the global economy. Critically, what we are witnessing today is not the *rise* of China since 1978, as is commonly assumed within IR and IPE, but the *return* of China to near the centre of the (second) global economy.[26] And, no less, we are witnessing the return of India and Japan – given that the former was a key player throughout the FGE while Japan became reasonably significant after c. 1530. Nevertheless, this is obscured by the Eurocentric vision in which European capitalism is treated as the originary benchmark against which modern Chinese – as well as Indian and Japanese – development is judged. But this misses the point that China, India and Japan had all been early developers, while Britain and the continental European countries were late developers.[27] Moreover, given that Britain not only borrowed numerous ideas, technologies and institutions particularly from China but also from Islamic West Asia and India, as noted earlier, then equally we might treat China or these other

---

[26] See also Jones *et al.* (1993) and Zhang (2020).
[27] Hobson (2004: chs. 3–4, 9, 11).

Asian countries as the originary benchmark against which British late-development should be judged. In reality though, neither benchmark position is feasible for replacing a Eurocentric with a Sinocentric or Asian centric benchmark would be no more appropriate than measuring China, Japan and India today according to a Eurocentric standard.

Thus, we need to ask 'what's in a word – rise or return'? As it turns out, a very great deal. For depicting China as 'rising' since 1978 leads back into Eurocentric thinking, insofar as its capitalist success is presumed to have been a function of China simply emulating, or conforming to, Western capitalist practices. Indeed, it is reminiscent of Marx's famous Eurocentric mantra that the '[European] country that is more developed industrially only shows, to the [non-Western] less developed, the image of its own future'.[28] Or in Martin Jacques' nice turn of phrase, Eurocentric thinking 'still sees [global] history as a one-way ticket to Westernization'.[29]

Eurocentrism paints China as a 'late-late-developer' whose early development is conjured into thin air as if it never happened. Moreover, it becomes meaningless to talk about Chinese developmental agency given that in this Eurocentric vision the late-late-developing state simply replicates the processes of Western capitalism. The reality, however, is that China has undergone multiple developmental paths to modernity rather than plying a singular passage to Westernisation. It began with its long *historical capitalist* path at the inception of the economically impressive Song dynasty (post-960 CE). Following its subsequent rise to near the centre of the FGE during the late Ming and Qing periods ('going global 1.0'), China then moved much later through its exceptional socialist path of closure and retreat under Mao to a more open *modern capitalist* path since 1978 under Deng Xiaoping, which has subsequently returned it to near the centre of the (second) global economy ('going global 2.0'). Thus, China's position near the centre of the global economy today is symptomatic of a key vital temporal capillary that links the first and second global economies. Three further points are necessary to clinch my claim.

First, reading contemporary China through a Eurocentric lens views its joining of the World Trade Organization in 2001 and its shift to freer trade following Mao's highly protectionist retreat, as a clear example of China's emulation of Western trade practice. But if we view this through a non-Eurocentric global historical–sociological lens, then China is simply returning to its post-1684 freer trading posture, following the limited

[28] Marx (1867/1954: 19).
[29] Jacques (2012: 564).

period of closure between 1661 and 1683 (see Chapter 2). Zhang Shizhi argues that China's 'managed (economic) liberalism' forms the lowest common denominator of the post-2001 and post-1684 periods.[30]

Second, although China has adapted various modern Western capitalist processes, nevertheless reducing China's development to the status of a mere follower or emulator of Western economic practices ignores the part presence of modern capitalist social relations of production in various industries such as porcelain, iron, tea, cotton and silk textiles well before 1850. Also significant here is the *cultural specificity* of its overseas lending programme in both Africa and Latin America today. Often the kind of scholars who ignore this buy into the monological notion that Western neoliberalism and the associated Washington Consensus is *the* master-socialising ideology of the (second) global age. Even if one rejects the salience of the notion of the 'Beijing consensus',[31] the fact is that China does not attach *economic conditions* to its lending programmes and nor does it use them as a vehicle for spreading Sinic civilisation around the world.[32] And, to the extent that any conditions are laid down, these are purely *political* in nature – specifically, the requirement that states accept both China's control over the Spratly Islands in the South China Sea and that Taiwan is Chinese.[33] Which is precisely why African and especially left-wing Latin American governments have been so keen to strike up deals with China as a preferable alternative to Western finance and its neoliberal structural adjustment programmes.[34] Accordingly, when compared with Western lending programmes, China does global capitalism differently. Thus, we are beginning to see the emergence of a global economy with Chinese characteristics.[35]

Third, it is notable that with the return of China and India we are moving back toward the future of the polycentric global economic order that existed after about 1500, having gone through a relatively brief but highly significant world historical-changing Western interlude between 1850 and c. 2008. This phenomenon finds its expression in various terms advanced by IR scholars, which include the shift to a 'multiplex world',[36] or from 'centred globalism' to 'decentred globalism',[37] or the emergence

---

[30] Zhang (2020).
[31] Ramo (2004).
[32] Jacques (2012: ch. 10).
[33] O'Keefe (2018: 138–9).
[34] Ramo (2004), Jacques (2012) and O'Keefe (2018: ch. 6).
[35] Jacques (2012: 596–608).
[36] Acharya (2018).
[37] Buzan and Lawson (2015).

of 'embedded pluralism',[38] or last, but not least, the rise of economic multipolarity in a post-Western world.[39] But, as Lily (L. H. M.) Ling has constantly reminded us in her pioneering postcolonial books, 'multiple worlds' have *always* co-existed though they have been drowned out by the noise of Eurocentric 'Westphalia world' in the Western imagination.[40] All in all, I would like to conclude this discussion by paraphrasing one of William McNeill's conclusions to his classic work, *The Rise of the West*, that

the return of China [and Japan and India] is accelerated not only when one or another Asian or African people throws off European [colonial] administration and not only when they adapt Western techniques, ideas and attitudes but also when they return to their own non-Western historical roots to forge their own way ahead.[41]

Paradoxically, though, this takes us to Peter Katzenstein's important claim that what we are witnessing today is not the 'return' of seventeenth-century China, as if history (and China) has undergone a linear or possibly a cyclical path, but a 'recombination' of a new and old China in a changed global context in which the West had more recently become the dominant civilization.[42]

The tenth capillary necessarily flows on from the ninth and reveals another Eurocentric great illusion that globalisation scholars have been rather too easily seduced by. For the alleged era of internationalisation between 1648 and 1945 is generally thought of as mercantilist and protectionist, whereas the post–1979 global economy is thought of as one that is increasingly moving towards freer trade. But, as I explained in detail in Chapter 7, this illusion is produced by a Eurocentric *camera obscura*, given that between 1500 and c. 1945 only in the West do we encounter generally moderate to high levels of protectionism given that the non-Western world on average likely achieved freer trade, notwithstanding various forms of non-tariff trade regulations. Thus, as the West moved towards freer trade in the 1970s and 1980s, it seems fair to say that it was 'catching up' with the non-Western freer trading norm that had been achieved hundreds of years earlier during the FGE. Seen from this angle, Sankaran Krishna's postcolonial-Marxist (Eurofetishist) claim, that '[p]olitical compulsion of weaker nations and peoples [by the West], and military coercion over them, has *always*

---

[38] Acharya and Buzan (2019).
[39] Stuenkel (2016).
[40] Ling (2014); also Agathangelou and Ling (2009).
[41] McNeill (1965: 878–9).
[42] Katzenstein (2012a, 2012b); also Jacques (2012: ch. 12).

overlain so-called free trade',[43] obscures the point that freer trade is *not* the creation of the West. The ironic double standard here is that it was the highly protectionist British who belatedly caught up with the non-West in 1846 only to disingenuously proclaim ownership of 'free trade', much as the highly protectionist Americans would do a century later. All of which means that with the exceptional period of Western protectionism, freer trade constitutes a continuity between the first and second global economies.

Last, but not least, I turn to the eleventh capillary, which comprises the continuity of forced/unfree labour. And, once again, this comes in the guise of yet another Eurocentric great illusion. As I discussed in Chapter 8, orthodox Marxism, most especially Political Marxism, shares with Smithian liberalism the assumption that modern capitalism is defined by free wage labour such that forced/unfree labour is assumed to necessarily die out as this mode of production deepens through time and space.[44] But as various authorities have shown, not least Nicola Phillips, Genevieve LeBaron and Sébastien Rioux, forced labour has increased in the last four decades as neoliberal global capitalism has deepened.[45] In the White Western imagination, we comfort ourselves with an image of Black slavery that not only consigns it to the deep historical past of the Atlantic slave trade where the average life expectancy was a mere seven years, but we congratulate ourselves that great Western humanitarians such as Abraham Lincoln and William Wilberforce mercifully brought this great human tragedy to an end. Unfortunately, not only does this miss the point that non-Western indentured labour became important after 1833 but that Black slavery continued in the Southern states' cotton plantations after 1865 through the more hidden medium of the US prison service, where life expectancy of Black convicts-as-slaves was a mere seven years.[46] Lest it be thought that this was an unfortunate, albeit temporary, hangover of the old system of slavery, it turns out that it continues today and has taken a potent form not least through the reintroduction of convict chain gangs in 1995 in numerous US southern states.[47] And what this specific context has in common with the wider development of forced labour across the global economy is the impact of global neoliberalism and, most notably, the accompanying Eurocentric

[43] Krishna (2009: 4).
[44] Rioux *et al.* (2019).
[45] Phillips *et al.* (2014), LeBaron and Ayers (2013), Rioux (2013) and Rioux *et al.* (2019).
[46] LeBaron (2012).
[47] Ibid. (243–4).

discourse that takes us back to the future of the FGE with its scientific racist discourses of Black inferiority.[48]

Conclusion

And so, finally, we arrive at the terminus of our long voyage. Much as Acharya and Buzan call for a 'Global IR',[49] so this book calls for a New Global Political Economy. As I noted in Chapter 1, prevailing conceptions of International Political Economy/Global Political Economy are mired in Eurocentrism, presenting the global as the provincial West masquerading as the universal. A good example of this lies in critical analyses of North–South relations, which are almost invariably presented in terms of a hyper-agential, all-powerful metropolitan Northern core dominating an agency-less, passive Southern periphery. By no means is this to deny the presence of a power gap in favour of the West since the late-nineteenth century. But the central challenge of New Global Political Economy is to begin the task of unveiling instantiations of agency within the Global South even though they clearly operate within global structural constraints. And, for this reason, potential critics of my focus on non-Western agency who view it as reflecting some kind of liberal voluntarism or liberal pluralism miss their target.

Moving beyond reductive conceptions of agency-as-power opens up new vistas of unexplored Southern agency. These include the manifold ways in which Southern agency interconnects with Northern agency in ways that shape both the Global North and South as well as the SGE. While the role of great economic powers such as China and India are obviously important, nevertheless, we also need to reach down to the micro-level of everyday agency within the Global South, as I have argued elsewhere.[50] Moreover, much more work needs to be undertaken on intra-Southern relations rather than presuming that North–South relations are the only ones that matter. It has been my intention in this book to begin such an analysis by exploring the historical instantiations of Western and non-Western agency in the making of the global economies. The task ahead, I believe, is to develop all this as it has played out in the twentieth and early-twenty-first century,[51] some of the cues for which I have pointed to in this chapter.

---

[48] See also Alexander (2012).
[49] Acharya and Buzan (2019).
[50] Hobson and Seabrooke (2007).
[51] See especially Stuenkel (2016).

Appendix 1: Guesstimating the Size of the Trade in Indian Cotton Textiles in the Seventeenth and Eighteenth Centuries

Here, I provide the background explanations, sources and calculations of the size of the export trade in Indian cotton textiles (ICTs) for the seventeenth and eighteenth centuries that I discussed in Chapter 5. Because estimating the size of the overland and seaborne trade in ICTs that was carried by Indian merchants is highly problematic given the general lack of available archival data, so I am forced to rely on derivative calculations. The majority of my focus will be on ascertaining the size of the overland trade. There are two methods that I use, the first of which counts the number of camels that traversed the overland routes while the second guesstimates the size of foreign trade as a percentage of total ICT production. And so to the camels.

The first problem here is that on the few occasions when some kind of figure is offered in the primary and secondary literatures, it is usually a single one for a single year. Not infrequently, this comprises the Dutch-reported figure of 20–25,000 camels on the Indian–Persian overland route in 1639,[1] or sometimes the Dutch-reported figure of 25–30,000 in the 1660s.[2] Notable in the latter context is Scott Levi's single estimate for the caravan trade to Isfahan in Persia from which he draws out an average annual figure:

European accounts of the seventeenth century suggest that ... between 25,000 and 30,000 camels annually transported Indian merchandise—principally cotton textiles—along the overland trade routes from Qandahar to Isfahan. Considering that the standard camels used in India carried loads that weighed in excess of 400 pounds, these figures suggest that India traders supplied Iranian markets with more than 5000 tons of merchandise each year.[3]

---

[1] For example, Van Santen (1991: 90).
[2] For example, Riello (2009b: 326, 2013: 23, 75).
[3] Levi (2016: 98).

From these figures, he derives a final annual average guesstimate of 72 million yards of cloth that were transported from India to Isfahan.[4] But if Indian camels could carry loads of 450 or 500 pounds (lbs) over these long distances,[5] then these calculations might err on the side of caution, assuming, of course, that we accept this number of camels as representative of the seventeenth-century trade more generally.

Here, however, I am cognisant of the point that Sinappah Arasaratnam makes: that we must avoid giving episodic observations a long-term significance unless these are validated over a sustained time period.[6] And what is clear from the available contemporary observations, which is all we have to go on, is that the number of camels arriving in Persia (mainly in the capital of Isfahan) varied considerably from year to year and from observer to observer. These vary from a low of 800 camels (2 million yards) in 1634,[7] to 3,000 camels (about 8 million yards) in 1615, though when wars disrupted the sea route, this figure would rise to 12–14,000 camels (about 34 million yards),[8] to 7–8,000 camels around 1610 (20 million yards),[9] to 10–20,000 pack animals that went from India to Kabul each year,[10] to 20,000 camels (59 million yards) in 1615,[11] to 25–30,000 camels (65 million to 79 million yards or an average of 72 million) in the 1660s, as noted earlier.

These extremely crude estimates fluctuate wildly in a range between 2 million and 72 million yards. But because they are based on the amounts that went from India to Persia so we also need to consider those amounts that were destined for the thriving overland markets in Afghanistan, Central Asia and Russia. One contemporary estimate suggests that as late as 1813, the number of Indian camels, which carried mainly ICTs from Bukhara in Central Asia to Russia, comprised 4–5,000 camels (or about 11–13 million yards).[12] This is significant because the Multānī trade in ICTs to Russia peaked well before 1813. Adding in this figure takes the aggregate volume of ICTs to anywhere between roughly 14

---

[4] The calculation is as follows: 27,500 camels multiplied by 400 equals 11 million lbs. Divided by 2,200 equals 5,000 tons and when multiplied by 14,400 equals 72 million yards (as there are 14,400 yards of cloth in one ton).

[5] See, respectively, Steensgaard (2007: 68) and Dale (1994: 48).

[6] Arasaratnam (1987: 95).

[7] Steensgaard (2007: 68–9). Curiously, Steensgaard quotes a figure of 2.1 million yards that he assumes is carried by about 5,500 camels, though this amount could have been carried by about 800 camels.

[8] Steele (1615/1824).

[9] Coverte (1612).

[10] Bābar cited in Levi (2016: 97–8, 145).

[11] Roe (1926: 446).

[12] Ullah (1843: 332).

million and 84 million yards. And although the amounts that were offloaded in central Asia were almost certainly larger than those that were sold in Russia, I shall assume that a further 12 m yards were sold there. Adding this on takes the aggregate figure to between 26 m and 96 m yards.

What then of overseas trade? Numerous scholars argue that the size of the seaborne trade probably surpassed that of the overland caravan routes,[13] though others suggest that trade was apportioned about equally.[14] Thus, if as much trade went by sea as by land, then this produces a range of between 52 million and 192 million yards that were carried by Indians and other Asians, including West Asian Muslims and Armenians.

Given that 192 million yards is an upper bound estimate and 52 million a lower bound figure, then if we take the median as a plausible guesstimate, we arrive at a figure of around 124 million yards of ICT exports. Still, so as to err on the side of caution, I shall assume a figure of 100 m yards in total. But how plausible is this?

Some have argued that between 4 and 12 per cent of the total ICT production was exported, with a mid-point being 8 per cent, though unfortunately no substantiation of these figures is provided.[15] It is certainly the case that the demand for ICTs was widespread among global consumers. Given that this was the single most important global trading item after 1500 and that much of the world's population became clothed in Indian cottons,[16] a figure of only 8 per cent of total Indian production destined for the global market would not be too high. For it would have been impossible to clothe so many people around the world with anything much below 100 million yards. If a cotton shirt weighs about a quarter of a lb of cotton and one yard of yarn weighs roughly the same, then 100 million yards coverts to about 100 million shirts. Interestingly, for example, it has been claimed that as early as 1602, there was, on average, one square metre sold to each person in Southeast Asia.[17] Given that the world's population in 1700 was around

---

[13] Dale (1994: 46), Alam (1994: 213) and Steensgaard (2007: 69–71).

[14] Barendse (2002: 245).

[15] Vries (2013: 276) suggests a range between 4 and 12 per cent for the year 1800. Jeffrey Williamson (2011: 76) suggests that in 1800, 'India's exports had dropped dramatically to 6 to 7 per cent of the domestic textile market, a fall of 20 percentage points … over the [previous] half century'. Which means that prior to 1750, the figure would have been around 8 per cent.

[16] Washbrook (2007: 90).

[17] Reid (2009: 36–7).

650 million, so this means that ICT exports could have clothed about 15 per cent of the world's population.

If about 8 per cent of ICT production was exported, then running with the figure of 100 million yards of exports yields a total Indian production figure of about 1.3 billion yards. How plausible is this? Broadberry and Gupta estimate that total ICT production destined for *domestic* markets in the first half of the seventeenth century was about 1.2 billion yards. So if we add to this a further 100 million yards that were exported this confirms my guesstimate, in that 8 per cent of 1.3 billion yards comes out at about 100 million yards. They then provide further estimates of the size of domestic textile production: 1.4 billion yards in 1700, 1.6 billion in 1751 and 1.7 billion in 1801.[18] If these figures of total production sound implausibly high, it is notable that the figure of 1.6 billion yards for 1751 is about a quarter of the Chinese production figure in that year.[19] So adding on 8 per cent to these figures of total Indian domestic production yields the following estimates of ICT exports: 96 million yards in 1650, 112 million in 1700, 128 million in 1750 and 136 million in 1801.

To guesstimate the size of the Asian trade in ICTs, I then subtract the guesstimates of the European share, which yields the following figures: 89 million yards (1600/50), 97 million yards (1700), 101 million yards (1750) and 93 million yards (1800). Interestingly, Parthasarathi dismisses as 'highly problematic and likely to be wildly off the mark' the figure of fifty million yards that Tirthankar Roy produced for 1800, which Roy used to support his claim that Indian exports in general were very low.[20] What then of the estimates of European sales of ICTs?

I guesstimated the British distribution of ICTs as three million yards (1600/50), six million yards (1690/1710), eleven million yards (1745/55) and twenty-four million yards (1795/1805). These were calculated in the following way. First, I took the robust East India Company (EIC)-import data from Chaudhuri, Riello and Bowen.[21] I then added the average re-export trade from the data in Wadsworth and de Lacy Mann,[22] though these figures are an extrapolation of the 1773/80 years. I then guesstimated Britain's share in the intra-Asian country trade to be half the size of the import trade into Britain, given that even as late as in the 1790s, the English East India Company (EEIC) country trade was worth about half of the value of its imports of ICTs into Britain.[23] Moreover,

---

[18] Broadberry and Gupta (2009: 21).
[19] Pomeranz (2000: 334).
[20] See Parthasarathi (2005: 10–11).
[21] Chaudhuri (2006: 540–5), Bowen (2007); and Riello (2009a: 265).
[22] Wadsworth and de Lacy Mann (1931: 162).
[23] Riello (2009b: 324).

it was the Vereenigde Oost-Indische Compagnie (VOC) rather than the EEIC that was most heavily engaged in the intra-Asian country trade.[24]

I guesstimated the *overall* European trade in ICTs as seven million yards (1600/50), fifteen million yards (1690/1710), twenty-seven million yards (1745/55) and forty-three million yards (1795/1805). These were calculated in the following way. First, I took the robust European company import data from Riello.[25] I then added the re-export trade, which I guesstimated as double the size of the British figure. Finally, I guesstimated the intra-Asian country trade to be the same size as the total import trade into Europe; and given that the VOC was the key player in the country trade, so this figure is certainly an exaggeration (given too that the VOC's distribution of ICTs in the country trade was about a quarter lower than its imports into Europe in 1712 – the year when we have a clear estimate of the size of this trade).[26]

[24] Chaudhuri (2006: 208–13) and Riello (2009b, 2013: 93–5).
[25] Riello (2009a: 265).
[26] Riello (2013: 95).

Appendix 2: Estimating the Size of the Revenues Generated by All Atlantic-based Colonial-related Activities that Potentially Funded British Industrial Investment

Here, I provide the background explanations that underpin the calculations I presented in Chapter 9 concerning the impact of Atlantic colonial-related profits on British industrialisation.

Aggregate Contribution of Slave-Related Activities to British Industrial Investment

The Marxist historian, Robin Blackburn, has most usefully drawn together a set of data that aggregates some of the key contributions of the so-called triangular system to British industrialisation for the year 1770,[1] which also includes the understated Anstey profit figure of £115,000 for the slave trade.[2] For 1770, which was an unexceptional year,[3] total profits for all Atlantic slave-based colonial production and related trading activities (including commissions, brokerage and insurance) were £4.3 million according to the Sheridan/Ward estimates and £2.8 million using the Thomas/Ward estimates.[4] So as not to bias the findings in favour of my hypothesis I will assume a final profit figure that stands mid-way between these two sets – i.e., £3.6 million. The critical issue is how significant these profits were for enabling investment in the British economy.

Blackburn argues that somewhere between 30 and 50 per cent of these profits would have been invested in the British economy given that they accrued to the richest individuals who had a high propensity to save and invest. On this basis, he suggests that reinvested profits could have financed between 21 and 55 per cent of Britain's domestic investment, measured as 'gross fixed capital formation' (GFCF).[5] Nevertheless, to

---

[1] Blackburn (2010: ch. 12).
[2] Anstey (1975).
[3] Blackburn (2010: 538).
[4] Ward (1978: 209), Sheridan (1969: 21) and Thomas (1968). Full computations are in Blackburn (2010: 531–42, especially 541).
[5] Blackburn (2010: 542).

affect the right direction of bias against my argument, I shall assume a much lower savings rate of 20 per cent (which is twice the British *average* savings rate for 1770),[6] on the basis that British absentee landlords lived notoriously extravagant lifestyles, coupled with the fact that not all of the profits would have been repatriated. This, then, yields a figure of £0.7 million that was available to reinvest (i.e., 20 per cent of £3.6 million). Using the Feinstein data of £4.0 million for GFCF in 1770,[7] the amounts that were available from the profits derived from slave-based production *could have financed about 18 per cent of investment (GFCF) in the British economy*. Paradoxically, this figure accords roughly with the one that Patrick O'Brien produced for Britain.[8] For this came in his well-known article, which argued that total European colonial trade with the periphery was inconsequential, adding perhaps only 1 or 2 per cent to aggregate European income and, therefore, could not account for the rise of European industrialisation.[9]

A second calculation that I present in Chapter 9 is the percentage of colonial-related moneys that might have been invested in the British iron and cotton textile industries. In the final few decades of the eighteenth century, fixed capital investment in the cotton and iron industries, which comprised machines and buildings, cost about £0.4 million per annum each, while one of the largest sources of capital investment – canals, docks and harbours – upon which the export of these products relied, averaged £0.28 million per annum between 1755 and 1815.[10] Aggregating all of this comes to an annual average figure of £1.1 million in fixed capital investment in the key industries.

Estimating the Contribution of the 'Imperial-Debt Military Multiplier' on British Investment

To quantify the imperial-military debt multiplier, four calculations are necessary. First, for 1770, I note that some £4.8 million was spent on interest payments on the national debt that was accrued from financing Britain's imperial wars. Because about 20 per cent of this figure was then remitted abroad to Dutch creditors, so this left a final figure of about £3.8 million. Note that I have not included the moneys that drained

---

[6] Crafts (1987: 248).
[7] Feinstein (1978: 40–1). Blackburn (2010: 540) also uses this source.
[8] O'Brien (1982: 5, 7).
[9] Ibid. (1–18) and Bairoch (1993: chs. 6–7).
[10] Calculated from Deane and Cole (1969: 262).

out of India that went into paying off the Dutch creditors.[11] On my earlier assumption that the savings rate stood at about 20 per cent for the richest investor groups in 1770, so this means that about £0.8 million was available for reinvestment in the British economy, *which comprised 19 per cent of GFCF.*

What then of the calculations regarding what I call the British policy of 'forced savings'? Of the £3.8 million that the state spent on interest payments that went to the City of London in 1770, about 60 per cent was paid by the lower income orders through the regressive tax system, which means that some £2.3 million was redistributed to the rich investor classes – or about 2.5 per cent of national income. Moreover, this 60 per cent figure can be increased to around 70 per cent when we factor in the amounts that were redistributed from the working *and* middle classes to the combined ranks of the landed and financial aristocracy, gentry, leading tradesmen and manufacturers,[12] which means that about £2.7 million was redistributed – or about 2.9 per cent of national income.

Finally, in the conclusion to Chapter 9, I argued that between 4.5 and 5.0 per cent of fixed capital investment might have been financed by all colonial-related activities. This is broken down into the following calculations. First, between 1760 and 1820 about 2 per cent of national income was channelled back into investment from the moneys that were accrued from the imperial-military debt multiplier. I also noted Inikori's claim that the credit and insurance facilities, which the banks provided, drummed up even more business than did the loans that the city provided for the state's imperial military spending. This then could have added another 2 per cent of national income to investment (in circulating rather than fixed capital). These two figures come to 4 per cent of national income. In addition, perhaps somewhere between 0.5 and 1 per cent of national income from the profits and trade that were derived from the Atlantic colonies could have gone back into investment within the British economy.

[11] See Esteban (2001). Indeed, as he put it, 'without the accumulated credits from India transfers since 1757, Britain's financing of land warfare during the French wars could have been compromised' (Esteban 2001: 58).

[12] Blackburn (2010: 564).

Bibliography

Abu-Lughod, Janet L. (1989) *Before European Hegemony*, Oxford: Oxford University Press.

Acemoglu, Daron, Simon Johnson, and James Robinson (2005) 'The Rise of Europe: Atlantic Trade, Institutional Change, and Economic Growth', *American Economic Review* 95(3): 546–79.

Acharya, Amitav (2018) *Constructing Global Order*, Cambridge: Cambridge University Press.

Acharya, Amitav, and Barry Buzan (2019) *The Making of Global International Relations*, Cambridge: Cambridge University Press.

Adelman, Jeremy (2017) 'What Is Global History Now?', *Aeon*. Posted at: https://aeon.co/essays/is-global-history-still-possible-or-has-it-had-its-moment

Adelman, Jeremy (2019) *Empire and the Social Sciences*, London: Bloomsbury.

Adenaike, Carolyn Keyes (2016) 'West African textiles, 1500–1800', in Maureen Fennell Mazzaoui (ed.), *Textiles: Production, Trade and Demand*, Aldershot: Varorium, 250–62.

Agathangelou, Anna, and L. H. M. Ling (2009) *Transforming World Politics*, London: Routledge.

Alam, Muzafar (1994) 'Trade, State Policy and Regional Change: Aspects of Mughal-Uzbek Commercial Relations, c.1550–1750', *Journal of the Economic and Social History of the Orient* 37(3): 200–27.

Al-Djazairi, S. E. (2017) *The Myth of Islamic Barbarism and Its Aims*, Bursa: MSBN Books.

Alejandro, Audrey (2019) *Western Dominance in International Relations?*, London: Routledge.

Alexander, Michelle (2012) *The New Jim Crow*, New York: The New Press.

Al-Hassani, Salim (2015) *1001 Inventions*, Washington, DC: National Geographic.

Allen, Robert C. (2009) *The British Industrial Revolution in Global Perspective*, Cambridge: Cambridge University Press.

Allen, Richard B. (2010) 'Satisfying the "Want for Labouring People": European Slave Trading in the Indian Ocean, 1500–1850', *Journal of World History* 21(1): 45–73.

Allinson, Jamie, and Alexander Anievas (2010) 'Approaching "the international": Beyond Political Marxism', in Anievas (ed.), 197–214.

Al-Rodhan, Nayef R. F. (2012) *The Role of the Arab-Islamic World in the Rise of the West*, Houndmills: Palgrave.

Amin, Samir (1989) *Eurocentrism*, London: Zed.

Anderson, Perry (1974) *Lineages of the Absolutist State*, London: Verso.

Anievas, Alexander (ed.) (2010) *Marxism and World Politics*, London: Routledge.

Anievas, Alexander, and Kerem Nişancioğlu (2015) *How the West Came to Rule*, London: Pluto.

Anievas, Alexander, Nivi Manchanda, and Robbie Shilliam (eds.) (2015) *Race and Racism in International Relations*, London: Routledge.

Anstey, Roger (1975) 'The volume and profitability of the British slave trade, 1761–1807', in Engerman and Genovese (eds.), 3–31.

Appadurai, Arjun (1996) *Modernity at Large*, Minneapolis: University of Minnesota Press.

Arasaratnam, Sinnappah (1987) 'India and the Indian Ocean in the seventeenth century', in Das Gupta and Pearson (eds.), *India and the Indian Ocean 1500–1800*, Oxford: Oxford University Press, 94–130.

Arrighi, Giovanni (1994) *The Long Twentieth Century*, London: Verso.

Arrighi, Giovanni (2007) *Adam Smith in Beijing*, New York: Verso.

Arrighi, Giovanni, Takeshi Hamashita, and Mark Selden (eds.) (2003) *The Resurgence of East Asia*, London: Routledge.

Arrighi, Giovanni, Po-keung Hui, Ho-fung Hung, and Mark Selden (2003) 'Historical capitalism, east and west', in Arrighi, Hamashita, and Selden (eds.), 259–333.

Ashman, Sam (2010) 'Capitalism, uneven and combined development and the transhistoric', in Anievas (ed.), 183–96.

Ashworth, William J. (2017) *The Industrial Revolution*, London: Bloomsbury.

Aslanian, Debouh David (2011) *From the Indian Ocean to the Mediterranean*, Berkeley: University of California Press.

Atwell, William S. (1982) 'International Bullion Flows and the Chinese Economy', *Past & Present* 95: 68–90.

Austen, Ralph A. (1979) 'The trans-Saharan slave trade: A tentative census', in H. A. Gemery and J. S. Hogendorn (eds.), *The Uncommon Market*, New York: Academic Press, 23–76.

Baber, Zaheer (1996) *The Science of Empire*, Albany: State University of New York Press.

Baer, Gabriel (1967) 'Slavery in Nineteenth Century Egypt', *Journal of African History* 8(3): 417–41.

Baines, Edward (1835/1966) *History of the Cotton Manufacture in Great Britain*, London: Fisher, Fisher and Jackson.

Bairoch, Paul A. (1982) 'International Industrialization Levels from 1750 to 1980', *Journal of European Economic History* 11(2): 269–333.

Bairoch, Paul A. (1993) *Economics and World History*, Chicago: University of Chicago Press.

Bala, Arun (2006) *The Dialogue of Civilizations in the Birth of Modern Science*, Houndmills: Palgrave Macmillan.

Balachandran, G., and Sanjay Subrahmanyam (2005) 'On the history of globalization and India: Concepts, measures and debates', in Jackie Assayag and Chris Fuller (eds.), *Globalizing India*, London: Anthem, 17–46.

Banaji, Jairus (2010) *Theory as History*, Delhi: Aakar Books.

Banaji, Jairus (2018) 'Globalising the History of Capital: Ways Forward', *Historical Materialism* 26(3): 143–66.

Baptist, Edward (2016) *The Half Has Never Been Told*, New York: Basic Books.

Barendse, René J. (2002) *The Arabian Seas*, Armonk: M. E. Sharpe.

Barendse, René J. (2009) *Arabian Seas 1700–1763*, Leiden: Brill.

Bartlett, Beatrice (1991) *Monarchs and Ministers*, Berkeley: University of California Press.

Barua, Pradeep P. (2011) 'Maritime Trade, Seapower and the Anglo-Mysore Wars, 1767–1799', *The Historian* 73(1): 22–40.

Bayly, Christopher (2002) '"Archaic" and "modern" globalization in the Eurasian and African Arena, c.1750–1850', in Hopkins (ed.), 47–73.

Beaujard, Philippe (2019) *The Worlds of the Indian Ocean*, Vol. II, Cambridge: Cambridge University Press.

Beckert, Sven (2015) *Empire of Cotton*, London: Penguin.

Beckett, J. V., and Michael Turner (1990) 'Taxation and Economic Growth in Eighteenth Century England', *Economic History Review* 43(3): 377–403.

Bell, Duncan (2019) *Empire, Race and Global Justice*, Cambridge: Cambridge University Press.

Benjamin, Thomas (2009) *The Atlantic World*, Cambridge: Cambridge University Press.

Bentley, Jerry H. (1996) 'Cross-Cultural Interaction and Periodization in World History', *American Historical Review* 101(3): 749–70.

Berg, Maxine (2004) 'In Pursuit of Luxury: Global History and British Consumer Goods in the Eighteenth Century', *Past & Present* 182: 85–142.

Berg, Maxine (2009) 'Quality, cotton and the global luxury trade', in Riello and Roy (eds.), 391–414.

Bernal, Martin (1991) *Black Athena, I*, London: Vintage.

Bhabha, Homi (1994) *The Location of Culture*, London: Routledge.

Bhambra, Gurminder K. (2007) *Rethinking Modernity*, Houndmills: Palgrave Macmillan.

Bhambra, Gurminder K. (2014) *Connected Sociologies*, London: Bloomsbury.

Bilgin, Pinar, and L. H. M. Ling (eds.) (2017) *Asia in International Relations*, New York: Routledge.

Biswas, Arun Kumar (1999) 'Minerals and metals in medieval India', in A. Rahman (ed.), *History of Indian Science: Technology and Culture, AD 1000–1800*, Oxford: Oxford University Press, 275–313.

Blackburn, Robin (2010) *The Making of New World Slavery*, London: Verso.

Blaney, David L., and Naeem Inayatullah (2010) *Savage Economics*, London: Routledge.

Blaney, David L., and Naeem Inayatullah (2021) *Within, Against, and Beyond Liberalism*, London: Rowman & Littlefield International.

Blaut, James M. (1993) *The Colonizer's Model of the World*, London: Guilford.

Bovill, E. W. (1933/2018) *Caravans of the Old Sahara*, London: Routledge.

Bowden, Brett (2009) *The Empire of Civilization*, Chicago: University of Chicago Press.

Bowden, Brett, and Leonard Seabrooke (eds.) (2006) *Global Standards of Market Civilization*, London: Routledge.

Bowen, H. V. (2002) '"So Alarming an Evil": Smuggling, Pilfering and the English East India Company, 1750–1810', *International Journal of Maritime History* 14(1): 1–31.

Bowen, H. V. (2007) *East India Company: Trade and Domestic Financial Statistics, 1755–1838* [computer file]. Colchester: UK Data Archive [distributor]. SN: 5690. Posted at: http://dx.doi.org/10.5255/UKDA-SN-5690-1

Bowen, H. V. (2009) 'British exports of raw cotton from India to China during the late eighteenth and early nineteenth centuries', in Riello and Roy (eds.), 115–37.

Braudel, Fernand (1992) *Civilization and Capitalism, 15th–18th Century, III*, Berkeley: University of California Press.

Bray, Francesca (1984) *Science and Civilisation in China, VI(2)*, Cambridge: Cambridge University Press.

Bray, Francesca (1999) 'Towards a critical history of non-western technology', in Timothy Brook and Gregory Blue (eds.), *China and Historical Capitalism*, Cambridge: Cambridge University Press, 158–209.

Brenner, Robert (1977) 'The Origins of Capitalist Development: A Critique of Neo-Smithian Marxism', *New Left Review* 104: 25–92.

Brenner, Robert (1982) 'The Agrarian Roots of European Capitalism', *Past & Present* 97(Nov.): 16–113.

Brewer, John (1989) *The Sinews of Power*, London: Unwin Hyman.

Brewer, John, and Roy Porter (eds.) (1993) *Consumption and the World of Goods*, New York: Routledge.

Brittlebank, Kate (1982) *Tipu Sultan's Search for Legitimacy*, Delhi: Oxford University Press.

Broadberry, Stephen, and Bishnupriya Gupta (2009) 'Lancashire, India, and Shifting Competitive Advantage in Cotton Textiles, 1700–1850: The Neglected Role of Factor Prices', *Economic History Review* 62(2): 279–305.

Broadberry, Stephen, B. M. S. Campbell, and B. van Leeuwen (2013) 'When Did Britain Industrialise? The Sectoral Distribution of the Labour Force and Labour Productivity in Britain, 1381–1851', *Explorations in Economic History* 50(1): 16–27.

Broadberry, Stephen, Johann Custodis, and Bishnupriya Gupta (2015) 'India and the Great Divergence: An Anglo-Indian Comparison of GDP Per Capita, 1600–1871', *Explorations in Economic History* 55(C): 58–75.

Bronson, Bennet (1982/1983) 'An Industrial Miracle in a Golden Age: The 17th-Century Cloth Exports of India'. Posted at: http://iref.homestead.com/textile.html

Bronson, Bennet (1986) 'The Making and Selling of Wootz, A Crucible Steel of India', *Archeomaterials* 1(1): 13–51.

Broome, André (2010) *The Currency of Power*, Houndmills: Palgrave Macmillan.

Bryant, Joseph (2006) 'The West and the Rest Revisited: Debating Capitalist Origins, European Colonialism, and the Advent of Modernity', *Canadian Journal of Sociology* 31(4): 403–44.

Bührer, Tanja, Flavio Eichmann, Stig Förster, and Benedikt Stuchey (eds.) (2017) *Cooperation and Empire*, New York: Berghahn.

Bull, Hedley (1977) *The Anarchical Society*, Houndmills: Macmillan.

Bull, Hedley, and Adam Watson (eds.) (1984a) *The Expansion of International Society*, Oxford: Oxford University Press.

Bull, Hedley, and Adam Watson (1984b) 'Introduction', in Bull and Watson (eds.), 1–9.

Burton, John W. (1972) *World Society*, Cambridge: Cambridge University Press.

Buzan, Barry, and George Lawson (2015) *The Global Transformation*, Cambridge: Cambridge University Press.

Callahan, William (2012) 'Sino-Speak: Chinese Exceptionalism and the Politics of History', *Journal of Asian Studies* 71(1): 33–55.

Camilleri, Joseph A., and Jim Falk (1993) *The End of Sovereignty?*, Aldershot: Edward Elgar.

Campbell, Gwyn (ed.) (2004) *The Structure of Slavery in Indian Ocean Africa and Asia*, London: Frank Cass.

Chakrabarty, Dipesh (2000) *Provincializing Europe*, Princeton: Princeton University Press.

Chandavarkar, Rajnarayan (1994) *The Origins of Industrial Capitalism in India*, Cambridge: Cambridge University Press.

Chang, Ha-Joon (2002) *Kicking Away the Ladder*, London: Anthem.

Chao, Kang (1977) *The Development of Cotton Textile Production in China*, Cambridge: Harvard University Press.

Chapman, Stanley D. (1972/2006) *The Cotton Industry in the Industrial Revolution*, London: Macmillan.

Chapman, Stanley D., and Serge Chassagne (1981) *European Textile Printers in the Eighteenth Century*, London: Ashgate.

Chase, Kenneth (2008) *Firearms: A Global History to 1700*, Cambridge: Cambridge University Press.

Chase-Dunn, Christopher K. (1989) *Global Formation*, Oxford: Blackwell.

Chaudhuri, Kirti N. (1974) 'The Structure of Indian Textile Industry in the Seventeenth and Eighteenth Centuries', *Indian Economic and Social History Review* 11(2–3): 127–82.

Chaudhuri, Kirti N. (1985) *Trade and Civilisation in the Indian Ocean*, Cambridge: Cambridge University Press.

Chaudhuri, Kirti N. (2006) *The Trading World of Asia and the English East India Company 1660–1760*, Cambridge: Cambridge University Press.

Chaudhury, Sushil (1995a) 'International Trade in Bengal Silk and the Comparative Role of Asians and Europeans, Circa 1700–1757', *Modern Asian Studies* 29(2): 373–86.

Chaudhury, Sushil (1995b) *From Prosperity to Decline: Eighteenth Century Bengal*, New Delhi: Manohar.

Chaudhury, Sushil, and Michel Morineau (eds.) (2007a) *Merchants, Companies and Trade*, Cambridge: Cambridge University Press.

Chaudhury, Sushil, and Michel Morineau (2007b) 'Introduction', in Chaudhury and Morineau (eds.), 1–18.

Chen, F. (1992) *Study on Military Expenditure in the Qing Period* (清代军费研究), Wuhan: Wuhan University Press.

Chen, Xuewen (1991) 'A Study of Sugar Production in Taiwan, Guangdong and Fujian During the Ming and Qing Periods (论明清时期粤闽台的蔗糖业)', *Journal of Social Science in Guangdong* 6: 30–5.

Choi, Jung-Bong (2003) 'Mapping Japanese Imperialism onto Postcolonial Criticism', *Social Identities: Journal for the Study of Race, Nation and Culture* 9(3): 325–39.

Chowdhry, Geeta, and Sheila Nair (2004) *Power, Postcolonialism and International Relations*, London: Routledge.

Christian, David (2004) *Maps of Time*, Berkeley: University of California Press.

Clarence-Smith, William Gervase (2013) 'The economics of the Indian Ocean and Red Sea slave trades in the 19th century: An overview', in W. G. Clarence-Smith (ed.), *The Economics of the Indian Ocean Slave Trade in the Nineteenth Century*, London: Routledge, 1–21.

Clarke, J. J. (1997) *Oriental Enlightenment*, London: Routledge.

Clingingsmith, David, and Jeffrey G. Williamson (2005) 'Deindustrialization in 18th and 19th Century India: Mughal Decline, Climate Shocks and British Industrial Ascent', *Explorations in Economic History* 45(3): 209–34.

Cohen, Benjamin J. (2008) *International Political Economy: An Intellectual History*, Princeton: Princeton University Press.

Cohen, Gerry A. (1980) *Karl Marx's Theory of History*, Oxford: Oxford University Press.

Cole, W. A. (1958) 'Trends in Eighteenth Century Smuggling', *Economic History Review* 10(3): 395–410.

Collins, Randall (1985) *Weberian Sociological Theory*, Cambridge: Cambridge University Press.

Cooper, Frederick (1977) *Plantation Slavery on the East Coast of Africa*, London: Yale University Press.

Coverte, Robert (1612) *A True and Almost Incredible Report of an Englishman*, London: Thomas Hall & Richard Redmer.

Cox, Robert W. (1987) *Power, Production and World Order*, New York: Columbia University Press.

Cox, Robert W. (1996) *Approaches to World Order*, Cambridge: Cambridge University Press.

Crafts, N. F. R. (1987) 'British Economic Growth, 1700–1850: Some Difficulties of Interpretation', *Explorations in Economic History* 24(3): 245–68.

Crafts, N. F. R., and Nikolaus Wolf (2012) 'The Location of the British Cotton Textiles Industry in 1838: A Quantitative Analysis', LSE Seminar Paper. Posted at: http://cep.lse.ac.uk/seminarpapers/13-01-12-NC.pdf

Crawford, Neta (2002) *Argument and Change in World Politics*, Cambridge: Cambridge University Press.

Crisp, Olga (1991) 'Russia', in Richard Sylla and Gianni Toniolo (eds.), *Patterns of European Industrialisation*, London: Routledge, 248–68.

Crosby, Alfred W. (1972) *The Columbian Exchange*, Westport: Greenwood Press.

Crowley, John E. (2016) 'Sugar Machines: Picturing Industrialized Slavery', *American Historical Review* 121(2): 403–36.

Cuno, Kenneth M. (2009) 'African Slaves in 19th-Century Rural Egypt', *International Journal of Middle East Studies* 41(2): 186–8.

Curtin, Philip D. (1984) *Cross-Cultural Trade in World History*, Cambridge: Cambridge University Press.

Dale, Stephen (1994) *Indian Merchants and Eurasian Trade 1600–1750*, Cambridge: Cambridge University Press.

Das, Gurcharan (2016) 'Introduction', in Scott Levi, *Caravans*, xi–xxxi.

Das Gupta, Ashin (2001) *The World of the Indian Ocean Merchant, 1500–1800*, New Delhi: Oxford University Press.

Das Gupta, Ashin, and M. N. Pearson (eds.) (1987) *India and the Indian Ocean 1500–1800*, Calcutta: Oxford University Press.

Datta, Karubaki (2008) 'Portuguese trade in Indian cotton textiles during the late eighteenth century', in S. Jeyaseela Stephen (ed.), *The Indian Trade at the Asian Frontier*, New Delhi: Gyan Publishing House, 281–94.

Davidson, Basil (1992) *Africa in History*, London: Orion.

Davidson, Lola Sharon (2012) 'Woven Webs: Trading Textiles Around the Indian Ocean', *PORTAL* 9(1): 1–21.

Davidson, Neil (2009) 'Putting the Nation Back into "the International"', *Cambridge Review of International Affairs* 22(1): 9–28.

Davis, Mike (2001) *Late Victorian Holocausts*, London: Verso.

Davis, Ralph (1962) 'English Foreign Trade, 1770–1774', *Economic History Review* 15(2): 285–303.

Davis, Ralph (1966) 'The Rise of Protection in England, 1689–1786', *Economic History Review* 19(2): 306–17.

Deane, Phyllis (1965) *The First Industrial Revolution*, Cambridge: Cambridge University Press.

Deane, Phyllis, and W. A. Cole (1969) *British Economic Growth 1688–1959*, Cambridge: Cambridge University Press.

Dellios, Rosita (1996) 'Mandalas of Security', *Culture Mandala* 2(1): 1–20.

Deng, Kent G. (1997) 'The Foreign Staple Trade of China in the Pre-Modern Era', *International History Review* 19(2): 253–85.

Deng, Kent G. (2004) 'Why Did the Chinese Never Develop a Steam Engine?', *History of Technology* 25: 151–71.

Deng, Kent G. (2008) 'Miracle or Mirage? Foreign Silver, China's Economy and Globalization from the Sixteenth to the Nineteenth Centuries', *Pacific Economic Review* 13(3): 320–58.

Deng, Kent G. (2012a) *China's Political Economy in Modern Times*, Abingdon: Routledge.

Deng, Kent G. (2012b) 'The continuation and efficiency of the Chinese fiscal state, 700 bc–ad 1911', in Yun-Casalilla and O'Brien (eds.), 335–52.

Dharampal (1983) *Dharampal Collected Writings, I: Indian Science and Technology in the Eighteenth Century*, Feira Alta: SIDH.

Dickson, Peter G. M. (1967) *The Financial Revolution in England*, London: St. Martin's Press.

Dikötter, Frank (1997) 'Racial discourse in China: Continuities and permutations', in Frank Dikötter (ed.), *The Construction of Racial Identities*, London: Hurst.

Dirlik, Arif (2007) *Global Modernity*, Boulder: Paradigm Publishers.

Dobb, Maurice (1959) *Studies in the Development of Capitalism*, London: Routledge & Kegan Paul.

Dobbin, Christine (1996) *Asian Entrepreneurial Minorities*, London: RoutledgeCurzon.

Drayton, Richard (2002) 'The collaboration of labour: Slaves, empires, and globalizations in the Atlantic World, c.1600–1850', in Hopkins (ed.), 98–114.

Du Bois, W. E. B. (1946/2015) *The World and Africa*, Mansfield Centre: Martino Publishing.

Duchesne, Ricardo (2012) *The Uniqueness of Western Civilization*, Leiden: Brill.

Duchesne, Ricardo (2016) 'The Underdevelopment of European Pride', Council of European Canadians. Posted at: www.eurocanadian.ca/2016/02/underdevelopment-of-european-pride.html

Dunne, Tim, and Chris Reus-Smit (eds.) (2017) *The Globalization of International Society*, Oxford: Oxford University Press.

Dunstan, Helen (1992) 'Safely Supplying with the Devil: The Qing State and Its Merchant Suppliers of Copper', *Late Imperial China* 13(2): 42–81.

Dutt, Romesh C. (1906) *The Economic History of India Under Early British Rule*, 2nd ed., London: Kegan Paul, Trench, Trübner & Co.

Dutt, Romesh C. (1916) *The Economic History of India in the Victorian Age*, 4th ed., London: Kegan Paul, Trench, Trübner & Co.

Duzgun, Eren (2018) 'Property, Geopolitics, and Eurocentrism: The "Great Divergence" and the Ottoman Empire', *Review of Radical Political Economics* 50(1): 24–43.

Earle, Edward Meade (1926) 'Egyptian Cotton and the American Civil War', *Political Science Quarterly* 41(4): 520–45.

Eley, Geoff (2007) 'Historicising the Global', *History Workshop Journal* 63: 154–88.

Elias, Norbert (1939/1994) *The Civilizing Process*, Oxford: Blackwell.

Eltis, David (2019) 'The Trans-Atlantic Slave Trade Data Base', Emory University. Posted at: www.slavevoyages.org/assessment/estimates

Elvin, Mark (1973) *The Pattern of the Chinese Past*, Stanford: Stanford University Press.

Engels, Friedrich (1952) *The Condition of the Working-Class in England in 1844*, London: Allen & Unwin.

Engerman, Stanley L. (1972) 'The Slave Trade and British Capital Formation in the Eighteenth Century: A Comment on the Williams Thesis', *Business History Review* 46(4): 430–43.

Engerman, Stanley L., and Eugene Genovese (eds.) (1975) *Race and Slavery in the Western Hemisphere*, Princeton: Princeton University Press.

Epstein, Charlotte (ed.) (2017) *Against International Relations Norms*, New York: Routledge.

Equiano, Olaudah (1789/2003) *The Interesting Narrative and Other Writings*, London: Penguin.

Esteban, Javier Cuenca (2001) 'The British Balance of Payments 1772–1820: Indian Transfers and War Finance', *Economic History Review* 54(1): 58–85.

Fage, J. D. (1969) 'Slavery and the Slave Trade in the Context of West African History', *Journal of African History* 10(3): 393–404.

Fage, J. D. (1995) *A History of Africa*, London: Routledge.

Fairbank, John K. (1942) 'Tributary Trade and China's Relations with the West', *Far Eastern Quarterly* 1(2): 129–49.

Fan, Jinming (2016) 'Anhui Merchants and the Jiangnan Cloth Industry During the Ming-Qing Dynasty', *Journal of Historical Research in Anhui* 2: 117–29.

Fan, Shuzhi (1990) *The Discovery and Study on Cities and Towns in Jiangnan Region During the Ming and Qing Periods (*明清江南市镇探微*)*, Shanghai: Fudan University Press.

Fanon, Frantz (1965/2001) *The Wretched of the Earth*, London: Penguin.

Faraday, Michael (1819) 'An Analysis of Wootz or Indian Steel', *Quarterly Journal of Science, Literature and the Arts* 14: 288–90.

Farnie, Douglas (1979) *The English Cotton Industry and the World Market, 1815–1896*, Oxford: Oxford University Press.

Farrell, William (2016) 'Smuggling Silks into Eighteenth-Century Britain: Geography, Perpetrators, and Consumers', *Journal of British Studies* 55(2): 268–94.

Feinstein, Charles H. (1978) 'Capital formation in Britain', in Peter Mathias and M. M. Postan (eds.), *The Cambridge Economic History of Europe*, Vol. VII, Cambridge: Cambridge University Press, 28–96.

Ferguson, Niall (2002) *Empire*, London: Allen Lane.

Ferguson, Niall (2011) *Civilization*, London: Allen Lane.

Feuerwerker, Albert (1970) 'Handicraft and Manufactured Cotton Textiles in China, 1871–1910', *Journal of Economic History* 30(2): 338–78.

Feuerwerker, Albert (1984) 'The State and Economy in Late Imperial China', *Theory & Society* 13(3): 297–326.

Finlay, Robert (1998) 'The Pilgrim Art: The Culture of Porcelain in World History', *Journal of World History* 9(2): 141–87.

Finlay, Robert (2010) *The Pilgrim Art*, Berkeley: University of California Press.

Flynn, Dennis O., and Arturo Giráldez (1994) 'China and the Manila Galleon', in Latham and Kawakatsu (eds.), 71–90.

Flynn, Dennis O., and Arturo Giráldez (1995a) 'Born with a "Silver Spoon": The Origins of World Trade in 1571', *Journal of World History* 6(2): 201–21.

Flynn, Dennis O., and Arturo Giráldez (1995b) 'Arbitrage, China, and World Trade in the Early Modern Period', *Journal of the Economic and Social History of the Orient* 38(4): 429–48.

Flynn, Dennis O., and Arturo Giráldez (2004) 'Path Dependence, Time Lags and the Birth of Globalisation: A Critique of O'Rourke and Williamson', *European Review of Economic History* 8: 81–108.

Flynn, Dennis O., and Arturo Giráldez (2006) 'Globalization began in 1571', in B. K. Gills and W. R. Thompson (eds.), 232–47.

Flynn, Dennis O., and Arturo Giráldez (2008) 'Born Again: Globalization's Sixteenth Century Origins (Asian/Global Versus European Dynamics)', *Pacific Economic Review* 13(3): 359–87.

Flynn, Dennis O., Arturo Giráldez, and Richard von Glahn (eds.) (2003) *Global Connections and Monetary History*, Aldershot: Ashgate.

Fogel, Robert W. (1989) *Without Consent or Contract*, New York: W. W. Norton.

Frank, Andre Gunder (1998) *ReOrient*, Berkeley: University of California Press.

Frank, Andre Gunder (2015) *Reorienting the 19th Century*, London: Paradigm Publishers.

Frank, Andre Gunder, and Barry K. Gills (eds.) (1996) *The World System*, London: Routledge.

Friedman, Thomas L. (1999) *The Lexus and the Olive Tree*, London: Harper Collins.

Friedman, Thomas L. (2005) *The World Is Flat*, London: Penguin.

Fry, Tony, and Anne-Marie Willis (2015) *Steel: A Design, Cultural and Ecological History*, London: Bloomsbury.

Fryer, Peter (1988) *Black People in the British Empire*, London: Pluto Press.

Fukuyama, Francis (1992) *The End of History and the Last Man*, London: Hamish Hamilton.

Gaastra, Femme S. (2007) 'Competition or collaboration? Relations between the Dutch East India Company and Indian merchants around 1680', in Chaudhury and Morineau (eds.), 189–201.

Gamble, Andrew (1995) 'The New Political Economy', *Millennium* 43(3): 516–30.

Gamble, Andrew, Anthony J. Payne, Ankie Hoogvelt, Michael Dietrich, and Michael Kenny (1996) 'Editorial: New Political Economy', *New Political Economy* 1(1): 5–11.

Gappah, Petina (2019) *Out of Darkness, Shining Light*, New York: Scribner.

Gaskell, Peter (1833) *The Manufacturing Population of England*, London: Baldwin and Cradock.

Gekas, Athanasios (2007) 'A global history of Ottoman cotton textiles 1600–1850', European University Institute, EUI Working Paper MWP No. 2007/30.

Gereffi, Gary, John Humphrey, and Timothy Sturgeon (2005) 'The Governance of Global Value Chains', *Review of International Political Economy* 12(1): 78–104.

Gernet, Jacques (1999) *A History of Chinese Civilization*, Cambridge: Cambridge University Press.

Gerritsen, Ann (2020) 'The view from early modern China: Capitalism and the Jingdezhen ceramics industry', in Yazdani and Menon (eds.), 306–26.

Gerritsen, Ann, and Stephen McDowall (2012) 'Material Culture and the Other: European Encounters with Chinese Porcelain, ca.1650–1800', *Journal of World History* 23(1): 87–113.

Gerschenkron, Alexander (1962) *Economic Backwardness in Historical Perspective*, Cambridge: Harvard University Press.

Ghazanfar, S. M. (2006) *Islamic Civilization*, Lanham: Scarecrow Press.

Giddens, Anthony (1985) *The Nation-State and Violence*, Cambridge: Polity.

Giddens, Anthony (1990) *The Consequences of Modernity*, Cambridge: Polity.

Gill, Stephen (1995) 'Globalisation, Market Civilisation and Disciplinary Neoliberalism', *Millennium* 24(3): 399–423.

Gills, Barry K., and William R. Thompson (eds.) (2006) *Globalization and Global History*, London: Routledge.

Gilpin, Robert (1981) *War and Change in World Politics*, Cambridge: Cambridge University Press.

Gilroy, Paul (1993) *The Black Atlantic*, London: Verso.

Glahn, Richard von (1996a) *Fountain of Fortune*, Berkeley: University of California Press.

Glahn, Richard von (1996b) 'Myth and Reality of China's Seventeenth Century Monetary Crisis', *Journal of Economic History* 56(2): 429–54.

Glahn, Richard von (2003) 'Money use in China and changing patterns of global trade in monetary metals, 1500–1800', in Flynn, Giráldez, and von Glahn (eds.), 187–205.

Glamann, Kristof (1958) *Dutch-Asiatic Trade 1620–1740*, Copenhagen: Martinus Nijhoff's Gavenhage.

Glamann, Kristof (1974) 'European trade 1500–1750', in Carlo M. Cipolla (ed.), *The Sixteenth and Seventeenth Centuries (The Fontana History of Europe)*, Vol. 2, London: Fontana, 427–526.

Go, Julian (2011) *Patterns of Empire*, Cambridge: Cambridge University Press.

Go, Julian (2016) *Postcolonial Thought and Social Theory*, Oxford: Oxford University Press.

Go, Julian, and George Lawson (2017) 'Introduction: For a global historical sociology', in Julian Go and George Lawson (eds.), *Global Historical Sociology*, Cambridge: Cambridge University Press, 1–34.

Goitein, Shelomo Dov (1967) *A Mediterranean Society*, Vol. I, Berkeley: University of California Press.

Gokhale, Balkrishna Govind (1979) *Surat in the Seventeenth Century*, London: Curzon.

Golas, Peter J. (1999) *Science and Civilisation in China, V(13)* Cambridge: Cambridge University Press.

Goldstone, Jack A. (2000) 'The "Rise of the West" or Not? A Revision to Socio-Economic History', *Sociological Theory* 18(2): 175–94.

Goldstone, Jack A. (2002) 'Efflorescences and Economic Growth in World History: Rethinking the "Rise of the West" and the Industrial Revolution', *Journal of World History* 13(2): 323–89.

Goldstone, Jack A. (2008) *Why Europe? The Rise of the West in World History, 1500–1850*, New York: McGraw Hill.

Goody, Jack (1996) *The East in the West*, Cambridge: Cambridge University Press.

Goody, Jack (2004) *Islam in Europe*, Cambridge: Polity.

Goonatilake, Susantha (1998) *Toward a Global Science*, New Delhi: Vistaar.

Gopal, Priyamvada (2019) *Insurgent Empire*, London: Verso.

Gordon, Murray (1989) *Slavery in the Arab World*, New York: New Amsterdam Books.

Gordon, Stewart (2008) *When Asia Was the World*, Philadelphia: Da Capo Press.

Goswami, Chhaya (2016) *Globalization Before Its Time*, London: Penguin.

Greif, Avner (2006) *Institutions and the Path to the Modern Economy*, Cambridge: Cambridge University Press.

Grey, Maggie (2001) 'Encountering the Mandala: The Mental and Political Cultures of Dependency', *Culture Mandala* 4(2): 1–13.

Griffiths, Trevor, Philip Hunt, and Patrick K. O'Brien (2008) 'Scottish, Irish, and Imperial Connections: Parliament, the Three Kingdoms, and the Mechanization of Cotton Spinning in Eighteenth-Century Britain', *Economic History Review* 61(3): 625–50.

Grinin, Leonid, and Andrey Korotayev (2015) *Great Divergence and Great Convergence*, London: Springer.

Grover, B. R. (1994) 'An integrated pattern of commercial life in rural society of North India during the seventeenth and eighteenth centuries', in Sanjay Subrahmanyam (ed.), *Money and the Market in India 1100–1700*, Delhi: Oxford University Press, 219–55.

Gruffydd-Jones, Branwen (ed.) (2006) *Decolonizing International Relations*, Lanham: Rowman & Littlefield.

Habib, Irfan (1960) 'Banking in Mughal India', in Tapan Raychaudhuri (ed.), *Contributions to Indian Economic History*, Vol. I, Calcutta: Firma K. L. Mukhopadhyay, 1–20.

Habib, Irfan (1990) 'Merchant communities in pre-colonial India', in James D. Tracy (ed.), *The Rise of Merchant Empires*, Cambridge: Cambridge University Press, 371–99.

Haider, Najaf (1996) 'Precious Metal Flows and Currency Circulation in the Mughal Empire', *Journal of the Economic and Social History of the Orient* 39(3): 298–364.

Haldén, Peter (2020) *Family Power*, Cambridge: Cambridge University Press.

Hall, Kenneth R. (1996) 'The Textile Industry and Southeast Asia', *Journal of the Economic and Social History of the Orient* 39(2): 87–135.

Halperin, Sandra (2013) *Re-envisioning Global Development*, New York: Routledge.

Halperin, Sandra, and Ronen Palan (eds.) (2015) *Legacies of Empire*, Cambridge: Cambridge University Press.

Hamashita, Takeshi (1994) 'The tribute trade system and modern Asia', in Latham and Kawakatsu (eds.), 71–90.

Hamashita, Takeshi (2003a) 'Tribute and treaties: Maritime Asia and treaty port networks in the era of negotiation', in Arrighi, Hamashita, and Selden (eds.), 17–50.

Hamashita, Takeshi (2003b) 'Ryukyu Networks in Maritime Asia', *Kyoto Review of Southeast Asia* 3. Posted at: https://kyotoreview.org/issue-3-nations-and-stories/ryukyu-networks-in-maritime-asia/

Harnetty, Peter (1970) 'The Cotton Improvement Program in India 1865–1875', *Agricultural History* 44(4): 379–92.

Harrison, Graham (2013) *The African Presence*, Manchester: Manchester University Press.

Hartwell, Robert M. (1966) 'Markets, Technology, and the Structure of Enterprise in the Development of the Eleventh-Century Chinese Iron and Steel Industry', *Journal of Economic History* 26(1): 29–58.

Harvey, David (1991) *The Condition of Post-Modernity*, Oxford: Blackwell.

Hasan, Mohibbul (1971) *History of Tipu Sultan*, Calcutta: The World Press.

Hay, Colin, and David Marsh (1999) 'Introduction: Towards a New (International) Political Economy', *New Political Economy* 4(1): 5–22.

Haynes, Douglas E. (2012) *Small Town Capitalism in Western India*, Cambridge: Cambridge University Press.

Held, David, Anthony McGrew, David Goldblatt, and Jonathan Perraton (1999) *Global Transformations*, Cambridge: Polity.

Helleiner, Eric (2014) *Forgotten Foundations of Bretton Woods*, Ithaca: Cornell University Press.

Helleiner, Eric (2015) 'Globalising the Classical Foundations of IPE Thought', *Contextio Internacional* 37(3): 975–1010.

Helleiner, Eric (2018) 'Sun Yat-Sen as a Pioneer of International Development', *History of Political Economy* 50(Supplement): 59–75.

Helleiner, Eric (2021) *The Diverse Origins of Neomercantilist Ideology*, Ithaca: Cornell University Press.

Helleiner, Eric, and Antulio Rosales (2017) 'Peripheral Thoughts for International Political Economy: Latin American Ideational Innovation and the Diffusion of the Nineteenth Century Free Trade Doctrine', *International Studies Quarterly* 61(4): 924–34.

Hersh, Jonathan, and Hans-Joachim Voth (2009) 'Sweet Diversity: Colonial Goods and the Rise of European Living Standards'. Posted at: https://papers.ssrn.com/sol3/papers.cfm?abstract_id=1402322

Hobsbawm, Eric J. (1969) *Industry and Empire*, London: Weidenfeld & Nicolson.

Hobson, John M. (1993) 'The Military-Extraction Gap and the Wary Titan: The Fiscal-Sociology of British Defence Policy 1870–1913', *Journal of European Economic History* 22(3): 466–507.

Hobson, John M. (1997) *The Wealth of States*, Cambridge: Cambridge University Press.

Hobson, John M. (2004) *The Eastern Origins of Western Civilisation*, Cambridge: Cambridge University Press.

Hobson, John M. (2012) *The Eurocentric Conception of World Politics*, Cambridge: Cambridge University Press.

Hobson, John M. (2013a) 'Part 1 – Revealing the Eurocentric Foundations of IPE: A Critical Historiography of the Discipline from the Classical to the Modern Era', *Review of International Political Economy* 20(5): 1024–54.

Hobson, John M. (2013b) 'Part 2 – Reconstructing the Non-Eurocentric Foundations of IPE: From Eurocentric "Open Economy Politics" to Inter-Civilizational Political Economy', *Review of International Political Economy* 20(5): 1055–81.

Hobson, John M., and Leonard Seabrooke (eds.) (2007) *Everyday Politics of the World Economy*, Cambridge: Cambridge University Press.

Hobson, John M., and J. C. Sharman (2005) 'The Enduring Place of Hierarchy in World Politics: Tracing the Social Logics of Hierarchy and Political Change', *European Journal of International Relations* 11(1): 63–98.

Hodgson, Marshall G. S. (1993) *Rethinking World History*, Cambridge: Cambridge University Press.

Holland, John (1833) *A Treatise on the Progressive Improvement and Present State of the Manufactures of Metal II: Iron and Steel*, London: Longman & Co.

Holsti, Kalevi J. (1991) *Peace and War*, Cambridge: Cambridge University Press.

Hoogvelt, Ankie (1997) *Globalisation and the Postcolonial World*, London: Macmillan.

Hopkins, A. G. (ed.) (2002) *Globalization in World History*, London: Pimlico.

Hsu, Wen-chin (1988) 'Social and Economic Factors in the Chinese Porcelain Industry in Jingdezhen During the Late Ming and Early Qing Period, ca. 1620–1683', *Journal of the Royal Asiatic Society* 120(1): 135–59.

Huang, Guosheng (1999) 'Historical Statues and Experience of the Opening and Customs Policy in the Early Qing Period (清代前期开海设关的历史地位与经验教训)', *Journal of Southeast Academic Research* 6: 86–95.

Hudson, Pat (1986) *The Genesis of Industrial Capital*, Cambridge: Cambridge University Press.

Huff, Toby E. (2011) *Intellectual Curiosity and the Scientific Revolution*, Cambridge: Cambridge University Press.

Hui, Po-keung (1995) 'Overseas Chinese Business Networks: East Asian Economic Development in Historical Perspective', PhD thesis, Sociology Department, State University of New York at Binghamton, New York.

Hui, Victoria Tin-bor (2005) *War and State Formation in Ancient China and Early Modern Europe*, Cambridge: Cambridge University Press.

Hung, Ho-fung (2000) 'Maritime capitalism in seventeenth-century China: The rise and fall of Koxinga revisited', IROWS Working Paper No. 72, University of California, Riverside.

Hung, Ho-fung (2001) 'Imperial China and Capitalist Europe in the Eighteenth-Century Global Economy', *Review* 24(2): 473–513.

Hunwick, John, and Eve Troutt Powell (2002) *The African Diaspora in the Mediterranean Lands of Islam*, Princeton: Markus Wiener.

Ibn Khaldūn, Abd al-Rahmān (1377/1958) *The Muqaddimah*, New York: Pantheon.

Ikeda, Satoshi (1996) 'The History of the Capitalist World-System vs. the History of East-Southeast Asia', *Review* 19(1): 49–77.

Imlah, Albert H. (1958) *Economic Elements in the Pax Britannica*, Cambridge: Harvard University Press.

Inayatullah, Naeem, and David L. Blaney (2004) *International Relations and the Problem of Difference*, London: Routledge.

Inikori, Joseph E. (2002) *Africans and the Industrial Revolution in England*, Cambridge: Cambridge University Press.

Inikori, Joseph E. (2009) 'English versus Indian cotton textiles: The impact of imports on cotton textile production in West Africa', in Riello and Roy (eds.), 85–114.

Inikori, Joseph E. (2020) 'The first capitalist nation: The development of capitalism in England', in Yazdani and Menon (eds.), 251–76.

Inikori, Joseph E., and Stanley Engerman (eds.) (1992) *The Atlantic Slave Trade*, London: Duke University Press.

Irwin, John (1959) 'Indian Textile Trade in the Seventeenth Century: Foreign Influences', *Journal of Indian Textile History* 4: 57–64.

Irwin, John, and Katharine B. Brett (1970) *Origins of Chintz*, London: H. M. S. O.

Jacob, Margaret (1997) *Scientific Culture and the Making of the Industrial West*, Oxford: Oxford University Press.

Jacques, Martin (2012) *When China Rules the World*, London: Penguin.

Jansen, Marius (1992) *China in the Tokugawa World*, Cambridge: Harvard University Press.

Jayasuriya, Shihan de Silva, and Richard Pankhurst (eds.) (2003) *The African Diaspora in the Indian Ocean*, Asmara: African World Press.

John, A. H. (1955) 'War and the English Economy, 1700–63', *Economic History Review* 7(3): 329–44.

Johnson, Marion (1990) 'Anglo-African trade in the eighteenth century', Leiden: Centre for the History of European Expansion.

Johnston, Alistair Iain (1995) *Cultural Realism*, Princeton: Princeton University Press.

Jones, Eric L. (1981) *The European Miracle*, Cambridge: Cambridge University Press.

Jones, Eric L., Lionel Frost, and Colin White (1993) *Coming Full Circle*, London: Routledge.

Joseph, George Ghergevese (1992) *The Crest of the Peacock*, London: Penguin.

Kang, David C. (2010) *East Asia Before the West*, New York: Columbia University Press.

Kanth, Rajani K. (ed.) (2009) *The Challenge of Eurocentrism*, New York: Palgrave Macmillan.

Kapoor, Ilan (2008) *The Postcolonial Politics of Development*, London: Routledge.

Kasaba, Reşat (1993) 'Treaties and Friendships: British Imperialism, the Ottoman Empire, and China in the Nineteenth Century', *Journal of World History* 4(2): 215–41.

Katzenstein, Peter J. (ed.) (2012a) *Sinicization and the Rise of China*, New York: Routledge.

Katzenstein, Peter J. (2012b) 'China's rise: Rupture, return or recombination?', in Katzenstein (ed.), 1–37.

Kavalski, Emilian (2018) *The Guanxi of Relational International Theory*, London: Routledge.

Kelly, Robert E. (2012) 'A "Confucian Long Peace" in Pre-Western East Asia?', *European Journal of International Relations* 18(3): 407–30.

Keohane, Robert O. (2009) 'The Old IPE and the New', *Review of International Political Economy* 16(1): 34–46.

Kerr, Rose, and Nigel Wood (2004) *Science and Civilisation in China*, 5(12), Cambridge: Cambridge University Press.

Kindleberger, Charles P. (1996) *World Economic Primacy*, Oxford: Oxford University Press.

Klein, Herbert S. (1999) *The Atlantic Slave Trade*, Cambridge: Cambridge University Press.

Klein, Herbert S. (2004) 'The Atlantic slave trade to 1650', in Schwartz (ed.), 201–36.

Klein, Martin A. (1990) 'The Impact of the Atlantic Slave Trade on the Societies of the Western Sudan', *Social Science History* 14(2): 231–53.

Knight, G. Roger (2014) *Sugar, Steam and Steel*, Adelaide: University of Adelaide Press.

Kobayashi, Kazuo (2019) *Indian Cotton Textiles in West Africa*, Houndmills: Palgrave.

Koehler, Benedikt (2014) *Early Islam and the Birth of Capitalism*, London: Lexington Books.

Kolff, Dirk H. A. (1990) *Naukar, Rajput & Sepoy*, Cambridge: Cambridge University Press.

Kraidy, Marwan M. (2005) *Hybridity, or the Cultural Logic of Globalization*, Philadelphia: Temple University Press.

Krasner, Stephen D. (1976) 'State Power and the Structure of International Trade', *World Politics* 28(3): 317–47.

Kreidte, Peter, Hans Medick, and Jürgen Schlumbohm (1981) *Industrialization Before Industrialization*, Cambridge: Cambridge University Press.

Kriedte, Peter (1981a) 'Proto-industrialization between industrialization and de-industrialization', in Kriedte, Medick, and Schlumbohm, 135–60.

Kriedte, Peter (1981b) 'The origins, the Agrarian context, and the conditions in the world market', in Kriedte, Medick, and Schlumbohm, 12–37.

Kriger, Colleen E. (2005) 'Mapping the History of Cotton Textile Production in Pre-Colonial West Africa', *African Economic History* 33: 87–116.

Kriger, Colleen E. (2006) *Cloth in West African History*, Lanham: AltaMira Press.

Kriger, Colleen E. (2009) '"Guinea Cloth": Production and consumption of cotton textiles in West Africa before and during the Atlantic slave trade', in Riello and Parthasarathi (eds.), 105–26.

Krishna, Sankaran (2009) *Globalization & Postcolonialism*, Boulder: Rowman & Littlefield.

Kuhn, Dieter (1988) *Science and Civilisation in China, V(9)*, Cambridge: Cambridge University Press.

Kwass, Michael (2014) *Contraband*, Cambridge: Harvard University Press.

Lach, Donald F., and Edwin J. Van Kley (1993) *Asia in the Making of Europe*, Vol. III, Chicago: Chicago University Press.

Lacher, Hannes, and Julian Germann (2012) 'Before Hegemony: Britain, Free Trade, and Nineteenth-Century World Order Revisited', *International Studies Review* 14(1): 99–124.

Landes, David S. (1969) *The Unbound Prometheus*, Cambridge: Cambridge University Press.

Landes, David S. (1998) *The Wealth and Poverty of Nations*, London: Little, Brown and Co.

Landrin, M. H. C. (1868) *A Treatise on Steel*, London: Trübner & Co.

Larson, Pier (2007) 'African diasporas and the Atlantic', in Jorge Canizares-Esguerra and Erik R. Seeman (eds.), *The Atlantic in Global History, 1500–2000*, Upper Saddle River: Prentice Hall, 129–47.

Latham, A. J. H., and Heita Kawakatsu (eds.) (1994) *Japanese Industrialization and the Asian Economy*, London: Routledge.

Laue, Theodore H. von (1963) *Sergei Witte and the Industrialization of Russia*, New York: Columbia University Press.

Laue, Theodore H. von (1987) *The World Revolution of Westernization*, Oxford: Oxford University Press.

Lauren, Paul Gordon (1996) *Power and Prejudice*, Boulder: Westview Press.

Leander, Anna (2009) 'Why We Need Multiple Stories About the Global Political Economy', *Review of International Political Economy* 16(2): 321–28.

LeBaron, Genevieve (2012) 'Rethinking Prison Labor: Social Discipline and the State in Historical Perspective', *Working USA: The Journal of Labor & Society* 15: 327–51.

LeBaron, Genevieve, and Alison J. Ayers (2013) 'The Rise of a "New Slavery"? Understanding African Unfree Labour Through Neoliberalism', *Third World Quarterly* 34(5): 873–92.

Lee, John (1999) 'Trade and Economy in Preindustrial East Asia, c.1500–c.1800: East Asia in the Age of Global Integration', *Journal of Asian Studies* 58(1): 2–26.

Lemire, Beverly (1990) 'The Theft of Clothes and Popular Consumerism in Early Modern England', *Journal of Social History* 24(2): 255–76.

Lemire, Beverly (1992) *Fashion's Favourite*, Oxford: Oxford University Press.

Lemire, Beverly (2009) 'Revising the historical narrative: India, Europe, and the cotton trade, c.1300–1800', in Riello and Parthasarathi (eds.), 205–26.

Lemire, Beverly (2011) *Cotton*, New York: Berg.

Levathes, Louise E. (1994) *When China Ruled the Seas*, London: Simon & Schuster.

Levi, Scott (2016) *Caravans: Punjabi Khatri Merchants on the Silk Road*, London: Portfolio.

Li, Bozhong (1998) *Agricultural Development in Jiangnan, 1620–1850*, Basingstoke: Palgrave Macmillan.

Li, Bozhong (2000) *Early Industrialization in Jiangnan, 1550–1850 (*江南早期的 工业化 *1550-1850)*, Beijing: Social Sciences Academic Press.

Li, Bozhong (2009) 'Involution and Chinese cotton textile production: Songjiang in the late eighteenth and early nineteenth centuries', in Riello and Parthasarathi (eds.), 387–95.

Li, Longqian (1983) 'The sprouts of capitalism in various handicraft industries in Guangdong in the early Qing Dynasty', in *A Collection of Articles on the Sprouts of Capitalism in China*, Jiangsu: Jiangsu People's Publishing (Ming and Qing History Research Office, Nanjing University), 400–19.

Lieberman, Victor (2003) *Strange Parallels*, Cambridge: Cambridge University Press.

Lin, Justin Yifu (1995) 'The Needham Puzzle: Why the Industrial Revolution Did Not Originate in China', *Economic Development and Cultural Change* 43(2): 269–92.

Ling, L. H. M. (2002) *Postcolonial International Relations*, Houndmills: Palgrave Macmillan.

Ling, L. H. M. (2014) *The Dao of World Politics*, London: Routledge.

Linklater, Andrew (2016) *Violence and Civilization in the Western States-Systems*, Cambridge: Cambridge University Press.

Linklater, Andrew (2020) *The Idea of Civilization in the Making of the Global Order*, Bristol: Bristol University Press.

Lippit, Victor D. (1987) *The Economic Development of China*, Armonk: M.E. Sharpe.

List, Friedrich (1841/1885) *The National System of Political Economy*, London: Longmans, Green & Co.

Liu, T. (2009) 'An Estimation of China's GDP from 1600 to 1840', *Economic Research Journal* 10: 144–55.

Logan, Frenise A. (1958) 'India – Britain's Substitute for American Cotton, 1861–1865', *Journal of Southern History* 24(4): 472–80.

Long, David, and Brian C. Schmidt (eds.) (2005) *Imperialism and Internationalism in the Discipline of International Relations*, New York: State University of New York Press.

Lord, John (1923) *Capital and Steam Power*, London: P. S. King & Son.

Lorge, Peter A. (2008) *The Asian Military Revolution*, Cambridge: Cambridge University Press.

Lovejoy, Paul E. (1983) *Transformations in Slavery*, Cambridge: Cambridge University Press.

Lovejoy, Paul E. (1989) 'The Impact of the Atlantic Slave Trade on Africa: A Review of the Literature', *Journal of African History* 30(3): 365–94.

Lovejoy, Paul E. (2002) 'Islam, Slavery, and Political Transformation in West Africa: Constraints on the Trans-Atlantic Slave Trade', *Outre-mers* 89(336–7): 247–82. DOI: 10.3406/outre.2002.3992

Lox, William (2009) 'Bintie: The Wootz Steel in Ancient China', *Indian Journal of History of Science* 44(3): 369–88.

Ma, Debin (2013) 'State Capacity and Great Divergence, the Case of Qing China (1644–1911)', *Eurasian Geography and Economics* 54(5–6): 484–99.

Macdougall, Philip (2011) 'British Seapower and the Mysore Wars of the Eighteenth Century', *Mariner's Mirror* 97(4): 299–314.

Machado, Pedro (2009a) 'Awash in a sea of cloth: Gujarat, Africa, and the West Indian Ocean 1300–1800', in Riello and Parthasarathi (eds.), 161–79.

Machado, Pedro (2009b) 'Clothes of a new fashion: Indian Ocean networks of exchange and cloth zones of contact in Africa and India in the eighteenth and nineteenth centuries', in Riello and Roy (eds.), 53–84.

Machado, Pedro (2014) *Ocean of Trade*, Cambridge: Cambridge University Press.

MacLeod, Christine (1988) *Inventing the Industrial Revolution*, New York: Cambridge University Press.

Maddison, Angus (2007) *Contours of the World Economy, 1–2030 AD*, Oxford: Oxford University Press.

Malik, Kenan (1996) *The Meaning of Race*, New York: Palgrave.

Manggala, Pandu Utama (2013) 'The Mandala Culture of Anarchy: The Pre-Colonial Southeast Asian International Society', *Journal of ASEAN Studies* 1(1): 1–13.

Mann, Michael (1986) *The Sources of Social Power*, Vol. I, Cambridge: Cambridge University Press.

Mantz, Felix (2019) 'Decolonizing the IPE Syllabus: Eurocentrism and the Coloniality of Knowledge in International Political Economy', *Review of International Political Economy* 26(6): 1361–78.

Markovits, Claude (2000) *The Global World of Indian Merchants 1750–1946*, Cambridge: Cambridge University Press.

Marks, Robert B. (1999) 'Maritime trade and the agro-ecology of South China, 1685–1850', in Dennis Flynn, Lionel Frost, and A. J. H. Latham (eds.), *Pacific Centuries*, London: Routledge, 85–109.

Marks, Robert B. (2002) *The Origins of the Modern World*, Lanham, MD: Rowman & Littlefield.

Marques, Leonardo (2020) 'New world slavery in the capitalist world-economy', in Yazdani and Menon (eds.), 71–94.

Marshall, P. J. (1987) 'Private British trade in the Indian Ocean before 1800', in Das Gupta and Pearson (eds.), 276–316.

Martin-Fox, Stuart (2003) *A Short History of China and Southeast Asia*, Crows Nest: Allen & Unwin.

Marx, Karl (1846/1975) 'Letter to Pavel Vasilyevich Annenkov', in Karl Marx and Frederick Engels (eds.), *Collected Works*, Vol. 38, New York: International Publishers, 95.

Marx, Karl (1852/2009) *The Eighteenth Brumaire of Louis Bonaparte*, Wokingham: Dodo Press.

Marx, Karl (1859/1977) 'Preface to the critique of political economy', in David McClellan (ed.), *Karl Marx: Selected Writings*, Oxford: Oxford University Press, 388–92.

Marx, Karl (1867/1954) *Capital*, Vol. I, London: Lawrence & Wishart.

Marx, Karl (1867/1959) *Capital*, Vol. III, London: Lawrence & Wishart.

Marx, Karl (1969) *Karl Marx on Colonialism and Modernization*, edited by Shlomo Avineri, New York: Anchor.

Marx, Karl, and Friedrich Engels (1846/2011) *The German Ideology*, Eastford, CT: Martino Fine Books.

Marx, Karl, and Friedrich Engels (1848/1977) *The Communist Manifesto*, Harmondsworth: Penguin.

Maskiell, Michelle (2002) 'Consuming Kashmir: Shawls and Empires, 1500–2000', *Journal of World History* 13(1): 27–65.

Masters, Bruce (1989) *The Origins of Western Economic Dominance in the Middle East*, New York: New York University Press.

Mathias, Peter, and Patrick K. O'Brien (1976) 'Taxation in Britain and France, 1715–1810. A Comparison of the Social and Economic Incidence of Taxes Collected for the Central Governments', *Journal of European Economic History* 5(3): 601–50.

Mathieu, Xavier (2020) *Sovereignty and the Denial of International Equality*, London: Routledge.

Matin, Kamran (2013) *Recasting Iranian Modernity*, London: Routledge.

Mazumdar, Sucheta (1998) *Sugar and Society in China*, London: Harvard University Press.

Mbeki, Linda, and Matthias van Rossum (2017) 'Private Slave Trade in the Dutch Indian Ocean World: A Study into the Networks and Backgrounds of the Slavers and the Enslaved in South Asia and South Africa', *Slavery and Abolition* 38(1): 95–116.

McCants, Anne E. C. (2007) 'Exotic Goods, Popular Consumption, and the Standard of Living: Thinking About Globalization in the Early Modern World', *Journal of World History* 18(4): 433–62.

McCants, Anne E. C. (2008) 'Poor Consumers as Global Consumers: The Diffusion of Tea and Coffee Drinking in the Eighteenth Century', *Economic History Review* 61(S1): 172–200.

McCarthy, Thomas (2009) *Race, Empire, and the Idea of Human Development*, Cambridge: Cambridge University Press.

McCloskey, Deirdre N. (2010) *Bourgeois Dignity*, Chicago: University of Chicago Press.

McEwan, Cheryl (2009) *Postcolonialism and Development*, London: Routledge.

McKendrick, Neil (1982) 'The consumer revolution of eighteenth-century England', in McKendrick, Brewer, and Plumb (eds.), 9–33.

McKendrick, Neil, John Brewer, and J. H. Plumb (eds.) (1982) *The Birth of a Consumer Society*, Indiana: Indiana University Press.

McMichael, Philip (1991) 'Slavery in Capitalism: The Rise and Demise of the U.S. Ante-Bellum Cotton Culture', *Theory & Society* 20(3): 321–49.

McNeill, William H. (1965) *The Rise of the West*, New York: Mentor.

McNeill, William H. (1982) *The Pursuit of Power*, Oxford: Blackwell.

Mearsheimer, John J. (2001) *The Tragedy of Great Power Politics*, New York: W. W. Norton.

Meek, Ronald L. (1976) *Social Science and the Ignoble Savage*, Cambridge: Cambridge University Press.

Mehta, Makrand (1991) *Indian Merchants and Entrepreneurs in Historical Perspective*, Delhi: Academic Foundation.

Meilink-Roelofsz, M. A. P. (1962) *Asian Trade and European Influence in the Indonesian Archipelago Between 1500 and About 1630*, The Hague: Martinus Nijhoff.

Menard, Russell R. (1991) 'Transport costs and long-range trade, 1300–1800: Was There a European "transport revolution" in the early modern era?', in J. D. Tracy (ed.), 228–75.

Mendels, Franklin F. (1972) 'Proto-Industrialization: The First Phase of the Industrialization Process', *Journal of Economic History* 32(1): 241–61.

Metzer, Jacob (1975) 'Rational Management, Modern Business Practices, and Economies of Scale in the Ante-Bellum Southern Plantations', *Explorations in Economic History* 12(2): 123–50.

Middleton, John (1992) *The World of the Swahili*, New Haven: Yale University Press.

Millar, Ashley Eva (2017) *A Singular Case*, Montréal: McGill-Queen's University Press.

Mintz, Sidney (1986) *Sweetness and Power*, London: Penguin.

Mitchell, B. R. (2011) *British Historical Statistics*, Cambridge: Cambridge University Press.

Mitchell, Timothy (2000) 'The stage of modernity', in T. Mitchell (ed.), *Questions of Modernity*, Minneapolis: University of Minnesota Press, 1–34.

Miyamoto, Matao, and Shikano Yoshiaki (2003) 'The emergence of the Tokugawa monetary system in East Asian perspective', in Flynn, Giráldez, and von Glahn (eds.), 169–86.

Mokyr, Joel (1990) *The Lever of Riches*, New York: Oxford University Press.

Mokyr, Joel (2002) *The Gifts of Athena*, Princeton: Princeton University Press.

Mokyr, Joel (2009) *The Enlightened Economy*, New Haven: Yale University Press.

Mooers, Colin (1991) *The Making of Bourgeois Europe*, London: Verso.

Moovsi, Shireen (1987) 'The Silver Influx, Money Supply, Prices and Revenue-Extraction in Mughal India', *Journal of the Economic and Social History of the Orient* 30(1): 47–94.

Moovsi, Shireen (2011) 'The World of Labour in Mughal India (c.1500–1750)', *International Review of Social History* 56(S19): 245–61.

Morris, Morris D. (1963) 'Towards a Reinterpretation of Nineteenth-Century Indian Economic History', *Journal of Economic History* 23(4): 606–18.

Moseley, K. P. (1992) 'Caravel and Caravan: West Africa and the World-Economies, ca. 900–1900 AD', *Review* 15(3): 523–55.

Mui, Hoh-Cheung, and Lorna H. Mui (1975) '"Trends in Eighteenth-Century Smuggling" Reconsidered', *Economic History Review* 28(1): 28–43.

Mukund, Kanakalatha (1992) 'Indian Textile Industry in 17th and 18th Centuries: Structure, Organisation and Responses', *Economic & Political Weekly* 27(38): 2057–65.

Mumford, Lewis (1934) *Technics and Civilisation*, London: Routledge.

Munck, Ronaldo, and Denis O'Hearn (eds.) (1999) *Critical Development Theory*, London: Zed.

Murphey, Rhoads (1974) 'The treaty ports and China's modernization', in Mark Elvin and George William Skinner (eds.), *The Chinese City Between Two Worlds*, Stanford: Stanford University Press, 17–72.

Murphey, Rhoads (1977) *The Outsiders*, Ann Arbor: University of Michigan Press.

Murphy, Craig. N. (2009) 'Do the Left-Out Matter?', *New Political Economy* 14(3): 357–65.

Murphy, Craig N., and Roger Tooze (eds.) (1991) *The New International Political Economy*, Boulder: Lynne Rienner.

Mushet, David (1805) 'Experiments on Wootz', *Philosophical Transactions of the Royal Society of London* 95: 163–75.

Mushet, David (1840/2011) *Papers on Iron and Steel, Practical and Experimental*, Cambridge: Cambridge University Press.

Naoroji, Dadabhai (1901) *Poverty and Un-British Rule in India*, London: Swan Sonnenschein.

Nash, Robert C. (1982) 'The English and Scottish Tobacco Trades in the Seventeenth and Eighteenth Centuries: Legal and Illegal Trade', *Economic History Review* 35(3): 354–72.

Needham, Joseph (1964) *The Development of Iron and Steel Technology in China*, Cambridge: W. Heffer & Sons.

Needham, Joseph (1969) *The Grand Titration*, London: George Allen & Unwin.

Needham, Joseph (1970) *Clerks and Craftsmen in China and the West*, Cambridge: Cambridge University Press.

Needham, Joseph, Wang Ling and Lu Gwei-Djen (1971) *Science and Civilisation in China*, Vol. IV(3), Cambridge: Cambridge University Press.

Needham, Joseph, Ho Ping-Yü, Lu Gwei-Djen, and Wang Ling (1986) *Science and Civilisation in China*, Vol. V(7), Cambridge: Cambridge University Press.

Nehru, Jawarhalal (1947) *The Discovery of India*, London: Meridian Books.

Nicolini, Beatrice (2012) *The First Sultan of Zanzibar*, Princeton: Markus Wiener.

Nierstrasz, Chris (2015) 'The popularization of tea: East India companies, private traders, smugglers and the consumption of tea', in M. Berg, F. Gottmann, H. Hodacs, and C. Nierstrasz (eds.), *Goods from the East, 1600–1800*, Houndmills: Palgrave Macmillan, 263–76.

North, Douglass C. (1991) 'Institutions, transaction costs, and the rise of merchant empires', in J. D. Tracy (ed.), 22–40.

North, Douglass C., and Robert P. Thomas (1973) *The Rise of the Western World*, Cambridge: Cambridge University Press.

North, Susan (2008) 'The Physical Manifestation of an Abstraction: A Pair of 1750s Waistcoat Shapes', *Textile History* 39(1): 92–104.

Northrup, David (1998) 'Vasco da Gama and Africa: An Era of Mutual Discovery, 1497–1800', *Journal of World History* 9(2): 189–211.

Northrup, David (2009) *Africa's Discovery of Europe*, Oxford: Oxford University Press.

Nunn, Nathan (2008) 'The Long-Term Effects of Africa's Slave Trades', *Quarterly Journal of Economics* 123(1): 139–76.

O'Brien, Patrick K. (1982) 'European Economic Development: The Contribution of the Periphery', *Economic History Review* 35(1): 1–18.

O'Brien, Patrick K. (1988) 'The Political Economy of British Taxation, 1688–1815', *Economic History Review* 41(1): 1–32.

O'Brien, Patrick K. (1989) 'The Impact of the Revolutionary and Napoleonic Wars, 1793–1815, on the Long-Run Growth of the British Economy', *Review* 12(3): 335–87.

O'Brien, Patrick K. (1991) 'Power with profit: The state and the economy, 1688–1815', Institute of Historical Research Working Paper, Senate House, University of London, 1–43.

O'Brien, Robert, and Marc Williams (2004) *Global Political Economy*, Houndmills: Palgrave Macmillan.

Ohmae, Kenichi (1990) *The Borderless World*, London: Collins.

O'Keefe, Thomas A. (2018) *Bush II, Obama, and the Decline of US Hegemony in the Western Hemisphere*, London: Routledge.

O'Leary, Brendan (1989) *The Asiatic Mode of Production*, Oxford: Blackwell.

Oliver, Roland (1999) *The African Experience*, London: Weidenfeld & Nicolson.

O'Rourke, Kevin H., and Jeffrey G. Williamson (2002a) 'When Did Globalization Begin?', *European Review of Economic History* 6(1): 23–50.

O'Rourke, Kevin H., and Jeffrey G. Williamson (2002b) 'After Columbus: Explaining Europe's Overseas Trade Boom, 1500–1800', *Journal of Economic History* 62(2): 417–56.

O'Rourke, Kevin H., and Jeffrey G. Williamson (2004) 'Once More: When Did Globalization Begin?', *European Review of Economic History* 8(1): 109–117.

Orwell, George (1929) 'How a Nation Is Exploited: The British Empire in Burma', *Le Progrès Civique*. Posted at: www.orwellfoundation.com/the-orwell-foundation/orwell/essays-and-other-works/how-a-nation-is-exploited-the-British-empire-in-Burma

Panikkar, Sardar K. M. (1959) *Asia and Western Dominance*, London: George Allen & Unwin.

Parthasarathi, Prasannan (2005) 'Cotton Textile Exports from the Indian Subcontinent, 1680–1780', GEHN Conference, University of Padova (17–19 November).

Parthasarathi, Prasannan (2011) *Why Europe Grew Rich and Asia Did Not*, Cambridge: Cambridge University Press.

Pasha, Mustapha Kamal (2006) 'Islam, "Soft" Orientalism and Hegemony: A Gramscian Rereading', *Critical Review of International Social and Political Philosophy* 8(4): 543–58.

Patterson, Orlando (1982) *Slavery and Social Death*, Cambridge: Harvard University Press.

Payne, Anthony J. (2006) 'The genealogy of new political economy', in Anthony J. Payne (ed.), *Key Debates in New Political Economy*, London: Routledge, 9–18.

Pearson, George (1795) 'Experiments and Observations to Investigate the Nature of a Kind of Steel, Manufactured at Bombay, and There Called Wootz', *Philosophical Transactions of the Royal Society of London* 85: 322–46.

Pearson, Michael N. (1988) 'Brokers in Western Indian Port Cities Their Role in Servicing Foreign Merchants', *Modern Asian Studies* 22(3): 455–72.

Pearson, Michael N. (1991) 'Merchants and states', in J. D. Tracy (ed.), 41–116.

Pearson, Michael N. (1998) *Port Cities and Intruders*, Baltimore: Johns Hopkins University Press.

Peng, Zeyi (1982) 'Characteristics of the Sprouts of Capitalism in the Tea Industry in the Early Qing Period (清代前期茶业资本主义萌芽的特点)', *The Journal of Chinese Social and Economic History* 3: 15–25.

Percy, John (1864) *Metallurgy*, London: John Murray.

Perdue, Peter (2004) 'Constructing Chinese property rights: East and West', in Huri Islamoğlu (ed.), *Constituting Modernity*, London: I. B. Tauris, 35–68.

Perdue, Peter (2005) *China Marches West*, Cambridge: Belknap Press.

Perdue, Peter (2015) 'The Tenacious Tributary System', *Journal of Contemporary China* 24(96): 1002–14.

Perdue, Peter (2017) 'The expansion of the Qing dynasty of China and the Zunghar Mongol State', in *Oxford Research Encyclopedia of Asian History*. DOI: 10.1093/acrefore/9780190277727.013.7

Perkins, Dwight (1967) 'Government as an Obstacle to Industrialization: The Case of Nineteenth-Century China', *Journal of Economic History* 27(4): 478–92.

Perlin, Frank (1983) 'Proto-Industrialization and Pre-Colonial South Asia', *Past & Present* 98: 30–95.

Perry, Felton E. (2009) 'Kidnapping: An Underreported Aspect of African Agency During the Slave Trade Era (1440–1886)', *Ufahamu: A Journal of African Studies* 35(2). Posted at: https://escholarship.org/uc/item/8kf4m24x

Persaud, Randolph B. (2001) *Counter-Hegemony and Foreign Policy*, New York: State University of New York Press.

Persaud, Randolph B. (2019) 'Killing the Third World: Civilisational Security as US Grand Strategy', *Third World Quarterly* 40(2): 266–83.

Phillips, Nicola (2005) *Globalizing International Political Economy*, Houndmills: Palgrave Macmillan.

Phillips, Nicola (2009) 'The Slow Death of Pluralism', *Review of International Political Economy* 16(1): 85–94.

Phillips, Andrew (2017) 'Making empires: Hierarchy, conquest and customization', in Ayşe Zarakol (ed.), 44–68.

Phillips, Andrew, and Jason C. Sharman (2015) *International Order in Diversity*, Cambridge: Cambridge University Press.

Phillips, Nicola, Resmi Bhaskaran, Dev Nathan, and C. Upendranadh (2014) 'The Social Foundations of Global Production Networks: Towards a Global Political Economy of Child Labour', *Third World Quarterly* 35(3): 428–46. DOI: 10.1080/01436597.2014.893486

Pieterse, Jan Nederveen (1990) *Empire and Emancipation*, London: Pluto.

Pieterse, Jan Nederveen (2006) 'Oriental globalization: Past and present', in Gerard Delanty (ed.), *Europe and Asia Beyond East and West*, London: Routledge, 61–73.

Pieterse, Jan Nederveen (2020) *Globalization and Culture*, London: Rowman & Littlefield.

Polanyi, Karl (1944/2001) *The Great Transformation*, Boston: Beacon Press.

Pomeranz, Kenneth (2000) *The Great Divergence*, Princeton: Princeton University Press.

Pomeranz, Kenneth, and Stephen Topik (2006) *The World that Trade Created*, Armonk: M. E. Sharpe.

Ponting, Clive (2000) *World History*, London: Chatto & Windus.

Postan, M. M. (1935) 'Recent Trends in the Accumulation of Capital', *Economic History Review* 6(1): 1–12.

Power, Marcus (2003) *Rethinking Development Geographies*, London: Routledge.

Prakash, Om (1985) *The Dutch East India Company and the Economy of Bengal*, Princeton: Princeton University Press.

Prakash, Om (2007) 'The Portuguese and the Dutch in Asian maritime trade: A comparative analysis', in Chaudhury and Morineau (eds.), 175–88.

Prakash, Om (2009) 'The Dutch and the Indian Ocean textile trade', in Riello and Parthasarathi (eds.), 145–60.

Prestholdt, Jeremy (2004) 'On the Global Repercussions of East African Consumerism', *American Historical Review* 109(3): 755–81.

Prestholdt, Jeremy (2008) *Domesticating the World*, Berkeley: University of California Press.

Price, Jacob (1991) 'Transaction Costs: A Note on Merchant Credit and the Organization of Private Trade', in J. D. Tracy (ed.), 276–97.

Qian, Jiang (1985) 'The Inflows of America Silver to China Through the Hispanic Philippines, 1570–1760 (1570–1760年西属菲律宾流入中国的美洲白银)', *Journal of Southeast Asian Affairs* 3: 96–106.

Qin, Yaqing (2018) *A Relational Theory of World Politics*, Cambridge: Cambridge University Press.

Quirk, Joel, and David Richardson (2014) 'Europeans, Africans and the Atlantic World, 1450–1850', in Suzuki, Zhang, and Quirk (eds.), 138–58.

Raju, C. K. (2007) *Cultural Foundations of Mathematics*, Vol. X(4), New Delhi: Pearson Education.

Ramo, Joshua (2004) *The Beijing Consensus*, London: The Foreign Policy Centre.

Ravenstein, E. G. (2016) *A Journal of the First Voyage of Vasco da Gama, 1497–1499*, London: Routledge.

Ray, H. Prabha (2004) 'Far-flung fabrics – Indian textiles in ancient maritime trade', in R. Barnes (ed.), *Textiles in Indian Ocean Societies*, New York: Routledge, 17–37.

Ray, Rajat Kanta (1995) 'Asian Capital in the Age of European Domination: The Rise of the Bazaar, 1800–1914', *Modern Asian Studies* 29(3): 449–554.

Raychaudhuri, Tapan (1982) 'Non-agricultural production', in Tapan Raychaudhuri and Irfan Habib (eds.), *The Cambridge Economic History of India*, Vol. I, Cambridge: Cambridge University Press, 261–307.

Raynal, Abbé (1777) *A Philosophical and Political History of the Settlements and Trade of the Europeans in the East and West Indies*, London: T. Cadell.

Reader, John (1998) *Africa: A Biography of the Continent*, London: Penguin.

Reid, Anthony (2009) 'Southeast Asian consumption of Indian and British cotton cloth, 1600–1850', in Riello and Roy (eds.), 31–51.

Reus-Smit, Christian (2013) *Individual Rights and the Making of the International System*, Cambridge: Cambridge University Press.

Ricardo, David (1819) *On the Principles of Political Economy and Taxation*, Georgetown: Joseph Milligan.

Richards, J. F. (2012) 'Fiscal states in Mughal and British India', in Yun-Casalilla and O'Brien (eds.), 410–41.

Riello, Giorgio (2009a) 'The globalization of cotton textiles: Indian cottons, Europe, and the Atlantic World, 1600–1800', in Riello and Parthasarathi (eds.), 261–87.

Riello, Giorgio (2009b) 'The Indian apprenticeship: The trade of Indian textiles and the making of European cottons', in Riello and Roy (eds.), 309–46.

Riello, Giorgio (2013) *Cotton: The Fabric that Made the Modern World*, Cambridge: Cambridge University Press.

Riello, Giorgio, and Prasannan Parthasarathi (eds.) (2009) *The Spinning World*, Oxford: Oxford University Press.

Riello, Giorgio, and Tirthankar Roy (eds.) (2009) *How India Clothed the World*, Leiden: Brill.

Rioux, Sébastien (2013) 'The Fiction of Economic Coercion: Political Marxism and the Separation of Theory and History', *Historical Materialism* 21(4): 92–128.

Rioux, Sébastien, Genevieve LeBaron, and Peter Verovšek (2019) 'Capitalism and Unfree Labor: A Review of Marxist Perspectives on Modern Slavery', *Review of International Political Economy*. DOI: 10.1080/09692290.2019.1650094

Roberts, John M. (1985) *The Triumph of the West*, London: BBC Books.

Roberts, John M., and Jonathan Joseph (2015) 'Beyond Flows, Fluids and Networks: Social Theory and the Fetishism of the Global Informational Economy', *New Political Economy* 20(1): 1–20. DOI: 10.1080/13563467.2013.861413

Robins, Nick (2012) *The Corporation that Changed the World*, London: Pluto.

Robinson, W. I. (2004) *A Theory of Global Capitalism*, Baltimore, MD: Johns Hopkins University Press.

Robson, Robert (1957) *The Cotton Industry in Britain*, London: Macmillan.

Rodger, N. A. M. (2010) 'War as an Economic Activity in the "Long" Eighteenth Century', *International Journal of Maritime History* 22(2): 1–18.

Rodinson, Maxime (2007) *Islam and Capitalism*, London: Saqi Essentials.

Rodney, Walter (1972/2012) *How Europe Underdeveloped Africa*, Oxford: Pambazuka Press.

Rodzinski, Witold (1979) *A History of China*, Oxford: Pergamon Press.

Roe, Sir Thomas (1926) *The Embassy of Sir Thomas Roe to India 1615–19*, London: Oxford University Press.

Roepke, Howard G. (1956) *Movements of the British Iron and Steel Industry 1720 to 1951*, Urbana: University of Urbana Press.

Rönnbäck, Klas (2009) 'Integration of Global Commodity Markets in the Early Modern Era', *European Review of Economic History* 13: 95–120.

Rosenberg, Justin (2006) 'Why Is There No International Historical Sociology?', *European Journal of International Relations* 12(3): 307–40.

Rosenberg, Justin (2008) 'Uneven and Combined Development: The Social-Relational Substratum of "the International"?', *Cambridge Review of International Affairs* 21(1): 77–112.

Rosenthal, Jean-Laurent, and Roy Bin Wong (2011) *Before and Beyond the Great Divergence*, London: Harvard University Press.

Roy, Kaushik (2005) 'Rockets Under Haidar Ali and Tipu Sultan', *Indian Journal of History and Science* 40(4): 635–55.

Roy, Kaushik (2011) 'The Hybrid Military Establishment of the English East India Company in South Asia 1750–1849', *Journal of Global History* 6(2): 195–218.

Roy, Tirthankar (2004) 'Economic History: An Endangered Discipline?', *Economic & Political Weekly* 39(29): 3238–3243.

Roy, Tirthankar (2009) 'Did Globalisation Aid Industrial Development in Colonial India? A Study of Knowledge Transfer in Colonial India', *Indian Economic and Social History Review* 46(4): 579–613.

Roy, Tirthankar (2012) *India in the World Economy*, Cambridge: Cambridge University Press.

Roy, Tirthankar (2013) *An Economic History of Early Modern India*, London: Routledge.

Russell-Wood, A. J. R. (1998) *The Portuguese Empire 1415–1808*, Baltimore, MD: Johns Hopkins University Press.

Said, Edward W. (1978/2003) *Orientalism*, Harmondsworth: Penguin.

Said, Edward W. (1994) *Culture & Imperialism*, London: Vintage.

Said, Edward W. (2004) *Power, Politics, and Culture*, London: Bloomsbury.

Sajed, Alina (2013) *Postcolonial Encounters in International Relations*, New York: Routledge.

Sajed, Alina, and Naeem Inayatullah (2016) 'On the Perils of Lifting the Weight of Structures: An Engagement of Hobson's Critique of the Discipline of IR', *Postcolonial Studies* 19(2): 201–9.

Sajed, Alina, and Randolph B. Persaud (2018) *Race, Gender and Culture in International Relations*, London: Routledge.

Satia, Priya (2018) *Empire of Guns*, London: Duckworth Overlook.

Saurin, Julian (2006) 'International relations as the imperial illusion: Or, the need to decolonize IR', in Branwen Gruffydd-Jones (ed.), 23–42.

Schlumbohm, Jürgen (1981) 'Relations of production – Productive forces – Crises in proto-industrialization', in Kriedte, Medick, and Schlumbohm, 94–125.

Schottenhammer, Angela (2010) 'Characteristics of Qing China's maritime trade policies, Shunzhi through Qianlong reigns', in A. Schottenhammer (ed.), *Trading Networks in Early Modern East Asia*, Wiesbaden: Harrassowitz Verlag, 101–53.

Schumpeter, Joseph (1943/2010) *Capitalism, Socialism and Democracy*, London: Routledge.

Schwartz, Stuart B. (ed.) (2004a) *Tropical Babylons*, Chapel Hill: University of North Carolina Press.

Schwartz, Stuart B. (2004b) 'Introduction', in Schwartz (ed.), 1–26.

Scott, Helenius (1790–1801) 'Aspects of Technology in Western India: Letters to Sir Joseph Banks', in Dharampal, 252–9.

Seabrooke, Leonard (2010) 'Bitter pills to swallow: Legitimacy gaps and social recognition of the IMF tax policy norms in East Asia', in S. Park and A. Vetterlein (eds.), *Owning Development*, Cambridge: Cambridge University Press, 137–59.

Segal, Ronald (2003) *Islam's Black Slaves*, London: Atlantic Books.

Selwyn, Benjamin (2015) 'Twenty-First-Century International Political Economy: A Class-Relational Perspective', *European Journal of International Relations* 21(3): 513–37.

Sen, Asok (1977) 'A Pre-British Economic Formation in India of the Late Eighteenth Century: Tipu Sultan's Mysore', in Barun De (ed.), *Perspectives in Social Sciences, Vol. I: Historical Dimensions*, Calcutta: Oxford University Press, 46–108.

Sen, Gautam (1984) *The Military Origins of Industrialisation and International Trade Rivalry*, London: Frances Pinter.

Sen, S. P. (1962) 'The Role of Indian Textiles in Southeast Asian Trade in the Seventeenth Century', *Journal of Southeast Asian History* 3(2): 92–110.

Seth, Sanjay (ed.) (2013) *Postcolonial Theory and International Relations*, London: Routledge.

Shambaugh, David (2004/5) 'China Engages Asia: Reshaping the Regional Order', *International Security* 29(3): 64–99.

Shammas, Carole (1993) 'Changes in English and Anglo-American consumption from 1550 to 1800', in Brewer and Porter (eds.), 177–205.

Shapiro, Seymour (1967) *Capital and the Cotton Industry in the Industrial Revolution*, Ithaca: Cornell University Press.

Sharman, Jason C. (2019) *Empires of the Weak*, Princeton: Princeton University Press.

Sheridan, Richard B. (1969) 'The Plantation Revolution and the Industrial Revolution, 1625–1775', *Caribbean Studies* 9(3): 5–25.

Shilliam, Robbie (ed.) (2011) *International Relations and Non-Western Thought*, London: Routledge.

Shilliam, Robbie (2015) *The Black Pacific*, London: Bloomsbury.

Shilliam, Robbie (2018) *Race and the Undeserving Poor*, Newcastle-upon-Tyne: Agenda Publishing.

Singh, Abhay Kumar (2006) *Modern World System and Indian Proto-Industrialization*, Vol. I, New Delhi: Northern Book Centre.

Singh, J. P. (2017) *Sweet Talk*, Stanford: Stanford University Press.

Shinjiro, Nagaoka (1960/1983), 'Sugar Industry Production and the Chinese in Batavia During the 17th and 18th Centuries (17, 18世纪巴达维亚的糖业与华侨)', *Southeast Asian Studies* (南洋资料译丛杂志) 3: 108–9.

Skinner, G. William (1977) 'Regional urbanization in nineteenth century China', in G. William Skinner (ed.), *The City in Late Imperial China*, Stanford: Stanford University Press, 211–49.

Slater, David (2004) *Geopolitics and the Post-Colonial*, Oxford: Blackwell.

Smiles, Samuel (1863) *Industrial Biography*, London: John Murray.

Smith, Adam (1776/1937) *The Wealth of Nations*, New York: The Modern Library.

Smith, Cyril S. (1960) *A History of Metallography*, Chicago: University of Chicago Press.

Snow, Philip (1989) *The Star Raft: China's Encounter with Africa*, Ithaca: Cornell University Press.

Solow, Barbara L. (1985) 'Caribbean Slavery and British Growth: The Eric Williams Hypothesis', *Journal of Development Economics* 17(1–2): 99–115.

Solow, Barbara L. (ed.) (1991) *Slavery and the Rise of the Atlantic System*, Cambridge: Cambridge University Press.

Solow, Barbara L., and Stanley L. Engerman (eds.) (1987) *British Capitalism & Caribbean Slavery*, Cambridge: Cambridge University Press.

Song, Nianshen (2012) '"Tributary" from a Multilateral and Multilayered Perspective', *Chinese Journal of International Politics* 5(2): 155–82.

Song, Yingxing (1637/2017) *Tiangong Kaiwu*, Beijing: Foreign Languages Press.

Srinivasan, Sharda, and Srinivasa Ranganathan (2014) *India's Legendary Wootz Steel*, Himayatnagar, Hyderabad: Universities Press (India).

Steele, Richard (1615/1824) 'Journey of Richard Steel and John Crowther, from Ajmeer in India, to Ispahan in Persia, in the years 1615 and 1616', in Robert Kerr (ed.), *A General History and Collection of Voyages and Travels*, Vol. IX, Edinburgh and London, 206–19. Posted at: https://depts.washington.edu/silkroad/texts/steel_crowther.html

Steensgaard, Niels (1974) *The Asian Trade Revolution of the Seventeenth Century*, Chicago: Chicago University Press.

Steensgaard, Niels (2007) 'The route through Quandahar: The significance of the overland trade from India to the West in the seventeenth century', in Chaudhury and Morineau (eds.), 55–73.

Stein, Burton (1985) 'State Formation and Economy Reconsidered: Part 1', *Modern Asian Studies* 19(3): 387–413.

Stodart, James (1818) 'A Brief Account of *Wootz*, or Indian Steel: Showing Its Fitness for Making Surgical Instruments, and Other Articles of Fine Cutlery', *Asiatic Journal and Monthly Register* 5: 570–1.

Stodart, James, and Michael Faraday (1822) 'On the Alloys of Steel', *Philosophical Transactions of the Royal Society of London* 112: 253–70.

Strange, Susan (1996) *The Retreat of the State*, Cambridge: Cambridge University Press.

Stuenkel, Oliver (2016) *Post-Western World*, Cambridge: Polity.

Styles, John (2000) 'Product Innovation in Early Modern London', *Past & Present* 168: 124–69.

Subrahmanyam, Sanjay (1997) 'Connected Histories: Notes Towards a Reconfiguration of Early Modern Eurasia', *Modern Asian Studies* 31(3): 735–62.

Subramanian, Lakshmi (2016) *Three Merchants of Bombay*, London: Portfolio.

Sugihara, Kaoru (2003) 'The East Asian path of economic development', in Arrighi, Hamashita, and Selden (eds.), 78–123.

Suzuki, Shogo (2007) 'The agency of subordinate polities: Western hegemony in the East Asian mirror', in Hobson and Seabrooke (eds.), 177–95.

Suzuki, Shogo (2014) 'Europe at the periphery of the Japanese world order', in Suzuki, Zhang, and Quirk (eds.), 76–93.

Suzuki, Shogo, Yongjin Zhang, and Joel Quirk (eds.) (2014) *International Orders in the Early Modern World*, London: Routledge.

Sweezy, Paul M., and Maurice Dobb (1950) 'The Transition from Feudalism to Capitalism', *Science & Society* 14(2): 134–67.

Tang, Jie (2018) 'The Chinese grand canal world heritage site: Living heritage in the 21st century', PhD thesis, Department of Landscape, University of Sheffield.

Tansel, Cemal Burak (2013) 'Breaking the Eurocentric Cage', *Capital & Class* 37(2): 299–307.

Tansel, Cemal Burak (2015a) 'Deafening Silence? Marxism, International Historical Sociology and the Spectre of Eurocentrism', *European Journal of International Relations* 21(1): 76–100.

Tansel, Cemal Burak (2015b) 'State formation and social change in modern Turkey', Unpublished PhD thesis, School of Politics and International Relations, University of Nottingham.

Tavernier, Jean Baptiste (1667/1889) *Travels in India*, London: Macmillan & Co.

Tharoor, Shashi (2017) *Inglorious Empire*, London: Penguin.

Thomas, Robert P. (1968) 'The Sugar Colonies of the Old Empire: Profit or Loss for Great Britain?', *Economic History Review* 21(1): 30–45.

Thomaz, Luis Filipe Ferreira Reis (1993) 'The Malay Sultanate of Melaka', in A. Reid (ed.), *Southeast Asia in the Early Modern Era*, Ithaca: Cornell University Press, 69–90.

Thompson, Edward P. (1965) *The Making of the English Working Class*, London: Victor Gollancz.

Thompson, Edwina A. (2011) *Trust is the Coin of the Realm*, Oxford: Oxford University Press.

Thornton, John K. (1998) *Africa and Africans in the Making of the Atlantic World, 1400–1800*, Cambridge: Cambridge University Press.

Thornton, John K. (2012) *A Cultural History of the Atlantic World, 1250–1820*, Cambridge: Cambridge University Press.

Tickner, Arlene B., and David L. Blaney (eds.) (2012) *Thinking International Relations Differently*, London: Routledge.

Tilly, Charles (1984) *Big Structures, Large Processes and Huge Comparisons*, New York: Russell Sage Foundation.

Tilly, Charles (1990) *Coercion, Capital and European States, AD. 990–1990*, Oxford: Blackwell.

Timberg, Thomas A. (2014) *The Marwaris*, Gurgaon: Portfolio.

Toby, Ronald P. (1984) *State and Diplomacy in Early Modern Japan*, Princeton: Princeton University Press.

Toffler, Alvin (1980) *The Third Wave*, New York: Bantam.

Tomich, Dale W. (2004) *Through the Prism of Slavery*, Lanham: Rowman & Littlefield.

Tracy, James D. (ed.) (1991) *The Political Economy of Merchant Empires*, Cambridge: Cambridge University Press.

Trotsky, Leon (1906/2010) *Results and Prospects*, Seattle: Red Letter Press.

Twomey, Michael J. (1983) 'Employment in Nineteenth Century Indian Textiles', *Explorations in Economic History* 20(1): 37–57.

Udovitch, Abraham L. (1962) 'At the Origins of the Western *Commenda*: Islam, Israel, Byzantium?', *Speculum* 37(2): 198–207.

Udovitch, Abraham L. (1970) *Partnership and Profit in Medieval Islam*, Princeton: Princeton University Press.

Uglow, Jenny (2003) *The Lunar Men*, London: Faber & Faber.

Ullah, Mir Izzet (1843) 'Travels Beyond the Himalayas', *Journal of the Royal Asiatic Society* 7(2): 283–342.

United States Department of Commerce (1975) *Historical Statistics of the United States*, Washington: Government Printing Office.

van Leur, Jakob (1955) *Indonesian Trade and Society*, The Hague: W. van Hoeve.

Vanina, Eugenia (2004) *Urban Crafts and Craftsmen in Medieval India*, New Delhi: Munshiram Manoharlal Publishers.

Van Santen, H. W. (1991) 'Trade between Mughal India and the Middle East, and Mughal Monetary Policy, c.1600–1660', in Karl R. Haellquist (ed.), *Asian Trade Routes*, London: Curzon Press, 87–95.

Vernet, Thomas (2009) 'Slave trade and slavery on the Swahili Coast (1500–1750)', in B. A. Mirzai, I. M. Montana, and P. Lovejoy (eds.), *Slavery, Islam and Diaspora*, Trenton: Africa World Press, 37–76.

Vitalis, Robert (2015) *White World Order, Black Power Politics*, Ithaca: Cornell University Press.

Vries, Jan de (2003) 'Connecting Europe and Asia: A quantitative analysis of the Cape-route trade, 1497–1795', in Flynn, Giráldez, and von Glahn (eds.), 35–106.

Vries, Jan de (2008) *The Industrious Revolution*, Cambridge: Cambridge University Press.

Vries, Jan de (2010) 'The Limits of Globalization in the Early Modern World', *Economic History Review* 63(3): 710–33.

Vries, Peer (2002) 'Governing Growth: A Comparative Analysis of the State in the Rise of the West', *Journal of World History* 13(1): 67–138.

Vries, Peer (2010) 'The California School and Beyond: How to Study the Great Divergence', *History Compass* 8(7): 730–51.

Vries, Peer (2013) *Escaping Poverty*, Goettingen: V&R Unipress.

Vries, Peer (2015) *State, Economy and the Great Divergence*, London: Bloomsbury.

Wade, Geoff (2004) 'Ming China and Southeast Asia in the 15th century: A reappraisal', Asia Research Institute, Working Paper Series No. 28, NUS, 1–42.

Wadsworth, A.P., and Julia de Lacy Mann (1931) *The Cotton Trade and Industrial Lancashire, 1600–1780*, Manchester: Manchester University Press.

Wagner, Donald B. (2008) *Science and Civilisation in China*, Vol. 2, Cambridge: Cambridge University Press.

Wallerstein, Immanuel (1974) *The Modern World-System*, Vol. I, London: Academic Press.

Wallerstein, Immanuel (1980) *The Modern World-System*, Vol. II, Berkeley: University of California Press.

Wallerstein, Immanuel (1984) *The Politics of the World-Economy*, Cambridge: Cambridge University Press.

Wallerstein, Immanuel (1987) 'The incorporation of the Indian subcontinent into the capitalist world economy', in Satish Chandra (ed.), *The Indian Ocean*, New Delhi: Sage, 222–53.

Wallerstein, Immanuel (1989) *The Modern World-System*, Vol. III, San Diego: Academic Press.

Wallerstein, Immanuel (1997) 'Eurocentrism and Its Avatars: The Dilemmas of Social Science', *New Left Review* I/226: 93–108.

Waltz, Kenneth N. (1979) *Theory of International Politics*, New York: McGraw Hill.

Walvin, James (1992) *Black Ivory*, London: HarperCollins.

Wang, Yuan-kang (2011) *Harmony & War*, New York: Columbia University Press.

Ward, J. R. (1978) 'The Profitability of Sugar Planting in the British West Indies, 1650–1834', *Economic History Review* 31(2): 197–213.

Washbrook, David (1988) 'Progress and Problems: South Asian Economic and Social History, c.1720–1860', *Modern Asian Studies* 22(1): 57–96.

Washbrook, David (1990) 'South Asia, the World System, and World Capitalism', *Journal of Asian Studies* 49(3): 479–508.

Washbrook, David (2007) 'India in the Early Modern World Economy: Modes of Production, Reproduction and Exchange', *Journal of Global History* 2(1): 87–111.

Washbrook, David (2020) 'The Cambridge history of capitalism: India', in Yazdani and Menon (eds.), 128–51.

Waters, Malcolm (1995) *Globalization*, London: Routledge.

Weber, Heloise (2015) 'Is IPE Just Boring, or Committed to Problematic Meta-Theoretical Assumptions? A Critical Engagement with the Politics of Method', *Contexto Internacional* 37(3): 913–44.

Weber, Max (1922/1978) *Economy and Society*, 2 vols, Berkeley: University of California Press.

Weiss, Linda, and John M. Hobson (1995) *States and Economic Development*, Cambridge: Polity.

Wendt, Ian C. (2009) 'Four centuries of decline? Understanding the changing structure of the South Indian textile industry', in Riello and Roy (eds.), 193–215.

Wertime, Theodore A. (1961) *The Coming of the Age of Steel*, Leiden: Brill.

Whatley, Warren (2017) 'The Gun-Slave Hypothesis and the 18th Century British Slave Trade', African Economic History Working Paper Series No. 35/2017, University of Michigan, 1–56. Posted at: www.aehnetwork.org/wp-content/uploads/2017/07/AEHN-WP-35.pdf

White, Colin (2011) *Understanding Economic Development*, Cheltenham: Edward Elgar.

Wilkinson, Henry (1837) 'On the Cause of the External Pattern, or Watering of the Damascus Sword-Blades', *Journal of the Royal Asiatic Society* 7(4): 187–93.

Wilkinson, Henry (1841) *Engines of War*, London: Longman, Orme, Brown, Green and Longmans.

Williams, Eric (1944/1964) *Capitalism and Slavery*, London: Andre Deutsch.

Williamson, Jeffrey G. (1984) 'Why Was British Growth So Slow During the Industrial Revolution?', *Journal of Economic History* 44(3): 687–712.

Williamson, Jeffrey G. (2011) *Trade and Poverty*, Cambridge: Massachusetts Institute of Technology Press.

Wills, John E. (1993) 'Maritime Asia, 1500–1800: The Interactive Emergence of European Domination', *American Historical Review* 98(1): 83–105.

Wink, André (1988) '"Al-Hind": India and Indonesia in the Islamic World-Economy, c.700–1800 AD', *Itinerario* 12(1): 33–72.

Wink, André (1990) *Al-Hind: The Making of the Indo-Islamic World*, Vol. I, Leiden: Brill.

Wolf, Eric R. (1982) *Europe and the People Without History*, Berkeley: University of California Press.

Wolf, Martin (2005) *Why Globalization Works*, London: Yale Nota Bene.

Wolters, O. W. (1967) *Early Indonesian Commerce*, Ithaca: Cornell University Press.

Wong, Roy Bin (1997) *China Transformed*, Ithaca: Cornell University Press.

Wong, Roy Bin (2002) 'The Search for European Differences and Domination in the Early Modern World: A View from Asia', *American Historical Review* 107(2): 447–69.

Wood, Ellen Meiksins (2002) *The Origin of Capitalism*, London: Verso.

Wright, John (2007) *The Trans-Saharan Slave Trade*, London: Routledge.

Wu, Jianhu (2004) 'On the Changes of Occupational Structures of Population in the Jiangnan Areas During the Ming–Qing Times', *Agricultural History of China* 4: 105–10.

Xian, J., and L. Tan (1994) 'Industry of Sugar Production in Guangdong During the Ming and Qing Periods (明清时期广东的制糖业)', *Social Science in Guangdong* 4: 91–7.

Xing, Fang (2000) 'The role of embryonic capitalism in China', in Xu Dixin and Wu Chengming (eds.), *Chinese Capitalism, 1522–1840*, London: Palgrave Macmillan, 402–29.

Xu, Dixin, and Chengming Wu (2003) *Development History of Chinese Capitalism, II (*中国资本主义发展史卷二：旧民主主义革命时期的中国资本主义*)*, Beijing: Peoples Publishing House.

Xu, Mingde (1995) 'China's Closed–Door Policy in the Period of 14th–19th Century', *Journal of Maritime History Studies* 1: 19–37.

Xu, Xinwu (1988) 'The Struggle of the Handicraft Cotton Industry Against Machine Textiles in China', *Modern China* 14(1): 31–49.

Xu, Xinwu (1992) *History of Cotton Cloth in Jiangnan (*江南土布史*)*, Shanghai: Shanghai Academy of Social Sciences Press.

Xu, Yingnan (2011) 'Industrialization and the Chinese Hand-Reeled Silk Industry (1880–1930)', *Penn History Review* 19(1): 27–46.

Yazdani, Kaveh (2017) *India, Modernity and the Great Divergence*, Leiden: Brill.

Yazdani, Kaveh (2019) 'South Asia in the great divergence', in *Oxford Research Encyclopedia of Asian History*. DOI: 10.1093/acrefore/9780190277727.013.354

Yazdani, Kaveh (2020) 'Mysore at war: The military structure during the reigns of Haidar Ali and Tipu Sultan', in Ravi Ahuja and Martin Christof-Füchsle (eds.), *A Great War in South India*, Oldenbourg: De Gruyter, 17–53.

Yazdani, Kaveh, and Dilip Menon (eds.) (2020) *Capitalisms: Towards a Global History*, New Delhi: Oxford University Press.

Yule, Henry (1875) *The Book of Ser Marco Polo*, London: John Murray.

Yun-Casalilla, Bartolomé, and Patrick K. O'Brien (eds.) (2012) *The Rise of Fiscal States*, Cambridge: Cambridge University Press.

Zarakol, Ayşe (ed.) (2017) *Hierarchies in World Politics*, Cambridge: Cambridge University Press.

Zelin, Madeleine (1984) *The Magistrate's Tael*, Berkeley: University of California Press.

Zelin, Madeleine (2005) *The Merchants of Zigong*, New York: Columbia University Press.

Zeng, Ling (1993) 'The "Outward" Feature of Handicraft Production in Fujian in the Ming-Qing Period (明清福建手工业生产的"外向型"特征)', *Journal of Fujian Tribune* (3): 54–8.

Zhang, Feng (2009) 'Rethinking the "Tribute System": Broadening the Conceptual Horizon of Historical East Asian Politics', *Chinese Journal of International Politics* 2(4): 545–74.

Zhang, Feng (2015) 'Confucian Foreign Policy Traditions in Chinese History', *Chinese Journal of International Politics* 8(2): 197–218.

Zhang, Shizhi (2020) 'The return of China: Historicising China in the global economy', PhD thesis, Department of Politics and International Relations, University of Sheffield.

Zhang, Yongjin, and Barry Buzan (2012) 'The Tributary System as International Society in Theory and Practice', *Chinese Journal of International Politics* 5(1): 3–36.

Zhao, Gang (2013) *The Qing Opening to the Ocean*, Honolulu: University of Hawai'i Press.

Zhao, Suisheng (2015) 'Rethinking the Chinese World Order: The Imperial Cycle and the Rise of China', *Journal of Contemporary China* 24(96): 961–82.

Zheng, Yangwen (2014) *China on the Sea*, Leiden: Brill.

Zhou, Fangyin (2011) 'Equilibrium Analysis of the Tributary System', *Chinese Journal of International Politics* 4(2): 147–78.

Zhuang, Guotu (1999) 'Tea Production, Sale and Social Impact in Fujian Before the Opium War (鸦片战争前福建外销茶叶生产和营销及对当地社会经济的影响)', *Journal of Chinese Historical Studies* 3: 145–56.

Zinkina, Julia, David Christian, Leonid Grinnin, Ilya Ilyin, Alexey Andreev, Ivan Aleshkovsk, Sergey Shulgin, and Andrey Korotayev (2019) *A Big History of Globalization*, Switzerland: Springer Nature.

Zurndorfer, Harriet T. (2009) 'The resistant fibre: Cotton textiles in imperial China', in Riello and Parthasarathi (eds.), 43–62.

Zwart, Pim de (2016) *Globalization and the Colonial Origins of the Great Divergence*, Leiden: Brill.

Index